Be My Disciples

Peter M. Esposito
President

Jo Rotunno, MA
Publisher

Susan Smith
Director of Project Development

Program Advisors
Michael P. Horan, PhD
Elizabeth Nagel, SSD

GRADE SIX
CATECHIST EDITION

The Subcommittee on the Catechism, United States Conference of Catholic Bishops, has found the doctrinal content of this manual, copyright 2013, to be in conformity with the *Catechism of the Catholic Church*.

NIHIL OBSTAT
Rev. Msgr. Robert Coerver
Censor Librorum

IMPRIMATUR
† Most Reverend Kevin J. Farrell DD
Bishop of Dallas
August 22, 2011

Toll Free   877-275-4725
Fax   800-688-8356

Visit us at www.RCLBenziger.com
and www.BeMyDisciples.com

20716 ISBN 978-0-7829-1581-5 (Catechist Edition)
20706 ISBN 978-0-7829-1575-4 (Student Edition)

1st printing
Manufactured for RCL Benziger in Cincinnati, OH, USA. March, 2012

Contents

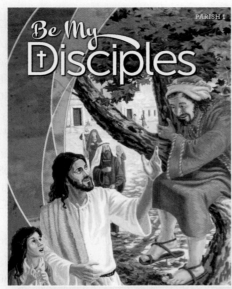

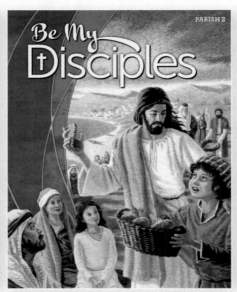

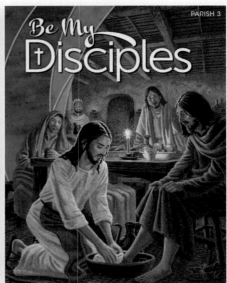

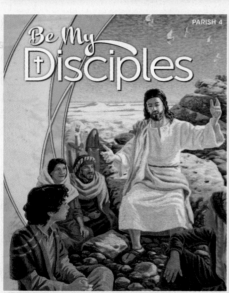

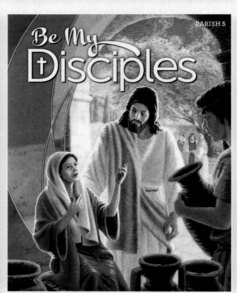

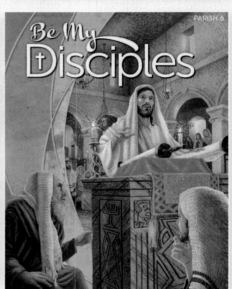

Be My ✝ Disciples

The innovative new program that leads Catholic children and their families to:

- grow in their conversion to Jesus Christ.
- develop the habits of discipleship.
- decide each day to choose life in Christ.
- live as active, committed members of the Catholic Church.

A Balanced Approach to Children's Catechesis

A BALANCED APPROACH

An innovative religion curriculum that empowers children and their families to answer Jesus' call to "Be My Disciples"

- **Invites** children to discipleship
- **Teaches** Scripture, Doctrine, and Celebration
- **Challenges** children to integrate faith and life

Invites
through its **Catechumenal Methodology**

Teaches
through its **Spiral Structure** of Scripture, Doctrine, and Celebration

Challenges
through Integration Activities and Faith Choices

A Child-Centered Catechesis

Be My Disciples shares the Christian story in a catechumenal methodology, using reflection on Scripture and doctrine, plus prayer celebration in every class and during all the major seasons of the Church year. It initiates children into the community of faith and challenges them to discipleship.

A Balanced Approach

- **Invites** children to discipleship through a dynamic methodology that incorporates the latest findings in brain research, psycho-social development, and emotional intelligence.

- **Teaches**, reinforces, and extends knowledge of Scripture, Catholic doctrine, and the Church year *every year in every grade* through RCL Benziger's unique **spiral structure**.

- **Challenges** children to a deeper integration of faith and life by leading them to higher levels of thinking and encouraging a weekly faith choice.

A Child-Centered Catechesis

Be My Disciples helps children know and live their faith through loving service to others. Week by week, children gather to:

- **Grow in Knowledge.** Through RCL Benziger's unique spiral structure, children are introduced to Scripture, Catholic Tradition, and the liturgical year, and reinforce and extend their knowledge year by year.

- **Connect Faith with Their Experience.** Through a process of presentation, application, reflection, and decision, children relate knowledge of the Catholic faith to their life experiences and commit themselves more deeply to the person and mission of Jesus Christ.

- **Practice the Skills of Discipleship.** By learning the gifts and qualities of discipleship and practicing its habits and virtues, children learn the skills required to follow Jesus.

www.BeMyDisciples.com

Unparalleled online resources for children, parents, catechists, and catechetical leaders invite and deepen discipleship.

Student Book Features

Innovative features develop religious literacy and invite the integration of faith and life.

The child's book is divided into six units of four chapters each. The structure of each eight-page chapter invites the children to Explore, Discover, and Decide on a life-centered response to the lesson content.

Unit Opener

- An opening Scripture story grounds the unit content in the Word of God. Each grade uses a unique art style to engage the children's imagination from year to year.

- The second page activates the child's prior knowledge of the unit content.

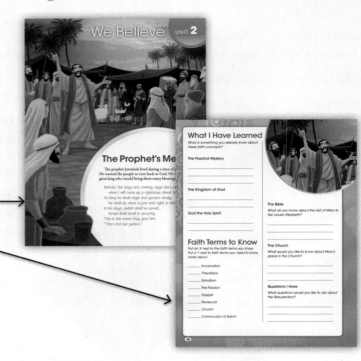

EXPLORE

Chapter Opener

The Chapter Opener invites reflection on life experience and Scripture to engage the child's interest and ground the chapter content in the Word of God. A combination of word and image helps to illuminate the core concepts the child is learning.

The Church Follows Jesus

The second page tells the story of a saint, holy person, or ministry of the Church that has made a difference in the world. By learning more about a person or group that has lived the values of Jesus, children begin to learn the habits of discipleship.

- A key character formation feature teaching virtues, gifts, or qualities that build disciples

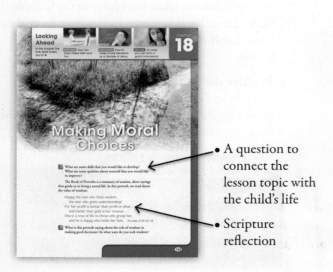

- A question to connect the lesson topic with the child's life

- Scripture reflection

- Stories of Catholics who have made a difference

DISCOVER

A question predicting the key chapter teaching, plus clear definitions of chapter terms

A related saint or holy person who models the way of discipleship

Highlights a Catholic doctrine or practice to help build Catholic identity

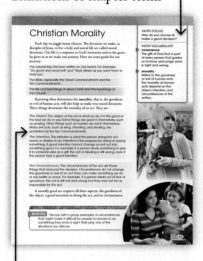

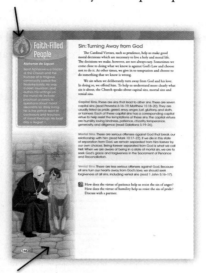

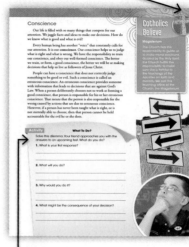

Doctrinal presentations and Scripture quotations

Photos and illustrations to provide visual cues

Application activities to check comprehension

DECIDE

I Follow Jesus

This response page summarizes the lesson teaching, provides an integration activity, and invites the child to make a faith choice.

An integration activity to connect faith and life

CONCLUDING THE LESSON

A review to check understanding of key concepts

A tear-out page in each chapter to assist parents

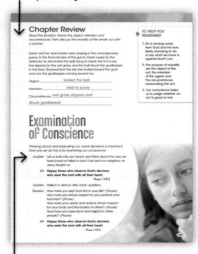

A weekly challenge to live as a disciple

A variety of prayer styles to help children celebrate their faith

A chapter summary, family activities, and background on the Church's tradition of prayer

Build Religious Literacy

A variety of resources activates prior knowledge and measures the children's progress.

Unit Openers

The second page of the Unit Opener activates the child's prior knowledge of the unit content and forecasts key concepts and vocabulary.

Unit Reviews

In addition to the short Chapter Reviews, the Unit Reviews offer variety of strategies help children to reinforce key concepts and identify their own faith discoveries.

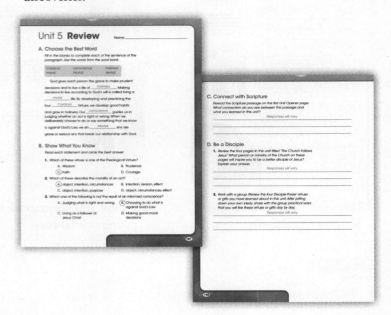

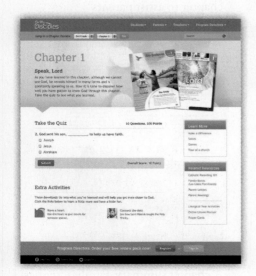

Assessment Tools Booklet

A resource of reproducible masters available in both print and online versions helps you create an assessment portfolio for each student. It includes chapter and unit tests, and suggests other informal ways to assess the ongoing faith growth of your students.

Online Chapter Reviews

Children's interactive reviews for every chapter of every grade level are available at BeMyDisciples.com. This tool reinforces learning and invites parental involvement.

A Lesson Process That Works!

In **Be My Disciples** you will follow
a simple, effective three-part process for each chapter.

▶ EXPLORE	▶ DISCOVER	▶ DECIDE

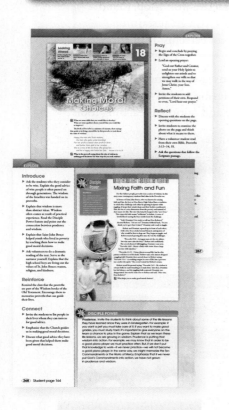

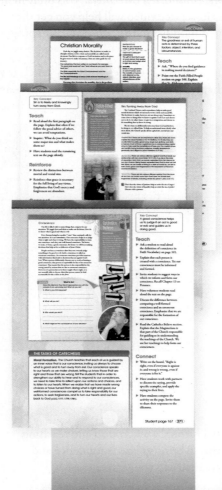

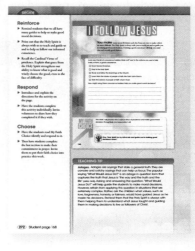

1. Explore

You will lead the class through an opening process that engages their life experiences, grounds the chapter content in Scripture, and invites reflection on it. A second page titled The Church Follows Jesus helps you share a story from the Church's Tradition about a saint, holy person, or ministry that illustrates discipleship.

2. Discover

These doctrinal teaching pages are the building blocks of your lessons and will make the core doctrinal content accessible to the children. Each page of the teaching plan names the core concept for the page and provides you with simple teaching steps.

3. Decide

This page shows you how to assist the children in integrating the content with their own lives and making a clear faith choice for the coming week to continue their journey of discipleship.

Be My Disciples Catechist Guides offer
Front-to-Back Catechist Formation.

From Day One

Your starting point for confident, capable, committed catechesis. This built-in interactive workshop, found on pages 17–34, and the *Be My Disciples* in-service video will help you get the year off to a great start *from Day One*. It includes a correlation to related modules in the *Echoes of Faith* program for catechist formation.

A short theological essay, practical teaching advice, and quotes from Church documents focused on the chapter theme.

A clear focus and outline for each part of the three-step lesson process, including materials you'll need and optional teaching tools

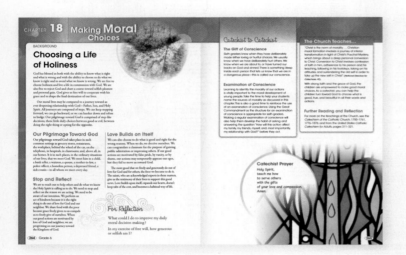

A concise point-by-point plan that leads you page by page through a creative teaching process

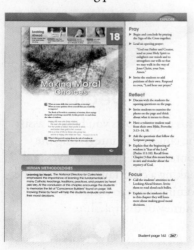

Additional background and teaching tips to bring greater confidence and creativity to your catechesis

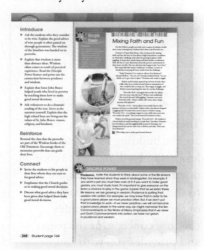

Three optional activities to enrich or extend the learning for each chapter

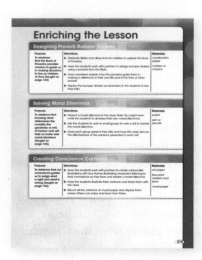

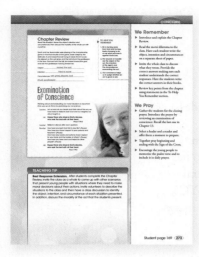

CONCLUDING THE LESSON

We Remember

Guidelines for leading the children in

- a brief review of chapter content through the To Help You Remember feature
- a short Chapter Review activity

We Pray

Your lessons end as they began—with prayer. The lesson plan provides clear instructions for leading the prayer, along with ideas for involving the students and enhancing their prayer experiences.

With My Family

The With My Family page that ends each chapter assists the family in guiding faith formation at home. It includes:

- A summary of the chapter's doctrine concepts
- Suggestions for reading the Bible at home
- Ideas for family activities
- A spirituality feature to deepen knowledge of the Church's spiritual tradition and prayer practices for the home

Catholic Social Teaching

The last teaching box in each unit highlights a principle of Catholic Social Teaching that was addressed in the unit. A related Enriching the Lesson activity on the facing page reinforces this teaching for the children.

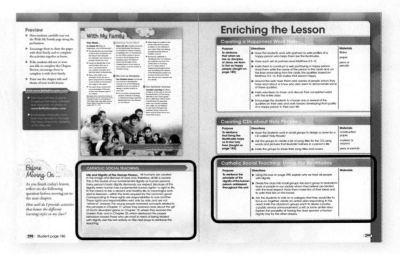

Be My Disciples Supplements

Resources designed to enrich and extend your sessions!

A Complete Music Program for Grades 1–8

The *Be My Disciples* Music Program for Grades 1–8 was directed by well-known Catholic performing artist Steve Angrisano. A veteran musician, composer and youth minister who has been featured at six World Youth Days, several National Catholic Youth Conferences (NCYC), LA Congress, the March for Life Rally, and many diocesan youth conventions and conferences, Steve brings a fresh, youthful perspective to the *Be My Disciples* Music Program. He is the composer of the *Be My Disciples* theme song and is featured in several other tracks on each CD.

Eight Music CDs for Grades 1–8

Each music CD contains:

- A program theme song
- Six hymns (one for each unit) sung by young voices that help children build a musical repertoire of liturgical music as they advance through the grades
- Sung Mass parts reflecting the *Roman Missal*
- Instrumental music for classroom meditation

Music Accompaniment Book

Complete lyrics and accompaniment for guitar and piano complete the *Be My Disciples* Music Program.

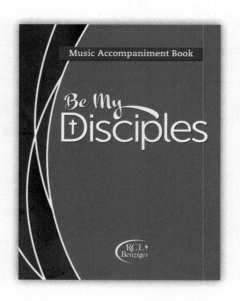

Additional Resources

Assessment Tools — ? Where?

Use these reproducible masters to create an assessment portfolio with chapter and unit tests and other assessment instruments. Available in print and downloadable versions.

Additional Activities

Enhance your lessons with time-saving reproducible activities that extend learning in class or at home. Available in print or downloadable versions.

Be My Disciples @ Home

An at-home companion to the *Be My Disciples* program will help parents either teach or reinforce the content of the children's text. Suitable for homeschoolers as well.

Be My Disciples Summer Program

A complete resource to help parish catechetical leaders adapt the *Be My Disciples* curriculum for use in a summer program format.

Program Director's Manual

This accessible e-resource includes everything the catechetical leader needs to implement *Be My Disciples* in your parish, including ideas for catechist training and parent support, meeting and retreat models, and much, much more.

Sow Seeds of Discipleship from Preschool through Grade 8!

*The **Be My Disciples** family of texts provides a comprehensive and complete program for parish religious education.*

Stories of God's Love for Children, Ages 3–5

Age-appropriate religion readiness lessons prepare preschool and kindergarten children for a lifetime of faith through an introduction to the Word of God. This program has been found to be in conformity with the *Catechism of the Catholic Church.*

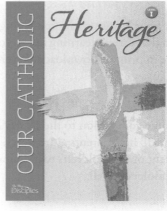

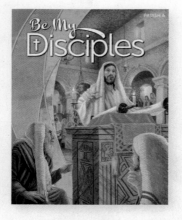

Be My Disciples for Grades 1–6

A Christ-centered and balanced approach to catechesis focuses on an exciting exploration of our Catholic faith using a catechumenal methodology. Found to be in conformity with the *Catechism of the Catholic Church.*

Our Catholic Heritage

This comprehensive and engaging two-level program for intermediate-age and junior high students is designed for older students who are just beginning formal catechesis on their journey of faith. It includes a number of features from *Be My Disciples* to prepare the children to enter the regular basal curriculum in the following year.

Coming in 2013!

Be My Disciples Junior High

Four semester texts make it easy for you to design your own two-year course of study—one that meets your scheduling needs. Each text treats a category of doctrine and also includes special Church History chapters that help students see how the development of doctrine has occurred within the history of the Church.

Bilingual Editions for Grades 1–6 and for Our Catholic Heritage coming in 2013!

BeMyDisciples.com

BeMyDisciples.com offers the best possible support for children, families, catechists, and program directors.

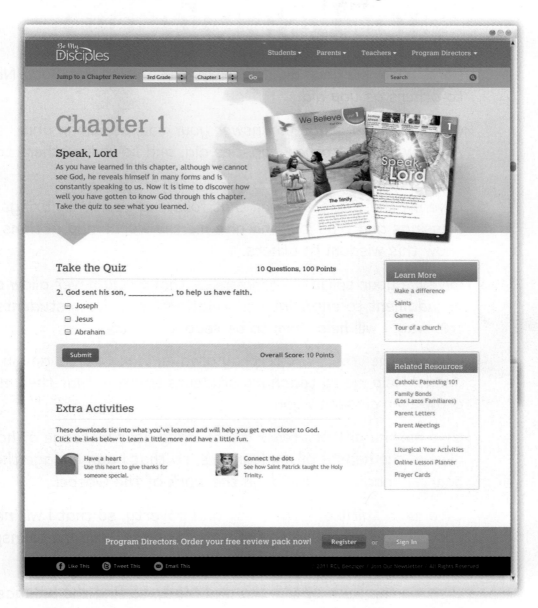

- Connections between the textbooks and the Web site enhance the learning experience in the classroom and at home.

- Social networking opportunities offer safe, faith-filled venues for sharing faith beyond the printed page.

- Easy access for catechists and program directors encourages the use of the extensive practical and creative resources.

- Downloadable activities and assessment tools support busy catechists and catechetical leaders.

A Catechist's Prayer for Discipleship

Lord, make me your disciple. Help me to bring the Good News to others as you did.

Give me the courage to answer your call, as Simon and Andrew and the other Apostles did, and to invite others to answer bravely too.

Give me the wisdom to see that following your Way brings blessings and true joy, and give me the words and actions to show this wisdom to others.

Give me your spirit of forgiveness, that I may never allow anger or judgment to enter into my relationship with my students. In this way, I will help them to be reconcilers too.

Give me the reverence to pray always, in my words and in my deeds. Help me to teach my students to pray, that they may grow ever closer to you.

Give me the gift of creativity, to bring your message of hope alive in the hearts of my learners, so that I can engage their hearts, heads, and hands in the work of the Gospel.

Give me a spirit of generosity and poverty, so that I will never become too attached to the world's goods. Help me to inspire my students to see the emptiness of material things.

Give me the faith of Martha and Mary, to find the balance between prayerfulness and my good works for the Gospel. In this way I will lead my students to greater works than my own.

Spirit of Love, help me to proclaim the Good News to all I meet, so that I can hasten the day when your Reign will come in its fullness. I ask this in the name of your Son, Jesus Christ. Amen.

From Day One

Your starting point for confident, capable, committed catechesis

Welcome to Be My Disciples!

Thank you for answering Jesus' call to discipleship! You have agreed to serve in the Church's ministry of the Word as a catechist. Your decision is a sign of your faith commitment to the young people and their families, to your fellow catechists, and to your parish.

RCL Benziger not only wants to support you, but also to empower you with the knowledge, skills, and spirituality needed to be a confident, capable and committed catechist. From day one, as *Be My Disciples* was being developed, great consideration was given to the learner, the learning process, and to you—the catechist.

This built-in interactive workshop and the *Be My Disciples* in-service video will help you get the year off to a great start *from Day One*. You'll also find a correlation to related modules in the Echoes of Faith program for catechist formation that will increase your confidence still further.

For Reflection

From Day One, think about the ways you have answered the call to discipleship and who has nurtured you along the way. Now think of the ways you can help the young people in your class to be engaged learners as they answer Jesus' call to discipleship.

Be Confident:
You Are a Catechist!

As a catechist, you are joining a long line of dedicated believers stretching back through the ages who have answered God's call to share the Catholic faith with others. Like them, you have been touched by your experience of Jesus Christ and are unable to keep the Good News to yourself.

Dr. Thomas Groome speaks of the catechist as a "leading learner." This image can help you remember that you do not need to have all the answers. You are still learning yourself, and that process will continue for the rest of your life, as a catechist and as a Christian. But you are indeed a leader for the young people in your care. They look to you for information, but even more, they look to you as a role model. This is both an honor and a great responsibility.

As important as your role is, it is not the most important one in the faith formation of the children. That role is reserved for their parents; your role is to support them. Ideally, the home is the "domestic Church" in which the Catholic faith is nurtured on a daily basis. In others, family pressures may get in the way and make your classroom the best experience the children have of the Church, at least for a time. The best attitude to have toward the families of your learners is to assume that, at heart, all parents want the best for their children and that they are grateful for your assistance.

Your role in children's faith formation is to make more explicit for them the Scripture and doctrine of the Catholic Tradition and to give them opportunities to integrate their new knowledge into their daily lives. It is to help children celebrate the great events in the life of Jesus Christ, his mother Mary, and the great saints of the Church throughout the year. In this role you are helping the children establish their Catholic identity.

For Reflection

How well equipped are you to be a "leading learner" in your catechetical setting? What do you see as your strengths and weaknesses? Discuss your assessment with your parish catechetical leader. He or she can help you establish a growth plan for continued learning throughout the year.

Be Confident...The Six Tasks of Catechesis

[T]he definitive aim of catechesis is to put people not only in touch but in communion [and] intimacy with Jesus Christ.

On Catechesis in Our Time 5

Just as some actors play multiple roles in a drama, so will you in your role as a catechist. At times, you are a storyteller, at others a facilitator, a presenter, or a leader of prayer. At all times, you are a witness to your own faith in Jesus Christ. The Catholic Church defines six key tasks for you to fulfill in your role as a catechist.

The *General Directory for Catechesis*, published in 1987, guides the worldwide Church in its catechetical mission. It identified six important tasks of catechesis (*GDC* 85–87). These tasks are reiterated in the *National Directory for Catechesis*, published in 2005 (*NDC* 20). Reflect on the list on the next page and assess your abilities in each of these areas before you begin the year.

The Six Tasks of Catechesis

1. **Promoting knowledge of the faith.** Catechists introduce their learners to all that has been revealed through Jesus Christ by initiating them gradually into the whole truth revealed through Scripture and Tradition.

2. **Liturgical education.** As a catechist, you will help children understand the Church's sacramental life and give them an experience of the signs, symbols, gestures, prayers, and creeds of the Church.

3. **Moral formation.** Moral catechesis involves both the announcement of the Good News through your proclamation of the Gospel call to moral living and your presentation of what the Church's Tradition teaches about this message. The Disciple Power feature in every chapter helps you introduce to the young people to the gifts, virtues, and habits of Christian living.

4. **Teaching to pray.** Every chapter begins and ends with prayer. *Be My Disciples* will provide you with a wide variety of prayer experiences to introduce the children to the Church's tradition of prayer. The last chapter in the child's book teaches and extends the young people's knowledge of the Our Father every year.

5. **Education for community life.** You are leading children into a way of life that you have already been privileged to experience. You invite them to join a loving community of faith, to live simply and humbly, to care for the poor and alienated, to forgive as they wish to be forgiven, and to join in common prayer. Your classroom will become a weekly experience of Christian community for the children.

6. **Missionary initiation.** Catechesis prepares children to live the Gospel in daily life and to prepare the way for the coming of the kingdom of God. *Be My Disciples* is filled with suggestions for outreach activities and service projects to help children begin to participate in the Church's mission. Be sure to note the Catholic Social Teaching feature at the end of each unit.

FOR FURTHER STUDY

See the *Echoes of Faith Plus* "Roles of the Catechist" and the "Person of the Catechist" modules. Go to EchoesofFaith.com for more information.

For Reflection

For which task of catechesis do you feel most qualified? Which seems most daunting? Share with another catechist what strengths and concerns you bring to the catechetical vocation.

Be Capable...
The Be My Disciples Approach

A BALANCED APPROACH

An innovative religion curriculum that empowers children and their families to answer Jesus' call to "Be My Disciples"

- **Invites** children to discipleship
- **Teaches** Scripture, Doctrine, and Celebration
- **Challenges** children to integrate faith and life

Invites
through its **Catechumenal Methodology**

Teaches
through its **Spiral Structure** of Scripture, Doctrine, and Celebration

Challenges
through Integration Activities and Faith Choices

A Child-Centered Catechesis

You feel confident as a catechist when you know what our role is. You will feel more and more capable as you develop the skills to facilitate the catechetical process effectively. **Be My Disciples** uses a unique balanced approach to children's catechesis rooted in the mandate of the *General Directory for Catechesis* that all catechesis include formation as well as information, so that the life of the learner may be transformed (see *GDC* 29).

A BALANCED APPROACH that

- **invites** children to discipleship through a dynamic methodology that incorporates the latest findings in brain research, psycho-social development, and emotional intelligence.

- **teaches,** reinforces, and extends knowledge of Catholic doctrine, and the Church's seasons *every year in every grade* through RCL Benziger's unique spiral structure.

- **challenges** children to a deeper integration of faith and life by leading them to higher levels of thinking and encouraging a weekly faith choice.

Be My Disciples helps children to know and live their faith through loving service to others. Here is what they will experience through the balanced approach.

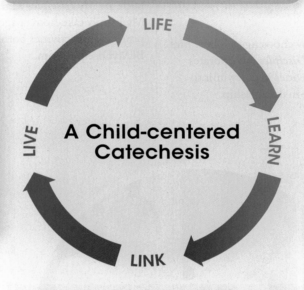

1 Begin with Life.
Each chapter begins with a question to relate the faith concepts to the child's experience. By following this question with a Scripture passage, the children can see that the Bible, too, is related to life. It reflects the life experience of people who came to see God as active in their midst.

4 Practice the Skills of Discipleship.
By learning gifts and qualities of discipleship and practicing its habits and virtues, children learn the skills of daily living required to follow Jesus, and are challenged to integrate them into their daily lives.

2 Grow in Knowledge.
Through RCL Benziger's unique spiral structure, children are introduced to Sacred Scripture, the four pillars of the *Catechism of the Catholic Church* and the celebrations of the liturgical year. Every year at every grade, their core knowledge is both reinforced and extended.

3 Connect Faith with their Experience.
Through a process of presentation, application, reflection, and decision, children relate knowledge of the Catholic faith with their life experience and commit themselves more deeply to the person and mission of Jesus Christ.

For Reflection

Which do you think is more important in catechesis—the teaching of the truths of the faith, or facilitating the integration of faith and life?

For which of these tasks are you the most qualified? What could you do to balance your strengths and challenges?

Be Capable... The Eight Human Methodologies

The *National Directory for Catechesis* describes eight methodologies, or avenues through which individuals come to faith. **Be My Disciples** incorporates these methodologies in a consistent way throughout the program.

1. Learning through Human Experience

We respond to God's invitation through our human experience. Every **Be My Disciples** chapter begins by engaging the child's interest and imagination and helping them relate the lesson concept to their experience.

2. Learning by Discipleship

We learn the Way of Jesus Christ by choosing to follow him and do what he asks of us. **Be My Disciples** incorporates New Testament reflection and activities in every unit to assist in the young people's growth in discipleship.

3. Learning within the Christian Community

The witness of the Church shows children how to believe, worship, and to take up the Gospel call to service. Each week, **Be My Disciples** invites children to make concrete faith choices for the Kingdom of God.

4. Learning within the Christian Family

The Christian family is often the first experience the child has of what it means to live in a Christian community. The family offers the first and best environment for growth in faith. **Be My Disciples** engages the family through the With My Family take-home pages, and through a variety of other projects and activities both within the text and online at BeMyDisciples.com.

5. Learning through the Witness of the Catechist

You will be a powerful influence on your learners' faith formation this year, both by the faith knowledge you will share with them and, most importantly, by your witness of the Catholic faith. Your words and actions model for the children what it means to live a Christian life. Your *Be My Disciples* Catechist Guide offers you front-to-back catechist formation to assist you every step of the way.

6. Learning by Heart

When we "learn by heart," we make knowledge or a skill our own. Memorization of key definitions, doctrinal formulations, and prayers plays an important role in building religious literacy and identity. *Be My Disciples* highlights faith vocabulary and reinforces key concepts in every chapter through student book sidebar features and Catechist Guide strategies.

7. Making a Commitment to Live the Christian Life

Our acts of commitment to live the faith, made again and again throughout our lives, are how we learn what it means to have faith. *Be My Disciples* invites young people to make a faith choice at the end of every chapter so that they can live the faith more deeply in the coming week.

8. Learning by Apprenticeship

Learning by apprenticeship allows us to learn from an experienced Catholic, a mentor, who can give us insight into the Christian life. You are such a person for your learners this year. *Be My Disciples* also provides activities at every grade inviting young people to begin modeling for younger children actions of a disciple.

Look for a box in every chapter's lesson plan that will assist you in incorporating the human methodologies into your sessions. The boxes provide you with helpful background information, activities, and lesson strategies.

FOR FURTHER STUDY

Review the *Echoes of Faith Plus* Methodology module for grades 5 and 6. Look for activities and teaching techniques that utilize the eight human methodologies. Go to EchoesofFaith.com for more resources.

For Reflection

Which of the human methodologies has most helped you grow in faith? How will utilizing the different methodologies help you to be a more effective catechist?

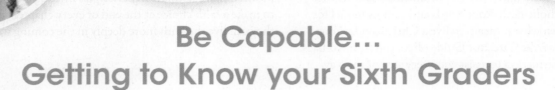

Be Capable...
Getting to Know your Sixth Graders

"Catechesis, therefore, is given by right on the basis of diverse and complementary age groups, on account of the needs and capacity of its recipients."

General Directory for Catechesis 171

Sixth graders exhibit high energy balanced with a need for much rest. They experience mood swings but have an increased level of self-control and tolerance. These adolescents recognize their peers for their behavior standards so life centers around their peers. As their independence increases, they still require adult guidance and support. Intellectually, these sixth graders are transitioning from concrete to abstract thinking. They appreciate humor and at the same time they love to argue! Eleven and twelve - year olds have grown to become empathetic, they are more self-aware and often quite insightful. Because there are vast differences in developmental growth, the only unifying characteristic is change. Look forward to a year with highly intellectual and inquisitive young people who demonstrate a heightened sense of justice!

Growing in Discipleship

In their journey of faith, sixth graders have a strong sense of fairness and perceive God as more rational and less judgmental. With the emergence of adolescence, these young persons have more of a questioning nature in religious matters. They especially want to know what it means to be a Catholic. They are growing spiritually in their prayer life, their sense of right and wrong and are capable of deep feelings of love for God. Sixth graders often seek guidance from God in their everyday lives. As these relationships with God are developed so is their response to the call of discipleship.

Physical Characteristics

Rapid and irregular physical growth

Changes in physical growth increase tiredness

Rapid brain growth

Is active and curious

Cognitive/Learning Skills

Inquisitive and questions adult concepts

Transitioning from concrete to abstract thinking

Prefers learning experiences with peers

Exhibits varied ability levels

Relationships

Peer acceptance is important

Desires independence

Focuses on role models

Accepts responsibility

Religious Growth

Developing a value system

Exhibits a strong sense of justice

Seeks guidance from God for everyday decisions

Questions matters of faith

Enjoys a variety of prayer forms

Relates Bible messages to life experiences

Desires to participate in liturgical celebrations in a more meaningful way

FOR FURTHER STUDY

The module entitled "The Learner" in *Echoes of Faith Plus* provides a good overview of the human stages of growth and development. Go to EchoesofFaith.com for more resources.

For Reflection

- What do you remember about your experiences as a sixth grader? What are the similarities and differences between your experiences and today's sixth graders?

- How does this help you understand your sixth graders to enjoy them and plan for your religion classes this year?

Be Capable... Helping My Sixth Graders Learn

For as in one body we have many parts, and all the parts do not have the same function, so we, though many, are one body in Christ and individually parts of one another.   Romans 12:4-5

God has given each of us variety of spiritual gifts to help us to grow individually and in the community. Each gift is unique and each person and gift is needed. It is through these diverse spiritual gifts that we are one body in Christ!

Knowing your own gifts will assist you in helping your sixth graders discover their own gifts. The way you learn and the way each young person learns is also unique and these are gifts from God. How are you smart? How do you prefer to learn? How do you respond emotionally to help you think and form relationships?

Learning Smart

A well-known educator, Howard Gardner, believes that each of us is born with at least eight different ways of processing and responding to new information that he calls multiple intelligences. All of us possess each of these kinds of 'smart' in one degree or another. The particular combination of these intelligences is what makes each of us unique; there is usually one or several of these intelligences that is dominant for each person. Refer to the *"Eight Kinds of Smart"* on the next page.

Digital Disciples

Young people today are also digital learners. They access information quickly from multimedia sources; primarily utilizing the internet, laptops and cell phones. Learning takes place through multitasking while processing pictures, sound, color and video before text. Digital learners are graphic thinkers! They respond to learning that is relevant, instant, active, useful, and fun.

Learning Heart

How do your recognize your own emotions and how do they affect your thoughts and behaviors? How do you manage your emotions and adapt to change? How do you understand the emotions, needs, and concerns of other people? How do you develop and maintain good relationships and communicate clearly? The research of Daniel Goleman on 'Emotional Intelligence' is an important part of understanding who you are and who you are in relationship with others. The 'heart' must be a part of learning in order to grow in a faith response that lets you share why you love being Catholic!

As children grow in relationship with others and Jesus, they need to know how to express their own feelings and knowledge to have common ground with their family, classmates, and people from other cultures and religions. Learning heart will help children to be engaged and active members of the Church.

Be My Disciples provides a variety of strategies that respect the many gifts of children as they learn smart, learn ways to grasp the knowledge and learn heart to grow spiritually.

To assist you in engaging all your learners, here are some activities related to the eight intelligences that support the different ways children can learn and express their relationship with God and one another.

FOR FURTHER STUDY

The "Methods for Grades 5 & 6" module of *Echoes of Faith Plus* will help you provide activities that will assist many kinds of learners. See EchoesofFaith.com for more resources.

For Reflection

- Knowing your own gifts will assist you in helping your sixth graders discover their own gifts. How do you learn "smart" and what are your preferences for learning? How does this help you understand the young people in your class so that your catechesis will engage them more?

- How will you nurture and incorporate the emotional intelligence of the young people so that their faith response will be more authentic?

8 Kinds of Smart

WordSmart

LogicSmart

ImageSmart

SelfSmart

BodySmart

PeopleSmart

NatureSmart

SoundSmart

Language and Music-Related Activities

- Researching word meanings
- Word games and puzzles
- Reading and Bible search activities
- Storytelling and journal writing
- Learning hymns and Mass responses
- Writing prayers or songs
- Using background music for activities

Object-Related Activities

- Learning "how many?" of different categories
- Celebrating the liturgical seasons
- "You are there" activities such as placing oneself in the action of a Bible story
- Using maps and models
- Using or creating graphic organizers
- Posters and art activities
- Crafts and classroom dramas
- Using gestures with songs and prayers
- Expressing response through dance
- Nurturing plants and animals
- Creating gardens or nature areas

Person-Related Activities

- Cooperative learning activities
- Peer tutoring and sharing
- Teaching other students
- Games and simulations
- Quiet prayer times
- Writing and drawing in journals
- Creating autobiographies
- Self-assessment activities

Teaching Trends

- Build in more discovery.
- Put content in context.
- Pose problems first and teach second.
- Give fewer conclusions.
- Integrate digital learning.
- Utilize higher-level thinking techniques.

Be Capable ...Designing the Environment

The most important task of the catechesis of children is to provide, through the witness of adults, an environment in which young people can grow in faith. National Directory for Catechesis 48E 2

The learning process can occur in any place, anywhere, at any time. Our master teacher, Jesus, taught while he was walking, sitting on a hillside, preaching in the synagogue, or conversing in a home. Jesus modeled a variety of ways to teach through telling stories, asking questions, offering compassion, and challenging others. He also knew that the physical needs of people must be met so they can focus on God's message. A caring, child-centered environment helps invite young people to discipleship. Since passing on faith is a sacred task, it deserves the creation of sacred space.

Prayer Space

Every catechetical space should be focused around an age-appropriate prayer space. Here are some suggestions:

- Cover the table with an attractive cloth that matches the liturgical season.

- Place a crucifix at the highest point in the prayer space.

- Place a candle on the surface of the table as a sign of the light of faith. Light the candle only during the prayer service. Use an electric candle if school fire regulations require it.

- Enthrone an open Bible on the table. The opening lesson in your student book includes a prayer service for enthroning the Bible on the first day of class.

- Place a plant or other objects in the prayer space to symbolize the lesson theme or the liturgical season.

- You may want to consider placing a cell phone, laptop, or another type of technology in the prayer space. Make sure it is turned off! This can indicate to your learners that digital media, when used properly, can be used to communicate the Christian message.

Learning Space

Now it's time for careful consideration of the other aspects of your sacred learning space. How will you create a distinctive space for catechesis? Here are some questions to help you create a child-centered learning environment that will encourage faith reflection:

- Are chairs or desks arranged in such a way to promote cooperative learning? Is the arrangement flexible to allow for individual, small, and large group learning experiences?

- Can you easily transition the young people to the prayer space for a more solemn reading of Bible stories and prayer services?

- Can you adjust lighting during reflective activities or prayer services?

- How can you display student activities? Is there a way to use liturgical colors in the learning area beyond the prayer space?

- Do you have some reflective music available for use in prayer services and reflective activities? As you know, music can help to set the mood appropriately to signal that the class is moving into a more sacred time. Consider utilizing the *Be My Disciples* Music Program to enhance the learner's knowledge of liturgical music and experience of prayer.

Learning Materials

You will need certain classroom essentials: pencils, pens, paper, and some art supplies. Here are a few other items you will want to have available to enhance your religion classes:

- Materials for the prayer space
- A class set of Bibles
- Maps of the Bible lands
- Photos and posters that match the lesson themes
- General literature titles connected to the lesson themes
- A DVD/CD player

How will you incorporate digital learning solutions to engage these young learners and where can they be incorporated into the physical space? Discuss with your parish catechetical leader what resources are available and learn how to use them. If you have a smart phone or laptop and have Internet access in the classroom, there are many resources at BeMyDisciples.com that could enhance your classroom sessions. The Churchs asks us to "proclaim the Gospel to the world of youth with courage and creativity" (*General Directory for Catechesis* 181). Jesus used all the means available to him in his own time to invite others to conversion, and so should you!

FOR FURTHER STUDY

Take a look at the *Echoes of Faith Plus* module "Getting Started" for ideas on creating a positive environment for catechesis. Go to EchoesofFaith.com for more resources.

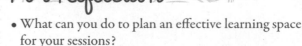

For Reflection

- What can you do to plan an effective learning space for your sessions?

- How can you create an inviting climate for prayer that will deepen the experience for your learners?

Be Committed: Being A Person of Prayer

Liturgical formation . . . must explain what the Christian liturgy is, and what the sacraments are. It must also however, offer an experience of the different kinds of celebration and it must make symbols, gestures, etc., known and loved.

General Directory for Catechesis 87

To teach others to pray requires, first of all, that you are a person of prayer yourself. Children look to you as an example of what a prayerful person looks like. Prayer is listening with openness to God's word, and responding in faith, hope, and love. Our response involves a willingness to spend time with God, to ponder the words of Scripture, to discern God's message to us, and to respond with our whole selves—body, mind, and heart. Spending daily time alone with God in an attitude of openness and thanksgiving will transform you and prepare you to be the inspiration to the children that you hope to be and that they deserve.

Worship is simply the prayer of the Church. We gather together to lay our lives before God the Father, to praise him and give thanks for the gift of his love, and to join with his Son in offering our lives for his service. That is why the *Catechism of the Catholic Church* refers to liturgy as "the participation of the People of God in the work of God" (CCC 1069). Liturgical celebrations weave together signs and symbols drawn from our human experience—words and actions, singing and music, and sacred images. An artful blending of these elements produces a worship experience that can evoke for us the mystery of God and lead us to a fruitful response.

As children experience such gestures as signing, anointing, blessing, and kneeling within the intimacy of your classroom setting, you will be preparing them to participate more fully in the worship of the whole community. Just as you have certain ways of praying with which you are most comfortable, you will find that children have their preferences too. The many approaches that are included in the *Be My Disciples* program will provide a true school of prayer for your learners.

How *Be My Disciples* Will Help You

- Beginning and closing prayer experiences in every lesson

- A rich variety of prayer experiences using the signs, symbols, and gestures of the Church's liturgy whenever appropriate

- An exposition of the rich variety of the Church's tradition of prayer, liturgy, and sacraments

- Tips for enhancing the classroom prayer experiences

- A closing chapter on the Our Father that summarizes the year's Gospel message

FOR FURTHER STUDY

See the *Echoes of Faith Plus* "Prayer and Spirituality" and "Liturgy and Sacraments" modules. Go to EchoesofFaith.com for more resources.

For Reflection

- How do you create opportunities in your daily life to hear the voice of God speaking to you?

- What forms of prayer will you most enjoy leading for your learners?

Scope and Sequence | Grade 6

CHAPTER 7—The Holy Spirit
Faith Concepts:
- The Holy Spirit is at work bringing about God's plan of Salvation within the Church.
- The Holy Spirit strengthens the Church to be a sign of Christ's love for humanity and enables us to proclaim the Gospel.
- With the Gifts of the Holy Spirit, we can help continue the mission of the Church.

Sacred Scripture: Psalm 143:10 (Lord, teach me to do your will.); Matthew 28:16–20 (Go make disciples of all nations and baptize them.); Luke 24:48–49 (Jesus announces the Spirit is with him.); John 19:26–27 (Jesus gives Mary to the Church as our mother.); Acts 1:4–5, 14–41, 2:1–4 (Events of Pentecost); 1 Corinthians 6:19 (Your body is a temple of the Holy Spirit.)
Disciple Power: counsel (Gift of the Holy Spirit)
Faith Vocabulary: charism, Gospels, Pentecost
Faith-Filled People: the Spiritans
Catholics Believe: social teachings of the Church
The Church Follows Jesus: Saints Benedict and Scholastica
Prayer: a liturgy of the Word: John 17:20–21
Catechism of the Catholic Church (CCC): 683–747, 963–975
U.S. Catholic Catechism for Adults (USCCA): pp.102–110, 141–149

CHAPTER 8—The Mystery of the Church
Faith Concepts:
- Jesus Christ is the Head of the Church, the Body of Christ.
- The Holy Spirit strengthens the Church to be one, holy, catholic, and apostolic.
- The Kingdom of God is mysteriously present in the Church and will come about in fullness at the end of time.

Sacred Scripture: Psalm 28:7–9 (Lord, you are the strength of your people.); Matthew 28:19–20 (Make disciples of all nations.); Ephesians 4:5–6 (There is one Lord, one faith, one Baptism, one God and Father of all.); 1 Peter 2:9 (You are a chosen race, a holy nation.)
Disciple Power: peace (Fruit of the Holy Spirit)
Faith Vocabulary: Church, Kingdom of God
Faith-Filled People: Saint Timothy
Catholics Believe: the Last Judgment
The Church Follows Jesus: Saint Marguerite Marie Alacoque
Prayer: a prayer of vocations
Catechism of the Catholic Church (CCC): 748–962, 988–1060
U.S. Catholic Catechism for Adults (USCCA): pp. 111–139, 151–162

UNIT 3: WE WORSHIP, PART ONE

CHAPTER 9—Celebrating the Liturgy
Faith Concepts:
- The celebration of the liturgy is the Church's work of worshipping God.
- The Seven Sacraments are the center of the Church's liturgy.
- Throughout the year, the Church praises God the Father for what he has done and continues to do for us.

Sacred Scripture: 1 Samuel 16:1–13 (The anointing of David); Acts 2:2–4 (Pentecost); Galatians 5:22–26 (The Fruit of the Holy Spirit)
Disciple Power: fortitude (Cardinal Virtue)
Faith Vocabulary: Confirmation, consecrate
Faith-Filled People: USCCB
Catholics Believe: Gifts of the Holy Spirit
The Church Follows Jesus: martyrs in China
Prayer: a liturgy of the Word: Galatians 5:22–26
Catechism of the Catholic Church (CCC): 1285–1321
U.S. Catholic Catechism for Adults (USCCA): pp. 201–211

CHAPTER 10—Baptism
Faith Concepts:
- A person becomes fully initiated into the Church through the celebration of the Sacraments of Christian Initiation.
- Baptism is the first sacrament and is the doorway to new life in the Holy Spirit and salvation in Christ.
- Through Baptism we receive the gift of the Holy Spirit and are made sharers in God's divine life.

Sacred Scripture: Genesis 7:6–23 (Noah and the Flood); Exodus 14:26–31 (Crossing of the Red Sea); Mark 1:9–11 (Baptism of Jesus); John 19:31–37 (Water and blood out of Jesus' pierced side.)
Disciple Power: modesty (Fruit of the Holy Spirit)
Faith Vocabulary: Baptism, Christian Initiation, sanctifying grace
Faith-Filled People: the Old Testament prophets
Catholics Believe: Sacred Chrism
The Church Follows Jesus: Saint Charles Lwanga
Prayer: recalling our anointing at Baptism
Catechism of the Catholic Church (CCC): 1210–1284
U.S. Catholic Catechism for Adults (USCCA): pp. 181–199

CHAPTER 11—Confirmation
Faith Concepts:
- The Sacrament of Confirmation perfects the grace of Baptism.
- The Rite of Confirmation includes the laying on of hands and anointing with oil by the bishop.
- Strengthened by Confirmation, we are called to be living witnesses for Christ.

Sacred Scripture: 1 Samuel 16:1–13 (The anointing of David); Acts 2:2–4 (Pentecost); Galatians 5:22–26 (The Fruit of the Holy Spirit)
Disciple Power: fortitude (Cardinal Virtue)
Faith Vocabulary: Confirmation, consecrate
Faith-Filled People: USCCB
Catholics Believe: Gifts of the Holy Spirit
The Church Follows Jesus: martyrs in China
Prayer: Galatians 5:22–26
Catechism of the Catholic Church (CCC): 1285–1321
U.S. Catholic Catechism for Adults (USCCA): pp. 201–211

CHAPTER 12—The Eucharist
Faith Concepts:
- Many events in the Old Testament prefigure the mystery of the Eucharist.
- The Mass recalls and makes present the one sacrifice of Christ.
- The Eucharist is a memorial of the Paschal Mystery.

Sacred Scripture: Genesis 14:17–20 (Melchizidek); Exodus 12:1–20 (Passover in Egypt); Exodus 16:1–15 (Manna in the desert); Psalm 105:39–41 (God provided bread from heaven.)
Disciple Power: faithfulness (Fruit of the Holy Spirit)
Faith Vocabulary: Eucharist, Mass
Faith-Filled People: Saint Dominic de Guzman
Catholics Believe: the Altar
The Church Follows Jesus: Archbishop Óscar Romero
Prayer: a liturgy of the Word: John 6:32–35
Catechism of the Catholic Church (CCC): 1322–1419
U.S. Catholic Catechism for Adults (USCCA): pp. 215–232

UNIT 4: WE WORSHIP, PART TWO

CHAPTER 13—Penance and Reconciliation
Faith Concepts:
- The Sacraments of Healing include the Sacrament of Penance and Reconciliation and the Sacrament of Anointing of the Sick.
- The Rite of Penance has a movement of conversion that includes repentance, confession, and absolution.
- In Reconciliation, we receive God's forgiveness for sins committed after Baptism.

Sacred Scripture: Matthew 25:41–43 (Whatever you do to the least of people you do to Jesus.); Luke 7:47–50 (Jesus forgives the repentant woman.)
Disciple Power: self-control (Fruit of the Holy Spirit)
Faith Vocabulary: mortal sin, venial sin
Faith-Filled People: Saint Mary Magdalene
Catholics Believe: forgiveness
The Church Follows Jesus: Saint Monica
Prayer: an act of contrition
Catechism of the Catholic Church (CCC): 1420–1498
U.S. Catholic Catechism for Adults (USCCA): pp. 233–247

CHAPTER 14—Anointing of the Sick
Faith Concepts:
- The Church continues Jesus' ministry of healing in the Sacraments of Healing.
- Anointing of the Sick is the sacrament that strengthens our faith and trust in God when we are seriously ill or dying.
- The Rite of Anointing consists of the prayer of faith, laying on of hands, and the anointing with oil.

Sacred Scripture: Numbers 21:4–9 (Moses heals the ill in the desert.); Psalm 102:2–6 (Prayer to God in time of distress); Matthew 9:35 (Jesus heals people.); Mark 6:12–13 (The Apostles drove out many demons and anointed the sick with oil and healed them.); James 5:14–15 (If you are sick, call upon the presbyters of the Church to pray over, anoint, and heal them.)
Disciple Power: gentleness (Fruit of the Holy Spirit)
Faith Vocabulary: Anointing of the Sick, hospice care
Faith-Filled People: Saint Rafqa
Catholics Believe: respect for the terminally ill
The Church Follows Jesus: Catholic hospice care
Prayer: a litany of saints
Catechism of the Catholic Church (CCC): 1499–1532
U.S. Catholic Catechism for Adults (USCCA): pp. 249–259

CHAPTER 15—The Sacrament of Holy Orders
Faith Concepts:
- Every Christian is joined to Christ in Baptism and is called to live a life of generous service to God and others as Jesus did.
- Holy Orders consecrates a baptized man to serve the whole Church as a bishop, priest, or deacon.
- A bishop has received the fullness of the Sacrament of Holy Orders.

Sacred Scripture: Matthew 9:35–38 (Pray for vocations.); Mark 10:44–45 (To serve as Jesus did means to serve others.); Matthew 19:11–12 (Some give up marriage for the sake of the Kingdom.)
Disciple Power: patience (Fruit of the Holy Spirit)
Faith Vocabulary: Communion, Ordination
Faith-Filled People: Venerable Jean Gailhac
Catholics Believe: male ordination
The Church Follows Jesus: Blessed John Henry Newman
Prayer: a prayer for vocations
Catechism of the Catholic Church (CCC): 1533–1600
U.S. Catholic Catechism for Adults (USCCA): pp. 261–275

CHAPTER 16—The Sacrament of Matrimony
Faith Concepts:
- Marriage is part of God's plan for love and life in which a man and a woman form a lifelong bond with openness to life.
- Spousal love is to be exclusive, permanent, unbreakable, and faithful.
- Matrimony unites a baptized man and a baptized woman to be a living sign of Christ's love for the Church.

Sacred Scripture: Tobit 7:11–13 (Marriage of Tobiah and Sarah); Isaiah 54:5–8 (God is like a husband to Israel.); Hosea 2:21–25 (God's covenant between himself and Israel is like a marriage.); Matthew 19:6 (What God has joined together, no one can separate.); 1 Corinthians 13:4–7, 13 (Love is the greatest.); Ephesians 5:21–27 (Relationship of husband and wife)
Disciple Power: chastity (Fruit of the Holy Spirit)
Faith Vocabulary: complementarity, conjugal love, Matrimony
Faith-Filled People: Blesseds Louis and Zélie Martin
Catholics Believe: marital love
The Church Follows Jesus: solemn blessing of marriage
Prayer: adaptation from the Rite of Marriage
Catechism of the Catholic Church (CCC): 1601–1666
U.S. Catholic Catechism for Adults (USCCA): pp. 277–292

UNIT 5: WE LIVE, PART ONE

CHAPTER 17—Our Call to Holiness
Faith Concepts:
- The Theological Virtues are gifts from God that connect us with him and strengthen us to live lives of holiness.
- The grace of the Holy Spirit helps us grow in our ability to freely make choices to grow in holiness.
- Living the Works of Mercy is a sign that we are trying to live holy lives.

Sacred Scripture: Leviticus 11:44–45 (Be holy for God is holy.); Psalm 99:4, 7, 9 (God loves justice.); 1 Corinthians 13:13 (Faith, hope, and love remain, but love is the greatest.); Colossians 3:12–14 (Love, the bond of perfection.)
Disciple Power: understanding (Gift of the Holy Spirit)
Faith Vocabulary: holiness, Theological Virtues, Works of Mercy
Faith-Filled People: Job
Catholics Believe: sacramentals
The Church Follows Jesus: the Gleaning Network
Prayer: adaptation of *The Road Ahead* by Thomas Merton
Catechism of the Catholic Church (CCC): 1699–1715, 1730–1748, 1803–1845, 1987–2029
U.S. Catholic Catechism for Adults (USCCA): pp. 307–313, 315–321, 328–330

CHAPTER 18—Making Moral Choices
Faith Concepts:
- Sin is turning away from God and his love, freely choosing to do or say what we know is against God's Law.
- The sources of morality are the object of the act, the intention of the agent, and the circumstances surrounding the act.
- Our consciences help us to judge whether an act is good or evil.

Sacred Scripture: Proverbs 3:13–14, 18 (Value of wisdom); Proverbs 6:16–19 (The Lord hates the dishonest and those who stir up discord.); Proverbs 11:19 (Virtue leads to life.); Proverbs 15:4 (Speak kindly to others.); Proverbs 16:8 (It is better to have a little with virtue than a lot through dishonesty.); Proverbs 24:3, 29:8 (Seek wisdom.); Matthew 15:18–20 (Concern over committing sin); Mark 10:17–22 (Jesus tells rich young man to sell everything and follow him.); 1 John 5:16–17 (Pray for those who are sinning.)
Disciple Power: prudence (Cardinal Virtue)
Faith Vocabulary: conscience, morality
Faith-Filled People: Saint Alphonse de Liguori
Catholics Believe: the Magisterium
The Church Follows Jesus: the Don Bosco system
Prayer: an examination of conscience
Catechism of the Catholic Church (CCC): 1750–1761, 1776–1876
U.S. Catholic Catechism for Adults (USCCA): pp. 311–321

CHAPTER 19—The Law of Love
Faith Concepts:
- Do good and avoid evil is a principle of the Natural Law
- Love of God and love of neighbor is essentially the Great Commandment.
- The Law of Love is the way we are called to be friends with Jesus and with one another.

Sacred Scripture: Sacred Scripture: Deuteronomy 6:4–5 (The Lord is your God, the Lord alone.); Tobit 4:15 (Do to no one what you dislike.); Matthew 5:44–47 (Love your enemies.); Matthew 7:12 (Do to others what you want them to do to you.); Matthew 22:37–40 (Jesus teaches the Great Commandment.); Matthew 25:31–40 (Judgment of the Nations); Luke 6:31 (Do unto others as you would have them do to you.); John 13:34–35 (The New Commandment); John 15:9–15 (Remain in God's love and keep his commandments.)

Disciple Power: charity (Theological Virtue)
Faith Vocabulary: Golden Rule, Natural Law, Shema
Faith-Filled People: Canossian Sisters
Catholics Believe: the New Law
The Church Follows Jesus: Saint Josephine Bakhita
Prayer: The Shema (English and Hebrew)
Catechism of the Catholic Church (CCC): 1949–2029
U.S. Catholic Catechism for Adults (USCCA):
   pp. 310–311, 315–318, 327–330

CHAPTER 20—Ways of Happiness
Faith Concepts:
- The Beatitudes are teachings of Jesus from his Sermon on the Mount.
- Living the Beatitudes is the way to follow the Law of Love.
- The spirit of joy comes from the love of God being the treasure kept in our hearts.

Sacred Scripture: Matthew 5:3–11 (The Beatitudes); Philippians 4:4, 8, 13 (Rejoice in the Lord always. Think about only good and holy things.)

Disciple Power: joy (Fruit of the Holy Spirit)
Faith Vocabulary: Beatitudes, canonization
Faith-Filled People: Blessed Chiara Badano
Catholics Believe: Communion of Saints
The Church Follows Jesus: Blessed Pope John XXIII
Prayer: Psalm 146:2, 5, 10
Catechism of the Catholic Church (CCC):
   1716–1729, 1812–1819, 1830–1845, 1965–2029
U.S. Catholic Catechism for Adults (USCCA):
   pp. 307–311, 318

UNIT 6: WE LIVE, PART TWO

CHAPTER 21—Love of God
Faith Concepts:
- The First Commandment teaches us to worship only God and to love and serve him above all else.
- The Second Commandment teaches us to use the name of God reverently and respectfully.
- The Third Commandment teaches us to keep the Lord's Day a holy day.

Sacred Scripture: Exodus 20:1–17 (The Ten Commandments); Psalm 19:8–9 (The Law of the Lord is perfect and refreshes the soul.)

Disciple Power: piety (Gift of the Holy Spirit)
Faith Vocabulary: idolatry, worship
Faith-Filled People: Moses
Catholics Believe: sins against the honor of God
The Church Follows Jesus: the collection at Mass
Prayer: Psalm 103:1
Catechism of the Catholic Church (CCC): 2083–2195
U.S. Catholic Catechism for Adults (USCCA): pp. 337–371

CHAPTER 22—Commandments of Love
Faith Concepts:
- The Fourth Commandment teaches about our responsibilities as family members, neighbors, and citizens.
- The Fifth Commandment teaches that we are to build a culture of life.
- The Sixth and Ninth Commandments teach us to express our friendship and love in respectful ways.

Sacred Scripture: Exodus 20:12–17 (God gives the Fourth, Fifth, Sixth, and Ninth Commandments.); Mark 10:5–9 (Jesus teaches there is no divorce in God's plan.)

Disciple Power: temperance (Cardinal Virtue)
Faith Vocabulary: covet, murder
Faith-Filled People: Ruth
Catholics Believe: male and female God created us
The Church Follows Jesus: culture of life
Prayer: Prayer of St. Francis of Assisi
Catechism of the Catholic Church (CCC):
   2196–2400, 2514–2533
U.S. Catholic Catechism for Adults (USCCA):
   pp. 373–416, 439–446

CHAPTER 23—Love of Neighbor
Faith Concepts:
- The Seventh and Tenth Commandments teach us to respect the resources God has provided and the goods belonging to others.
- The Eighth Commandment teaches us that we are to speak the truth and honor the good name of others.
- We all have the obligation to make use of our talents and to use them for the common good.

Sacred Scripture: Exodus 20:15–17 (God gives the Seventh, Eighth, and Tenth Commandments.); Luke 21:3–4 (The poor widow's contribution was generous.)

Disciple Power: generosity (Fruit of the Holy Spirit)
Faith Vocabulary: almsgiving, reparation, stewardship
Faith-Filled People: Saint Paul of Tarsus
Catholics Believe: poverty of heart
The Church Follows Jesus: Venerable Henriette Delille
Prayer: a prayer for peace (Sign Language)
Catechism of the Catholic Church (CCC):
   2401–2513, 2534–2557
U.S. Catholic Catechism for Adults (USCCA):
   pp. 417–438, 447–457

CHAPTER 24—The Summary of the Gospel
Faith Concepts:
- The Lord's Prayer is a prayer of all Christians
- The Lord's Prayer teaches us how to live the Gospel.
- Traditionally there are three forms of prayer: vocal prayer, prayers of meditation, and contemplation.

Sacred Scripture: Psalm 33:20–22 (Hope in the Lord); Matthew 6:9–13 (Jesus teaches the Our Father.); John 12:27–28 (Jesus' prayer in the Garden of Gethsemane)

Disciple Power: hope (Theological Virtue)
Faith Vocabulary: adoration, contemplation, meditation
Faith-Filled People: Sarah
Catholics Believe: ecumenism
The Church Follows Jesus: Saint Hildegard of Bingen
Prayer: The Lord's Prayer
Catechism of the Catholic Church (CCC): 2558–2865
U.S. Catholic Catechism for Adults (USCCA): pp. 461–495

WE CELEBRATE THE CHURCH YEAR

See the Table of Contents for a listing of the lesson titles.

Be My Disciples

Peter M. Esposito
President

Jo Rotunno, MA
Publisher

Susan Smith
Director of Project Development

Program Advisors
Michael P. Horan, PhD
Elizabeth Nagel, SSD

GRADE SIX
PARISH EDITION

Contents

4

5

Welcome to Be My ✝ Disciples

God's Plan of Salvation

Just as the story of your life happens over time, so has the story of God's love for his people unfolded in history. This year you will learn many new things about God and the story of his people. Complete the activities below and on the next page to see what you already know, and to find out the kinds of things you will learn this year.

1. We Believe, Part One

God revealed himself as a Triune God. Who are the Three Persons of the Trinity? God the __Father__, God the __Son__, and God the __Holy Spirit__

Look on page 30 to check your answer.

2. We Believe, Part Two

This year in Unit 2 you will learn about Jesus' Passion, Death, and Resurrection. What is another name for Jesus' passion, Death, and Resurrection? __The Paschal Mystery__

Look on page 57 to check your answer.

6

Welcome

To the Catechist

Creating an inviting environment is an important part of everything you do with the students. Before your first meeting, prepare name tags for them. Greet each student as they arrive. This will help them feel safe and ready to learn. This first session provides the opportunity for you to get to know the group. By setting realistic expectations, introducing them to their new books, and creating an atmosphere of prayer and hospitality, they will know they are welcome.

Invite

Give each child a name tag with their name on it. You can find additional introduction activities at www.BeMyDisciples.com.

Discover and Involve

▶ Introduce the book and allow the students to look through it and find a favorite picture.

▶ Have them share their favorite picture with the child beside them.

Involve

▶ Read the activity to the group. Have them turn to the page to complete the sentence for each unit.

▶ Have them find the name of the season when the Church celebrates that Jesus was raised from the dead. *(Easter)*

▶ Ask the children to work together in pairs to discover the most important celebration of the Church. *(Easter)*

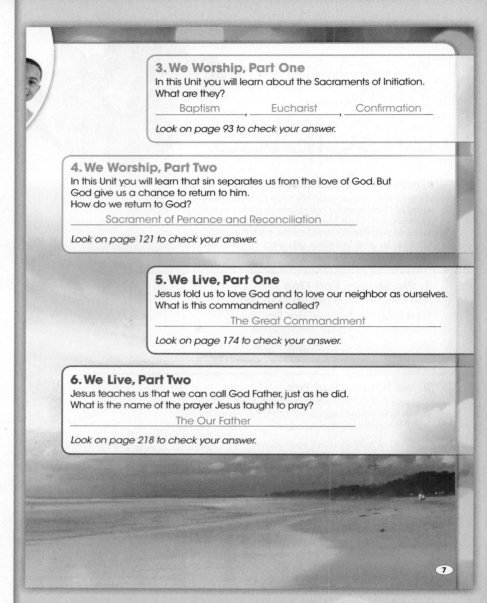

3. We Worship, Part One
In this Unit you will learn about the Sacraments of Initiation. What are they?

_____Baptism_____ , _____Eucharist_____ _____Confirmation_____

Look on page 93 to check your answer.

4. We Worship, Part Two
In this Unit you will learn that sin separates us from the love of God. But God give us a chance to return to him.
How do we return to God?

_____Sacrament of Penance and Reconciliation_____

Look on page 121 to check your answer.

5. We Live, Part One
Jesus told us to love God and to love our neighbor as ourselves. What is this commandment called?

_____The Great Commandment_____

Look on page 174 to check your answer.

6. We Live, Part Two
Jesus teaches us that we can call God Father, just as he did. What is the name of the prayer Jesus taught to pray?

_____The Our Father_____

Look on page 218 to check your answer.

7

To Bring Glad Tidings

The leader walks at the head of the procession to the prayer space, holding the Bible high for all to see.

Leader: Lord, we gather today to honor the gift
Of your Word. We remember your love
for us and that you are always with us.

All: **We praise you, O Lord.**

Leader: The Lord be with you.

All: **And with your spirit.**

Leader: A reading from the holy Gospel according to Luke.

All: **Glory to you, O Lord.**

Leader: [Jesus] unrolled the scroll [of the prophet Isaiah]
And found the passage where it was written:

"The Spirit of the Lord is upon me,
because he has anointed me
to bring glad tidings to the poor.
He has sent me to proclaim liberty to captives
And recovery of sight to the blind,
To let the oppressed go free,
And to proclaim a year acceptable to the Lord."

The Gospel of the Lord.

All: **Praise to you, Lord Jesus Christ.**

BASED ON PSALM LUKE 4:17-19

* All come forward and reverence the Bible.

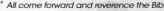

Pray

▶ Invite the students to prepare for prayer. Reverently hold a Bible slightly above your head and lead them in procession to the prayer space.

▶ After a moment of silence, lead the class in praying To Bring Glad Tidings. Use a hand gesture to invite the students to join in when you want them to pray their parts of the prayer.

▶ After the prayer, place the Bible on the prayer table and reverence the Bible by standing before it and slightly bowing your head. Invite each student to come forward and do the same.

▶ Thank the students for being good learners and remind them to have a good week.

TEACHING TIP

Creating a Prayer Space. Having a prayer space that is decorated in a special way will help the children realize the importance of prayer. Display the Bible in your prayer space in such a way that shows its importance. Talk about respecting the Bible. Always hold the Bible reverently when you proclaim God's word. Before you pray together, allow a moment of quiet time and share with the group that God is with them.

We Believe
Part One

Objectives

In this unit the students will learn that:

▶ Faith is the gift from God to believe in him, and the grace to respond freely to that gift by knowing, loving and serving him

▶ Through the Bible, God reveals himself and his loving plan of salvation for the world and all people

▶ God has revealed himself to be the mystery of one God in three Divine Persons

▶ Jesus Christ, the Son of God, taught us that God is our loving Father

Spiritual Insights

God makes himself known to us through Revelation in order to both give us something and to draw a response from us. Both this gift of God and our response to his Revelation are called faith. By faith, we are able to give our minds and hearts to God, to trust in his will, and to follow the direction he gives us" (*United States Catholic Catechism for Adults* Washington, D.C.: USCCB, 2006).

"It is impossible for us not to speak about what we have seen and heard" (Acts 4:20).

Living the Six Tasks of Catechesis

Promoting Knowledge of the Faith: Saint Robert Bellarmine (1542–1621)

Even as a young boy in Italy, Robert felt called to serve God as a priest. After years of study, he was ordained a Jesuit priest. His first assignment was teaching Greek at a boys' school. Robert was successful only because he first taught himself the language by staying one lesson ahead of his students in the textbook.

Robert had a gift for preaching. People traveled great distances to hear him explain the Scriptures and to defend the faith during the challenges of the Reformation. He also wrote two catechisms to help people grow in their understanding of the Catholic doctrine. Although he became a bishop and then a cardinal, he never lost his thirst for learning and teaching.

Cardinal Bellarmine lived a very simple life, even when he lived in a lavish apartment in the Vatican while serving as the Pope's official theologian. It is said that he took down the hangings that decorated his walls and donated the fabric to clothe the poor. When he was quizzed about his empty walls, he showed his sense of humor by declaring, "The walls won't catch cold."

Saint Robert Bellarmine is an excellent model for catechists. His life encourages us to know our faith well so that we can share it with our learners. He reminds us to be proud of our calling to profess our faith in Jesus and the Church.

Sharing Your Faith

Find a partner to work with: a spouse, a friend, a fellow catechist. Come together at the beginning or end of each unit for shared prayer and discussion. Use the questions below as a starting point. As an alternative, record your thoughts in a personal journal.

▶ What three words describe your journey of faith?

▶ How has God made himself known to you?

▶ What prompted you to become a catechist?

We Believe
UNIT 1
Part One

God Calls Abraham

The Lord called Abraham:
"Go forth from your home
  to a land I will show you.
I will make you a great nation,
  and I will bless you.
I will make your name great,
  so that you will be a blessing.
All nations shall find blessing in you."

Abraham did as the Lord said. He took his wife Sarah, his nephew Lot, and all their possessions. They set out for the land of Canaan. When they got there, others were living there. But God said, "I will give this land to those who will be descended from you."

BASED ON GENESIS 12:1–7

9

What I Have Learned
What is something you already know about these faith concepts?

Divine Revelation
_____
_____
_____

The Covenant
_____
_____

God the Father
_____
_____

Faith Terms to Know
Put an X next to the faith terms you know. Put a ? next to faith terms you need to learn more about.

_____ faith

_____ creed

_____ canon

_____ inspiration

_____ original holiness

_____ Redemption

_____ Original Sin

_____ temptation

The Bible
What do you know about the two accounts of creation in Genesis?
_____
_____
_____

The Church
What would you like to know about the creed we say at Mass?
_____
_____
_____

Questions I Have
What questions would you like to ask about the mystery of God?
_____
_____
_____

10

Unit 1 Opener

The Unit 1 opener pages assess the young people's prior knowledge about the key faith concepts in the unit. Processing these pages should take no more than fifteen minutes.

Opening Page

Invite the students to tell you what they see in the image on the page. Proclaim the Scripture story, God Calls Abraham. Ask: "How hard would it be to leave for an unknown place as Abraham did? What did Abraham receive for God as a result of his faith?" Facilitate a discussion, but do not respond to their answers at this time.

Getting Ready

▶ Invite the young people to write their responses to the questions and directions under What I Have Learned, Faith Terms to Know, and the other headings in the second column.

▶ Invite a few volunteers to share their responses, but do not correct them at this time. Tell the students that they will return to this page to check their learning at the end of the unit.

▶ For Questions I Have, you might write their questions on the board or on a piece of newsprint so that you can refer to them when the topics come up in the unit.

▶ Ask the class to look at the next page and begin Chapter 1.

The Gift of Faith

The Divine Invitation to Faith

Think about this: God the Father has created us, addresses us as his children, and moves among us; he has revealed himself to us, given us access to him through his Son, and invites us to share in his life. And if that isn't enough, God the Son freely sacrifices his bodily life for our Salvation, calls himself our friend and servant; God the Holy Spirit is our constant companion, our helper and Advocate.

Invitation to a Life of Faith

How do we respond to such an extraordinary and loving God? Our primary response is faith. This faith is exemplified in Mary's response to God the Father's invitation to be the Mother of his Son, Jesus: "May it be done to me according to your word" (Luke 1:38).

Faith is saying, "Yes, I do believe. Do with me as you will." Faith is our willingness to believe that God first loves us. This faith is a willingness to give our lives and will to his divine care. Faith implies obedience, that is, a desire to hear and listen to God and trust in his divine Providence. Faith implies a relationship characterized by trust in the One who has shown himself constant in love, true to his word, and trustworthy in his care for us.

Our faith in God the Father, the Son, and the Holy Spirit is not something we can possess, much less sustain, without his invitation and grace to respond freely to that invitation. Here is the challenging part: God does not force us to believe in him. He does not coerce us to submit to his loving will. God's grace empowers us to freely choose to respond, with a truly human freedom, to his invitation.

The Free Human Response of Faith

God desires our cooperation; thus, faith is a very human act. We are free to say no to him and reject his invitation and grace. We can first believe and then lose our faith, which tells us that faith requires work on our part. Like the gifts of our intellect or our physical strength, faith requires exercise and proper nourishment.

Growing in faith is a very vital to our life. Think about it. What do our human dignity, our Salvation, our being one with God, our charitable activity and our wisdom depend upon? The answer is always "the graced response of faith." Responding to God's invitation to be part of our lives and cooperating with the grace that he lavishes upon us is faith in action. The world will consistently test our faith. By holding steadfastly to our faith in God we will emerge as stronger, more loving and life-giving members of the Church and of the human family.

For Reflection

When has my faith been the strongest and the weakest?

What trials have severely tested my belief and trust in God?

Catechist to Catechist

Faith Sharing

The sharing of faith is a holy moment. Saint Paul tells us that faith comes from hearing. When you share your faith, you celebrate God's presence in your life. You show the importance of faith and the difference faith can make in your life. God is at work in many ways during your time with the students. As they listen to you and watch you, as they interact with you and with one another, God is at work leading each one of you to a deeper love for him. Trust in that presence as you share faith with the students this year.

A Daily Faith

Share with the students the importance of your own faith in your daily life. Remember to keep your faith stories simple and appropriate. Use the faith vocabulary that the students are learning. This will help them put "flesh and blood" on the faith concepts that they are learning and make connections between those concepts and their own lives. Be sure to invite the students to share ways that faith is important for their own lives. Always respect their need for confidentiality and their desire not to share what is personal to them.

The Church Teaches...

[The Christian faith] is the fruit of God's grace and the free response to the prompting of the Holy Spirit. It raises from the depths of the human person and involves such a profound transformation of heart and mind that it causes the believer to change radically both internally and externally (*National Directory for Catechesis*, 17B).

By approaching religious studies as a mystery to unravel, you can use each chapter to elicit excitement in the children and help them build an enduring relationship with God. In this chapter, the children will learn how our response to God's invitation to know and believe in him is the gift of faith. Encourage them to seek the promptings of the Holy Spirit to open their hearts and minds to his Word.

Further Reading and Reflection

For more on the teachings of the Catholic Church on the gift of faith, see *Catechism of the Catholic Church*, 26–49, 142–197; and the *United States Catholic Catechism for Adults*, pages 2–9, 36–47.

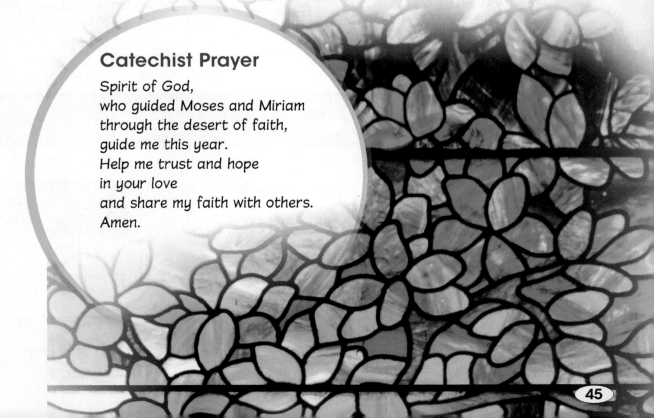

Catechist Prayer

Spirit of God,
who guided Moses and Miriam
through the desert of faith,
guide me this year.
Help me trust and hope
in your love
and share my faith with others.
Amen.

Lesson Planner

Chapter 1 The Gift of Faith

Focus To discover how we can grow in our faith in God

LESSON PART	PROCESS	MATERIALS and RESOURCES
EXPLORE **Focus** To explore a psalm as a response to God's invitation to faith ⏱ 10 minutes **Pages** 11–12	▶ Proclaim and discuss Psalm 148:7–13 (Praise the Lord from the earth). ▶ Share the story of World Youth Day. **Disciple Power:** Perseverance **Activity:** Name ways parish youth celebrate, grow in, and live their faith.	Bible Pencils
DISCOVER **Focus** To discover ways to grow in faith and to express our faith ⏱ 30 minutes **Pages** 13–15	▶ Explore ways to respond and grow in faith. ▶ Learn the relationship between belief and trust. ▶ Distinguish between the Apostles' Creed and the Nicene Creed. **Activities:** Choose ways for the Apostles' Creed.	Journals or notebooks, one per student (optional) Crayons or markers **Additional Activities Booklet:** Activities 1a–1b, or see BeMyDisciples.com.
DECIDE **Focus** To decide on a way to express faith in God through words and actions ⏱ 10 minutes **Page** 16	**Activity:** Identify people who help us grow in faith. **My Faith Choice:** Choose ways to profess faith in God through words and actions.	**Enriching the Lesson Activities:** Catechist Edition, page 55 • Creating Bookmarks • Honoring God's Word • Living Our Faith

Concluding the Lesson   10 minutes

We Remember	We Pray	Preview
Page 17 ▶ Review concepts and do the review activity. ▶ **Assessment Tools Booklet:** Chapter Test 1a–1b, or see BeMyDisciples.com.	▶ **Prayer:** a profession of faith **Materials:** Bible, candle, cross for prayer space ▶ Grade 6 Music CD	Point out resources for this chapter at **www.BeMyDisciples.com** ▶ Preview the With My Family page and next week's lesson theme.

Looking Ahead

In this chapter the Holy Spirit invites you to ▶

EXPLORE how Catholic youth around the world respond to the gift of faith.

DISCOVER that the gift of faith involves trusting in God's love.

DECIDE how you will profess your faith in word and in action.

CHAPTER **1**

The Gift of Faith

[?] We get to know a person gradually. How did you get to know your best friend?

God has made himself known to us in many ways. Read and think about these words:

Praise the LORD from the earth,
   you sea monsters and all deep waters . . .
You mountains and all hills,
   fruit trees and all cedars;
You animals wild and tame,
   you creatures that crawl and fly . . .
Young men and women too,
   old and young alike.
Let them all praise the LORD's name,
   for his name alone is exalted,
   majestic above earth and heaven.   PSALM 148: 7–13

[?] How can viewing a scenic landscape help you to know more about God?

(11)

HUMAN METHODOLOGIES

Learning by Heart. The *National Directory for Catechesis* explains that memorization of the basic formulas of the faith helps to develop a unified prayer and faith vocabulary among the People of God (*see NDC* 29F). In this chapter, the students will learn about both the Apostles' Creed and the Nicene Creed, which is usually prayed at Mass. The students may confuse the wording of the Apostles' Creed with that of the Nicene Creed. Encourage your students to memorize the Apostles' Creed and pray it frequently as a class. This will help them differentiate between the two creeds. You will find the full wording of the two creeds in the back of the student text in "Catholic Prayers and Practices."

Pray

▶ Gather the students for prayer. Remind them that they are in the presence of God. Begin and end with the Sign of the Cross.

▶ Begin with a prayer of spontaneous petitions for family and friends. After each petition, invite the children to respond, "Lord, hear our prayer."

Reflect

▶ Ask the students to respond to the question at the top of the page.

▶ Use the opening paragraph to introduced the Scripture passage. Have the students take a moment of silence and quietly read Psalm 148:7–13.

▶ Then use the follow-up question to dialogue with the students about their impression of the psalm they just read.

▶ Point out that the faith of the psalmist allows him to recognize God in the world around him and to offer praise and thanks.

Focus

▶ Use the Looking Ahead box to forecast the lesson content.

▶ Tell the children that on the next page they will learn how some young people have expressed their faith.

Introduce

▶ Invite the students to read World Youth Day to discover more about this event.

▶ If you have Internet access review with students the latest World Youth Day Web site to discover the logo, slogan, and themes. Ask the students about the appeal and effectiveness of such a gathering.

▶ Read Disciple Power. Have students suggest reasons why people today can benefit from practicing this virtue.

Reinforce

Point out that one way in which the Word of God is constantly in our lives is through events like World Youth Day.

Connect

▶ Have volunteers share what it means to them when a friend shares their faith with them.

▶ Discuss some ways that your parish brings or can bring youth together to celebrate and grow in the Catholic faith. Complete the activity on the page.

▶ Ask volunteers to compare their responses.

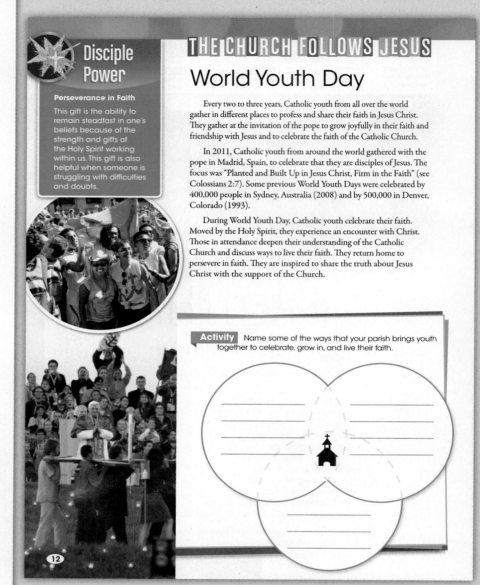

Disciple Power

Perseverance in Faith

This gift is the ability to remain steadfast in one's beliefs because of the strength and gifts of the Holy Spirit working within us. This gift is also helpful when someone is struggling with difficulties and doubts.

THE CHURCH FOLLOWS JESUS
World Youth Day

Every two to three years, Catholic youth from all over the world gather in different places to profess and share their faith in Jesus Christ. They gather at the invitation of the pope to grow joyfully in their faith and friendship with Jesus and to celebrate the faith of the Catholic Church.

In 2011, Catholic youth from around the world gathered with the pope in Madrid, Spain, to celebrate that they are disciples of Jesus. The focus was "Planted and Built Up in Jesus Christ, Firm in the Faith" (see Colossians 2:7). Some previous World Youth Days were celebrated by 400,000 people in Sydney, Australia (2008) and by 500,000 in Denver, Colorado (1993).

During World Youth Day, Catholic youth celebrate their faith. Moved by the Holy Spirit, they experience an encounter with Christ. Those in attendance deepen their understanding of the Catholic Church and discuss ways to live their faith. They return home to persevere in faith. They are inspired to share the truth about Jesus Christ with the support of the Church.

Activity Name some of the ways that your parish brings youth together to celebrate, grow in, and live their faith.

DISCIPLE POWER

Perseverance in Faith. Whether one is participating at Mass or involved in various parish-sponsored activities, it is sometimes easier to express our faith when we are actively involved in the Church. In everyday life, too, it is easier to remain faithful to God's Word and to God's commands when our family members, classmates, and friends are people of faith.

✳ Ask students to make a list of the people who are a part of their lives at home, school, and through their extracurricular activities. Have them circle the names of those whom they consider to be people of faith, and invite them to explain their choices.

Growing in Faith

God places his Word in our hearts. He plants his love deep in our souls. Jeremiah the Prophet shared this truth about God and us when he wrote:

[God said:] "I will give them a heart with which to understand that I am the Lord." JEREMIAH 24:7

Whether we are happy or sad, successful or in trouble, God is always with us and speaking to us. His Word within us acts like the sun to light up our days and like the moon to help us see at night. God's Word within us is his grace. The grace of God helps us to recognize and to accept his love. Our challenge is to respond and grow in faith.

Here are some ways to help us respond and grow in faith:

1. **Pray to the Holy Spirit.** The Holy Spirit lives in our hearts and gives us the power to call God "Abba, Father."

2. **Personally know Jesus Christ, the Incarnate Word of God.** Faith in Jesus Christ, the only Son of God and our Lord, is necessary for salvation. Everything God wants to say to us is revealed through Jesus Christ.

3. **Study the Bible, the inspired Word of God.** We can better understand who God is by reading his Divine Revelation in Sacred Scripture.

4. **Learn the teachings of the Church.** Sacred Tradition and Sacred Scripture are sources of the Word of God. Together they are like a mirror in which the Church looks and contemplates God.

5. **Listen to the pope, the bishop in your diocese, and the priests in your parish.** Through their writings, speeches, and homilies, they teach us in the name of Christ to help us understand God's Revelation more clearly and live it in practical ways.

? What ways have you responded to God's invitation to grow in faith?

FAITH FOCUS
How can you persevere and grow in your faith?

FAITH VOCABULARY
creed
A creed is a statement of beliefs, a profession of faith, a summary of the principal beliefs of the Church.

faith
Faith is one of the three Theological Virtues. It is the gift of God's invitation to us that enables us to know and believe in him, and the power God gives us to respond freely to his invitation.

[handwritten notes: faith / hope / Love/charity]

Key Concept
God's grace helps us grow in faith and love of God.

Teach

▶ Ask a student to read aloud the Faith Focus question. Then invite all students to think about how they might respond.

▶ Paraphrase the introductory paragraph, and read the Scripture passage from Jeremiah.

▶ Invite students to share what Jeremiah's passage means to them.

▶ Paraphrase the next paragraph and then have the students silently read the rest of the text on the page to learn ways in which we can grow in faith.

▶ Call attention to he definition of *faith* in Faith Vocabulary. Recall the three Theological Virtues of faith, hope, and charity.

Connect

Ask the students to select one of the five ways listed and to discuss with a partner how they could grow in that way.

TEACHING TIP

Providing Options for Assignments. Try to meet the needs of all students. Assignments that give them some influence over the outcome can be highly motivating. Provide activities for the students that give them options. For example, instead of having them write down responses and ideas, give them the option to act out their ideas, draw a picture, or share their responses with a partner.

Provide opportunities for quiet reflection or journaling. Encourage students to journal their faith using various media: writing in a private notebook, blogging online, or digital scrapbooking. Vary large and small group activities to include techniques such as Scripture searches, research, use of charts and graphs, and interviews.

Key Concept
God calls us to accept the
gift of faith and trust in him.

Teach

▶ Tell the students to listen for words about faith as volunteers read The Gift of Faith.

▶ Remind students that Scripture includes many stories about people of faith. Have students brainstorm, naming people in history who are models of faith. Discuss what they do and say that reflects their faith.

▶ Refer to Faith-Filled People. Share additional facts about Miriam from the box on this page.

Reinforce

▶ Discuss responses to the first question. Remind students that although God places his Word within us, we are free to accept or reject it. *free will*

▶ Emphasize that Jesus shows us how to grow in faith and in the love of God.

Connect

Give the students time to think about the last questions on the page. Ask volunteers to share responses.

Faith-Filled People

Miriam

Miriam the Prophet was the sister of Moses and Aaron. After the Israelites crossed the Red Sea during the Exodus, Miriam gathered the women of Israel. With tambourine in hand, she led the women in song and dance as she sang, "Sing to the Lord, for he is gloriously triumphant" (Exodus 15:21).

The Gift of Faith

Faith is a supernatural gift, meaning a gift from God. It is one of the three Theological Virtues, which are **faith,** hope, and charity. Faith is not something that we can earn or deserve. We cannot achieve a deep faith through only our own efforts. We need the grace, or help, of the Holy Spirit. We must pray for his grace to truly know God and respond to his love. This kind of faith is not easy or automatic.

God created us with a desire for him in our hearts. God also gave us the freedom to choose or reject him and his love. Accepting the gift of faith often seems difficult; however, God gives us his grace to encourage and strengthen us. God's grace helps us to persevere, or remain strong, in our faith. We can grow in faith by learning more about God. We can also choose to accept his love by living a Christian life. Ultimately, God calls us to accept the gift of faith by opening our hearts and minds to live according to his will.

? Why did God place his Word in your heart?

Trust in God   *belief vs. trust?*

Believing in God relates to trusting God. Jesus revealed that God is our Father who created us out of love, for love, and to be loved. In his love, God reveals himself to us as Father, Son, and Holy Spirit. God knows everything about us and knows our needs before we do. He wants only what is best for us.

The Gospel tells us that Jesus' whole life on Earth showed us that God wants our happiness. Our happiness is ultimately found in God. He created us to live in communion with him now on Earth and forever in Heaven. God gave us the Church to help and support us in our journey of faith.

? Describe someone whom you trust who has helped you grow in faith. What did this person do to help you? How did you respond?

FAITH-FILLED PEOPLE

Miriam, the Sister of Moses. The Book of Exodus describes Miriam, the sister of Moses and Aaron, as a prophet leading the Hebrews in worship. "The prophetess Miriam, Aaron's sister, took a tambourine in her hand, while all the women went out after her with tambourines, dancing; and she led them in the refrain: /Sing to the LORD, for he is gloriously triumphant; /horse and chariot he has cast into the sea" (Exodus 15: 20–21). The word *prophecy*, the highest form of authoritative speech in the Old Testament, was used to personify Miriam as a spokesperson for God. A woman of faith, Miriam modeled for others faith and trust in the Lord.

Professing Our Faith

From the beginning, the Church has proudly proclaimed her faith in God in the form of a **creed**. A creed includes the language of the faith as a heartfelt expression of the Church's faith. As members of the Church, we profess our faith together through statements of faith in a creed. We celebrate and pass on the Word of God alive in our hearts and minds. The Apostles' Creed and the Nicene Creed are the two main creeds of the Church.

The Apostles' Creed is one of the earliest creeds of the Church. It is divided into three parts:

- The first part professes our faith in God the Father, who created all that exists, Heaven and Earth.

- The second part professes our faith in God the Son, Jesus Christ, who redeemed humanity from the eternal death of sin.

- The third part professes our faith in God the Holy Spirit and speaks of our sanctification. Our sanctification is the gift of sharing in God's life and love. This is possible by growing in friendship with God.

The Nicene Creed is more detailed than the Apostles' Creed, yet both equally express the faith of the Church. When we proclaim the Nicene Creed, we offer our hearts in faith to God, the Holy Trinity. Because we profess the Nicene Creed together as the Body of Christ, we unite ourselves with Christians throughout the world.

Each time that we profess our faith, God seals in our hearts the gift of faith. This seal is a symbol of our faith and a reminder of God's love in our lives.

Catholics Believe

Nicene Creed

The Nicene Creed is the creed we usually profess at Mass on Sundays. This creed was written by the Church at the Council of Nicaea in A.D. 325 and the Council of Constantinople in A.D. 381. The Nicene Creed clearly states that the Father, Son, and Holy Spirit are one God in three Divine Persons. Jesus Christ is true God and true man and is equally God as the Father is God.

Activity In the circles, draw a symbol for each part of the Apostles' Creed. Tell partner how the symbol relates to that part of the Creed.

Father

Son

Holy Spirit

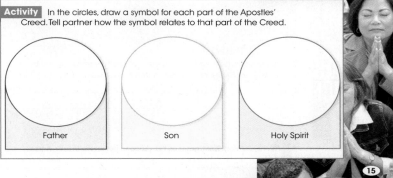

15

CATHOLICS BELIEVE

The Creeds of the Church. The Church's earliest profession of faith was "Jesus is Lord." The first ecumenical council of the Church was held at Nicaea, in what is now Turkey, in A.D. 325. At Nicaea, the Church affirmed the apostolic teaching that Jesus Christ is true God and true man. This teaching about Jesus was further affirmed at the First Council of Constantinople in A.D. 381 and Chalcedon in A.D. 451. The Nicene Creed that we pray at Mass is based on the teachings of these councils.

Teach

- Ask a student to read aloud the first paragraph of Professing Our Faith.

- Read aloud Catholics Believe. Explain that a creed is a statement of faith and reminds a person of faith how their actions are to follow what they believe.

- Invite volunteers to the sections about the Apostles' and Nicene Creeds.

Reinforce

Reinforce that both the Nicene Creed and the Apostles' Creed are a summary of the faith of the Church. By praying the creed, we unite ourselves together as the Church throughout the world.

Connect

- Explain that each time we profess our faith, God seals in our hearts the gift of faith.

- Have the students complete the activity on the page. Then invite volunteers to share their responses with the class.

- Encourage the students to pray the Apostles' Creed every day this week.

Reinforce

Remind the students that the Holy Spirit always helps them to live the gift of faith.

Respond

Introduce the activity and allow the students time to complete it. Ask several volunteers to share their responses.

Choose

▶ Have students individually complete the My Faith Choice section on the page.

▶ Ask the students to pray silently the short prayer to the Holy Spirit.

I FOLLOW JESUS

Jesus promised the disciples that he and the Father would send the Holy Spirit to be our teacher and helper. You received the gift of the Holy Spirit at Baptism. The Holy Spirit continuously invites you to grow in your faith and friendship with God. The Holy Spirit helps you to persevere and to live the gift of faith with all of your heart, mind, and spirit.

I BELIEVE IN GOD

Read the full text of the Apostles' Creed on page 258. Then write a short reflection about your faith in God the Father, God the Son, and God the Holy Spirit.

I Believe in God

1. _____
_____
_____

2. _____
_____
_____

3. _____
_____
_____

MY FAITH CHOICE

I profess my faith in God the Holy Trinity each day both by my words and by my actions. This week I will profess my faith in God through words and actions. I will

_____
_____

Pray, "O Holy Spirit, grant us the grace to persevere in faith. Amen."

16

THE TASKS OF CATECHESIS

Liturgical Education. During the liturgical season of Lent, the elect (those preparing to celebrate the Sacraments of Christian Initiation at the Easter Vigil) receive the Creed. Explain this rite to the young people: At Sunday Mass the elect are called forward to stand and face the assembly of the baptized. The assembly then presents the Creed to the elect by professing it aloud. The Creed is one of two prayers that the elect receive during the liturgical season of Lent. The other is the Lord's Prayer. They are among the most ancient formulations of the Church.

Chapter Review

Match each term in column A with its definition in column B.

Column A

_A_ **1.** faith

_E_ **2.** Holy Trinity

_D_ **3.** Nicene Creed

_C_ **4.** redemption

_B_ **5.** sanctification

Column B

a. our acceptance of God and our willingness to receive his Revelation

b. the gift of sharing in God's life and love

c. the saving activity of God through Christ, delivering humanity from the eternal death of sin

d. a summary of the principal beliefs of the Church that we profess at Mass

e. the mystery of one God in three Divine Persons

TO HELP YOU REMEMBER

1. God placed in our hearts a desire to know, love, and serve him.

2. Jesus' whole life on Earth invited us to have faith in God. Faith is the gift from God to believe in him, and the grace to respond freely to that gift.

3. The creeds of the Church are both a profession and a summary of the Church's faith in God.

We Believe in God

At Baptism, we first profess our faith in God with the Church. Pray this profession of faith, which is taken from the Rite of Baptism.

Leader: Let us profess our faith. Do you reject sin so as to live in the freedom of God's children?

All: I do.

Leader: Do you reject the glamour of evil and refuse to be mastered by sin?

All: I do.

Leader: Do you reject Satan, father of sin and prince of darkness?

All: I do.

Leader: Do you believe in God the Father?

All: I do.

Leader: Do you believe in Jesus Christ, his only Son, our Lord?

All: I do.

Leader: Do you believe in the Holy Spirit?

All: I do.

Leader: This is our faith. This is the faith of the Church. We are proud to profess it, in Christ Jesus our Lord.

BASED ON THE "PROFESSION OF FAITH," RITE OF BAPTISM

(17)

LITURGY CONNECTION

Renewal of Baptismal Promises. The renewal of baptismal promises or making a profession of faith is an ancient tradition of the Church. Today, we continue that tradition at Easter liturgies. We also renew our baptismal promises and profess our faith as part of the Rite of Confirmation and on other occasions, such as at the close of a parish mission. Remind the students that when they renew their baptismal promises and profess their faith in the closing prayer, they are also renewing their faith in Christ and their promise to live their Baptism.

We Remember

▶ Have the students close their books and write on a piece of paper three important things that they learned from this chapter.

▶ Invite the students to open their books and compare what they wrote with summary list, To Help You Remember.

▶ Have all students complete the Chapter Review activity. Then review the answers as a class.

We Pray

▶ Gather the students to conclude the chapter with prayer.

▶ Explain that in the prayer today they will renew the promises and profession of faith that they made or their parents and godparents made for them at Baptism.

▶ Ask the students to quiet themselves for prayer.

▶ After a moment of prayerful silence, lead the students in praying the closing prayer.

Preview

▶ Have students carefully tear out the With My Family page along the perforation.

▶ Encourage them to share the pages with their family and to complete the activities together at home.

▶ If the students did not complete the chapter review, encourage them to complete it with their family.

▶ Point out the title and theme of next week's chapter to the children.

Visit www.BeMyDisciples.com

▶ Take time with the students to explore the many activities and resources available at the Web site, **www.BeMyDisciples.com.**

▶ Encourage them especially to visit it with their families during the week.

Before Moving On ...

As you finish today's lesson, reflect on the following question before moving on to the next chapter.

How have I created an atmosphere of trust in my classroom?

With My Family

This Week...

In chapter 1, The Gift of Faith, your child learned:

▶ God invites us to know him and believe in him. God invites us to make him the center of our lives and to discover the experience and meaning of true happiness.

▶ The whole life of Jesus Christ on Earth most clearly and fully reveals that divine invitation. God created us to know, love, and serve him and to be happy with him now on Earth and forever in Heaven.

▶ The Apostles' Creed and the Nicene Creed are the two principal creeds of the Church.

▶ The virtue of perseverance strengthens us to remain strong and steadfast in our faith.

For more about related teachings of the Church, see the *Catechism of the Catholic Church,* 26–49, 142–197; and the *United States Catholic Catechism for Adults,* pages 2–9, 36–47.

▨ Sharing God's Word

Read together Jeremiah 24:7. Emphasize that God created us and his Word is alive in our hearts and his love deep in our souls.

▨ We Live as Disciples

The Christian home and family is a school of discipleship. Choose one of the following activities to do as a family, or design a similar activity of your own:

▶ Make a puzzle to help your child learn the Apostles' Creed by heart. Write the words of the Creed on a piece of paper. Then cut the paper into pieces, and together assemble the puzzle pieces.

▶ Share ideas on ways that your family shows that God is at the center of the life of your family. Discuss how family members are signs to others that they are disciples of Christ.

▶ Visit BeMyDisciples.com. Look up the profiles of several martyrs of the Church. Discuss how they persevered in their faith, even to freely suffering death for their faith.

▨ Our Spiritual Journey

In this chapter, your child prayed a profession of faith based on the "Profession of Faith" in the Rite of Baptism. Read and pray together this prayer on page 17.

For more ideas on ways your family can live as disciples of Jesus, visit **www.BeMyDisciples.com**

18

PARTNERING WITH PARENTS

The Word of God. In your communication with parents, share with them that the Word of God is an important part of their child's faith formation. Emphasize that reading the Bible together as a family further reinforces the importance of God's Word in the life of the Christian. Point out that a good place to begin is by reading together the Gospel for the upcoming Sunday. Encourage parents to go to www.BeMyDisciples.com and click on Gospel Reflections for a list of the upcoming Sunday Gospel readings and related family-appropriate reflection and discussion questions. They can also find a "Question of the Week" related to the Sunday readings and a link to the text for the readings.

Enriching the Lesson

Creating Bookmarks

Purpose

To reinforce that everything God wants to say to us can be found in Jesus Christ (taught on page 13)

Directions

Point out that John's Gospel gives us several "I am" images to help us express our faith in Jesus. For example: "I am the bread of life" (John 6:35), "I am the light of the world" (John 8:12), "I am the good shepherd" (John10:11), "I am the gate" (John 10:9), "I am the resurrection" (John 11:25), "I am the way and the truth and the life" (John 14:6), "I am the true vine" (John 15:1).

▶ Invite students to look up and read about these images in the Bible and together discuss how each of the images helps us live as Jesus wants us to live.

▶ Have the students design a bookmark for one of the images as a reminder to live as Jesus wants us to live.

Materials

strips of tag board

markers or crayons

Honoring God's Word

Purpose

To reinforce that it is our job to seek out and understand the light of God's Word (taught on page 13)

Directions

▶ Have the students work in small groups to conduct discussions on the challenge of spending time with God's Word in the Scriptures.

▶ Have each member of the panel speak to a truth of the faith of the Church that the Scriptures helped them to understand.

▶ Invite each group to share one interesting way a young person in their group came to understand a truth of their faith through something they learned in the Bible.

Materials

Living Our Faith

Purpose

To reinforce that we need to celebrate our faith with others (taught on page 15)

Directions

Use parish bulletins or other resources to help the students learn more about the ways the parish celebrates and lives its faith.

▶ Brainstorm ways the students can participate in service projects that are already happening in the parish.

▶ Have the students select one project and prepare a checklist of what needs to be accomplished to participate in the project.

▶ Have the young people accept different tasks to make this project a success.

▶ Invite the young people to write a letter to the pastor or an appropriate parishioner sharing their commitment to live their faith by taking part in the project.

Materials

parish bulletins

pens or pencils

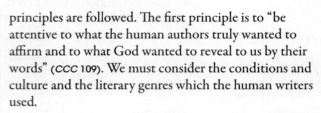

BACKGROUND

The Living Word of God

The words of Scripture are like one long utterance from God, revealing himself and his plan for our Salvation. There may be numerous human authors, but there is only one Holy Spirit inspiring them all.

The Inspired Word of God

The human writers of the Bible used a variety of literary genres, or writing forms, to communicate faithfully God's word. They employed poetry, songs, narration, allegory, storytelling, prophecy, and proverbs to convey God's own word to us.

Using their own historical and cultural situations, the inspired human writers of the Bible conveyed the stunning reality of our heavenly Father lovingly meeting his children and talking with them. Faith tells us that

> all that the inspired authors, or sacred writers, . . . affirm should be regarded as affirmed by the Holy Spirit . . . [and] that the books of Scripture, firmly, faithfully and without error, teach that truth which God, for the sake of our salvation, wished to see confided to the sacred Scriptures.
>
> Vatican II, *Dogmatic Constitution on Divine Revelation* [Dei verbum] 11

Understanding God's Word

How do we interpret Scripture? The interpretation of Sacred Scripture is not a private, personal, individualistic task. It is the responsibility of the Church.

> The task of interpreting the Word of God authentically has been entrusted solely to the Magisterium of the Church, that is, to the Pope and to the bishops in communion with him (*Catechism of the Catholic Church* [CCC] 100).

As the Magisterium seeks to interpret the Scriptures under the guidance of the Holy Spirit, certain principles are followed. The first principle is to "be attentive to what the human authors truly wanted to affirm and to what God wanted to reveal to us by their words" (*CCC* 109). We must consider the conditions and culture and the literary genres which the human writers used.

A second and equally important principle is to realize that God is the true author of Sacred Scripture (see Vatican II *Dogmatic Constitution on Divine Revelation* [Dei verbum] 12). What this means is that we need to be attentive to the unity of Scripture. There are certainly many different books in the Bible, but there is also a unifying theme that unites them. This theme is the unity of God's plan, with Jesus Christ at its heart.

Stay close to Christ and the Holy Spirit and stay close to the Church. For "Sacred Scripture is written principally in the Church's heart rather than in documents and records . . ." (*CCC* 113).

Remember that Christianity is rooted in the Word of the living God, a word not just written, but the Word of God alive and in our midst. We must listen to this living Word with the guidance of the Holy Spirit to allow it to truly come alive in our hearts and lives.

For Reflection

What place does Sacred Scripture have in my faith life?

In what ways do I invite the living Word of God to enter my heart and transform my life?

Catechist to Catechist

God's Ever-Present Love

Continuity and consistency describe the love God has for each of us. God's love is always constant, always faithful. If the Bible reveals anything about him, it is that divine love does not change or alter. God is love. You can count on it.

Consistency and Continuity

Sixth-graders crave continuity and consistency, especially in a world that is often topsy-turvy. The ebb and flow of the catechetical process guides you in providing these qualities during your time with the students.

Take the time to become comfortable with that process. Open with an invitation to listen and respond to the Word of God in prayer. This form of prayer, named *lectio divina*, invites people to place themselves within the Scripture passage, listen to what God's Word is saying to them, connect it to their life experiences and respond. The students will discover the wonderful effects that faith has in the life of the Catholic Church and in their own lives. Conclude as you began, by praying together.

The Church Teaches...

God's Revelation is the self-disclosure of the loving communion of Father, Son, and Holy Spirit in which he makes known the mystery of his divine plan. . . . God's self-communication is realized gradually through his actions and his words. It is most fully achieved in the Word made flesh, Jesus Christ (*National Directory for Catechesis*, 28).

It is so important to help children begin to reflect on their experiences. That is why every chapter begins by helping the children to prayerfully situate the chapter concepts in their own life experience through prayerful reflection on Scripture.

Further Reading and Reflection

For more on the teachings of the Catholic Church on the mystery of Divine Revelation, see *Catechism of the Catholic Church*, 50–73, 101–141; and the *United States Catholic Catechism of Adults*, pages 12–27.

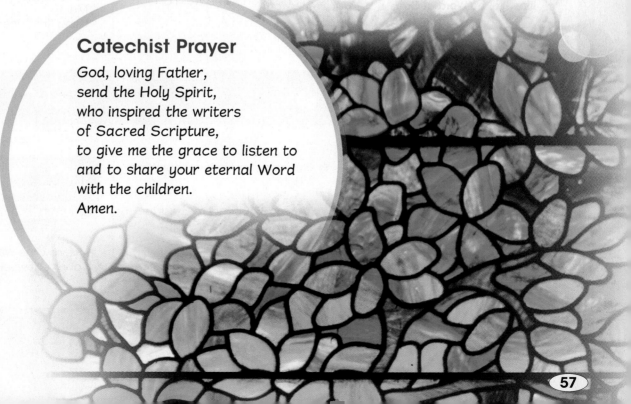

Catechist Prayer

God, loving Father,
send the Holy Spirit,
who inspired the writers
of Sacred Scripture,
to give me the grace to listen to
and to share your eternal Word
with the children.
Amen.

Lesson Planner

Chapter 2 The Word of God

Focus To identify that God has revealed himself and his love for all people through the Bible

LESSON PART	PROCESS	MATERIALS and RESOURCES
EXPLORE **Focus** To explore the power of God's Word 🕐 10 minutes **Pages** 19–20	▶ Proclaim and discuss Psalm 119:105–106, 111–116 (Your word is a lamp for my feet). ▶ Learn the story of the prophet Baruch. **Disciple Power:** Knowledge **Activity:** Describe what images come to mind when you pray to God.	Bible Pencils Crayons or markers
DISCOVER **Focus** To discover that the Bible is the inspired Word of God in which he reveals himself and his love for his people 🕐 30 minutes **Pages** 21–23	▶ Learn about God's names in the Scriptures. ▶ Explore the contents of the Old and New Testaments. ▶ Review the story of the Covenant. **Activity:** Complete a Scripture Search about the Covenant.	Journals Bibles for each student Crayons or markers **Additional Activities Booklet:** Activities 2a–2b, or see BeMyDisciples.com.
DECIDE **Focus** To decide on a way to read and listen to the Word of God 🕐 10 minutes **Page** 24	**Activity:** Explore the impact of reading the Bible. **My Faith Choice:** Choose a way to read and listen to the Word of God.	**Enriching the Lesson Activities:** Catechist Edition, page 67 • Creating a Baruch Tableau • Designing Messenger of Hope Murals • Using Time Lines

Concluding the Lesson 10 minutes

We Remember

Page 25

▶ Review concepts and do the review activity.

▶ **Assessment Tools Booklet:** Chapter Test 2a–2b, or see BeMyDisciples.com.

We Pray

▶ **Prayer:** a meditation, "Your Word is Light"

Materials: Bible, candle, cross for prayer space

▶ Grade 6 Music CD

Preview

Point out resources for this chapter at

www.BeMyDisciples.com

▶ Preview the With My Family page and next week's lesson theme.

Looking Ahead

In this chapter the Holy Spirit invites you to ▶

EXPLORE how Baruch called the Israelites to know God's plan.

DISCOVER that God reveals himself and his plan in Scripture.

DECIDE how you can respond to God's Word proclaimed at Mass.

CHAPTER **2**

The Word of God

? With the Internet, seeking and finding information today is literally at our fingertips. To what extent do you trust all of the information available to you?

You can trust God's Word in the Bible. Take a few moments to read these words from the Bible carefully. Listen to what the writer of this psalm is saying about the Word of God:

> Your word is a lamp for my feet,
>   a light for my path.
> I make a solemn vow
>   to keep your just edicts . . .
> Your decrees are my heritage forever;
>   they are the joy of my heart . . .
> Sustain me by your promise that I may live;
>   do not disappoint me in my hope.
>
> PSALM 119:105–106, 111–116

[handwritten note: edict = decree = laws of God]

? How does this passage from Sacred Scripture help you to grow in faith?

(19)

THE TASKS OF CATECHESIS

Liturgical Education. If you asked most Catholics how many Scripture readings are proclaimed in the Liturgy of the Word at Sunday Mass, many would say three. The First Reading, the Second Reading, and the Gospel are those that would most likely come to mind. We often forget that the Responsorial Psalm, sung between the First and Second Readings, is also Sacred Scripture. That is why the cantor will often proclaim the Responsorial Psalm from the ambo. The Psalms, too, are the inspired Word of God.

Pray

▶ Invite students to quiet themselves for prayer. Begin and end with the Sign of the Cross.

▶ Ask the class to repeat after you:

"Lord God, send the Holy Spirit to open our minds and hearts to your holy word. May we share the good news of your love with all we meet today."

Reflect

▶ Have the students read and respond to the question at the top of the page.

▶ Paraphrase the opening paragraph and ask a volunteer read aloud Psalm 119:105–106, 111–116.

▶ Have the students quietly reread the Scripture passage on the page. Then have them personally reflect on the questions provided on the page. Invite responses.

Focus

▶ Preview the chapter content by reading or paraphrasing the Looking Ahead box.

▶ Tell the students that on the next page they will learn about the Old Testament prophet Baruch and how he led the people to remember their faith in God.

Introduce

▶ Remind students that all biblical prophets shared a common calling: to remind the people of the Covenant and to call them to repent.

▶ Explain that God chose them to speak in his name. Point out that the prophets delivered a message of hope during the Exile, a time when the Israelites seemed to have little hope.

▶ Have the students silently read the text on the page to learn about the prophet Baruch.

▶ Divide the class into two groups. Explain that the class will do a choral reading of the Scripture passage on the page. Have the two groups alternately read aloud the verses of the passage.

▶ Have a volunteer read aloud Disciple Power. Point out that knowledge helps us respond in faith to God.

Reinforce

Reinforce the teaching of Baruch that if we cling to God's way, we will have peace in our hearts.

Connect

▶ Have the students complete the activity on the page individually and then share their pictures as a class.

▶ Invite student groups chosen above to list decisions that people make that lead to happiness and unhappiness.

Disciple Power

The Gift of Knowledge

Part of the gift of faith is the desire to know God better. By accepting God's gift of faith, the Holy Spirit perfects our faith with gifts, such as wisdom, knowledge, and understanding. In other words, part of our response in faith is to know God more fully. The light of reason aids us in our journey to love, serve, and know God.

THE CHURCH FOLLOWS JESUS

The Prophet Baruch

There was a time when God's people seemed to have very little hope. They were confused about life, and they had difficulty in understanding God's Word. It was a time of great infidelity by the Israelites to the Covenant. It was a time known as the Exile.

During the Exile, the Israelites were forced to leave their homeland and live in the country of their conquerors, the Assyrians and the Babylonians. During this time of suffering, God sent Baruch the Prophet and other prophets to speak to his people in Babylonia.

Baruch's message is found in the Book of Baruch. This six-chapter book contains different kinds of writing. This passage is part of a poem:

> Hear, O Israel, the commandments of life:
> listen, and know prudence! . . .
> You have forsaken the fountain of wisdom!
> Had you walked in the way of God,
> you would have dwelt in enduring peace. . . .
> All who cling to [wisdom] will live,
> but those will die who forsake her.
> Turn, O Jacob, and receive her:
> walk by her light toward splendor.
>
> BARUCH 3:9, 12–13; 4:1–2

In this poem, Baruch tried to help God's people understand both how their suffering had happened and how they could find true happiness in God. So even in difficult times, you can find comfort in knowing that if you cling to God's way, peace will endure. This means that the grace of faith can open your eyes to God's plan of saving love. The gift of knowledge will help you to recognize how what happens in your life can help you understand God's plan of saving love.

Activity When you pray to God, what image comes to your mind? Draw it here.

DISCIPLE POWER

The Gift of Knowledge. One of a prophet's roles is to proclaim God's plan of saving love and to offer hope in difficult times. We might not see ourselves as prophets, but there are many ways in which we can be God's messengers of love and hope each and every day. Encourage your students to stop and think of people whom they know who are discouraged and fearful today. Ask them to remember those who are ill, the unemployed, the elderly, the poor, parents, peers, students, and ministers of the Church. Discuss the specific things that they can say and do to offer others God's gift of understanding, love, and hope today to these people.

Divine Revelation

Through Sacred Scripture, God reveals himself and his plan of salvation. By the gift of faith, we seek to understand better his Revelation. As we grow in our understanding, we also grow in faith.

In the Book of Exodus, one of the books in the Pentateuch, God reveals his name to Moses and reestablishes the **Covenant**, or solemn commitment of fidelity between God and his Chosen People, the Israelites.

One day while he was tending sheep, Moses saw a bush that was in flames yet was not consumed by the fire. Curiously approaching this strange sight, Moses heard a voice coming from the bush, saying

"Moses! Moses! . . . I am . . . the God of Abraham, the God of Isaac, the God of Jacob. . . . Come, now! I will send you to Pharaoh to lead my people, the Israelites, out of Egypt."

EXODUS 3:4, 6, 10

You can just imagine how confused Moses must have been. So he asked,

"[W]hen I go to the Israelites and say to them, 'The God of your fathers has sent me to you,' if they ask me, 'What is his name?' what am I to tell them?" God replied, "I am who am. . . . [T]ell the Israelites: I AM sent me to you."

EXODUS 3:13–14

Through this Old Testament story, God shares his name with Moses, with the Israelites, and with all people. He says, "I am who am." In Hebrew, that name is YHWH. By naming himself YHWH, God is letting us know that he alone is the Creator and source of all that exists. In revealing his name to Moses, God also established a personal relationship with the Israelites through Moses. Therefore, God reveals to all people that he is always with us. Wherever we are, God is.

? Look up and read Deuteronomy 6:4–9. What is God asking of you?

21

FAITH FOCUS
In what ways did God reveal himself and his love for all people through the Bible?

FAITH VOCABULARY
biblical inspiration
This is the Holy Spirit guiding the human writers of Sacred Scripture so that they would faithfully and accurately communicate what God intended to reveal.

canon
The word itself means "standard" or "official list." Thus, the canon of Scripture is the official list of books included in the Bible.

Covenant
This is the solemn *promise* commitment of fidelity that God and the People of God made with one another, which was renewed in Christ, the new and everlasting Covenant.

SACRED SCRIPTURE

Covenant. Entering into a covenant was part of the life of the people of ancient Israel and her neighbors. In ancient times, a covenant was a solemn agreement in which people made serious commitments to each other. These commitments entailed accepting and fulfilling serious responsibilities. Such covenants were most often spoken, not written down, but the spoken words held great power. Once given, they could not be broken or taken back. The inspired writers of the Bible used the covenant, which the people of God knew well, to describe the relationship between God and his people.

Key Concept
With faith we seek to understand God's Revelation in Scripture.

Teach

▶ Ask a student to read aloud the Faith Focus question.

▶ Ask volunteers to read aloud the text on the page.

▶ Ask the students what they recall about God's Covenant with the Israelites. Review their understanding by reading aloud the second paragraph.

▶ Ask students to use their imagination to recreate the scene in their minds as volunteers proclaim the two passages from Exodus.

▶ Read and discuss the terms and definitions in Faith Vocabulary.

Reinforce

▶ Invite students to share why they think God revealed himself through a burning bush. Discuss the significance of the bush's not being consumed by the fire.

▶ Remind students that God reveals himself throughout Scripture.

Connect

Invite the class to look up the Scripture passage from Deuteronomy and reflect on the question. Ask volunteers to share their responses.

Key Concept
Sacred Scripture is the inspired Word of God.

Teach

▶ Read aloud to the students the first two paragraphs. Point out that biblical inspiration does not imply dictation.

▶ Divide the class into two groups. Have one group read the Old Testament section and the other group to read the New Testament section. Ask volunteers from the two groups to share some things they learned.

Reinforce

▶ Recall with the students the list of books in the Bible. Tell them this list is called the canon of Scripture.

▶ Have the students read the last paragraph silently then ask for volunteers to comment on it.

Connect

▶ On the board, make two columns headed *Old Testament* and *New Testament*.

▶ Using their Bibles, have each group locate the various groupings which make up the Old and New Testaments.

▶ Then have the students close their Bibles and books and jot down from memory the kinds of books included in the Bible.

▶ Discuss responses to the questions at the bottom of the page

---

Faith-Filled People

People of God

The People of God are the descendants of Abraham to whom God made the promise, "I will make of you a great nation, / and I will bless you.... / All the communities of the earth / shall find blessing in you" (Genesis 12:2, 3). We, the Church, are the People of God by right of our Baptism. A person who has faith in Jesus Christ is a member of the Church, the People of God.

The Inspired Word of God

The Bible, or Sacred Scripture, is the inspired Word of God. This means that God inspired or guided human authors so that they wrote what he intended to reveal. We call this **biblical inspiration.** The various human writers of Sacred Scripture wrote only the truths about God and his plan of love for us that God revealed for our salvation.

The Bible contains seventy-three books in its **canon**, or official list. These books, or writings, make up the Old Testament and the New Testament.

OLD TESTAMENT. The forty-six books of the Old Testament are often grouped this way:

The Pentateuch The first five books of the Bible are called the Pentateuch, a term that means "five containers." These books, which are also called the written Torah, tell of God revealing himself and establishing the Covenant with the Chosen People, the Hebrews or Israelites.

The Historical Books The sixteen historical books tell of how God's people sometimes lived the Covenant well and at other times did not.

The Wisdom Books The seven books of wisdom share advice on how to live the Covenant.

The Prophetic Books The eighteen prophetic books remind God's people to be faithful to the Covenant and that God will always be faithful to them.

NEW TESTAMENT. The twenty-seven books of the New Testament are grouped this way:

The Gospels The four written accounts of the Gospel are the heart of Sacred Scripture, because Jesus Christ is their center.

The Acts of the Apostles The Acts of the Apostles tells the story of the early Church.

The New Testament Letters The thirteen epistles, or letters, of Saint Paul help us to understand our faith in Jesus and how to live that faith.

The Catholic Letters Eight other letters in the New Testament also help us to understand and live our faith.

The Book of Revelation This final book of the Bible encourages Christians to remain faithful to Jesus when they suffer because of their faith in him.

 How would you describe, in your own words, what biblical inspiration is? What does God reveal to us in the Pentateuch? In the Gospels?

(22)

FAITH-FILLED PEOPLE

People of God. Through Ezekiel the Prophet, God assured his people that they would be his people and he would be their God (Ezekiel 36: 28). The Church is the new People of God. Through the Church, God calls the entire human family into the unity of the new People of God, gathered in Christ. We encounter Christ, who is the way to the Father, through the Church community. When we gather to celebrate the sacrifice of the Mass, our unity with Christ and one another is deepened. God unites us in prayer, charity, and peace, and sends us forth to renew the face of the Earth.

The Covenant

The story of the Covenant begins in the Book of Genesis, the first book of the Bible. It continues to unfold with more and more detail even to the last book of the Bible, the Book of Revelation. The following are some highlights found in the Old Testament:

- God promised that from Eve's descendants would come one who would conquer the tempter, the devil (read Genesis 3:14–16).

- God entered a Covenant with Noah and promised that all living things will continue as long as the world lasts (read Genesis 9:9–17).

- God promised Abraham that he would be the father of a great people (read Genesis 12:1–3).

- At Mount Sinai, God promised Moses and the Israelites that he would be their God. They promised that they would be his people and live the Law he revealed to them (read Exodus 19:4–6).

- The prophets chosen by God reminded his people to live the Covenant and announced a new and everlasting Covenant in the Messiah (read Jeremiah 32:36–43 and Ezekiel 37:26–28).

In the New Testament, Jesus revealed that he is the Christ, the Anointed One or Messiah, the new and everlasting Covenant. In him and through his work all people can live faithfully according to the will of God. In Jesus Christ, God's final Covenant with the world has been made now and forever.

Even though God reveals himself through Sacred Scripture and through the Sacred Tradition of the Church, he remains a mystery beyond our full comprehension. Because God is the source of all, he is due our worship. We are to praise and thank him for initiating and maintaining the Covenant.

Activity

Look up and read one of these three passages. Then write one word or image that tells something about the Covenant.

GENESIS 9:9–17   **GENESIS 12:1–3**   **EXODUS 19:4–6**

_____

_____

_____

Catholics Believe

Sacred Scripture

God is the author of Sacred Scripture because he inspired human authors to communicate faithfully the covenantal relationship between God and humanity. The Church therefore acknowledges that Scripture firmly, faithfully, and without error teaches the truth about God's plan of salvation.

23

Key Concept
Jesus Christ is the new and everlasting Covenant.

Teach

▶ Ask volunteers to read aloud The Covenant.

▶ Divide the class into five groups. Ask each group to read one passage found at the end of each bullet.

▶ Starting with Genesis 3:14–16, have the students share details about the Covenant, which they found in reading their Scripture passage.

Reinforce

Summarize the lesson thus far by reviewing the Catholics Believe feature on the page. Explain that the People of God are God's chosen people who, because of Christ, have a share in the Covenant.

Connect

▶ Have students work individually to complete the Scripture search on the page. Invite volunteers to share their responses with the class.

▶ As a class, identify major qualities of living the Covenant. *Follow 10 Commdmts*

▶ Explain that at the heart of the Covenant is loving fidelity, which involves both loyalty and mercy. *Be Faithful Be Forgiving*

▶ Have students brainstorm ideas describing a world today in which people live the Covenant.

Reinforce

Remind the students that through Sacred Scripture, God communicates his saving love for us, enabling us to grow in faith. Thus, the Bible is a vital source of inspiration and guidance that helps us put faith into practice.

Respond

Have the class brainstorm ways in which their lives could be transformed by reading, listening, or studying Sacred Scripture.

Choose

▶ Have students complete the activity on the page and ask volunteers to share their responses.

▶ Invite the young people to complete their Faith Choice. Ask them to conclude by praying the closing prayer.

I FOLLOW JESUS

God wishes for all people to respond to him in faith. We can use the gift of knowledge to assist us in growing in faith. The Scriptures reveal to us God's plan of everlasting love.

THE WORD OF THE LORD

Write three ways your life could be changed by reading, listening to, and studying the Bible.

1. _____
_____

2. _____
_____

3. _____
_____

MY FAITH CHOICE

This week I will read and listen to the Sunday Gospel and respond to it. I will
_____
_____

Pray: "Lord, fill my mind and heart so that I may proclaim your Word to others. Amen."

24

CATHOLIC DOCTRINE

Liturgy of the Word. God speaks to us through Sacred Scripture in a human way. "The Church has always venerated the divine Scriptures as she venerated the Body of the Lord, in so far as she never ceases, particularly in the sacred liturgy, to partake of the bread of life and to offer it to the faithful from the one table of the Word of God and the Body of Christ" (Vatican II, *Dogmatic Constitution on Divine Revelation* [Dei Verbum] 21).

Chapter Review

Write a paragraph describing the Church's teaching about Sacred Scripture. Be sure to include at least these terms: Bible, canon, covenant, and inspiration.

Canon = official list
Covenant = promise/agreemnt
Inspiration = HS guides the author
Bible = sacred scripture

Your World Is Light

Lectio divina, or "divine reading," is an ancient prayer of meditation. Along with vocal prayer and contemplation, it forms the three main expressions of prayer. Follow these steps to spend quiet time with God, reading and listening to his Word.

1. Open your Bible to a favorite passage or one from this chapter. Sit quietly.

2. Be aware that God is present by the indwelling presence of the Holy Spirit within you. Sign your forehead, lips, and chest over your heart with a small Sign of the Cross.

3. Imagine yourself in a safe place where you can talk and listen to God.

4. Reverently and slowly read the Scripture passage you selected.

5. Speak to God with words, images, or ideas. Take time to talk and listen to God. Say, "Your word, LORD, is a light for my path" (based on Psalm 119:105).

6. After a few quiet moments, ask the Holy Spirit, "What is your Word saying to me?" Write down any key words or phrases that you remember. Listening with an open heart can help you to be receptive to God speaking to you through his Word.

7. Make a faith decision, and put God's Word into action. Realize that the goal of *lectio divina* is simply being with God by praying the Scriptures.

TO HELP YOU REMEMBER

1. The Holy Spirit guided the human writers of Sacred Scripture to faithfully and accurately tell what God intended to reveal.

2. Through the Bible, God reveals himself and his loving plan of salvation for the world and all people.

3. The Bible tells the story of the Covenant into which God entered with his people. In his only Son, Jesus Christ, God established his Covenant forever.

25

TEACHING TIP

Finding and Choosing Scripture Passages. Depending on their familiarity with the Bible, young people may or may not have difficulty in finding and choosing a Scripture passage to use in a prayer of meditation such as *lectio divina*. Here are some passages from the Gospels that you might suggest:

Matthew 5: 13–16 (Salt and Light)

Mark 4: 35–41 (Jesus Stills a Storm)

Luke 13: 18–19 (Parable of the Mustard Seed)

John 10: 1–14 (The Good Shepherd).

We Remember

▶ Ask the students to write a paragraph using the instructions on the page. Review any concepts that need clarification before they begin to write.

▶ Invite volunteer students to read aloud their paragraphs.

▶ Have the students then close their books. Write on the board the first part of each summary statement in the To Help You Remember section. Then have students complete the statements on the board.

▶ Have students open their books to compare their completed statements on the board with those on the page. Point out and clarify any corrections necessary.

We Pray

▶ Gather the students to conclude the chapter with prayer. Explain that in the prayer today they will learn about and practice *lectio divina*, a form of praying the Scriptures.

▶ Make sure that each student has a Bible and is able to select a Scripture passage. You might even suggest a common passage for all students to use. See the Teaching Tip for suggestions. Have the students write their thoughts and key words in their journals.

▶ Ask the students to quiet themselves for prayer. After a moment of prayerful silence, lead the students in praying a short closing prayer.

Preview

▶ Have students carefully tear out the With My Family page along the perforation.

▶ Encourage them to share the pages with their family and to complete the activities together at home.

▶ If the students did not complete the chapter review, encourage them to complete it with their family.

▶ Point out the title and theme of next week's chapter to the children.

Visit www.BeMyDisciples.com

▶ Take time with the students to explore the many activities and resources available at **www.BeMyDisciples.com.**

▶ Encourage especially students and their families to discover the many resources available at the Web site during the week.

Before Moving On ...

As you finish today's lesson, reflect on the following question before moving on to the next chapter.

Which young people seem to work best in groups?

With My Family

This Week...

In chapter 2, The Word of God, your child learned:

▶ The Holy Spirit inspired the writers of Scripture to express God's Word faithfully and truthfully as a gift to all people.

▶ The heart of Sacred Scripture is the Gospel because Jesus Christ, the Incarnate Word of God, is the heart and fullness of God's Revelation.

▶ Sacred Scripture firmly, faithfully, and without error teaches the truth about God's plan for salvation.

▶ Sacred Scripture reveals God's Covenant, or solemn commitment of fidelity, with his Chosen People, the Israelites.

▶ The gift of knowledge, one of the seven Gifts of the Holy Spirit, gives us the grace to deepen our understanding of Sacred Scripture.

For more about related teachings of the Church, see the *Catechism of the Catholic Church,* 50–73, 101–141; and the *United States Catholic Catechism of Adults,* pages 12–27.

■ Sharing God's Word

Read together 1 Thessalonians 2:13 and 2 Timothy 3:16–17. Emphasize that the Bible is the inspired Word of God.

■ We Live as Disciples

The Christian home and family is a school of discipleship. Choose one of the following activities to do as a family, or design a similar activity of your own:

▶ Make a special place in your home to display a Bible. This is called "enthroning" the Bible. Open the Bible each day to a selected passage. This practice can help the family recall the importance of the Word of God in our daily lives.

▶ Include the reading of Scripture to begin your family mealtime prayers. Invite a different family member to select a passage each day. During the meal, have family members share what the passage means to them.

▶ As a family, carefully watch and listen to the news events that are making the headlines. Now imagine that you are a prophet called to remind others about the Covenant. As a family, discuss how you would encourage one another to live as a family according to God's will.

■ Our Spiritual Journey

Praying together is one of the main practices of a disciple of Jesus. In this chapter, your child practiced the *lectio divina* form of prayer. Read about this prayer on page 25. Make this a form of prayer that your family regularly prays together.

For more ideas on ways your family can live as disciples of Jesus, visit **www.BeMyDisciples.com**

(26)

PLANNING AHEAD

Art Appreciation. A variety of art forms have always been used to teach and inspire people to know and love God. Next week's lesson explores the many art forms used in the building of cathedrals and churches. Consider taking the class on a tour of your parish church. During the visit, have the group jot down notes about the art forms that they see. Focus on the architecture, statues, Stations of the Cross, altar, tabernacle, stained-glass windows, mosaics, paintings, and other art forms.

Enriching the Lesson

Creating a Baruch Tableau

Purpose	Directions	Materials
To reinforce the prophet Baruch's message to God's people found in the Book of Baruch (taught on page 20)	▶ Divide the class into groups and assign each group a part of the poem from Baruch on page 20 of the student text. ▶ Have each group work together to create a silent snapshot, or tableau, of its section of the reading. ▶ Have each group present its tableau as the rest of the class reads aloud that section of the poem.	student text

Designing Messenger of Hope Murals

Purpose	Directions	Materials
To reinforce that the gift of wisdom helps keep God at the center of our lives (taught on page 20)	▶ Have the students work in small groups. Assign one group Job 28:1–28 to read. Assign the second group Psalm 90 to read. ▶ Have each group read and discuss the passage assigned to them. ▶ Invite the students to use watercolors or another art medium to illustrate their understanding of the Scripture passage by creating a mural. ▶ Have the students share their murals and discuss their illustrations.	Bibles shelf paper water colors or pastels or crayons

Using Time Lines

Purpose	Directions	Materials
To reinforce that the story of the Covenant begins in the first book of the Bible and unfolds with more details in each of the other books of the Bible (taught on page 23)	▶ Have the students work in small groups, using a roll of white shelf paper, to write and illustrate a time line of the major events of the story of the Covenant found in this chapter. ▶ Have each group share their time line with the entire class. ▶ Tell the class that in subsequent weeks they will continue to fill in and illustrate their time lines with the different key events as they study the Scripture.	rolls of shelf paper markers or crayons containers to store the time lines

BACKGROUND

The Mystery of Mysteries

"I believe in God the Father Almighty. . . . I believe in Jesus Christ, the only begotten Son of God. . . . I believe in the Holy Spirit, the Lord and Giver of life." This profession of faith, seemingly so simple, is profound in its significance.

Surrender to the Mystery of the Living God

By truly professing faith in God, we open the door to an entire reorienting of our lives. We acknowledge that One greater than ourselves exists. We profess that God created us, loves us, and desires that we be united with him.

When we profess, "I believe in God," we profess faith in the mystery of God, who is beyond our full comprehension. We could spend a lifetime of study, delving into the writings of saints and mystics, scholars and prophets, and still have only a mere glimpse of him who is inviting us to love him with our whole hearts, minds, and souls.

Our minds can only take us so far into the Mystery, who alone is God, until, at some point, he engages our hearts. Once we surrender our hearts, we will no longer live, but he will live in us. God will no longer be a mystery to be solved, but the One who embraces us and to whom we surrender.

The One Who Always Is

When we profess, "I believe in God," we address our Father, the Creator who makes us sharers in his life and love. He is our Abba, the Father who knows us, calls us his adopted children, reflects our goodness in his gaze, protects us in the shadow of his wings, and accompanies us from birth through death and beyond.

When we profess, "I believe in God," we stand in awe of him who transcends history and time, Heaven, and earth. All else in our lives will pass away—loved ones will die, material possessions will prove useless, but he always IS. When we live in God and he lives in us, we live in the hope of life forever with him.

When we profess, "I believe in God," we affirm that we believe in love because "God is love" (1 John 4:8). By loving God and others, we remain in him and he in us. Hatred is love's opposite.

If anyone says, "I love God," but hates his brother, he is a liar; for whoever does not love a brother whom he has seen cannot love God whom he has not seen (1 John 4:20).

When we profess, "I believe in God," we declare our trust in the One who will not deceive us. He is Truth and Love. His promises of faithfulness and abiding kindness will all come true. In a world where fidelity, honesty, and integrity are under siege, we have in God the steadfast and eternal source of Love and Truth who will never let us down or betray our trust.

For Reflection

When I stand and join in the profession of faith at Mass, what do I mean when I pray, "I believe in God"?

How do I describe the qualities of my relationship with God?

Catechist to Catechist

The Quest for God

Young people love mysteries. They enjoy seeking answers to the questions mysteries evoke. They are drawn into solving the dilemmas mysteries present. You will find that most sixth-graders have a natural interest in the mysteries of our faith. God is the greatest mystery of faith. He has created us to know, love, and serve him. He is the source of the greatest quest of the human heart and human mind. The depths of his beauty, truth and goodness are inexhaustible. You will want to point out to the young people that God is a mystery who cannot be known completely. There will always be something more to discover about God.

An Awareness of God's Presence

During your time with the students this session, find ways to invite them to respond to God's revelation of himself. Since many sixth-graders are concrete thinkers, you might begin by displaying some gifts of creation—a flower, a picture of a brilliant sunset, an interesting stone, and other appropriate examples. Ask the students to describe what these "gifts" tell them about God.

The Church Teaches...

"The Christian message is inherently Trinitarian because its source is the incarnate Word of the Father, Jesus Christ, who speaks to the world through his Holy Spirit" (*National Directory for Catechesis*, 25B). This is why the mystery of the Trinity is introduced early, helping the children to center themselves in a Trinitarian faith.

Further Reading and Reflection

For more on the teachings of the Church, see the *Catechism of the Catholic Church*, 198–231, 249–267, 355–387 and from the *United States Catholic Catechism for Adults*, pages 50–53, 56–69.

Catechist Prayer

Come, Holy Spirit,
create a new heart in me.
Guide me to seek out
and to find your love
and to share it enthusiastically
with the young people.
Amen.

Lesson Planner

Chapter 3   The Mystery of God

Focus To discover why we say that God is the mystery of mysteries

LESSON PART	PROCESS	MATERIALS and RESOURCES
EXPLORE **Focus** To explore the mystery of God 🕐 10 minutes **Pages** 27–28	▶ Proclaim and discuss John 1:1–5 (In the beginning was the Word). ▶ Explore the story of Christian mosaic art. **Disciple Power:** Wonder and awe **Activity:** Create mosaics depicting the mystery of God.	Bible Pencils Colored paper Glue Pieces of cardboard Crayons or markers
DISCOVER **Focus** To discover the Church's teaching on the mystery of the Holy Trinity and the creation of people in the image of God 🕐 30 minutes **Pages** 29–31	▶ Review Divine Revelation and explore some attributes of God. ▶ Learn the relationship of the Holy Trinity to Creation. ▶ Introduce the works of the Holy Trinity. **Activity:** Use a graphic to describe the work of the Holy Trinity.	Journals **Additional Activities Booklet:** Activities 3a–3b, or see BeMyDisciples.com.
DECIDE **Focus** To decide a way to be a sign of God's love to others 🕐 10 minutes **Page** 32	**Activity:** Create a collage of words and images that are signs of God's love. **My Faith Choice:** Choose a way to be a sign of God's love.	**Enriching the Lesson Activities:** Catechist Edition, page 79 • Writing Acrostic Poems • Creating Paper Mosaics • Literature Connection

Concluding the Lesson 10 minutes

We Remember

Page 33

▶ Review concepts and do review activity.

▶ **Assessment Tools Booklet:** Chapter Test 3a–3b, or see BeMyDisciples.com.

We Pray

▶ **Prayer:** an antiphonal prayer

Materials: Bible, candle, cross for prayer space

▶ Grade 6 Music CD

Preview

Point out resources for this chapter at

www.BeMyDisciples.com

▶ Preview the With My Family page and next week's lesson theme.

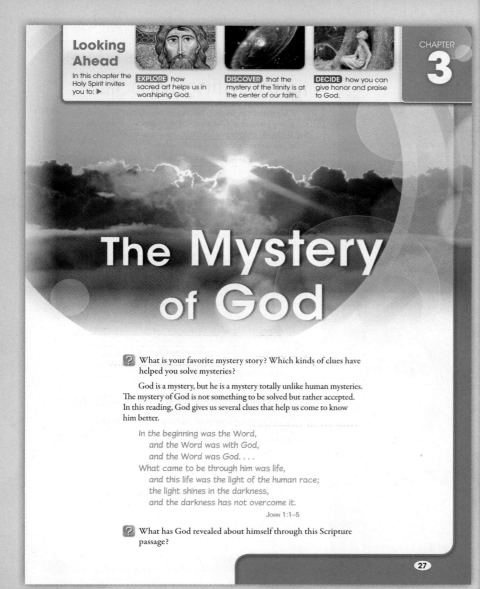

Looking Ahead

In this chapter the Holy Spirit invites you to: ▶

EXPLORE how sacred art helps us in worshiping God.

DISCOVER that the mystery of the Trinity is at the center of our faith.

DECIDE how you can give honor and praise to God.

CHAPTER **3**

The Mystery of God

? What is your favorite mystery story? Which kinds of clues have helped you solve mysteries?

God is a mystery, but he is a mystery totally unlike human mysteries. The mystery of God is not something to be solved but rather accepted. In this reading, God gives us several clues that help us come to know him better.

> In the beginning was the Word,
>   and the Word was with God,
>   and the Word was God. . . .
> What came to be through him was life,
>   and this life was the light of the human race;
>   the light shines in the darkness,
>   and the darkness has not overcome it.
>
> JOHN 1:1–5

? What has God revealed about himself through this Scripture passage?

27

HUMAN METHODOLOGIES

Learning within the Christian Family. The *National Directory for Catechesis* reminds us that the Christian family is a place where the child experiences Christian community and is the main community where a child's faith is nurtured and grows (*NDC* 29D). As you explore the mystery of God with the students this week, invite them to reflect on their early childhood experiences of learning about God and Jesus within their families. Give the students opportunities to name and pray for the people in their families who helped them grow in their awareness of God's presence. Be sensitive to those children who may have had few, if any, of these experiences.

Pray

▶ Gather students into two groups for prayer. Begin and end with praying the Sign of the Cross.

▶ Ask the class to repeat after you:

"You are great, O God. All creation bows before you. Amen."

Reflect

▶ Invite students to reflect on the image on the page. Inquire, "How does this image evoke a sense of mystery?"

▶ Have the students read the questions at the top of the page. Allow time for them to respond.

▶ Read or paraphrase the opening paragraph. Then invite a student to proclaim the Scripture passage from the Gospel of John.

▶ Proclaim the Scripture passage on the page. Then have them personally reflect on the questions.

▶ Ask volunteers to share what is the most important thing they have come to believe about the mystery of God.

Focus

▶ Refer to the Looking Ahead feature to forecast the chapter content.

▶ Tell the students to turn the page to learn how Christians have expressed their wonder at the mystery of God through art.

Introduce

▶ Have the students silently read the text on the page to learn about mosaics.

▶ Examine the image on the page an example of a mosaic.

▶ Lead a discussion about how sacred art, mosaics in particular, aids a person in worshipping God.

▶ Have students read aloud Disciple Power. Point out that fear of the Lord means having wonder and awe before God the Almighty.

Reinforce

▶ Remind students that God has revealed himself to be the mystery of one God in three Divine Persons: Father, Son, and Holy Spirit. Reread the last paragraph to expand on this understanding.

▶ Point out that throughout history, Christians have used art in many forms to express their faith in God.

Connect

▶ Invite students to list forms of art used for religious purposes (for example, statues, icons, frescoes, murals, music, poetry, architecture, stained-glass windows, furniture). Be sure to highlight those works of art found at your parish.

▶ Have students complete the activity on the page. Invite all students to display the sketches for their mosaics.

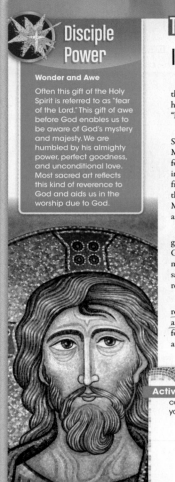

Disciple Power

Wonder and Awe

Often this gift of the Holy Spirit is referred to as "fear of the Lord." This gift of awe before God enables us to be aware of God's mystery and majesty. We are humbled by his almighty power, perfect goodness, and unconditional love. Most sacred art reflects this kind of reverence to God and aids us in the worship due to God.

28

THE CHURCH FOLLOWS JESUS
Illuminating Mosaics

Christian artists can help us to know more about the mystery of the loving presence of God within us and among us. Long before we had Bibles for everyone to read, Christians used art to help people "hear" the story of creation and redemption.

Mosaics are one of the earliest forms of art used by Christians. Some of the earliest Christian mosaics date back to A.D. 320, in the Mausoleum of Santa Costanza in Rome, Italy. Mosaics are an art form consisting of colored pieces of material called *tesserae* pressed into soft plaster to form pictures. Often the material used comes from glass or ceramic tiles. The *tesserae* often reflect light. This gives the viewer the impression that the image is shimmering or glowing. Mosaics can help people enter into the mystery of God and see him as the source of all that is true, good, and beautiful.

Mosaics often decorate the ceilings and walls of Churches. They give drama and life to scenes from the Bible that reveal the story of God's love for us. They instruct the faithful about the majesty and mystery of God, the life of Jesus, and the lives of Mary and other saints. They illuminate God's plan of creation and redemption as revealed to us by the Word of God, Jesus Christ.

Christian art, like all the sacramentals of the Church, helps us respond in faith to the mystery of the one God, who is Father, Son, and Holy Spirit. Such art invokes in us a sense of wonder and awe for God. It sparks a desire within us to spread the story of God's love and to be his living images in the world.

Activity Using small pieces of colored paper, glue, and a piece of cardboard, create a mosaic depicting the mystery of God. Sketch your idea for your mosaic here.

DISCIPLE POWER

Wonder and Awe. When is the last time something took your breath away—a time you knew that God was revealing himself to you in a powerful way? Was it at the sight of a beautiful sunrise or a starry sky? A baby's cry? A beautiful song or movie? Be especially mindful of God's awesome presence and majesty today. Let your breath be taken away by the beauty of everyday moments that reveal God's glory and power. Invite your students to enter into these experiences of wonder and awe by taking time to notice a beautiful sky or sunset, to listen to the rain on a stormy day, or to enjoy the birds singing right outside your classroom.

The Nature of God

Our minds can never fully understand the holy mystery of God. God is like, and at the same time unlike, anyone or anything we know. God is one, and there is only one God. He is truth and love.

We can come to know something about God through our reason. For example, we can know that God exists. However, we cannot fully understand who God is on our own. We need God to reveal himself to us. We need **Divine Revelation**—God making himself and his divine plan of creation and salvation known over time. We therefore depend on God revealing himself to us. Through the Word of God, we believe that he has done just that.

Here are some of the qualities or attributes that God has revealed about himself through Sacred Scripture:

Faithful. God is the One who is always faithful to his people (read Exodus 34:6).

Truth. God's Word is true, and all his promises come true (read 2 Samuel 7:28 and Deuteronomy 7:9). God the Son came to bear witness to the truth (read John 18:37).

Merciful. God's merciful love endures forever, and in his mercy all sins are forgiven (read Psalm 136, Ephesians 2:4, and Jude 1:21).

Love. God is love (read 1 John 4:8,16). God loves us with an everlasting love (see Jeremiah 31:3). Moreover, God so loved the world that he sent his only Son (see John 3:16).

God has revealed these qualities, or attributes, and many others about himself. Each quality helps us to know something more about him. God has revealed himself to be Father, Son, and Holy Spirit.

? What other qualities of God have you learned?

FAITH FOCUS
Who has God revealed himself to be?

FAITH VOCABULARY
Divine Revelation
Divine Revelation is God making himself and his divine plan of creation and salvation known over time.

original holiness
Original holiness is that first state of grace in which Adam and Eve shared in God's divine life. They were therefore in a perfect state of grace before the Fall.

original justice
Original justice is that first state of grace before the Fall, when Adam and Eve and all of creation were in harmony.

sanctify
To sanctify is to put one in that state of grace in which sin is removed and we are made holy.

CATHOLIC DOCTRINE

The Meaning of Mystery. In a world where we have come to expect answers, facts, and understanding in an instant, it is increasingly difficult to live with the concept of mystery. The mystery of God is unlike any other mystery. God is revealed to us in many ways. He makes himself known to us, invites us to share in his love and goodness, and to live in communion with him. Yet there is still much about God that will always remain a mystery to us. There will always be more about God to learn, to know, and to love. The mystery of God is simply beyond our human understanding and beyond our words to express (*CCC*, 206, 230).

Key Concept
God has revealed attributes of himself through Sacred Scripture.

Teach

▶ Ask students to read quietly the Faith Focus question. Then invite all students to share their response with the class.

▶ Write on the board, Attributes of God. Explain that attributes are qualities. Have the students listen for them as a volunteer reads aloud the text on the page.

▶ Have the students form three groups. Using their Bibles, ask them to find Psalm 103:1–18. Assign each group a section (I, II, III) to find and share additional attributes of God. Record these on the board.

▶ Invite volunteers to read each of the definitions of each of the terms in Faith Vocabulary. Mention that we will continue to grow in our understanding of these terms.

Reinforce

Remind students that God is the mystery of mysteries. Using the image on the page discuss how it relates to the mysteries of God.

Connect

Ask the students to share which attribute they have experienced through their relationship with God.

Key Concept
The mystery of the Trinity
is at the center of our faith.

Teach

▶ Have several volunteers read the text on the page. Ask "What has God done to show his love for us?" *(God created us, sent his Son to save us, and sent the Holy Spirit to sanctify us.)*

▶ Point out that the belief in the Holy Trinity is central to our faith.

▶ Explore the state of original holiness. Ask the students to visualize and describe what such a world might have been like.

Reinforce

▶ Point out that God did not create us as gods, but in his image, to be like him. Inquire, "How are we to be like God?" *(By loving and caring for others as God has done for us)*

▶ Point out the vocabulary words on the page and review their meaning.

▶ Invite a volunteer to read aloud Faith-Filled People. Explain that St. Thomas Aquinas had a deep faith in the Holy Trinity.

Connect

Have students answer the question, "Which qualities of a holy person do others see in you?"

Faith-Filled People

Saint Thomas Aquinas

Thomas Aquinas was such a quiet student that some people soon named him "the dumb ox." But Thomas was far from dumb. The question "Who is God?" was always on his mind and he spent many years sharing his answers to that question as a university professor. Today Saint Thomas Aquinas is honored as a Doctor, or great teacher, of the faith of the Church. His feast day is celebrated January 28.

The Most Holy Trinity

God has also revealed himself to be the mystery of one God in three Divine Persons: Father, Son, and Holy Spirit. This is who God is. This is the mystery of the Holy, or Blessed, Trinity. The Church has passed on this Divine Revelation in Sacred Scripture and in the Sacred Tradition of the Church. The mystery of the Most Holy Trinity is at the very center of our faith. Believing in God the Holy Trinity is essential to Christian living.

Many other mysteries of faith have their beginning in this mystery of mysteries. For example, the story of the human family begins with God creating us out of love in a state of **original holiness** and **original justice**. In the Fall, humanity then lost that original state of grace because of Original Sin. Eventually God the Father sent God the Son, who became fully human. The Son became like us in all ways but sin, so that we could become sharers in his divinity. The Father and the Son have sent the Holy Spirit to make us holy, or **sanctify** us. He reconciles us with God, who created us to live eternally with him.

In God's plan of creation, human beings have an extraordinary and unique place. The greatness of every person rests on this revealed truth:

> God created man in his image; in the divine image he created him; male and female he created them.
> GENESIS 1:27

God created each person with a soul. The soul bears the imprint of God's image and is the innermost spiritual part of us. The soul is immortal, or never dies. Our soul gives us the ability to share in God's life and love forever.

? Which qualities of a holy person do others see in you?

In the Son and through the Spirit, God the Father reveals the innermost aspect of who God is. The Holy Trinity is a perfect, eternal exchange of love. When we choose to live as images of God, we tell others about his love and give honor and glory to God. In our loving relationships with one another, we reflect the love within the Holy Trinity.

The Trinity, painted by the Russian artist Andrei Rublev around 1410

30

FAITH-FILLED PEOPLE

Saint Thomas Aquinas. Saint Thomas Aquinas was born in 1226. In 1243, at the age of seventeen, he joined the Order of Saint Dominic. He studied at Cologne under Saint Albert the Great. At the age of twenty-two, he was appointed to teach at the same university and began to publish his first works. Saint Thomas's greatest writing is his *Summa Theologica*. He was canonized in 1323 and declared Doctor of the Church by Pope Pius V.

God the Creator

The very first words of the Bible begin with God's love:

In the beginning, when God created the heavens and the earth . . .

GENESIS 1:1

If we listen carefully to the Word of God revealed in the Book of Genesis, we come to know something about God the Creator. We also understand more about the world and ourselves. Here are three things we learn about God the Creator and his Creation:

"In the beginning" means that the world had a beginning. The world was not always in existence.

"God created" means that only God creates. Only he makes everyone and everything, out of nothing, without any help.

"Heavens and the earth" is another way of saying "everything, visible and invisible," as in the Nicene Creed. Angels, part of God's unseen Creation, are spiritual beings who always give glory to God. They serve his saving plan for all creatures.

In creation, God reveals his plan. Because God the Father, the Son, and the Holy Spirit are inseparable, they are one in being and act as one. Each Divine Person of the Trinity has a unique role. God the Father not only created the universe out of love but also keeps it in existence by his Word, the Son, and by the Holy Spirit, the Giver of Life. Thus, Creation is the work of the Holy Trinity.

Catholics Believe

Faith in God

Faith leads us to turn to God alone as our origin and our ultimate goal. We are neither to prefer anything to him nor to substitute anything for him. Scripture and Tradition never cease to teach and celebrate this fundamental truth: "The world was made for the glory of God." (*Catechism of the Catholic Church* 229, 293–394).

Activity In each part of the triangle, write a phrase about the Holy Trinity's work as Creator.

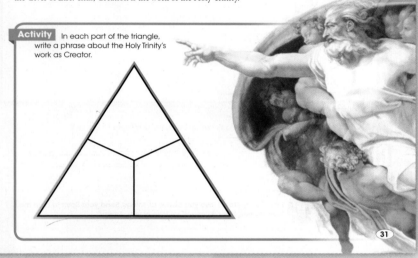

(31)

SCRIPTURE BACKGROUND

The Creation Stories. The young people may be confused about headings in the Bible that read "First Story of Creation" and "Second Story of Creation." They might wrongly conclude that there are two versions of the story of Creation and then wonder which is the true one. The book of Genesis had its roots in a long oral tradition and in three main strands of source material known as the Yahwist (J), Elohist (E), and Priestly (P) traditions. All this eventually became the masterpiece that we now know as the book of Genesis and accept as the Word of God. The first story of Creation has a foundation in the Yahwist source and emphasizes the creation of the physical world. The second story has its roots in the Priestly (P) Source and emphasizes the creation of man and woman and their fall from grace. The two chapters are closely related and both reveal a fundamental truth about God's relation to his Creation.

Teach

▶ Invite students to write on the board words or phrases that describe God as Creator.

▶ Divide the class into two groups. Have one group read and report on the first creation account in Genesis 1:1–31, 2:1–3. The other group should then read and report on Genesis 2:4b–25.

▶ Ask the groups to compare what they found in their readings.

Reinforce

▶ Read the Catholics Believe box aloud. Point out that in God's plan, humans have a unique place because God creates all people in his image and likeness.

▶ Paraphrase the text on the page to summarize the students' reflection on the accounts of Creation. Point out that all of creation is the work of the Holy Trinity.

Connect

▶ Have students then work individually to complete the activity on the page. Invite volunteers to share their responses with the class.

▶ Explain that as stewards of the gift of creation, we are to use it as a way to give honor and glory back to God.

Reinforce

Recall with the students that signs of God's love are all around us. Point out that these signs give us a glimpse into the mystery of God. Refer to the various images and photographs in this chapter and unit.

Respond

▶ Introduce the collage activity. Invite the young people to work in groups of three to complete it. Provide magazines and art supplies to assist them.

▶ Ask each group to share their collage and display it in the classroom.

Choose

▶ Invite the students to complete My Faith Choice.

▶ Ask them to spend a moment offering a silent prayer.

I FOLLOW JESUS

God always manifests his love. God never stops giving you signs of his love. If you look closely, there are many clues that give you a glimpse into the mystery of God.

SIGNS OF THE MYSTERY OF GOD

Make a collage of words and pictures of people, places, things, and events that have come to be signs of God and his love for you.

MY FAITH CHOICE

This week I will reflect God's love for me in the way I treat others, I will

_____

_____

 Pray, "O my God, I love you above all things. Send your Spirit to help me love my neighbor as myself for love of you. Amen."

32

THE TASKS OF CATECHESIS

Education for Community Life. Many of us grew up hearing our parents say, "You can't judge a book by its cover!" This adage invites us to look beyond what we see on the outside. Many of us have a tendency to judge others by their outer appearance. A person's height, weight, clothing, way of walking, hairstyle, accent, or skin color may determine whether he or she will be "in" or "out" with his or her peers. Your classroom should be a microcosm of Christian community life. Work to develop a classroom atmosphere where all feel safe, welcome, included, and appreciated for who they are. Look for and acknowledge the gifts that you see in each student. The story of Saint Thomas reminds us that every person is a child of God with a gift to share and a role to play in building God's Kingdom.

Chapter Review

Complete the sentences to decipher the hidden message below. Unscramble the highlighted letters to discover the belief about God that is at the center of our faith.

1. God has revealed himself to be the m y s **t** e **r** **y** of one God in three Divine Persons.

2. Divine R e v e l a t **i** o **n** is God making himself and his plan of creation and redemption known over time.

3. C r e a **t** i o n is God making everyone and everything, visible and invisible, out of nothing and without any help.

4. O r i g **i** n a l Sin is the name given to the first sin.

The central belief about God is the mystery of the

T R I N I T Y .

> **TO HELP YOU REMEMBER**
>
> 1. God is the Mystery of mysteries who has revealed himself and his plan of creation and redemption.
>
> 2. Creation is the work of the Holy Trinity. God is the source of all truth, goodness, and beauty.
>
> 3. The mystery of the most Holy Trinity is at the center of our faith.

Give Thanks to God

The Church prays the Psalms each day in the Liturgy of the Hours. The Liturgy of the Hours is the official daily prayer of the Church. One way we can pray a psalm is by alternately praying the verses aloud. We call this praying a psalm antiphonally.

All: **Come and see the works of God, awesome in the deeds done for us.**

Group 1: Shout joyfully to God, all you on earth;

Group 2: sing of his glorious name.

All: **Come and see the works of God, awesome in the deeds done for us.**

Group 1: All on earth fall in worship before you;

Group 2: they sing of you, sing of your name!

All: **Come and see the works of God, awesome in the deeds done for us.**

BASED ON PSALM 66:1–2, 4

33

LITURGY CONNECTION

Ways to Pray. Make a conscientious effort to engage the students in classroom prayer by incorporating some of the following suggestions:

- Divide a prayer into parts and assign each part to a different group.
- Use gestures or other movements.
- Echo parts of the prayer.
- Use appropriate music during prayer time to create a prayerful mood.
- Invite the students to serve as leaders of prayer and as the readers of Scripture.

We Remember

▶ Read aloud each summary statement in the To Help You Remember section on the page, leaving a key word or phrase out. Have students complete the statements from memory, without looking at their books.

▶ Review any concepts that need clarification before they begin the review section.

▶ Have students privately complete the top section to decipher the message. For the final statement, have students write their answer on a small piece of paper and exchange papers with a peer.

▶ Invite volunteer students to read aloud their responses for the first four statements.

We Pray

▶ Gather the students to conclude the chapter with prayer.

▶ Explain that in the prayer today they will learn about the Liturgy of the Hours which is the official daily prayer of the Church.

▶ Place the students into two groups for prayer.

▶ Together, pray the prayer on the page according to the instructions. Pray the "All" responses together as a class.

Preview

▶ Have students carefully tear out the With My Family page along the perforation.

▶ Encourage them to share the pages with their family and to complete the activities together at home.

▶ If the students did not or were not able to complete the chapter review, encourage them to complete it with their family.

▶ Point out the chapter title and theme of next week's lesson.

Visit www.BeMyDisciples.com

▶ Take time with the students to explore the many activities and resources available at **www.BeMyDisciples.com**.

▶ Encourage them to join with their families to discover the many resources available at the Web site.

Before Moving On ...

As you finish today's lesson, reflect on the following question before moving on to the next chapter.

How have I accepted that God is the mystery of mysteries?

With My Family

This Week...

In chapter 3, The Mystery of God, your child learned:

▶ God is the Mystery of mysteries. We receive the gift and grace of wonder and awe, or fear of the Lord, to help us give praise and thanks to God.

▶ Although we can come to know with certainty that God exists by reason, we depend on his Divine Revelation. Through Sacred Scripture and Sacred Tradition in the Church, God has revealed himself to be the most Holy Trinity—the Mystery of one God in three Divine Persons: God the Father, God the Son, and God the Holy Spirit.

▶ Jesus Christ, the Incarnate Son of God, has revealed this truth about God to us. This mystery of the Holy Trinity is at the center of our faith.

For more about related teachings of the Church, see the *Catechism of the Catholic Church*, 198–231, 249–267, 355–387; and the *United States Catholic Catechism for Adults*, pages 50–53, 56–69.

■ Sharing God's Word

Read together Exodus 34:6, Deuteronomy 7:9, and 1 John 4:8. Emphasize that through Sacred Scripture, God reveals who he is and his plan of loving goodness for the world. The teachings of the Church help us to understand the true meaning of Sacred Scripture, God's Word.

■ We Live as Disciples

The Christian home and family is a school of discipleship. Choose one of the following activities to do as a family, or design a similar activity of your own.

▶ Invite family members to take turns completing the sentence, "God is . . ." Continue until no one is able to complete the sentence. Distribute art materials, and create tablemats displaying words and phrases that your family used to describe God.

▶ Recall that all people are created in the image and likeness of God. Share ideas about how your family is an image of God.

▶ Discuss as a family how religious art in your home can help you keep God and prayer at the center of family life. Start with a family crucifix as a central and important reminder of Catholic family living.

■ Our Spiritual Journey

Daily prayer is vital to the life of a Christian family. In this chapter, your child prayed a prayer based on Psalm 66. Read and pray together this prayer on page 33.

For more ideas on ways your family can live as disciples of Jesus, visit **www.BeMyDisciples.com**

(34)

PARTNERING WITH PARENTS

Enriching Daily Prayer in the Home. Inform parents that the United States Conference of Catholic Bishops has provided an excellent resource for prayer in the home: *Catholic Household Blessings and Prayers* (Washington, D.C: USCCB, 2007). It contains traditional Catholic prayers, prayers to be said during the liturgical seasons of the Church's year, devotional prayers, and prayers for important moments and times of transition in a family's life.

Enriching the Lesson

Writing Acrostic Poems

Purpose

To reinforce that God revealed himself to be YHWH (taught on page 30)

Directions

▶ Have the students work with partners to write an acrostic.

▶ Remind them of how an acrostic is written: (1) Stack the letters of a word vertically, that is, one on top of the other. (2) Use each letter to begin the line of the acrostic.

▶ An appropriate word for this session is *TRINITY*. They might begin by writing "Three in one" for the "T" in Trinity.

▶ Have the students share their acrostics, mount them on construction paper, and place them where other people can enjoy them.

Materials

poster or art paper 8-1/2" x 11"

pens or pencils

Creating Paper Mosaics

Purpose

To reinforce that mosaics help us enter the mystery of God (taught on page 28)

Directions

▶ As an alternative to the activity on page 28, invite the students to create more elaborate paper mosaics to represent the Holy Trinity. Ask them first to refer to the ideas they wrote on page 31.

▶ Have them work in small groups to cut out squares of many different colors from construction paper and glue the squares together to create mosaics of a symbol of the Holy Trinity. Note: You may wish to pre-cut the squares using a paper cutter to save time.

▶ Have the young people share their mosaics and discuss the meaning of their symbols.

Materials

scissors and glue sticks

construction paper of many colors

Literature Connection

Purpose

To extend the teaching about St. Thomas Aquinas in Faith-Filled People (taught on page 30)

Directions

▶ You may wish to borrow or purchase the *Loyola Treasury of Saints: From the Time of Jesus to the Present Day*, by David Self (Loyola Press, 2003). This excellent and beautifully illustrated book for young people contains the stories of many saints that the young people are learning about.

▶ Read the story of St. Thomas Aquinas to the class and discuss the life of this giant of Catholic theology with them. The story is very accessible in this book's format.

▶ Invite interested young people to browse through the book at the beginning or end of class or borrow it to learn more about saints they have been studying.

▶ Suggest that they research more about favorite saint or their patron saint in libraries or on the Internet and create a short report for the class.

Materials

Loyola Treasury of Saints by David Self

God, Father and Creator

The Mysteries of Christ's Life

Blessed Kateri Tekawitha remarked that she often went into the woods because it was there that she felt God's presence with her. Creation is the work of God, and he manifests himself and his love for us in the divine work of creation.

God the Father and Creator

God is Creator of heaven and earth, as we boldly proclaim in the Apostles' Creed. The awesome, wonderful, and almighty Creator of the universe, of all that is, seen and unseen, the One who created humanity in the divine image and likeness, has imprinted his image on creation. Through that creation he invites us to know and love him.

> In the creation of the world and of man, God gave the first and universal witness to his almighty love and his wisdom, the first proclamation of the "plan of his loving goodness," which finds its goal in the new creation in Christ.

Catechism of the Catholic Church 315

After he created the whole world out of love, "God looked at everything he had made, and he found, it very good" (Genesis 1:31). Everything God created reveals his infinite goodness and love. This truth about creation is our hope for the future.

At the end of time, there will be a new heaven and a new earth in Christ (Revelation 21:1). God's plan of goodness, intended from the beginning of creation, will be restored in Christ and will give glory and honor to him forever.

Thy Kingdom Come! Deliver Us from Evil!

All creation struggles and groans in hope for the future — indeed for a future. Not everyone is loving. Evil and sin and death mar the goodness of the world. People suffer. Violence, disorder, and fear tear nations apart.

In and through all of this we live as people of faith, the People of God. We believe with all our hearts that God created a very good world. We believe in Jesus Christ. Through him we obtain the grace to unite our suffering and to live as adopted sons and daughters of God. In faith and hope we pray:

> "Great and wonderful are your works,
> Lord God almighty.
> Just and true are your ways,
> O king of the nations.
> Who will not fear you, Lord,
> or glorify your name?
> For you alone are holy.
> All the nations will come
> and worship before you,
> for your righteous acts have been revealed."

Revelation 15:3–4

For Reflection

What are my favorite images of God? What do they say to me about God?

What can I do to help the children appreciate that each one of them is an image of God?

Catechist to Catechist

Growing in Holiness

God the Father can be difficult for sixth-graders to understand. Many of your students might just be starting to understand their relationship with God. This is a good age to help them understand what it means to grow in holiness and to become better at living and celebrating their faith. Many young people think of a holy person as someone who is perfect or someone who is almost perfect. In truth, holiness is a trait of a person who is growing and striving to become perfect as God our Father is perfect. Let the love of God the Father be their guidance in growing in holiness.

A Prayer Space

The prayer area in your learning space is a concrete reminder of God's presence with you and your students. Change the colors that decorate it according to the Liturgical Year. Enthrone a Bible so the presence of God's Word dominates the environment. Hang symbols of the faith of the Church that the students have created. Adding something new on a regular basis will attract attention to the prayer area.

The Church Teaches...

"Human experiences provide the sensible signs that lead the person, by the grace of the Holy Spirit, to a better understanding of the truths of the faith" (*National Directory for Catechesis*, 29A). That is why every chapter begins by helping the children situate the lesson concepts in their own life experiences. In this chapter, the children will explore some of the attributes of God, attributes they have already come to know through study and prayer and living their faith each day. Furthermore every chapter includes a feature on how the children can grow virtuously as a disciple of Jesus.

Further Reading and Reflection

For more on the teachings of the Church, see the *Catechism of the Catholic Church*, 1232–248, 268–354, 388–421 and from the *United States Catholic Catechism for Adults*, pages 53–56, 68–75.

Catechist Prayer

Holy Spirit,
bless the young people this week.
Help them understand and share
 more deeply and more abundantly
in the Paschal Mystery,
as they grow in the relationship
with Jesus Christ.
Amen.

Lesson Planner

Chapter 4 God, Father and Creator

Focus To explore the meaning of calling God Father and Creator

LESSON PART	PROCESS	MATERIALS and RESOURCES
EXPLORE **Focus** To explore the concept of the Kingdom of God 🕐 10 minutes **Pages 35–36**	▶ Proclaim and discuss Matthew 6:9–13 (Our Father in Heaven). ▶ Hear a story about the Kingdom of God. **Disciple Power:** Justice	Bible Pencils Crayons or markers
DISCOVER **Focus** To discover our relationship to God as Father and Creator 🕐 30 minutes **Pages 37–39**	▶ Learn to distinguish between the two Creation accounts. **Activity:** Do a Scripture search about our relationship with God. ▶ Learn the meaning of Original Sin. ▶ Explore God's plan of salvation. **Activity:** Describe three ways that Jesus is a sign of God's love.	Pencils Crayons or markers **Additional Activities Booklet:** Activities 4a–4b, or see BeMyDisciples.com.
DECIDE **Focus** To decide on a way to prepare for the Kingdom of God 🕐 10 minutes **Page 40**	**Activity:** Create a Web home page about the Kingdom of God. **My Faith Choice:** Choose a way to build the Kingdom of God.	Pencils Journals **Enriching the Lesson Activities:** Catechist Edition, page 91 • Writing Diamantes • Creating a Scripture Service • Catholic Social Teaching: Charting Our Stewardship Process

Concluding the Lesson 10 minutes

We Remember

Page 41

▶ Review concepts and do review activity.

▶ **Assessment Tools Booklet:** Chapter Test 4a–4b, or see BeMyDisciples.com.

We Pray

▶ **Prayer:** a responsorial psalm

Materials: Bible, candle, cross for prayer space

▶ Grade 6 Music CD

Preview

Point out resources for this chapter at

www.BeMyDisciples.com

▶ Preview the With My Family page and next week's lesson theme.

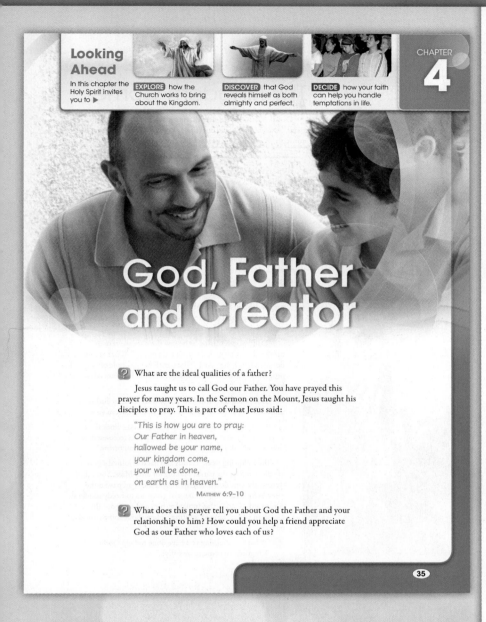

Looking Ahead

In this chapter the Holy Spirit invites you to ▶

EXPLORE how the Church works to bring about the Kingdom.

DISCOVER that God reveals himself as both almighty and perfect.

DECIDE how your faith can help you handle temptations in life.

CHAPTER 4

God, Father and Creator

❓ What are the ideal qualities of a father?

Jesus taught us to call God our Father. You have prayed this prayer for many years. In the Sermon on the Mount, Jesus taught his disciples to pray. This is part of what Jesus said:

*"This is how you are to pray:
Our Father in heaven,
hallowed be your name,
your kingdom come,
your will be done,
on earth as in heaven."*

MATTHEW 6:9–10

❓ What does this prayer tell you about God the Father and your relationship to him? How could you help a friend appreciate God as our Father who loves each of us?

35

Pray

▶ Gather students for prayer. Begin and end with praying the Sign of the Cross.

▶ Ask the children to repeat after you:

"God and Father of all, we praise you. You are the source of all we have and are. Amen."

Reflect

▶ Ask the opening question and jot the students' responses on the board.

▶ Invite students to reflect on the image on the page. Inquire, "What are some attributes of being a father that reflect the love of God the Father?"

▶ Introduce the Scripture passage and invite a student to proclaim it for the class. Then have them personally reflect on the closing questions. *(Accept all appropriate responses.)*

▶ Spend some time discussing the students' understanding of how Jesus revealed the merciful love of God the Father.

Focus

Call attention to Looking Ahead. What is it that the Holy Spirit is inviting students to do?

HUMAN METHODOLOGIES

Learning Through Human Experience. The *National Directory for Catechesis* notes that our human experiences and the Holy Spirit teach us and help us grow in our understanding of the truths of the faith (*NDC*, 29A). As this chapter's Scripture story suggests, Adam and Eve learned that their unwise choices had serious negative consequences. Invite students to write a story about a student their age who learned from an unwise choice. Ask them to describe how the experience of making the wrong choice later helped them to understand why it was wrong. Remind them that relying on God's grace can guide us in making choices.

Introduce

▶ Invite volunteers to read aloud each paragraph of Thy Kingdom Come.

▶ Ask, What do you think of Carlos' Father's concern about helping to bring the Kingdom of God? Where have you seen similar needs? Discuss your responses together.

Reinforce

▶ Ask the students to underline a definition of the Kingdom of God in the text.

▶ Have students read aloud the Disciple Power section. Point out that justice happens when our words and actions reflect God's love. Bringing justice to others is part of the work of bringing the Kingdom of God.

Connect

▶ Have students reflect on the questions on the page silently, and then to share their responses with a partner.

▶ Remind the students that acting justly extends to the way we talk to or about others and about God. Profanity, name-calling, and gossip are all examples of injustice. They do nothing to build the Kingdom of God.

Disciple Power

Justice

Justice is one of the four Cardinal Virtues. Justice is the habit of consistently giving what is due to God and to our neighbor. We give God what is due to him when we worship him alone. Our worship of God includes loving our neighbor and respecting the dignity of every human person. Through Christian justice, we participate in preparing the way for the coming of the Kingdom of God.

THE CHURCH FOLLOWS JESUS
Thy Kingdom Come

Carlos and his father were driving home for church. Carlos asked, "Dad, are we going out for pancakes today?" His father did not reply. "Dad, did you hear me? What about pancakes today?"

"What was that Carlos?" asked Mr. Sanchez, absent-mindedly.

"Pancakes, Dad. Are we going for pancakes? You seem as if you are a million miles way," said Carlos.

"Sorry, Carlos. I guess I was thinking about the Our Father." Carlos looked at his father, bewildered. "The Our Father?"

"Yes. Each week at Mass we pray, 'thy kingdom come.' I was just thinking as we drive through this neighborhood that I don't see God's Kingdom coming much around here."

Carlos looked out the window. Some of the houses looked abandoned. At others, a few people sat on their front steps. Two boys were throwing a ball in a yard behind a chain-link fence.

His dad continued, "Most of the people in this neighborhood have no jobs. Then last year that bad storm blew through and did a lot of damage. It doesn't look like some of these roofs have ever been repaired."

"Dad," began Carlos, as he saw the pancake restaurant up ahead. But his father continued talking. "What are we doing to help?" he asked. "The parish has a couple of outreach programs, but what are we doing to help?" He glanced over at his son.

"Dad, what does this have to do with the Our Father?" asked Carlos, as the pancake restaurant faded from view.

"It has everything to do with it, son. God's work is our work too. Our job is to help God's Kingdom to come in its fullness. I think I'll give Father Tom a call tomorrow."

The following week, Carlos and his dad joined a group of volunteers in the parish parking lot after Mass. Soon they were in the run-down neighborhood they had passed the week before, handing out bags of groceries to needy residents. Afterwards, Carlos' dad looked at him and smiled. "Thy kingdom come," he said, smiling. "How about some pancakes now?"

? What is something you have done to help God's Kingdom to come more fully?

36

DISCIPLE POWER

Justice. Clothing and food drives, house building and repair efforts, rallies for life, and responses to natural disasters are acts of justice we often see in the media. People seldom think of justice in terms of respect for and consideration of our neighbor—the person next to us at home, work, parish, or school. Justice demands that we look out for our neighbor's most basic needs. We do so when we shovel a snowy walk, mow a lawn, share a meal, welcome a new neighbor with a plate of cookies, invite the new coworker to lunch, or sit next to the unpopular classmate. These are everyday acts of justice. What other examples can you and your students add?

Almighty Love

Abba, Father

The Book of Genesis, the first book of the Bible, contains two accounts of creation. In the first creation account, you learned that God is Creator. He is almighty and omnipotent (read Genesis 1:1–2:4). God is the Father, the Almighty, the Creator of all that is visible and invisible. This means that God created everything and that creation is good. We read, "God looked at everything he had made, and he found it very good" (Genesis 1:31). God is the source of everything that is good, true, and beautiful.

The second account of creation emphasizes the personal relationship that God has with humanity (read Genesis 2:4–25). The events of this account reveal God's presence and his love for us. When we address God as "Abba, Father," as Jesus did and taught us to do, we acknowledge God's presence with us and his deep personal love for each of us.

Through Baptism in Jesus Christ, the Son of God, we become adopted sons and daughters of God our Father. God the Father is perfect in his love for us. Jesus constantly taught about the love of the Father. Jesus wants us to know the parental tenderness that God has for us. God desires for all of us to be with him forever (see Matthew 18:10–14).

FAITH FOCUS
What is our relationship to God the Creator?

FAITH VOCABULARY

▶ **Original Sin**
Original Sin is the sin of Adam and Eve by which they lost the state of original holiness, and by which death, sin, and suffering entered into the world.

▶ **sin**
Sin is freely choosing to do what we know is against God's will or freely choosing not to do something that we know God wants us to do.

▶ **temptation**
Temptation is anything that tries to move us to do or say something that we know is wrong, or prevents us from doing something that we know is good and that we ought to do.

Activity Look up and read the following Scripture passages. Think about what God is telling you about himself and your relationship with him. Write your responses here. Share your thoughts with a partner.

John 14:6 _____

_____

Romans 8:15 _____

_____

Galatians 4:5 _____

_____

37

TASKS OF CATECHESIS

Promoting Knowledge of the Faith. Each and every day we are bombarded by words and images that seek to define what is beautiful and good in today's world. The latest styles, the most current gadgets, and the best sensational movies catch our attention. Invite your students to reflect on beauty that is a reflection of God the Creator's loving hand. Have them make collages of God's beautiful creation, especially people. Invite them to include images from popular culture that they think reflect Catholic values. As the students work on their projects, play quiet instrumental music or nature sounds. Take time to appreciate each student's work of beauty.

Key Concept
God is the Father, the Almighty, the Creator of all that is visible and invisible.

Teach

▶ Recall what was discussed about the creation accounts in the previous chapter.

▶ Have students quietly read the text on the page. Ask students to respond to the "Faith Focus" question.

▶ Ask the students to read silently to recall the distinction between the two Creation accounts. Ask volunteers to identify the differences.

▶ Have the students close their books. Ask for volunteers to define the terms in Faith Vocabulary. Then examine the definitions with their responses. Clarify any questions the students may have.

Reinforce

Inquire, "What are examples of God the Father's perfect love?"

Connect

Distribute Bibles to the students. Have the students complete the activity and share their responses.

Key Concept
Original Sin is the turning away from God and his plan for Creation.

Teach

▶ Have students take turns reading paragraphs of the text on the page. Have them identify what sin and evil are.

▶ Explain that sin is essentially refusing to do the will of God. The first time human beings rejected God's will is referred to as Original Sin.

▶ Explain that the disobedience of Adam and Eve to God's commandment has become part of our human nature. By rejecting God's loving commandment, we reject God himself.

▶ Point out The New Eve in Faith-Filled People. Discuss why Mary is called the new Eve.

Reinforce

Remind students that in the beginning, God created humanity in a state of friendship with him. State again that our relationship with God could only be restored through Jesus Christ.

Connect

Explain that through the sacramental grace of Baptism, God gives us the strength to resist temptations and choose to do what is good and avoid what is evil. Invite the students to share their response to the question on the page with a partner.

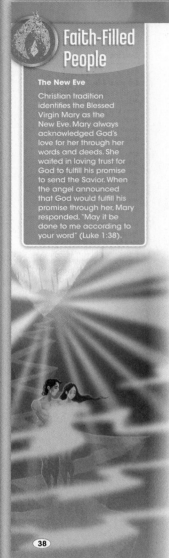

Faith-Filled People

The New Eve

Christian tradition identifies the Blessed Virgin Mary as the New Eve. Mary always acknowledged God's love for her through her words and deeds. She waited in loving trust for God to fulfill his promise to send the Savior. When the angel announced that God would fulfill his promise through her, Mary responded, "May it be done to me according to your word" (Luke 1:38).

Separated from God

You have learned that God created humanity in a state of original holiness and justice, or friendship with him. **Sin** and evil, the Bible tells us, made their way into the good world of God's creation when the first humans turned away from God. We give the name **Original Sin** to this turning away from God and his plan of Creation.

Adam and Eve freely chose to do what they knew God did not want them to do. They sinned, and by their sin, all of humanity lost original holiness and original justice, except Mary, the Mother of God, who was born without Original Sin. Mary remained free from personal sin throughout her entire life. The name given to this unique grace and privilege that God gave to Mary is the Immaculate Conception.

The Scripture story of humanity's fall from grace and loss of original holiness began with the **temptation** of Adam and Eve. Prior to the Fall, God had commanded Adam and Eve:

"You are free to eat from any of the trees of the garden except the tree of knowledge of good and bad. From that tree you shall not eat; the moment you eat from it you are surely doomed to die."

GENESIS 2:16–17

Then the serpent, representing Satan, the Evil One, tempted Adam and Eve by telling them that they would not die. The serpent lied to Eve:

"You certainly will not die! No, God knows well that the moment you eat of it your eyes will be opened and you will be like gods who know what is good and what is bad."

GENESIS 3:4–5

Adam and Eve gave in to temptation and sinned. They rejected God by rejecting his loving commandment (read Genesis 3:1–7). The loss of original holiness has become part of our fallen human nature. We now share in the effects of Original Sin. The world and all of us in the human family are marked by sin. From the very first moment of our existence, or conception, we need to be reconciled with God.

Through the Sacrament of Baptism, we become adopted sons and daughters of God. We are reborn in Christ with the forgiveness of Original Sin at Baptism. We receive the gift and grace of the Holy Spirit to live as children of God the Father.

 What does being an adopted son or daughter of God means to you?

38

FAITH-FILLED PEOPLE

The New Eve. The *New Eve* is one of the many names by which Christians address the Blessed Virgin Mary. In the Litany of the Blessed Virgin Mary she is also addressed as Mother of our Creator, Mirror of justice, Cause of our joy, Health of the sick, Comfort of the troubled, Queen of all saints, and Queen of peace (*Catholic Household Blessings and Prayers.* Washington, DC: USCCB, 2007). Discuss with your students why Mary has been given each of these titles, including the New Eve. Invite them to share what they know about Mary and to use their knowledge and imagination to create other titles for Mary. Use those names in a litany to conclude this week's session or on one of Mary's feasts during the year.

Promise of Salvation

God did not reject Adam and Eve after they turned away from him. He approached them as a loving and good father. God promised to send someone to heal the relationship between him and humanity. This is God's plan of salvation (read Genesis 3: 15).

All of God's promises in the Old Testament point to Jesus Christ, the Savior whom God promised to send. In truth, God's promise of eternal life begins with Jesus. In Christ, all of God's promises are fulfilled. Jesus did not abolish the Law and Covenant of Sinai. The Son of God fulfilled and perfected these promises (read Matthew 5:17–18). Jesus Christ is the new and everlasting Covenant (read 1 Corinthians 11:25). Jesus is the Savior of all people. Christ is the center of God's plan of salvation.

The Son of God, Jesus Christ, became a man, lived on earth, and was raised from the dead to save us and redeem us from sin and death. In Jesus Christ, we have been healed, or reconciled, with God, with one another, and with all of creation.

What about those who have not heard of Jesus? The answer to that question is very important. God wants everyone to share in his life and love both now and forever. The Church teaches that through the grace of the Holy Spirit, God works quietly and mysteriously to draw all people to himself, even those who have not heard of Jesus. All people can be saved who seek to serve and love God with all their hearts. This is both the promise and desire of God (read John 17:1–26).

Catholics Believe

Salvation is the deliverance of humanity from the power of sin and death through Jesus Christ. The Incarnate Son of God, Jesus Christ, died for our sins and revealed God's power over death in the Resurrection. Our faith in Christ is necessary for our salvation.

Activity Describe three acts that Christ has done for us that show the love of the Father for all people. Share your responses with others.

Signs of God's Love

1. _____
   _____

2. _____
   _____

3. _____
   _____

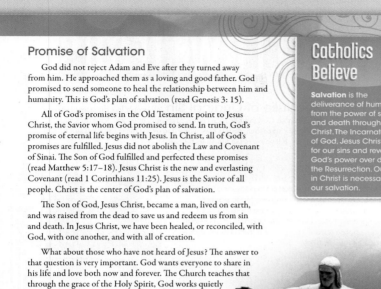

39

CATHOLICS BELIEVE

Salvation and the Unbaptized. The Church holds that "Baptism is necessary for salvation for those to whom the Gospel has been proclaimed and who have had the possibility of asking for this sacrament" (*CCC*, 1257). In addition, the Church holds that salvation is possible for "those who suffer death for the sake of the faith without having received Baptism" (*CCC* 1258); for "catechumens who die before their Baptism" (*CCC* 1259); for "[e]very man who is ignorant of the Gospel of Christ and of his Church, but seeks the truth and does the will of God in accordance of his understanding of it" (*CCC* 1260); and for "children who have died without Baptism" (*CCC* 1261).

Key Concept
Salvation is necessary and possible for all people.

Teach

▶ Invite students to share what they know about God's plan of salvation. Ask what they recall about God's Covenant.

▶ Have students silently read the text on the page, stopping when they reach a Scripture passages reference. Have volunteer students read those passages from their Bibles to extend learning.

▶ Ask, "Is salvation necessary for even those who have not heard of Jesus?" (*Yes. God wants everyone to share in his life and love both now and forever. All people can be saved who love and serve God with their whole heart.*)

Reinforce

▶ Have a student read the Catholics Believe feature. Reinforce that salvation is necessary because sin has separated us from God.

▶ Remind students that God has initiated his loving plan of salvation by sending his only Son for our salvation.

Connect

Have students work individually to complete the activity on the page. Invite volunteers to share their responses with the class.

Reinforce

Ask a student to read aloud the opening paragraph.

Respond

- ▶ Invite students to share how they use the Internet and online social networking sites.

- ▶ Explain that these online sites can be both beneficial and detrimental to our relationships.

- ▶ Reinforce that technology itself is not good or bad, but how we use it can lead us to do something good or choose to commit sin.

- ▶ Give the students time to complete the activity and invite them to show their work.

Choose

- ▶ Have students privately complete My Faith Choice. Invite students to share their responses to the activity with the class.

- ▶ Invite them to pray the Our Father silently and reverently.

I FOLLOW JESUS

Because of Original Sin, all people lost the state of original holiness that God intended, except for Mary and, of course, Jesus. In every generation since then, people have worked to overcome temptation and to help bring the Kingdom of God in all its fullness.

I BELIEVE IN GOD

John and Alison want to start a fan page for a famous person. At first they are thinking of a movie star, but they decide to choose a famous person known for humanitarian efforts to build the Kingdom of God. Help them choose a worthy person, and then design a home page for their Web site.

MY FAITH CHOICE

This week I will do something each day to build the Kingdom of God. I will

_____

_____

 Place yourself in the presence of God the Father. Pray the Our Father in the silence of your heart. Pause after each petition of the prayer.

40

TEACHING TIP

Resisting Temptation. Today's Web activity calls to mind the many temptations on the Internet. Remind students that temptation is anything that draws our attention away from God or causes us to turn away from God's commands. Have students work in small groups to discuss sources of temptation in the lives of young people today (i.e., peer pressure and the desire to be popular), and healthy habits that they can develop to resist temptation (i.e., talking to God in prayer, reading God's Word, or consciously choosing to avoid people who try to pressure them into habits or activities they know are wrong). Invite the entire group to share their thoughts regarding sources of temptation and ways to avoid it.

Chapter Review

Complete each sentence using one of the terms provided in the word bank.

Father	presence	justice	salvation	almighty

1. Jesus Christ, the Son of God, taught us that God is our loving
_____ Father _____

2. Through the cardinal virtue of _____ justice _____ we
participate in the Kingdom of God by following God's Law of Love.

3. In the first account of creation, God reveals that he is
_____ almighty _____ and omnipotent.

4. In the second account of creation, God reveals his
_____ presence _____ in a personal way as goodness and love.

5. Our _____ salvation _____ is deliverance from the power of sin
and eternal death, made possible by God.

> **TO HELP YOU REMEMBER**
>
> 1. God reveals himself as Father and Creator, the source of all that is visible and invisible.
>
> 2. Original Sin is the sin that Adam and Eve committed by freely turning away from God's love and friendship.
>
> 3. In Jesus Christ, the Savior promised by God, we have been healed, or reconciled, with God, with one another, and with all of creation.

Sing to the Lord

In the Liturgy of the Word, the Church as a whole assembly prays the psalms in the Responsorial Psalm. In a similar way, this psalm is structured for a leader and the whole class to pray together.

Leader: Sing to the Lord, bless his name;
announce his salvation day after day.

All: **Sing to the Lord, bless his name;
announce his salvation day after day.**

Leader: Tell God's glory among the nations;
among all peoples, God's marvelous deeds.

All: **Sing to the Lord, bless his name;
announce his salvation day after day.**

Leader: For great is the Lord and highly to be praised,
to be feared above all gods . . .
Let the heavens be glad and the earth rejoice.

All: **Sing to the Lord, bless his name;
announce his salvation day after day.**

PSALM 96:2, 3–4, 11

41

We Remember

▶ Read aloud each summary statement in the To Help You Remember section on the page, leaving a key word or phrase out. Then have students complete the statements from memory without looking at their books.

▶ Review any concepts that need clarification before they begin the review section.

▶ Have students privately complete the Chapter Review.

▶ Invite volunteer students to read aloud their responses for the five statements. Review any points that are not clear.

We Pray

▶ Gather the students to conclude the chapter with prayer. Select a volunteer to be the leader.

▶ Together, pray the prayer on the page according to the instructions. Pray the "All" responses together as a class.

LITURGY CONNECTION

Leaders of Prayer. The liturgical name for a leader of prayer is *presider.* The presider's task is to lead prayer with confidence and reverence, and in a clear, strong voice. The presider also paces the prayer by allowing time for silence before beginning to pray and between the various parts of the prayer. As you invite students to serve as leaders of prayer this year, help them to develop these qualities of a good presider. Encourage good preparation as a leader of prayer or as a reader of Sacred Scripture by appointing students a week or more in advance. Give everyone who wishes to do so an opportunity to take part as a presider, a leader of prayer.

Preview

▶ Have students carefully tear out the With My Family page along the perforation.

▶ Encourage them to share the pages with their family and to complete the activities together at home.

▶ If the students did not or were not able to complete the Chapter Review, encourage them to complete it with their family.

▶ Point out the chapter title and theme of next week's lesson.

Visit www.BeMyDisciples.com

▶ Take time with the students to explore the many activities and resources available at **www.BeMyDisciples.com.**

▶ Encourage students and their families to discover the many resources available at the Web site.

Before Moving On ...

As you finish today's lesson, reflect on the following question before moving on to the next chapter.

How do I appreciate God as our Father?

With My Family

This Week...

In chapter 4, God, Father and Creator, your child learned:

▶ The Kingdom of God is the fulfillment of God's plan for all creation in Christ at the end of time when Christ will come again in glory. Each of us is called to help bring the Kingdom of God to its fullness by our words and actions.

▶ The Book of Genesis contains two accounts of creation. In the first, God is revealed as Creator and almighty Father, maker of all that is. The second emphasizes the personal relationship of love that God has with humanity.

▶ God created humanity in a state of original holiness and justice, but our first parents freely sinned. Their Original Sin lost for us the original state of grace.

▶ Through Baptism we are reborn in Christ and the effects of Original Sin are forgiven. We receive the gift and grace of the Holy Spirit to live as children of God the Father.

▶ God freely entered into a Covenant with humanity, and that Covenant reached its fullness in Jesus Christ, the new and everlasting Covenant. Jesus is the center of God's plan for salvation.

For more about related teachings of the Church, see the *Catechism of the Catholic Church*, 51232–248, 268–354, 388–421; and the *United States Catholic Catechism for Adults*, pages 53–56, 68–75.

■ Sharing God's Word

Read together John 17:1–26. Emphasize that through Sacred Scripture, God reveals himself as "our Father." In Jesus Christ, the Incarnate Son of God, we have salvation and redemption. We have been healed, or reconciled, with God, with one another, and with all of creation.

■ We Live as Disciples

The Christian home and family is a school of discipleship. Choose one of the following activities to do as a family, or design a similar activity of your own.

▶ Choose one of the Scripture passages from this chapter and design a family prayer banner. Display this banner prominently in your home. Use it during family prayer time as a way to focus on God, who loves us and sustains us.

▶ Discuss as a family ways that you experience the fatherly love of God. Choose one way to honor God the Father for all that he provides.

▶ As a family, develop a stewardship plan on how each family member will help take care of the gift of creation that God has given to everyone. Realize that caring for creation involves practicing the virtue of justice.

■ Our Spiritual Journey

Listening to and praying the Scriptures has a long tradition in the Church. In this chapter, your child prayed a prayer based on Psalm 96. Read and pray together this prayer on page 41.

For more ideas on ways your family can live as disciples of Jesus, visit **www.BeMyDisciples.com**

(42)

CATHOLIC SOCIAL TEACHING

Care for God's Creation. We show our respect for God the Creator by caring for all that he created. Care for creation is, in fact, a requirement of Christian faith. First of all, we are called by God to show care and respect for all people, since we are all created in his image. This is the foundation of our human dignity. We are to be stewards of the earth as well. Christians must measure every choice by the impact it has on human life and on the environment. This principle was taught in this unit in Chapter 4, where students explored the concept of the Kingdom of God that calls us to care for all that God has created and to cooperate in bringing it to perfection. The last activity on the facing page, reinforces this concept.

Enriching the Lesson

Writing Diamantes

Purpose

To reinforce that in Jesus Christ we have been reconciled with God, with one another, and with all creation (taught on page 39)

Directions

Review with the students that a diamante is a form of verse consisting of seven lines and sixteen words, contrasting two words.

▶ Review the structure of a diamante—Line 1: one word of a pair of opposites; Line 2: two words describing the word; Line 3: three action words ending in "ing" describing the word; Line 4: two words describing the word in Line 1 followed by a dash and two words describing the contrasting word, which will appear in Line 7; Line 5: three action words ending in "ing" describing the contrasting word; Line 6: two words describing the contrasting word; Line 7: name the contrasting word.

▶ Have the students work with partners to create diamantes using the names Jesus and Adam.

▶ Invite the young people to share their diamantes.

Materials

paper and pens or pencils

Creating a Scripture Service

Purpose

To reinforce that the Church encourages participation in Scripture services, or services of the word (illustrated on page 41)

Directions

▶ Have the students plan an Advent service for the fifth grade.

▶ Brainstorm a list of everything that needs to happen, for example, opening and closing prayers, a ritual action, the selection of readings, invitations to the fifth graders, and music.

▶ Have the students create a checklist of what they can do each week to make this Scripture service a success.

Materials

paper

pens or pencils

Catholic Social Teaching: Charting Our Stewardship Progress

Purpose

To respond to the teaching that we are to be the stewards of God's Creation (taught in Chapter 4)

Directions

▶ Remind the children of the words in Genesis 1:28, where God told Adam and Eve to "fill the earth and subdue it." Recall also the words of Genesis 2:15: "The LORD God then took the man and settled him in the garden of Eden, to cultivate and care for it." Tell the class that this work of stewardship is ours today.

▶ Invite the class to work in groups brainstorming ways to do a better job of caring for earth in their parish, school, or neighborhood.

▶ Once you have recorded their ideas on the board, invite a team to create a progress chart listing areas of concern, actions steps, and a column where progress can be noted.

▶ Set a deadline for the project and post the poster where it can be updated weekly.

Materials

sticky notes

pens or pencils

The Unit Review provides the opportunity to assess the students' understanding of the faith concepts presented in the unit and to affirm them in their growing knowledge and love of God. Here are a few suggestions for using these pages.

▶ Share that the next two pages are an opportunity to stop and review what they have learned.

▶ Provide time for the students to ask questions.

▶ Have the students complete the review alone or with partners.

A. Choose the Best Word

▶ Read the directions for this section.

▶ Then have the student work alone or with a partner to complete the section.

▶ Invite volunteers to share their responses. Clarify and correct responses as needed.

B. Show What You Know

▶ Read the directions for this section. Answer the first question together as a class.

▶ Then have the student continue working alone or with a partner to complete the section.

▶ Invite volunteers to share their responses. Clarify and correct responses as needed.

Unit 1 **Review** Name _____

A. Choose the Best Word

Fill in the blanks to complete each of the sentences. Use the words from the word bank.

| Bible | Creation | Father |
| Redemption | sanctification | salvation |

1. __Creation__ is God creating everyone and everything, seen and unseen, out of nothing and without any help.

2. Jesus Christ, the Son of God, taught us that God is our loving __Father__.

3. Through the __Bible__, God reveals himself and his loving plan of __salvation__ for the world and all people.

4. Through Christ's act of __redemption__, God delivered humanity from the eternal death of sin.

5. The gift of sharing in God's life and love is called __sanctification__.

B. Show What You Know

Match the items in column A with those in column B.

Column A

A. faith

B. creed

C. the Holy Trinity

D. Original Sin

E. justice

Column B

_A_ 1. A supernatural gift from God

_C_ 2. The mystery of one God in three Divine Persons

_D_ 3. The result of the fall of Adam and Eve

_E_ 4. One of the Cardinal Virtues that is the habit of giving what is due to God and to our neighbor

_B_ 5. Summary of the principal beliefs of the Church

43

TEACHING TIP

Assessing Learning. Throughout the year, use multiple forms of assessment at the end of each unit. Students learn and communicate their understanding in multiple ways. Some forms of communication, for example, writing paragraphs, work better for some students. Other forms of communication, for example, artwork and verbal responses, work better for others. Asking questions, observing small group interactions, and using different activities throughout the chapter will provide you with multiple ways of identifying the students' understanding of the truths of the faith.

C. Connect with Scripture

Reread the Scripture passage on the first Unit Opener page. What connection do you see between this passage and what you learned in this unit?

_____ Responses will vary.

_____

_____

D. Be a Disciple

1. *Review the four pages in this unit titled "The Church Follows Jesus." What person or ministry of the Church on these pages will inspire you to be a better disciple of Jesus? Explain your answer.*

_____ Responses will vary.

_____

_____

2. *Work with a group. Review the four Disciple Power virtues or gifts you have learned about in this unit. After jotting down your own ideas, share with the group practical ways that you will live these virtues or gifts day by day.*

_____ Responses will vary.

_____

_____

44

C. Connect with Scripture

▶ Invite the students to reflect on the Scripture passage in the Unit Opener and to write their understanding of how this passage connects with the doctrinal content of the unit they have just completed.

▶ Ask volunteers to share their responses, now or after completion of the entire Unit Review.

D. Be a Disciple

▶ Invite the young people to work independently on the first question about The Church Follows Jesus. Ask volunteers to share their responses.

▶ Divide the students into small groups of three or four for the second part of this section. Ask them to write their personal reflections first, and then to share with their group practical ways of living the Disciple Power virtues or qualities of discipleship in everyday life.

▶ Ask for feedback from the small groups as time allows.

TEACHING TIP

Sensitivity to All Learners. As you complete this Unit Review, be sensitive to all types of learners. Those students with special learning needs as well as those who may be hesitant to share their ideas aloud in a group may need particular encouragement and support. Remember that this Unit Review is only one way to access the students' understanding of the faith concepts as presented in this unit. Alternative assessments can be found online at www.BeMyDisciples.com.

We Believe

Part Two

Objectives

In this unit, the students will learn that:

▶ The Incarnation is the belief that the Son of God became fully human in all ways except sin, while remaining fully divine.

▶ The Paschal Mystery is the Passion, Death, Resurrection, and Ascension of Jesus Christ.

▶ The Holy Spirit is at work bringing about God's plan of Salvation within the Church.

▶ God the Father has called the Church, the People of God, together in Jesus Christ by the power of the Holy Spirit.

Spiritual Insights

"When we speak of the Paschal Mystery, we refer to Christ's death and Resurrection as one inseparable event. It is a mystery because it is a visible sign of an invisible act of God. It is paschal because it is Christ's passing through death into new life. For us it means that we can now die to sin and its domination of our lives, and we pass over into divine life already here on earth and more completely in heaven" (*United States Catholic Catechism for Adults*, page 93).

"Remain in me, as I remain in you . . . I am the vine, you are the branches" (John 15:4–5).

Living the Six Tasks of Catechesis

Liturgical Education: Saint Elizabeth Ann Seton (1774–1821)

Elizabeth was raised in a wealthy Episcopalian family in New York. The family read the Scriptures and prayed together often. Her parents also encouraged Elizabeth to participate in charitable activities.

Elizabeth fell in love with and married Will Seton when she was nineteen. They had five children together. Then Will contracted tuberculosis. He was unable to work and his successful business failed. Family friends in Italy invited the Seton family to stay with them while William recovered. They also wanted to help Elizabeth with the responsibility of caring for her children.

Elizabeth was deeply moved by her friends' Catholic faith. She began to visit Catholic churches to pray before the Blessed Sacrament. She had no doubt that Jesus was truly present in the bread and consecrated wine at Mass. Elizabeth also felt drawn to our Blessed Mother, especially after Will died. She knew that Mary had suffered the loss of her beloved son, Jesus. As she knelt before the tabernacle praying to Jesus and his mother, Elizabeth felt the Lord calling her to join the Catholic Church.

A year later, back in America, she professed her faith as a Catholic although many friends and family turned their backs on her. She decided that the best way she could support herself and her children was to open a Catholic boarding school for girls. In this way, she could provide both faith and education for the girls.

In time, Elizabeth formed a religious order for women called the American Sisters of Charity. With Elizabeth's leadership, the nuns opened orphanages and schools for the poor. Mother Seton, as she became known, was one of the first to reach out to developmentally challenged children. Her nuns also worked in hospitals and homes for the elderly.

We honor Elizabeth Ann Seton as the first American-born saint. As catechists, we respond to the gift of Jesus' Body and Blood in the Eucharist through our service to others, as Saint Elizabeth did.

Sharing Your Faith

Find a partner to work with: a spouse, a friend, a fellow catechist. Come together at the beginning or end of each unit for shared prayer and discussion. Use the questions below as a starting point. As an alternative, record your thoughts in a personal journal.

▶ Why are the Cross and the Resurrection inseparable for us as Jesus' disciples?

▶ Describe an experience of the Holy Spirit inspiring or encouraging you.

▶ How do you build up the Body of Christ, the Church?

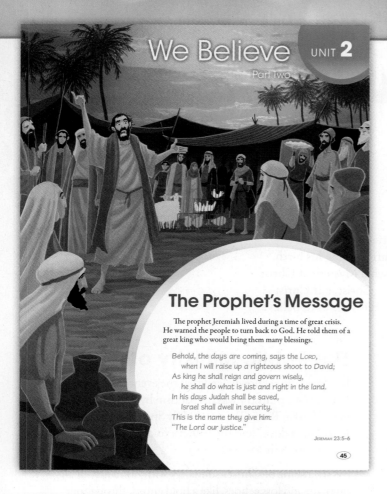

We Believe UNIT 2
Part Two

The Prophet's Message

The prophet Jeremiah lived during a time of great crisis. He warned the people to turn back to God. He told them of a great king who would bring them many blessings.

> Behold, the days are coming, says the LORD,
>   when I will raise up a righteous shoot to David;
> As king he shall reign and govern wisely,
>   he shall do what is just and right in the land.
> In his days Judah shall be saved,
>   Israel shall dwell in security.
> This is the name they give him:
> "The Lord our justice."
>
> JEREMIAH 23:5–6

45

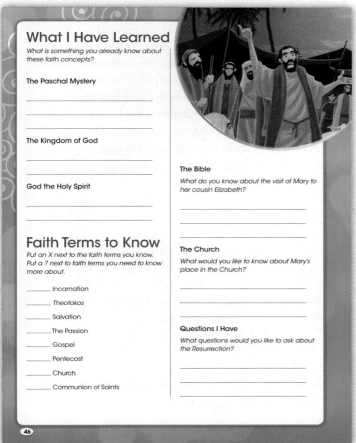

What I Have Learned

What is something you already know about these faith concepts?

The Paschal Mystery

_____
_____
_____

The Kingdom of God

_____
_____
_____

God the Holy Spirit

_____
_____
_____

Faith Terms to Know

Put an X next to the faith terms you know. Put a ? next to faith terms you need to know more about.

_____ Incarnation

_____ *Theotokos*

_____ Salvation

_____ The Passion

_____ Gospel

_____ Pentecost

_____ Church

_____ Communion of Saints

The Bible

What do you know about the visit of Mary to her cousin Elizabeth?

_____
_____
_____

The Church

What would you like to know about Mary's place in the Church?

_____
_____
_____

Questions I Have

What questions would you like to ask about the Resurrection?

_____
_____
_____

46

Unit 2 Opener

Opening Page

▶ Invite the young people to tell you what they see in the illustration. *(The prophet Jeremiah is speaking to the people.)*

▶ Ask a volunteer to read the Scripture story aloud. Then ask: "About whom is Jeremiah speaking?" *(Accept all reasonable responses.)*

Getting Ready

▶ Invite the young people to write their responses to the questions and directions under What I Have Learned, Faith Terms to Know, and the other headings in the second column.

▶ Invite a few volunteers to share their responses, but do not correct them at this time. Tell the students that they will return to this page to check their learning at the end of the unit.

▶ For Questions I Have, you might write their questions on the board or on a piece of newsprint so that you can refer to them if or when the topics come up in the unit.

▶ Ask the class to look at the next page and begin Chapter 5.

BACKGROUND

The Mysteries of Christ's Life

When you speak the name Jesus Christ, which memories does it evoke? Most of our attention will likely focus on the events surrounding his birth, Death, and Resurrection. The Incarnation and the Paschal Mystery of Christ are indeed the central mysteries of the Church's faith in Christ, but Christ's whole life on earth reveals the mystery of God's love and invites us to believe in and share in that love.

The Mystery of Redemption

"Christ's whole life is a mystery of redemption. Redemption comes to us above all through the blood of the cross, but this mystery is at work throughout Christ's entire life" (*Catechism of the Catholic Church,* 517). Reflecting on the other mysteries of Christ's life is also important as we try to come to know and love him and grow as his disciples.

The Hidden Life of Christ

For most of his life on earth, Jesus was hidden from view. It is reasonable to assume that he led a life very similar to those of his contemporaries during the early years. He woke up, worked, ate meals with his parents, and gave little evidence of greatness (see Matthew 13:55). Jesus obeyed Mary and Joseph and observed the laws of the Jewish religion.

His home at Nazareth, with its routines of family life, work, and parental instruction, is something with which we can easily identify. Jesus was a young boy. He was, in some ways, much like us or the young people sitting in a sixth-grade classroom who are advancing in "wisdom and age and favor before God and man" (Luke 2:52).

The Public Ministry of Jesus

It is generally acknowledged that the event that initiated Jesus' public ministry was his baptism by John the Baptist in the Jordan River. There the Holy Spirit descended on Jesus "like a dove," and the Father's voice declared, "This is my beloved Son" (Matthew 3:17).

The theme of Christ's solidarity with humanity in all our pain and loss echoes, like a bold chord, throughout his short ministry. Jesus reached out to everyone and preached a kingdom where we are all restored to God's image and likeness. He made it clear that the kingdom belongs to the poor and the lowly who accept his kingdom with humble hearts. It belongs to people who struggle to turn their lives and wills over to God's provident care. He worked miracles not to impress people, but to invite people to faith in God and to demonstrate the power of divine love at work in the world amid hunger, injustice, poverty, illness, death, and sin.

For Reflection

How do I respond to Jesus' question, "Who do you say that I am?"

How does my reflection on the mysteries of Christ's entire life on earth influence my daily decisions?

Catechist to Catechist

Planting the Seeds of Faith

Saint Paul the Apostle wrote, "I planted, Apollos watered, but God caused the growth" (1 Corinthians 3:6). Saint Paul's description of his ministry describes your work as a catechist in many ways. You plant the seeds of faith; someone else waters it; God, in his good time, brings the harvest. Growth in faith in Jesus Christ is more than simply learning more about Jesus; it is encountering Christ. It is growing in friendship and intimacy with him through study and prayer. It is growing in a relationship with Jesus that becomes so central to who you are that it gives direction to all that you say and do.

Modeling a Life of Faith

As Mary is the model of faith for all Christians, you are a model of faith for your students. Your actions, as well as your words, manifest your faith and the difference living a life of faith makes in a person. The students will see your love and patience and your compassion and understanding as signs of God's loving patience, compassion, and understanding of them. They will come to trust in God's love when they trust your love for them.

The Church Teaches...

"The incarnation of the only Son of God is the original inculturation of God's word. The mystery of the incarnation is also the model of all evangelization by the Church" (*National Directory for Catechesis*, 21A). It is important that catechists introduce their students to the Person of Jesus so that they may develop a personal relationship with him and grow in intimacy with him.

Further Reading and Reflection

For more on the teachings of the Church, see the *Catechism of the Catholic Church*, 422–570; and the *United States Catholic Catechism for Adults*, pages 77–87.

Catechist Prayer

Holy Spirit,
bless the young people
this week.
Help them understand
and share
more deeply and more
abundantly
in the Paschal Mystery.
Amen.

Lesson Planner

Chapter 5 Son of God, Son of Mary

Focus To learn more about the meaning of the Incarnation

LESSON PART	PROCESS	MATERIALS and RESOURCES
EXPLORE **Focus** **To explore the faith and humility of Mary** 🕐 10 minutes **Pages 47–48**	▶ Proclaim and discuss Luke 1:35, 38 (the angel Gabriel visits Mary). ▶ Learn why Mary is the model disciple. **Disciple Power:** Humility **Activity:** Write a prayer of praise to God for his blessings.	Bible Pencils
DISCOVER **Focus** **To discover the mystery of the Incarnate Word who is Savior and Messiah** 🕐 30 minutes **Pages 49–51**	▶ Deepen understanding of the Incarnation. ▶ Explore the meaning of Jesus Christ as Messiah and Savior. ▶ Explore the mysteries of the Rosary. **Activity:** Design a poster for the Month of the Holy Rosary.	Crayons or markers Art paper **Additional Activities Booklet:** Activities 5a–5b, or see BeMyDisciples.com.
DECIDE **Focus** **To decide on a way to practice humility** 🕐 10 minutes **Page 52**	**Activity:** Write a story about Mary. **My Faith Choice:** Choose a way to be humble.	Journals **Enriching the Lesson Activities:** Catechist Edition, page 107 • Role-playing Saying "Yes" to God • Designing Symbols for Mary • Writing in Journals

Concluding the Lesson 10 minutes

We Remember

Page 53

▶ Review concepts and do the review activity.

▶ **Assessment Tools Booklet:** Chapter Test 5a–5b, or see BeMyDisciples.com.

We Pray

▶ **Prayer:** Hail Holy Queen

Materials: Bible, candle, cross for prayer space

▶ Grade 6 Music CD

Preview

Point out resources for this chapter at

www.BeMyDisciples.com

▶ Preview the With My Family page and next week's lesson theme.

Looking Ahead

In this chapter the Holy Spirit invites you to ▶

EXPLORE how Mary demonstrates the virtue of humility.

DISCOVER that God the Son has human to reconciled us with God.

DECIDE on how you can commit to living with humility.

CHAPTER **5**

Son of God, Son of Mary

? When someone asks you to do something, how do you respond?
Let us listen to what Saint Luke tells us about Mary's response to the angel's message to her.

"The holy Spirit will come upon you, and the power of the Most High will overshadow you. Therefore the child to be born will be called holy, the Son of God. . . ." Mary said, "Behold, I am the handmaid of the Lord. May it be done to me according to your word."

Luke 1:35, 38

Microphone

? Why do you think that Mary responded "yes" to God? What is the name that the Church gives to this event of the angel Gabriel's announcement to Mary?

Annunciation

47

HUMAN METHODOLOGIES

Learning by Discipleship. The *National Directory for Catechesis* states that Mary is the first disciple and a model for all followers of Christ (NDC 29B). This week, as you discuss Mary's faith and trust in God, consider conducting a walking tour of the parish grounds, looking for statues and other depictions of Mary. Ask the students what these works of art tell us about our Blessed Mother and how we can grow as disciples by following her example. Conclude the tour by gathering at a favorite statue. As the students stand or kneel, invite them to offer silent prayers asking Mary to help them grow in discipleship. Pray the Hail Mary together.

Pray

▶ Gather students for prayer. Begin and end with praying the Sign of the Cross.

▶ Lead the class in praying the Hail Mary.

▶ Conclude with, "Father, may Mary be a source of joy through all ages. Amen."

Reflect

▶ Ask the opening question and invite responses.

▶ Invite a student to read the Scripture passage aloud. Spend time discussing the questions following the Scripture passage on the page.

▶ Inquire, "What if God called on *Noah story* you to accept something that you never thought possible? How would you respond? What is God inviting you to do today?" Discuss with the young people.

▶ Explain that when we honor Mary in prayer, she can help us focus on Christ, her son.

▶ Ask students which details they recall about the Annunciation.

▶ Have a volunteer student read aloud the Annunciation from Luke 1:26–38.

▶ Tell the young people that on the next page they will learn more about how Mary responded to God's call.

Focus

Call attention to Looking Ahead to highlight what they will explore, discover and decide in this chapter.

Introduce

▶ Point out that Mary can help us learn how to love as God loves.

▶ Have a volunteer read aloud the text on the page. Prepare a female student to take the part of Mary and proclaim the Scripture passages at the appropriate times.

▶ Inquire: How would you have responded if you were Mary?

Reinforce

▶ Remind students that Mary is a perfect model of faith.

▶ Invite students to examine the image of Mary on the page. Ask them to describe what characteristics of Mary are represented.

Connect

▶ Have students complete the activity on the page in groups. The prayers of praise will be used at the end of this chapter for a closing prayer.

▶ Ask students what it means to be humble. Have them read the Disciple Power box.

▶ Point out that Mary is a perfect model of one who is humble.

▶ Conclude with a discussion on ways we can show humility.

Disciple Power

Humility

Humility helps us see and accept the truth about God and ourselves. A humble person acknowledges that God is the source of life and author of all that is good. Humility is often described as "poverty in spirit" when the humble person completely trusts in God.

THE CHURCH FOLLOWS JESUS

Mary, the First and Model Disciple

Imagine the teenage Mary's surprise and confusion when God invited her to be the mother of his Son. Mary did not understand why God had chosen her. She was a virgin and asked, "How can that be?" Yet, she responded, "May it be done to me according to your word" (Luke 1:38).

Full of humility at what God was asking from her, Mary set out to visit her relative Elizabeth, who was also pregnant. It was not an easy journey from Nazareth to the home of Elizabeth. When Mary arrived, she was perhaps once again surprised when the much older Elizabeth greeted her,

"Most blessed are you among women, and blessed is the fruit of your womb . . . Blessed are you who believed that what was spoken to you by the Lord would be fulfilled." Luke 1:42, 45

Mary responds to Elizabeth with great faith. Mary proclaims,

"My soul proclaims the greatness of the Lord;
my spirit rejoices in God my savior . . .
The Mighty One has done great things for me,
and holy is his name." Luke 1:46–47, 49

Mary told Elizabeth that all blessings come from God. She realized that her being "blessed" in the eyes of Elizabeth and future believers was not of her own doing. Hers was the response of a true and faithful Israelite, one who knew her part in the Covenant that God made with Abraham and Moses, "God alone is God" (see Psalm 62:2). Mary's humble "yes" models for us what it means to be a true disciple of her Son, Jesus. She is the model for the whole Church of how to follow Jesus.

Activity Reflecting on Mary's faith and humility, write a short prayer of praise to God for how he has blessed you this week.

_____

_____

_____

DISCIPLE POWER

Humility. Many people want recognition for their achievements. Being recognized for one's achievement can be a good thing, yet when we desire to be the center of attention, we lose sight of the purpose for achieving good. Motivation of a humble person comes from the desire to honor and love God. Invite volunteers to share examples of people who are humble, quiet servants, doing good without seeking praise or reward. Examples might include parents, grandparents, teachers, catechists, or a helpful neighbor. Ask students to name acts of service that they might do this week to honor God, and challenge them to act with a humbled servant's heart.

Jesus the Christ

God the Father chose the Blessed Virgin Mary to be the mother of his Son. She is the handmaid of the **Lord**, who was a virgin her whole life.

The Incarnation

The Virgin Mary conceived Jesus by the power of the Holy Spirit. He is the Son of God. Jesus is the Second Person of the Trinity, who took on flesh and became fully human in all things except sin. This great event is called the **Incarnation**. Thus the Virgin Mary, mother of Jesus, is truly the *Theotokos*, the Mother of God. The Greek word *theotokos* means "God-bearer."

In the opening passages of the Gospel of John, we read,

And the Word became flesh and made his dwelling among us, and we saw his glory, the glory as of the Father's only Son, full of grace and truth.

JOHN 1:14

God has revealed to us, through Sacred Scripture and Sacred Tradition, that his only begotten Son assumed our human nature while remaining fully God.

The early Church called Jesus the New Adam. The Incarnation was the beginning of the new Creation, the beginning of restoring God's plan of creation. The Word of God became a man so that we could be redeemed and share in the divine life. In him, God's plan of salvation and redemption came true.

Because Jesus was fully human, he experienced joy and sadness, peace and suffering. He thought with a human mind, acted with a human will, worked with human hands, and loved with a human heart. Jesus is a divine Person with both a human and divine nature. This is a great mystery of faith.

FAITH FOCUS
What is the meaning the Incarnation?

FAITH VOCABULARY
Christ
This title of Jesus identifies him as the Messiah, the Anointed One, whom God sent to save all of humanity.

Incarnation
The Incarnation is the belief of the Church that the Son of God became fully human in all ways except sin, while remaining fully divine.

Lord
This title of Jesus indicates his divine sovereignty, or power.

Activity Read the following Scripture passage. Tell a partner whether each passage reminds you more of the human or divine nature of Jesus.
John 1:1–5
John 11:32–36

(49)

TEACHING TIP

Theotokos. There are many beautiful icons of the *Theotokos*. In preparation for this week's lesson, take time to do an Internet search for pictures of these icons. Pay particular attention to details such as the placement of the hands, the direction in which the eyes of both Mary and Christ are gazing, the facial expressions, and other symbols hidden in the details of the icon. In the most common iconic portrayals of the *Theotokos*, for example, Mary's right hand points to Jesus. In this simple gesture, she is telling us that Jesus is the way and we are to follow him. Both she and Jesus are looking at us, the observers of the icon. Looking at an icon with this attention to detail is actually referred to as "reading the icon."

Key Concept
In the Incarnation, Jesus, the Son of God, took on flesh and became human in all things except sin.

Teach

▶ Write the Faith Focus question on the board.

▶ Point out the terms and definitions in the Faith Vocabulary box.

▶ Ask, "What does the Prologue of John's Gospel remind you of?" Point out that the Gospel of John opens up similarly to the Book of Genesis. Explain that John is revealing that Jesus Christ is the eternal Son of God.

▶ Divide the class into two groups. Invite a group to read about Jesus as the New Adam. Invite the second group to read about the human and divine natures of Jesus. Ask each group to share with the other what they learned.

Reinforce

▶ Write the word "*theotokos*" on the board. Ask the class to read the first two paragraphs to learn the meaning of this term.

▶ Ask a volunteer to proclaim the Scripture passage.

Connect

▶ Point out the image on the page.

▶ Ask: "Which events in the life of Jesus was Mary present?" *(For example, the Annunciation, The Nativity, The Marriage at Cana.)*

▶ Have students complete the Scripture activity on the page with partners.

Teach

▶ Invite a volunteer to read the introductory paragraph.

▶ Have the students work in four groups. Assign one of the four, shaded statements about Jesus to each group. Have each group read their statement and discuss what they understand about the content and select one person to report back to whole group.

▶ Distribute Bibles and have each group read the Scripture passages that relate to their statement.

Reinforce

▶ Remind the students that Jesus is the Savior of all people. Point out that while Jesus lived on Earth, not everyone came to believe this.

▶ Read the Faith-Filled People box to highlight someone who did come to believe that Jesus is the Savior and gave his life for it.

Connect

▶ Conclude by asking each group to discuss how they would respond to Jesus' question, "Who do you say that I am?"

▶ If time allows, have each of the four groups decorate a piece of art paper with the words of their response and share with the class.

 **Faith-Filled People**

Saint Lawrence

Lawrence, deacon and martyr, served the Church during the persecution under Emperor Valerian (A.D. 257–260). Lawrence had the responsibility to care for the "treasures" of the Church. He was ordered to bring these treasures to his sentencing for execution. Lawrence arrived accompanied by a large number of blind, sick, and poor people. He declared, "Here are the treasures of the Church."

In His Name

While Jesus lived on Earth and did the work his Father sent him to do, not everyone came to believe he was **Christ**, the Savior and Messiah. Some people were confused and hesitant to believe. Others were hostile. On one occasion when Jesus asked his disciples, "Who do you say that I am?" only Peter the Apostle spoke out and confessed his faith in Jesus. Simon Peter said in reply,

> *"You are the Messiah, the Son of the living God."*
> MATTHEW 16:16

Like Peter we too, led by the Holy Spirit, confess our faith in Jesus. We believe in the faith as handed down to us by the Apostles:

Jesus is Lord. In Sacred Scripture, the word *Lord* is used for God. Jesus is the Son of the living God. He is the Second Person of the Holy Trinity and is intimately one with the Father in the Holy Spirit (see John 12:44–45; 1 Corinthians12:3).

Jesus is true God and true man. The Son of God became true man without giving up his divinity. The Son of God became like us in all things but sin. We call this the mystery of the Incarnation (see John 1:14).

Jesus is the One whom God promised to send to deliver his people and to lead them to live the Covenant faithfully. The name of Jesus means "God saves." Jesus is the Messiah and Savior. The title Messiah, or Christ, means "Anointed One."

Jesus Christ is the one and only Mediator, or "go-between," who links God and the human family. He alone reconciles the human family with God (see 1 Timothy 2:5–6; Hebrews 9:15–28).

Being a Christian is not only knowing and believing that Jesus is Lord, the Son of God, the Savior of the World but also living as his faithful disciples, as Saint Lawrence did.

 Who do you say Jesus is?

FAITH-FILLED PEOPLE

Saint Lawrence, Deacon and Martyr. Saint Lawrence, who died for Christ in 258, was a deacon under Pope Saint Sixtus II. Four days after the pope was put to death, Lawrence, the only living deacon in Rome, was arrested by the Emperor Valerian. After his arrest, the greedy emperor demanded that Lawrence surrender the church's wealth to Rome. Lawrence asked for three days to do so. On the third day, he explained, "Here is all the church's treasure." Lawrence then presented hundreds of lepers, orphans, the blind, and the lame to Valerian. The emperor was enraged and ordered Lawrence to be tortured and put to death. For more information on St. Lawrence, go to the Saint Resource at www.BeMyDisciples.com.

The Mysteries of Salvation

Mary is the first disciple of Jesus. She is the first and greatest saint of the Church. Mary always points us to Christ. We can look to Mary to teach us and help keep our eyes fixed on Jesus. Mary gazed on the human face of her son, Jesus, and saw God. She kept in her heart the beautiful mystery of her son, Jesus Christ, the Son of God. We are to honor Mary as our mother too, and our hearts are to be like hers.

The Church has given us the Rosary to help us join with Mary and always keep our lives centered on Jesus. There are twenty Mysteries of the Rosary. The word *mysteries* points to the mystery of Salvation. There are five Joyful Mysteries, five Sorrowful Mysteries, five Luminous Mysteries, and five Glorious Mysteries. Here is a list of the Joyful Mysteries:

1. The Annunciation of Gabriel the Archangel to the Blessed Virgin Mary (see Luke 1:26–38)

2. The Visitation of the Blessed Virgin Mary to Saint Elizabeth (see Luke 1:39–49)

3. The Nativity of Jesus in Bethlehem (see Luke 2:1–14)

4. The Presentation of Jesus in the Temple (see Luke 2:22–38)

5. The Finding of Jesus in the Temple (see Luke 2:41–52)

Because of Mary's unique role in God's plan of Salvation, at the end of her earthly life, she was taken up, body and soul, into Heaven. The Church encourages us to pray the Rosary in her honor. It is one way we can bless and honor God with Mary. The Church celebrates October as the Month of The Holy Rosary.

Activity Design a poster encouraging classmates to participate in the Month of The Holy Rosary. Include events, and reasons that will motivate students to take part.

Catholics Believe

The Rosary

The Church honors Mary as Our Lady of the Rosary each year on October 7. Praying the twenty mysteries of the Rosary helps us to reflect on the main events, or mysteries, of salvation. This kind of meditative prayer helps puts us in touch with the heart of our faith in Christ.

(51)

THE TASKS OF CATECHESIS

Promoting Knowledge of the Faith. In addition to the Marian holy days (January 1, August 15, and December 8) and Marian feasts (October 7, May 31, and December 12), the events of Mary's life are celebrated on many other days during the liturgical year. List the following feasts and dates on the board. Have the students research one on the Marian Feasts at www.BeMyDisciples.com: the Birth of the Blessed Virgin Mary (September 8), Our Lady of Sorrows (September 15), The Presentation of the Blessed Virgin Mary (November 21), The Annunciation of the Blessed Virgin Mary (March 25), The Immaculate Heart of Mary (Saturday after Corpus Christi), and the Queenship of Mary (August 22). Ask the students to write a one-paragraph summary of what they learned about the feast day that they chose.

Key Concept
The mysteries of the Rosary help us reflect on the life and work of Jesus.

Teach

▶ Have students quietly read the text on the page. As they read, ask them to note how Mary points us to Christ.

▶ Divide the class into five groups, assigning each group one of the five Joyful Mysteries. Have each group read the related Scripture passage, and share why this mystery is considered joyful.

▶ Explain that many believe praying the Joyful Mysteries provides the spiritual strength of humility. Ask the students why they think this is the case. *(They show the example of Mary's trust in God.)*

Reinforce

▶ Remind students that the Blessed Virgin Mary has a favored and unique place in God's loving plan of Salvation.

▶ Invite the students to read the Catholics Believe box. Explain that the Church honors Mary throughout the year. List the major Marian feasts on the board using the box on this page to assist you.

Connect

Distribute art paper and supplies. Have students complete the activity on the page and share their work.

Reinforce

▶ Discuss how Mary is the perfect model of discipleship for us.

▶ Brainstorm as a class various actions that demonstrate the virtue and attitude of humility.

Respond

Invite the students to complete the story activity. Encourage them to sketch an illustration for their story. You may wish to provide a small piece of white art paper for this activity and display their work.

Choose

▶ Invite the students to complete My Faith Choice.

▶ Remind the students to pray the prayer to ask God to help them act with a humble heart.

I FOLLOW JESUS

Mary teaches us how to be humble disciples of Jesus. She is the virgin Mother of Jesus. Because Jesus is the Son of God, Mary is the Mother of God.

THE STORY OF MARY

Review what you learned about Mary in this chapter. Use the Gospel Stories and Mysteries of the Rosary to assist you in writing a story about Mary. Give your story a title and illustrate it.

MY FAITH CHOICE

Having reflected on Mary's humility, I will try to be humble this week. I will
_____
_____

Pray, "Heavenly Father, I praise you for giving me this opportunity to act with a humble heart. Amen."

52

SACRED TRADITION

Marian Devotion. The Rosary is the most widely popular Catholic devotion honoring Mary. Although the exact origins of the Rosary are not certain, the Dominicans, followers of Saint Dominic, have traditionally known for promoting it. Until 2002, when Pope John Paul II added the five Luminous Mysteries, there were fifteen mysteries of the Rosary. At that time the pope explained the meaning of the "mysteries" of the rosary. He wrote: "in the course of those mysteries we contemplate important aspects of the person of Christ as the definitive revelation of God." When we pray the Rosary, we both honor Mary and join her in giving honor and praise to God for the gift of Salvation in Christ.

Chapter Review

Complete the crossword puzzle.

Down

1. The Son of God, the Messiah and Savior

2. The belief that the Son of God became man

3. The Mother of Jesus, the Mother of God

Across

4. The prayerful meditation on events in the life of Jesus and Mary

5. The virtue related to "poverty in spirit"

Crossword puzzle:
- 2 Down: INCARNATION
- 1 Down: JESUS
- 3 Down: MARY
- 4 Across: ROSARY
- 5 Across: HUMILITY

TO HELP YOU REMEMBER

1. God the Father chose the Blessed Virgin Mary to be the mother of his Son.

2. Jesus is the Second Person of the Trinity who is the Messiah, Christ, or "Anointed One." He is true God and true man.

3. The Rosary is a prayer in which we reflect on the Mysteries of Salvation.

Hail, Holy Queen

We conclude the praying of the Rosary by praying the prayer, Hail, Holy Queen. Catholics have been praying this prayer since the 1100s. Originally written in Latin, it is now prayed around the world.

Here is the Hail, Holy Queen in Polish. You will find the Hail, Holy Queen in English on page 262 of your book. Pray the Hail, Holy Queen together in the language you know.

Witaj Królowo, Matko Miłosierdzia,
życie, słodyczy i nadziejo nasza, witaj!
Do Ciebie wołamy
wygnańcy, synowie Ewy,
do Ciebie wzdychamy jęcząc i płacząc
na tym łez padole.
Przeto, Orędowniczko nasza,
one miłosierne oczy Twoje na nas zwróć,
a Jezusa, błogosławiony owoc żywota Twojego,
po tym wygnaniu nam okaż.
O łaskawa, o litościwa, o słodka Panno Maryjo!

(53)

TEACHING TIP

Music in the Classroom. In addition to biblical texts, holy images, and traditional prayers, music also reveals much about what we believe as Catholics. Consider using a traditional Marian hymn ("Immaculate Mary", "Sing of Mary", or "Hail, Holy Queen") to close this week's session or see the Grade 6 Music CD. Choose a hymn found in your parish hymnal or missalette so that the students can look at the text of the song that you choose. Ask the students to share what the text teaches us about Mary's life.

We Remember

▶ Ask the students which images best represent from what they recall included in the chapter.

▶ If they do not recall all of the bulleted summary statements under the To Help You Remember section, then be sure to review them with the students.

▶ Have students review the chapter by filling in the crossword puzzle.

We Pray

▶ Gather the students to conclude the chapter with prayer.

▶ If rosaries are available, distribute one to each student.

▶ Choose one of the Mysteries of the Rosary to pray. See page 262 for a list of the Mysteries. You may consider the following:

- Joyful Mysteries (Mon., Sat.)
- Luminous Mysteries (Thurs.)
- Sorrowful Mysteries (Tue., Fri.)
- Glorious Mysteries (Wed. Sun.)

▶ Together pray the Hail, Holy Queen.

▶ Consider singing or just listening to a traditional Marian hymn to close the lesson.

Preview

▶ Have students carefully tear out the "With My Family" page along the perforation.

▶ Encourage them to share the pages with their families and to complete the activities together at home.

▶ If the students did not or could not complete the chapter review, encourage them to complete it with their families.

▶ Point out the title and theme of next week's chapter to the children.

Visit www.BeMyDisciples.com

▶ Take time with the students to explore the many activities and resources available at www.BeMyDisciples.com.

▶ Encourage them and their families to discover the many resources available at the Web site.

Before Moving On ...

As you finish today's lesson, reflect on the following question before moving on to the next chapter.

How well do I allow silent time for children to reflect on what I am teaching?

With My Family

This Week...

In chapter 5, Son of God, Son of Mary, your child learned:

▶ God the Father chose the Blessed Virgin Mary to be the mother of Jesus, the Son of God, who became one of us without giving up being God.

▶ In Jesus Christ, the Son of God and the Son of Mary, God's promise and plan of salvation are fulfilled.

▶ In praying the Rosary, we can honor Mary and meditate on the life of Christ.

▶ Mary is the first and model disciple of her son. She demonstrates the virtue of humility in her words and deeds, acknowledging that all her blessings are from God.

For more about related teachings of the Church, see the *Catechism of the Catholic Church*, 422–570; and the *United States Catholic Catechism for Adults*, pages 77–87.

■ Sharing God's Word

Read Hebrews 2:8–18 together. Emphasize that Jesus is Lord, yet became human even unto death. In Christ, we are adopted children of God. Christ has reconciled us with God, who promises us eternal life if we live according to the Gospel.

■ We Live as Disciples

The Christian home and family is a school of discipleship. Choose one of the following activities to do as a family, or design a similar activity of your own:

▶ Talk about some of the choices your family has made. How are these choices signs of your faith in Jesus Christ? Reflect on your celebration of the Christmas season. Decide as a family what Christian choices you can make amid the popular consumerism of the season.

▶ Humility can be a difficult virtue for pre-adolescent sixth-graders, who are trying to maintain independence and autonomy. Discuss practical ways your family can live this virtue. Remind your child that humility is not a sign of weakness, but of a strong faith and relationship with God.

▶ Pray the Rosary as a family at home, especially on a feast of Mary, making sure each family member has his or her own rosary. Also participate in a family Rosary at your parish, if and when it is prayed.

■ Our Spiritual Journey

Praying the Rosary helps us see how Mary always points us to Jesus. In this chapter, your child prayed part of the Rosary. Read and pray together the prayer on page 53.

For more ideas on ways that your family can live as disciples of Jesus, visit **www.BeMyDisciples.com**

54

PARTNERING WITH PARENTS

Praying the Rosary. The month of October is the month of the Rosary. Build on today's lesson by encouraging parents to pray the Rosary with their children, especially during the month of October. Suggest that they continue this tradition during the month of May and on Marian feast days throughout the liturgical year. Provide parents with those dates, as listed in the "Tasks of Catechesis" box in this chapter on page 103. A list of Marian feasts can also be found at www.BeMyDisciples.com. Send or e-mail directions for praying the Rosary to the parents, refer them to the back of the student book, or ask them to visit or www.BeMyDisciples.com.

Enriching the Lesson

Role-playing Saying "Yes" to God

Purpose

To reinforce the Gospel account of the Annunciation in Luke 1:26–38, especially Mary's response of faith (taught on page 47–48)

Directions

▶ Focus on the response of Mary to Gabriel, "Behold, I am the handmaid of the Lord. May it be done to me according to your word" (Luke 1:38). Point out that we call this "Mary's yes to God."

▶ Have the students work in small groups to create role plays using real-life situations that illustrate saying yes to God.

▶ Invite the groups to present their role plays.

▶ Discuss the role plays with the entire class.

▶ Encourage the students to pray and put their trust in God when they make decisions to live their faith.

Materials

Designing Symbols for Mary

Purpose

To reinforce the Joyful Mysteries of the Rosary taught on page 51.

Directions

▶ Have the students work individually to list the Joyful Mysteries that they learned in this chapter.

▶ Invite them to create symbols for one of the mysteries or for Mary as a disciple of Jesus.

▶ Have the students share their symbols.

Materials

construction paper

markers or crayons

Writing in Journals

Purpose

To reinforce Saint Peter's response to Jesus when Jesus asked his disciples, "Who do you say that I am?" (taught on page 50)

Directions

▶ Discuss with the class ways that they believe young people today would respond to Jesus' question, "Who do you say that I am?"

▶ Next have the students write their own personal responses to Jesus' question.

Materials

journals or paper

pens or pencils

The Suffering Servant

BACKGROUND

Jesus, Messiah and Servant

God first chose the Israelites to be the people of the Covenant, the People of God. Their history is full of ups and downs. In their hearts they knew and believed that God had made the Covenant with them. They expected God to save them, despite their many acts of infidelity to the Covenant. There were times, however, when that expectation, or hope, grew weak because of the oppressive nature of political events, such as the oppression both of their own kings and of the kings of nations that overran and conquered Israel.

God Speaks through the Prophets

During those times, when the belief of the Israelites in the value of being God's people was fading, God manifested his fidelity to the promises that he had made to them. He sent prophets to the Israelites. Through the words and actions of the prophets, God made it clear to the Israelites that he would always be their God and they would be his people. He reached out to strengthen their faith and enliven their hope. Along with that message came another: Israelites must repent, and they would be saved.

Isaiah was one of the prophets of Israel. He lived at a critical time in Israel's history and proclaimed that a messiah would come who would be, paradoxically, majestic and glorious, yet weak and ridiculed by his enemies. He would be known as the suffering Servant of God.

Jesus, the Messiah

In the New Testament, *Christ* is the title most frequently used to describe Jesus. The use of this title professes the faith of the apostolic Church that Jesus is the Christ, the Messiah. *Christos* is the Greek translation of the Hebrew word for messiah, which literally means "anointed one." In ancient Israel, those who were consecrated to God for a special mission were anointed in his name. Kings, priests, and, in some instances prophets were thus anointed.

The Servant King

At the time of Jesus, there was an expectation among Jews for the coming of the Messiah, the One anointed by God to save them, as Isaiah and the other prophets had announced. Jesus did not fit the profile of the Messiah whom many expected and yearned for, however. They were looking for a savior to lead them to freedom from Roman rule. Most were not looking for a messiah who would have to suffer and die as Jesus did. They were not looking for the establishment of the kingdom of God that Jesus announced.

Jesus Christ, the Messiah, came not to be served but to serve. Like Jesus, we place our lives at the service of God's people and work for the coming of the kingdom. When we do, we become living signs of hope among the people of our time.

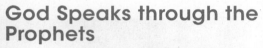

For Reflection

During times when I feel oppressed, where do I find hope?

When have I placed my life at the service of the kingdom and been a messenger of hope for others?

Catechist to Catechist

Ministers of the Word

God chose the prophets to speak in his name. In a sense, they were ministers of his Word, making it clearly known in the concrete situations in which his people were living. The prophets were a constant reminder to God's people of his faithful presence among them. You, too, share in the ministry of the Word. You pass on to the students the teachings and traditions of the Catholic Church. You make known the power of knowing and believing in God and trusting in his Word, Jesus Christ.

Growing in Faith

In addition to new faith concepts, the students will be reinforcing and expanding what they have previously learned about the faith of the Church. Before beginning this session, it is important for you to be in touch with what the students already know about Jesus—about the Incarnation and the Paschal Mystery.

The Church Teaches...

"Catechesis that is centered on Christ presents Christ first and presents everything else with reference to him, for he is the center of the Gospel message . . . [Christ] is the point in salvation history toward which the created order proceeds from the beginning of time and the final event toward which it converges" (*National Directory for Catechesis*, 25A).

Through living and sharing your faith in Jesus, you can help the children come to know the Lord, their Savior and Redeemer. Encourage them to read Scripture and learn more about Jesus this year.

Further Reading and Reflection

For more on the teachings of the Church, see the *Catechism of the Catholic Church*, 571–682; and from the *United States Catholic Catechism for Adults*, pages 90–110.

Catechist Prayer

God, our loving Creator,
who spoke through
Saint Paul and other writers of the
New Testament, speak through me
to the young people.
Give me the words that will
help them come to know you.
Amen.

Lesson Planner

Chapter 6   The Suffering Servant

Focus To explore the Paschal Mystery of Jesus and why he fulfills God's promises

LESSON PART	PROCESS	MATERIALS and RESOURCES
EXPLORE **Focus** To explore St. Paul's message of faith and mercy ⏱ 10 minutes **Pages 55–56**	▶ Proclaim and discuss Isaiah 52:13–15 (the Suffering Servant). ▶ Explore the story of St. Paul of the Cross. **Disciple Power:** Mercy	Bible
DISCOVER **Focus** To discover and explain the events and meaning of the journey of Jesus' Passion, Death, Resurrection, and Ascension ⏱ 30 minutes **Pages 57–59**	▶ Learn that the Paschal Mystery is the center of the work God the Father sent Jesus to do. **Activity:** Draw a symbol reflecting faith in the Paschal Mystery. ▶ Learn more about the Paschal Mystery. ▶ Relate the Passover to Jesus' work of salvation. **Activity:** Create a montage about The Resurrection.	Pencils Crayons or markers **Additional Activities Booklet:** Activities 6a–6b, or see BeMyDisciples.com. Designing Crosses and Expressing Faith through Art
DECIDE **Focus** To decide on a response to the lesson on the Suffering Servant ⏱ 10 minutes **Page 60**	**Activity:** Share a story from your life that shows your faith in Jesus. **My Faith Choice:** Choose a way to show mercy.	**Enriching the Lesson Activities:** Catechist Edition, page 119 • Developing a TV Episode • Designing Crosses • Expressing Faith through Art

Concluding the Lesson   ⏱ 10 minutes

We Remember
Page 61
- ▶ Review concepts and do the review activity.
- ▶ **Assessment Tools Booklet:** Chapter Test 6a–6b, or see BeMyDisciples.com.

We Pray
- ▶ **Prayer:** the Stations of the Cross

Materials: Bible, candle, cross for prayer space

- ▶ Grade 6 Music CD

Preview
Point out resources for this chapter at

www.BeMyDisciples.com ▶

- ▶ Preview the With My Family page and next week's lesson theme.

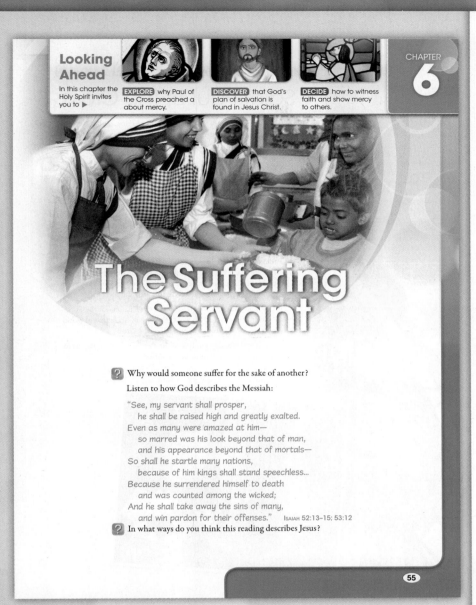

55

Pray

▶ Gather students for prayer. Begin and end with praying the Sign of the Cross.

▶ Ask the class to pray with you: "Praise to you, Lord Jesus Christ."

Reflect

▶ Invite the class to reflect on the image on the page. Be sure that they can identify the women as Missionaries of Charity. Then read aloud the passage from Isaiah on the page.

▶ Ask the question at the top of the page and invite responses.

▶ Ask the closing question and invite responses.

▶ Discuss what it means to be a servant. Inquire, "How did Jesus act like a servant?"

▶ Explain that Jesus' attitude of humility and acts of love point to him being a servant and calls us to do the same. This is what it means to be a disciple of Jesus.

Focus

▶ Invite students to read aloud the Looking Ahead section. Explain that in this chapter they will learn how Jesus fulfilled God's promise of salvation.

▶ Tell the students to turn the page to learn about a man whose life work was a response to his faith in Jesus, the suffering servant.

HUMAN METHODOLOGIES

Learning by Human Experience. The *National Directory for Catechesis* makes clear the importance of being able to make the connections between the Gospel and everyday life experiences (NDC 29A). This chapter focuses on our faith in Jesus Christ and the great gift of God's love for us revealed in the Paschal Mystery of Christ's Passion, Death, Resurrection, and Ascension. In preparing for this week's lesson, take time to consider how you have experienced the Paschal Mystery in your life. Recall some of your own experiences of suffering and sorrow. Looking back, how was God present to you then? How was God's love revealed to you? Which new life has come as a result of those experiences?

Introduce

▶ Paraphrase the text on the page. Emphasize St. Paul of the Cross' compassion for those who suffer.

▶ Call attention to the images on the page. Ask, "How might you reach out with compassion toward others today?" How might your faith in Christ help them as it did St. Paul of the Cross?"

Reinforce

▶ Inquire, "Do you think suffering is punishment?" Recall that some people think suffering is a punishment for something done wrong. The ancient Israelites believed this too.

▶ Explain that Christ's suffering and death reveals that often the innocent suffer. We can offer our own innocent suffering with that of Christ.

Connect

▶ Have a volunteer read aloud "Disciple Power." Explain that mercy means "loving kindness" to those who suffer.

▶ Explain that because of sin, suffering in the world does exist, yet this does not mean that personal suffering is a direct result of personal sin. Point out that even if a person sins and causes harm to another, God calls us to reconciliation and forgiveness.

▶ Ask the closing question. *(Accept all responses that are consistent with the text.)*

Disciple Power

Mercy

This fruit of charity is the loving kindness and compassion shown to one who offends us. Even though our sins damage our relationship with God, he still loves us. Throughout his life, Jesus taught how the love of God is one of mercy. Jesus, the Son of God, suffered and died for our sake. Truly, the Paschal Mystery reveals the depths of God's mercy for us.

THE CHURCH FOLLOWS JESUS

Saint Paul of the Cross

The Paschal Mystery (the Passion, Resurrection, and Ascension of Jesus Christ) is the heart of the Gospel. For Paolo (Paul) Francesco Daneo, the Passion and Resurrection of Christ was the greatest work of divine love. He understood the depths of God's merciful love revealed in the Paschal Mystery.

Paolo lived in northern Italy during the early 1700s, where there was great neglect of the hungry and the poor. He noticed that people were ungrateful for God's love. Paolo believed neglect and ungratefulness were signs that people had forgotten the meaning of God's love for all people, revealed in the Paschal Mystery. He wrote, "The world lives unmindful of the sufferings of Jesus which are the miracle of miracles of the love of God."

Paolo decided to help people become more aware of God's love working in the world, especially the Passion of our Lord Jesus Christ. Dressed in a black robe, he traveled tirelessly for many years throughout Italy, preaching a message of faith and mercy.

Paolo founded the "Congregation of the Passion," or the Passionists, to help him in his work. Because of his faith and work, the Church honors Paolo as Saint Paul of the Cross.

? Why does an understanding of the Paschal Mystery help us to reach out to assist those who are suffering?

DISCIPLE POWER

Mercy. The Penitential Rite is one of the parts of the Introductory Rites of the Mass. In this rite we acknowledge our sinfulness, and we call on God to have mercy on us. We do so again in the Communion Rite, when we say or sing the Lamb of God. At each of these points in the Mass, we stand humbly before God as both individual persons and as a community of faith. Explain that there are times when the faith community as a whole damages its relationship with God by ✗ sinful choices and needs God's compassion, healing, and mercy. Remind the students that God will always forgive us when we express sorrow for our sins.

✗ example? ——

The Paschal Mystery

Believe it or not, the Gospels were not the first written books of the New Testament. Because of their importance, however, the Church placed them at the beginning of that part of the Bible.

At the heart of the Gospels is the **Paschal Mystery** of Jesus. The Paschal Mystery is the center of the work that God the Father sent Jesus, his Son, to do on Earth. The word *paschal* comes from a Hebrew word meaning "the passing over." The Paschal Mystery is Jesus' passing over from life on Earth to a new and glorified life with God the Father and God the Holy Spirit.

The Mission of Jesus

The New Testament reveals the fulfillment of God's plan of **salvation** for all people in Jesus Christ. Jesus shows us how we can respond to God the Father by the way we know, love, and serve him.

While the Old Testament records the events that prepared humankind for the coming of the Messiah, all Scripture is centered on the Person of Jesus Christ. Jesus is the Son of God, the Messiah, the Chosen One, who saved humanity from sin (read Matthew 27:54, Mark 14:61–62; John 19:24). The Gospels are the heart of all Sacred Scripture, and the mission of Jesus is the centerpiece of the Gospels.

> **FAITH FOCUS**
> Why is Jesus the fulfillment of all of God's promises?
>
> **FAITH VOCABULARY**
> ▶ **Paschal Mystery**
> The Paschal Mystery is Jesus' passing over from life on Earth through his Passion, Death, Resurrection and Ascension to a new and glorified life with the Father.
>
> ▶ **Passion**
> The Passion is the suffering of Jesus on his way to the cross and his death on the cross.
>
> ▶ **salvation**
> Salvation is the deliverance of humanity from the power of sin and death by God through Jesus Christ, who died for our sins in accordance with the Scriptures.

Activity The ⊂× (fish) is an ancient Christian symbol for Jesus Christ. Reflect on the meaning of the Paschal Mystery. Draw a symbol that expresses your faith in this mystery.

(57)

DOCTRINE BACKGROUND

The Mystery of Christ's Whole Life. Jesus' entire life was a life of mystery, a life of sacrifice, and the Revelation of the mystery of divine love. We learn from all that he said and did. His parables and miracles, his love of children and sinners, his care of the sick and people in need, his prayer, his suffering, and his whole earthly life is the Revelation of the Father. Because the Son of God became man in order to do his Father's will, even the least characteristcs of his mysteries manifest "God's love…among us" (1 JOHN 4:9. See also *CCC* 516).

> **Key Concept**
> The Paschal Mystery is the center of Jesus' mission on earth.

Teach

▶ Have students share examples of their actions that most represent who they are.

▶ Explain that these actions are symbols that remind us of the most important aspects of their life.

▶ Invite students to read the first two paragraphs silently to review miracles that reveal the meaning of the Paschal Mystery.

▶ Invite students to read aloud the Faith Focus question and the Faith Vocabulary.

Reinforce

▶ Ask volunteers to define the Paschal Mystery in their own words. Reread the text definition aloud.

▶ Explain to students that a fish image is an ancient Christian symbol for Jesus Christ. It comes from the Greek word *ΙΧΘΥΣ* (ICHTHUS), an acrostic, or word formed by the first letter of other words. It represents the Greek words for "Jesus Christ, Son of God, Savior."

Connect

Allow time for the students to complete the activity and share their work.

Key Concept
Jesus freely suffered death for our salvation.

Teach

▶ Allow time for students to read the text silently.

▶ Emphasize that Jesus loved us so much that he died for our sake. Clarify that Jesus did not wish to die, because he agonized over it (see Luke 22:39–46).

▶ Recall the meaning of the Jewish Passover: The Jews would offer their best young lamb to God in an animal sacrifice, and then smear its blood on their doorway to avoid death's entering their homes. Jesus is the Lamb of God who takes away sin and death.

▶ Paraphrase Faith-Filled People. Invite students to learn more about the Passionists on the Internet.

Reinforce

▶ Explain that each year at the end of Lent on Palm Sunday of the Lord's Passion, the Church proclaims the Gospel by reading from the Passion narrative.

▶ Discuss how your parish usually proclaims the Gospel on Palm Sunday.

Connect

Ask the closing question and allow time for discussion.

Faith-Filled People

The Passionists

Today, thousands of Passionist priests, men and women religious, and lay people preach the message of the Cross to a suffering world across the globe. They see Jesus in people, especially those who are suffering. They believe that when they help the suffering, they are helping Jesus, who said. "Amen, I say to you, whatever you did for one of these least brothers of mine, you did for me" (Matthew 25:40).

He Freely Suffered Death

Each of the four Gospels includes a Passion narrative (see Matthew 27:32; Mark 15:21; Luke 23:26–32; John 19:17–18). These narratives tell of the suffering and death of Jesus as he made his way to the cross and was crucified on it. During Holy Week in the season of Lent, we recall Jesus' love for us in his suffering and death.

Jesus sacrificed his life by freely accepting death on a cross; he was buried and three days later rose from the dead. Christ went down to the dead and opened the gates of Heaven for the just who had gone before him and for those who would come after him.

The **Passion** and Resurrection of our Lord Jesus Christ took place during the Jewish feast of Passover. Just as a lamb was sacrificed to save the Israelites, Jesus freely sacrificed his life on the cross to save all people from the power of sin and death (read John 1:29).

The Last Supper was a Passover meal, but Jesus gave it new meaning. At the Last Supper, Jesus blessed the bread and wine, and then distributed them as his Body and Blood. The Eucharist is a memorial of Jesus' Passover—his work of salvation through his suffering, Death, Resurrection, and Ascension. His Body and Blood would enable his followers to be redeemed from sin and find eternal happiness in the Kingdom of God.

? What does it mean to you that Jesus suffered death for your sake?

58

FAITH-FILLED PEOPLE

Saint Paul of the Cross and the Passionists. Paolo (Paul) Francesco Daneo was born on January 3, 1694 in Ovada, Italy. As a teenager, he was so moved by God's great love manifested in the Passion and death of Jesus that he decided to show his love in return by living a life of prayer, preaching, and penance. Adults recognized his exemplary qualities of holiness and wisdom and came to him for advice. Paul wrote a rule, which was approved by the Church in 1741, that guided the way in which he and his followers would live the Gospel. His followers are known as Passionists. The Church celebrates the feast of Saint Paul of the Cross on October 19. For more information on Saint Paul of the Cross, go to the Saint Resource at www.BeMyDisciples.com.

The Risen Lord

Three days after he died and was buried, Christ rose from the dead with a new and glorified body. All four accounts of the Gospel clearly teach that this event took place. The Resurrection of Jesus is at the heart of our faith in Christ (see 1 Corinthians 15:3–5).

Forty days after the Resurrection, the Risen Christ ascended to the Father in Heaven. God's domain, Heaven, is where Jesus, the Son of God, reigns gloriously at the right hand of God the Father (see Luke 24:50–53). From there, Christ, who is hidden from our eyes, will come again in glory at the end of time to judge the living and the dead (see Matthew 25:31–46). Through Christ's Ascension and exaltation in glory, all humanity has been given an unbreakable promise of everlasting life of happiness with the Trinity, with the angels, and with Mary and all the saints (see Revelation 22:4–5).

? When you think of Heaven, what do you picture in your mind?

This great mystery of God's love for us is the center of the Gospel, or Good News. Through the Paschal Mystery, all things have been justified, or made right, in Christ with God. Through him, we are saved and will rise to life everlasting.

Activity Create a montage of images and symbols that represent the Resurrection of Christ. Sketch your ideas here.

Catholics Believe

The Paschal Mystery

The Paschal Mystery has two aspects: by his Death, Christ liberates us from sin; by his Resurrection, he opens for us the way to a new life. Christ's Resurrection is the principle and source of our future resurrection. The Risen Christ lives in the hearts of his faithful while they await that fulfillment.

The Resurrection
by Anton Laurids Johannes Dorph

59

LITURGY CONNECTION

The Liturgical Cycle. If asked to name the most important liturgical season of the Church's year, many Catholics would reply "Christmas." We would not celebrate Christmas if it were not for Easter, however. The highest point of the Church year is the Easter Triduum, which encompasses Holy Thursday (beginning with the Mass of the Lord's Supper on Holy Thursday evening), Good Friday, the Easter Vigil, and Easter Sunday (ending with Evening Prayer on Easter Sunday evening). In these three days, counted from sundown to sundown, the Paschal Mystery unfolds in Scripture, symbol, ritual, and song. The Easter Season, which follows the celebration of the Easter Triduum, lasts for fifty days, ending with the great feast of Pentecost.

Key Concept
The Resurrection is at the heart of our faith in Christ.

Teach

▶ Divide the class into four groups, and assign each group one of the Gospel accounts of the Resurrection (Matthew 28:1–20; Mark 16:1–20; Luke 24:1–49; John 20:1–31).

▶ Have the class chart the four accounts to find out what is unique and similar about them. Give attention to those who witnessed the Risen Lord, and what they had to say about it.

Reinforce

▶ Explain that because the Son of God became human, suffered, died, and was raised from the dead, we too will suffer, die, and be raised from the dead. If we live and die in Christ, then we will share in the life of God forever.

▶ Invite volunteers to share their ideas about Heaven.

▶ Summarize by reading the last paragraph aloud to the class.

▶ Inquire, "How is the Ascension of Christ a sign of the unbreakable promise of everlasting life?" (*Jesus has promised that if we believe, we too, will join the Father in heaven.*)

Connect

Invite a volunteer to read the Catholics Believe box, and then have students complete the activity on the page.

Reinforce

▶ Recall with students the virtue of mercy previously covered in this chapter.

▶ Discuss what we mean by "carrying our crosses in life."

▶ Remind the students that living our faith can be challenging.

▶ Ask, "Who was a model of God's mercy and preached a message of faith and mercy?" *(St. Paul of the Cross)*

▶ Tell the young people that the following activity will help them recall both large and small ways that they have lived their faith.

Respond

▶ Explain the directions and have students complete the activity on the page.

▶ Pair up students so that they can share their stories.

▶ Invite a few volunteers to share their partner's story with the class.

Choose

Have students individually and privately write in My Faith Choice how they will choose to show mercy today. Ask them to silently pray the prayer.

I FOLLOW JESUS

The Paschal Mystery is at the center of the Gospel. Jesus asks us today to witness to others our faith in what he has done for all people. Through his actions we are saved and will rise to eternal life. We, in turn, are to show mercy to others.

LIVING OUR FAITH IN JESUS

You are to be interviewed by a reporter for a Catholic magazine about your faith in Jesus. What example from your life would you like to share? Write your notes for the interview here.

_____

_____

_____

_____

_____

_____

_____

_____

MY FAITH CHOICE

Mercy is one of the virtues of a disciple. I will show mercy to others this week. I will

_____

_____

 Pray, "Lord help me to show mercy to others in my words and actions. Amen."

60

THE TASKS OF CATECHESIS

Education for Community Life. Before having the students complete their My Faith Choice, discuss some of the crosses that others throughout the world are carrying today. These might be the crosses of poverty, war, and prejudice, or the crosses of loneliness, fear, and illness. Discuss the situations in which people, acting individually and as a community, have responded to a crisis by showing mercy for those affected (e.g., any recent response to a natural disaster). Point out that as the People of God, we are called individually and communally to be merciful in our daily lives. Ask the students to keep that in mind as they write a specific plan for being merciful in their faith choice.

Chapter Review

Write a sentence using all of these words.

| Salvation | Passion | Crucifixion | Resurrection | Ascension |

_____

_____

_____

TO HELP YOU REMEMBER

1. The Paschal Mystery is the Passion, Death, Resurrection, and Ascension of Jesus Christ.

2. Jesus Christ suffered death for the redemption and salvation of humanity.

3. The Resurrection is the principle and source of our future resurrection.

Station of the Cross

This Scripture based version of the Stations has been given to us by Blessed Pope John Paul II. It differs slightly from the traditional Stations, found on page 263. Prayerfully journey in silence the way of the Cross with Jesus.

Leader: Lord Jesus, be with us as we remember your Passion and Death.

1. Jesus in the Garden of Gethsemane.
2. Jesus, betrayed by Judas, is arrested.
3. Jesus is condemned by the Sanhedrin.
4. Jesus is denied by Peter.
5. Jesus is judged by Pilate.
6. Jesus is scourged and crowned with thorns.
7. Jesus takes up his cross.
8. Jesus is helped by Simon of Cyrene to carry his cross.
9. Jesus meets the women of Jerusalem.
10. Jesus is crucified.
11. Jesus promises redemption to the good thief.
12. Jesus is on the cross, with his mother and Saint John at the foot of the cross.
13. Jesus dies on the cross.
14. Jesus is placed in the tomb.

Leader: (after each station)
We adore you, O Christ, and we bless you.

All: By your holy cross you have saved us and set us free.

(61)

TEACHING TIP

The Stations and the Gospels. In addition to the traditional Stations of the Cross that we often pray on the Fridays of Lent, many Catholics use the Gospel to help them reflect on the last hours of Jesus' earthly life. You may want to pray the Stations in this new way with your class during Lent. The Scriptural Stations of the Cross are based on the following Bible passages:

1. Matthew 26:36–48
2. Matthew 26:14–15
3. Matthew 26:57–68
4. Matthew 26:69–75
5. Matthew 27:15–26
6. Matthew 27:26, 29
7. John 19:17
8. Matthew 27:32
9. Luke 23:27
10. Matthew 27:45–50
11. Luke 23:39–42
12. John 19:25–27
13. Matthew 27:45–50
14. Matthew 27:57–60.

We Remember

▶ Invite the students to complete the chapter review activity.

▶ Ask volunteers to share their understanding of the words that they found.

▶ Read to the students the bulleted summary in the To Help You Remember section. Have students circle all the terms here that correspond to those they found in the puzzle.

▶ Be sure to clarify any misunderstandings or questions related to the content of the chapter.

We Pray

▶ Gather the students for prayer and introduce the closing prayer. If it is convenient, have the group go to the sanctuary or chapel.

▶ Paraphrase the introduction to the prayer. Then gather in a line for a procession. Lead the procession yourself holding a crucifix aloft.

▶ Pause for the naming of each station by a class member. Explain that after each station is read aloud, there will be a moment of reflection, which will be followed by the prayer.

▶ If time allows, include the Scripture readings named in the Teaching Tip box.

Preview

▶ Have students carefully tear out the With My Family page along the perforation.

▶ Encourage them to share the pages with their families and to complete the activities together at home.

▶ If the students did not or could not complete the chapter review, encourage them to complete it with their families.

▶ Point out the title and theme of next week's chapter to the children.

Visit www.BeMyDisciples.com

▶ Take time with the students to explore the many activities and resources available at **www.BeMyDisciples.com**.

▶ Encourage them to explore the site with their families.

Before Moving On ...

As you finish today's lesson, reflect on the following question before moving on to the next chapter.

How do I show mercy, especially to students who may have crosses to bear?

With My Family

This Week...

In chapter 6, The Suffering Servant, your child learned:

▶ God's plan of salvation is fulfilled in Jesus Christ, the Son of God.

▶ Through the Paschal Mystery, Christ has saved and redeemed all of humanity, revealing the depths of God's mercy for us.

▶ Three days after he died and was buried, Christ rose from the dead with a new and glorified body.

▶ We have received the promise of eternal life made possible by Jesus Christ, the Son of God.

▶ The virtue of mercy is the loving kindness and compassion shown to one who offends. The Paschal Mystery reveals the depths of God's mercy for us.

For more about related teachings of the Church, see the *Catechism of the Catholic Church*, 571–682; and the *United States Catholic Catechism for Adults*, pages 90–110.

■ Sharing God's Word

Read together Hebrews 9:15–28. Emphasize that Jesus, the Savior of the world, alone reconciles the human family with God.

■ We Live as Disciples

The Christian home and family is a school of discipleship. Choose one of the following activities to do as a family, or design a similar activity of your own:

▶ Talk about some of the choices that your family has made recently. How are these decisions signs of your faith in Jesus Christ?

▶ Discuss why standing up for one's faith is sometimes difficult? When would you be willing to stand up for your faith?

▶ When we pray the Sign of the Cross, we profess our faith in Jesus, who freely died on the cross to save us from sin and death. This week, pray the Sign of the Cross every time you begin to pray.

■ Our Spiritual Journey

Praying the Stations of the Cross helps us meditate on Jesus' loving sacrifice, both individually and as a community. In this chapter, your child prayed the scriptural Stations of the Cross. Read and pray together the prayer on page 61. Consider taking your children to Church to walk the Way of the Cross.

For more ideas on ways your family can live as a disciples of Jesus, visit **www.BeMyDisciples.com**

62

PARTNERING WITH PARENTS

The Home: A School for Discipleship. In a note or e-mail to parents, offer the following practical suggestions for raising disciples. Invite parents to add to the list by sharing things that they do or other ideas they have for making their home and their family a school of discipleship.

1. Pray together every day (morning, evening, mealtimes, bedtime).

2. Read and reflect on God's word as a family.

3. Attend Mass together on Sundays and holy days.

4. Take part in special gatherings of the parish community.

5. Choose an act of service to do as a family.

Enriching the Lesson

Developing a TV Episode

Purpose

To reinforce living a life of faith in Jesus taught in this chapter.

Directions

▶ Have the students work in small groups to identify three or four people who encountered Jesus when he was on earth.

▶ Have each group develop a scenario that shows one of the characters demonstrating their belief in Jesus.

▶ Invite the groups to present their scenarios and discuss how meeting Jesus changed their lives.

Materials

paper

pens or pencils

Designing Crosses

Purpose

To reinforce the students' understanding that Jesus sacrificed his life by freely accepting death on the Cross (taught on page 58)

Directions

▶ Discuss with the students the importance of the symbol of the cross for Christians.

▶ Invite the students to create and design crosses, using a variety of different resources, such as twigs, paper, stones, or yarn.

▶ Have the students share their crosses with the class. Encourage them to put their crosses in a place that will help them remember that the Paschal Mystery is the source of their hope and joy.

Materials

twigs

stones

yarn

paper

Expressing Faith through Art

Purpose

To reinforce that the Resurrection narratives pass on to us the love of God and the Good News of the Paschal Mystery (taught on page 59)

Directions

▶ Have the students work in small groups to create a mural or other art form (e.g. clay sculptures) that illustrates the Resurrection of Jesus Christ.

▶ Have the groups share their works of art.

Materials

clay

shelf paper

markers or crayons

The Holy Spirit

Think about this for a minute: God the Father could have provided another scenario with which to complete Christ's mission. He could have declared, "I have said all that needs to be said through my Son. Go and do as he did." Following that declaration, God the Father could have left us on our own, but he chose to do otherwise.

God Is Ever Present

In his wisdom and love, God the Father did not leave us on our own. He sent the Holy Spirit to dwell with us and within us. Without the guidance of the Holy Spirit, Christ's life and message could have easily faded from human memory or been distorted beyond all recognition. Instead it has been passed on authentically and without error for nearly 2,000 years.

Christ, the Spirit, and the Church

The mission of Christ and the Holy Spirit is brought to completion in the Church, which is the Body of Christ and the Temple of the Holy Spirit. . . . [T]he Church's mission is not an addition to that of Christ and the Holy Spirit, but is its sacrament" (*Catechism of the Catholic Church 737, 738*).

The Church has been an authentic witness for Christ for 2,000 years because of the Holy Spirit's presence with and in her. Through periods of persecution, human weakness, wars, and schism, the Church has endured and prospered by the grace of God.

Biblical Images for Church

Some of the biblical images of the Church can give us insight into her role in the divine plan. The Church has been called a sheepfold, with Christ himself as the Shepherd. Granted, we are governed by human shepherds with their assorted strengths and weaknesses, but ultimately it is Christ, the Good Shepherd, who leads and cares for the Church.

The Church has also been described as a cultivated field, with the Father acting as the heavenly cultivator. In this holy ground, the Father has planted Christ and continues to tend the soil of the Church, planting and sowing year after year. Despite sin, the storms of history, and the poor stewardship of human workers, he continues to bring forth a rich harvest.

The Church is also described as the building of God, with Jesus at its cornerstone. The Church is the house and household of God, in which his family dwells. With the exception of the Holy Family, no family that has walked this earth has always been faithful to God.

Do not expect either the local or universal family of the Church to be perfectly faithful either. Do expect and trust the Holy Spirit to bring the mission of Christ to completion in the Church, the Body of Christ and the Temple of the Holy Spirit.

For Reflection

Where do I sense that the Holy Spirit is at work in the life of the Church?

What are some of the ways that I can become more aware of the Holy Spirit at work in my life?

Catechist to Catechist

Our Faith Journey

Any physical journey takes strength and requires guidance if the destination is to be successfully reached. Our faith journey takes strength and needs clear guidance too. At Baptism, we receive that strength and guidance from the Holy Spirit, the Third Person of the Holy Trinity, who is the Advocate, Helper, and Teacher. With his grace, we are able to reach our destination—eternal life. During your time with the students trust in the Holy Spirit, who is the primary catechist in your group.

A Faith Journey Notebook

You might have each student create a My Faith Journey notebook. Each time your class meets, ask the students to add something to their notebook that describes one way they grew in faith and friendship with Jesus that week. At the end of the year, they can look back and enjoy seeing the progress they made on their journey of faith. This notebook would be an excellent place for the young people to record their faith choices and to reflect on how will they followed through on them.

The Church Teaches...

"The Holy Spirit unfolds the divine plan of salvation within the Church. With Christ, the Holy Spirit animates the Church and directs her mission. The Holy Spirit makes the Paschal Mystery of Christ present in the human mind to accept Christ, converts the human heart to love Christ, and encourages the human person to follow Christ" (*National Directory for Catechesis,* 28A.3).

This chapter introduces the children to the work of the Holy Spirit at work in the Apostles as they shared the message of the Gospel. Help the children understand how the Holy Spirit can animate them into following Jesus.

Further Reading and Reflection

For more on the teachings of the Church, see the *Catechism of the Catholic Church,* 683–747, 963–975; and the *United States Catholic Catechism for Adults,* pages 102–110, 141–149.

Catechist Prayer

Holy Spirit,
breathe new life and
new love into me.
Help me to know and recognize
you in new and vibrant ways,
especially as you live and breathe
in the Church.
Amen.

Lesson Planner

Chapter 7   The Holy Spirit

Focus To identify the work of the Holy Spirit in the Church

LESSON PART	PROCESS	MATERIALS and RESOURCES
EXPLORE **Focus** **To explore the Holy Spirit's gift of counsel** 🕐 10 minutes **Pages 63–64**	▶ Proclaim and discuss Psalm 143:10 (Teach me to do your will). ▶ Explore the story of St. Benedict of Nursia. **Disciple Power:** Counsel	Bible
DISCOVER **Focus** **To discover that the work of Jesus and the Holy Spirit cannot be separated** 🕐 30 minutes **Pages 65–67**	▶ Discover that the work of the Holy Spirit is to proclaim the Gospel. **Activity:** Scripture search— Compare the same event in different Gospels. ▶ Explore ways that the Holy Spirit has been revealed in human history. ▶ Learn how the Holy Spirit dwells within the Church. **Activity:** Create a storyboard describing a Spirit-filled town.	Journals Bibles Pencils Crayons or markers **Additional Activities Booklet:** Activities 7a–7b, or see BeMyDisciples.com.
DECIDE **Focus** **To decide a response to the lesson on the Holy Spirit** 🕐 10 minutes **Page 68**	**Activity:** Name how the parish reflects the Gifts of the Holy Spirit. **My Faith Choice:** Choose a way to use the gift of counsel or right judgment.	**Enriching the Lesson Activities:** Catechist Edition, page 131 • Decoding a Gospel Message • Celebrating the Holy Spirit • Portraying Life in the Holy Spirit

Concluding the Lesson 10 minutes

We Remember

Page 69

▶ Review concepts and do the review activity.

▶ **Assessment Tools Booklet:** Chapter Test 7a–7b, or see BeMyDisciples.com.

We Pray

▶ **Prayer:** from the Gospel of John 17:20–21.

Materials: Bible, candle, cross for prayer space

▶ Grade 6 Music CD

Preview

Point out resources for this chapter at

www.BeMyDisciples.com ▷

▶ Preview the With My Family page and next week's lesson theme.

Looking Ahead

In this chapter the Holy Spirit invites you to ▶

EXPLORE how the Holy Spirit guided St. Benedict to use the gift of counsel.

DISCOVER the work of the Holy Spirit within the Church.

DECIDE how you will take part in the work of the Church.

CHAPTER **7**

The Holy Spirit

? Why is it sometimes difficult to obey rules?

The writer of Psalm 143 may have realized that he needed God's help to obey his laws. Join with him as he prays:

"[Lord,] teach me to do your will,
   for you are my God.
May your kind spirit guide me
   on ground that is level." PSALM 143:10

? How do you know that the Holy Spirit will guide you to do what is right and good?

63

Pray

▶ Gather students for prayer. Begin and end with praying the Sign of the Cross.

▶ Remind them that God is always with us and when we pray we acknowledge his presence.

▶ Lead the class in prayer with, "God our Father, may your Church always be a sign of your holiness for all people."

Reflect

▶ Have a volunteer read aloud the opening question.

▶ Discuss as a class how obeying good rules can help someone do what is right and just. Have students cite examples.

▶ Have the class then prayerfully read Psalm 143:10 in their books.

▶ Using the final two questions lead the class in a discussion about the guidance of the Holy Spirit.

Focus

▶ Explain that in this chapter they will learn about the work of the Holy Spirit in the Church. Invite students to read aloud the Looking Ahead section.

▶ Tell the young people that on the next page they will learn about what a great Saint of the Church was guided by The Holy Spirit to do.

HUMAN METHODOLOGIES

Learning by Heart. The *National Directory for Catechesis* states that learning by heart is an important part of catechesis (NDC 29F.4). This includes learning the rules by which all Christians are called to live, such as the Ten Commandments (page 210), the Beatitudes (page 260), and the precepts of the Church (page 261). This week's lesson includes a discussion on the Rule of St. Benedict and an opportunity to examine the principles of Catholic Social Teaching. Help the students to appreciate that we are called to go beyond simply knowing or memorizing these moral teachings. We are called to incorporate them into our daily actions. Emphasize that knowing these important moral principles is the first step in living as Jesus calls us to live.

Introduce

Paraphrase or read aloud the text on the page. Emphasize how Saint Benedict used the gift of counsel in his set of rules to help guide his religious community to live the Gospel.

Reinforce

▶ Remind the students of the importance of supporting one another in living the Gospel.

▶ Point out that Saints Benedict and Scholastica established religious communities whose members supported one another in living the Gospel.

Connect

▶ Have a volunteer read aloud the Disciple Power section. Explain that the gift of counsel involves the guidance of the Holy Spirit within the Church.

▶ Invite the students to respond to the question on the page. Explain that the Church has sets of good and just rules to help guide us in life. Some of these are the Ten Commandments, the Beatitudes, and basic principles from the Social Doctrine of the Church.

▶ Name some of the rules you follow and then ask the students to share some of the ones they listed.

▶ Discuss how the Holy Spirit guides us to follow different kinds of rules each day.

Disciple Power

Counsel

Counsel, or right judgment, is one of the seven Gifts of the Holy Spirit. This gift, or grace, helps a person sense the moral truth about how to live. The gift of counsel is the ability to judge correctly the daily activity of our lives according to God's will. The source of this gift is the Holy Spirit, who empowers us to form our consciences properly.

THE CHURCH FOLLOWS JESUS
Saint Benedict and Saint Scholastica

Christians need one another to live the Gospel. Saint Benedict lived in Nursia, Italy, from A.D. 480–547. He wrote a rule of life that spelled out a clear way to live the Gospel in a monastic setting. A monastery is a place where a group of religious people lives and works together under a common set of rules. The Rule of St. Benedict is based on a life of peace as one works and prays in imitation of Christ.

Benedict's rules were so helpful that people came from many places to live together and follow them. Saint Scholastica (A.D. 480–543), Benedict's twin sister, was the first woman to choose to follow his rule of life. Soon other women came to live together to follow the same rules.

The followers of Saint Benedict and Saint Scholastica are baptized Christians who consecrate their lives to God. They are known as Benedictines. According to the rules, Benedictines are led by an abbot (for male communities) or a prioress (for female communities). The leader, guided by the Holy Spirit, is responsible for counseling the members on how to live a Christian life.

The Holy Spirit guided Benedict in his own personal life and empowered him to establish his set of rules through the gift of counsel or right judgment. With the aid of the Rule of St. Benedict, Benedictines today live as disciples of Christ.

? What are good rules to live by at home, at school, and in your neighborhood? Talk about them with a partner.

64

DISCIPLE POWR

Counsel. The ability to make decisions according to God's will requires both knowledge and practice. We must first know the rules for Christian living as revealed in Sacred Scripture and the teachings of the Church and then apply them to our everyday life. Brainstorm with the class a list of everyday life scenarios. For example, being asked by a parent to do something they don't want to do; being tempted to cheat on a test; or seeing several kids picking on a classmate who doesn't seem to have any friends. Ask students how they can respond in each situation using the gift of counsel. Discuss what the wisest choice is in each situation, according to what they have learned as disciples. Encourage the students to explain how Church teaching (e.g., the Beatitudes, the Ten Commandments, or the precepts of the Church) applies in each situation.

The Holy Spirit at Work

In the New Testament, there are four written accounts of the Gospel. They are the **Gospels** according to Matthew, Mark, Luke, and John. Through the guidance of the Holy Spirit, each passes on the faith of the Church in Jesus Christ, and in the saving events of the Paschal Mystery. Each announces the good news of Salvation in Jesus, who is the Lord and Savior of the world.

The four Gospels formed over three different stages. The first stage belongs to the very words and deeds of Jesus. The second stage belongs to the time of the Apostles' preaching about Jesus after the Holy Spirit descended upon them at **Pentecost**. The third stage belongs to the four evangelists—Matthew, Mark, Luke, and John. Under the inspiration of the Holy Spirit, each evangelist, a name that means "announcer of good news," wrote their account of the Gospel that the Apostles had passed on about Jesus.

Each of the four accounts of the Gospel passes on the faith of the Church in Jesus from four individual perspectives:

Matthew pays special attention to the rich Jewish heritage of the Church, and to the great teachings of Jesus.

Mark emphasizes what it means to be a disciple of Jesus and to walk with him toward the cross.

Luke shows how salvation in Jesus embraces all people, especially those who are most in need.

John reflects on the inner meaning of Jesus' words and deeds, and writes in a very poetic style.

FAITH FOCUS
What is the work of the Holy Spirit in the Church?

FAITH VOCABULARY
charism
A charism is a grace of the Holy Spirit given to build up the Church and to help the Church fulfill her work in the world.

Gospels
The Gospels are the first four books of the New Testament which pass on the faith of the Church in Jesus Christ and in the saving events of the Paschal Mystery.

Pentecost
Pentecost is the liturgical feast and holy day when the Church celebrates the coming of the Holy Spirit on the disciples and the birth of the Church.

Activity

Read Matthew 26: 6-13, Mark 14: 3-9, Luke 7: 36-50 and John 12: 1-8. Compare how the same event is reported in different ways.

Matthew _____

Mark _____

Luke _____

John _____

(65)

SCRIPTURE BACKGROUND

The Four Evangelists. The four evangelists are often symbolically depicted as the four creatures that surround God's throne (see Ezekiel 1: 4–10, 10:14–15 and Revelation 4:6–8). Matthew is depicted as a human, representing humanity and reason. Matthew's Gospel focuses on the humanity of Christ. Mark is depicted as a lion, representing royalty and courage. The Gospel of Mark focuses on the kingship of Christ. Luke is depicted as an ox, representing sacrifice and strength. Luke writes of Christ's priesthood and Christ's sacrifice for humankind. John is depicted as an eagle, representing the heavens, the sky, and the Spirit. The Gospel of John reveals Christ's divine (heavenly) nature.

Key Concept
The work of the Holy Spirit within the Church is to proclaim the Gospel.

Teach

▶ Read the Faith Focus question. Invite several students write their answers on the board.

▶ Read aloud the introductory paragraph on the page.

▶ Invite the students to look at the symbols on the page that represent the four evangelists. Have them speculate on the connection between the symbol and the Gospel. *(See the explanation in the Scripture Background box on this page.)*

▶ Have the students silently read the rest of the text to learn about the formation of the Gospels.

▶ Write each word in the Faith Vocabulary on the board and invite three students to read the definitions.

Connect

▶ Place students in four groups; assign each group one of the four Gospels.

▶ Have them then read the account of a woman anointing Jesus in their assigned Gospel (Matthew 26:–13; Mark 14:3–9; Luke 7:36–50; John 12:1–8).

▶ Have each group write a synopsis of the story and write a summary in the appropriate space on the page. As each group reports, have the other students fill in the rest of their boxes.

Key Concept
The Holy Spirit strengthens the Church to be a sign of Christ's love for humanity.

Teach

▶ Write *Holy Spirit* on the board. Invite students to list all of the Biblical events they know of in which the Holy Spirit is mentioned.

▶ Have the students read the text on the page, looking for mention of the work of the Holy Spirit. See if there are any other events that should be added to the list after the reading; if so add them.

▶ Read Faith-Filled People. Invite students to learn more about how this group helps those in need by living according to the just rules of the Church (like the principles of social teaching).

▶ Invite a volunteer to read the Catholics Believe box.

Reinforce

Ask the students to read the event of Pentecost in Acts 2:1–13. Invite them to dramatize what happened at Pentecost.

Connect

▶ Invite the students to examine the details of the image on the page and how it relates to the biblical account of Pentecost.

▶ Ask the closing question and accept all reasonable answers. Discuss how the Holy Spirit animates the Church to proclaim the Gospel boldly.

▶ You might have students record their responses in their journal.

Faith-Filled People

The Spiritans

The Spiritans, or the Congregation of the Holy Spirit, is a religious community of priests and lay brothers approved by the Church. Guided by the unifying presence of the Holy Spirit, Spiritans seek to transform the hearts and minds of those who suffer. Their **charism** or special gift, is bringing hope and compassion to those in need among the culturally diverse.

The Age of the Spirit

After his Resurrection, Jesus appeared to his disciples and promised to send the Holy Spirit to guide them and to be their advocate, or helper (read Luke 24:48–49; Acts 1:4–5).

Fifty days after Jesus rose from the dead, the Holy Spirit came to the disciples as promised. This was during the Jewish feast of Pentecost, a time to celebrate God's blessings (read Acts 2:1–4). Filled with enthusiasm, Peter the Apostle and the other disciples went into the streets of Jerusalem. There Peter boldly proclaimed the Gospel. People who had come to Jerusalem from many countries to celebrate the Jewish feast of Pentecost listened to Peter and heard him in their own language. Moved by the Holy Spirit, thousands were baptized (read Acts 1:14–41).

When Christians think of the Holy Spirit, we might think that the Holy Spirit waited until Pentecost to begin working among the people of God. The truth is that the Holy Spirit has always been at work in the world. We read about the Holy Spirit in the story of Creation (see Genesis 2:7; Psalm 104:30), and with the prophets of the Old Testament (see Zechariah 4:5–6). We also read about the work of the Holy Spirit in the life of Mary and all of the disciples.

The Holy Spirit was always with Jesus, the Son of God. When he began his public ministry, Jesus announced in the synagogue at Nazareth,

"The Spirit of the Lord is upon me."

LUKE 4:18

The mission of Jesus, the Son of God, and the Holy Spirit always go together. The Holy Trinity always works together. The Father, Son, and the Holy Spirit cannot be separated.

Today on Pentecost, we celebrate the beginning of the work that Jesus commissioned the Church to do (read Matthew 28:16–20). The Church is a sign and instrument of God's communion with all humanity and a sign in the world of the unity of the whole human race. God's promise made to Abraham came true in Christ. The Holy Spirit inspires the Church to boldly proclaim the Gospel.

? In what ways can the Holy Spirit help you in your daily life?

FAITH-FILLED PEOPLE

The Spiritans. "One Heart, One Spirit" is the motto of the Spiritans, who seek to follow the promptings of the Holy Spirit in every aspect of their daily living and ministry. They seek to go where the Holy Spirit leads and to improve the world through their work in education, the missions, and parish ministry. The Spiritans were founded in 1703 by Claude des Places. Claude was destined for service in the government until he was shocked by the poverty and homelessness that he witnessed on the streets of Paris. He left his exclusive college and entered a seminary. He founded the Spiritans even before he was ordained. The ministry of the Spiritans first took them to Africa, but today their ministry is worldwide. In the United States they serve mostly African American and Hispanic parishes.

Temple of the Holy Spirit

The Gospel of John tells us that when the crucified Jesus saw his mother and the disciple he loved standing by the cross, he said,

> " 'Woman, behold, your son.' Then he said to the disciple, 'Behold, your mother.' "
>
> JOHN 19:26–27

The "beloved disciple" who is at the foot of the cross stands for all who are Jesus' disciples. Mary, the Mother of God, is the mother of all who follow her Son, Jesus. Mary is the Mother of God and the Mother of the Church, the Body of Christ.

Mary is the first among all followers of Jesus. She was truly a temple of the Holy Spirit. We praise her to be blessed among all women because of the fruit of her womb, Jesus. The Holy Spirit is always with her (see Luke 1:35).

? What does it mean to say Mary is a "temple of the Holy Spirit?

In his First Letter to the Corinthians, Saint Paul asks the Christian community in Corinth,

> "Do you not know that your body is a temple of the holy Spirit within you, whom you have from God?"
>
> 1 CORINTHIANS 6:19

The Holy Spirit dwells within each of the baptized and within the whole Church. The Church is the Temple of the Holy Spirit.

The Holy Spirit is the source of the Church's life, and of her unity as the one People of God. The Holy Spirit is also the one source of the richness of the Church's many gifts and charisms.

Activity Imagine that you could live in a city or town where the Holy Spirit guides everyone. Describe the look of this city or town. Create a story board showing three things that would happen there.

Catholics Believe

Social Teachings

The Social Teachings of the Catholic Church are a set of teachings which provide the basic principles to guide us in how we are to build up the Church and fulfill her work in the world. If we open our hearts and minds to the guidance of the Holy Spirit, living according to these principles will lead us to holiness and a just society. The first and most fundamental principle is the life and dignity of the human person.

(67)

THE TASKS OF CATECHESIS

Moral Formation. The last verse of 1 Corinthians 6:12–20 requires us to glorify God in our bodies. Take time to discuss with the students what this means in everyday terms. All that we choose to look at and listen to, the words that we choose to speak, the actions that we choose to do, and the places that we choose to go, should be in accordance with what is right and pleasing to God. Invite the students to make a private list of the choices they've made today and to consider whether they have glorified God in those choices. In light of God's rules for our lives, be mindful of your own choices and actions, remembering that you are a living witness of the Gospel for your students.

Teach

▶ Share that the Temple of the Holy Spirit and the Body of Christ are two important images for the Church.

▶ Ask the students to read quietly the text on the page to answer this question: "What does it mean to understand that your body is a temple of the Holy Spirit?"

▶ Explain that when we are baptized we are made holy by the presence of the Holy Spirit. This makes us a temple, a holy place for God to dwell.

Reinforce

▶ Have students read aloud 1 Corinthians 6:12–20.

▶ Discuss practical ways that young people can make choices to reflect their belief that they are temples of the Holy Spirit.

Connect

▶ Have students complete the activity on the page.

▶ Invite students to share their City of God storyboards and suggest Social Teachings of the Church that would guide their city.

▶ Explain that part of the Church's mission in the world is to remind society of what is right and good.

Reinforce

▶ Inquire, "In what ways can the Church help guide or counsel you to do what is good and right? How does your parish help you in specific ways?"

▶ Invite the students to reflect how they individually use the Gifts of the Holy Spirit to bear fruit in the world.

Respond

Place students in groups of three or four. Explain the directions for the activity. Invite volunteers to share their profiles.

Choose

▶ Have students complete their faith choices and to pray the final prayer. Affirm the gifts and talents of each student.

▶ Explain that God has given each person a purpose and mission. We are called to gather together as the Church, the Body of Christ, to be instruments of the Holy Spirit.

I FOLLOW JESUS

As a member of the Church, the Holy Spirit dwells within you, giving you the grace to live the Gospel. Among the graces we receive at Baptism are the seven Gifts of the Holy Spirit. These Gifts, which are strengthened at Confirmation, help you to take part in the life and work of the Church.

GIFTS OF THE HOLY SPIRIT

Review the seven Gifts of the Holy Spirit found below. Choose three of them and think of people in your family, school, or neighborhood who have these gifts. Name the three people and what gift they exhibit. Then write a profile (short description) of one of these people.

wisdom	understanding	knowledge
counsel	piety	fortitude
fear of the Lord		

Name _____ Gift _____
Name _____ Gift _____
Name _____ Gift _____
Profile of _____
_____

MY FAITH CHOICE

This week, I will use the gift of counsel, or right judgment, to help the Church fulfill her mission of proclaiming the Gospel. I will
_____
_____

Pray, "Come Holy Spirit, fill my heart and enkindle in me the fire of your love. Amen."

68

TEACHING TIP

Taking a Spiritual Inventory. After reviewing the seven Gifts of the Holy Spirit, distribute lined paper and have the students list the names of the gifts, one on each line. Reiterate that the Gifts of the Holy Spirit strengthen us to take part in the life and work of the Church. Ask them to rate themselves for each gift on a scale of 1 to 5, 5 being "strongly living this gift in my life" and 1 being "not living this gift in my life." Tell the students that you will not ask them to share their personal ratings with the class. Encourage students to make an effort to improve in those areas that were a 1 or a 2 on their list. You may also want to poll the class by secret ballot to see if there are certain Gifts of the Spirit that they are living more faithfully as a class than others.

Chapter Review

Use the code to discover this important message about the Gospel.

A	B	C	D	E	F	G	H	I	J	K	L	M
1	2	3	4	5	6	7	8	9	10	11	12	13

N	O	P	Q	R	S	T	U	V	W	X	Y	Z
14	15	16	17	18	19	20	21	22	23	24	25	26

T H E   G O S P E L
4x5 12-4 10÷2   12-5 3x5 24-5 4x4 10÷2 6+6

A N N O U N C E S
6-5 2x7 12÷2 3x5 22-1 9+5 3+0 10÷2 24-5

T H E
4x5 12-4 10÷2

K I N G D O M
21-10 3x3 28÷2 19-12 2x2 5x3 26÷2

O F   G O D
3+12 18-12   13-6 8+7 19-15

TO HELP YOU REMEMBER

1. The Holy Spirit is at work bringing about God's plan of salvation within the Church.

2. The Holy Spirit strengthens the Church to be a sign of Christ's love for humanity and enables us to proclaim the Gospel.

3. With the Gifts of the Holy Spirit, we can help continue the mission of the Church.

Prayer of Intercession

In a prayer of intercession, we pray for others. Jesus constantly prayed for his followers. Let us listen to the prayer of Jesus in the Gospel of John, and pray for others to the Father as Jesus did.

Leader: Lord, we gather to listen to your Word. May we always live as the one People of God.

Reader: A reading from the holy Gospel according to John.

All: Glory to you, O Lord.

Reader: Proclaim John 17:20–21. The gospel of the Lord.

All: Praise to you, Lord Jesus Christ.
(Pause to pray for those who need God's help.)

Leader: Lord God, Father of all, fill all who call upon you with the love of the Holy Spirit. Make us one in the fullness of faith and fellowship of love. We ask this through Jesus Christ, your Son, who lives and reigns with you and the Holy Spirit, one God, for ever and ever.

All: Amen.

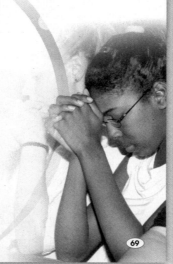

69

We Remember

▶ Invite the students to complete the chapter review and check the answers.

▶ Read the bulleted summary in the To Help You Remember section. Have students identify content that they are not clear about.

▶ Clarify any misunderstandings or questions related to the content of the chapter.

We Pray

▶ Gather the students for prayer, and introduce the closing prayer. Point out the meaning of prayers of intercession.

▶ Be sure to prepare a volunteer student to read the passage from the Gospel of John. If permitted, you can also include a lighted candle as sign of God's presence.

▶ Together pray this liturgy of the Word.

▶ If time allows, pray for various vocations to help build up the Kingdom of God.

LITURGY CONNECTION

Prayers of Intercession. At every Mass, during the Prayer of the Faithful, the Church offers prayers of intercession for the Church and her leaders, the world and its leaders, the gathered community, those in need, and those who are sick or dying. This pattern of intercessory prayer is an excellent format for both private and group prayer and a good reminder that we are called to pray for other people and their needs. Be mindful of honoring this pattern of prayer when you lead your students in prayers of intercession.

Preview

▶ Have students carefully tear out the With My Family page along the perforation.

▶ Encourage them to share the pages with their families and to complete the activities together at home.

▶ If the students did not or could not complete the chapter review, encourage them to complete it with their families.

▶ Point out the title and theme of next week's chapter to the children.

Visit www.BeMyDisciples.com

▶ Take time with the students to explore the many activities and resources available at the **www.BeMyDisciples.com.**

▶ Especially encourage them and their families to discover the many resources available at the Web site.

Before Moving On ...

As you finish today's lesson, reflect on the following question before moving on to the next chapter.

Where have I noticed the Holy Spirit at work in the actions of students in my class?

With My Family

This Week...

In chapter 7, The Holy Spirit, your child learned:

▶ The Gospel is the announcement of the good news of salvation in Jesus Christ. The four Evangelists—Matthew, Mark, Luke, and John—wrote their accounts under the inspiration of the Holy Spirit.

▶ The Holy Spirit, the Third Person of the Holy Trinity, is at work within the Church. The Holy Spirit dwells within each of us as members of the one Body of Christ.

▶ As one Church, God calls all the baptized to use the gift of counsel and the other Gifts of the Holy Spirit to take part in the Church's mission, or work, of proclaiming the Gospel.

For more about related teachings of the Church, see the *Catechism of the Catholic Church,* 683–747, 963–975; and the *United States Catholic Catechism for Adults,* pages 102–110, 141–149.

■ Sharing God's Word

Read together I Corinthians 6:19. Emphasize that the Holy Spirit is the source of the Church's life and her unity as the holy People of God.

■ We Live as Disciples

The Christian home and family is a school of discipleship. Choose one of the following activities to do as a family, or design a similar activity of your own:

▶ Look at the many things you do as a family. Discuss how each of these helps you take part in the life and work of the Church.

▶ At a family meal, name and talk about the people who help you live the Gospel. Take time to thank God for the gifts they share with your family.

▶ Choose the Gospel of Matthew, Mark, or Luke. As a family, take a short passage and share together your reflection on it.

■ Our Spiritual Journey

Discernment is a spiritual discipline of the Church that relates to counsel, or right judgment, which is one of the Gifts of the Holy Spirit. Review the steps you take to arrive at a serious decision. Be sure that you are including prayer to the Holy Spirit in your process. Your family decision-making is a way of unifying your family's efforts to live the Gospel. In this chapter, your child prayed a prayer of intercession, or praying for others. Read and pray together the prayer on page 69.

For more ideas on ways that your family can live as disciples of Jesus, visit **www.BeMyDisciples.com**

70

PARTNERING WITH PARENTS

We Live as Disciples. Encourage parents to go beyond the "We Live as Disciples" suggestions on the With My Family page. For example, suggest that families take time to write thank-you cards to those people who help them live the Gospel. Help facilitate this concrete action by sending home a blank thank-you card or two, or cards that the students have designed and created in class, with directions for the activity attached. In a later session, offer prayers of petitions for these people, and encourage families to do the same.

Enriching the Lesson

Decoding a Gospel Message

Purpose	Directions	Materials
To reinforce that each of the four Evangelists tells about Jesus from a different perspective (taught on page 65)	▶ Ask the students to review the different perspectives of the four Evangelists that they learned on page 65. ▶ Have the students work with partners to summarize the message of each Gospel and develop a number code for their summary statements. ▶ Have partners exchange their codes with another set of partners and invite them to decode the messages.	Bible paper pens or pencils

Celebrating the Holy Spirit

Purpose	Directions	Materials
To reinforce that the Holy Spirit came to the disciples as Jesus promised (taught on page 66)	▶ Have the students work in small groups to create a dance that expresses how their life is filled with the Holy Spirit, who helps them share their faith in Jesus with others. ▶ Encourage the students to include the use of streamers made out of crepe paper in their dance routines. ▶ Have the groups present their dances. ▶ Conclude by praying together to the Holy Spirit to continue to help them share their faith in Jesus Christ with others.	crepe paper scissors music

Portraying Life in the Holy Spirit

Purpose	Directions	Materials
To reinforce that we are temples of the Holy Spirit (taught on page 67)	▶ Have the students work together on a Scripture mural. ▶ On a large piece of shelf paper, have them write the headline "The Holy Spirit Gives Us Life." ▶ Next, using words and pictures from magazines, newspapers, or their own illustrations, have them portray ways in which we are temples of the Holy Spirit. ▶ Display the mural for others to see.	shelf paper markers or crayons scissors and glue sticks

The **Mystery** of the **Church**

All Are One

We are members of the Body of Christ, the Church. Our holiness and happiness are inextricably bound up with the holiness and happiness of others. God did not just choose a few Israelite people; he chose the entire Israelite people. He did not establish the Covenant with only Moses, Miriam, and some select friends. He entered into the Covenant with all the people of Israel.

The New and Everlasting Covenant

The Covenant with the people of Israel prepared the world for the new and everlasting Covenant. Jesus Christ, the Incarnate Son of God, at the Last Supper proclaimed, "Drink [of] it, all of you, this is my blood of the covenant, which will be shed on behalf of many for the forgiveness of sins" (Matthew 26:27-28). In Christ, the Incarnate Son of God, God the Father enters the new and everlasting Covenant with the new People of God, the Church. The new and everlasting Covenant transcends cultural differences, political boundaries, and ethnic divisions. It is the act of the One God, who is Father, Son, and Holy Spirit, calling all people in history to be one.

The Church Is a Sacrament

The Church is the Sacrament of Salvation through which God works to convoke his new People. The Church is a visible society founded by Christ under the leadership of Saint Peter the Apostle and his successors. She is commissioned to be the salt of the earth and a light of truth for all people. She is to be "a most sure seed of unity, hope and salvation for the whole human race" (*Vatican II, Dogmatic Constitution on the Church* [*Lumen gentium*] 9). As the new People of God, the Church acknowledges that God is the God of all people, extending his saving grace to all who sincerely seek him and love him above all else and love their neighbors as they love themselves.

We become members of the Church by being joined to Christ and being born anew through water and the Holy Spirit in Baptism. This gives us the status of adopted daughters and sons of God the Father and the responsibility to live the Covenant that we have entered into with him at Baptism. We are to live Christ's new commandment and to love as he has loved us. We are to manifest his love in our daily lives by comforting our sisters and brothers. We are to be merciful and kind. We are to mourn injustice and suffering. In homes, schools, and workplaces, we are to treat people with tenderness and goodness, and with patience, courage, and trust. In this way others will come to know that we are Christ's disciples.

For Reflection

What does belonging to the new People of God, the Church, mean to me?

How am I a living sign of the love of Christ for all people?

Catechist to Catechist

A Community of Believers

When someone asks you "What is the Church?" what is your first response? The truth is that if students were to ask a variety of Catholic adults that question, they probably would hear a wide variety of responses. Because the Church is a mystery, Scripture uses many images to help us understand the Church. The "new People of God" is one of the key biblical images emphasized by the Second Vatican Council (1962–1965). The Church is the new People of God whom God the Father has chosen in Jesus Christ, his Son, to be his very own people. The Church is a community of people who share in the life of Christ and receive the responsibility to continue the work of Christ.

Building a Learning Community

Build your learning group into a learning community. Create a learning environment that welcomes everyone to participate. One strategy you might use to assure that you involve everyone is to create a volunteer box. Write each student's name on an index card and place the cards in the box. Whenever you need a volunteer, draw a card from the box. This will enable you to include all of the students.

The Church Teaches…

"The Gospel message of salvation in Jesus Christ has a distinctly historical character. Jesus Christ is a historical figure who preached the Good News of the coming of the Kingdom of God in time. The Incarnation, passion, death, and Resurrection of Christ are real historical events. Jesus Christ poured out his Holy Spirit and established the Church on Pentecost, thereby ushering in a new era of salvation history: the age of the Church" (*National Directory for Catechesis,* **25E**).

Your students are learning the cost and responsibility of being members of the Body of Christ and to serve others as Jesus did. By doing so, we cooperate in helping the Church transmit her memory of God's plan of salvation from generation to generation.

Further Reading and Reflection

For more on the teachings of the Church, see the *Catechism of the Catholic Church,* 748–962, 988–1060; and the *United States Catholic Catechism for Adults,* pages 111–139, 151–162.

Catechist Prayer

God, our loving Creator, help me prepare for the coming of the kingdom in all its fullness through the choices I make this day. Amen.

Lesson Planner

Chapter 8   The Mystery of the Church

Focus To identify the images that help us understand the mystery of the Church

LESSON PART	PROCESS	MATERIALS and RESOURCES
EXPLORE **Focus** To explore the power of peace 🕐 10 minutes **Pages** 71–72	► Proclaim and discuss Psalm 28:7–9 (the Lord is my strength and shield). ► Learn the story of St. Marguerite Marie Alscoque. **Disciple Power:** Peace	Bible
DISCOVER **Focus** To discover that the Church as the Body of Christ and explain how we prepare for the coming of the Kingdom of God 🕐 30 minutes **Pages** 73–75	► Review and expand understanding of the Marks of the Church. **Activity:** Decorate a banner about a mark of the Church. ► Discover ways that the Church fulfills the mission of Jesus. ► Learn the doctrine of eternal life. **Activity:** Prepare a skit about service to others.	Index cards Pencils Crayons or markers **Additional Activities Booklet:** Activities 8a–8b, or see BeMyDisciples.com.
DECIDE **Focus** To decide a way to be a peacemaker 🕐 10 minutes **Page** 76	**Activity:** Create a billboard advertisement about the Church as a sign of peace in the world. **My Faith Choice:** Choose a way to be a peacemaker.	**Enriching the Lesson Activities:** Catechist Edition, page 143 • Sharing Faith • Role-Playing a Journey • Catholic Social Teaching: Kingdom of God Triptych

Concluding the Lesson 10 minutes

We Remember

Page 77

► Review concepts and do the review activity.

► **Assessment Tools Booklet:** Chapter Test 8a–8b, or see BeMyDisciples.com.

We Pray

► **Prayer:** a prayer of vocations.

Materials: Bible, candle, cross for prayer space

► Grade 6 Music CD

Preview

Point out resources for this chapter at

www.BeMyDisciples.com

► Preview the With My Family page and next week's lesson theme.

Looking Ahead

In this chapter the Holy Spirit invites you to ▶

EXPLORE the life of Saint Marguerite Marie Alacoque.

DISCOVER how the Church is the sacrament of salvation.

DECIDE how your life will be an image of the Church for others.

CHAPTER **8**

The Mystery of the Church

[?] If you were describing a member of your family or a friend, what image would you use to help others understand that person's best qualities?

In this prayer, the psalmist used an image to describe God. Quietly read and reflect on this passage.

> The LORD is my strength and my shield,
>   in whom my heart trusted and found help.
> So my heart rejoices;
>   with my song I praise my God.
> LORD, you are the strength of your people . . .
> Save your people, bless your inheritance;
>   feed and sustain them forever!
>
> PSALM 28:7–9

[?] What image would you use to describe God?

(71)

TEACHING TIP

The Power of Symbols. Symbols point beyond themselves to a deeper meaning than meets the eye or the other senses. They stimulate our imagination and help us learn in ways beyond using just words. As you teach this chapter, take time to review with students the power of symbols. Include concrete examples of symbols and images that the Church uses to help us grasp the meaning of Divine Revelation and in celebrating the Liturgy. Use a variety of examples, such as a crucifix, palms, ashes, water, oil, candles, the altar, a wedding ring, incense, liturgical colors, or clothing.

Pray

▶ Write on the board: "God our Father, may your Church be a leaven in the world, transforming us into your family. Amen."

▶ Gather students in silence for prayer. Begin with the Sign of the Cross. Pray together the prayer you have written.

Reflect

▶ Discuss various images or symbols that society uses to communicate when words are not enough. *(a heart for love, clasped hands of different skin tones to show diversity, the dove for peace.)* Then ask the opening question.

▶ Read the Scripture passage on the page, and then discuss the questions that follow.

▶ As a class, brainstorm images of God that the students have. Challenge them to explain how their images describe God.

Focus

▶ Have a volunteer read Looking Ahead.

▶ Tell the students that on the next page they will learn the story of a woman who introduced the Church to a powerful image for Jesus Christ.

Introduce

▶ Invite the students to reflect on which image of Christ would resonate best with them: a lamb, a cross, or a heart. Encourage them to explain their reflection.

▶ Explain that many holy people have had images or visions of Jesus as a result of their strong faith. One such person was Saint Marguerite Marie Alacoque.

▶ Read aloud the text on the page. Emphasize the image of her and of the Sacred Heart of Jesus on the page.

Reinforce

Ask why the image of a heart is a good one to represent Jesus. *(His great love for us; The peace he brings.)*

Connect

▶ Have a volunteer read Disciple Power. Ask: "How does the Church reflect the peace and love of Christ to the world?"

▶ Invite students to respond to the question on the page. Have them share with a partner.

▶ Discuss as a class the value of honoring the Sacred Heart of Jesus on First Fridays of the Month.

Disciple Power

Peace

Peace is one of the twelve Fruits of the Holy Spirit. Peace on Earth is a reflection of the peace of Christ. Christ has reconciled humanity with God and made the Church the sacrament of unity and peace. Disciples of Jesus are called to be peacemakers.

THE CHURCH FOLLOWS JESUS

Saint Marguerite Marie Alacoque

When Marguerite Marie Alacoque was a child in Burgundy, France, more than 360 years ago, she had a strong devotion to the Blessed Sacrament. In fact, she preferred to pray in the peace of silence before the Blessed Sacrament, instead of playing with other children. At one point she became ill and was paralyzed. After four years of being confined to her bed, she decided to devote her life to the service of God and the Church. As a result, she was instantly cured and began her life's work.

At the age of twenty-five, Marguerite joined the Salesian Sisters. At a young age, she had visions of Christ and of Mary. While a Salesian Sister, Marguerite Marie had visions of Christ's heart. In these visions, the Lord told Marguerite Marie to set aside a special time for peaceful prayer, a holy hour, in honor of the Sacred Heart of Jesus.

When the Catholic Church honors the Sacred Heart of Jesus, the Church is honoring Jesus and his intense love for all of us. The Church honors the Sacred Heart of Jesus with traditional practices of praying before the Blessed Sacrament on the first Friday of the month. It celebrates the Solemnity of the Most Sacred Heart of Jesus on the Friday following the Second Sunday after Pentecost.

We can also honor Jesus with acts of charity toward those who suffer. This is a Christian way of bringing a sense of peace to those in need.

? What images remind you of Christ's love and peace? Tell a partner.

72

DISCIPLE POWER

Peace. Have the students work in groups of three or four. Invite each group to discuss concrete ways to be peacemakers in one of the following situations: at home, at school, with friends, or in the community. After allowing sufficient time for discussion, ask each group to share their ideas with the entire class and make a written list of their suggestions on the board. Before students complete their "My Faith Choice" later in the chapter, invite them to review this list for ideas and inspiration.

The Kingdom of God

Jesus Christ established the **Church** with his Apostles and disciples. After the Ascension, the Holy Spirit became the principal guide within the Church. In his writings, Saint Paul teaches that the Church is the Body of Christ, a community of saints, the Temple of the Holy Spirit, and the Bride of Christ (see 1 Corinthians 12:27).

These images help us to understand the mystery of the Church as the sacrament of salvation. We, as members of the Church, are a communion of "holy people" who participate in God's plan of salvation. The Church is the Communion of Saints. The Communion of Saints includes all of the faithful members of the Church on Earth and those who have died. The Church has four essential characteristics, or marks. The Church is one, holy, catholic, and apostolic.

The Church is *one*. She professes there is "one Lord, one faith, one baptism; one God and Father of all" (Ephesians 4:5–6).

The Church is *holy*—a "holy nation" living in communion with God the Father, the Son, and the Holy Spirit (see I Peter 2:9). We share in the Seven Sacraments, above all the Eucharist.

The Church is *catholic*, or universal, inviting all people to become disciples of Jesus, who is the Savior of all people. We share with all people the goods and the blessings that God bestows on us.

The Church is *apostolic*, that is, rooted in what the Apostles taught in the name of Jesus. The baptized members of the Church share in the charisms of the Holy Spirit. There is an unbroken connection, called apostolic succession, made visible by the pope, the successor of Saint Peter the Apostle, and the other bishops who are the successors of the other Apostles.

> **FAITH FOCUS**
> What is the Church?
>
> **FAITH VOCABULARY**
> **Church**
> The Church is the new People of God, the Body of Christ, the Temple of the Holy Spirit, and the Bride of Christ, called together in Jesus Christ by the power of the Holy Spirit.
>
> **Kingdom of God**
> The Kingdom of God is the fulfillment of God's plan for all Creation in Christ at the end of time when Christ will come again in glory.

Activity Choose one of the marks of the Church. Decorate a banner with words and images that symbolize that mark.

73

CATHOLIC DOCTRINE

Images of Church. There are many names and images by which the Church is known: the *Body of Christ, Bride of Christ, Temple of the Holy Spirit,* and *People of God.* The Church is also known as *Mother* and *Teacher. Magisterium,* a Latin word meaning teacher, is the term used to identify the Church as Teacher. The pope and the bishops are authentic teachers, that is, teachers endowed with the authority of Christ, who preach the faith to the people entrusted to them, the faith to be believed and put into practice (see Vatican II, *Dogmatic Constitution on the Church* [Lumen gentium] 25). For a more extended treatment of the Church as Mother and Teacher, see the *Catechism of the Catholic Church* 2030–2046.

Key Concept
The Church is one, holy, catholic and apostolic.

Teach

▶ Ask the Faith Focus question. Write the word Church on the board and create a word map of the students responses.

▶ Pair up students, and have them read the text on the page. Have them work together to identify ourselves to these questions: What is the Church? What is the Communion of Saints? What are the marks of the Church? Ask for responses from the whole class.

Reinforce

Emphasize the Four Marks of the Church. Explain that these are the key characteristics of the Church. Read aloud the definition of the Church in Faith Vocabulary.

Connect

Place students in four groups. Assign each group one of the four marks. Invite them to decorate a banner with symbols to represent their mark. Discuss and display the banners.

Key Concept

The whole Church is responsible for continuing the work of Christ on earth.

Teach

▶ As a class, discuss modern-day models of Christian living. List them on the board, and talk about how they demonstrate what it means to be a Christian. Use the Faith-Filled People section as an example.

▶ Divide the class into groups, and assign each group a paragraph of text from the page. Tell them they will be asked to report to the others what they have learned.

Reinforce

▶ Invite volunteers to write one responsibility of the Pope on the board.

▶ Explain what we mean when we say that one day we will experience the fullness of God's reign of holiness. Refer to the Lord's Prayer.

▶ Read the definition of The Kingdom of God from the previous page.

Connect

Ask the closing question and invite responses.

Faith-Filled People

Saint Timothy

Timothy was the child of a Greek father and Jewish mother. Paul baptized him. Timothy traveled with Paul on missionary journeys and became the first bishop of Ephesus. There are two letters in the New Testament addressed to Timothy. He was stoned to death in A.D. 97 because he refused to worship the Roman Emperor Dionysius.

God's Reign of Holiness

Like our Old Testament ancestors in faith, who journeyed from slavery in Egypt to freedom in the Promised Land, the Church is a people on a journey of faith. Our destination is the **Kingdom of God**. It will come to completion by God himself at the end of time when Christ will come again in glory.

The Church is both physical and spiritual, both human and divine. Christ is the Head of the Body, and we are the members. All baptized members of the Church—the ordained, the consecrated, and the laity—make up the one Body of Christ. Each member has unique gifts and different responsibilities to build up the Church.

All the baptized, according to their role in the Church, share in the responsibility to evangelize, and proclaim the truth of God revealed in Jesus Christ to those who have not heard it, or need to hear it again. We are to be Christ to others by living the commandments and the Beatitudes. Jesus commanded,

"Go, therefore, and make disciples of all nations, baptizing them in the name of the Father, and of the Son, and of the holy Spirit, teaching them to observe all that I have commanded you. And behold, I am with you always, until the end of the age."

MATTHEW 28: 19–20

Jesus gave Saint Peter a unique responsibility in the Church (read Matthew 16:18–19). This unique responsibility is known as the Petrine ministry. Today, the pope continues this ministry as the successor of Saint Peter and the bishop of Rome. The pope is the immediate and universal pastor, or shepherd, of the whole universal Church.

The pope's ministry includes the responsibility to keep the Church together as one Body of Christ. The pope also insures that the teachings of the Church are faithful to the truth of Jesus handed down by the Apostles. The pope supports and encourages all members of the People of God to faithfully proclaim the Gospel.

? What are you doing to build the Kingdom of God?

74

FAITH-FILLED PEOPLE

Saint Timothy. Saint Timothy was summoned by Saint Paul the Apostle to help build the early Church in places such as Corinth, Thessalonica, and Ephesus, where he eventually served as bishop. Saint Paul wrote two letters to Saint Timothy, which are in the New Testament. Both letters provide guidelines and encouragement to Saint Timothy to do the difficult work of being a minister of the Gospel at the risk of suffering and death. Saint Timothy was martyred in A.D. 97 while opposing a pagan festival. Saint Paul's words of encouragement to Saint Timothy inspire us to be enthusiastic followers of Jesus (read 2 Timothy 2:12). For more information on Saint Timothy, go to the Saint Resource at www.BeMyDisciples.com.

Life After Death

The Gospel proclaims that God invites all people to live with him forever. When a person dies, life is changed not ended. At the moment of death, Christ will judge the way that person has lived his or her life (read Matthew 25:31–32). This is called the particular judgment.

Those who have been faithful to God on Earth will be invited into the Kingdom of God (see Matthew 25:34–40). This is everlasting life in communion with God, the Holy Trinity, and with the Blessed Virgin Mary, the angels, and all the holy men and women who have lived before us. This perfect life with God is called Heaven.

Some people who die are not ready to receive the gift of eternal life in Heaven. After death, they are purified of their weakness and given the opportunity to grow in their love for God. This is called Purgatory.

Sadly, some people choose to turn themselves completely away from God's love. They do this by sinning seriously and not asking God for forgiveness. When people do this and die, they choose to stay separated from God forever (read Matthew 25:41–46). This eternal separation from God is called Hell.

Catholics Believe

Last Judgment

On the last day, at the end of time, the lives of everyone will be judged. This is called the Last Judgment. On this day, God will invite all the faithful to everlasting life in the Kingdom. Our risen bodies will be reunited with our immortal souls. We will rise from the dead just as Christ was raised from the dead.

Activity Read Matthew 25:31–40. List the actions Jesus names as ways to minister to others in his name. Working with a partner, prepare a skit illustrating a way to serve others in one of these ways.

_____

_____

_____

_____

_____

_____

75

HUMAN METHODOLOGIES

Making a Commitment to Live the Christian Life. The *National Directory for Catechesis* reminds us that participating in acts of charity promotes learning by doing (NDC 29G). The Corporal Works of Mercy (listed on page 261) invite us to share love with others by caring for their physical or bodily needs. The first six are listed in Matthew 25:31–40, and the seventh is identified in Tobit 1:16–20. Discuss with the class how caring for the needs of others helps us to grow as disciples of Jesus. Explore with the students what we learn about living as Catholics when we participate in charitable acts.

Teach

▶ Write on the board the following terms: *Purgatory, Hell,* and *Heaven.* Explain that they will learn about these important concepts.

▶ Read the text on the page. Be sure to pause and write on the board a simple definition of each term as you read about it.

▶ Invite a volunteer to read the Catholics Believe box.

Reinforce

▶ Explain that when people die, the way that they have freely chosen to live their life will determine the way they will live eternally.

▶ Remind the students that God gives us many graces through the sacraments and the guidance of the Holy Spirit to help us be united with him forever in Heaven.

▶ Review and answer any questions about the difference between the particular judgement and the last judgement.

Connect

Read Matthew 25:31–40 as a class, and then have students complete the activity on the page and discuss what the students have prepared.

Reinforce

▶ Remind the students that we follow Jesus by living according to his teachings, guided by the power of the Holy Spirit.

▶ Point out that as people of a parish, we help people as Jesus taught us to do. In this way we are a sign or image of the Church.

▶ Discuss how the people of your parish are a sign of peace.

Respond

▶ Review with students the Works of Mercy found on page 261. Explain that these acts demonstrate how we can make a real difference in the lives of others.

▶ Explain that any good and just activity can work toward peace.

▶ Review the activity on the page with the students. Encourage them to sketch their ideas on the page.

▶ As a class, develop one large billboard to tell others about the Church and her mission in the world.

Choose

▶ Have students complete in their journal the call to action and prayer from My Faith Choice. Remind them to pray the Glory Be prayer silently.

▶ Explain that the Beatitudes help us to understand that before we can make peace, we must have an attitude of peace within ourselves.

I FOLLOW JESUS

You are a sign, or image, of the Church. At Baptism, you received the responsibility and the grace to help bring about the Kingdom of God. Peace is one essential characteristic of the Kingdom. As Jesus is the Prince of Peace, the Church is to be a people of peace.

SEEING THE CHURCH

Use symbols, images, and words to create a billboard advertisement that tells others about the Church and how she is a sign of peace in the world.

MY FAITH CHOICE

This week, I will be a peacemaker. I will be a clear image of what the Church is. I will

_____

_____

Think of yourself as an image of the Church. Pray, "Glory be to the Father, and to the Son, and to the Holy Spirit: As it was in the beginning, is now and ever shall be, world without end."

(76)

TEACHING TIPS

The Prayer of Saint Francis. The Prayer of Saint Francis is one of the best-known prayers for peace. As the students work on the billboard activity and decide on their faith choice, play one of the many recorded versions of the Prayer of Saint Francis as background music. Your catechetical leader or music minister might have some suggestions of specific recordings that you can play for the students.

Chapter Review

Use the words below to complete each sentence. Not all words will be used.

Blessings	Charisms	Communion of Saints
Kingdom of God	ordained ministers	Petrine ministry

1. Bishops, priests and deacons are ___ordained___ ___ministers___.

2. ___Charisms___ are graces of the Holy Spirit given to help the Church fulfill her work in the world.

3. The ___Petrine___ ___ministry___ is the special ministry of the pope.

4. The ___Communion___ ___of___ ___Saints___ includes all the faithful members of the Church, those on earth and those in Heaven and in Purgatory.

5. The ___Kingdom___ ___of___ ___God___ is all people and creation living in communion with God.

TO HELP YOU REMEMBER

1. Jesus Christ is the Head of the Church, the Body of Christ. The laity, the ordained, and members of the consecrated life are her members.

2. The Holy Spirit strengthens the Church to be one, holy, catholic, and apostolic.

3. The Kingdom of God begun by God the Father and announced in the Gospel is mysteriously present in the Church and will come about in fullness at the end of time.

Prayer of Vocation

Each member of the Church, young people and adults, is called to continue the work of Jesus. We all have the vocation to live our life in Christ.

Leader: God calls each member of the Church to share in the work of Christ. All the baptized have the responsibility to prepare the way for the coming of the Kingdom of God. Let us pray that we hear and respond to God's invitation to spread the Gospel.

Reader: *Proclaim Matthew 9:35–38.*

All: **Praise to you, Lord, Jesus Christ.**

Leader: Lord God, we pray that all the members of the Church may hear your call to serve your people. We ask this in the name of Christ, our Lord.

All: **Amen.**

77

THE TASKS OF CATECHESIS

Teaching to Pray. Explain to the students the important Church tradition of praying for vocations. Point out the different ways that this may be done. For example, in some parishes people gather before the Blessed Sacrament all day and night to pray for vocations to the priesthood, religious life and lay ecclesial ministers. In other parishes, a different family each week prays daily for vocations, incorporating the "Traveling Chalice" program. Remind the students that God calls each of the baptized to live the Gospel in a specific way. Encourage the students to pray regularly to learn how God is calling them to take part in the work of the Church in the world.

We Remember

▶ Invite the students to do the Chapter Review and have them check each others' answers.

▶ Read to the students the bulleted summary in the To Help You Remember section. Be sure to clarify any misunderstandings or questions related to the content of the chapter.

▶ Have the students underline all the words or phrases in the bulleted statements that describe the Church or are images of the Church.

We Pray

▶ Gather the students for prayer, and introduce the closing prayer.

▶ Explain that this prayer is for vocations. Remind them that all of the baptized share the vocation to love and serve God by loving and serving one another.

▶ Choose a leader and a reader. Invite the class to collect petitions for specific vocations or family members who are considering becoming a priest or religious brother or sister or a lay person dedicated to Church ministry.

▶ Pray the prayer together.

Preview

▶ Have students carefully tear out the With My Family page along the perforation.

▶ Encourage them to share the pages with their families and to complete the activities together at home.

▶ If the students did not or could not complete the chapter review, encourage them to complete it with their families.

▶ Point out the title and theme of next week's chapter to the children.

Visit www.BeMyDisciples.com

▶ Take time with the students to explore the many activities and resources available at **www.BeMyDisciples.com.**

▶ Especially encourage them and their families to discover the many resources available at the Web site.

Before Moving On ...

As you finish today's lesson, reflect on the following question before moving on to the next chapter.

Which student could use more praise from me?

With My Family

This Week...

In chapter 8, The Mystery of the Church, your child learned:

▶ The Church is the new People of God, the Temple of the Holy Spirit, and the Communion of Saints.

▶ Called by God the Father, all the baptized are joined to Christ through the power of the Holy Spirit.

▶ The whole Church, Christ the Head, and all the members (the laity, the ordained, consecrated religious and lay ecclesial ministers) are the Body of Christ.

▶ There are four marks, or characteristics of the Church. The Church is one, holy, catholic, and apostolic.

▶ Peace is a fruit of the Holy Spirit. Peacemaking is the call of every Christian.

For more about related teachings of the Church, see the *Catechism of the Catholic Church*, 748–962, 988–1060; and the *United States Catholic Catechism for Adults*, pages 111–139, 151–162.

■ Sharing God's Word

Read together Matthew 25:31–40. Emphasize that Jesus clearly teaches that those who faithfully follow his teachings will be invited to join him in the Kingdom of God.

■ We Live as Disciples

The Christian home and family is a school of discipleship. Choose one of the following activities to do as a family, or design a similar activity of your own:

▶ Discuss the Four Marks of the Church: one, holy, catholic, and apostolic. Talk about the meaning of each and the ways each of the marks of the Church is a characteristic of your family.

▶ Read Matthew 25:31–40 at the beginning of a family meal. Decide how your family can join with other members of your parish to follow the teachings of Jesus.

▶ Discuss a way that your family can be an image of the Church in your neighborhood. Put your idea into action.

■ Our Spiritual Journey

Sharing our material and spiritual blessings helps bring about the peace that Christ proclaimed, the peace that comes from all people living in right relationship with God and with one another. What might your family do to bring about this peace within your family and among others?

For more ideas on ways your family can live as a disciples of Jesus, visit **www.BeMyDisciples.com**

78

CATHOLIC SOCIAL TEACHING

Call to Family, Community, and Participation. The worldwide Catholic Church is a community of many races, languages, and ethnic groups, yet we are one community of faith. As the one People of God we are concerned about issues affecting human dignity and the ability of all people to grow through equitable, just, and fair participation in community life. Therefore, we have an obligation and the responsibility to participate in society and to work to promote the common good. This principle was taught in Chapter 7 in the activity about the Gifts of the Holy Spirit building up the community of faith, and in this chapter, where the students reflected on the Communion of Saints and our call to be peacemakers in our families and communities. The activity at the bottom of the next page reinforces this teaching.

Enriching the Lesson

Sharing Faith

Purpose

To reinforce that the whole Church must work together as the one People of God (taught on page 76).

Directions

▶ Discuss with the students the relationship between elderly and younger people. Emphasize the wisdom and experience that elderly people have to share with younger generations and the energy and vitality that younger generations have to share with older people.

▶ Divide the students into two groups, namely, "Elderly Generation" and "Younger Generation."

▶ Invite the two groups to share with each other the gifts and talents that each of the generations can share with the other.

▶ Brainstorm as a class how both generations might work together to do the work of the Church.

Materials

newsprint

pens or pencils

Role-Playing a Journey

Purpose

To reinforce that as our Old Testament ancestors in faith journeyed from slavery in Egypt to freedom, the Church is also on a journey of faith, one that involves life after death (taught on page 75)

Directions

▶ Write the phrase "Journey of Faith" on the board.

▶ Have the students work in small groups to role-play something that they might do on their journey of faith to the Kingdom of God. Their role play should demonstrate a way of building The Kingdom of God.

Materials

Catholic Social Teaching: Kingdom of God Triptych

Purpose

To reinforce that Jesus proclaimed and often taught about the Kingdom of God (taught on page 74)

Directions

▶ Recall with the students the second account of creation in the Book of Genesis. Point out that the peace and harmony that filled God's creation in the beginning is an image of the Kingdom of God that will come again at the end of time, when Christ's work will be completed.

▶ Divide the class into three groups. Have each group create a panel for a triptych depicting the Kingdom of God.

▶ Have one panel show the original state of creation prior to the Fall (Original holiness, see Chapter 3), the second illustrate people working to prepare the way for the coming of the Kingdom, and the third feature the Kingdom at the end of time. Be sure that the third group includes Christ in their panel illustration.

▶ Join the three panels together to form a triptych.

▶ Display the triptych for other members of the parish to see so that the students can help others to see the responsibility of all to build up the Kingdom of God.

Materials

poster board

tape for hinging the panels together

markers, crayons, or other suitable art media

The Unit Review provides the opportunity to assess the students' understanding of the faith concepts presented in the unit and to affirm them in their growing knowledge and love of God. Here are a few suggestions for using these pages.

▶ Share that the next two pages are an opportunity to stop and review what they have learned.

▶ Provide time for the students to ask questions.

▶ Have the students complete the review alone or with partners.

A. Choose the Best Word

▶ Read the directions for this section.

▶ Then have the student work alone or with a partner to complete the section.

▶ Invite volunteers to share their responses. Clarify and correct responses as needed.

B. Show What You Know

▶ Read the directions for this section. Answer the first question together as a class.

▶ Then have the student continue working alone or with a partner to complete the section.

▶ Invite volunteers to share their responses. Clarify and correct responses as needed.

Unit 2 **Review**

Name _____

A. Choose the Best Word

Read each statement and circle the best answer.

1. Where in the Bible do you find stories about the early Church?
- A. Wisdom Books
- B. New Testament
- C. Old Testament
- D. Pentateuch

2. The events of Jesus' life that make up the Paschal Mystery are his:
- A. Public ministry
- B. Arrest and Passion
- C. Passion, Death, Resurrection, and Ascension
- D. Birth, baptism, healing miracles, and parables

3. Which of the following is not an image of the Church?
- A. Breath of God
- B. Body of Christ
- C. Communion of Saints
- D. Temple of the Holy Spirit

4. Which of the following is not one of the canonical Gospels?
- A. Matthew
- B. Thomas
- C. John
- D. Luke

5. The four marks of the Church are:
- A. one, holy, catholic and apostolic
- B. death, judgment, hell and Heaven
- C. prudence, justice, fortitude and temperance
- D. Matthew, Mark, Luke and John

B. Show What You Know

Match the items in column A with those in column B.

Column A	Column B
A. Jesus Christ	_E_ **1.** The creed we usually profess at Mass
B. Incarnation	_D_ **2.** One of the earliest creeds
C. Hail, Holy Queen	_A_ **3.** The center of God's plan of salvation
D. Apostles' Creed	_C_ **4.** The prayer at the end of the Rosary
E. Nicene Creed	_B_ **5.** The belief that the Son of God became man

79

TEACHING TIP

Assessment as Affirmation. Assessment is a time of affirmation more than correction. Take the time to affirm the students in all that they have learned. Be sure to acknowledge their many efforts at living the faith that they have been learning about. Do not use this time to overemphasize the ways the ways they have fallen short. If you discover areas that they have not learned well, take time to re-teach key concepts at the appropriate time, or perhaps encourage the parents to review the material with their children at home. Remember that throughout the program, many key concepts are reinforced to help students to retain and reinforce the key concepts. They will also have opportunities in succeeding years to extend their knowledge of all key faith concepts.

C. Connect with Scripture

Reread the Scripture passage on the first Unit Opener page. What connection do you see between this passage and what you learned in this unit?

_____ Answers will vary. _____

_____

D. Be a Disciple

1. *Review the four pages in this unit titled "The Church Follows Jesus." What person or ministry of the Church on these pages will inspire you to be a better disciple of Jesus? Explain your answer.*

_____ Answers will vary. _____

_____

2. *Work with a group. Review the four Disciple Power virtues or gifts you have learned about in this unit. After jotting down your own ideas, share with the group practical ways that you will live these virtues or gifts day by day.*

_____ Answers will vary. _____

_____

C. Connect with Scripture

▶ Invite the students to reflect on the Scripture passage in the Unit Opener and to write their understanding of how this passage connects with the doctrinal content of the unit they have just completed.

▶ Ask volunteers to share their responses, now or after completion of the entire Unit Review.

D. Be a Disciple

▶ Invite the young people to work independently on the first question about The Church Follows Jesus. Ask volunteers to share their responses.

▶ Divide the students into small groups of three or four for the second part of this section. Ask them to write their personal reflections first, and then to share with their group practical ways of living the Disciple Power virtues or qualities of discipleship in everyday life.

▶ Ask for feedback from the small groups as time allows.

TEACHING TIP

Recall Faith Choices. As you complete this unit, remember to take the time to reinforce the importance of the faith choices that the students have made in each chapter. Invite volunteers to share more success stories about putting their faith choices into action. Perhaps you might also invite a discussion of some challenges the students faced in their efforts to implement their faith choices. Summarize by affirming their good choices, and encouraging them to continue their journey in faith.

We Worship

Part One

Objectives

In Unit 3, you will help the children learn that:

▶ The Seven Sacraments are the center of the Church's liturgy and make us sharers in the life of God through the power of the Holy Spirit.

▶ Baptism, the first sacrament that we receive, is the doorway to new life in the Holy Spirit and salvation in Christ.

▶ In Confirmation, the grace of Baptism is strengthened, and our new life in Christ is sealed by the gift of the Holy Spirit.

▶ The Eucharist is the Sacrament of the Body and Blood of Christ in which we receive the real presence of Christ and are most fully joined to Christ and the Church.

Spiritual Insights

"Liturgy is centered on the Holy Trinity. At every liturgy the action of worship is directed to the Father, from whom all blessings come, through the Son in the unity of the Holy Spirit. We praise the Father who first called us to be his people by sending us his Son as our Redeemer and giving us the Holy Spirit so that we can continue to gather, to remember what God has done for us, and to share in the blessings of salvation" (*United States Catholic Catechism for Adults,* page 167).

"For where two or three are gathered together in my name, there am I in the midst of them" (Matthew 18:20).

Living the Six Tasks of Catechesis

Moral Formation: Saint Martin De Porres (1579–1639)

Martin grew up in poverty in the slums of Lima, Peru. His father was a Spanish nobleman, and his mother was a former slave. She was left to raise Martin after his father abandoned them. As poor as the family was, Martin saw that other people were in greater need. Even as a young boy, he gave his food and clothing away to the poor.

When he was twelve, Martin took a job as an apprentice to a barber. In those days in Peru, many barbers also served as surgeons for their villages, and so in addition to learning how to cut hair, Martin learned how to treat to wounds and injuries.

A few years later, Martin volunteered to work as a lay helper at the local Dominican monastery. He was given menial jobs, which he did cheerfully. He also spent many hours in prayer—in the chapel, in the kitchen while he was cleaning up after serving meals, or in the fields while he tended crops. Martin managed to find God in everything he did. The Dominicans noticed his great faith and invited him to become a brother. Martin knew that being a member of the Dominican order would help him do more good in the world and so he eagerly accepted. He took his vows when he was twenty-four.

Martin began to reach out to Lima's poor through his ministry at the monastery. He served leftover food to the hungry each day and brought the sick into the monastery for treatment until every available space was taken. When the Dominicans complained, Martin found lodging for people in abandoned buildings. He also opened a home for homeless children. He arranged for the children to be cared for by a paid staff of teachers, doctors, nurses, cooks, and even counselors. Martin and his helpers raised the money to pay the workers so that they would receive a just wage. Martin's children's home is believed to be the first of its kind in both North and South America.

Martin de Porres was canonized a saint in 1962 by Pope John XXIII. The pope named Martin the patron of interracial justice. Saint Martin was a living example of the Corporal and Spiritual Works of Mercy. As we share the moral teachings of the Catholic Church with our students, we can ask God to help us emulate Martin's example. Like Martin, we can teach them what it means to follow Jesus' command: "Love one another" (John 13:34).

Sharing Your Faith

Find a partner to work with: a spouse, a friend, or a fellow catechist. Come together at the beginning or end of each unit for shared prayer and discussion. Use the questions below as a starting point. As an alternative, record your thoughts in a personal journal.

▶ How do you follow Jesus' command to "love one another"?

▶ How do the moral teachings of the Catholic faith inspire you to live your Baptism?

▶ When and where do you most feel Christ's presence?

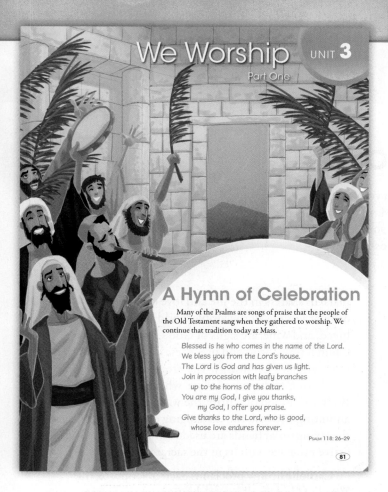

We Worship · UNIT 3
Part One

A Hymn of Celebration

Many of the Psalms are songs of praise that the people of the Old Testament sang when they gathered to worship. We continue that tradition today at Mass.

Blessed is he who comes in the name of the Lord.
We bless you from the Lord's house.
The Lord is God and has given us light.
Join in procession with leafy branches
    up to the horns of the altar.
You are my God, I give you thanks,
    my God, I offer you praise.
Give thanks to the Lord, who is good,
    whose love endures forever.

PSALM 118: 26–29

81

What I Have Learned
What is something you already know about these faith concepts?

liturgy

_____
_____
_____

The Sacraments of Christian Initiation

_____
_____
_____

sanctifying grace

_____
_____
_____

Faith Terms to Know
Put an X next to the faith terms you know. Put a ? next to faith terms you need to learn more about.

_____ the Mass
_____ sacrament
_____ vocation
_____ Baptism
_____ consecrate
_____ Confirmation
_____ Real Presence
_____ the Eucharist

The Bible
What do you know about the event of Pentecost from the Acts of the Apostles?

_____
_____
_____

The Church
What would you like to know about the Church's liturgy?

_____
_____
_____

Questions I Have
What questions would you like to ask about the liturgical year?

_____
_____
_____

82

Unit 3 Opener

Opening Page

▶ Invite the young people to tell you what they see in the illustration. *(Old Testament figures entering a temple in a mood of celebration.)*

▶ Proclaim the Scripture passage for the class. Ask: "When you go to Mass this week, what will you want to praise God for?" Accept the children's answers, but do not comment on them.

Getting Ready

▶ Invite the young people to write their responses to the questions and directions under What I Have Learned, Faith Terms to Know, and the other headings in the second column.

▶ Invite a few volunteers to share their responses, but do not correct them at this time. Tell the students that they will return to this page to check their learning at the end of the unit.

▶ For Questions I Have, you might write their questions on the board on a piece of newsprint so that you can refer to them if or when the topics come up in the unit.

▶ Ask the class to look at the next page and begin Chapter 9.

Celebrating the Liturgy

BACKGROUND

Worshipping God

When you hear the word *liturgy*, what first comes to your mind? Most of us quickly, even instinctively, focus on the Mass, or Eucharist. Perhaps this is so because Eucharist is the source and summit of Christian life, but Eucharist is also our most common experience of the liturgy.

Rendering Worship to God

It is important, however, not to equate the liturgy of the Church with the Eucharist. The liturgy of the Church is her work of participating in the Paschal Mystery of Christ. "Through the liturgy Christ our high priest continues the work of our redemption through the Church's celebration of the Paschal Mystery by which he accomplished our salvation" (*Catechism of the Catholic Church*, "Glossary"; see also 1067–1069). This work is accomplished through the celebration of the Seven Sacraments as well as the Liturgy of the Hours, or Divine Office.

The Work of the Whole Church

The liturgy of the Church is the work of the whole Church. It is the work of both Christ, the Head of the Church, and her members. When the Church celebrates the liturgy, Christ, our High Priest, is present, leading her. For example, when the Church anoints the sick, it is Jesus Christ who anoints the sick and invites them to faith in God. When the Church celebrates the Eucharist, Christ is present in a unique way. He is truly and really present under the appearances of bread and wine, which have become his Body and Blood.

Sacramental Signs

The Seven Sacraments are signs of God's love given to us by Christ, the Incarnate Son of God, that make us sharers in the life and love of God. The ordinary things of the visible world, such as water, oil, bread, and wine, are signs of God's love for us. The Church transforms and uses these natural signs in the celebration of her liturgy. The breaking of bread and the sharing of the cup of wine, which have become the Body and Blood of Christ, the washing with water, the anointing with oil, the exchanging of promises, and the laying on of hands are used to visibly affirm God's active presence with us in the sacraments.

Catholic liturgy proclaims Sacred Scripture, the Word of God, in all her celebrations of the sacraments (see *Catechism of the Catholic Church*, 1154). God is present in his word. Hearing his word helps us recall the divine plan of creation and salvation. It affords us the opportunity to give our assent to God's own word to us.

As we prepare for the celebration of the liturgy, we need to be aware that it is through Christ, in Christ, and with Christ, in the unity of the Holy Spirit, that we give honor and glory to the Father.

For Reflection

Which of the many signs, the words and actions, used in the celebration of the sacraments manifests most clearly for me the presence of God at work in the Church and in my life?

What might I do to increase my active participation in the celebration of the Eucharist?

Catechist to Catechist

(handwritten: young → & old)

The Work of the Church

The liturgy is the work, or activity, of the whole Church. This is an important concept for sixth-graders. The Church clearly teaches that "all the faithful should be led to that full, conscious, and active participation in liturgical celebrations which is demanded by the very nature of the liturgy" (*Vatican II, Constitution on the Sacred Liturgy* 14). The word *all* includes young people as well as adults.

Encouraging Participation

To help the children appreciate that the liturgy is a communal activity, or the work of the whole Church, list the names of all the participants in the celebration of the Mass. Explain the roles of the worshiping assembly, priest and deacon, ministers of the Word, extraordinary ministers of Holy Communion, cantor, organist, choir, altar servers, and ministers of hospitality. Talk about how young people can more fully participate in the liturgy.

The Church Teaches...

"Catechesis both precedes the Liturgy and springs from it. It prepares people for a full, conscious, and active participation in the Liturgy by helping them understand its nature, rites, and symbols. It stems from the Liturgy insofar as it helps people to worship God and to reflect on their experience of the words, signs, rituals, and symbols expressed in the Liturgy; to discern the implications of their participation in the Liturgy; and to respond to its missionary summons to bear witness and offer service"

(*National Directory for Catechesis*, 33).

That is why throughout every chapter, prayer from the liturgical traditions and prayerful experiences of the Church are included as a regular part of its curriculum.

Further Reading and Reflection

For more on the teachings of the Church, see the *Catechism of the Catholic Church*, 1076–1109, 1136–1186, 1206; and from the *United States Catholic Catechism for Adults*, pages 165–179.

(handwritten list: priest, deacon, lectors, eucharistic server, cantor, organist, choir, altar servers)

(handwritten: says people of church participate in the worship of God (work of liturgy))

Catechist Prayer

God our Father,
you chose Mary to be
the mother of your Son.
Her faith in your great love
gave her the courage to say yes
to your will for her.
Help me to say yes to your will
each and every day.
Amen.

Lesson Planner

Chapter 9 Celebrating the Liturgy

Focus To explain why the Church celebrates the liturgy and the sacraments

LESSON PART	PROCESS	MATERIALS and RESOURCES
EXPLORE **Focus** **To explore the way we celebrate the Lord's Day** ⏱ 10 minutes **Pages 83–84**	▶ Proclaim and discuss Psalm 57:9–11 (in praise of the Lord's steadfastness and faithfulness). ▶ Hear a story about the Lord's Day. **Disciple Power:** Diligence	Bible
DISCOVER **Focus** **To discover the Catholic Church's teaching on the liturgy and the sacraments** ⏱ 30 minutes **Pages 85–87**	▶ Discover that the Seven Sacraments are the heart of the liturgy of the Church. **Activity:** Analyze words, objects, and actions used at Mass. ▶ Learn how many of the Church's rituals are rooted in the Old Testament. **Activity:** Explain stained-glass images related to the Sacraments. ▶ Riview liturgical year.	Pencils Optional Materials: Crayons and markers Glue and scissors Colored paper **Additional Activities Booklet:** Activities 9a–9b, or see BeMyDisciples.com.
DECIDE **Focus** **To decide how to participate more fully in the Mass** ⏱ 10 minutes **Page 88**	**Activity:** Plan a ritual prayer celebration. **My Faith Choice:** Choose a way to prepare to participate at Mass.	**Enriching the Lesson Activities:** Catechist Edition, page 159 • Creating Greetings of Joy • Designing Symbols for the Sacraments • Making a Liturgical Seasons Mural

Concluding the Lesson   ⏱ 10 minutes

We Remember

Page 89

▶ Review concepts and do the review activity.

▶ **Assessment Tools Booklet:** Chapter Test 9a–9b, or see BeMyDisciples.com.

We Pray

▶ **Prayer:** the Doxology

Materials: Bible, candle, cross for prayer space

▶ Grade 6 Music CD

Preview

Point out resources for this chapter at

www.BeMyDisciples.com

▶ Preview the With My Family page and next week's lesson theme.

Looking Ahead

In this chapter the Holy Spirit invites you to ▶

EXPLORE why the Church keeps Sunday as the Lord's Day.

DISCOVER why the Church celebrates the liturgy.

DECIDE on how you can better take part in the Mass.

CHAPTER **9**

Celebrating the Liturgy

Which routines are part of your life each day? How would describe these daily routines?

Let us listen to the psalmist describe his daily life.

"My heart is steadfast, God,
   my heart is steadfast.
   I will sing and chant praise.
Awake, my soul;
   awake, lyre and harp!
   I will wake the dawn.
I will praise you among the peoples, Lord;
   I will chant your praise among the nations.
For your love towers to the heavens." Psalm 57:8–11

What do these words tell you the psalmist included in his daily life?

83

HUMAN METHODOLOGIES

Learning through the Witness of the Catechist. The *National Directory for Catechesis* states: "Catechists must make the words of Christ their own: 'My teaching is not my own but is from the one who sent me,' and they confess with St. Paul, 'I handed on to you . . . what I also received' " (John 7: 16, 1 Corinthians 15:3, *NDC* 29E). As a catechist, you have the opportunity to make the Church year come alive for your students. The atmosphere and environment that you provide, the attitude that you foster, and the example that you give all help you pass on the teachings of Christ.

Pray

▶ Ask the children to gather and quiet their minds and hearts for prayer.

▶ Begin and conclude the prayer by praying the Sign of the Cross.

▶ Read aloud to the class the Scripture passage on the page. As you read Psalm 57:8–11, invite the children to hold their hands over their heart for the first part, and then take the orans posture for the second half.

Reflect

▶ Have the children respond to the question at the top of the page.

▶ Reread Psalm 57:8–11 and discuss with the young people how certain gestures can enhance the words prayed and proclaimed. For example, hands over heart while reading "My heart is steadfast . . ."

▶ Discuss some of the rituals of the Church that they have experienced. Inquire of them which rituals they enjoy. Discuss the last questions.

Focus

▶ Explain that in this chapter they will learn more about the Liturgy of the Catholic Church, especially the Latin Rite.

▶ Invite them to read aloud each bullet in the Looking Ahead feature.

Introduce

▶ Remind the young people that the liturgy is the Church's work of worshipping God. Point out that wherever they go in the world the Catholic Church celebrates the sacraments in essentially the same way.

▶ Invite volunteers to read aloud One Faith, One Lord.

▶ Ask volunteers to compare the similarities and differences of the celebrations with the way their home parish celebrates liturgy.

Reinforce

Ask the students to look at the photos on the page. Discuss what the photos show about the worldwide celebration of Catholic liturgy.

Connect

▶ Ask the students the closing question and invite them to share their experiences.

▶ Read aloud the Disciple Power box. Remind the students that full participation in the liturgy requires our diligence. Remind them that sitting closer to the altar and participating in the prayers and gestures of liturgy will help them to have a fuller experience of the Mass.

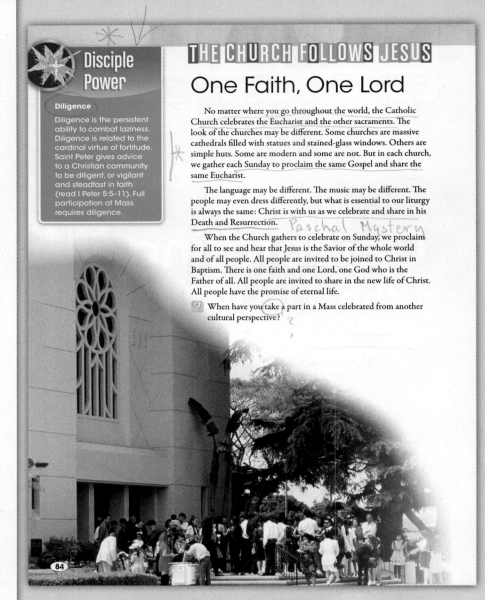

Disciple Power

Diligence

Diligence is the persistent ability to combat laziness. Diligence is related to the cardinal virtue of fortitude. Saint Peter gives advice to a Christian community to be diligent, or vigilant and steadfast in faith (read I Peter 5:5–11). Full participation at Mass requires diligence.

THE CHURCH FOLLOWS JESUS
One Faith, One Lord

No matter where you go throughout the world, the Catholic Church celebrates the Eucharist and the other sacraments. The look of the churches may be different. Some churches are massive cathedrals filled with statues and stained-glass windows. Others are simple huts. Some are modern and some are not. But in each church, we gather each Sunday to proclaim the same Gospel and share the same Eucharist.

The language may be different. The music may be different. The people may even dress differently, but what is essential to our liturgy is always the same: Christ is with us as we celebrate and share in his Death and Resurrection. *Paschal Mystery*

When the Church gathers to celebrate on Sunday, we proclaim for all to see and hear that Jesus is the Savior of the whole world and of all people. All people are invited to be joined to Christ in Baptism. There is one faith and one Lord, one God who is the Father of all. All people are invited to share in the new life of Christ. All people have the promise of eternal life.

❓ When have you take a part in a Mass celebrated from another cultural perspective?

84

DISCIPLE POWER

Diligence. Ask the children to share what they hope to become when they grow up. Choose two or three responses, and as a class, talk about what a person would have to do to achieve those goals. Responses might include: make good grades, go to college, or practice sports or music every day. Point out that any goal that we choose requires diligence, or constant work, to achieve. The same is true for growing in faith. Ask the young people which things they can do to remain diligent in their faith. Emphasize that keeping Sunday as the Lord's Day by going to Mass is one of the key things we do to be diligent, or steadfast, in faith.

diligence = constant work to achieve a goal

How? to be "diligent" in faith?

The Work of God's People

The **liturgy** is the work of the Church, the People of God. In the liturgy, the Church worships God the Father through the ritual actions in the liturgy. A ritual is similar to a routine, something that we repeat over and over again. The rituals of the Church include words, objects, and actions in the celebration of the liturgy.

The Church worships God because he alone is God. He is the source of all the blessings of creation and salvation. We praise and thank God. We worship him as the one Body of Christ. With Christ, the Head of the Church, and with the Holy Spirit animating our hearts and minds, we give honor and glory, praise and thanksgiving to God our Father, together with Christ through the power of the Holy Spirit.

The Sacraments

The Seven **Sacraments** are at the heart of the liturgy of the Church. When we celebrate the sacraments, we join with the whole Church on Earth and in Heaven. The sacraments are the seven main liturgical signs of the Church, given to us by Jesus Christ. They make his saving work present to us and make us sharers in the life of God, the Holy Trinity.

In every celebration of the sacraments, God proclaims in our midst the story of his loving plan of creation and salvation. That is why the Liturgy of the Word is always part of celebrating the sacraments. In the Liturgy of the Word, the Holy Spirit prepares the worshiping assembly to encounter Christ, the Word of God. God speaks and we listen attentively and respond diligently with open hearts.

FAITH FOCUS
Why does the Church celebrate the liturgy?

FAITH VOCABULARY
liturgy
Liturgy is the work by the Church of worshipping God. Liturgy includes words, signs, symbols, and actions used to give praise and thanks, and honor and glory to God the Father.

Sacraments
Sacraments are the seven sacred signs and causes of grace given to the Church by Christ to continue his saving action among us through the power of the Holy Spirit.

1. Baptism
2. Confirmation
3. Reconcilliation/confession
4. Eucharist
5. Annointing/last rites
6. Marriage
7. Holy Orders

Activity Think of some words, objects, and actions within the Mass. Discuss why each of your choices is important to the celebration of the liturgy.

Ritual	Importance
Words: *In name of Father/Son/HS*	
Object: *Greeting/Opening of ritual*	
Action: *Sign o' Cross @ begining of Mass*	

85

LITURGY CONNECTION

Liturgical Vestments. Among the objects used in the celebration of the liturgy are liturgical vestments. Review with the young people the names of the vestments worn by the priest and deacon during the celebration of the Eucharist:

▶ **Alb:** A long, white vestment tied at the waist with a cincture, or cord, worn by priests and deacons.

▶ **Stole:** A long strip of cloth in the color of the liturgical season, worn over the alb by priests and deacons.

▶ **Chasuble:** The outer liturgical garment worn by the priest. It matches the liturgical color of the season.

▶ **Dalmatic:** The outer liturgical garment worn by the deacon. It also matches the liturgical color of the season.

Key Concept
Liturgy is the work of the Church, the People of God.

Teach

▶ Read the Faith Focus question aloud and ask the young people to reflect silently on how they would respond.

▶ Point out that the sacraments make us sharers in the life of Christ through the power of the Holy Spirit.

Reinforce

▶ Forecast the chapter by reviewing the Faith Vocabulary. Invite the children to make word cards.

▶ Have the youth read the text on the page. Ask them to highlight key words and phrases that help them to define the concepts in the heading. Share some of these with the group.

Connect

▶ Introduce the activity. Help them point out some of the key words, signs, and symbols in the rites.

▶ Explain that what we say and do in the rites reflects what we believe. For example, the baptismal font is often in or near the entrance of the church. This points to Baptism as the entrance into the Church.

▶ Inquire, "How have some of the ritual aspects of the liturgy helped you to better understand the Mass?" *(Accept all reasonable answers.)*

Key Concept
Each sacrament includes essential words, signs, and symbolic actions.

Teach

▶ Read the Faith-Filled People feature. Explain that Abraham is the father of three major faiths (Judaism, Islam, and Christianity).

▶ Remind the group that every celebration of the liturgy and sacraments is a celebration of the universal Church with Christ as the Head.

▶ Read The Book of Leviticus aloud to the students. Discuss how the Old Testament can help us learn about our liturgy. Point out that the Holiness Code begins with the Sabbath.

▶ Discuss how celebrating rituals reminded the Israelites about their Covenant with God.

Reinforce

Ask the students to give an example of a changeable and an unchangeable aspect of the Rite of the Mass. (*Unchangeable: words of Consecration; Changeable: music.*)

Connect

▶ Ask volunteers to share why celebrating the Sacraments is important to them.

▶ Have the group complete the activity and share their responses.

Option: Have the group design their own stained-glass image of one of the Seven Sacraments.

Faith-Filled People

Abraham

At Mass during Eucharistic Prayer I, the Church proclaims Abraham to be "our father in faith." God and Abraham entered into the Covenant. Abraham believed that God was always present with him. Abraham trusted God and lived a life of hope in the future God promised to him and his family. You can find out more about Abraham in Genesis 12:1–7; 22:2–18.

The Book of Leviticus

Some of the rituals of the Catholic Church have developed from the traditions and laws of God's people in Old Testament times. That is why reading the Old Testament can help us to learn more about the liturgy.

The Book of Leviticus, the third book of the Pentateuch, served as a liturgical handbook for the Levites, the priests of the Israelites. Leviticus contains a section called the Holiness Code. In this section, we find the rituals and rules for celebrating the Sabbath. The Holiness Code begins with the Sabbath:

> The LORD said to Moses, ". . . For six days work may be done; but the seventh day is the [S]abbath rest, a day for sacred assembly, on which you shall do no work. The [S]abbath shall belong to the LORD wherever you dwell."
> LEVITICUS 23:1, 3

The Book of Leviticus then details the rituals for the observance of the feasts of Passover and unleavened bread. Celebrating the Sabbath and Passover rituals helped the Israelites to share in the love of God. It helped them remember all that God had done for them, and to live their Covenant with God.

Sacramental Signs

The sacraments of the Catholic Church also include rituals. They include prayerful words with signs and symbolic actions. Some of these words, signs, and symbolic actions cannot be eliminated or changed in its celebration. For example, the words the priest says at the Consecration during Mass should not be eliminated or changed. However, other parts of the celebration of a sacrament, such as the music can change.

[handwritten: ritual helps to remind us of our promise to Xrist]

Activity Look at the stained-glass images for some of the Seven Sacraments on this page. Write what each of the images tells about that sacrament.

[handwritten:]
1) Baptism
2) Eucharist
3) Holy Orders

86

FAITH-FILLED PEOPLE

Abraham. In Eucharistic Prayer I, the Church proclaims Abraham to be our father in faith. Abraham is honored as a person of deep faith by Jews, Christians, and Muslims. Genesis 12:1–9 tells us that God revealed himself to Abraham and called Abraham to take his family and leave his homeland. God promised Abraham that if he did so, God would make of him father of a great nation (**Genesis 12:2**). Abraham's assent in faith to God was unconditional. Not fully understanding God's request and promise, Abraham set forth, trusting God.

The Liturgical Year   *6 seasons*

The Church celebrates her liturgy throughout the year. She celebrates it every day throughout the day somewhere in the world. The Church celebrates the liturgy in the languages spoken by people all over the world.

Just as the calendar year has different seasons and is filled with many holidays, so too the Church's liturgical year is composed of different seasons and feasts. The liturgical feasts are moments for us to commemorate those events and people who help us to encounter Christ. For Catholics, the liturgical year is a time of receiving grace—a yearlong celebration of our life in Christ.

1 **Advent.** Advent is a liturgical season to prepare for Christ's coming among us. This is the beginning of the liturgical year typically marked by the color purple.

2 **Christmas.** This season celebrates that the Son of God became one of us without giving up his divinity and is the Savior of the world. During this season, the colors white or gold are used.

3 **Lent.** Lent is a liturgical season that calls us to change our hearts, seek God's forgiveness, prepare candidates for Baptism, and renew our commitment to live our Baptism. The color purple is used during this season to represent penance and reconciliation.

4 **Easter Triduum.** The Easter Triduum, or "the three days," is the center of the entire liturgical year. This period of time begins on Holy Thursday evening, continues on Good Friday, and concludes with the celebrations of the Easter Vigil and Easter Sunday.

5 **Easter.** The fifty days of the Easter season, which culminates on Pentecost, are a time of proclaiming the mystery of the new life that we have in the Risen Christ.

6 **Ordinary Time.** During this period of time, we hear the story of Jesus from one of the four accounts of the Gospels—Matthew, Mark, Luke, or John. We learn the meaning of being a disciple of Jesus in the daily activity of life. Green is used to indicate the growth of discipleship during this time.

Feasts. The solemnities and feasts of the Lord and of Mary, the Apostles, martyrs, and other holy men and women deepen our sharing in God's work in our world.

? Which are your favorite parts of the Church's liturgical year?

Catholics Believe

Rites of the Catholic Church

There are different approved rites celebrated within the Catholic Church. These rites witness the diverse liturgical traditions of the Church around the world. Most Catholics in the United States celebrate the Latin Rite. Other rites include the Byzantine, Alexandrian (or Coptic), Syriac, Armenian, Maronite, Ukrainian, Syrian, Romanian, Russian, Malabar, and Chaldean rites. Such diversity does not distract from the unity of the Church, but rather points to her universality in celebrating the mystery of Christ for all people.

87

SCRIPTURE BACKGROUND

The Liturgical Seasons. Share these Gospel passages with each group before they prepare their statement on the segment of the liturgical year assigned to them. Each passage helps reinforce their understanding of the liturgical year.

▶ **Advent:**   Luke 1:26–38 (Annunciation)

▶ **Christmas:**   Luke 2:1–14 (Nativity)

▶ **Ordinary Time:**   Luke 19:1–10 (Zaccheus and Jesus, Thirty-first Sunday in Ordinary Time, Cycle C)

▶ **Lent:**   Matthew 4:1–11 (Temptation of Jesus in the Desert)

▶ **Triduum:**   John 13:1–15 (Washing of the Apostles' Feet)

▶ **Easter:**   Matthew 28:1–10 (Resurrection)

▶ **Feasts:**   Matthew 5:1–12 (All Saints)

> **Key Concept**
> Each Liturgical year is a celebration of the grace of our life in Christ.

Teach

▶ Recall with the group that using words, signs and symbolic action, the Church celebrates the liturgy.

▶ Explain that the Church celebrates the liturgy every day. We call the yearlong celebration the liturgical year. It comprises a cycle of seasons and feasts.

▶ Read the Catholics Believe section aloud. Ask if the children know anyone who belongs to one of these rites.

▶ Divide the class into seven small groups. Give each group a card with the name of one of the parts of the liturgical year.

▶ Have each group read silently the text about their assigned part and to formulate a statement about it and report to the class.

Reinforce

Refer the students to the graphic of The Liturgical Year on page 225 to review learning.

Connect

Have students then name their favorite feasts and seasons of the liturgical year.

Reinforce

▶ Recall with the youth that Jesus always leads the Church in celebrating the Seven Sacraments.

▶ Point out that the Church always prays in, with, and through Christ in union with the Holy Spirit. With the grace of the Holy Spirit, we can be diligent about our participation in the life of the Church, especially in the liturgy and the Seven Sacraments.

Respond

▶ Explain the directions to the activity on the page. Invite the students to complete the chart.

▶ Ask volunteers to share with the class their responses.

▶ Emphasize that our unified actions within the liturgy enable everyone to participate as a sign of our one faith in one God.

Choose

▶ Have students complete My Faith Choice. Allow them time to reflect on how they can better praise and honor God our Father in the Mass.

▶ Encourage the young people to put their faith choice into practice this week by remembering something concrete and practical that they have learned during this chapter to help them be diligent in their participation.

▶ Remind them to offer the silent prayer on the page.

I FOLLOW JESUS

The Holy Spirit prepares you to celebrate the sacraments. Jesus is always there, leading the Church in her celebration of the Seven Sacraments. The words, objects, and actions used in these celebrations help us to participate and express our faith more fully.

A RITUAL CELEBRATION

Plan a ritual prayer celebration for your class. Choose words, objects, and actions that will involve your classmates in the celebration. Tell how these help us participate.

Theme: _____

Words (Including Scripture): _____

_____

Objects: _____

_____

Actions: _____

_____

What the Church Does	How These Help Us Participate
_____	_____
_____	_____
_____	_____

MY FAITH CHOICE

Before participating in Mass this week, I will remember that we encounter Christ during Mass. At Mass, I will:

_____

_____

 Pray, "O Eternal Father, grant that I may remain steadfast in faith, and diligent in giving you honor and praise. Amen."

88

THE TASKS OF CATECHESIS

Liturgical Education. To help students remember what the Church does during every Mass, take time to review the We Celebrate The Mass section on pages 396–402 of the student text. As you review this section, ask the youth to name all of the opportunities that they have to take an active part in the celebration of the Mass. Conclude this review by inviting the students to name other things they've seen done during Mass (i.e., dismissal of children for Children's Liturgy of the Word, celebrations of Baptisms, or special collections for the poor).

Chapter Review

Match the terms in column A with their meanings in column B.

Column A

1. __E__ liturgy

2. __B__ Paschal Mystery

3. __D__ Sacraments

4. __A__ Liturgical Year

5. __C__ Easter Triduum

Column B

A. The Church's yearly cycle of seasons and feasts that make up the Church's year of worship.

B. Christ's Passion, Death, Resurrection, and glorious Ascension

C. The three-day celebration that is at the center of the liturgical year of the Church

D. The seven main celebrations of the Church's liturgy given to us by Christ that makes us sharers in the life of God

E. The Church's work of worshiping God

TO HELP YOU REMEMBER

1. The celebration of the liturgy is the Church's work of worshiping God.

2. The Seven Sacraments are the center of the Church's liturgy. They make us sharers in the life of God through the power of the Holy Spirit.

3. Throughout the year, the Church praises God the Father for what he has done and continues to do for us.

Give Glory to God!

A doxology is a prayer of praise to God the Father in the name of Jesus through the power of the Holy Spirit. Conclude with this ritual prayer from the conclusion of the Eucharistic Prayer.

Leader: Let us acknowledge that all of our blessings come from God our Father. *(Pause.)*
Let us join with Christ and give glory to God the Father.

All: **Through him, and with him, and in him, O God, almighty Father, in the unity of the Holy Spirit, all glory and honor is yours, for ever and ever. Amen.**

Doxology, Eucharistic Prayer, Roman Missal

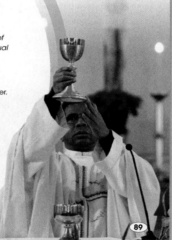

89

We Remember

▶ Read to the group the bulleted summary in the To Help You Remember section. Be sure to clarify any misunderstandings or questions related to the content of the chapter.

▶ Have the young people highlight one statement that was most significant for them.

▶ Invite the students to complete the matching activity. Review their answers.

We Pray

▶ Gather the youth for prayer, and introduce the closing prayer.

▶ Read the introductory paragraph. Point out that Saint Paul frequently ended his letters with a doxology. Explain that at Mass the priest prays the doxology and we proclaim what is called the Great Amen.

▶ Pray the prayer together, beginning and ending with the Sign of the Cross.

LITURGY CONNECTION

Sung Prayers. The closing prayer for this lesson is the doxology that is prayed at the conclusion of the Eucharistic Prayer at every Mass is prayed or sung by the priest. In the case of a concelebrated Mass the celebrants say or sing the doxology together. The people's part is the Great Amen.

Preview

▶ Have the participants carefully tear out the With My Family page along the perforation.

▶ Encourage them to share the pages with their families and to complete the activities together at home.

▶ If the students did not or could not complete the chapter review, encourage them to complete it with their families.

▶ Point out the title and theme of next week's chapter to the children.

Visit www.BeMyDisciples.com

▶ Take time with the group to explore the many activities and resources available at the Web site.

▶ Especially encourage them and their families to discover the many resources available at **www.BeMyDisciples.com.**

Before Moving On ...

As you finish today's lesson, reflect on the following question before moving on to the next chapter.

Which opportunities do I give the students to express themselves through prayer?

With My Family

This Week...

In chapter 9, Celebrating the Liturgy, your child learned:

▶ The liturgy is the Church's work of worshiping God. It centers on the Eucharist and the other sacraments.

▶ The whole Church gathers with Christ to share in the life of the Holy Trinity. We bless, give praise and thanks, and honor and glory to the Father.

▶ Through the power of the Holy Spirit, we, as members of the Church, remember and are made sharers in the Paschal Mystery.

▶ Throughout the liturgical year, we join with Christ to share in his work of Salvation.

▶ Each of us is called by God to be diligent and steadfast in faith.

For more about related teachings of the Church, see the *Catechism of the Catholic Church*, 1076–1109, 1136–1186, 1206; and the *United States Catholic Catechism for Adults*, pages 165–179.

■ Sharing God's Word

Read Psalm 95:1–7 together. Emphasize that the Seven Sacraments are signs and sources of God's grace through which we are made sharers of the life and work of Jesus Christ, the Son of God. Talk about your family's diligent participation in the celebration of the Eucharist and the Sacrament of Penance and Reconciliation.

■ We Live as Disciples

The Christian family and home is a school of discipleship. Choose one of the following activities to do as a family, or design a similar activity of your own:

▶ When you take part in the Mass this week, notice the liturgical decorations and the priest's vestments. Talk about what they tell you about which liturgical season is being celebrated.

▶ Create a doorknob hanger or wreath for the front door of your home. Decorate it so that it is a reminder for the current liturgical season.

■ Our Spiritual Journey

The Church has always prayed doxologies, short formulaic prayers praising God, within the rites. Memorize the doxology on page 89. Pray it as a mantra or a simple spontaneous prayer throughout the day. This will help focus your living the dismissal at Mass, "Go in peace, glorifying the Lord with your life" (Revised Roman Missal).

For more ideas on ways that your family can live as disciples of Jesus, visit **www.BeMyDisciples.com**

90

ENRICHING THE LESSON

The Liturgical Calendar. Liturgy Training Publications annually publishes a beautiful, poster-sized liturgical calendar intended for classroom use. The calendar is a wonderful visual aid for teaching the liturgical seasons of the Church year. In addition, the calendar includes the holy days and feast days of the saints. Consider purchasing a poster through Liturgy Training Publications, (1-800-933-1800; www.ltp.org.) A smaller version of the calendar is available in packs of ten, and makes an inexpensive gift for families when the new liturgical year begins on the first Sunday of Advent.

Enriching the Lesson

Creating Greetings of Joy

Purpose

To reinforce that every celebration of the liturgy and the Sacraments is a celebration of the whole Body of Christ (taught on page 85)

Directions

► Have the youth develop a list of joyful greetings they can use to welcome people as they gather for the Mass.

► Have the students sign up to be ministers of hospitality and greet parishioners, using the greetings they have created. Be sure to get permission for this activity.

► Gather together after the young people have had the experience of being ministers of hospitality to talk about what it was like to greet parishioners coming to celebrate the liturgy.

Materials

paper

pens or pencils

Designing Symbols for the Sacraments

Purpose

To reinforce that each celebration of the sacraments combines words, signs, and symbolic actions (taught on page 86)

Directions

► Show the group water, oil, and bread. Encourage them to eat the bread, to bless themselves with the water, and to dip their fingers in the oil and rub it on the palms of their hands.

► Next, invite the participants to work in small groups and use words and images to design a symbol to represent a sacrament that they have received.

► Have the students share their symbols with the class.

Materials

construction paper

markers or crayons

Making a Liturgical Seasons Mural

Purpose

To reinforce that the liturgical year of the Church is composed of seasons and feasts (taught on page 87)

Directions

► Divide the class into six groups, and assign a liturgical season to each group.

► Have the students work together to create a mural depicting what the Church celebrates in each of the liturgical seasons.

► Remind the groups to use words, symbols, and the liturgical colors for each season.

► Display the completed mural in your learning space, or with proper permission, in a public place in the parish.

Materials

large mural paper

different colors of construction paper

scissors

glue sticks

markers, crayons, or colored chalk

BACKGROUND

Sacrament of Baptism

The sacraments are rich in importance and inspiration for Catholics. They accompany us through all the stages and transitions in our lives. Baptism is the gateway to all of the other sacraments. Baptism joins us to Christ and incorporates us into the Church. We receive the gift of the Holy Spirit, new life in Christ, and become adopted sons and daughters of God the Father. Through Baptism we are made sharers in the divine plan of Salvation. Original Sin and all personal sins are forgiven. An indelible sign, or character, is marked on the soul of the newly baptized, identifying us as belonging to Christ forever.

Triple Immersion

The most expressive way to be baptized is by triple immersion into the sacred water. Three times we enter into the water and rise from it to new life. This signifies our baptism into the death and Resurrection of Christ. From its earliest days, however, the Church has also used the rite of a triple pouring of water over the head as an expression of a person's being baptized. In both Baptism by immersion and by the pouring of water, the celebrant baptizes as Christ commanded, "In the name of the Father, and of the Son, and of the Holy Spirit" (see Matthew 28:19).

Baptism by Desire

You might ask, "Is Baptism by water the only form of Baptism? Does a person have to be baptized in water to be saved?" The answer is no. A person who truly desires to be baptized and does not have the opportunity to receive the sacrament can be saved through the baptism of desire. The Church also teaches that those who have not come to know and believe in Christ and who sincerely seek God and strive to lead a virtuous life can be saved even though they have not been baptized. God loves all people and desires all to live in communion with him forever.

Images of Baptism

Baptism constitutes the foundation for the whole Christian life. As a Sacrament of Christian Initiation, it accomplishes what it implies—it initiates a person into the life of Christ and into the life of the Church, the Body of Christ.

The word *baptism* comes from a Greek word that means "to plunge" or "immerse" into water. This description of Baptism points to the reality that when we are baptized, we are immersed in Christ's death and Resurrection. In Baptism we die to sin and rise to new life in Christ.

Baptism has also been described as a "washing." The reality captured by this image is one of purification. By Baptism, all sins, both Original Sin and personal sins, are washed away. We are washed clean of all that separates us from God.

The words *renewal* and *enlightenment* have also been applied to Baptism. These words point to the activity of the Holy Spirit, who gives us the power of hope and love to embrace life. Baptism is also called a "gift." In other words, it is something we neither earn nor deserve.

For Reflection

When I reflect on my initiation into Christ and the Church, what is my most vivid memory?

What does this memory say to me about my identity?

Catechist to Catechist

we are X's friend

Belonging to Christ

Baptism joins a person to Christ and marks that person as belonging to Christ forever. Being baptized gives us the identity of a friend and disciple of Christ. He will forever consider us his friends and trust us with the responsibility of continuing his work on earth. "I have called you friends, because I have told you everything I have heard from my Father. It was not you who chose me, but I chose you and appointed you to go and bear fruit that will remain" (John 15:15–16).

Rituals

The Church's rituals, the combination of words, actions, and objects that are used in the celebration of the liturgy, and invite us into a life of holiness. Take the time to unlock the meaning of these sacramental rituals. Generously use gestures, such as laying on of hands, in your prayers. Understanding the meaning of the rituals of the sacraments will help the students become more aware of God acting in their lives through the celebration of the sacraments.

The Church Teaches...

"Catechesis has a distinctly ecclesial character because the Christian community transmits the Gospel essentially as it has received it, understands it, celebrates it, lives it, and communicates it. . . . Although the community of the disciples of Jesus Christ is spread throughout the world, the Gospel message that binds them together is one; it is the same faith that is transmitted in many different languages and through many cultures" (*National Directory for Catechesis,* 25D).

This chapter helps the children deepen their knowledge of and faith in the Holy Spirit, who is ever present to them, guiding them to live their Baptism. This knowledge or awareness in faith has a spirit of being invited and welcomed into the Church.

Further Reading and Reflection

For more on the teachings of the Church, see the *Catechism of the Catholic Church,* 1210–1284; and from the *United States Catholic Catechism for Adults,* pages 181–199.

"cannot be un-baptized" marked as belonging to X forever

Catechist Prayer

Holy Spirit,
fill me with the desire
to proclaim
the Good News
by the way I live,
love, and speak.
Amen.

Lesson Planner

Focus To discover the meaning of the Sacrament of Baptism as a Sacrament of Christian Initiation

LESSON PART	PROCESS	MATERIALS and RESOURCES
EXPLORE **Focus** To explore ways of living the faith ⏱ 10 minutes **Pages** 91–92	▶ Proclaim and discuss Mark 1:9–11 (Jesus is baptized by John). ▶ Learn the story of St. Charles Lwanga. **Disciple Power:** Modesty	Bible
DISCOVER **Focus** To discover more about the Sacrament of Baptism ⏱ 30 minutes **Pages** 93–95	▶ Emphasize that in the Sacrament of Baptism, water is a symbol of new life. **Activity:** Write or draw ideas for a mural. ▶ Expand understanding of the Rite of Baptism. ▶ Identify the graces of Baptism. **Activity:** Create an image of Baptism.	index cards water colors (optional) crayons or markers butcher paper pencils **Additional Activities Booklet:** Activities 10a–10b, or see BeMyDisciples.com.
DECIDE **Focus** To decide a way to serve Christ and act with modesty ⏱ 10 minutes **Page** 96	**Activity:** Use a word web to decide how to serve and protect the dignity of others. **My Faith Choice:** Choose a way to serve God and others and act modestly.	**Enriching the Lesson Activities:** Catechist Edition, page 171 • Making Oral Presentations • Creating Welcome-to-the-Church Cards • Creating Faith Family Trees

Concluding the Lesson 10 minutes

We Remember	We Pray	Preview
Page 97 ▶ Review concepts and do the review activity. ▶ **Assessment Tools Booklet:** Chapter Test 10a–10b, or see BeMyDisciples.com.	▶ **Prayer:** a prayer of anointing **Materials:** Bible, candle, cross for prayer space, container of oil and water ▶ Grade 6 Music CD	Point out resources for this chapter at **www.BeMyDisciples.com** ▶ Preview the With My Family page and next week's lesson theme.

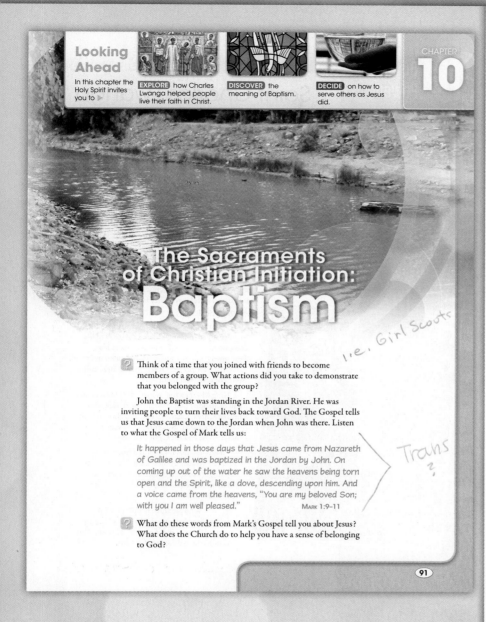

Looking Ahead

In this chapter the Holy Spirit invites you to ▶

EXPLORE how Charles Lwanga helped people live their faith in Christ.

DISCOVER the meaning of Baptism.

DECIDE on how to serve others as Jesus did.

CHAPTER **10**

The Sacraments of Christian Initiation: Baptism

i.e. Girl Scouts

[?] Think of a time that you joined with friends to become members of a group. What actions did you take to demonstrate that you belonged with the group?

John the Baptist was standing in the Jordan River. He was inviting people to turn their lives back toward God. The Gospel tells us that Jesus came down to the Jordan when John was there. Listen to what the Gospel of Mark tells us:

It happened in those days that Jesus came from Nazareth of Galilee and was baptized in the Jordan by John. On coming up out of the water he saw the heavens being torn open and the Spirit, like a dove, descending upon him. And a voice came from the heavens, "You are my beloved Son; with you I am well pleased."   MARK 1:9–11

Trans ?

[?] What do these words from Mark's Gospel tell you about Jesus? What does the Church do to help you have a sense of belonging to God?

(91)

HUMAN METHODOLOGIES

Making a Commitment to Live the Christian Life. The *National Directory for Catechesis* states that all of the baptized are called to share in the sanctification of the world *(NDC 29G)*. As you study this chapter, which focuses on the Sacrament of Baptism, remind the students that we are called to be faithful to our baptismal commitment to live as followers of Jesus Christ each and every day. Discuss the many simple, practical ways that a sixth grader can do so, and share examples from your own life. As an added activity, have students study the parish bulletin or diocesan newspaper to identify ways that the Church as a whole is being faithful to its baptismal responsibilities.

Pray

▶ Call the students to prayer by having them stand and join hands. Begin and end with the Sign of the Cross.

▶ Lead the class in prayer: "Lord God, send your Holy Spirit to help us see one another as your sons and daughters. Amen."

Reflect

▶ Have a volunteer read aloud and discuss the opening question.

▶ Invite one volunteer to read the Scripture introduction and another to read the Scripture passage.

▶ Discuss the questions related to the Scripture. Invite the students to determine the top three ways that the Church helps them have a sense of belonging to God.

▶ Invite two volunteers to demonstrate some of the ways in which people demonstrate their connection with others. (*for example, a common handshake or emblem on clothing*)

Focus

▶ Call the students' attention to the Looking Ahead feature. Invite them to read aloud each bulleted item.

▶ Invite a volunteer to describe how the image on the page relates to the content of the chapter.

▶ Explain that in this chapter they will learn more about the Sacrament of Baptism.

Introduce

▶ Point out the Faith-Filled People box on page 94 and read it aloud. Remind the students that baptism by water that John the Baptist practiced is different from the Sacrament of Baptism in the Holy Spirit.

▶ Introduce the story of Saint Charles Lwanga by reading aloud Disciple Power. Emphasize that modesty is more about inner understanding than outward expression.

▶ Tell students about how Saint Charles Lwanga was a model of modesty because he followed a code of conduct that showed that he belonged to God.

▶ Preface the reading by stating that Saint Charles demonstrates how to protect the dignity of the human person even if it means becoming a martyr.

▶ Invite volunteers to read aloud the text on the page.

Reinforce

Remind the students that martyrs sacrifice their lives to defend their belief in Jesus Christ.

Connect

Give the students time to reflect on the questions at the bottom of the page. Facilitate a large group discussion about people they know who protect the dignity of others, and how their actions demonstrate their love for Christ.

Disciple Power

Modesty

Modesty is one of the Fruits of the Holy Spirit. These are signs that a person is cooperating with the grace of the Holy Spirit. A modest person protects his or her inner self. Modesty encourages a person to respect the dignity of every human person, including oneself.

THE CHURCH FOLLOWS JESUS

Saint Charles Lwanga

Charles Lwanga, like Saint John the Baptist, called people to conversion. He called people to change their lives. He called them to turn back to God. He called them to be steadfast in their living as God wants them to live.

In the late 1800s, Catholic missionaries were successfully spreading the Gospel in central Africa, including modern day Uganda. One of these Catholic missionary groups was the Society of Missionaries of Africa. These missionaries were so successful that many people converted and were baptized. One such convert was Charles Lwanga.

Charles lived in a kingdom violently ruled by a ruthless man, King Mwanga. He was cruel to children, especially teenage boys, who were his servants. In secret, Charles taught the Catholic faith to many of these young boys. He taught them that they belonged to God, and that Jesus Christ is the Son of God and Savior. Charles taught them to protect themselves from Mwanga's violent and sinful ways. They must respect their God-given dignity.

King Mwanga became furious with Charles. In great anger, the king ordered the gates of his compound closed so that no one could leave. Fear spread. Charles gathered those who were Christians for prayer. Others joined them and were baptized that night.

King Mwanga summoned all of his servants and demanded that they choose to side with him or Christ. Charles stood and chose Christ. Others followed. This enraged Mwanga even more, so he had them put to death.

Saint Charles Lwanga and his companions suffered because of their faith. They protected the dignity of their bodies with their lives. They were the first canonized saints from modern Africa.

 Who are three people you know or have heard about who have stood up to protect the dignity of people? How do their actions show their love for Christ?

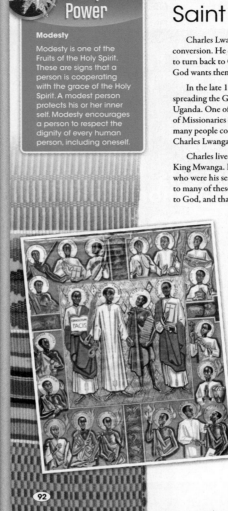

92

DISCIPLE POWER

Modesty. Young people today can understand modesty as it relates to three areas of their lives—modesty of speech, modesty of dress, and modesty of behavior. Discuss with students what it means to be modest in each of these three areas. Invite them to name famous persons (e.g., sports heroes, music figures, actors and actresses) who exhibit these qualities in both positive and negative ways. Refer back to this discussion when students complete this week's My Faith Choice.

The Sacrament of Baptism

Baptism, Confirmation, and the Eucharist are the three Sacraments of **Christian Initiation**. Through the celebration of these three sacraments, beginning with **Baptism**, a person is joined to Christ and his Body, the Church. The unity of all three Sacraments of Christian Initiation is required for the complete initiation of a person into the Body of Christ, the Church.

The first Sacrament of Christian Initiation uses baptismal water. Water can be both a sign of life (as in a flowing stream) and of destruction (as in a raging flood). Throughout the history of God's people, water has been a sign of cleansing from sin and being reborn into new life. The Church has understood the events of Noah's ark (read Genesis 7:6–23), the Crossing of the Red Sea (read Exodus 14:26–31), and the Jordan River as moments when God provided a new beginning for his Chosen People.

New Life in Christ

Christ instituted, or gave the Church, the Sacrament of Baptism and the six other sacraments. Jesus showed us the beginning of new life in him when he allowed John to baptize him in the Jordan River.

On the cross, the crucified Jesus is a sign of new life with his pierced side flowing with blood and water (read John 19:31–37). Christ makes possible our entrance into the Kingdom of God by giving the Church this sacrament. In Baptism, we die to sin and are reborn into a new life with God the Holy Trinity. Since the early days of the Church, both adults and children have been baptized. Baptism is the gateway, or doorway, to new life in the Holy Spirit and to salvation in Christ.

FAITH FOCUS
What does the Church teach about the Sacrament of Baptism.

FAITH VOCABULARY

Baptism
Baptism is the Sacrament of Christian Initiation in which we are joined to Jesus Christ, become members of his Church, and are reborn as God's adopted children. We receive the gift of the Holy Spirit, and Original Sin and personal sins are forgiven.

Christian Initiation
Christian Initiation is the liturgical process by which a person becomes a full member of the Church.

sanctifying grace
Sanctifying grace is the grace that heals our human nature wounded by sin by giving us a share in the divine life of the Holy Trinity.

Activity Write or draw some of your ideas for a mural about Baptism.

93

CATHOLIC DOCTRINE

The Social Teachings of the Catholic Church emphasize that because we are one human and global family, all people have the right to the material goods of the world and to conditions that contribute to the health and safety of everyone. We are called to share the common goods of the world. Among the basic needs of every human being is the need for clean drinking water and water to use for cooking, bathing, and cleaning. Hundreds of children die each day of diseases stemming from unclean water. Catholic Relief Services works throughout the world to improve water supplies for domestic, productive, and environmental purposes.

Key Concept
Baptism is the gateway to new life in the Holy Spirit and Salvation in Christ.

Teach

▶ Have students recall the Biblical stories of Noah (Genesis 7:6–23) and the Crossing of the Red Sea (Exodus 14:26–31). Focus on the significance of water in both stories.

▶ Read the Faith Focus question aloud, and ask students to describe the use of water in the sacrament.

▶ Ask the students to name words that describe the characteristics and qualities of water. *(liquid, clear, cleansing, abundant, necessary for life)*

▶ Have students read the text on the page. Inquire, "How does the use of water in Baptism help you to understand the process of initiation into the Church?" *(Accept all reasonable answers.)*

Reinforce

Review the Faith Vocabulary. Encourage students to maintain all their vocabulary cards.

Connect

▶ Gather the students together to create a mural about Baptism using watercolors. Allow them to be creative with the materials. Explain that the point of the mural is to celebrate the power of water in Baptism.

▶ Point out that as they create the mural, they are participating in a common activity that can help unify them as they work together.

Teach

If possible, have the students visit
the parish baptismal font, or provide
photographs of the area and font itself.

▶ Have a volunteer student read
aloud the first two paragraphs.

▶ Invite other students to share their
personal experiences of witnessing
a Baptism. See how many elements
(e.g., words, signs, and symbols) the
students can identify that are used
in the rite of Baptism.

▶ Write the words *chrism, white
garment,* and *lighted candle* on the
board. Ask for volunteers to use the
text to find what each signifies.

▶ If possible, read some of the
accompanying prayers from the
rite itself.

Connect

▶ Read the remaining text on the
page. Inquire, "What would you
like to ask a person who recently
was baptized?"

▶ Discuss why the Easter candle is
always lighted at a Baptism.

▶ Read the Faith-Filled People feature
about prophets.

Faith-Filled People

The Prophets

The Old Testament
prophets received
the grace to be living
witnesses for God. Their
words and actions called
God's people to live the
Covenant. When the
prophetic preacher John
the Baptist baptizes Jesus,
the Old Testament time of
promise ends and Jesus'
ministry and the time of
fulfillment begin.

The Rite of Baptism

In different ways, the sign of water in the Old Testament
prepared for its use in the Sacrament of Baptism. In the prayers for
the blessing of the water used in Baptism, we hear of why water
is a symbol of the story of Salvation. For example, in the Book of
Exodus, we read that God led his people through the water of the
Red Sea, saving them from slavery.

God saves us from sin in the water of Baptism. By hearing the
words and following the actions the Church uses in the celebration
of Baptism, we can come to know the meaning of this sacrament.

The Rite of Baptism in the Latin Church always includes the
minister of the sacrament immersing a person three times into the
baptismal water or pouring the water three times over the person's
head. The minister of Baptism does this action saying, "I baptize you
in the name of the Father, and of the Son, and of the Holy Spirit."
These are the essential elements of the celebration. Without these
words and actions, there is no Baptism.

The celebration of the Baptism also has these parts, or
ritual actions:

Anointing with Chrism: The minister anoints the baptized person
with Sacred Chrism. This signifies that the person shares in the work of
Christ the Priest, Prophet, and King.

Clothing with a white garment: The baptized person is given a
white garment to wear. This is a sign that the newly baptized person
has the new dignity of one who has been joined to the Risen Christ.

Presentation of a lighted candle: A baptismal candle that has
been lighted from the Easter candle is presented to the newly
baptized or to the parents and godparents of a newly baptized
infant. This symbolizes that the baptized person is to walk always with
Christ and always keep the flame of faith alive in his or her heart.

? What would you ask an adult who recently became a member
of the Catholic Church?

94

FAITH-FILLED PEOPLE

The Prophets. The biblical prophets, whose messages are recorded
in the prophetic books of the Old Testament, were chosen by God
to speak in his name to the people of God. The word prophet means
"one who speaks before others." Sometimes the prophets welcomed
God's call. At other times they feared the consequences of bringing
an unwelcome message from God to the people. No matter which
weaknesses they had, the prophets kept the light of faith alive in
Israel. There are eighteen prophetic books in the Old Testament. A list
of these books can be found at www.BeMyDisciples.com. (For more
information, see *Catechism of the Catholic Church* 64, 120, 522, 702, and 2581.)

The Graces of Baptism

What happens when we are baptized? The term *sacramental graces* is used to tell us what happens. It tells us what effects that Baptism has on a person who is baptized. These are the sacramental graces a person who is properly baptized receives.

- We are joined to Christ in his dying and rising. We receive new birth in Christ and we become adopted sons and daughters of God the Father.
- We receive the gift of the Holy Spirit.
- We become members of the Church, the Body of Christ, and are made sharers in the priesthood of Christ.
- We receive the gift of **sanctifying grace**. We are freed from all sin—Original Sin and personal sins.
- We are spiritually marked as belonging to Christ forever. This mark, which no sin can erase, is called a sacramental character. This mark means that Baptism can be received only one time and can never be repeated.

Baptism, as with all sacraments, is the work of the Church. It is the work of Christ and the members of the Church.

Activity Create an image for Baptism that includes one or more of its ritual elements.

Catholics Believe

Chrism

Sacred Chrism is one of the three oils that the Church uses in her rituals. Chrism is primarily used to consecrate (to set aside for a holy purpose) people, places, and things for the service of God and his people. Chrism is used in the Sacraments of Baptism, Confirmation, and Holy Orders. It is also used to consecrate churches and altars.

95

LITURGY CONNECTION

Blessed Oils. The Catholic Church uses three blessed oils in her celebration of the liturgy. They are Chrism, Oil of the Sick, and Oil of Catechumens. Traditionally, these oils are blessed by the bishop at the Chrism Mass on Holy Thursday. In the prayer of consecration of the Chrism, the bishop prays in part, "And so Father, we ask you to bless this oil you have created. / Fill it with the power of your Holy Spirit / through Christ your Son. / It is from him that chrism takes its name / and with chrism you have anointed / for yourself priests and kings, / prophets and martyrs" (see *Rites of the Blessing of Oils* and *Consecrating the Chrism*, paragraph 25).

Key Concept
The sacramental graces of Baptism tell us what effects it has on us.

Teach

▶ Inform the students that they will be asked to present a short summary about the Sacrament of Baptism. They should include (1) significance of the sacrament, (2) key aspects of the rite, and (3) the effects of the Sacrament.

▶ Invite volunteers to read the text on the page. Pause between paragraphs to clarify the main point for each paragraph.

▶ Place the students in groups to write their short summaries of the Sacrament of Baptism.

Connect

Have students complete the activity on the page. Explain that they are to illustrate the difference between washing and cleansing. See how the students make a distinction between the two. Suggest that the result of being washed is being cleansed.

Reinforce

Remind students that during the celebration of their Baptism, they were anointed with Chrism. Point out that the anointing with Chrism in Baptism is a sign that they are called to serve others as Jesus did.

Respond

▶ Introduce and explain the directions to the Anointed to Serve activity on the page.

▶ Ask volunteers to share with the class their responses.

Choose

▶ Share photographs or stories of your own Baptism. Describe how you try to "put on Christ" and serve others as part of your own baptismal call.

▶ Recall the full meaning of modesty (inner and outward understanding). Explain that part of "putting on Christ" means to think and act with modesty.

▶ Have the young people read the last section. Allow them time to reflect on how they can serve others as Christ did, especially with modesty.

▶ Have students individually complete the last section to make their faith choice. Encourage students to ask God to help them put their faith choice into practice this week. Remind them to take a moment & pray the final prayer silently.

I FOLLOW JESUS

In Baptism, the minister (priest or deacon) anointed the crown of your head with chrism. He said that God was now anointing you to serve others as Jesus did. Remembering that Jesus served others with humility and modesty, complete the activity below.

ANOINTED TO SERVE

In the circle, write one thing you can do to serve others as Jesus did. On each of the four lines coming out from the circle, write how that action helps protect the dignity of the person you are serving.

MY FAITH CHOICE

This week I will remember how I was chosen by God and anointed with Chrism in Baptism to serve him and others as Christ did. I will put on Christ and will act modestly by _____

 Pray, "Jesus you are the Son of God, the One who shows us how to love and serve God. Help me to be humble and modest like you."

96

THE TASKS OF CATECHESIS

Moral Formation. Closely related to modesty is the moral virtue of temperance, the spiritual habit that helps one exercise self-control. Self-control invites us to be humble about our awards and achievements when we are tempted to boast. It even invites us to bring under control any bad habits in areas of our lives such as excessive money, unhealthy eating, profane speech, and immodest dress. As the students prepare to complete their My Faith Choice, it may be helpful to invite them to think of modesty in terms of temperance, the spiritual habit of self-control.

Chapter Review

Write T if the statement is true. Write F if the statement is false.

1. __T__ The Sacrament of Baptism is our gateway to life in the Holy Spirit.

2. __T__ Through Baptism, we are spiritually marked as belonging to Christ.

3. __F__ Baptism frees us from all future sins.

4. __T__ In the Rite of Baptism, both water and oil are used.

5. __F__ Baptism is a sacrament that can be repeated.

> **TO HELP YOU REMEMBER**
>
> 1. A person becomes fully initiated into the Church through the celebration of the Sacraments of Christian Initiation: Baptism, Confirmation, and Eucharist.
>
> 2. Baptism is the first sacrament we receive; it is the doorway to new life in the Holy Spirit and salvation in Christ.
>
> 3. Through Baptism, we receive the gift of the Holy Spirit. God makes us sharers in his divine life. We are called to serve others as Christ did.

Bless Us Today, Lord

In the Old Testament, kings and priests were anointed with oil. This was a sign that they were chosen by God for a special service to God's people. Anointing with oil was also a sign that God would be with them to help them in their work. Use this prayer to recall God's presence with us.

Leader: In Baptism, we were anointed with Chrism as members of the Body of Christ, the Church. Let us recall our anointing at Baptism. *(Pause.)*
Lord, you freed us from sin in the water of Baptism. *(Raise a clear bowl of water.)*

All: **Bless us today, Lord.**

Leader: Lord, you anointed us as members of Christ's Body. *(Raise a container of oil.)*

All: **Bless us today, Lord.**

Leader: Lord, you are the Light of the world. *(Lift up a candle.)*

All: **Bless us today, Lord.**

97

We Remember

▶ Have students share three main points that they learned in this chapter.

▶ Use the bulleted summary in the To Help You Remember section as a way to assess their knowledge informally. For example, read aloud the statement, leaving key terms blank for the students to fill in orally.

▶ Invite the students to complete the Chapter Review activity and check their responses with a partner.

We Pray

▶ Gather the students for prayer. Introduce the closing prayer by pointing out that the prayer includes the use of water, oil, and a candle.

▶ Lead the class in the prayer, beginning and ending with the Sign of the Cross.

TEACHING TIP

Affirming the Gifts of All the Students. All of the baptized are blessed with gifts that the Holy Spirit invites us to use in contributing to the work of the Church. Be sure to acknowledge and affirm the gifts of *all* students. When you regularly invite young people with special needs to contribute and be fully included in the class, the entire class benefits. All of your students will grow in valuing every member of the class as an integral member of the Body of Christ. When all are invited to use their gifts and share their faith, all students will grow in mutual respect, understanding, and self-confidence.

Preview

▶ Have students carefully tear out the With My Family page along the perforation.

▶ Encourage them to share the pages with their families and to complete the activities together at home.

▶ If the students did not or could not complete the Chapter Review, encourage them to complete it with their families.

▶ Point out the chapter title and theme of next week's lesson.

Visit www.BeMyDisciples.com

▶ Take time with the students to explore the many activities and resources available at www.BeMyDisciples.com.

▶ Especially encourage them and their families to discover the many resources available at **www.BeMyDisciples.com.**

Before Moving On ...

As you finish today's lesson, reflect on the following question before moving on to the next chapter.

How well am I using the students unique gifts and talents?

With My Family

This Week...

In chapter 10, The Sacraments of Christian Initiation: Baptism, your child learned:

▶ Through Baptism, we first receive new life and salvation in Christ, and become members of the Church, the Body of Christ.

▶ Through the baptismal water and the grace of the Holy Spirit, Original Sin and everything that separates us from God is washed away.

▶ In Baptism, we are sealed with the gift of faith helping us to participate in the life and work of the Church.

▶ As disciples of Jesus, we are to be modest in all aspects of life.

For more about related teachings of the Church, see the *Catechism of the Catholic Church*, 1210–1284; and the *United States Catholic Catechism for Adults*, pages 181–199.

■ Sharing God's Word

Read together John 3:3–6. Emphasize that through the Sacrament of Baptism, we are reborn of water and the Holy Spirit.

■ We Live as Disciples

The Christian family and family is a school of discipleship. Choose one of the following activities to do as a family, or design a similar activity of your own:

▶ Water can symbolize many things. Talk about what water symbolizes for you. Share ideas about how water helps you understand what happens in Baptism.

▶ Place a dish of holy water in a convenient location in your home. Bless each other and yourselves as you come and go during the day and before bedtime. Remember that in Baptism we are made sharers in the life of God.

■ Our Spiritual Journey

Daily rituals that involve the use of water fill our life each day. These can be sacred moments. Stop and pause as you wash your hands or take a drink of water. Remember the gift of living water that you received and that is vital to your life as a follower of Jesus.

For more ideas on ways that your family can live as disciples of Jesus, visit **www.BeMyDisciples.com**

98

PARTNERING WITH PARENTS

Sharing Baptism Day Stories. Encourage parents to continue this class discussion on Baptism by taking time to share with their child memories of his or her Baptism. Offer parents the following discussion starters:

▶ Why was your child's Baptism a special event in your family's life?

▶ Who was present at the celebration of Baptism?

▶ Why did you give your child his or her name?

▶ How was your child baptized? (Did the priest pour water over your child's head, or was your child immersed in the water?)

Suggest that parents also share any photos, notes, and cards saved from the Baptism, and that they show their child his or her baptismal candle and garment.

Enriching the Lesson

Making Oral Presentations

Purpose

To reinforce that through the celebration of the Sacraments of Christian Initiation, a person becomes a full member of the Church, fully joined to Christ (taught on pages 94 and 95)

Directions

▶ Divide the class into three smaller groups and ask each group to prepare an oral presentation on one of the following aspects of being a follower of Jesus:

- Why have so many people followed Jesus for the last 2,000 years?
- What does it mean to be a follower of Jesus today?
- How can we support one another and work together to be witnesses for Jesus Christ?

▶ Have the groups make their presentations to the entire class.

▶ Write the key points of each presentation on newsprint and display this in your learning space for several weeks.

Materials

newsprint

Creating Welcome-to-the-Church Cards

Purpose

To reinforce what happens when a person is baptized (taught on page 95)

Directions

▶ Contact the pastor or a staff member of the parish. Ask for the names of both the adults and young people in the RCIA program who will be initiated into the Church at the Easter Vigil and also the names of the infants who will be baptized within the next few months.

▶ Invite the students to create welcome cards for these people. The cards should include a message welcoming them into the Church.

▶ Have the students decorate the cards with signs and symbols of the Sacrament of Baptism.

▶ Have the students share their cards with one another, and then give the cards to the pastor or parish staff member for delivery to the appropriate people.

Materials

construction, art, or poster paper

envelopes

pens or pencils

crayons or markers

Creating Faith Family Trees

Purpose

To reinforce the effects of Baptism, especially becoming a member of the Church (taught on page 95)

Directions

▶ Invite the students to create a personal Faith Tree, similar to a family tree.

▶ Have them make a year-by-year time line from their birth to their present age, marking all of the important faith events and people of faith who had a positive influence on their growth as Catholics.

▶ Have the students share their Faith Trees with one another. Encourage them to share their Faith Tree with their families.

Materials

shelf paper

pens or pencils

BACKGROUND

Gift of the Holy Spirit

Christ promised the gift of the Holy Spirit. At Pentecost, not only was that promise fulfilled, but the Apostles also received the ability to give the Holy Spirit to others. "This we read in the Acts of the Apostles. When Saint Paul placed his hands on those who had been baptized, the holy Spirit came upon them, and they began to speak in other languages and in prophetic words" *(Rite of Confirmation*, 73).

The Sacrament of Confirmation

Confirmation perfects the graces of Baptism. Sealed with the gift of the Holy Spirit in Confirmation, the baptized are united more firmly to Christ and the Church and strengthened with the Gifts of the Holy Spirit. We are confirmed to be faithful witnesses to the word planted in us at Baptism. (See *Catechism of the Catholic Church* 1302–1305.) As Baptism does, Confirmation seals our souls with a spiritual mark and thus can be received only once.

Baptism and Confirmation are ordered to participation in the Eucharist, which is the third Sacrament of Christian Initiation. Eucharist unites us most fully with Christ and the members of the Body of Christ, the Church. (See *Catechism of the Catholic Church* 1275.)

Images for Confirmation

First, Confirmation has been called an "outpouring of the Holy Spirit." As the Apostles at Pentecost were, those who receive this sacrament are filled and sealed with the gift of the Holy Spirit and receive the power to be witnesses for Christ.

Second, Confirmation has also been described as "anointing with oil." When we relate this image to the many ways that we use oil, such as to cleanse after a bath and to limber up for an athletic event, we get a glimpse of the mystery of God's presence in Confirmation.

In Confirmation we are cleansed, healed, made radiant in Christ, and limbered up for the struggle to be witnesses for Christ in a world that often rejects his message.

Finally, Confirmation is called the "completion of Baptism." The word *confirmation* suggests ratification. In Confirmation our initiation into new life in Christ is deepened. We are sealed with the gift of the Holy Spirit, and the graces of Baptism are strengthened. Confirmation unites us more firmly to Christ, increases the Gifts of the Holy Spirit in us, renders our bond with the Church more perfect, and gives us a special strength of the Holy Spirit to spread and defend the faith. (See *Catechism of the Catholic Church* 1303.)

For Reflection

What does it mean for me that I am joined to Christ and marked as belonging to him forever?

How do Baptism and Confirmation empower me to be a witness for Christ?

Catechist to Catechist

The Kingdom of God

At the beginning of his public ministry, Jesus announced, "The kingdom of God is at hand. Repent, and believe in the gospel" (Mark 1:15). Jesus returned to this proclamation time and time again, often using parables to help his listeners understand the true nature of the Kingdom of God. The image of the Kingdom of God describes the way people are to relate to God and to one another. The Sacrament of Confirmation strengthens us in our resolve to help build the Kingdom of God. As disciples of Jesus we are called to invite all people to come to the heavenly banquet in the Kingdom of God.

Celebrating Friendship

Having friends is important for sixth graders, as it is for all people. Help the students discover the sacramental rituals as celebrations of their friendship and union with God. Have them rub oil on the palms of their hands and talk about how anointing with oil in Confirmation shows that the Holy Spirit strengthens them to live in friendship with God.

The Church Teaches...

"God draws every human being toward himself, and every human being desires communion with God. Prayer is the basis and expression of the vital and personal relationship of a human person with the living and true God . . . His initiative comes first; the human response to his initiative is itself prompted by the grace of the Holy Spirit. That human response is the free self-surrender to the incomprehensible mystery of God. In prayer, the Holy Spirit not only reveals the identity of the Triune God to human persons, but also reveals the identity of human persons to themselves" (*National Directory for Catechesis,* **34**). In teaching about the Sacrament of Confirmation, focus on the role of the Holy Spirit in the lives of the youth. The Holy Spirit guides each of us on our faith journey, prompting us to follow Jesus.

Further Reading and Reflection

For more on the teachings of the Church, see the *Catechism of the Catholic Church*, 1285–1321; and from the *United States Catholic Catechism for Adults*, pages 201–211.

Catechist Prayer

Holy Spirit,
you guide the Church.
Help me bring the wonder
of my senses,
the longing of my heart,
 and the goodness of my soul
to the celebration of the liturgy.
Amen.

Lesson Planner

Focus To discover the meaning of Confirmation as a Sacrament of Christian Initiation

LESSON PART	PROCESS	MATERIALS and RESOURCES
EXPLORE **Focus** **To explore the role of the gift of courage in imitating Christ** 🕙 10 minutes **Pages** 99–100 *Fortitude*	▶ Proclaim and discuss Acts 2:2–4 (the descent of the Holy Spirit). ▶ Learn the story of martyrs in China. **Disciple Power:** Fortitude **Activity:** Create on acrostic of the word *martyr*.	Bible Pencils
DISCOVER **Focus** **To discover more about the meaning and practice of the Sacrament of Confirmation** 🕧 30 minutes **Pages** 101–103	▶ Learn the requirements for Confirmation. ▶ Review the Rite of Confirmation. ▶ Learn the effects of Confirmation. **Activity:** Write a profile of a witness for Christ.	Index cards Crayons or markers **Additional Activities Booklet:** Activities 11a–11b, or see BeMyDisciples.com.
DECIDE **Focus** **To decide a way to exhibit the gift of courage** 🕙 10 minutes **Page** 104	**Activity:** Choose and assign a motto describing being a witness for Christ. **My Faith Choice:** Choose a response to the gift of fortitude, or courage. ▶ Pray for strengthening the gifts needed to be a witness for Christ.	**Enriching the Lesson Activities:** Catechist Edition, page 183 • Writing an Advice Column • Creating Acrostics • Defining True Followers of Christ

Concluding the Lesson 🕙 10 minutes

We Remember	We Pray	Preview
Page 105 ▶ Review concepts and do the review activity. ▶ **Assessment Tools Booklet:** Chapter Test 11a–11b, or see BeMyDisciples.com.	▶ **Prayer:** a prayer to the Holy Spirit **Materials:** Bible, candle, cross for prayer center ▶ Grade 6 Music CD	Point out resources for this chapter at **www.BeMyDisciples.com** ▶ Preview the With My Family page and next week's lesson theme.

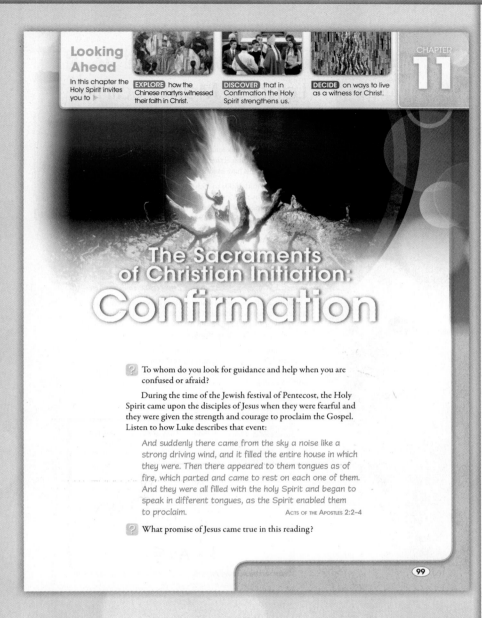

Looking Ahead

In this chapter the Holy Spirit invites you to ▶

EXPLORE how the Chinese martyrs witnessed their faith in Christ.

DISCOVER that in Confirmation the Holy Spirit strengthens us.

DECIDE on ways to live as a witness for Christ.

CHAPTER **11**

The Sacraments of Christian Initiation: Confirmation

❓ To whom do you look for guidance and help when you are confused or afraid?

During the time of the Jewish festival of Pentecost, the Holy Spirit came upon the disciples of Jesus when they were fearful and they were given the strength and courage to proclaim the Gospel. Listen to how Luke describes that event:

And suddenly there came from the sky a noise like a strong driving wind, and it filled the entire house in which they were. Then there appeared to them tongues as of fire, which parted and came to rest on each one of them. And they were all filled with the holy Spirit and began to speak in different tongues, as the Spirit enabled them to proclaim. ACTS OF THE APOSTLES 2:2–4

❓ What promise of Jesus came true in this reading?

(99)

HUMAN METHODOLOGIES

Learning by Discipleship. The *National Directory for Catechesis* affirms that catechesis helps promote an active, vibrant faith life as a disciple of Jesus Christ (*see NDC* 29B). At Baptism and Confirmation, we are anointed with Chrism as a sign that the Holy Spirit strengthens us to live as disciples of Christ. If you have not yet done so, take time to visit the church with the class and point out the ambry, the place where the three holy oils—Chrism, the Oil of the Sick, and the Oil of Catechumens—are kept. Briefly explain that oils are blessed and presented to every parish at the Chrism Mass, which is usually celebrated on Holy Thursday morning. Ask volunteers to give an example of the Holy Spirit strengthening a sixth-grader to live as a disciple of Jesus.

Pray

▶ Gather and have the students quiet themselves for prayer. Begin and end with the Sign of the Cross.

▶ Lead the class in prayer:

"Lord God, send your Holy Spirit to encourage us to be witnesses for Christ. Amen."

Reflect

▶ Recall the previous chapter's focus on having a sense of belonging. Explain that part of having that sense is knowing someone in whom you can trust. Have a volunteer read aloud the opening questions and invite responses.

▶ Explain that in this chapter they will learn more about the Sacrament of Confirmation.

▶ Invite one volunteer to read the Scripture introduction and another to read the Scripture passage.

▶ Discuss the question related to the Scripture.

▶ Call the students' attention to the Looking Ahead feature. Invite them to read aloud each bulleted item.

▶ Invite a volunteer to describe how the image on the page relates to the Sacrament of Confirmation.

Introduce

▶ Explain that in Baptism and Confirmation, God gives us the unique graces to be witnesses for Christ.

▶ Point out that the saints of the Church are excellent examples of being a witness for Christ.

Reinforce

Read aloud Land of Martyr Saints. Have the students underline the names and ages of the children who are among the martyrs. Emphasize how these Chinese Catholics were living witnesses for Christ by demonstrating the cardinal virtue of fortitude. Read the definition of fortitude in the Disciple Power feature.

Connect

▶ Explain that the virtue of fortitude or courage is a habit that is developed as a result of facing adversity correctly. Often the act of fortitude involves sacrifice, but it need not include sacrificing one's life for another. These martyrs were definitely heroes and saints because they imitated Christ to the highest level, by giving their lives for their faith.

▶ Have students complete the activity on the page. Ask volunteers to share their responses.

Disciple Power

Fortitude

Fortitude is one of the four Cardinal Virtues. It is the strength of mind and will to do what is good in the face of adversity or difficulty. It enables a person to be a steadfast witness for Christ.

THE CHURCH FOLLOWS JESUS
Land of Martyr Saints

For centuries, Catholics in China have responded to the call of the Holy Spirit to be witnesses for Christ. In the 500s, the Gospel was preached in China, and the first church was built there around the year A.D. 600. The Jesuit missionary Saint Francis Xavier arrived in China and preached the Gospel there in the 1600s. Through the centuries, the Catholics in China have lived and died for their faith with great courage.

From the mid-1600s to 1930, 120 Chinese martyrs have been named saints by the Church. The first of these martyrs was the Dominican priest and missionary Father Francisco Fernández de Capillas. He was killed in 1648 by the invading Manchu Tartars. They imprisoned him, and then tortured and beheaded him while he was praying the Sorrowful Mysteries of the Rosary.

The courage of Catholics in China only grew stronger and from 1796 to 1856, twelve more Chinese Catholics died for their faith in Christ. Among these were Agnes Cao Guiying, Peter Liu, Jerome Lu Tingmei, Lawrence Wang Bing and Agatha Lin Zao, who were all catechists.

In the 1900s, beginning with the Boxer Rebellion, the courage of more than ninety Catholics in China cost them their lives. Among these martyrs were Paulus Lang Fu and Andreas Wang Tianqing, age 9; Maria Zeng Xu, age 11; and Anna Wang and Simon Qin Chunfu, age 14.

The English word *martyr* comes from the Greek word meaning "witness." The Church in China is a courageous living witness to the power of the Holy Spirit at work leading the Church to fulfill Jesus' command to preach the Gospel to all nations.

Activity Reflect on the meaning of the word "martyr." Use the letters of the word to write words or phrases (such as courageous) describing the qualities or works of a martyr.

M
A   Witness
COURAGEOUS
T
Y
B R AVE

DISCIPLE POWER

Fortitude. Martyrs are people who are killed because they will not forsake or compromise their beliefs. Do an Internet search to learn the stories of Archbishop Oscar Romero and Sister Dorothy Stang, SNDdeN, who are modern martyrs of the faith. Share their stories with the students, and ask how each person showed fortitude in the face of difficulty and danger. If you have access to a liturgical calendar, conclude this discussion by working with the youth to identify the many saints of the Church who have been martyred for their faith. Create a litany of these saints' names. Read each name, and invite the students to respond, "Pray for us."

Confirmed in Christ

Most Roman Catholics today are baptized as infants and are confirmed many years later. In the Eastern Catholic Churches, **Confirmation** is administered immediately after Baptism and is followed by participation in the Eucharist.

The Sacrament of Confirmation perfects and strengthens the graces of Baptism. The baptized receive and accept important Christian responsibilities and the graces to fulfill those responsibilities. They accept the grace and make the commitment to join Christ in his mission to prepare for the coming of the Kingdom of God. They cooperate with the grace of the Holy Spirit and bring healing and reconciliation to the world as members of the Church.

Requirements for Confirmation

In the Roman Catholic Church, there are unique requirements for a baptized person preparing to receive the Sacrament of Confirmation. These requirements are:

- **Faith:** The person must be baptized. Candidates for Confirmation must profess their faith with the Church.
- **Age:** Today, young people who are Roman Catholic are confirmed at various ages, usually when they are young teens.
- **Grace:** Candidates must also be in a state of grace. They must be free of mortal sin. Their relationship with God must be close.
- **Will:** Candidates must have a clear and deliberate intention to receive the sacrament. In other words, they are to accept the responsibilities of being a witness for Christ.

Confirmation marks our lifelong commitment to be witnesses for Christ. With the help of the Holy Spirit, we prepare ourselves for Confirmation. This preparation includes prayer, service, and reception of the Sacrament of Penance and Reconciliation.

It also includes choosing a sponsor. A sponsor is someone who gives spiritual help and encouragement to a person preparing to receive Confirmation.

? What spiritual qualities would you want to have if you were a Confirmation sponsor for someone?

FAITH FOCUS
Why does the Church celebrate the Sacrament of Confirmation?

FAITH VOCABULARY
Confirmation
Confirmation is the Sacrament of Christian Initiation that strengthens the grace of Baptism and in which our life in Christ is sealed by the gift of the Holy Spirit.

consecrate
To consecrate is to set aside and dedicate for a holy purpose.

(101)

THE TASKS OF CATECHESIS

Missionary Initiation. Baptized and confirmed members of the Church can help bring healing and reconciliation to the world by caring for those in need, by being peacemakers, and by working for justice. The Corporal and Spiritual Works of Mercy (student page 261), the Beatitudes (student page 260) and the social teachings of the Church highlight practical things that the Body of Christ can do to bring about the Kingdom of God. Invite the students to share ways that they or their families are fulfilling these responsibilities given to us by God and by the Church. Affirm the youth for the Kingdom-building work in which they and their families are taking part.

Key Concept
Confirmation strengthens the grace necessary to be a witness for Christ.

Teach

Review the Faith Vocabulary. Encourage students to maintain their vocabulary cards on the Seven Sacraments. Also highlight the term *consecrate*.

Reinforce

- Have students read the text on the page to find out why the Church celebrates the Sacrament of Confirmation. It perfects baptismal grace and strengthens the person to be a witness for Christ.
- Inquire, "What are the unique requirements for a baptized person preparing to receive the Sacrament of Confirmation?"

Connect

- Have the class imagine that they are asking to be confirmed. Invite volunteers to see if they would be able to fulfill the requirements. Explain the age for Confirmation in your diocese.
- Point out that sponsors help candidates prepare for Confirmation and continue in the Christian journey of being a witness for Christ.
- Inquire, "If you were asked to be a sponsor for a candidate, what spiritual qualities would you want to have? What kind of guidance could you provide?" *(Accept all reasonable responses.)*

Key Concept
Confirmation consecrates a person as a disciple of Christ.

Teach

Have students read about the anointing of the King of Israel in I Samuel 10:1 and I Samuel 16:1–13. Explain that the anointing consecrated the person.

Reinforce

▶ Have a volunteer read the first paragraph aloud. Emphasize that the anointing both consecrated the person and gave him strength. Inquire, "What did David's anointing signify?"

▶ Read aloud to the students the remaining text on the page. If possible, read some of the prayers from the rite itself.

▶ Emphasize that Confirmation is conferred through the anointing on the forehead, done by the laying on of hands, and through the words: "Be sealed with gift of the Holy Spirit." The ordinary minister is the bishop because he references the Apostles, who were the first to receive the Holy Spirit on Pentecost.

Connect

▶ List the parts of the rite of Confirmation on the board and ask volunteers to summarize what happens in each part.

▶ Read the Faith-Filled People section. Use information from the box at the right to supplement the student book.

Faith-Filled People

United States Conference of Catholic Bishops (USCCB)

The bishops are anointed to lead the Church in worshiping God, proclaiming the Gospel to all people and living as disciples of Christ. The U.S. bishops work together as a conference to fulfill their responsibilities. Together they work to unify, coordinate, encourage, promote, and carry out Catholic activities in the United States of America.

Anointing in the Old Testament

Anointing with oil is essential to the Rite of Confirmation. Oil is used as a sign to **consecrate** a person, or set that person aside for a holy purpose. In different ways, the ritual of anointing with oil in the Old Testament prepared for its use in the sacraments of the Church. In the First Book of Samuel, for example, we read about the anointing of David, the shepherd boy whom God had chosen to be king of Israel (read 1 Samuel 16:1–13). This anointing was a sign that the Spirit of God lived within David and would help him to do the work that God had chosen him to do.

The Rite of Confirmation

The Rite of Confirmation is usually celebrated during the Eucharist. This helps point out to the unity of the three Sacraments of Christian Initiation. When Confirmation is celebrated during Mass, it begins after the reading of the Gospel. The parts of the Rite of Confirmation when celebrated during Mass and separated from Baptism are:

Presentation of the Candidates: The pastor or a representative of the parish presents the candidates, if possible, by name to the bishop.

Homily: The bishop preaches a homily to help the candidates understand the mystery of Confirmation.

Renewal of Baptismal Promises: The *confirmandi* (those to be confirmed) renew the profession of faith that they made at Baptism or that their parents and godparents made in union with the whole Church at that time.

The Laying on of Hands: In the Roman Rite, the bishop or the priest delegated by him extends his hands over the confirmandi. Since the time of the Apostles, this gesture has signified the gift of the Holy Spirit. The minister of the sacrament prays invoking the gifts of the Holy Spirit.

Anointing with Chrism: The candidates come forward with their sponsors. The sponsor places his or her right hand on the candidate's shoulder. The bishop places, or lays, his hand on the head of the one being confirmed and says, "Be sealed with the Gift of the Holy Spirit" as he anoints the forehead of the baptized person being confirmed. At the same time, the bishop anoints the person's forehead with the Sacred Chrism.

The Sacraments of Christian Initiation celebrate our becoming members of the Church and our sharing in the life of God. Confirmation, like Baptism, imprints a spiritual mark on our soul. For this reason, it can be received only one time.

 How does the symbol of oil in the Old Testament help us understand Confirmation?

FAITH-FILLED PEOPLE

United States Conference of Catholic Bishops. The USCCB was formed in 2001, when the National Conference of Catholic Bishops (NCCB) and the United States Catholic Conference (USCC) merged. Among its many works, the USCCB sees as its main emphasis the work of evangelization. It carries on this work in four ways:

▶ Promoting Catholic activities in the United States

▶ Organizing and carrying out religious and social justice work at home and abroad

▶ Supporting education

▶ Caring for immigrants

For more information on the work of the USCCB, go to www.usccb.org.

The Effects of Confirmation

At Confirmation, we receive and accept some important responsibilities and graces to fulfill those responsibilities. The graces and responsibilities, or the effects of, Confirmation are:

- We receive the grace of the outpouring of the Holy Spirit in our lives.
- We accept grace and commit to join Christ in his mission to prepare for the coming of the Kingdom of God.
- We cooperate with the grace of the Holy Spirit and bring healing and reconciliation into the world.
- The grace of the Holy Spirit strengthens our bond with the Church and her mission to defend the faith.
- The grace of the Holy Spirit guides us to live as signs of the Covenant as the prophets did.

We receive the seven-fold Gifts of the Holy Spirit to remain witnesses for Christ, even in the face of misunderstanding, ridicule, and suffering. The confirmed person receives the strength and power to confidently profess his or her faith in Jesus, the Lord and Savior of the world, and to live as a witness for him.

Catholics Believe

Gifts of the Holy Spirit

The Rite of Confirmation identifies the seven-fold Gifts of the Holy Spirit as wisdom, understanding, right judgment and counsel, knowledge and reverence, and wonder and awe. The more traditional names for these gifts are wisdom, understanding, counsel, fortitude, knowledge, piety, and fear of the Lord.

Activity Write a brief description of a person (real or fictional) who is living the call to be a witness for Christ. What kind of person is he or she?

_____
_____
_____
_____
_____
_____
_____

103

TEACHING TIP

Confirmation. Confirmation strengthens the graces of Baptism. Have the students read Isaiah 11:1–3 and 1 Corinthians 12:4–7 to learn more about some of the important gifts and responsibilities that Confirmation confers. (See also *Catechism of the Catholic Church* 1302–1305.)

Key Concept
Confirmation seals us with the strength to profess and live our faith.

Teach

▶ Inquire, "What gives you confidence? Does it come from inside or outside yourself? How do you feel if someone whom you look-up to is proud of you?"

▶ Have students describe the image on the page.

▶ Read the Catholics Believe section. Review the meaning of each of the Gifts of the Holy Spirit.

▶ Ask the students to read the text to learn the effects of Confirmation. Check comprehension, and jot their responses on the board. Correct any misunderstandings.

Connect

▶ Affirm the diligent work that the students have done thus far. Tell them that now it is time to have some creative fun.

▶ Have young people complete the activity on the page. Explain that their witness for Christ can be fictional but must have the qualities necessary. To get them started, inquire, "How is a witness for Christ a hero?" Ask volunteers to read their profiles aloud.

Reinforce

See how well the students can list from memory the cardinal virtues (prudence, justice, temperance and fortitude) and the Gifts of the Holy Spirit(listed in Catholics Believe on page 103). Note that fortitude is included in both.

Respond

▶ Introduce and explain the directions to the Sealed by the Holy Spirit activity on the page. Invite the students to complete the activity.

▶ Have the young people proudly proclaim their mottos. To help relax the class, offer your own motto first, and proclaim it like a superhero. The motto should represent what you stand for as a witness for Christ.

Choose

Have the students individually complete the last section to make their faith choice and to pray for God's help. Encourage the young people to put their faith choices into practice this week. Ask them to pray the final prayer on page 104 silently.

I FOLLOW JESUS

You are called to be a living witness for Christ. Strengthened with the Gifts of the Holy Spirit, you continue the work of Christ, as a member of the Church, in your home, school, neighborhood—or wherever you are.

SEALED BY THE HOLY SPIRIT

Create a motto or brief statement describing you and what you can do right now to be a witness for Christ.

MY FAITH CHOICE

With the gift of courage, or fortitude, I can be strong in my stance as a witness for Christ. I will put my witness motto into action this week. I will:

_____

 Pray, "Lord and Giver of life, continue to strengthen me with your gifts so that I may be a witness for Christ."

(104)

TEACHING TIP

Respecting Different Learning Styles. Remember to use a variety of activities to engage learners with different learning styles. On this page, for example, have the young people think about the mottos or statements that they have suggested for being a witness for Christ. Provide the option of having the students work with partners or in small groups to design a cheer or rap that encourages them to live their faith choice. Use their cheers or raps throughout the year to reinforce their commitment to be witnesses for Christ.

Chapter Review

Compare and contrast the Sacraments of Baptism and Confirmation. Write the unique features of each sacrament in the large circles. In the center space tell how they are the same.

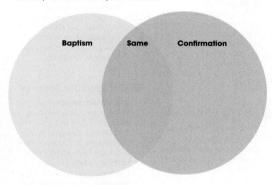

Baptism   Same   Confirmation

TO HELP YOU REMEMBER

1. The Sacrament of Confirmation perfects the grace of Baptism.

2. Like Baptism, the Holy Spirit marks us with his seal in Confirmation. This sacramental character leaves an indelible spiritual mark imprinted on our soul.

3. In the Latin rite of Confirmation, the bishop or priest-delegate rests his hands on the top of each candidate's head as he anoints each candidate's forehead with Chrism.

Come, Holy Spirit

We first receive the gift of the Holy Spirit at Baptism and are sealed with the gift of the Holy Spirit at Confirmation. Pray together for the strength of the Holy Spirit.

Leader: On the day of Pentecost, tongues of fire parted and came to rest on the disciples. They were all filled with the Holy Spirit.

Reader: *Proclaim* Galatians 5:22–26

Leader: Remember that the Holy Spirit dwells within us. Let us ask the Holy Spirit to give us the grace to be living witnesses for Christ.

All: **Come, Holy Spirit,
fill the hearts of your faithful.
And kindle in them the fire of your love.
Send forth your Spirit
and they shall be created.
And you will renew the face of the earth.
Amen.**

105

We Remember

▶ Have students share three main points they learned in this chapter.

▶ Use the bulleted summary in the To Help You Remember section as a way to assess their knowledge informally. For example, read aloud the statement, leaving key terms blank for the group to fill in orally.

▶ Have the students complete the compare and contrast activity in the Chapter Review as a class. Allow them to use their books if necessary.

▶ If necessary, explain that a Venn diagram is a graphic way to show the relationship between two different concepts. Point out that the overlay is how Baptism and Confirmation are similar.

We Pray

▶ Gather the young people for prayer. Introduce the closing prayer by pointing out that the prayer concludes with a doxology, one of the Church's traditional prayers to the Holy Spirit.

▶ Prepare a volunteer student to proclaim Galatians 5:22–26.

▶ Lead the class in the prayer, beginning and ending with the Sign of the Cross. Invite all students to pause after the reading to recall their faith choice made in this chapter.

Preview

▶ Have students carefully tear out the With My Family page along the perforation.

▶ Encourage them to share the pages with their families and to complete the activities together at home.

▶ If the students did not or could not complete the chapter review, encourage them to complete it with their families.

▶ Point out the chapter title and theme of next week's lesson.

Visit www.BeMyDisciples.com

▶ Take time with the young people to explore the many activities and resources available at **www.BeMyDisciples.com.**

▶ Especially encourage them and their families to discover the many resources available at the Web site.

Before Moving On ...

As you finish today's lesson, reflect on the following question before moving on to the next chapter.

Do I provide alternatives to reading and writing activities for students with verbal deficits?

With My Family

This Week...

In chapter 11, The Sacraments of Christian Initiation: Confirmation, your child learned:

▶ In the Sacrament of Confirmation, the graces of Baptism are strengthened by the Gifts of the Holy Spirit.

▶ The Holy Spirit marks, or seals, the confirmed with an indelible spiritual mark. Confirmation therefore may be received only one time.

▶ The confirmed person receives the strength and fortitude to profess and confidently give witness to his or her faith in Jesus Christ.

For more about related teachings of the Church, see the *Catechism of the Catholic Church*, 1285–1321; and the *United States Catholic Catechism for Adults*, pages 201–211.

■ Sharing God's Word

Read together I Samuel 16:1–13. Emphasize that the Spirit came upon David, who was chosen by God, to serve his people as king. Recall the anointing of your family members in Confirmation and relate that anointing to the story of David.

■ We Live as Disciples

The Christian family and home is a school of discipleship. Choose one of the following activities to do as a family, or design a similar activity of your own:

▶ Invite family members to name someone they know who is confirmed and is living as a witness for Christ. Describe what this person does that reflects Christian living.

▶ When you participate in Mass this week, find the ambry in your parish. The ambry is where the blessed oils are kept. These oils are used in the sacraments. Talk about how you are living out your baptismal anointing.

■ Our Spiritual Journey

Jesus proclaimed in the synagogue in Nazareth that the Spirit of God was upon him. That same Spirit came upon the disciples in the upper room in Jerusalem. The Spirit came upon you when you were baptized and continues with you wherever you are and will be with you wherever you go. We can look to the Holy Spirit in prayer to give us the gifts we need to follow Christ.

For more ideas on ways that your family can live as disciples of Jesus, visit **www.BeMyDisciples.com**

106

TEACHING TIP

Planning Ahead. Next week's lesson focuses on the Eucharist. Consider going on a tour of the sacristy. If possible arrange with one of the sacristans or someone in the parish liturgy office to show the students some of the following:

▶ the packages of wafers as they are shipped

▶ the bottles of wine

▶ the ciborium (or containers) from which the ministers of the Eucharist distribute communion

▶ the cups for the wine

▶ the chalices

▶ the censor and the incense

▶ the purificators and other linens

Have the sacristan explain how he prepares for every Mass.

Enriching the Lesson

Writing an Advice Column

Purpose

To reinforce that Catholics mature in their faith with the aid of grace and as we grow in our faith (taught on page 101)

Directions

▶ Invite the students to write an advice column, pretending that the Holy Spirit is responding to the questions. In their column, have them write the response to these questions: "How does your grace perfect us, making us more like Christ? How does celebrating our faith make us more aware of your love for us?"

▶ Invite volunteers to share their responses with the entire class.

Materials

paper

pens or pencils

Creating Acrostics

Purpose

To reinforce that at Confirmation we receive and accept important responsibilities and the graces to fulfill those responsibilities (taught on page 103)

Directions

▶ Have the students write acrostics, using the word *Confirmation*. Remind the group that an acrostic can be a poem, free verse, phrases, or statements.

▶ Have the students mount their acrostics on construction paper because they will be displayed where others can enjoy them.

▶ Invite partners to share their acrostics with the entire class.

Materials

paper or construction paper

glue sticks

pens, pencils, or fine-tipped markers

Defining True Followers of Christ

Purpose

To reinforce how those confirmed are to be witnesses for Christ (taught on page 100)

Directions

▶ Have the students work in small groups to discuss the way Christians are sometimes treated in China and other places they know about.

▶ Suggest that they use these questions as starters:

• Which qualities do Christians need to withstand criticism?

• What are things that a Christian can do to help him or her persevere in faith?

• Which role does reading the Bible play in the life of a witness for Christ?

• Which role does prayer play in the life of a witness for Christ?

▶ Ask a member from each group to take turns summarizing the group's discussion by listing key points on the board.

Materials

BACKGROUND

The Last Passover Supper

Was it just coincidence, or was it part of God's life-giving plan that the Last Supper occurred? For those of us viewing the unfolding drama of Christ's Passover from the vantage point of the present day, it is obvious that God's planning, not coincidence, situated our own passover from inevitable death to eternal life within the context of the Jewish Passover.

The Divine Plan

It is remarkable to contemplate the beauty of the divine plan. The people of Israel celebrated Passover to commemorate the astonishing actions of God's saving and liberating an enslaved nation. Using the exact same feast, we are given a meal to celebrate, remember, and take part in the divine plan of salvation for all people.

At the Last Supper, Jesus told his Apostles, "I have eagerly desired to eat this Passover with you before I suffer, for, I tell you, I shall not eat it [again] until there is fulfillment in the kingdom of God" (Luke 22:15-16). He then took bread and wine and, aware that his own passover was imminent, transformed the Passover meal into a memorial meal of his death and Resurrection, commanding, "Do this in remembrance of me" (1 Corinthians 11:24).

When we step back and reflect on the significance of Christ's actions and words at the Last Supper, we better appreciate what an incredible gift we have in the Eucharist. By choosing to celebrate this supper as a Passover meal, Jesus was underlining the fact that this meal, now and forever, provides the food of life. We are saved.

Christ in Our Midst

It is important that we never lose sight of the significance of our sharing in the Eucharist as the early Church in Corinth did. (See 1 Corinthians 11:27-34.) For example, our concerns about getting our family dressed for Mass cannot obscure the reality that we are about to be clothed with eternal life; our attention cannot be so directed at the trappings of the liturgy—the music, the quality of the sermon, the lack of heat or air conditioning—that we fail to attend to Christ in our midst.

The Source and Summit of the Christian Life

The Eucharist is "the source and summit of the Christian life" (Vatican II, *Dogmatic Constitution on the Church [Lumen gentium]* 11). The whole spiritual good of the Church is contained in the sharing of the Body and Blood of Christ. Christ touches us, becomes one with us, and loves us in a very tangible way. By receiving the Eucharist we receive Christ's Body and Blood and the pledge of eternal life. Sharing in the Eucharist is the single most important act of our life—it is the source and summit of our life in Christ.

For Reflection

How well do I prepare myself to share in the Eucharist?

How does this help me not lose sight of the significance of what I am sharing?

Catechist to Catechist

The Bread of Life

Blessed Mother Teresa of Calcutta has been honored with the title "Saint of the Gutter." This title succinctly describes her work with the poor and dying, a ministry that she began with people left to die in the streets of Calcutta, India. Mother Teresa said that she would simply be unable to minister to the poor and dying without the Body and Blood of Christ to sustain her. That is true for all Catholics. We need Christ, the Bread of Life, in our lives to nourish and give us the strength necessary to be his disciples in the world.

Love and Serve the Lord

There is a vital connection between the Eucharist and the mission of the Church. Use the example of Blessed Mother Teresa, who also received the Nobel Prize for Peace, to help the students make the connection between their own regular participation in the Eucharist and their daily lives as young disciples of Christ. Remind them that the Eucharist is the source and summit of the Christian life.

The Church Teaches...

"[T]he Eucharist constitutes the principal liturgical celebration of the Paschal Mystery of Christ and the ritual memorial of our communion in that mystery. . . . Since the Eucharist is the 'source and summit of the Christian life,' catechesis for the Eucharist recognizes it as the heart of Christian life for the whole Church" (*National Directory for Catechesis,* 36A.3).

This chapter presents a catechesis on the Eucharist. This helps the young people to grow in their love for the Eucharist, and to participate regularly in the celebration of this "Sacrament of sacraments."

Further Reading and Reflection

For more on the teachings of the Church, see the *Catechism of the Catholic Church,* 1322–1419; and from the *United States Catholic Catechism for Adults,* pages 215–232.

Catechist Prayer

*God of the Israelites,
who instructed your people
to put you first in their lives,
help me to find you
at the center of my life.
Amen.*

Lesson Planner

Chapter 12   The Sacraments of Christian Initiation: The Eucharist

Focus To identify what the Church celebrates and shares at Mass

LESSON PART	PROCESS	MATERIALS and RESOURCES
EXPLORE **Focus** **To explore the importance of faithfulness** 🕐 10 minutes **Pages 107–108**	▶ Proclaim and discuss Psalm 105:39–43 (God gave them food from heaven). ▶ Learn the story of Archbishop Oscar Romero. **Disciple Power:** Faithfulness	Bible Pencils Journals
DISCOVER **Focus** **To discover more about the Sacrament of Eucharist** 🕐 30 minutes **Pages 109–111**	▶ Learn how the Eucharist was prefigured in the Old Testament. ▶ Review the Mass and The Real Presence of Christ. ▶ Discover the graces of Eucharist. **Activity:** Develop strategies for active participation in Eucharist.	Pencils **Additional Activities Booklet:** Activities 12a–12b, or see BeMyDisciples.com.
DECIDE **Focus** **To decide on a way to be faithful to Jesus** 🕐 10 minutes **Page 112**	**Activity:** Complete a reflection on the Bread of Life and being a disciple of Jesus. **My Faith Choice:** Choose a way to live the Mass and glorify God during the week.	**Enriching the Lesson Activities:** Catechist Edition, page 195 • Creating Worship Aids • Designing a Web Page for Living the Eucharist • Catholic Social Teaching: The Dignity of the Disciple

Concluding the Lesson   10 minutes

We Remember

Page 113

▶ Review concepts and do the review activity.

▶ **Assessment Tools Booklet:** Chapter Test 12a–12b, or see BeMyDisciples.com.

We Pray

▶ **Prayer:** from the Gospel of John 6:32–35

Materials: Bible, candle, cross for prayer space

▶ Grade 6 Music CD

Preview

Point out resources for this chapter at

www.BeMyDisciples.com

▶ Preview the With My Family page and next week's lesson theme.

Looking Ahead

In this chapter the Holy Spirit invites you to ▶

EXPLORE how Óscar Romero gave praise and thanks to God.

DISCOVER how the Eucharist is a memorial.

DECIDE on how Jesus' presence helps you to glorify God.

CHAPTER **12**

The Sacraments of Christian Initiation: The Eucharist

❓ Symbols and signs point to something beyond themselves. For example, smoke may be a sign of a fire. What symbols and signs you have seen or heard, and what do they point to?

In this psalm, God is praised for remaining faithful to his chosen people by keeping his promises:

> He spread a cloud as a cover,
>   and made a fire to light up the night.
> They asked and he brought them quail;
>   with bread from heaven he filled them.
> He split the rock and water gushed forth;
>   it flowed through the desert like a river.
>
> PSALM 105:39–41

❓ What signs are used in this psalm to remember God's love for his people?

107

HUMAN METHODOLOGIES

Learning within the Christian Family. The *National Directory for Catechesis* points out, "[A]ll the members make up the family, and each can make a unique contribution to creating the basic environment in which a sense of God's loving presence is awakened and faith in Jesus Christ is confessed, encouraged, and lived" (*NDC* 29D). Surveys show that because of busy schedules, many families find it difficult to gather for family meals. Family meals have great potential for sharing faith and deepening family bonds. Encourage the students' families to make family meals a priority at home at least once or twice a week.

Pray

▶ Invite a volunteer to lead the class in prayer and give him or her a moment to prepare. Ask this student to open prayer in his or her own words, a brief one-sentence call to prayer focused on the Eucharist.

▶ Call the students to quiet themselves for a moment of silent prayer. Begin and end with the Sign of the Cross.

Reflect

▶ Have a volunteer read aloud the opening question about naming symbols and signs in everyday life. Invite discussion.

▶ Invite one volunteer to read the Scripture introduction and another to read the Scripture passage.

▶ Discuss the questions related to the Scripture. Explain that many symbolic actions have religious meanings. Recall that many symbols represent something real; for example, the symbol of the cross represents the real event of Jesus' redemptive death.

Focus

▶ Explain that in this chapter they will learn more about the Sacrament of the Eucharist, especially in the celebration of the Mass.

▶ Invite a volunteer to describe how the image on the page relates to the Sacrament of the Eucharist.

▶ Call the students' attention to the Looking Ahead feature. Invite them to read aloud each bullet.

Introduce

▶ Remind students that all of the sacraments give grace that is necessary for living the Christian life.

▶ Point out that the Eucharist is a unique source of grace that nourishes us to be faithful to Christ.

Reinforce

▶ Have four students each read a paragraph of the text on the page.

▶ Paraphrase the Disciple Power feature and highlight how Archbishop Oscar Romero was faithful to Christ and his ministry to bring justice to the oppressed.

▶ Explain that life involves both what is enjoyable and what is not. Our response to what is difficult in life can help or hinder our journey to God.

Connect

▶ Have students complete the activity on the page and expand their reflections in their journals.

▶ Encourage the young people to share their ideas. Suggest ways they might put them into practice.

▶ Discuss the importance of committing ourselves to following through on our impulses to serve.

Disciple Power

Faithfulness

This fruit of the Holy Spirit is the steadfast commitment a Christian demonstrates as an act of his or her faith in Jesus Christ as the Son of God, Lord, and Savior. Often faithfulness to God involves a struggle, but Jesus shows us the way to remain faithful to God, especially when it involves sacrifice.

THE CHURCH FOLLOWS JESUS

Archbishop Óscar Romero

Christians since the early days of the Church have given their lives out of love for God and others. Óscar Romero, the Archbishop of San Salvador, gave up his life serving Christ and the people of San Salvador. On March 24, 1980, as he began to raise the consecrated bread in his hands, he was shot through his heart and killed. He was assassinated because he truly lived the command we all receive during the concluding rite of the Mass, "Go in peace glorifying the Lord by your life."

During his homily at that Mass, Archbishop Romero said, "Those who give their lives to the service of the poor through love will live like the grain of wheat that dies. The harvest comes from the grains that die. We know that every effort to improve society, when society is so full of injustice, is an effort that God blesses, God wants, and God demands of us. I am bound by God's command to give my life for all the people of El Salvador, even those who want to kill me."

Archbishop Romero was faithful to Jesus Christ and his message. He believed that the Gospel demanded that he serve the poor and be their voice. He was truly bread of life for the poor. Like the grain of wheat, he died to bring a harvest of justice to the people of his country.

Activity List three ways that you can assist the poor in your community.

1. _____
   _____

2. _____
   _____

3. _____
   _____

DISCIPLE POWER

Faithfulness. Ask the students to share which specific things Jesus did to show that he was faithful to God his Father (e.g., he prayed, he cared for others, he preached the Good News to all). Continue the discussion by asking the students which difficulties Jesus encountered because he was faithful to God. Help them make connections with their own lives. Which specific things can they do to show that they are faithful to God? What helps them remain faithful to God? What makes it difficult for them to remain faithful to God? Emphasize that living as a faithful disciple is not always easy; sometimes we must make sacrifices to follow the Lord.

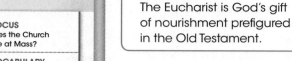
The Sacrament of the Eucharist

The Gift of Nourishment

Many of the Old Testament events point to, or prefigure, the mystery of the **Eucharist**, which we celebrate at **Mass**. Three accounts in the Old Testament, in particular, provide excellent examples of how God provided nourishment for his Chosen People, who in return offered thanksgiving to God. These are the stories of Melchizedek, the Passover, and the story of manna from Heaven.

Melchizedek

Upon settling in Canaan, Abram (Abraham) celebrated victory over an enemy ruler with Melchizedek, king of Salem. This story has a deep meaning for Christians. Three elements in this Old Testament story prefigure Christ's giving of himself to us in the Eucharist (read Genesis 14:17–20). These elements are the inclusion of bread and wine, the offering of bread and wine as gifts to God, and the grateful remembrance of what God has done for his people.

Passover

During the events of the Exodus, God protected and saved his people from slavery and plagues. In remembrance of God's saving power, the Israelites celebrated Passover each year with unleavened bread, the Passover lamb, bitter herbs, and wine (read Exodus 12:1–20). Jesus Christ, the Lamb of God, gave us a new Passover meal in the Eucharist.

Manna

While the Israelites wandered in the desert searching for the Promised Land, God gave them manna to eat (read Exodus 16:1–15). Manna is a bread-like substance produced on a shrub. This account reveals how God continually provided nourishment to his people. The Church teaches that manna prefigured the Eucharist, the Bread of Life God gives us.

? In what ways is the story of Melchizedek similar to how we celebrate Mass?

FAITH FOCUS
What does the Church celebrate at Mass?

FAITH VOCABULARY
Eucharist
The Eucharist is the Sacrament of the Body and Blood of Christ; the Sacrament of Christian Initiation in which we receive the Real Presence of Christ and are most fully joined to Christ and to the Church.

Mass
Mass is the main sacramental celebration of the Church at which we gather to listen to God's Word and through which we share in the saving Death of Christ and give praise and glory to God the Father.

109

TEACHING TIP

The Eucharist. Remind the students that the Catholic Church uses unleavened wheat bread and wine made from grapes for the celebration of the Eucharist, as Jesus did at the Last Supper. We break and share consecrated bread that is the Body of Christ. We share the consecrated wine that is the Blood of Christ. Sharing in the one Bread and drinking from the one Cup is an ancient and powerful sign that we are the one Body of Christ, the Church.

Key Concept
The Eucharist is God's gift of nourishment prefigured in the Old Testament.

Teach

▶ Read aloud the Faith Focus question, and have students respond.

▶ Explain that Jesus Christ fulfills the promises made by God in the Old Testament. Many events prefigure this fulfillment in the Eucharist.

▶ Read aloud to the class Genesis 14:17–20, and then read the second paragraph on the page.

▶ Have students read the rest of the text on the page silently to learn the connection between Melchizedek, Passover, and Manna.

Reinforce

Invite a volunteer to explain the connection between Passover and the Eucharist. Read Exodus 12:1–20 to help if needed.

Connect

▶ Have the class form four groups where each group is to take a portion of Exodus 16:1–18 and dramatize it.

▶ Summarize the page by reading the last paragraph on the page aloud to the class.

▶ Review by asking the closing question.

Key Concept
Christ is present Body and Blood, in the Eucharist through the priest's words of consecration, by the power of the Holy Spirit.

Teach

▶ Discuss the students' view of the Mass. Ask them if they have difficulty participating in the Mass, and why. Mention that finding joy often begins with a change in attitude.

▶ Read aloud to the students the first two paragraphs on the page. Ask them to listen to learn why celebrating the Eucharist at Mass is called a sacrifice.

▶ Inquire, "Which aspect of the Mass do you enjoy the most? Why?"

▶ Read the Faith-Filled People section and connect Saint Dominic to The Liturgy of The Word.

▶ Have students read the remaining text on the page.

▶ Time permitting, use the materials in the back of the student's book to review the various parts of the Mass.

Connect

Ask a volunteer to define the Real Presence. Remind the students that Christ remains present in the consecrated hosts reserved in the tabernacle. Encourage prayerful visits to the Blessed Sacraments.

Faith-Filled People

Saint Dominic de Guzman

Dominic gave his life to preaching the Gospel and explaining the meaning of the Word of God. So important was this work for Dominic that many soon joined him. They became the Order of Preachers and today are known as Dominicans. The Church celebrates the feast day of Saint Dominic on August 8.

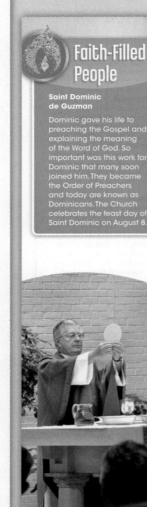

The Mass

The Eucharist, prefigured by the manna, the offering of Melchizedek, and the Passover meal, is the great sacrament of God's love. Celebrating the Eucharist at Mass recalls and makes present the one sacrifice of Christ. This is why we talk about the sacrifice of the Mass.

The two parts of the Mass are the Liturgy of the Word and the Liturgy of the Eucharist. These two parts make up one single act of worship that we call the Mass. The proclamation of God's very own Word in the Scriptures is the center of the Liturgy of the Word. The Word of God feeds us, nourishing our minds and hearts. It also inspires us to praise and thank God for showing us a path for living.

Blessing and Thanksgiving

In the Liturgy of the Eucharist, the Church celebrates the great prayer of blessing and thanksgiving to God the Father. God calls each of us to participate through our prayers of praise and thanksgiving. We all have the essential role of participating in the Mass. Together we celebrate a memorial—we remember what God makes present through our actions in the Liturgy. The presiding priest has a unique role. For example, only the priest can consecrate the bread and wine which become the Body and Blood of our Lord. This is because Christ, the High Priest, acts through the presiding priest and offers the sacrifice of the Mass.

During the Eucharistic Prayer, the priest pronounces the words of consecration. Through his words, and by the power of the Holy Spirit, the bread and wine are truly changed into the Body and Blood of Christ. Christ is truly present in the Eucharist. Then the consecrated bread is broken for us to share. The faithful in the state of grace are invited to process forward and receive Holy Communion. In this way, we receive Christ himself. This is what we mean by the Real Presence of Christ.

 What aspect of the Mass do you enjoy most?

FAITH-FILLED PEOPLE

Saint Dominic de Guzman. Saint Dominic (1170–1221) was born at Caleruega, Spain. In 1203, after he was ordained a priest, he became convinced that the Church needed an order of priests dedicated to preaching the Gospel. Dominic founded the Order of Preachers, which was approved by Pope Honorius III in 1216 and is known today as the Dominicans. Dominic's commitment to prayer and study, his concern for the salvation of souls, and his life of apostolic poverty became the foundation stones of the Order of Preachers. Saint Dominic died in Bologna, Italy, on August 6, 1221. To learn more about Saint Dominic, go to the Saint Resource at www.BeMyDisciples.com.

Holy Communion

In and through the Mass, Christ is present. We encounter Christ in the faithful assembled, in the Word of God proclaimed, in the priest who is minister of the Mass, and most importantly in the Eucharist that unites us. In Holy Communion, we are united more closely to Christ and to one another. The Eucharist preserves the life of grace received at Baptism. In this state of grace, we are separated from sin. We are strengthened to live our faith and be witnesses for Christ.

Therefore, the Church calls us to obligate ourselves to receive the Eucharist at least once a year. Strengthened and united as the Body of Christ, the Church professes the Eucharist as the source and summit of her life. This is truly a celebration to give thanks and praise to God. The amazing effect of the Eucharistic liturgy is that the Eucharist makes us the Body of Christ. We receive Holy Communion and become a holy communion, a people united in Christ.

Catholics Believe

Table of the Lord

The altar is the table of the Lord. From this table we are fed with the Body and Blood of our Lord Jesus. The altar is also a symbol of Christ. It reminds us that Jesus sacrificed his life for us on the cross. That is why at the beginning of the Mass and at the end of the Mass, the priest venerates, or honors, the altar by kissing and bowing before it. We too are to honor the altar through our own reverence before the altar.

Activity What are some ways that you actively participate in the Mass? After the Mass, how do you continue to glorify the Lord by your life?

_____
_____
_____
_____
_____
_____
_____
_____
_____
_____

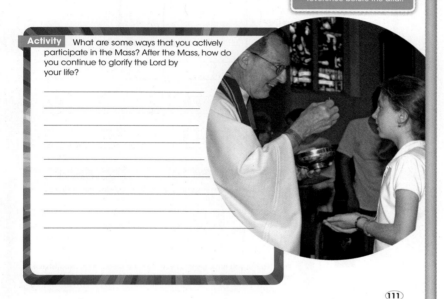

(111)

THE TASKS OF CATECHESIS

Promoting Knowledge of the Faith. The obligation to receive the Eucharist at least once a year is one of the Precepts of the Church. The Precepts of the Church are positive laws meant to encourage the faithful to continue to develop a life of prayer, service, love of God and neighbor, and morality through participation in the Church's liturgical and sacramental life. Each of the precepts has its own goal or guarantee (*see CCC* 2042). The Precepts of the Church are listed on page 261 of the student text. Discuss with the students why receiving the Eucharist is an important part of living our faith.

Key Concept
The Eucharist unites us with Christ, making us the Body of Christ.

Teach

▶ Inquire, "What do you think "active participation" means?" Explain that the Church invites us to actively participate in the Mass.

▶ Read the Catholics Believe section. Have students list furniture used in the liturgy that points to participation by someone or by a group of people. Emphasize that all assembled with the priest participate in the Mass before the altar.

Reinforce

▶ Invite volunteers to read the text on the page. Have the students highlight those parts of the Mass in which we encounter Christ.

▶ Explain that through the Eucharist, the work of salvation accomplished by the one sacrifice of Christ is made present and that we are made sharers in it.

▶ Review the Faith Vocabulary on page 109 in light of the discussion about the Eucharist. Have students write a new definition for each term in their own words.

Connect

Have students complete the activity on the page. Inquire, "How can your active participation in the Mass demonstrate your faithfulness to Christ?"

Reinforce

▶ Recall with students that Archbishop Romero made the ultimate sacrifice by giving up his life in service to Christ.

▶ Point out that each time we receive the Eucharist in Holy Communion we are strengthened to love and serve the Lord more faithfully.

▶ Review the Concluding Rite of the Mass in the back of the student's book on page 271.

Respond

Introduce and explain the directions to the activity on the page. Invite the students to complete the activity on the page. Invite volunteers to share with the class what they wrote. Provide time for the students to record more of their thoughts in their journals.

Choose

▶ Have the young people individually complete the last section to make their faith choices. Encourage students to put their faith choice into practice this week.

▶ If you desire, today invite the whole class to pray the reflection prayer on the bottom of the page. This might serve to reinforce the communal participation of celebrating the Eucharist as the Body of the Christ.

I FOLLOW JESUS

Receiving the Eucharist in Holy Communion strengthens your union with Jesus and the Church. Each time you participate in the Mass, you receive the call and the grace of the Holy Spirit to faithfully love and serve the Lord.

THE BREAD OF LIFE

Quietly read these words of Jesus. Reflect on what they tell you about being a disciple of Jesus:

Jesus said, "I am the bread of life; whoever comes to me will never hunger, and whoever believes in me will never thirst" (John 6:35). Describe how the Bread of Life helps you to be a disciple of Christ.

_____
_____
_____
_____
_____
_____

MY FAITH CHOICE

Through the week, I will live the Mass and glorify God. I will stay faithful to Jesus by:

_____
_____

 Pray, "Father, you have given us your Son, the Bread of Life. Nourish me with your Word so that I may remain faithful. Amen."

(112)

LITURGY CONNECTION

The Dismissal. To help the students prepare for "The Bread of Life" activity, review the four forms of dismissal used by the Catholic Church at the end of Mass. Read each of the forms of dismissal aloud. Pause after each, giving the students the opportunity to reflect on the meaning of each for their own lives:

▶ Go forth, the Mass is ended.

▶ Go and announce the Gospel of the Lord.

▶ Go in peace, glorifying the Lord by your life.

▶ Go in peace.

(Concluding Rites, Roman Missal)

Chapter Review

Read each sentence and unscramble the words to complete it.

1. The Sacrament of the ___Eucharist___ is the sacrament
   shaucErit
   of the Body and Blood of Christ.

2. The ___Passover___ meal prefigures the Last Supper
   sPaersov
   and the Eucharist.

3. During the Eucharistic Prayer, the priest pronounces the words

   of ___consecration___. These are the words Jesus spoke at
   crcontionsea
   the Last Supper.

TO HELP YOU REMEMBER

1. Many events in the Old Testament prefigure, or point to, the mystery of the Eucharist.

2. We encounter Christ in and through the Mass. The two parts of the Mass are the Liturgy of the Word and the Liturgy of the Eucharist. These two parts make up one single act of worship that we call the Mass.

3. The Eucharist is a memorial of the Paschal Mystery.

Praise to You, Lord!

The Eucharist nourishes us to live the Gospel. Celebrate the following Liturgy of the Word. Then go forth and be bread for the world.

Leader: Heavenly Father, giver of all blessings, thank you for the gift of your Son, Jesus, the Bread of Life. Send the Holy Spirit to help us serve others as your Son did.

Reader: *Proclaim John 6:32–35.* The gospel of the Lord.

All: **Praise to you, Lord Jesus Christ.**

Leader: Let us now pray to God the Father as Jesus taught.

All: **Our Father . . .**

Leader: Let us offer one another a sign of peace. (Pause.)

All: **Thanks be to God.**

(113)

We Remember

▶ Introduce the activity as the chapter review by reading the directions aloud. Have the students complete each sentence individually.

▶ Invite volunteers to share their answers.

▶ Read aloud the To Help You Remember statements to the class. Have students underline on the page and share with the class which statement had the greatest significance for them.

We Pray

▶ Gather the young people for prayer. Introduce the closing prayer and select a student leader and reader. Provide both a moment to practice their reading.

▶ Lead the class in the prayer, beginning and ending with the Sign of the Cross.

TEACHING TIP

Emphasize Learning Skills. Hearing the Scriptures proclaimed at Mass demands that we listen attentively. Attentive listening is an important life skill. Before celebrating the Liturgy of the Word with the students, discuss the art of listening attentively. Interestingly, young people have plenty of firsthand experience with listening. They know when others are listening to them and not listening to them. Ask the students to list three signs that someone is listening attentively to them and three signs that someone is not listening to them.

Preview

▶ Have students carefully tear out the With My Family page along the perforation.

▶ Encourage them to share the pages with their families and to complete the activities together at home.

▶ If the students did not or could not complete the chapter review, encourage them to complete it with their families.

▶ Point out the chapter title and theme of next week's lesson.

Visit www.BeMyDisciples.com

▶ Take time with the students to explore the many activities and resources available at **www.BeMyDisciples.com.**

▶ Especially encourage them and their families to discover the many resources available at the Web site.

Before Moving On ...

As you finish today's lesson, reflect on the following question before moving on to the next chapter.

As you finish today's lesson, ask, "What am I doing to involve students who never volunteer?"

With My Family

This Week...

In chapter 12, The Sacraments of Christian Initiation: The Eucharist, your child learned:

▶ The Old Testament stories of Melchizedek, Passover, and the Manna prefigure the Eucharist.

▶ The Eucharist is the sacrament of the Body and Blood of our Lord, Jesus Christ.

▶ In the Mass, the bread and wine truly become the Body and Blood of Christ through the power of the Holy Spirit and the words of the priest.

▶ At the end of Mass, we are sent forth to go glorify God by our lives.

▶ Faithfulness is a fruit of the Holy Spirit. It is our steadfast commitment to Jesus Christ.

For more about related teachings of the Church, see the *Catechism of the Catholic Church,* 1322–1419; and the *United States Catholic Catechism for Adults,* pages 215–232.

■ Sharing God's Word

Read together 1 Corinthians 11:17–34. Emphasize that the Eucharist is the sacrament of the Body and Blood of Christ. Sharing in the Eucharist nourishes us and strengthens us to love and serve God and one another.

■ We Live as Disciples

The Christian home and family is a school of discipleship. Choose one of the following activities to do as a family, or design a similar activity of your own.

▶ Find a favorite bread recipe and make homemade bread as a family. Talk about the unique ingredients needed to make bread rise. Use the bread for a special meal.

▶ When you take part in the Mass this week, listen and think carefully about the readings and prayers. After Mass, discuss what you heard and thought about during Mass.

▶ Talk about some ways you can participate in Mass more actively. Invite each family member to share how the family can help encourage conscious, active participation in Mass.

■ Our Spiritual Journey

Fasting helps us deepen our awareness of our dependence on God. The eucharistic fast deepens our desire for receiving the Body and Blood of Christ. It helps strengthen our union with him and the Church. A faithful Catholic receives Holy Communion frequently. It acknowledges that we are not alone.

For more ideas on ways that your family can live as disciples of Jesus, visit **www.BeMyDisciples.com**

(114)

CATHOLIC SOCIAL TEACHING

Dignity of Work and the Rights of Workers. Work has dignity because of the dignity of the worker, who is created in the image and likeness of God. Through our work we express and fulfill our humanity, share in God's work of creation, and contribute to the world through our work. We all have the obligation and the right to make use of our talents and work for the common good. The young people learned of the work of Saint Charles Lwanga in Chapter 10, the Chinese Martyrs in Chapter 11, and Archbishop Oscar Romero in Chapter 12. Each of these men and women died because they answered God's call to serve him and work for the Kingdom of God. These stories have prepared them for the activity on the next page about the call to service as the noblest work.

Enriching the Lesson

Creating Worship Aids

Purpose

To reinforce the Liturgy of the Word and the Liturgy of the Eucharist (taught on page 110)

Directions

▶ Have the students work in small groups to create and illustrate a worship aid for the children in the parish who will be receiving First Communion.

▶ The booklets should include the responses the children will say aloud during each part of the Mass.

▶ Tell the students to use the We Celebrate the Mass section on pages 265 of their textbook as a guide.

▶ Present the booklets to the appropriate staff person, who can distribute them to the children who will be celebrating First Communion.

Materials

construction paper

white paper

markers and crayons

Designing a Web Page for Living the Eucharist

Purpose

To reinforce that each time we participate in Mass, we receive the call and the grace of the Holy Spirit to love and serve the Lord (taught on page 111)

Directions

▶ Have the students work in small groups to create a design for a new parish Web page, "Living the Eucharist."

▶ Ask each group to come with several images, an appropriate message, and appropriate symbols.

▶ Display the Web pages. Share them with the pastor, and make them available for the parish to use.

Materials

paper

markers

pencils or pens

Catholic Social Teaching: The Dignity of the Disciple

Purpose

To reinforce the principle that the dignity of a Christian is related to the work they do to serve others (taught throughout Unit 3)

Directions

▶ Place two headings on the board: Work the World Values and Work that God Values. Brainstorm with he class various jobs that are valued and celebrated in our society. In the second column list jobs that they think God values. In each case, ask the students to give reasons for their answer.

▶ Divide the class into four groups and distribute poster paper and art supplies to each group. Tell each group to choose a job from the second column. Ask them to list all the reasons why that person's job is consistent with Jesus' call to discipleship. What does that person do that helps to build the Kingdom of God? Have the students decorate their posters with images and symbols and give it a title.

▶ Invite each group to present their poster to the class.

▶ Remind them that the work of a disciple is the noblest work because it is the work God asks of each of us.

Materials

poster board

crayons or markers

glue

magazines or newspapers

The Unit Review provides the opportunity to assess the students' understanding of the faith concepts presented in the unit and to affirm them in their growing knowledge and love of God. Here are a few suggestions for using these pages.

▶ Share that the next two pages are an opportunity to stop and review what they have learned.

▶ Provide time for the students to ask questions.

▶ Have the students complete the review alone or with partners.

A. Choose the Best Word

▶ Read the directions for this section.

▶ Then have the student work alone or with a partner to complete the section.

▶ Invite volunteers to share their responses. Clarify and correct responses as needed.

B. Show What You Know

▶ Read the directions for this section. Answer the first question together as a class.

▶ Then have the student continue working alone or with a partner to complete the section.

▶ Invite volunteers to share their responses. Clarify and correct responses as needed.

Unit 3 Review

Name _____

A. Choose the Best Word

Fill-in the blanks within the paragraph by using the terms in the word bank.

| Last Supper | salvation | Holy Communion |
| Word | sacraments | Paschal Mystery |

The story of God's loving plan of creation and __salvation__ in Jesus Christ is proclaimed and celebrated by the Church in the __sacraments__. Through rituals, the Church celebrates the liturgy, and we are made sharers in the __Paschal Mystery__ of Jesus Christ. The Sacrament of the Eucharist is celebrated at Mass. During the Liturgy of the __Word__, we listen to readings from Scripture. During the Liturgy of the Eucharist, we do what Jesus did at the __Last Supper__.

B. Show What You Know

Read each statement and circle the best answer.

1. Which season of the Church's year celebrates the Resurrection of Jesus?

A. Advent   B. Christmas

C. Lent   (D.) Easter

2. What is a sacrament?

A. Words and actions used in the Liturgy   B. Ways of living the Commandments

(C.) A sacred sign and cause of grace in the Church   D. Codes for happiness

3. Which sacrament is not a Sacrament of Christian Initiation?

(A.) Ordination   B. Baptism

C. Confirmation   D. Eucharist

4. What are the two main parts of the Mass?

A. Eucharistic Prayer and Communion Rite   (B.) Liturgy of the Word and Liturgy of the Eucharist

(115)

TEACHING TIP

Student Directed Assessment. Part of varying the type of assessment might include inviting students to develop, implement and facilitate the unit reviews. Placing them in the forefront of the learning process is a way not just to empower them in their learning, but a vital way of learning retention. When students teach what they have learned, the knowledge is retained and appreciated at a deeper level of understanding. Rotate through the year, volunteer students to lead the class in the unit reviews. Be sure to guide the students along the way.

C. Connect with Scripture

Reread the Scripture passage on the first Unit Opener page. What connection do you see between this passage and what you learned in this unit?

Responses will vary.

_____

_____

_____

D. Be a Disciple

1. Review the four pages in this unit titled "The Church Follows Jesus." What person or ministry of the Church on these pages will inspire you to be a better disciple of Jesus? Explain your answer.

Responses will vary.

_____

_____

_____

2. Work with a group. Review the four Disciple Power virtues or gifts you have learned about in this unit. After jotting down your own ideas, share with the group practical ways that you will live these virtues or gifts day by day.

Responses will vary.

_____

_____

_____

(116)

C. Connect with Scripture

▶ Invite the students to reflect on the Scripture passage in the Unit Opener and to write their understanding of how this passage connects with the doctrinal content of the unit they have just completed.

▶ Ask volunteers to share their responses, now or after completion of the entire Unit Review.

D. Be a Disciple

▶ Invite the young people to work independently on the first question about The Church Follows Jesus. Ask volunteers to share their responses.

▶ Divide the students into small groups of three or four for the second part of this section. Ask them to write their personal reflections first, and then to share with their group practical ways of living the Disciple Power virtues or qualities of discipleship in everyday life.

▶ Ask for feedback from the small groups as time allows.

TEACHING TIP

Memorization. Throughout the year, encourage the students to learn key concepts and teachings through the use of memorization. Expressing the faith is not something to be reduced to mere statements robotically mimicked. Memorizing important Scripture verses and traditional faith formulas are important as an essential learning strategy to help activate the mind in keeping to heart the key teachings of the faith. For example, Hebrew 11:1 can help one remember what faith is—"the assurance of things hoped for, the conviction of things not seen."

UNIT 4 We Worship

Part Two

Objectives

In Unit 4, you will help the children learn that:

▶ In the Sacrament of Reconciliation we receive God's mercy and forgiveness through the ministry of a priest for sins we have committed after Baptism.

▶ The Sacrament of the Anointing of the Sick strengthens our faith, hope, and love for God when we are seriously ill, weakened by old age or dying.

▶ In the Sacrament of Holy Orders, a baptized man is consecrated to serve the Church as a bishop, priest or deacon.

▶ Matrimony is the Sacrament of the Church that unites a baptized man and a baptized woman in a lifelong bond of faithful love as a sign of Christ's love for the Church.

Spiritual Insights

Jesus gave us the Sacraments to call us to worship God, to build up the Church, to deepen our faith, to show us how to pray, to connect us with the living Tradition of the Church, and to sanctify us. While God works primarily through the Sacraments, he also touches us through the community of the Church, through the lives of holy people, through prayer, spirituality, and acts of love" (*United States Catholic Catechism for Adults*, page 170).

"Through these, he has bestowed on us the precious and very great promises, so that through them, you may come to share in the divine nature" (2 Peter 1:4).

Living the Six Tasks of Catechesis

Teaching to Pray:
Saint Thérèse of Lisieux (1873–1897)

Marie Martin was raised in France. Her older sister Pauline raised her after her mother's death when Marie was only four years old. As a result, Marie was somewhat spoiled and used to getting her own way.

Pauline entered the Carmelite order when Marie was nine. Marie longed to join her, but she was too young. Five years later, when she was granted an audience with Pope Leo XIII, Marie boldly asked the Holy Father for special permission to enter Carmel. The Pope replied that she could enter if it was God's will for her. Finally, when Marie was fifteen, her bishop relented. She eagerly gave her life to God by entering the Carmelite cloister. Marie was given the name Sister Thérèse.

Sister Thérèse was given dull work—washing floors, scrubbing pots, and cleaning the chapel. Sister Thérèse did not mind because she had put away her selfish ways. She tried to do every task with love. She called it her "Little Way" of serving God. She knew that because she was small and often sickly, she would never do great things. Her daily work became a prayer to God. Thérèse called herself Jesus' little flower. That is how she got her nickname: "The Little Flower."

Sister Thérèse Marie was asked to write about her "Little Way." After her death, her autobiography was published. Its title was as humble as Thérèse was: *The Story of a Soul*. It is still read today by people who want to lead a more spiritual life. Shortly before she died, Sister Thérèse told her beloved Carmelite sisters that she wanted to "spend her heaven doing good on earth." Thérèse died when she was only twenty-four. She was canonized in 1925.

In 1997, Pope John Paul II declared Saint Thérèse a Doctor of the Church, a title given to the greatest teachers of our faith. Her life teaches us that prayer can transform us if we are open to the presence of the Holy Spirit's action in our lives.

Sharing Your Faith

Find a partner to work with: a spouse, a friend, a fellow catechist. Come together at the beginning or end of each unit for shared prayer and discussion. Use the questions below as a starting point.

▶ What can be done to increase participation in weekly Sunday liturgy among Catholics in our parish?

▶ How have you experienced the transforming power of prayer in your life?

▶ Name two ways that teaching about the sacraments has deepened your faith.

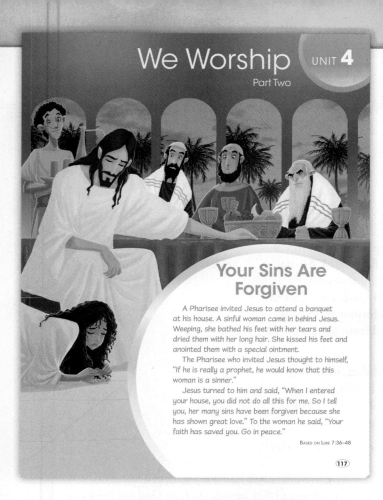

We Worship
Part Two
UNIT 4

Your Sins Are Forgiven

A Pharisee invited Jesus to attend a banquet at his house. A sinful woman came in behind Jesus. Weeping, she bathed his feet with her tears and dried them with her long hair. She kissed his feet and anointed them with a special ointment.

The Pharisee who invited Jesus thought to himself, "If he is really a prophet, he would know that this woman is a sinner."

Jesus turned to him and said, "When I entered your house, you did not do all this for me. So I tell you, her many sins have been forgiven because she has shown great love." To the woman he said, "Your faith has saved you. Go in peace."

BASED ON LUKE 7:36–48

(117)

What I Have Learned
What is something you already know about these faith concepts?

Examination of Conscience

_____

The Sacraments of Healing

_____

The Sacraments at the Service of Communion

_____

The Bible
What do you know about the healing miracles of Jesus?

_____

Faith Terms to Know
Put an X next to the faith terms you know. Put a ? next to faith terms you need to learn more about.

_____ mortal sin

_____ venial sin

_____ penance

_____ hospice care

_____ Ordination

_____ bishop

_____ spousal love

_____ complementarity

The Church
What would you like to know about the Church's authority?

_____

Questions I Have
What questions would you like to ask about the vocation to the priesthood religious life, or lay ecclesial ministry?

_____

(118)

Unit 4 Opener

Opening Page

▶ Invite the young people to tell you what they see in the illustration. *(A woman is kneeling and washing Jesus' feet with her hair.)*

▶ Ask a volunteer to read the Scripture story "Your Sins Are Forgiven" aloud. Then ask: "What do you think Jesus means when he says, 'Your sins are forgiven because you have shown great love?'" *(Accept all reasonable responses.)*

Getting Ready

▶ Invite the young people to write their responses to the questions and directions under What I Have Learned, Faith Terms to Know, and the other headings in the second column.

▶ Invite a few volunteers to share their responses, but do not correct them at this time. Tell the students that they will return to this page to check their learning at the end of the unit.

▶ For Questions I Have, you might write their questions on the board and on a piece of newsprint so that you can refer to them if, or when, the topics come up in the unit.

▶ Ask the class to look at the next page and begin Chapter 13.

BACKGROUND

Healing and Forgiveness

Sin is a two edged sword. When we sin, it not only separates us from God but it also separates us from the Church, that is, from the Christian community. Because of the reality of sin, Jesus' public ministry was centered on forgiving sins and reconciling people with God. The heart of that work was his Passion, Death, Resurrection, and glorious Ascension to the Father. Through him we are forgiven and healed from the pain and suffering sin has created.

> The Lord Jesus Christ, physician of our souls and bodies, who forgave the sins of the paralytic and restored him to bodily health, (Mark 2:1-12) has willed that his Church continue, in the power of the Holy Spirit, his work of healing and salvation, even among her own members.
>
> *Catechism of the Catholic Church* 1421

Forgiveness of Christ

Remaining faithful to God and the Covenant has always been a great struggle for humanity. Through these experiences we come up against our own sinfulness and our own powerlessness against sin but also experience the forgiveness of Christ that infuses us with grace. Such experiences can be events of conversion that lead us to God.

The four Gospels attest that Jesus had a real compassion for the sick and sinners. He had the power to heal people who were ill and to forgive their sins. At times he coupled the works of physical healing with the forgiveness of sin. Such healings were "signs of . . . the victory over sin and death through his Passover" *(Catechism of the Catholic Church* 1505).

Conversion

Through the Sacrament of Penance and Reconciliation, Christ continues his healing work in the Church and we are made sharers in it. While Baptism washes us clean of all sin, it does not take away our human frailty or our inclination to sin. We must continually strive, with the help of the Holy Spirit, to deepen our conversion to Christ.

This work of conversion is a work of healing, of overcoming all that separates us from God and from one another. Conversion is not merely a human endeavor. It is also the work of the Holy Spirit living within us. Conversion is motivated by a contrite heart in which the seeds of God's abundant and merciful grace are planted. It is a heartfelt turning back to the Lord God, who loves us so much that his Son, Jesus Christ, freely suffered and died for our salvation.

Christ's ultimate work of healing is the work of salvation. Salvation is a gift freely given to us in Christ. It includes the healing and forgiveness that come from God alone and are mediated through the ministry of the Church in the sacraments. Through the Sacrament of Penance and Reconciliation we are forgiven of our sins and are returned to a state of grace. We experience the greatness of God and are once again made full sharers in this salvation in Christ.

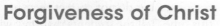

For Reflection

How might the regular celebration of Reconciliation help me strengthen my relationship with God and with others?

When have I been an agent of God's healing for others?

Catechist to Catechist

The Grace of Forgiveness

The Sacrament of Penance and Reconciliation accomplishes what its name implies. It heals the divisions sin has made between the sinner and God, between the sinner and the Church, and between the sinner and others. Help your students see the inner healing that comes from the grace found in this sacrament. Through his grace, God brings us a deep serenity and sense of peace. Just like in the Parable of the Forgiving Father, God the Father gives us a welcomed return to our true spiritual family.

Overcoming Obstacles

Even at this age, some of your students might be shy or hesitate about going to Confession. Some students might be more nervous than others because they are not use to talking to anyone, let alone a priest, about the things they have done wrong. Help your students by pointing out that many people, even adults, feel this way. Assure them that the priest will help them too.

The Church Teaches...

"Christ's methodology was multi-dimensional. It included his words, his signs, and the wonders he worked. He reached out to the poor, to sinners, and to those on the margins of society. He proclaimed insistently the coming of the Kingdom of God, the forgiveness of sins, and reconciliation with the Father . . . Christ invited his listeners to a whole new manner of life sustained by faith in God, encouraged by hope in the kingdom, and animated by the love for God and neighbor" (*National Directory for Catechesis,* 28A.2).

As a catechist and an evangelist, it is your responsibility in partnership with the parents to share the Gospel message and guide the children in discipleship. A key element in discipleship is reconciliation with God and with one another. Invite the children to find comfort in knowing the loving mercy of God.

Further Reading and Reflection

For more on the teachings of the Church, see the *Catechism of the Catholic Church,* 1420–1498; and from the *United States Catholic Catechism for Adults,* pages 233–247.

Catechist Prayer

Come Holy Spirit,
open my heart anew to accept
the gift of your love in all the
moments of my life.
Amen.

Lesson Planner

Chapter 13   Penance and Reconciliation

Focus To learn about forgiveness and the Sacrament of Reconciliation

LESSON PART	PROCESS	MATERIALS and RESOURCES
EXPLORE **Focus** **To explore the power of forgiveness** ⏱ 10 minutes **Pages** 119–120	▶ Proclaim and discuss Luke 7:47–50 (Jesus with the Sorrowful Woman). ▶ Learn the story of Saint Monica. **Disciple Power:** Self-control **Activity:** Demonstrating self-control throughout the day	Bible Pencils Crayons or markers
DISCOVER **Focus** **To discover the meaning and rite of the Sacrament of Reconciliation** ⏱ 30 minutes **Pages** 121–123	▶ Identify the Sacraments of Healing. ▶ Review the Rite of Penance. ▶ Discover the graces of the Sacrament of Reconciliation. **Activity:** Inventory the things distracting us from discipleship.	Index cards **Additional Activities Booklet:** Activities 13a–13b, or see BeMyDisciples.com
DECIDE **Focus** **To decide on a response to the lesson on forgiveness** ⏱ 10 minutes **Page** 124	**Activity:** Create an examination of conscience. **My Faith Choice:** Connect self-control and Works of Mercy.	**Enriching the Lesson Activities:** Catechist Edition, page 211 • Writing in Journals • Designing Reconciliation Guides • Creating Scenarios about Forgiveness

Concluding the Lesson 10 minutes

We Remember

Page 125

▶ Review concepts and do the review activity.

▶ **Assessment Tools Booklet:** Chapter Test 13a–13b, or see BeMyDisciples.com

We Pray

▶ **Prayer:** an Act of Contrition.

Materials: Bible, candle, cross for prayer space

▶ Grade 6 Music CD

Preview

Point out resources for this chapter at

www.BeMyDisciples.com

▶ Preview the With My Family page and next week's lesson theme.

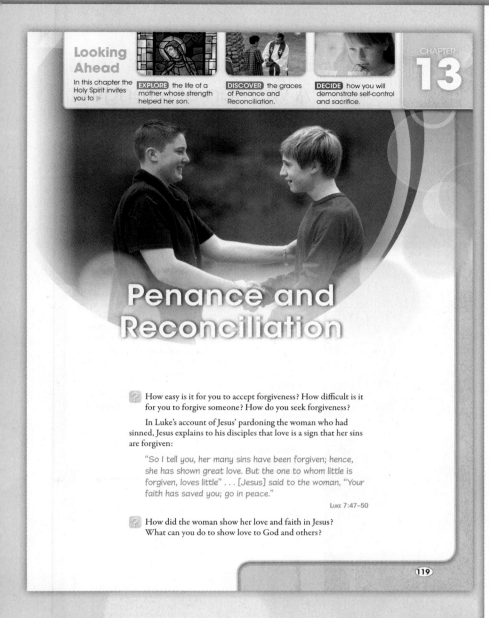

Looking
Ahead

In this chapter the
Holy Spirit invites
you to ▶

EXPLORE the life of a
mother whose strength
helped her son.

DISCOVER the graces
of Penance and
Reconciliation.

DECIDE how you will
demonstrate self-control
and sacrifice.

CHAPTER
13

Penance and Reconciliation

How easy is it for you to accept forgiveness? How difficult is it for you to forgive someone? How do you seek forgiveness?

In Luke's account of Jesus' pardoning the woman who had sinned, Jesus explains to his disciples that love is a sign that her sins are forgiven:

"So I tell you, her many sins have been forgiven; hence, she has shown great love. But the one to whom little is forgiven, loves little" . . . [Jesus] said to the woman, "Your faith has saved you; go in peace."

LUKE 7:47–50

How did the woman show her love and faith in Jesus? What can you do to show love to God and others?

(119)

HUMAN METHODOLOGIES

Learning through Human Experience. The *National Directory for Catechesis* explains: "Human experiences provide the sensible signs that lead the person, by the grace of the Holy Spirit, to a better understanding of the truths of the faith" **(NDC 29A)**. As the students learn about the Sacrament of Reconciliation in this chapter, review the process for celebrating Reconciliation, which is found on page 272 in the student text. Familiarize the students with the similarities and differences in the Individual Rite and the Communal Rite. Be sure to point out opportunities within the parish for students and their families to celebrate the Sacrament of Reconciliation.

Pray

▶ Tell the class that they will incorporate the gift of silence in prayer today. Provide a personal testimony to how silence has helped you focus in prayer. Begin prayer with the Sign of the Cross.

▶ Ask the class to spend a few quiet moments reflecting on God's presence with them.

Reflect

▶ Ask and discuss the opening questions. Proclaim Luke 7:47–50. Invite the students to picture in their minds what is happening in this Scripture passage.

▶ Allow a few minutes of silence.

▶ Invite one volunteer to read the Scripture introduction and another to read the Scripture passage.

▶ Discuss the follow-up questions. Remind the students that they are still in prayer as they discuss the questions.

▶ Emphasis that prayer can be more than memorized prayer. Often prayer can be part of our daily activity. End the prayer with the Sign of the Cross.

Focus

▶ Explain that in this chapter they will learn more about the healing ministry of Jesus, especially in the Sacrament of Penance and Reconciliation

▶ Call the students' attention to the Looking Ahead feature. Invite them to read aloud each bullet.

Introduce

▶ Recall with the students the meaning of forgiveness.

▶ Explain that love necessary for forgiveness comes from accepting God's mercy and love for ourselves. As we remain committed to God, we can be more Christ-like.

▶ Point out the Disciple Power box on the page. Explain that the students will learn about a woman whose faith demonstrated love through self-control.

▶ Have several students volunteer to read the text aloud.

▶ Discuss how St. Monica might have felt with a family who didn't show her the love she showed them. Inquire: How hard do you think it was for St. Monica to forgive her husband?

Reinforce

Point out that virtues are habits we form through daily practice. And with the grace of the Holy Spirit, our virtuous habits can bear fruit and result in something good and wonderful.

Connect

▶ Invite each student to work with a partner. Have students complete the activity on the page. Help them understand the importance of self control throughout the day.

▶ If time allows, invite several pairs to present their skits.

Disciple Power

Self-control

Self-control is a fruit of the Holy Spirit that comes from a steadfast commitment to God. A person with self-control demonstrates that God's will comes first in life. Self-control helps us do what is good and just. When others see self-control in us, we become witnesses for Christ by placing the needs of others before our own and following the will of God the Father, in whom we place our trust.

THE CHURCH FOLLOWS JESUS

A Woman of Strength

Faith and love are at the center of the life of Saint Monica. As a young girl, Monica was strong willed and devoted to her Christian faith. Born in Tagaste, North Africa (modern-day Algeria) in A.D. 332, her determination carried over into her adult life. As was customary then, Monica had an arranged marriage with a man named Patricius, who was not a Christian. Together they had three children, one of whom was named Augustine.

As a wife and a mother, Monica had a tough time. Patricius led a sinful and violent lifestyle, and Augustine was a reckless teenager. Despite this, Monica prayed patiently for their conversion.

Under the guidance of Ambrose, Monica remained strong in her faith and devoted to her family. Patricius witnessed his wife's commitment. He eventually changed his sinful ways and was baptized into the Church.

As for Augustine, he was not interested in God or religion as a young man. In fact, he led a wild life. His mother never gave up on him, however, praying for him every day. Augustine saw her discipline and grace-filled ability to allow God to lead her in life. Her daily example of self-control gradually influenced Augustine, and he too changed his life and was baptized. Augustine eventually became one of the foremost religious people of his time. His writings have inspired millions of Catholics.

Today many see Saint Monica as an example of a strong African Christian woman. Her faith in God gave her self-control. No matter how frustrating life seemed, she was true to her understanding of God's plan for her. Had it not been for Monica's faith and commitment to her family, the world may not ever have known her or her son. The Church celebrates the life of Saint Monica on her feast day, August 27.

Activity Work with a partner. Prepare a skit in which self-control is needed. Write a summary of your idea here and share it with your class.

_____

_____

_____

DISCIPLE POWER

Self-Control. Explain to the young people that one important aspect of self-control is doing the good and just thing independently without being asked, when no one is watching us. Expand upon the activity by creating a tracking chart on the board or a poster. Use the headings "place," "home," "school," and "church." Ask the students to list examples of how they exhibit self-control by following the will of God and doing the good and just thing in each of these places. For example, at home they do their chores without being told to do so. At school they do not speak unless they are called upon by the teacher. At church they join in singing the hymns.

God's Forgiveness

The self-control of Saint Monica shows how understanding God's plan for you can keep you true to the faith and love of God. Some people do not stay true to this love, however.

When we sin, we turn away from the love of God and of other people. We hurt ourselves, and we need spiritual healing. In the Sacraments of Healing, our relationship with God and with the Church is renewed. Both the Sacrament of Penance and Reconciliation and the Sacrament of Anointing of the Sick are Sacraments of Healing. We need the healing given by God, who alone can forgive sins. In his mercy and goodness, God shares his power to forgive sins with the Church, the Body of Christ. He shares this forgiveness through the celebration of the sacraments.

Sacraments of Forgiveness

Baptism is the first sacrament of forgiveness. In Baptism, Original Sin and all personal sins are forgiven. Jesus also gave the Church the Sacrament of Penance and Reconciliation for the forgiveness of sins committed after Baptism. He said to his disciples,

> "Receive the holy Spirit. Whose sins you forgive are forgiven them, and whose sins you retain are retained."
>
> JOHN 20:22–23

This work of forgiveness is continued through the ministry of bishops and priests.

The Eucharist is also a sacrament of forgiveness. Sharing in the Eucharist joins us more closely to Christ and to others. **Venial sins** are forgiven. **Mortal sins**, however, must be confessed in the Sacrament of Penance and Reconciliation. Celebrating Reconciliation and receiving the Eucharist regularly helps us deepen our relationship with God and others.

❓ When have you experienced God's mercy and forgiveness?

FAITH FOCUS
What does the Church teach about forgiveness?

FAITH VOCABULARY

mortal sin
A mortal sin is a serious failure in our love and respect for God, our neighbor, and ourselves. For a sin to be mortal, it must be gravely wrong, we must know it to be gravely wrong, and we must freely choose it.

venial sin
A venial sin is less serious than a mortal sin; it is a sin that does not have all three things necessary for a sin to be mortal.

TEACHING VOCABULARY

Reconciliation. The word "reconciliation," from the root word *reconcile* and the Latin *reconciliare*, means to restore friendship or harmony. Through the celebration of the Sacrament of Reconciliation, our right relationship, or harmony of living, with God and with the Church, is restored (see "Introduction," Rite of Penance 5).

Key Concept
The Sacrament of Penance and Reconciliation is for the forgiveness of sins committed after Baptism.

Teach

▶ Discuss the Faith Focus question as a class.

▶ Have the students identify the two Sacraments of Healing (*Penance and Reconciliation, and Anointing of the Sick*). Then invite students to explain what they know about each.

▶ Validate the accuracy of their statements.

▶ Read aloud Matthew 16:15–20. Explain that Jesus entrusted to the Church through Peter the gift of reconciling others with God. Then read aloud John 20:22–23. Explain that Jesus clearly expected the Church to continue his ministry of healing and forgiveness through the sacraments.

▶ Discuss how the Eucharist is also a sacrament of forgiveness.

▶ Have students read the text on the page. Invite them to recall their personal experiences of celebrating Baptism, Reconciliation, and the Eucharist.

Reinforce

Ask volunteers to read aloud the definitions of the Faith Vocabulary words. Invite them to make word cards for these words.

Connect

Inquire: When have you experienced God's mercy and forgiveness in the sacraments?

Key Concept
The Rite of Penance demonstrates a movement of conversion.

Teach

▶ Invite students to describe a recent moment in which they forgave someone or when they received forgiveness from someone.

▶ Discuss how there is a process or movement when forgiveness is involved. *(Ask for their ideas. If necessary, explain that it might include: wrong being done, harm being felt, desire to make amends, actions to make things right, reconciliation.)*

▶ Explain that when we sin, we do wrong against God and the Church, and need to seek forgiveness if we are to reconcile with God and the Church.

▶ Have volunteers read the text on the page aloud.

▶ Read the Faith-filled People section. Explain how Mary Magdalene is a great example of a person who experienced God's mercy and forgiveness.

Reinforce

Ask volunteers to name five things that happen in the Rite of Penance.

Connect

Point out that during an examination of conscience, a person begins the process of forgiveness. We reflect on harm done and our desire to make amends. Inquire: What kind of questions do you ask when you examine your conscience?

Faith-Filled People

Mary Magdalene

Some people think that the sinful woman pardoned by Jesus in Luke's account was Mary Magdalene. However, Luke refers to her as the woman whom Jesus cleansed from seven demons (see Luke 8:2). All the Gospel accounts place Mary as one of the first witnesses of Jesus' Resurrection. Mary Magdalene is a witness to God's mercy.

Reconciling Our Relationships

We can celebrate Reconciliation whenever we express our need for God's mercy and are sorry for our sins. The sacrament includes both the priest, who is the minister of the sacrament, and the penitent, who is seeking reconciliation with God and the Church.

Before confessing our sins to the priest, we first prepare for the sacrament through an examination of conscience. This is a reflection on our lives in light of the Gospel. It expresses our desire to enter into a deeper relationship with God. When we examine our conscience in this way, we are opening ourselves to God's grace. Reconciliation heals and transforms us into a new life with Christ.

? Which kinds of questions do you ask yourself when you examine your conscience?

The Rite of Penance

Another name for the Sacrament of Penance and Reconciliation is Confession. When we meet the priest in Confession, he welcomes us in the name of Jesus and the Church, inviting us to repentance. He may read a story or passage from the Bible, and then individually we confess, or tell the priest our sins, and express our sorrow.

The Church teaches that the penitent must confess to the priest all grave sins committed and not yet confessed. The Church forbids a priest ever to tell anything he hears in Confession. This frees us to be open and honest with God. The Church does not require that venial sins be confessed, but it is strongly recommended.

Next, the priest may suggest ways to grow closer to God. He then asks us to perform an act of penance. This way we can take responsibility for what we have done, and atone for the wrong we have committed. This penance might include a prayer, acts of charity, or works of mercy. The priest then asks us to tell God that we are sorry for our sins by praying the Act of Contrition.

On behalf of the Church, the priest then extends his hands over us and says a prayer of absolution. Through absolution by the priest, God heals us and grants pardon for our sins. Since we are sorry and willing to change, the Holy Spirit re-sanctifies us as temples of God. Finally, with the priest, we praise God for his mercy, and the priest encourages us to go in peace as a living sign of God's redeeming love.

122

FAITH-FILLED PEOPLE

Saint Mary Magdalene. Saint Mary Magdalene is often referred to as the "Apostle to the Apostles," for it was she who first announced news of the Resurrection of Jesus to the Apostles themselves. Sacred images and icons of Saint Mary Magdalene often depict her holding a red egg. Tradition states that, while at a dinner with the emperor Tiberius Caesar, Mary Magdalene was talking about the Resurrection. The emperor told her that the Resurrection could no more have happened than the egg in her hand could turn red. Upon making this statement, the egg in her hand did indeed turn red! For more information on Saint Mary Magdalene, go to the Saint Resource at www.BeMyDisciples.com.

The Graces of Reconciliation

Celebrating Reconciliation heals you spiritually. The grace of this sacrament is reconciliation. The Sacrament of Penance:

- restores and strengthens the life of grace with God, which sin has caused us to lose or weaken.

- renews our relationship with the Body of Christ, the Church.

- frees us from eternal separation from God.

- gives us the gift of peace and forgiveness, and the grace to follow Jesus Christ faithfully—even in the face of difficulties.

Jesus teaches that there is punishment connected with sin. In the Gospel he tells his disciples that when he comes again, he will separate the good from the wicked. To the evil ones he will say,

"Depart from me, you accursed, into the eternal fire prepared for the devil and his angels. . . . For I was thirsty and you gave me no drink, a stranger and you gave me no welcome, naked and you gave me no clothing, ill and in prison, and you did not care for me." MATTHEW 25:41–43

Punishment for sin is one of the consequences of our sinful acts. That punishment may be eternal or it may be temporary. Through prayers, good works, and indulgences, the faithful can obtain remission, or release, from this temporary punishment caused by sin. The baptized members of the Church can do this for us and for the souls in Purgatory. When we stray from God through sin, he calls us back with his mercy into his loving embrace within the Church.

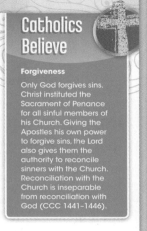

Catholics Believe

Forgiveness

Only God forgives sins. Christ instituted the Sacrament of Penance for all sinful members of his Church. Giving the Apostles his own power to forgive sins, the Lord also gives them the authority to reconcile sinners with the Church. Reconciliation with the Church is inseparable from reconciliation with God (CCC 1441–1446).

Activity Inventory the unnecessary material things in your life—those things you could really live without. Compare your list with others, and discuss how having too much can distract us from what is most important in life and lead us far from God.

_____

_____

_____

_____

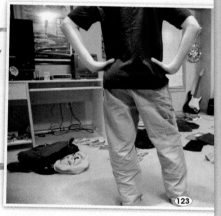

(123)

CATHOLICS BELIEVE

Celebrating Reconciliation. Regular participation in the Sacrament of Penance and Reconciliation is a vital way to prepare our minds and hearts for the coming of the Lord into our lives each day. When we celebrate Reconciliation, we strengthen our Baptismal promises to reject evil and live as children of God. Parishes commonly celebrate the communal rite of this sacrament during Advent and Lent. Check the parish bulletin for the dates and times of these celebrations in your parish. Pass this information on to the young people and their parents. Encourage them to take part in the celebrations.

Teach

▶ Have students silently read the definition of Reconciliation in the Faith Vocabulary section. Emphasize that the Sacrament of Penance and Reconciliation restores and strengthens our friendship with God and the Church, which we have broken or weakened by our sins.

▶ Have students read the text on the page. Reread the bullet points as a way to explain the importance of the Church in maintaining our relationship with God.

▶ Invite students to ask questions about any part they do not understand.

Reinforce

Then read aloud the Catholics Believe section. Have students explain in their own words why reconciliation with God is inseparable from reconciliation with the Church.

Connect

▶ Discuss how unnecessary material things can negatively impact a relationship with God.

▶ Have students complete the activity on the page and discuss their work.

Reinforce

▶ Recall with students that St. Monica had to commit daily to following Jesus.

▶ Point out that each of us is also called to be mindful of our actions and need the grace of the Holy Spirit to help us.

Respond

Introduce and explain the directions to the Examination of Conscience activity. Invite the students to complete the activity on the page. Explain to the young people that they do not have to share with the class what they wrote.

Choose

▶ Have students read My Faith Choice. Allow them time to reflect in silence about their commitment to God, especially in their daily activities. Encourage students to put their faith choice into practice this week.

▶ Time permitting, you can also teach the class the prayer, "Lord Jesus Christ, Son of the Living God, have mercy on me, a sinner." Explain that this prayer is known as the Jesus Prayer, as explained in the box on the next page.

I FOLLOW JESUS

Jesus gave the Church the Sacrament of Penance and Reconciliation so that you could have a way to seek and celebrate God's forgiveness for your sins. You can prepare to celebrate this sacrament by examining your conscience. Ask the Holy Spirit to help your take an honest look at your words and actions so that you can have better control of them and ask for God's forgiveness.

EXAMINATION OF CONSCIENCE

Work with a partner. Refer to the lists of Ten Commandments, Beatitudes, and Works of Mercy in the back of your textbook. From these references and from your knowledge of what God asks you to do, make a list of five questions that Christians should ask themselves in order to evaluate their daily words and actions. Record your questions below.

1.

2.

3.

4.

5.

MY FAITH CHOICE

This coming week, I will show my commitment to God through Works of Mercy and love. I will

_____

_____

 Pray, "Lord, let me be a witness for Christ through self-control and sacrifice. I ask this in Jesus' name. Amen."

(124)

TEACHING TIP

Examination of Conscience. Before having the students complete "Examination of Conscience," talk to them about cultivating the habit of reflecting on their day and the moral decisions they have made. Help them to develop questions to use in examining their conscience, using the Great Commandment (found on page 261), the Ten Commandments (page 261), and the Beatitudes (page 260) as guides. Direct them to write five or more reflection questions in their faith journals or on a separate piece of paper based on these moral teachings. Encourage them to examine their consciences using the questions at the end of each day for the next week. Begin next week's session by asking volunteers to share their experience of the daily examination of conscience.

Chapter Review

The words needed to complete the sentences are hidden in the puzzle. Find and circle the words. Then complete the sentences.

1. The first sacrament of forgiveness is _____Baptism_____.

2. _____Mortal_____ sins must be confessed in the Sacrament of Penance and Reconciliation.

3. Through the _____grace_____ received in Reconciliation, our relationship with God and the Church is restored and renewed.

4. In the Sacrament of Penance and Reconciliation, we receive the _____healing_____ needed from God, who alone can forgive sins.

5. Through _____absolution_____ by a priest, God heals us and grants pardon for our sins.

> ### TO HELP YOU REMEMBER
>
> 1. The Sacraments of Healing include both the Sacrament of Penance and Reconciliation and the Sacrament of Anointing of the Sick.
>
> 2. The Rite of Penance has a movement of conversion that includes repentance, confession, and absolution.
>
> 3. The Sacrament of Reconciliation is the sacrament through which we receive God's forgiveness for the sins that we commit after we have been baptized.

The Act of Contrition

In the Rite of Penance, before we receive absolution, the priest asks us to express our sorrow for our sins with the Act of Contrition. Take a moment of silence to examine your conscience using the questions you wrote for today's activity. Then pray together the Act of Contrition.

My God,

I am sorry for my sins with all my heart.

In choosing to do wrong

and failing to do good,

I have sinned against you

whom I should love above all things.

I firmly intend, with your help,

to do penance,

to sin no more,

and to avoid whatever leads me to sin.

Our Savior Jesus Christ

suffered and died for us.

In his name, my God, have mercy.

Amen.

(125)

THE TASKS OF CATECHESIS

Teaching to Pray. Paragraph 2616 of the *Catechism of the Catholic Church* reminds us that Jesus hears our prayers of faith whether they are offered aloud or in the silence of our hearts. Two such prayers of faith recorded in Scripture were offered by blind men seeking healing and forgiveness: "Son of David, have pity on us!" (Matthew 9:27) and "Son of David, have pity on me" (Mark 10:48). They are the foundation for a third prayer of faith often offered in silence: "Lord Jesus Christ, Son of God, have mercy on me, a sinner!" This prayer is known as the Jesus Prayer. Traditionally, the person praying the prayer breathes in on the words "Lord Jesus Christ, Son of God" and out on the words "have mercy on me, a sinner!" Before reciting the Act of Contrition in today's Closing Prayer, lead your students in praying the Jesus Prayer.

We Remember

▶ Review the major themes and concepts of the chapter using the To Help You Remember section. As you read the statements aloud, leave blank key terms and concepts for students to orally fill in.

▶ Introduce the Chapter Review activity by reading the directions aloud. Have the students complete the puzzle individually or in groups.

We Pray

▶ Gather the students for prayer. Introduce the prayer. Emphasize that we can pray the Act of Contrition anytime, not just during the Rite of Penance. Note that students may have learned a different wording for the Act of Contrition. There is no need to learn a new one.

▶ Allow time for students to examine their conscience using the questions they developed on page 124.

▶ Begin and end with the Sign of the Cross.

▶ Invite the students to write a short personal prayer of sorrow on a slip of paper and place in a basket on the prayer table.

▶ Lead the class in the Act of Contrition.

Preview

- Have students carefully tear-out the With My Family page along the perforation.

- Encourage them to share the pages with their family and to complete the activities together at home.

- If the students did not or were not able to complete the chapter review activity, encourage them to complete it with their family.

- Point out the title and theme of next week's chapter to the children.

Visit www.BeMyDisciples.com

- Take time with the students to explore the many activities and resources available at **www.BeMyDisciples.com.**

- Encourage especially them and their families to discover the many resources available at the Web site.

Before Moving On ...

As you finish today's lesson, reflect on the following question before moving on to the next chapter.

What do I do to affirm the sense of humor I see in the students?

With My Family

This Week...

In chapter 11, Penance and Reconciliation, your child learned:

- God shares his power to forgive sins with the Church through the Sacrament of Penance and Reconciliation.
- Through Reconciliation, we receive forgiveness for the sins committed after Baptism.
- Confession of sins, contrition (or sorrow), penance, and absolution are always part of the Rite of Penance.
- Discipline and self-control demonstrate our commitment to God.

For more about related teachings of the Church, see the *Catechism of the Catholic Church*, 1420–1498; and the *United States Catholic Catechism for Adults*, pages 233–247.

◼ Sharing God's Word

Read together John 20:21–23. Emphasize that Jesus gave the Church the power to forgive sins.

◼ We Live as Disciples

The Christian home and family form a school of discipleship. Choose one of the following activities to do as a family, or design a similar activity of your own:

- When your family has strife in your relationships, practice the movement of conversion: seek repentance, identify the harm done, express contrition and forgiveness, and pray for God's grace to renew the relationship.

- During mealtime or bedtime prayers, include occasionally the prayer of the penitent: "Lord Jesus, Son of God, have mercy on me a sinner."

◼ Our Spiritual Journey

Living a life more pleasing to God includes seeking his forgiveness and mercy. Conditioning our hearts to accept God's mercy often involves sacrifice and putting the needs of others before our own. This is possible by practicing self-control. How can you, as a family, practice self-control so that sacrifice is a priority?

For more ideas on ways that your family can live as disciples of Jesus, visit **www.BeMyDisciples.com**

(126)

PARTNERING WITH PARENTS

Focus on Reconciliation. As a follow-up to this session, contact parents through e-mail or a written note. Provide the instructions below for them to complete the Media Watch activity as a family.

Media Watch

1. During the coming week, list all TV shows watched together as a family.

2. Put a star by those shows that illustrate the importance of reconciliation. Name specific reasons for giving a star to those shows.

3. Using the same list, put an "x" by the shows that illustrate what happens when people sin or fail to make peace. Again, name specific reasons for putting an "x" by the names of those shows.

Enriching the Lesson

Writing in Journals

Purpose

To reinforce that Jesus taught about God's mercy, forgiveness and healing (taught on page 121)

Directions

▶ Have the students select one of these Gospel passages, look it up in their Bible, and prayerfully read it as a prayer of meditation.

- Matthew 6:9–15 (The Lord's Prayer)
- Mark 2:1–12 (The Healing of the Paralytic)
- Luke 6: 27–37 (Love of Enemies)
- John 20:19–23 (Appearance to the Disciples)

▶ Have them write their reflections in their journal and make a faith choice to live Jesus' ministry of forgiveness.

Materials

Bibles

journals

pens or pencils

Designing Reconciliation Guides

Purpose

To reinforce the movement of conversion that occurs during the Rite of Penance (taught on page 122)

Directions

▶ Have the students work with partners or in small groups to create Reconciliation Guides. Help them imagine how their guide can be like a travel guide, intended to help a person navigate their way through celebrating the Sacrament of Penance and Reconciliation.

▶ Brainstorm with the class a list of descriptive action words and phrases that tell about the movement of conversion during the Rite of Penance; for example, repentance, confession, and absolution.

▶ Ask each group to choose words or phrases from this master class list to create their travel guide. Then find images that reflect these words or phrases as well as the physical environment of a confessional.

▶ Invite the groups to share their guide.

▶ Optional: instead of producing a paper guide made of construction paper, you might invite your class or some students to build a digital e-guide with video and/or music.

Materials

construction paper

magazine images

digital camera

pens or pencils

(optional) computer

Creating Scenarios about Forgiveness

Purpose

To reinforce that Reconciliation bestows sacramental graces (taught on page 123)

Directions

▶ Present a scenario in which a young preteen, Tom, intentionally destroys a favorite possession of another young preteen, Ashley.

▶ Have small groups plan and present scenarios showing what happens next.

▶ Ask the students to discuss the question in detail before preparing their skits.

▶ Ask the students to judge how each skit does or does not reflect Jesus' teaching about forgiveness.

▶ Summarize with the class the importance of true sorrow and making reparation as elements of forgiveness.

Materials

newsprint

pens or pencils

BACKGROUND

A Faith That Heals

Sometimes our own personal experiences of suffering or witnessing and sharing in the sufferings of others can weaken or even shake our trust and hope in God (see *Catechism of the Catholic Church* 164). When this happens, there is a long litany of our ancestors in faith to whom we might turn to renew our faith and hope. For example, Abraham and Sarah bore many hardships. Mary, Our Lady of Sorrows, stood at the foot of the cross as her son died.

Trust in God

Our ancestors in faith testify by the example of their lives that they trusted God in the midst of tremendous hardship and pain. That trust gave them the strength to cope with suffering. The stories of so many men and women of faith today likewise reveal the same response of steadfast trust in God in the face of human suffering, misery, and evil.

God is not the author of suffering, nor does God bring about evil. The deprivation and pain involved in mental, physical, spiritual, or emotional suffering are present in our world as a result of original sin and continue to be a part of the human experience. Some suffering can be attributed to natural, worldly processes. If we put our hands into a fire, we will experience intense, immediate pain and often long-term discomfort and scarring. Other types of suffering result from the tragedy of sin and the evil choices humans continue to make.

Blessed Are Those Who Suffer in Faith

Christ did not come to do away with suffering. He came to take away the sting of suffering and death and replace it with the joy of eternal life. Suffering and death no longer have the final say. Jesus instructed his disciples that they would bear many crosses (see Matthew 5:11–12).

Christ has redeemed the world and has freed us from the power of suffering, death, and sin. Many of the miracle stories in the Gospels invite us to believe that God is with us in our suffering and pain. The Good News of Christ, who entered into our experience of suffering and pain, and who, indeed, took on the burden of our suffering, is that we ultimately have been saved in Christ.

Through his loving self-sacrifice, Christ heals our sinfulness. By the power of his own suffering and cross, Jesus Christ makes possible the transformation of every debilitating experience we undergo. Believers have the grace to respond to the difficulty and pain of human suffering. We personally appropriate through prayer, the sacraments, and Christian solidarity, the healing power of Christ's Paschal Mystery, knowing that when we suffer we share in the suffering of Christ. Our experience will ultimately be redemptive.

For Reflection

How aware am I of the presence of the God of compassion who willingly suffers with me?

When have I willingly suffered on behalf of another?

Catechist to Catechist

The Problem of Suffering

Some of your students may have experienced the death or long-term suffering of a loved one or friend. They may have heard about the sudden death of a classmate or a high school student from an automobile accident or overdose of drugs. They may have experienced the sudden and hurtful break-up of a friendship. These experiences wound our hearts. In the search for healing, we naturally ask, "Why?" Jesus revealed that God the Father's healing love is always present and active among us and within us. We need to reach out in faith and hope to the healing power of divine love that is always present to us.

Why? — lessons — ?

Accepting God's Healing Grace

Jesus Christ is the ever-present source of healing in times of suffering. As you present this lesson on the Sacrament of Anointing of the Sick, retell the account of Jesus in the Garden of Gethsemane. Give the students time to reflect on the ways that Jesus dealt with suffering—suffering that came from his Passion and Death. Help the students discover that Jesus found strength in trusting his Father.

solitary prayer

The Church Teaches...

"Human beings are unique in creation because they alone can offer God a response of faith to his initiative of love. The response of faith has two integral dimensions: the faith by which one believes and the faith which one believes. . . . The faith by which one believes is itself a gift from God. It is God's grace that moves and assists the individual to believe" (*National Directory for Catechesis*, 16C).

Through miracles, Jesus invited his followers to believe and trust in God. His miracles continue to invite us to that same faith and trust. By communicating God's gentle love and mercy, the children will come to know the healing power of his love in the Sacrament of Anointing of the Sick.

Further Reading and Reflection

For more on the teachings of the *Church,* see the *Catechism of the Catholic Church,* 1499–1532; and from the *United States Catholic Catechism for Adults,* pages 249–259.

Catechist Prayer

Holy Spirit,
help me serve others
as Christ did.
Amen.

Lesson Planner

Chapter 14   Anointing of the Sick

Focus To learn about healing and the Sacrament of the Anointing of the Sick

LESSON PART	PROCESS	MATERIALS and RESOURCES
EXPLORE **Focus** **To explore the power of gentleness and healing** 🕐 10 minutes **Pages** 127–128	▶ Proclaim and discuss Psalm 102:2–6 (Do not hide your face from me). ▶ Hear the story about a Catholic hospice. **Disciple Power:** Gentleness	Bible Pencils Crayons or markers
DISCOVER **Focus** **To discover the meaning and rite of the Sacrament of the Anointing of the Sick** 🕐 30 minutes **Pages** 129–131	▶ Learn about the Sacrament of the Anointing of the Sick. **Activity:** Act out a Gospel story. ▶ Review the Rite of Anointing. **Activity:** Create a Service of Healing Poster. ▶ Identify the graces of the Sacrament of the Anointing of the Sick.	Card stock paper **Additional Activities Booklet:** Activities 14a–14b, or see BeMyDisciples.com.
DECIDE **Focus** **To decide on a response to the lesson on Jesus' healing love** 🕐 10 minutes **Page** 132	**Activity:** Make a gentle offer of hope. **My Faith Choice:** Connect healing and gentleness.	**Enriching the Lesson Activities:** Catechist Edition, page 223 • Creating Healing Songs • Writing in Journals • Illustrating a book

Concluding the Lesson 10 minutes

We Remember

Page 133

▶ Review concepts and do the review activity.

▶ **Assessment Tools Booklet:** Chapter Test 14a–14b, or see BeMyDisciples.com.

We Pray

▶ **Prayer:** a Litany of Saints for the sick

Materials: Bible, candle, cross for prayer space

▶ Grade 6 Music CD

Preview

Point out resources for this chapter at

www.BeMyDisciples.com

▶ Preview the With My Family page and next week's lesson theme.

Looking Ahead

In this chapter the Holy Spirit invites you to ▶

EXPLORE gentleness that people experience from hospice care.

DISCOVER the healing ministry of Jesus in the Anointing of the Sick.

DECIDE on a moral way of caring for one who is suffering.

CHAPTER **14**

Anointing of the Sick

? What helped you feel better the last time you were sick? What do you think is necessary for someone to feel healed spiritually?

In this psalm of lament, the person is severely afflicted and pours out his anguish and pain before the Lord:

> LORD, hear my prayer;
>   let my cry come to you.
> Do not hide your face from me
>   now that I am in distress...
> For my days vanish like smoke;
>   my bones burn away as in a furnace . . .
> From my loud groaning
>   I become just skin and bones.   PSALM 102:2–6

? How do you think the Lord who is love and mercy responds to those who are suffering?

(127)

HUMAN METHODOLOGIES

Learning through the Witness of the Catechist. The *National Directory for Catechesis* emphasizes the importance of the witness of the catechist, most especially through the example they set by their own Christian living (*NDC* 29E). One dimension of ministering to the sick is ministering to ourselves so that we do not become ill. In order to be instruments of God's healing love and service to others, we need to take the time to pray and to nurture our own body and soul. Caring for ourselves enables us to be more effective models of Christ, bringing his healing presence to others, including the young people we serve. Model a healthy lifestyle for your sixth graders and encourage them to eat healthy meals and get enough sleep.

"Minister" to sick (and others) via caring for self.

Providing healthy snacks.

Pray

▶ Establish a sense of calmness by inviting the students to close their eyes and relax in silence.

▶ Open and close with the Sign of the Cross.

▶ Pray:
Dear God, be with us today. Show your mercy to those who are suffering in our world. Amen.

Reflect

▶ Explain to the students that in this chapter they will learn and discuss a very difficult topic: how to deal with suffering and caring for the sick.

▶ Help students prepare to focus on the topic of suffering by asking the opening questions and inviting responses.

▶ Read aloud Psalm 102:2–12.

▶ Invite volunteers to respond to what they heard.

▶ Discuss the questions related to the Scripture. You might also invite the students to discuss the images on the page as relevant to the chapter topic.

Focus

▶ Explain that in this chapter they will learn more about the healing ministry of Jesus, especially in the Sacrament of Anointing of the Sick.

▶ Call the students' attention to the Looking Ahead feature. Invite them to read aloud each bullet.

Introduce

▶ Point out the Disciple Power box on the page. Ask a student to read the box aloud.

▶ Explain that the story on the page is a snapshot of a grandson visiting his grandfather in hospice care.

▶ Inquire if any students have ever visited a hospice center. Ask them to share what it was like.

▶ Explain that it is OK to feel uncertain and even scared when they visit people who are ill.

Reinforce

Have students read the definition of hospice care on the following page and make a word card for it. Then have students read aloud the text on the page.

Connect

▶ Invite the students to discuss the closing question. Explain that experiencing the caring warmth of a loving family is beneficial to those who suffer.

▶ Have students read the question on the page and share their responses.

Disciple Power

Gentleness

When we exercise the virtue of temperance, the Holy Spirit provides us with this fruit, which is related to self-control. A gentle person is one who pardons injury and is free from harshness, even in the face of injury or illness. A sense of gentleness is a sense of calming peace and care in the way we treat others and ourselves.

THE CHURCH FOLLOWS JESUS

The Caring Warmth of Family

Everyone, at some point in his or her life, experiences sorrow and pain. With the support of family and faith in God, we can find comfort during such times of difficulty. Here is what one teen named Edgardo recently experienced.

"This past weekend was a really hard time," he told his friend, Tom, at school. "My family and I visited my grandfather, who was receiving **hospice care**".

Edgardo told Tom that Lolo, his grandfather, had been living at Sunrise Community for the past two years. His family visited Lolo almost every Sunday after Mass. "This time was different," he said. "I knew it as soon as we walked into his room."

Tom asked what was so different this time. "I know you love your grandfather," he said, "but you've said it can be hard visiting him sometimes because he is so sick."

"This time was different" Edgardo replied. "This time there was a strange sense of peace and calm, even though Lolo was feeling weak, and was still in bed. He asked me over to tell me something." Tom interrupted, "What did he say?"

"Edgardo," he said, "remember that there is no bread too hard for warm coffee."

Tom asked, "What did he mean by that?"

Edgardo told Tom, "Lolo would say that often to me. Years ago, I asked my father what Lolo meant. My father said it is a wise Filipino saying. And that I will learn what it means as I grow older."

"What else happened?" Tom asked.

"That was it." Lolo smiled. "The priest came and anointed him with oil and we prayed together. Lolo then closed his eyes. My father held Lolo's strong hands, and then Lolo passed away. It felt so peaceful and calm, even though I was crying."

 What do you think Edgardo's grandfather meant when he said, "Remember that there is no bread too hard for warm coffee"?

(128)

DISCIPLE POWER

Gentleness. Write each of the situations listed below, or other examples you may think of, on individual slips of paper. Divide the students into small groups of three or four. Have each group choose one of the paper slips and discuss possible gentle and harsh responses to the situation they chose. Have each group share their ideas with the class.

1. Your sister or brother breaks one of your favorite toys.

2. Your teammate commits an error that causes your team to lose the game.

3. Your mom or dad is unable to keep their promise to take you to the mall.

4. Your best friend tells someone else something you asked them to keep secret.

Healing the Sick

In the Old Testament, we read the story of how the people of Israel became ill in the desert (see Numbers 21:4–9). At God's direction, Moses lifted up a bronze serpent, and all who looked on it were healed. The Church has understood that lifting up the bronze serpent prefigured the lifting up of Jesus on the cross. By his suffering, Death, and Resurrection, Jesus heals the whole human family. Each of us is called to embrace Jesus' healing by receiving grace in the sacraments.

Throughout his life on Earth, Jesus healed those who were sick physically and spiritually. Matthew tells us,

Jesus went around to all the towns and villages, teaching in their synagogues, proclaiming the gospel of the kingdom, and curing every disease and illness. MATTHEW 9:35

In the Gospel of Luke, people flocked to Jesus in the hope that he would cure them of their various diseases (read Luke 4:40). This work of Jesus invited people both to see how much God loves them and to place their trust and faith in him. Jesus also sent his disciples to carry out his ministry of healing in his name.

So [the Twelve] went off and preached repentance. They drove out many demons, and they anointed with oil many who were sick and cured them. MARK 6:12–13

Today, the Church continues Jesus' ministry of healing through the Sacraments of Healing, including the **Anointing of the Sick**. Anyone who is seriously ill can receive the Sacrament of Anointing of the Sick. For those who are in danger of death because of illness or old age, the sacrament is especially important.

FAITH FOCUS
How does Jesus continue his healing ministry in the Church today?

FAITH VOCABULARY
Anointing of the Sick
The Anointing of the Sick is the Sacrament of Healing that strengthens our faith, hope, and love for God when we are seriously ill, weakened by old age, or dying.

hospice care
Hospice care is a ministry of caring for the terminally ill by offering them gentle end-of-life care that respects the dignity of the human person, according to Church teachings.

Activity
Choose one of the following Gospel accounts of Jesus' healing ministry. Act it out with a group of your classmates.

Healing a blind man: John 9:1–7, 35–38
Healing a sick man: John 5:1–8
Healing an official's son: John 4:43–53 or Luke 7:1–10
Healing a crippled man: Luke 5:17–25
Healing a dying girl and a sick woman: Luke 8:40–55; Matthew 9:18–26; or Mark 5:21–43
Healing two blind men: Matthew 20:29–34

129

THE TASKS OF CATECHESIS

Liturgical Formation. Have your students read and discuss the passage from James 5:14–16. Then help them to understand the Church Tradition of care for the sick by paraphrasing the following information for them. "The Lord himself showed great concern for the bodily and spiritual welfare of the sick and commanded his followers to do likewise. This is clear from the Gospels, and above all from the existence of the Sacrament of the Anointing of the Sick, which Christ instituted and which is made known in the Letter of James. Since then the Church has never ceased to celebrate this sacrament for its members by the anointing and the prayer of its priests, commending those who are ill to the suffering and glorified Lord, that he may raise them up and save them" (*General Introduction, Pastoral Care of the Sick 5*).

Key Concept
The Church continues the healing ministry of Christ in the Sacrament of Anointing of the Sick.

Teach

▶ Discuss the "Faith Focus" question as a class.

▶ Have the students read Numbers 21:4-9 silently. Then read the first paragraph. Ask: What connection can you see between lifting up the serpent and The Cross of Christ?

▶ Have students read the rest of the text on the page. Discuss how the Church continues Jesus' ministry of healing today.

Reinforce

Read aloud and make a word card for Anointing of the Sick.

Connect

▶ Recall who can receive the Sacrament of the Anointing of the Sick. Ask anyone who has ever witnessed this sacrament to share his or her experience.

▶ Distribute Bibles. Have the students work in small groups to complete the activity on the page.

▶ Emphasize that Jesus came to heal the whole person, both the physical and spiritual. To respect the dignity of the whole person, we must do the same.

Key Concept
Anointing of the Sick includes three statements: prayer, laying on of hands, and anointing with oil.

Teach

▶ Have students read the text on the page. Invite them to identify other ways in which the Church uses oil (*Baptism, Confirmation, RCIA, Chrism Mass, Dedicating a new church*). Explain that the Church has three holy oils: Sacred Chrism, Oil of the Sick, and Oil of the Catechumens. These are reserved in the ambry of the parish.

▶ Discuss the three aspects of the celebration of the Rite of Anointing. List these on the board.

Reinforce

▶ Pass around a small bottle of olive oil. Allow students to smell and touch the oil.

▶ Invite students to describe their sensation of handling the oil. Point out that oil has always been considered an element of strength.

▶ Read the Faith-filled People section.

Connect

Invite the students to complete the activity and share their work.

Faith-Filled People

Saint Rafqa

During her life, Rafqa experienced personal suffering and witnessed bloody conflict while living in war-torn Lebanon in the mid-1800s. By 1871, Rafqa had joined a monastic order, which she remained with until the last few years of her life. Having experienced intense pain and paralysis, she responded with humility, believing her suffering was united with Christ's. Despite her condition, Rafqa remained patient and uncomplaining.

Ministering to the Sick

From her very beginning, the Church has ministered to the sick in a special way. The New Testament Letter of James states:

Is anyone among you sick? He should summon the presbyters of the church, and they should pray over him and anoint [him] with oil in the name of the Lord, and the prayer of faith will save the sick person, and the Lord will raise him up. If he has committed any sins, he will be forgiven.
JAMES 5:14–15

Anointing of the Sick may be received each time we become seriously ill. We also may receive this sacrament more than once during the same illness if our sickness becomes worse. Those who are to undergo surgery are also encouraged to receive this sacrament.

Rite of Anointing

In the Rite of Anointing, there are three essential aspects to the celebration of the sacrament: the prayer of faith, the laying on of hands, and the anointing with oil. Only the priest is the minister of the sacrament.

The oil used to anoint is blessed by the bishop, or if necessary, blessed by a delegated priest. The priest usually anoints the forehead and hands of the sick, but other parts of the body may also be anointed, if deemed necessary.

The Church uses oil because of its natural healing powers and because anointing oil is soothing and comforting. The oil is a sign of healing and signifies the comforting presence of God for the sick person. When the priest is generous in its use, the sick person can better experience the sign of the Holy Spirit's healing and strengthening presence.

Through the celebration of the Sacrament of Anointing of the Sick, Christ's work of healing continues in the world today. His healing presence helps the sick and dying find courage, strength, and hope.

> **Activity** Work with a group. Create a poster to publicize a Service of Healing that your parish is having. Include a slogan that will encourage the whole parish community to attend. Write your idea for a slogan here.
>
> _____
>
> _____
>
> _____

(130)

FAITH-FILLED PEOPLE

Saint Rafqa. Rafqa was born in Lebanon on the feast of Saint Peter, June 29, 1832. Her baptismal name, Boutrosiya, is—when pronounced in Arabic—the feminine of Peter. When she was 21, she became a nun in the Marian Order of the Immaculate Conception of Bikfaya, and chose the religious name Anissa, or Agnes. Later, she joined the Lebanese Order of Saint Anthony of the Maronites and took the religious name of Rafqa, or Rebecca. Rafqa's deepest desire was to share in the sufferings of Christ, and she did suffer much physical pain in the last 29 years of her life. It is said that she never complained about her sufferings and that she remained joyful in Christ. Rafqa died on March 23, 1914, and was canonized by Pope John Paul II on June 10, 2001. For more information on Saint Rafqa, go to the Saint Resource at BeMyDisciples.com.

The Graces of Holy Anointing

In the Sacrament of Anointing of the Sick, we receive many graces. Some of the important graces of this sacrament are:

Our sufferings are united with those of Jesus, and in this union, we find strength and consolation, knowing that the Lord is with us.

We receive peace and courage to face our sufferings as a gift from the Holy Spirit.

We can receive the forgiveness of our sins if we are unable to celebrate the Sacrament of Penance and Reconciliation.

Our health may be restored; however, equally important, we receive a spiritual healing by the intercession of the Church.

We are prepared for our final journey to eternal life when we are very ill and near death.

Through the celebration of the Sacrament of Anointing of the Sick, Christ continues his work of healing among us. Having our close family and friends by our side when we receive this sacrament is beneficial in experiencing the support and love of the whole Church. With faith and trust in God, we can face our suffering by offering it up as our sacrifice, in imitation of Christ's suffering on the cross.

? What are some of the ways your parish works with people who are sick? Talk with your friends about things you and they can do to help.

Catholics Believe

Respect for Those Who Suffer

Those who suffer illness or physical limitations deserve special respect. Even if death is imminent, the normal care of a sick person should not be interrupted, nor is it morally permissible to intentionally end someone's life if they are suffering greatly or are terminally ill. Neither are we to prolong a person's natural death through the overzealous use of medical treatment.

131

CATHOLIC DOCTRINE

The Life and Dignity of Every Person. All humans are created in the image and likeness of God. Therefore, all human life is sacred. This truth is the source of the fundamental dignity of every person. The ministry of the Catholic Church to the sick, dying, and elderly is one significant way she implements this social teaching.

Tip: Work with the appropriate parish staff person to help organize practical ways the students can visit or minister to the elderly of the parish who are homebound or being cared for in a healthcare residence.

Teach

▶ Have students reread the definition of Anointing of the Sick in the "Faith Vocabulary" section. Emphasize that this Sacrament strengthens our faith, hope and love for God.

▶ Then read aloud the "Catholics Believe" section. Emphasize that intentionally ending the life of someone who is suffering or terminally ill is morally wrong. This is euthanasia.

▶ Have students read the text on the page.

Reinforce

Reread the bullet points as a way to explain the importance of God's comforting and healing presence in our lives.

Connect

Discuss in small groups how they can help people in their parish who are sick.

Reinforce

Then invite a student to read the opening paragraph at the top of the page.

Respond

▶ Invite the young people to work alone to complete the activity. Ask volunteers to save their work.

▶ Option: Have students decorate "get-well" cards for those within the parish who are sick.

▶ If the card option is chosen, invite the students to make this activity of decorating the cards a prayer that they can offer for the healing of those who are sick. After the cards are completed, offer a prayer of petition, listing the names of the people for whom the cards were made.

▶ Give the cards to the appropriate person on the parish staff to deliver to the sick.

Choose

▶ Have students complete the last section to make their faith choice.

▶ Encourage students to pray for all who are suffering in any way, using the prayer at the bottom of the page.

I FOLLOW JESUS

One of the important characteristics of Jesus' healing was his gentle touch. The Church sees his gentle touch as a sign of respecting the dignity of the human person, especially in times of pain and suffering.

GENTLE OFFER OF HOPE

Think of people in your family, your neighborhood, school, or parish who may be physically or spiritually suffering. Choose a way you could help to ease their pain—a card, a poem, or a drawing that would offer them hope and encouragement in the name of Jesus. Use this space to outline or sketch your idea.

MY FAITH CHOICE

This week, I will be more aware of people and situations that need healing and offer a gentle hand when I can. I will

_____

_____

Pray, "Lord Jesus, may your gentle touch restore those who are suffering and lead them to your glory. Amen."

(132)

TEACHING TIP

Moral Dilemmas. Offering young people hypothetical moral situations to discuss and resolve is an effective strategy in developing their skills for making moral decisions. When you use moral dilemmas, do not be too disappointed, however, if the students do not come to obvious conclusions. When they come to a conclusion that is off the mark, ask a clarifying question, such as "Can anyone else see another option?" It is always a good idea to summarize by clearly stating the moral principles that were used to correctly resolve the dilemma.

Chapter Review

Read each sentence, and choose the best answer to complete it. Circle the corresponding letter to the correct answer.

1. The Sacrament of Anointing of the Sick is especially for
   a. those who are in danger of death because of illness or old age.
   b. those who have already died.
   c. those who are not feeling well.

2. In the Rite of Anointing, who anoints the body of the sick person?
   a. the doctor
   b. the priest
   c. the closest family member

3. Which of the following is an essential element used in the celebration of the Sacrament of Anointing of the Sick?
   a. Holy water
   b. Bread
   c. Blessed oil

TO HELP YOU REMEMBER

1. The Church continues Jesus' ministry of healing in the Sacraments of Healing, including the Sacrament of Anointing of the sick.

2. Anointing of the Sick is the sacrament that strengthens our faith and trust in God when we are seriously ill or dying.

3. The Rite of Anointing consists of the prayer of faith, the laying on of hands, and the anointing with oil.

Prayer for the Sick

Saint James tells us to pray for the sick. During the care for the sick and dying, the Church prays a brief form of the Litany of the Saints. Think of people you know or have heard about who are sick, and write in their names to include in this prayer.

Leader:	All:
Holy Mary, Mother of God,	pray for _____.
Saint Joseph,	pray for _____.
Saint Peter,	pray for _____.
Saint James,	pray for _____.
Saint Mary Magdalene,	pray for _____.
Saint Lawrence,	pray for _____.
Saint Paul of the Cross,	pray for _____.
Saint Benedict of Nursia,	pray for _____.
Saint Teresa of the Andes,	pray for _____.
Saint Rafqa,	pray for _____.

(133)

Litany. The litany is a form of prayer in which a leader offers a series of invocations, alternating with responses recited by the assembly. There are many litanies that have developed through the centuries. Probably the best known is the Litany of the Saints sung at the Easter Vigil and sometimes at celebrations of Baptism during Sunday Mass. Since the form of the litany is simple, it is an easy form of prayer for young people to learn. If possible, sing the litany in today's closing prayer. Use a familiar chant sung at your parish. Take a moment to practice the sung response with the students by using an example one or two from the names they wrote.

We Remember

▶ Introduce the Chapter Review activity by reading the directions aloud. Have the students complete the sentences individually.

▶ Review the major themes and concepts of the chapter using the To Help You Remember section. As you read aloud the statements to the class, have students identify something new they learned about that particular point.

We Pray

▶ Gather the students for prayer. Introduce the prayer by reading the introductory paragraph.

▶ Lead the class in the prayer, beginning and ending with the Sign of the Cross.

▶ Invite the students to offer names of people they know who are sick or elderly. Invite the students to write these names on the lines so that all can pray for one another's intentions.

Preview

▶ Have students carefully tear-out the With My Family page along the perforation.

▶ Encourage them to share the pages with their family and to complete the activities together at home.

▶ If the students did not or were not able to complete the Chapter Review activity, encourage them to complete it with their family.

▶ Point out the title and theme of next week's chapter to the children.

Visit www.BeMyDisciples.com

▶ Take time with the students to explore the many activities and resources available at **www.BeMyDisciples.com.**

▶ Encourage especially them and their families to discover the many resources available at the Web site.

Before Moving On ...

As you finish today's lesson, reflect on the following question before moving on to the next chapter.

What am I doing to involve every student to actively participate in class?

With My Family

This Week...

In chapter 14, Anointing of the Sick, your child learned that:

▶ The healing ministry of Jesus was directed to those physically and spiritually in need.

▶ The Church continues Christ's healing ministry to those who are seriously sick and weak because of old age through the Sacrament of Anointing of the Sick.

▶ The Church extends the gentle touch of Jesus through other ministries, like hospice care. Gentleness is a fruit of the Holy Spirit, that brings peace to others.

For more about related teachings of the Church, see the *Catechism of the Catholic Church,* 1499–1532; and the *United States Catholic Catechism for Adults,* pages 249–259.

■ Sharing God's Word

Read James 5:14–15. Emphasize that the Church continues Jesus' ministry of healing in the Sacrament of Anointing of the Sick.

■ We Live as Disciples

The Christian home and family form a school of discipleship. Choose one of the following activities to do as a family, or design a similar activity of your own:

▶ Talk about the ways in which your family cares for one another when sick. Include extended family members like grandparents, aunts, uncles, and other relatives.

▶ Form the habit of having your child accompany you when you visit someone who is elderly or experiencing an extended convalescence. Have your child make a small gift to bring cheer to that person. Teach by your example to be thoughtful, gentle, and kind.

■ Our Spiritual Journey

Dealing with end-of-life issues can be very difficult for both children and adults. Experiencing the support of family and the Church community is vital and can help prepare us. Celebrate frequently the heritage of your family, and recall fond memories of previous generations.

For more ideas on ways that your family can live as disciples of Jesus, visit **www.BeMyDisciples.com**

(134)

PLANNING AHEAD

Classroom Visit. Next week's chapter focuses on the Sacrament of Holy Orders. Invite a parish priest or deacon to come to speak with the young people about his experience of receiving the Sacrament of Holy Orders and his ministry to the Church community.

Enriching the Lesson

Creating Healing Songs

Purpose

To reinforce that each of us can contribute to the physical and spiritual healing of someone who is ill or in need (taught on page 129)

Directions

▶ Have the students work in small groups to write chants or simple melodies that would encourage or support a person who is ill or in need. Encourage them to re-read Scripture passages mentioned in this chapter for inspiration.

▶ Invite groups to write their songs on the board or on newsprint. Then have them sing their chants or read the words aloud.

▶ Invite the groups to create a CD cover for their songs. Have them choose a title for the CD, illustrate the front cover, and include a list of songs on the reverse side.

▶ Have groups share their CD cover.

▶ (Optional) if possible have student record their music to play for someone they know who is ill or in need.

Materials

construction paper

markers or crayons

(optional) computer with microphone

Writing in Journals

Purpose

To reinforce God's gift of healing (taught on page 130)

Directions

▶ Ask the students to think silently about their own or someone in their family, experience of being healed (physically and spiritually).

▶ Then have them look up, read, and prayerfully meditate on a miracle of healing from Scripture, for example, the Healing of the Blind Beggar (Luke 18:35–43).

▶ Ask the students to write their reflections in their journal.

▶ Have them include a prayer of thanksgiving to God for the gift of his mercy and the power of healing.

Materials

Bibles

journals

pens or pencils

Illustrating a Book

Purpose

To reinforce that the Holy Spirit gives each person the grace to respond to his invitation to share in Jesus' work of healing (taught on page 131)

Directions

▶ Brainstorm with the students ways they can reach out to a young child who is ill.

▶ Have the students work with partners to create a booklet that contains appropriate jokes, riddles, codes, and other fun activities that can be shared with a child in the parish who is sick at home or in the hospital.

▶ Gather the pages and have the class work together to create the booklet.

▶ Check with the pastor or other appropriate parish staff person to have the booklet delivered to the parents of the child.

Materials

construction paper

pens or pencils

markers or crayons

BACKGROUND

Called to Serve the Church

Christ did not only institute the Eucharist at the Last Supper. He did another remarkable thing. He revealed the nature of the service he requires of his disciples. Jesus Christ, the Servant King, wrapped a towel around his waist and washed and dried his disciples' feet. Making sure that no one missed the point of what he was doing, he said:

> "If I, . . . the master and teacher, have washed your feet, you ought to wash one another's feet. I have given you a model to follow, so that as I have done for you, you should also do."
>
> John 13:14–15

Vocation

As baptized Christians we are all called to serve God. The Holy Spirit strengthens all believers for the Church's mission of service. Apart from the universal vocation to which we are all called, some members of the Church are invited to help build up the Church on earth into the new People of God, the Body of Christ, and the Temple of the Holy Spirit in a different manner. The work they are to carry out is marked by the two Sacraments at the Service of Communion, Matrimony, and Holy Orders. "Those among the faithful who have received Holy Orders are appointed to nourish the Church with the word and grace of God in the name of Christ" (*Dogmatic Constitution on the Church* 11).

Holy Orders

Holy Orders is the sacrament by which Christ's mission that was entrusted to the Apostles is carried on in the Church until he returns. In Holy Orders baptized men are consecrated as bishops and priests to serve the whole Church in the name and person of Christ by teaching, leading divine worship, and governing the Church as Jesus, the Good Shepherd, did. Deacons

are ordained and configured to Christ, the servant of all (see *Catechism of the Catholic Church,* 1570). They are chosen from among the people. Christ remains the one true priest and ministers through those ordained in his name. Through bishops, priests, and deacons the presence of Christ, the Head of the Church, is made visible in the midst of the Church around the world.

Three Degrees of Holy Orders

The bishops and the priests participate in the priesthood of Christ. In the order of bishop the fullness of the Sacrament of Holy Order is conferred. The priest is a co-worker of the bishop. He is entrusted to offer the Eucharist, to bless, to govern, to preach, and to baptize in the name of the bishop. The Order of Deacon is to serve and assist the bishop and the priest with various rites, at the altar, and with ministries of charity.

For Reflection

Who are bishops, priests, and deacons, I know who exemplify this kind of holiness?

Where am I called to service in my life as a disciple of Jesus?

Catechist to Catechist

The Meaning of Success

In the Gospel of Mark, the Apostles James and John asked Jesus for grandeur (see Mark 10:35–45). Jesus responded that greatness comes from serving others. What is the standard for success for a Christian? Is making it to the top of one's career or having wealth contrary to the Gospel? The standard for Christian living is that we commit ourselves and our blessings to the generous service of the Gospel by serving others, especially those in most need.

Seeking Success

Young people enthusiastically join in projects that serve others. When a need arises in your local community or parish, bring the needs to the attention of the students. There are also many other smaller ways young people can serve others as Jesus did. Take advantage of these smaller moments as they occur during your sessions. It is important to awaken the students' sensitivity to recognizing the many small and unseen ways they can serve—and be truly successful in living the Gospel.

The Church Teaches...

"Learning by apprenticeship ordinarily includes the profession of faith, education in the knowledge of the faith, celebration of the mysteries of the faith, practice of the Christian moral virtues, and dedication to the daily patterns of Christian prayer. It is a guided encounter with the entire Christian life, a journey toward conversion to Christ" (*National Directory for Catechesis*, 30H).

The Church is the new People of God who has the mission and responsibility to serve as Christ served. In this chapter, the children will reflect on the Church's ministry of service given to her by Christ through the Sacrament of Holy Orders.

Further Reading and Reflection

For more on the teachings of the Church, see the *Catechism of the Catholic Church*, 1533-1600; and from the *United States Catholic Catechism for Adults*, pages 261–275.

Catechist Prayer

Lord Jesus, you said, "This is my body." Help me to become the bread that feeds the needs of others. Amen.

Lesson Planner

Chapter 15 The Sacrament of Holy Orders

Focus To understand why we call Holy Orders a Sacrament at the Service of Communion

LESSON PART	PROCESS	MATERIALS and RESOURCES
EXPLORE **Focus** **To explore how proclaiming the Gospel is serving the Church** ⏱ 10 minutes **Pages** 135–136	▶ Proclaim and discuss Matthew 9:35–38 (the harvest is abundant, laborers are few). ▶ Learn about Blessed John Henry Newman. **Disciple Power:** Patience **Activity:** Discuss qualities necessary to be a priest.	Bible Pencils Crayons or markers
DISCOVER **Focus** **To discover how the Church celebrates the Sacrament of Holy Orders** ⏱ 30 minutes **Pages** 137–139	▶ Identify the ordained priesthood as celebrating those men called to serve the Church. ▶ Preview the three degrees of Holy Orders. ▶ Explore the role of the bishop as teacher, priest, and shepherd. **Activity:** Interview the pastor or a priest.	Lists of local bishops, and bishops in the state **Additional Activities Booklet:** Activities 15a–15b, or see BeMyDisciples.com.
DECIDE **Focus** **To decide on a response to the lesson on the Sacrament of Holy Orders** ⏱ 10 minutes **Page** 140	**Activity:** Create an entry for a service diary. **My Faith Choice:** Connect to living the baptismal call.	**Enriching the Lesson Activities:** Catechist Edition, page 235 • Planning a Multi-Media Presentation • Charting and Comparing Works of Service • Searching the Bible

Concluding the Lesson 10 minutes

We Remember

Page 141

▶ Review concepts and do the review activity.

▶ **Assessment Tools Booklet:** Chapter Test 15a–15b, or see BeMyDisciples.com.

We Pray

▶ **Prayer:** a prayer for vocations

Materials: Picture of pope, local bishop(s) optional Bible, candle, cross for prayer space

▶ Grade 6 Music CD

Preview

Point out resources for this chapter at

www.BeMyDisciples.com

▶ Preview the With My Family page and next week's lesson theme.

Looking Ahead

In this chapter the Holy Spirit invites you to ▶

EXPLORE how a priest sought out the truth of the Church.

DISCOVER the three degrees of Holy Orders.

DECIDE on how you can live in Christ by serving others.

CHAPTER **15**

The Sacrament of Holy Orders

? In what ways do you serve others?

Jesus was not alone when he went out to proclaim the Gospel, nor did he minister to those in need by himself. Read about how Jesus ministered to the people:

Jesus went around to all the towns and villages, teaching in their synagogues, proclaiming the gospel of the kingdom, and curing every disease and illness. At the sight of the crowds, his heart was moved with pity for them because they were troubled and abandoned, like sheep without a shepherd. Then he said to his disciples, "The harvest is abundant but the laborers are few; so ask the master of the harvest to send out laborers for his harvest." MATTHEW 9:35–38

? If you think of God as the "master of the harvest," who might his laborers be?

(135)

HUMAN METHODOLOGIES

Learning within the Christian Community. The *National Directory for Catechesis* points out that for many, "the parish, under the leadership of the pastor, is the door to participate in the ordinary Christian community" (NDC 29C). Invite a parish priest or deacon to share with the students their experience of preparing to be ordained, their memories of the celebration of the Sacrament of Holy Orders, and the many ways they serve God and God's people, the Church.

Pray

▶ Open and close with the Sign of the Cross. Remind students that we can make study a form of prayer too. Pray together:

> Dear Jesus,
> Help me to live
> the call of my
> Baptism today
> and every day.
> Amen.

Reflect

▶ Discuss the opening question on the page.

▶ Then invite a volunteer to read the Scripture passage on the page.

▶ Ask the questions related to the Scripture. You might also invite them to discuss the images on the page as relevant to the chapter topic.

▶ Explain that "the master" from the passage is God who calls each of us to our unique vocation. And each of us is called to be his laborers. Note that Christ called a unique group of 12 men to be special laborers in his ministry— the Apostles.

Focus

▶ Call the students' attention to the Looking Ahead feature. Invite them to read aloud each bullet.

▶ Help students prepare to focus on the topic of vocation by inviting them to brainstorm ways in which God calls people to serve the Church.

▶ Point out that the organization of the Church has developed over the years as a direct result of seeking to meet the needs of people.

Introduce

▶ Inquire with the students if they know anyone who has converted to the Catholic Church as an adult.

▶ Explain that the story on the page is about a famous man, John Henry Newman, who converted to Roman Catholicism, having been an Anglican priest.

▶ Read aloud the text on the page. Pause occasionally to invite students to consider how they might have felt if they were Newman at different stages of his life.

▶ Ask the students if they know what "full communion" means. Point out that validly baptized Christians who join the Catholic Church are not baptized again. After a period of preparation, they are accepted into "full communion" with the Church.

Connect

▶ Discuss the Disciple Power feature. Ask: "In what way was Cardinal Newman a patient man?" (*He patiently listened for God's will for him.*)

▶ Encourage students to consider Blessed Newman as an example of someone who is actively patient in seeking the truth of God.

▶ Have students complete the activity on the page and encourage them to thank their parish priests for what they do for the Church and serving everyone in the parish.

Disciple Power

Patience

One of the fruits of the Holy Spirit is patience, which is the result of virtuous living. Being patient does not mean doing nothing. Patience involves the wisdom of knowing how to wait for truth while actively seeking grace.

THE CHURCH FOLLOWS JESUS
Seeking to Serve

Every Catholic priest, as he ministers to people in need, travels on his own journey of faith. In the 1800s, John Henry Newman started one such faith journey. He began his journey as an evangelical Christian, then became an Anglican priest, and finally a Catholic cardinal. Throughout his life, Newman actively sought out the truth of God and the Church with humility and patience.

While still in his early twenties, Newman became a leader of the Oxford Movement. This was a movement of some Anglican scholars, at the University of Oxford, who sought to settle the differences between the Anglican Church and the Roman Catholic Church. Newman became an Anglican priest, an accomplished writer, and respected scholar.

In 1845, Newman's journey of faith continued when he was accepted into full communion with the Catholic Church. He was ordained a Roman Catholic priest a year later. He would go on to help Catholics in Ireland and England and continue to write about theological matters. Father Newman was instrumental in helping to expand the Catholic Church in England during a time when Catholics there faced prejudice and persecution. For this reason, the Church bestowed on him the honor of cardinal. A year before his death, Cardinal Newman celebrated his last Mass on Christmas Day, 1889.

Cardinal Newman patiently served the Church throughout his faith journey in various roles. In his heart, John Henry Cardinal Newman preferred the life of a parish pastor. In Birmingham, England, where he was a parish priest for more than 30 years, Pope Benedict XVI beatified John Henry Newman on September 19, 2010.

136

> **Activity** Which qualities do you think are necessary to be a priest? Discuss your ideas with a partner and make your list here.
>
> _____
> _____
> _____
> _____

DISCIPLE POWER

Patience. Ask the young people if they have recently had to wait for anyone or anything. List their responses on the board or a poster. If need be, share an example or two from your own life, such as waiting in line at the store or waiting for Christmas to come. Review the list of examples with the children, and ask them to describe how waiting in each circumstance made them feel. Anxious? Mad? Excited? Explain that, as People of God, we are to remain peaceful and patient when we are waiting. When we're tempted to get mad at a person we're waiting for, we can count to ten. When we are tired of waiting for something good to happen in our lives, we can talk to God about it in prayer.

Consecrated in Christ's Name

True success comes from happiness—the happiness of a servant's heart. Jesus has set the standard for success, and it is quite different from the standards sometimes seen in the world. Jesus taught,

[W]hoever wishes to be first among you will be the slave of all. For the Son of Man did not come to be served but to serve and to give his life as a ransom for many.

MARK 10:44–45

To serve God and others means that we must serve as Christ did. Success built on material goods, self-centeredness, and self-interests is not in God's plan. We must build a community and be ready to make sacrifices. Christian service means that we serve others by giving ourselves as Jesus did. In doing so, we share in the unity of Christ.

The Priesthood of Christ

Jesus Christ is the one true priest. The baptized can share in the priesthood of Christ is two ways. There is the priesthood of all the faithful and of the ordained priesthood. Every Christian is joined to Christ in Baptism and is called to live a life of generous service to God and others as Jesus did. We are a people set apart, consecrated to serve God and others. This is what we mean by the common priesthood of the faithful.

How do you live out your baptismal call to share in the priesthood of Christ?

The Ordained Priesthood

Those men who receive the Sacrament of Holy Orders share in the ordained ministry of service or the ministerial priesthood. This means that these ordained men are at the service of the common priesthood—they are consecrated in Christ's name for the good of all the faithful. Their solemn promises are a sign of being consecrated for the sake of the Kingdom of God (see Matthew 19:11–12). Through them, Christ continues to build up and serve the Church.

FAITH FOCUS
Why are Holy Orders and Matrimony called Sacraments at the Service of Communion?

FAITH VOCABULARY
Communion
Communion is the unity in Christ of all the members of the Church, the Body of Christ; the word is from two Latin words meaning "sharing with." Full communion refers to full initiation into the Church.

Ordination
Ordination is the Sacrament of Holy Orders in which a baptized man is consecrated to serve the Church as a bishop, priest, or deacon.

cardinal?

137

THE TASKS OF CATECHESIS

Missionary Initiative. Share with the students that holiness is the vocation of all the baptized. We fulfill that vocation in one of four ways, called our state of life:

▶ **Ordained life:** bishops, priests, or deacons.

▶ **Religious life:** members of the Church who live the evangelical counsels of obedience, chastity, and poverty in a religious community approved by the Church.

▶ **Married life:** a baptized man and a baptized woman who receive the Sacrament of Matrimony.

▶ **Single life:** the baptized who serve the Church directly as single persons and who do not belong to one of the other three states of life.

Key Concept
The Church celebrates those men called to serve the Church through the ordained ministry.

Teach

▶ Discuss the Faith Focus question as a class. Explain that through loving service we are in communion with one another.

▶ Have the students read Mark 10:44–45. Invite students to discuss what it means to lead by being a servant.

▶ Have students read the text on the page. As they read, ask them to underline the text that emphasizes *leading through service*.

▶ Invite the class to list on the board what they underlined from the text.

▶ Explain that living our call to share in the priesthood of Christ means that we live as Christ did. God calls us to think and act like Christ. This means we lead with a servant's heart.

Reinforce

Review the Faith Vocabulary words for a better understanding of the key concepts in this chapter. If you are having the children keep vocabulary cards, have them stop now to make them for these words.

Connect

Ask the question on the page. Challenge the class to list as many activities as they can to point out the variety of ways in which they can serve the Church and others. Label this "Christian Service and Catholic Communion."

Key Concept

The three degrees of Holy Orders include bishops, priests, and deacons.

Teach

▶ Have students work with partners to discuss the work of bishops, priests, and deacons. Tell them to read the text on the page together and discuss it.

▶ Ask the class what they learned through their discussion. Explain that before a man can become an ordained minister as either a deacon or priest, he must go to school to study theology and Scripture. This school is a called a seminary. Read Faith-filled People to learn about a famous seminary in Korea.

▶ Ask the question about apostolic succession. *(It insures that all bishops are handing on the teaching and authority of the bishops through the laying on of hands.)*

Reinforce

Explain that deacons are helpers to the bishop in serving the needs of the Church. Therefore, they often serve in parishes by proclaiming the Gospel, minister to the sick, and officiating at Baptism and the Sacrament of Matrimony.

Connect

▶ Inquire among students whose family members are deacons, priests, and/or bishops.

▶ Explain that these three degrees of Holy Orders help the Church best serve the various needs within the Church.

Faith-Filled People

Venerable Jean Gailhac

Jean Gailhac was born in France in 1802. In his early work as a priest he served the poor and most marginalized of society. After starting his first shelter, a wealthy widow, Appolinie Cure, joined him in his work and became the leader of a new religious community he founded, the Institute of the Religious of the Sacred Heart of Mary. She took the name of Mother Saint Jean. She transformed the shelter for women into a place of safety for young girls at risk and started a boarding school. Today, the sisters serve in educational and social ministries in fourteen countries around the world, including France, Ireland, the United States, Brazil, and Zimbabwe.

138

Degrees of Holy Orders

The Sacrament of Holy Orders and the Sacrament of Matrimony are the two Sacraments at the Service of **Communion**. Holy Orders, or **Ordination**, is the sacrament in which a baptized man shares in a unique way the priesthood of God as a bishop, priest, or deacon.

The three degrees of Holy Orders are the episcopate (bishops), the presbyterate (priests), and the diaconate (deacons). An ordained man becomes a member of the "order" of bishop, priest, or deacon through the Rite of Ordination as conferred by a bishop.

Unbroken Powers

Holy Orders is celebrated by the laying on of hands by a bishop on the head of a man to be ordained, which is followed by a prayer of consecration. Holy Orders, like Baptism and Confirmation, can be received only once and marks the man who is ordained with a spiritual character forever.

During the Ordination of a bishop, the powers conferred on the Apostles by Christ himself remain unbroken through the centuries by the laying on of hands. The Church refers to this passing on of the gift of the Holy Spirit as the apostolic succession, making a bishop the guardian of the work of Christ.

? Why is the apostolic succession important to understanding Church authority?

Bishops and priests share in the priesthood of Christ in a unique way. The Sacrament of Holy Orders enables bishops and priests to act in the person of Christ. When they serve the Church, Christ himself is present to the Church. For example, at Mass when the priest says, "This is my body," he is not referring to his own body, but Christ's. Through the priest or bishop, Christ says, "This is my body."

Through the ordained ministry, the presence of Christ as head of the Church is made visible to the faithful; however, this does not mean that the ordained man is not without fault or sin. This means that priests and bishops remind us of the reality that Christ himself is present when they exercise the office of their ministry.

FAITH-FILLED PEOPLE

Venerable Jean Gailhac. Fr. Jean Gailhac was born in France in 1802. In his early work as a priest, he served the poor and most marginalized of society. After starting his first shelter, a wealthy widow, Appolinie Cure, joined him in his work and became the leader of a new religious community he founded, the Institute of the Religious of the Sacred Heart of Mary. She took the name of Mother Saint Jean. She transformed the shelter for women into a place of safety for young girls at risk and started a boarding school. Today, the sisters serve in educational and social ministries in fourteen countries around the world, including France, Ireland, the United States, Brazil, and Zimbabwe.

Shepherds of the Flock

During the Rite of Ordination, the bishop is entrusted with the care of the Church. He is appointed by the Holy Spirit to attend to the whole flock, or the faithful of his particular diocese.

A bishop is a teacher, priest, and shepherd. He promises to guide his people in the way of salvation, showing kindness and compassion. Bishops seek out people who are lost and gather them into the fold for the Lord. With the help of God and until the end of his life, the bishop is to be faithful and constant in proclaiming the Gospel.

Continuing Apostolic Ministry

When a bishop is ordained, he receives the fullness of the sacrament and continues the ministry of the Apostles. At the same time, bishops work in communion with the pope, who is the bishop of Rome and successor of Saint Peter. A bishop serves as the visible head of a diocese and is a sign of her unity.

Bishops also have the duty to teach the faith; celebrate divine worship, above all the Eucharist; and guide their local churches as true pastors. The priests are the co-workers of the bishops, whereas the deacons are the helpers of the bishops. Each bishop shares the responsibility for the universal Church with the pope.

Catholics Believe

Male Ordination

As with all vocations, the life of the priest is a calling. The Church recognizes herself to be bound by Christ's choice of only men to form the ministerial priesthood. The priesthood is a sacramental sign of Christ. Men, called to this vocation in the Catholic Church, humbly submit to the authority of the Church in service to her.

Activity

Ask the Pastor

Brainstorm with a small group some questions you would like to ask your pastor about his work. Write your questions here. If possible, invite the pastor to visit your class so you can all ask your questions in person.

_____

_____

_____

_____

_____

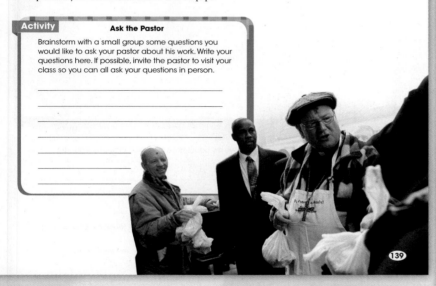

(139)

CATHOLIC DOCTRINE

Apostolic Succession. The Apostles were chosen by Jesus and "sent out" to spread the Good News. They were ministers of the Word and responsible for the well-being of the whole Church. The Church teaches that all the bishops of the Church are connected with the Apostles. This is called apostolic succession. The Church of every age is connected to the Church of apostolic times. We affirm this when we pray the Creed and say "I believe in one, holy, catholic, and apostolic Church."

Key Concept
The bishop receives the fullness of the Sacrament of Holy Orders.

Teach

▶ Explain that among the three degrees of Holy Order, the episcopate (bishops) receive the fullness of the Sacrament. They represent the Apostles today. Thus they are responsible for overseeing the mission of the Church.

▶ Read aloud the Catholics Believe section. Explain that male-only ordination is a clear teaching of the Catholic Church. Emphasize that in all sacraments, the Church is doing the work of Christ. The Church understands that since Christ appointed only males as Apostles, she does not have the ability to ordain women. Have students read the text on the page.

Reinforce

Emphasize that the fullness of the Sacrament comes from being in communion with Christ through the Apostles. The Apostles and then in turn Bishops are responsible for handing on the faith to others. This is the unique grace of this sacrament.

Connect

Have students complete the activity on the page. Arrange to have your pastor visit the class if possible to answer questions about his ministry.

Reinforce

▶ Remind students that all are called to fulfill their Baptismal vocation to live a life of holiness.

▶ Point out that the Church needs many more vocations to the priesthood and religious life.

Respond

▶ Introduce and explain the My Service Diary activity on the page.

▶ Have students complete the activity, inviting them to share their responses with a partner.

Choose

▶ Have students read My Faith Choice. Allow them time to reflect in silence about their commitment to serve God patiently.

▶ Invite them to pray the closing prayer silently and encourage students to put their faith choice into practice this week.

I FOLLOW JESUS

Every Christian is joined to Christ in Baptism and is called to live a life of generous service to God and others as Jesus did. The Church needs many more priests and religious sisters and brothers to meet the needs of the People of God.

MY SERVICE DIARY

Imagine that you are a priest or religious sister serving others here or in a missionary land. Write an entry in your journal describing a typical day in your life.

DATE

MY FAITH CHOICE

This week, I will patiently live my baptismal call to serve others as Jesus did.
I will

Pray, "Lord Jesus Christ, true High Priest of all, teach me how to serve others out of love for you. Amen."

(140)

TEACHING TIP

Give a Helping Hand. Sixth graders can work very well independently. However, as they work on their own to complete an activity, be sure to walk about the classroom to observe their progress. If you notice a student struggling with an activity, offer a suggestion or two to jog their imagination and memory. Always do so in a way that fosters a student's confidence and self-esteem and does not take away their independence and motivation.

Chapter Review

Fill-in the circle next to the word or phrase that completes each sentence correctly.

1. The word _____ is used to point out the sharing of Christians in the life of Christ.

○ sacrifice ● communion ○ service ○ Gentiles

2. The priesthood of all the faithful refers to the Sacrament of _____.

○ Marriage ○ Eucharist ● Baptism ○ Holy Orders

3. The ordained priesthood refers to the Sacrament of _____.

○ Marriage ○ Eucharist ○ Baptism ● Holy Orders

4. The _____ serves as the visible head of a diocese and is a sign of her unity.

○ apostle ● bishop ○ cardinal ○ pastor

TO HELP YOU REMEMBER

1. Every Christian is joined to Christ in Baptism and is called to live a life of generous service to God and others as Jesus did.

2. Holy Orders consecrates a baptized man to serve the whole Church as a bishop, priest, or deacon.

3. When a bishop is ordained, he receives the fullness of the Sacrament of Holy Orders.

Prayer for Vocations

Throughout the many dioceses in the United States, parishes pray for vocations to the priesthood and religious community life. Here is one from the U.S. Conference of Catholic Bishops that you can pray as a class.

God our Father,
you will all men and women to be saved
and come to the knowledge of your Truth.
Send workers into your great harvest
that the Gospel may be preached
to every creature
and your people, gathered together
by the word of life
and strengthened by
the power of the sacraments,
may advance in the way
of salvation and love.
I ask this through our Lord Jesus Christ, your Son,
who lives and reigns with you
and the Holy Spirit, one God, forever and ever.
Amen.

(141)

We Remember

▶ Review the major themes and concepts of the chapter using the To Help You Remember section. After you read aloud the statements to the class, have students add one of their own to the page.

▶ Then have each student read aloud what they added to the bulleted list on the page.

▶ Introduce the Chapter Review activity by reading the directions aloud. Have the students complete the sentences individually.

We Pray

▶ Gather the students for prayer. Introduce the prayer by reading the introduction. You can find more prayers for vocations at the Web site, www. USCCB.org.

▶ Lead the class in the prayer, beginning and ending with the Sign of the Cross.

SACRED TRADITION

The Elijah Cup. Elijah Cup, sometimes called the "Traveling Chalice" is the name of a new ministry in Catholic parishes in the United States. It has its roots in the story of Elijah and the poor widow of Zarapeth (1 Kings 17). The widow used the last of her flour to bake bread to feed Elijah. Because of her great faith, her supplies did not run out for a full year. The Elijah Cup is a chalice used at Sunday Mass. The cup is purified, and then given to a family, individual, or couple to take home for the week. They put the cup in a place of honor where it serves as a visual reminder to pray for an increase in vocations, trusting that if we pray with the faith of the widow our cup will not run dry. A journal is also sent home with the Elijah Cup. Participants are asked to write a prayer, a Scripture verse, or words of inspiration as a written record of a parish's ongoing commitment to fostering priestly vocations.

Preview

▶ Have students carefully tear-out the With My Family page along the perforation.

▶ Encourage them to share the pages with their family and to complete the activities together at home.

▶ If the students did not or were not able to complete the activities, encourage them to complete it with their family.

▶ Point out the title and theme of next week's chapter to the children.

Visit www.BeMyDisciples.com

▶ Take time with the students to explore the many activities and resources available at **www.BeMyDisciples.com.**

▶ Encourage especially them and their families to discover the many resources available at the Web site.

Before Moving On ...

As you finish today's lesson, reflect on the following question before moving on to the next chapter.

What student could use more attention or affirmation from me?

With My Family

This Week...

In chapter 15, The Sacrament of Holy Orders, your child learned that:

▶ God calls some members of the Church to live their baptismal calling by serving the whole Church through the Sacraments at the Service of Communion.

▶ Responding to one's vocation takes virtuous living. Patience, a fruit of the Holy Spirit, involves the wisdom of knowing how to wait for truth while actively seeking grace.

▶ In Holy Orders, a baptized man is ordained as a bishop, priest, or deacon to serve the whole Church by continuing the unique work of Jesus that was entrusted to the Apostles.

For more about related teachings of the Church, see the *Catechism of the Catholic Church,* 1533–1600; and the *United States Catholic Catechism for Adults,* pages 261–275.

■ Sharing God's Word

Read together Mark 10:42–45. Emphasize that each of us receives a special call or vocation from God to serve him and the whole community of the People of God, the Church.

■ We Live as Disciples

The Christian family and family form a school of discipleship. Choose one of the following activities to do as a family, or design a similar activity of your own:

▶ Review your parish bulletin or Web site to see in which ministries each family member can serve. Take time to find out about each, and discern the best match.

▶ Include in your family prayers a particular blessing for your parish priests and local bishop. Remember also the pope who serves the universal Church.

■ Our Spiritual Journey

The use of the spiritual discipline of discernment enables us to come to know both our vocation and how to live it. Discernment is the prayerful reflection on our gifts and talents. It is coming to know who God created us to be and how we can live the dismissal command given at the end of Mass to glorify God by our lives.

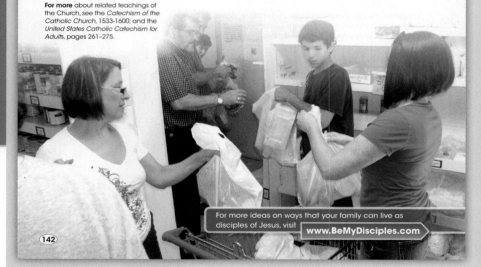

For more ideas on ways that your family can live as disciples of Jesus, visit **www.BeMyDisciples.com**

(142)

PARTNERING WITH PARENTS

Serving Others. One of this week's With My Family suggestions invites families to talk about ways they serve others as Jesus did. Through a written communication with parents, suggest that for the coming week, they make this a part of every evening meal discussion or bedtime prayer. You might also encourage families to look through family photo albums for pictures that show family members serving others by raking leaves together, serving a holiday meal, shoveling snow, or similar activities.

Enriching the Lesson

Planning a Multimedia Presentation

Purpose

To reinforce Holy Orders as the sacrament in which a baptized man shares in the ministerial priesthood of Christ in a unique way as a bishop, priest, or deacon (taught on page 138)

Directions

▶ Have the students plan a multimedia presentation on how a parish priest serves the people of the parish.

▶ Have the class create ten slides that share ways a parish priest serves the people. You may choose to have student-partners create one of the ten slides.

▶ Encourage them to include photos or images that they take in the parish to illustrate the ten points.

▶ Together, perhaps with the help of a parent or the parish technology coordinator, create the presentation and present it to the parish priest(s).

Materials

computer

paper

pens or pencils

Charting and Comparing Works of Service

Purpose

To reinforce that serving the Church means that we strive to serve others as Jesus did (taught on page 137)

Directions

▶ Have the students work in small groups to create a service chart. Each chart should have three columns, namely, "How Sixth Graders Live a Life of Service," "How Priests Live a Life of Service," and "How Christian Married People Live a Life of Service."

▶ Have volunteers list under the columns on the chart what they have learned.

▶ Share the concepts listed on the chart and compare matching ideas.

▶ Summarize together what it means to serve God and others as Jesus did.

▶ Option: You could vary this activity by giving groups the option of delivering their report with artwork or through a role-play activity.

Materials

chart paper or newsprint

pens or pencils

Searching the Bible

Purpose

To reinforce that the bishop is to be a teacher, priest and shepherd of his people (taught on page 139)

Directions

▶ Distribute Bibles to the students.

▶ Have each group search the Bible for stories and passages about shepherds and choose pertinent ones to compose and illustrate a brief explanation of how a bishop is like a shepherd.

▶ Suggested passages: Psalm 23, Luke 2:8–18, and John 10:1–9.

▶ Have each group share its work with the class.

▶ Make the reports available in the parish library for others to read and see.

Materials

Bibles

paper

pens, markers or crayons

BACKGROUND

Created from Love to Love

When God created humanity, he created us in his image and likeness out of love (Genesis 1:26–31). Thus love is our origin. We were created out of divine love and created to love God and others. Love is our constant calling. Love is our fulfillment in Heaven. The kind of love that Christians are called to is a love that acts on behalf of others because of our love for God.

Matrimony

Man and woman are both equally made in the image and likeness of God. Man and woman were created for each other (see Genesis, 2:18–25). As a result, once they enter into marriage "their mutual love becomes an image of the absolute and unfailing love with which God loves man" (*Catechism of the Catholic Church*, 1604).

Sin does not stem from the nature of humanity but from the disobedience of our first parents, Adam and Eve. Their sin brought discord into human experience. Since marriage is the union of human beings of course discord can enter it as well. God does not leave us alone to overcome this discord. Beginning with the Old Testament covenants we entered into with God, he has prepared the way for the "wedding feast for the Lamb" (Revelation 19:7–9).

The Sacrament of Matrimony instituted by Christ at the Wedding at Cana (see John 2:11) dedicates and strengthens a baptized man and a baptized woman to live as a special sign of the unity and love that binds Christ and the Church. It is a pledge of committed love, publicly declared before God, family and friends, and the Church that cannot be dissolved until death. It gives the spouses the grace to love each other with the love that Christ loves his Church.

Mutual Consent

The heart of the Sacrament of Matrimony is the mutual consent spouses give to each other in their exchange of marriage promises. The couple freely and unconditionally promises to love and honor each other all the days of their lives. They pledge their openness to "accept children lovingly from God, and bring them up according to the law of Christ and his Church" (Rite of Marriage 24). Chosen to be living signs of Christ's love for the Church, they receive the graces to help each other and their children to attain holiness.

The Domestic Church

When the first Christians were converted, their experiences of love, community, and salvation moved them to desire all of the members of their household be saved (see *Catechism of the Catholic Church* 1655, and Acts of the Apostles 18:8).

The family is at the center of the Church's living faith. The family is the "domestic Church" where parents are the first examples of faith. The family is the first school of discipleship where we learn to love, forgive, and pray.

For Reflection

In what ways does my family show it is a sign of God's love?

Who are the married couples I know who exemplify this kind of holiness?

Catechist to Catechist

Households of Faith

Holiness can be an abstract term until our life is impacted by a holy person. The Church teaches that the family is a domestic Church, a community of holiness. The Christian family is a living sign of God's love for the world and of Christ's love for the Church. God lives within families, calling each member to become reflections of his love and holiness. God works through families and his holiness shines through the interaction of all family members.

Family Efforts

The students in your classroom come from various family backgrounds and structures. Some families take a more active role in the life of the Church than others. Some families participate in the Mass on a regular basis; others do not. As the catechist, you have the responsibility to point out the Church's teaching about Sunday Mass obligation. Affirm all families in their efforts to live healthy and holy lives, sharing their faith with others.

The Church Teaches...

"Within the Christian family, parents are the primary educators in the faith . . . but all members make up the family, and each can make a unique contribution to creating the basic environment in which a sense of God's loving presence is awakened and faith in Jesus Christ is confessed, encouraged, and lived" (*National Directory for Catechesis*, 29D).

The family is to be a sign of God's love in the world. You are engaged in a partnership in which you and the parents each have a unique role to play in the faith formation of their children.

Further Reading and Reflection

For more on the teachings of the Church, see the *Catechism of the Catholic Church*, 1601–1666; and from the *United States Catholic Catechism for Adults*, pages 277–292.

Catechist Prayer

Generous and loving God, help me to work for the coming of your Kingdom in all its fullness. Amen.

Lesson Planner

Chapter 16 The Sacrament of Matrimony

Focus To understand why we call Matrimony a Sacrament at the Service of Communion

LESSON PART	PROCESS	MATERIALS and RESOURCES
EXPLORE **Focus** To explore the blessing of marriage 🕐 10 minutes **Pages** 143–144	▶ Proclaim and discuss 1 Corinthians 13: 4–7, 13 (Hymn of love) ▶ Reflect on the marriage blessing **Disciple Power:** Chastity **Activity:** Make greeting cards for newly married couples.	Bible Pencils Crayons or markers Art paper
DISCOVER **Focus** To discover God's plan for love and life 🕐 30 minutes **Pages** 145–147	▶ Explore the unique and loving relationship between a man and woman in marriage. ▶ Learn the qualities of spousal love. **Activity:** Real scripture stories about marriage. *where? resource?*	Pencils Crayons or markers **Additional Activities Booklet:** Activities 16a–16b, or see BeMyDisciples.com.
DECIDE **Focus** To decide on a response to the lesson on the Sacrament of Matrimony 🕐 10 minutes **Page** 148	**Activity:** Imagine your family as "My Church of the Home." **My Faith Choice:** Express love for family and friends according to God's plan.	Pencils **Enriching the Lesson Activities:** Catechist Edition, page 247 • Developing a Television Pilot • Writing Diamantes • Catholic Social Teaching: An Advice Column for Families

Concluding the Lesson 🕐 10 minutes

We Remember

Page 149
▶ Review concepts and do the review activity.

▶ **Assessment Tools Booklet:** Chapter Test 16a–6b, or see BeMyDisciples.com.

We Pray

▶ **Prayer:** a prayer from the Rite of Marriage.

Materials: Bible, candle, cross for prayer space

▶ Grade 6 Music CD

Preview

Point out resources for this chapter at

www.BeMyDisciples.com

▶ Preview the With My Family page and next week's lesson theme.

Looking Ahead

In this chapter the Holy Spirit invites you to ▶

EXPLORE the Church's hopes for newly married couples.

DISCOVER God's plan for love and life, in marriage.

DECIDE how to be a true sign of Christ's love.

The Sacrament of Matrimony

? What qualities are necessary to maintain a close friendship with someone? How would you define love?

Here is the way Saint Paul described for the community at Corinth what love is and what it is not:

Love is patient, love is kind. It is not jealous, [love] is not pompous, it is not inflated, it is not rude, it does not seek its own interests, it is not quick-tempered, it does not brood over injury, it does not rejoice over wrongdoing but rejoices with the truth. It bears all things, believes all things, hopes all things, endures all things. . . . So faith, hope, love remain, these three, but the greatest of these is love.

1 Corinthians 13:4–7, 13

? Have you heard this passage before? What does it tell you about the challenges of loving your family members or your friends?

143

Pray

▶ Open and close with the Sign of the Cross. Pray aloud with the students: "God our Father, may your Church be for all the world a sign of your unity and holiness."

▶ Invite students to add petitions to the prayer.

Reflect

▶ Discuss the opening questions on the page.

▶ Then invite a volunteer to read the Scripture passage on the page.

▶ Ask the questions related to the Scripture. Ask the young people to compare with their earlier definitions of love.

▶ Time permitting, have students discuss how the image on the page relates to the topic of love and marriage.

Focus

▶ Call the students' attention to the Looking Ahead feature. Invite them to read aloud each bullet.

▶ Inform the students that in this chapter they will learn about the second Sacrament at the Service of Communion, Matrimony. Explain that on the next page they will learn how the Church speaks to couples on their wedding day.

TEACHING TIP

Using Bibles. Include the use of the Bible in your sessions with the young people. It is important that they become familiar with the Bible, grow in their ability to look up and find passages, and respect and reverence the Scriptures as the inspired Word of God. After having students respond to the opening questions in today's lesson, invite them to read the full passage from 1 Corinthians 13 before you proclaim the excerpt on the page. This is a very well-known passage this is used very often in marriage ceremonies. Discuss the rich imagery of this passage with the students—gong and cymbal, moving mountains, glass (mirror)—and how they help us know the importance of love.

Introduce

▶ Ask the students to recall Catholic celebrations of the Sacrament of Matrimony that they may have attended and to describe what they remember about them.

▶ Tell them that at celebrations of Matrimony within Eucharist, a Solemn Blessing is given to the couple.

▶ Divide the class into three sections and have them read the three selections from the blessing in chorus.

▶ Ask each group to describe what the Church wishes for the couple. Jot key words on the board.

Connect

▶ Introduce the activity and ask each student to reflect silently before sharing their ideas with a partner.

▶ Then distribute art paper and ask each student to make a greeting card for a newly married couple expressing their hopes for them.

▶ Encourage the students to deliver their cards to the married couples.

Disciple Power

Chastity

When we exercise self-control with God's grace in our relationships, the Holy Spirit forms the virtue of chastity in us. This means that we can appropriately integrate the gift of our human sexuality according to God's calling for us. In other words, we respect each other as persons and not as objects to be used.

THE CHURCH FOLLOWS JESUS

A Marriage Blessing

When a man and woman are married in the presence of a priest within the Celebration of the Eucharist, the rite concludes with a Solemn Blessing. Here is a portion of that beautiful blessing:

May the peace of Christ live always in your hearts and in your home.

May you have true friends to stand by you, both in joy and in sorrow.

May you be ready and willing to help and comfort all who come to you in need.

And may the blessings promised to the compassionate be yours in abundance. . . .

May you find happiness and satisfaction in your work.

May daily problems never cause you undue anxiety, nor the desire for earthly possessions dominate your lives.

But may your hearts' first desire be always the good things waiting for you in the life of heaven. . . .

May the Lord bless you with many happy years together, so that you may enjoy the rewards of a good life.

And after you have served him loyally in his kingdom on earth, may he welcome you to his eternal kingdom in heaven.

RITE OF MARRIAGE

Activity Think of an older married couple you know. Discuss with a partner what parts of the blessing seem to have been fulfilled in their life together. Then think of a newly married couple. Write a note or card to them expressing your hopes for them, letting the Solemn Blessing be your guide.

DISCIPLE POWER

Chastity. The *Catechism of the Catholic Church* states that upholding and supporting the virtue of chastity is both a personal and a cultural responsibility (*CCC* 2344). On the board or a poster, create four columns titled as follows:

1. Personal: Upholds the Virtue of Chastity (appropriate dress)

2. Personal: Temptations against Chastity (inappropriate dress)

3. Cultural: Upholds the Virtue of Chastity (chastity ring, signifying one's commitment to purity)

4. Cultural: Temptations against Chastity (R-rated movies).

Invite the students to suggest activities or decisions that can be added under each heading. If need be, provide an example for each column, or use the suggestions given in parentheses next to each heading listed above.

God's Plan for Love and Life

Just as there are different types of relationships, there are different kinds of love. For example, there is the love between friends and siblings. There is also the love between parents and children, and there is yet another unique kind of love between a man and a woman who commit to an exclusive and faithful love over a lifetime in marriage. These are the kinds of relationships planned by God since the creation of Adam and Eve, our first parents. Each kind of love expresses being a "gift of self" to another. Every expression of love has at its source the love of God.

? How do you express your love for your friends, for your siblings, or for your parents?

Expressions of Love

With each kind of relationship, there are certain appropriate ways to express love. The appropriateness of the expression depends on the kind of relationship. Friends, for example, might express their love with a handshake. This might demonstrate friends who walk on equal ground, enjoying each other's company.

Parents show love for their children, for example, by caring for them. This love can be expressed with a hug, kind words, or providing material needs and wants (like chocolate chip cookies!). Because parents are responsible for raising their children, the relationship is not one between equals.

There is also the love between spouses. When a man and woman have strong feelings and are sexually attracted to each other, God calls them to recognize this unique expression of their love in a marriage commitment (read Tobit 7:11–13). The unique expression of married love is called **conjugal love.**

For Catholic couples, they celebrate the Sacrament of **Matrimony** to become married. The Sacrament of Matrimony is the celebration of a baptized man and a baptized woman who join themselves to each other in a lifelong bond of spousal and mutual love. The Sacrament of Matrimony is one of the two Sacraments at the Service of Communion.

FAITH FOCUS
Why does marriage have a unique expression of love?

FAITH VOCABULARY
complementarity
Complementarity is living with and for each other as equal in dignity and unique in gender, helping each other according to God's plan for both genders.

conjugal love
Conjugal love is the unique expression of sexual love between a husband and a wife, who freely give their whole selves to each other.

Matrimony
The Sacrament of the Church that unites a baptized man and a baptized woman in a lifelong bond of faithful love as a sign of Christ's love for the Church.

TEACHING VOCABULARY

Communion. For many years religion texts referred to Matrimony and Holy Orders as Sacraments of Service. The Catechism now designates these two sacraments as Sacraments at the Service of Communion. The word *communion* describes the intimate and loving fellowship that characterizes all the People of God. Priests and married couples participate in a "particular mission in the Church and serve to build up the People of God" (*CCC* 1534).

Key Concept
The Sacrament of Matrimony celebrates the lifelong spousal bond of man and woman.

Teach

▶ Discuss the Faith Focus question as a class.

▶ Inquire: "How do you express your love for your friends, siblings, relatives, parents, etc.?"

▶ Paraphrase the opening paragraph. Ask: "Would you express love for a sibling in the same manner as the love for a casual friend?" Explain that a "loving" gesture could be the same, but the emotion of love is different according to the particular bond in the relationship.

▶ Ask the students to read the next section to learn more about the unique expression of married love.

Reinforce

▶ Emphasize that one unique aspect of marriage is that the couple does not express their love through the conjugal act before marriage.

▶ Ask: "How does vowing to one's love before fully expressing it show their love and respect for each other?" (*Conjugal love demonstrates the spouses' loving commitment to one another.*)

▶ Review the Faith Vocabulary words. Have the Students make word cards for these words.

Connect

Discuss with the young people their understanding of complementarity between men and women in marriage. What positive qualities does each gender bring?

Key Concept
Spousal love is to be exclusive, permanent, unbreakable, and faithful.

Teach

▶ Have students express what they believe to be the essential qualities of marriage. Then have students read the text.

▶ Ask them to add any qualities they learned from the text. Be sure they include *permanent unbreakable,* and *faithful.*

Reinforce

Tell the students that Christian married love is a sign of Christ's love for the Church. Invite the students to explain how the images on the page illustrate this point.

Connect

▶ Explain a "church of the home." Point out that Blessed Louis and Zélie Martin in Faith-Filled People are a good example.

▶ Ask and discuss the question on the page.

▶ Remind the students that no family is perfect, and that God dwells with every family.

Faith-Filled People

Blessed Louis and Zélie Martin

The parents of Saint Thérèse of Lisieux were only the second married couple beatified by the Catholic Church. They saw their engagement as being open to the will of God. Married in 1858, they dedicated their marriage to serve God. Blessed with nine children, they are honored as a true model of Christian spouses.

A Married Couple's Bond

Marriage is like no other loving relationship. Through marriage, a man and a woman make the promise to love before fully expressing their love. In doing so, they express their **complementarity** with respect to and exclusively for each other.

Marital love is expressed according to the two unique genders. In this expression of love, spouses honor the equal dignity of being male and female. Their vowed love is a complete giving of themselves to one another, the promise to love freely, faithfully, fully, and forever.

Conjugal love is to be exclusive, permanent, unbreakable, and faithful. Their love expresses two important aspects of their relationship: their bond as a couple, and their openness to accept and raise children.

The married couple becomes a sign of Christ's love for the Church. Christian married love, like Christ's love for the Church, is a sign of the faithful and unbreakable love of God for his people.

Essential Qualities

In the Letter to the Ephesians, Paul encourages husbands to love their wives as Christ loves the Church. He equally encourages wives to respect their husbands. This mirrors the love and respect that exists between Christ and his Church (read Ephesians 5:21–27).

When a husband and wife nurture and cherish each other in this way, they become a living sacrament. They are a living sign through which Christ works in the world. The married couple with their children are a domestic Church, or "church of the home." The family listens to God's Word, prays together, and serves one another with generosity and compassion. All baptized Christians are called to serve as Jesus did, to be a living sign of God's saving presence, as the one family of God.

 How does your family live like a "church of the home"? In what ways do you contribute?

When selfishness and materialism replace service and communion, marriages and families are not successful and can lead to separation or divorce. Because married love is mutual, it requires the cooperation of both spouses. Divorce is painful for not just the married couple, but for the entire family. Sadly, divorce is a reality in many families. Many divorced persons wish to remain faithful to the Church and to raise their children in the Catholic faith. The Church continues to support them as baptized members, and prays for a resolution of their difficulties.

146

FAITH-FILLED PEOPLE

Blessed Louis and Zélie Martin. Blessed Louis and Zélie Martin, the parents of Saint Thérèse of Lisieux, were the first parents of a saint to be beatified and the first husband and wife to be proposed for sainthood as a couple. Though they faced many tragedies in life—Zélie's early death, the infant deaths of four of their nine children, the pressures of living in a time of war, and Louis's later illness—they continually turned to God as their source of strength and courage. They are an inspiration for all married couples to create in their homes a "domestic Church," a place where faith can be nurtured and strengthened, where children will respond to the teachings of Jesus and to the call of God. We celebrate their feast day on July 12. For more information on Blessed Louis and Zélie Martin, go to the Saint Resource at www.faithfirst.com.

Sacred Union

In the Book of Genesis, God's plan for love and life is revealed when he created humanity in his image, both male and female as equal in dignity yet unique in gender (read Genesis 2:22–24). Christ the Lord raised marriage to the dignity of a sacrament (read John 2:1–11). Unlike any other sacrament in the Latin Rite, the couple to be married are the ministers of the sacrament. By their free consent before the Church, a baptized man and a baptized woman offer themselves as a gift to the other. They become one according to God's plan. Jesus echoed this when he reminded the Pharisees of the words from the Book of Genesis:

So they are no longer two, but one flesh. Therefore, what God has joined together, no human being must separate.

MATTHEW 19:6

A Saving Reality

The marital love between spouses is a "saving reality" (read Isaiah 54:5–8, 10). This means that a husband and wife are to work for the good of each other and be open to life, to accept and raise children. Acts such as adultery, contraception, divorce, and polygamy are contrary to the dignity of marriage.

Through the Sacrament of Matrimony, the married couple enters into a covenantal relationship in which their love is sealed and strengthened by the grace of God (read Hosea 2:21–25). The married couple is to become a communion of love, in the image of the Holy Trinity.

Activity With a partner, read one of these Scripture passages and report to your class what it taught you about Matrimony. Jot your notes for your report here.

Genesis 2:22–24

Hosea 2:21–22

_____

_____

_____

_____

(147)

THE TASKS OF CATECHESIS

Moral Formation. The *Catechism of the Catholic Church* states that all who have been baptized are called to chastity, for through Baptism we have died to ourselves and are raised to new life in Christ, our model of chastity. The Church recognizes three forms of chastity: the chastity of spouses; the chastity of widows or widowers; and the chastity of virgins. She calls us to cultivate chastity according to our various states of life, whether single, married, engaged to be married, professed virgin, or consecrated celibate. The Church also warns us to avoid the offenses against chastity (*CCC* 2348, 2349, and 2351–2356).

Key Concept
Christ raised marriage to the dignity of a sacrament.

Teach

▶ Have the students read the opening paragraph to learn what happens in the marriage rite.

▶ Emphasize the point of the Scripture passage that the marriage bond is life-giving.

▶ Ask the students to read the rest of the page silently. Ask: what are two aspects of marital love? *(mutual support and openness to raising children)*

▶ Ask a volunteer to read the Catholics Believe box aloud.

▶ Remind the students that all baptized Christians are called to observe the virtue of chastity by acting appropriately in their relationship with others.

Reinforce

Have students read the text. Emphasize that in the Latin Rite of Marriage, the ministers of the sacrament are the couple themselves, and that the priest or deacon is a witness on behalf of the Church.

Connect

▶ Have students complete the activity on the page.

▶ Invite volunteers to share what they learned from their passage.

Reinforce

Invite a student to read the opening paragraph at the top of the page to recall the meaning of the Church of the home.

Respond

▶ Introduce and explain the directions for the activity on the page, My Church of the Home, and have students complete the activity.

▶ Remind the students that their home life may or may not be ideal. But they will have the opportunity one day to create the home they would like, and they can begin to imagine it now.

▶ Ask volunteers to share their work.

Choose

▶ Have the students write their faith choice.

▶ Then have students complete the last section to make their commitment in prayer. Encourage students to put their faith choice into practice this week.

I FOLLOW JESUS

The domestic Church, or church of the home, is the model for every Catholic household of faith. A Catholic family can be a living sign of Christ in the world. God dwells in all families, even though no family is perfect. It is the responsibility of every family member to make Christ's love visible to those in and outside the home.

MY CHURCH OF THE HOME

What would your family be like if it was a true sign of Christ's love? Write or draw your dreams here. Include the good things that are happening and the things you would like to see. Be sure to express your role.

_____
_____
_____
_____
_____
_____
_____
_____
_____
_____

MY FAITH CHOICE

This week, I choose to express my love for my family and friends according to God's plan for love and life. I will

_____
_____ .

Pray, "Holy Spirit, guide me to be a chaste person who loves and serves other in your image. Amen."

(148)

HUMAN METHODOLOGIES

Learning within the Christian Family. The *National Directory for Catechesis* emphasizes the primary importance of the Christian family in modeling and nurturing the Christian faith, and the key role of parents as catechists in the domestic Church (*NDC* 27D). Furthermore, the *General Directory for Catechesis* states that parents receive the grace to fulfill this responsibility in the Sacrament of Marriage (*GDC* 227). Take time to consider how your ministry as a catechist can and does support parents and families so that they might fulfill this important ministry in the lives of their children.

Chapter Review

Answer the following questions in complete sentences.

1. What does the Catholic Church teach about the unique meaning and purpose of marriage?

The Sacrament of Marriage unites a baptized man and a baptized woman in a lifelong bond of faithful love. Their spousal love is to bond them out of mutual respect with an openness to life.

2. What are the essential qualities necessary for conjugal love?

The essential qualities are exclusive, permanent, unbreakable and faithful.

3. How is the sacred union of the marriage of a baptized man and a baptized woman like the love between Christ and the Church?

Christian married love, like Christ's love for the Church, is a sign of the faithful and unbreakable love of God for his people.

TO HELP YOU REMEMBER

1. Marriage is part of God's plan for love and life in which a man and a woman form a lifelong bond with openness to life.

2. Spousal love is to be exclusive, permanent, unbreakable, and faithful.

3. Matrimony unites a baptized man and a baptized woman to be a living sign of Christ's love for the Church.

Signs of Christ's Love

Our prayers for married couples help them live their vocation to be signs of Christ's love in the world. This prayer recalls that blessing.

Leader: Let us pray for all who have been consecrated in the Sacrament of Matrimony to serve the Church.

Reader 1: May the peace of Christ live in their homes.

All: **Bless them, O Lord.**

Reader 2: May they have true friends to help them.

All: **Bless them, O Lord.**

Reader 3: May they not care too much about material things.

All: **Bless them, O Lord.**

Reader 4: May they enjoy their work and solve their daily problems.

All: **Bless them, O Lord.**

Reader 5: May they be ready to help all who are in need.

All: **Bless them, O Lord.**

Leader: We now pray aloud for the married couples we know. *(Pause for students to add intentions.)* May God reward them with a long life and with eternal happiness.

All: **Amen.** BASED ON THE RITE OF MARRIAGE

(149)

TEACHING TIP

Rite of Marriage. Point out the reference to the Rite of Marriage at the close of the prayer, "Signs of Christ's Love." As part of your introduction to this chapter's closing prayer, share with the students that the prayer comes from the Rite of Marriage. Explain to the students that every sacrament needs to be celebrated according to the rite for celebrating that sacrament approved by the Church.

We Remember

▶ Assess students' retention of the content from this chapter by having them define: marriage, spousal love and Matrimony in their own words. Explain that marriage can be understood as the natural institution while Matrimony is the sacred union because of its being a sacrament.

▶ Now review the To Help You Remember section to affirm or clarify students' understanding.

▶ Introduce the Chapter Review activity by reading the directions aloud. Have the students complete the sentences individually. Then ask volunteers to share their answers by correcting misunderstandings.

▶ Encourage students to tell their families what they learned in this chapter.

We Pray

▶ Gather the students for prayer. Introduce the prayer by preparing students for each of the parts.

▶ Invite students to take a few moments to think about one or more married couples for whom they would like to pray.

▶ Lead the class in the prayer, beginning and ending with the Sign of the Cross.

Preview

▶ Have students carefully tear-out the With My Family page along the perforation.

▶ Encourage them to share the pages with their family and to complete the activities together at home.

▶ If the students did not or were not able to complete the activity on page 149, encourage them to complete it with their family.

▶ Point out the title and theme of next week's chapter to the children.

Visit www.BeMyDisciples.com

▶ Take time with the students to explore the many activities and resources available at **www.BeMyDisciples.com.**

▶ Encourage especially them and their families to discover the many resources available at the Web site.

Before Moving On ...

As you finish today's lesson, reflect on the following question before moving on to the next chapter.

How flexible am I in adjusting time frames if students are working well on an activity.

With My Family

This Week...

In chapter 16, The Sacrament of Matrimony, your child learned that:

▶ Marriage is a natural institution and sacred union between a man and a woman only, who share in a lifelong commitment.

▶ Spousal love is to be exclusive, permanent, unbreakable, and faithful.

▶ In Matrimony, a baptized man and a baptized woman are united in a lifelong bond of faithful love as a sign of Christ's love for the Church.

▶ Through the virtue of chastity, we respect each other as persons, not as objects to be used. We integrate the gift of our sexuality according to God's plan.

For more about related teachings of the Church, see the *Catechism of the Catholic Church,* 1601–1666; and the *United States Catholic Catechism for Adults,* pages 277–292.

■ Sharing God's Word

Read together Ephesians 5:1–32; 6:1–4. Emphasize that each of us is to live in the light of Christ. Husbands and wives are to imitate the sacrificial love between Christ and the Church. Parents and children are to love each other with honor and respect.

■ We Live as Disciples

The Christian home and family form a school of discipleship. Choose one of the following activities to do as a family, or design a similar activity of your own.

▶ During family talks, discuss with your children the joys and struggles in marriage and what you are doing to create a household of faith. Plan regular outings together to strengthen your family bonds.

▶ Help your child to be sensitive to their friends who may be experiencing difficulties at home. Allow them to participate in some of your activities.

■ Our Spiritual Journey

Christ's sacrifice is the paradigm of Christian living. Sacrifice, the giving of oneself freely out of love for another, gives expression to the paradox that Saint Francis of Assisi captured in the words, "It is in giving that we receive," which in turn reflects the infinite Self-Giving Love of the Trinity, One Divine Person to the Others.

For more ideas on ways that your family can live as disciples of Jesus, visit **www.BeMyDisciples.com**

(150)

CATHOLIC SOCIAL TEACHING

Option for the Poor and Vulnerable. An inordinate and self-centered attachment to wealth and possessions is contrary to living as a disciple of Christ. The Catholic Church teaches that we are obligated to share our material and spiritual blessings. We are to be detached from them and work together for the elimination of the inequitable distribution of material and spiritual goods among peoples. Working to meet the needs of the poor and vulnerable must be a priority. The young people were introduced to this principle in the story of the care for the elderly in Chapter 14, where they learned of the call to priests to serve the common good of the Church, and in this chapter, where they learned more about the responsibilities of parents to their children. The last activity on the facing page will reinforce this key element of Catholic Social Teaching.

Enriching the Lesson

Developing a Television Pilot

Purpose

To reinforce that a Christian family is a domestic Church, or "church of the home" (taught on page 146

Directions

▶ Have the students work in small groups to create the pilot of a TV series portraying the lives of Christian families who are living signs of God's love.

▶ Have the groups outline the pilot episode using characters, settings, problems, and solutions. They can choose the series to be a drama or a situational comedy (sit-com).

▶ Invite the students to present the outline of their pilot in words or storyboard drawings.

▶ Summarize by sharing the difference that Christian families can make in the world.

Materials

paper

pens or pencils

Writing Diamantes

Purpose

To reinforce that God created marital love as a sacred union between a man and woman (taught on page 147).

Directions

▶ Review with the students that a diamante is a form of verse consisting of seven lines and sixteen words, contrasting two words.

▶ Review the structure of a diamante—Line 1: one word of a pair of opposites; Line 2: two words describing the word; Line 3: three action words ending in "ing" describing the word; Line 4: two words describing the word in Line 1 followed by a dash and two words describing the contrasting word, which will appear in Line 7; Line 5: three action words ending in "ing" describing the contrasting word; Line 6: two words describing the contrasting word; Line 7: name the contrasting word.

▶ Have the students work with partners to create diamantes using the names of a man and a woman.

▶ Invite the students to share their diamantes.

Materials

paper and pens or pencils

Catholic Social Teaching: An Advice Column for Families

Purpose

To reinforce that Catholics remember and celebrate that marriage is God's plan for love and life (taught on page 145)

Directions

▶ Divide the class into groups of three. Invite the groups to write an advice column, pretending that Jesus is responding to the questions. In their column, Have them respond to these questions.

▶ How can our family respond to people's most urgent needs in our community?

▶ Who is our neighbor? What is our responsibility to those we do not know?

▶ What can one family do when so many need our help?

▶ Invite each group to share their responses with the entire class. You might ask if the best responses could be published in the Parish bulletin or on the Parish Web site.

Materials

paper

pens or pencils

The Unit Review provides the opportunity to assess the students' understanding of the faith concepts presented in the unit and to affirm them in their growing knowledge and love of God. Here are a few suggestions for using these pages.

▶ Share that the next two pages are an opportunity to stop and review what they have learned.

▶ Provide time for the students to ask questions.

▶ Have the students complete the review alone or with partners.

A. Choose the Best Word

▶ Read the directions for this section.

▶ Then have the student work alone or with a partner to complete the section.

▶ Invite volunteers to share their responses. Clarify and correct responses as needed.

B. Show What You Know

▶ Read the directions for this section. Answer the first question together as a class.

▶ Then have the student continue working alone or with a partner to complete the section.

▶ Invite volunteers to share their responses. Clarify and correct responses as needed.

Unit 4 Review

Name _____

A. Choose the Best Word

Read each statement and circle the best answer.

1. Which sacrament uses the rite of anointing?
- (A.) Holy Orders
- B. Reconciliation
- C. Matrimony
- D. Eucharist

2. Which sacrament strengthens our faith and trust in God when we are ill?
- A. Holy Orders
- (B.) Anointing of the Sick
- C. Reconciliation
- D. Matrimony

3. What are the Sacraments at the Service of Communion?
- A. Baptism and Holy Orders
- B. Confirmation and Holy Orders
- C. Baptism and Matrimony
- (D.) Matrimony and Holy Orders

4. Which of these does not include anointing with oil?
- A. Anointing of the Sick
- B. Holy Orders
- (C.) Eucharist
- D. Baptism

5. Which kind of love is to be exclusive, permanent, unbreakable and faithful?
- A. conjugal love
- B. marital love
- C. spousal love
- (D.) All of the above

B. Show What You Know

Match the items in column A with those in column B.

Column A	Column B
A. Holy Orders	_C_ **1.** a gravely wrong action
B. Reconciliation	_E_ **2.** God's plan for love and life
C. mortal sin	_A_ **3.** a sacrament at the Service of Communion
D. diaconate	_D_ **4.** degree of Holy Orders
E. Marriage	_B_ **5.** a Sacrament of Healing

(151)

TEACHING TIP

Selective Review. To use all sections of the unit review during class time may not be necessary and perhaps, depending on your circumstances, may not even be desirable. Choose one of the review sections to be completed at home. Send a note to encourage families to complete this section of the Unit Review along with the family take-home page. This selective review process can be a means of partnering with the parents to help their children grow and mature in their faith. Furthermore the families can use this Unit Review also as a faith-sharing tool.

C. Connect with Scripture

Reread the Scripture passage on the first Unit Opener page. What connection do you see between this passage and what you learned in this unit?

Responses will vary.

D. Be a Disciple

1. Review the four pages in this unit titled "The Church Follows Jesus." What person or ministry of the Church on these pages will inspire you to be a better disciple of Jesus? Explain your answer.

Responses will vary.

2. Work with a group. Review the four Disciple Power virtues or gifts you have learned about in this unit. After jotting down your own ideas, share with the group practical ways that you will live these virtues or gifts day by day.

Responses will vary.

(152)

C. Connect with Scripture

▶ Invite the students to reflect on the Scripture passage in the Unit Opener and to write their understanding of how this passage connects with the doctrinal content of the unit they have just completed.

▶ Ask volunteers to share their responses, now or after completion of the entire Unit Review.

D. Be a Disciple

▶ Invite the young people to work independently on the first question about The Church Follows Jesus. Ask volunteers to share their responses.

▶ Divide the students into small groups of three or four for the second part of this section. Ask them to write their personal reflections first, and then to share with their group practical ways of living the Disciple Power virtues or qualities of discipleship in everyday life.

▶ Ask for feedback from the small groups as time allows.

TEACHING TIP

Music Participation. As the time allows, contact your parish music director to find appropriate opportunities throughout the year to help the students learn the music for the upcoming Sunday Liturgy. This could help the students become more comfortable with the music, and encourage them to have a greater active participation in the Mass. This also could be an opportunity for the students to share with the parish music director appropriate songs that they would like to sing during Sunday Liturgy.

We Live

Part One

Objectives

In Unit 5, the students will learn that:

▶ The Theological Virtues are gifts from God that connect us with him and strengthen us to live a life of holiness in communion with God.

▶ Sin is turning away from God and his love, freely choosing to do or say what we know is against God's law.

▶ Doing good and avoiding evil is a principle of the Natural Law.

▶ The Beatitudes are teachings of Jesus from his Sermon on the Mount that describe the attitudes and actions of people blessed by God.

Spiritual Insights

"In Christ we have been called to a New Covenant and a New Law that fulfills and perfects the Old Law. We also are invited to experience God's love for us and to return that love to God and to our neighbor" (*United States Catholic Catechism for Adults*, page 325).

"Teacher, what good must I do to gain eternal life?"

Matthew 19:16

Living the Six Tasks of Catechesis

Education for Community Life: Blessed Peter To Rot (1912–1942)

Peter To Rot was born in Rakunai, a village in Papua New Guinea. Peter's father was the chief of the village. He invited missionaries to preach the Word of God to his people. Soon after, Peter and his whole family were baptized.

When he was 18, Peter was chosen to be a catechist. He was sent to a mission school to learn how to teach the truths of the Catholic faith and lead prayer services. Three years later, Peter became the chief catechist of his village. He was filled with joy as he helped others to know and love the Lord.

Peter married and he and his wife had three children. Their lives were filled with love and service to God and their village. Their happiness was shattered in 1942, during World War II, when Japanese soldiers invaded their island. The priests were arrested, as was Peter. Each time Peter was released, however, he continued to teach, baptize, and lead Communion services with hosts consecrated by the priests in jail.

The Japanese tried to get the Christians to turn away from their faith. They passed a law saying that the people could return to the practice of polygamy, which allowed men to have more than one wife. Peter spoke out against polygamy, reminding people that marriage was a sacred vow between one man and one woman.

Peter was arrested for the last time. The Japanese authorities wanted to make an example of him. Peter knew he was going to be killed in prison. He asked his wife to bring him his best clothes so that he would be dressed properly when he met God face to face in heaven.

Peter died as a martyr for the Catholic faith. We celebrate his feast day on July 7. Blessed Peter To Rot's life reminds us of our commitment as catechists to share our faith with the young people whom we teach. We are called to build community among them and to prepare them to participate actively in the life and the mission of the Church.

Sharing Your Faith

Find a partner to work with: a spouse, a friend, a fellow catechist. Come together at the beginning or end of each unit for shared prayer and discussion. Use the questions below as a starting point. As an alternative, record your thoughts in a personal journal.

▶ How does your parish community help you to live your faith?

▶ How do you demonstrate love for your neighbor on a regular basis?

▶ Explain how you put God first in your life.

We Live — UNIT 5
Part One

Put On Love

Put on, then, as God's chosen ones, holy and beloved, heartfelt compassion, kindness, humility, gentleness, and patience bearing with one another and forgiving one another. If one has a grievance against another; as the Lord has forgiven you, so must you also do. And over all these put on love, that is, the bond of perfection.

Colossians 3: 12–14

(153)

What I Have Learned
What is something you already know about these faith concepts?

Works of Mercy

_____

Natural Law

_____

The Beatitudes

_____

Faith Terms to Know
Put an X next to the faith terms you know. Put a ? next to faith terms you need to learn more about.

_____ holiness

_____ Cardinal Virtues

_____ Theological Virtues

_____ conscience

_____ capital virtues

_____ The Golden Rule

_____ The Shema

_____ canonization

The Bible
What do you know about Jesus' teaching on the greatest commandment?

_____

The Church
What would you like to know about the requirements for sainthood?

_____

Questions I Have
What questions would you like to ask about the moral decision-making?

_____

(154)

Unit 5 Opener

Opening Page

▶ Invite the young people to tell you what they see in the illustration. *(A man—Paul—is writing at a table.)*

▶ Proclaim the Scripture passage for the class. Ask: "What advice does Paul give the Christians? When have you seen Christians following this advice?" *(Accept all answers, but do not comment on them.)*

Getting Ready

▶ Invite the young people to write their responses to the questions and directions under What I Have Learned, Faith Terms to Know, and the other headings in the second column.

▶ Invite a few volunteers to share their responses, but do not correct them at this time. Tell the students that they will return to this page to check their learning at the end of the unit.

▶ For Questions I Have, you might write their questions on the board and on a piece of newsprint so that you can refer to them if or when the topics come up in the unit.

▶ Ask the class to look at the next page and begin Chapter 17.

Our Call to Holiness

BACKGROUND

A Life of Virtue

Growing in holiness is a cooperative effort that begins with God's grace and is followed by our free response to that grace. It is God showering us with his grace and our responding to that grace by maintaining our focus on whatever is true, honorable, just, pure, lovely, and gracious (see Philippians 4:8).

A Life of Holiness

Living a life of holiness involves decisions and choices. It involves the daily decisions and choices to cooperate with the Theological Virtues of faith, hope and charity, or love. These "gifts infused into the souls of the faithful" make them capable of living a holy life and attaining eternal life (see *Catechism of the Catholic Church*, 1813).

Living a life of holiness also involves the daily decisions and choices to develop habits of prudence, justice, fortitude, and temperance. These human habits, or Cardinal Virtues, must be exercised in the small details of daily living. On them hinge a wide range of virtues that provide us the habit of living a holy life.

The Cardinal Virtues

Prudence is basically the practice of good sense applied to our daily decisions about living. It is the practice of looking before we leap and of setting practical rules and limits on ourselves. Prudent people determine and direct their conduct according to the dictates of their conscience.

Justice involves the constant and firm decision to give God and our neighbor their due. Justice is about respecting and honoring God, who dwells in everyone. This cardinal virtue labors to establish harmony and equity in human relationships for the common good of all.

Fortitude is the virtue of remaining virtuous in the face of difficulties. It is the virtue that helps us resist the temptation to "chuck it all" when assaulted by the seeming success of the imprudence and injustice of others. Fortitude enables us to overcome discouragement and fear and to rely on God to be the source of our strength in times of trouble.

Temperance is our inner voice of moderation, telling us not to make our high times too high or our low times too low. This virtue helps us balance our use of material goods. It moderates our desires, directing them toward what is good. Temperance is rightly equated with healthy discretion and sobriety. A temperate person is one whose energies can be soberly and discretely directed to fulfilling God's work on Earth.

Theological Virtues

Constructed on a solid foundation of God's infused Theological Virtues of faith, hope, and charity, the Cardinal Virtues Strengthen us to forge good character. They help us live holy lives and to maintain our focus on whatever is true, honorable, just, pure, lovely, and gracious.

For Reflection

How aware am I that God has gifted me with the gifts of faith, hope, and charity? How do I see myself responding to these gifts?

How might I evaluate my efforts to live a life of prudence, justice, fortitude, and temperance?

Catechist to Catechist

The Invitation to Holiness

God has created us to be reflections of his holiness. God's holiness shines through the good actions of people. This is the way it should be. God created us to be holy. God created human beings in his image and likeness. He created us out of love to share in his life. God created us to share in his holiness. So what could be more human than to strive to be holy?

Works of Mercy

Each day God's holiness shines among us. We see reflections of his holiness in people's morally good actions. God's holiness is seen in people who practice the Works of Mercy, which are presented in this chapter. It is important that the sixth graders discover ways that they can integrate the Works of Mercy into their daily lives. Take the time to help them. Living the Works of Mercy needs to become part of the everyday lives of all followers of Christ.

The Church Teaches...

"Just as Christ instructed his followers according to their capacity to understand his message, the Church also must take serious account of the circumstances and cultures in which the faithful live in order to present the meaning of the Gospel to them in understandable ways. There is one saving word—Jesus Christ—but that word can be spoken in many different ways" (*National Directory for Catechesis*, 47).

As you teach this chapter, remember that God invites all people to live in his Kingdom. By respecting and honoring the diverse group of children before you, you will open their minds and hearts to the universal mission to make disciples of all people.

Further Reading and Reflection

For more on the teachings of the Church, see the *Catechism of the Catholic Church*, 1699–1715, 1730–1748, 1803–1845, 1987–2029; and from the *United States Catholic Catechism for Adults*, pages 307–313, 315–321, 328–330.

Catechist Prayer

God of compassion,
you sent us Jesus, your Son.
Help me bring your compassion
and mercy to those
in need of healing.
Amen.

Lesson Planner

Chapter 17   Our Call to Holiness

Focus To understand what it means to live a holy life

LESSON PART	PROCESS	MATERIALS and RESOURCES
EXPLORE **Focus** **To explore acts of justice as Works of Mercy** 🕐 10 minutes **Pages** 155–156	▶ Proclaim and discuss Psalm 99: 4, 7, 9 (the Lord loves justice). ▶ Learn the story of the Gleaning Network. **Disciple Power:** Understanding **Activity:** Choose to "glean" from our abundance.	Bible Pencils Crayons or markers
DISCOVER **Focus** **To discover the role of grace and freedom in living a holy life** 🕐 30 minutes **Pages** 157–159	▶ Review the Theological Virtues. **Activity:** Draw an image of the Theological Virtues. ▶ Understand the relationship between grace and freedom. ▶ Learn about ways to live the Works of Mercy. **Activity:** Identify and apply the Works of Mercy in specific situations.	Pencils Crayons or markers **Additional Activities Booklet:** Activities 17a–17b, or see BeMyDisciples.com.
DECIDE **Focus** **To decide on a response to the lesson on living a holy life** 🕐 10 minutes **Page** 160	**Activity:** Choose activities that help us live a holy life. **My Faith Choice:** Connect the understanding of God's will to holy life in action.	**Enriching the Lesson Activities:** Catechist Edition, page 263 • Creating Portraits of Holiness • A Job Description for Life • Organizing a Food Drive

Concluding the Lesson 10 minutes

We Remember

Page 161
▶ Review concepts and do the review activity.
▶ **Assessment Tools Booklet:** Chapter Test 17a–17b, or see BeMyDisciples.com.

We Pray

▶ **Prayer:** a prayer about living a holy life
Materials: Bible, candle, cross for prayer space
▶ Grade 6 Music CD

Preview

Point out resources for this chapter at
www.BeMyDisciples.com ▶
▶ Preview the With My Family page and next week's lesson theme.

Looking Ahead

In this chapter the Holy Spirit invites you to ▶

EXPLORE simple ways to work for justice.

DISCOVER how God calls us to live with grace and freedom.

DECIDE on how you can grow through the Works of Mercy.

CHAPTER **17**

Our Call to Holiness

? What is something unique about yourself?
What do your actions say about you?

God's actions among his people revealed something about God. Listen to the psalmist's prayer of praise of God.

*O mighty king, lover of justice,
    you alone have established fairness . . .
From the pillar of cloud God spoke to them;
    they kept the decrees, the law they received.
Exalt the L*ORD*, our God;
    bow down before his holy mountain;
    holy is the L*ORD*, our God.*   PSALM 99:4, 7, 9

? What examples of God's justice do you know from the Scriptures?

(155)

THE TASKS OF CATECHESIS

Teaching to Pray. Three prayers of the Church highlight the Theological Virtues of faith, hope, and charity, which are defined on page 157 of this chapter. Take time to review the three prayers—the Act of Faith, the Act of Hope, and the Act of Love—with your students in the Catholic Prayers and Practices section of the text. You may wish to begin or end today's class by praying one or more of these prayers aloud together.

Pray

▶ Gather the class for prayer. Begin and conclude by praying the Sign of the Cross together.

▶ Invite a volunteer to joyfully pray, "God our Father, you alone are holy. You sent your Son, Jesus, to restore us to holiness. Send the Holy Spirit to help us become your holy people."

Reflect

▶ Call the students' attention to the photo on the page. Invite them to imagine themselves in this person's place.

▶ Ask: "What is something unique about yourself?" Invite responses. Follow with the second question. Explain that every person is both different and unique. Everyone is created in the image and likeness of God.

▶ Have the students respond by praying Psalm 99 :4, 7, 9.

▶ Ask the concluding question and invite responses.

Focus

▶ Inform the students that in this chapter they will learn about what it means to be created in the image and likeness of God, thereby calling us to live a life of holiness.

▶ Call the students' attention to the Looking Ahead feature. Invite them to read aloud each bullet.

Introduce

▶ Remind students that God calls all members of the Church to serve others as Jesus commanded. Explain that this is a way in which we can use our unique gifts from God.

▶ Point out that each of us can respond to God's call of service individually or as a member of a group.

▶ Ask the students to read silently the text on the page to learn more about The Gleaning Network.

▶ Have the students examine the photo on the page. Then lead them in a discussion of how the Gleaners respond to their call to live a holy life.

Connect

▶ Have the class brainstorm other items than food that they might be able to glean from to address the needs of others.

▶ Invite the students to work in groups to complete the activity on the page. Ask them to share their ideas with the whole group.

▶ Read aloud the Disciple Power feature. Explain that the gift of understanding is a result of seeking to know God more, and in turn we come to better know ourselves.

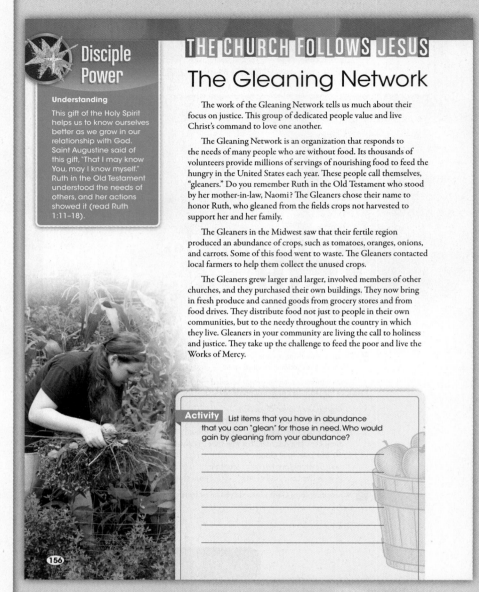

Disciple Power

Understanding

This gift of the Holy Spirit helps us to know ourselves better as we grow in our relationship with God. Saint Augustine said of this gift, "That I may know You, may I know myself." Ruth in the Old Testament understood the needs of others, and her actions showed it (read Ruth 1:11–18).

THE CHURCH FOLLOWS JESUS
The Gleaning Network

The work of the Gleaning Network tells us much about their focus on justice. This group of dedicated people value and live Christ's command to love one another.

The Gleaning Network is an organization that responds to the needs of many people who are without food. Its thousands of volunteers provide millions of servings of nourishing food to feed the hungry in the United States each year. These people call themselves, "gleaners." Do you remember Ruth in the Old Testament who stood by her mother-in-law, Naomi? The Gleaners chose their name to honor Ruth, who gleaned from the fields crops not harvested to support her and her family.

The Gleaners in the Midwest saw that their fertile region produced an abundance of crops, such as tomatoes, oranges, onions, and carrots. Some of this food went to waste. The Gleaners contacted local farmers to help them collect the unused crops.

The Gleaners grew larger and larger, involved members of other churches, and they purchased their own buildings. They now bring in fresh produce and canned goods from grocery stores and from food drives. They distribute food not just to people in their own communities, but to the needy throughout the country in which they live. Gleaners in your community are living the call to holiness and justice. They take up the challenge to feed the poor and live the Works of Mercy.

Activity List items that you have in abundance that you can "glean" for those in need. Who would gain by gleaning from your abundance?

_____

_____

_____

_____

_____

DISCIPLE POWER

Understanding. Ask the students to name the different subjects they are studying in school this year. Invite them to share things they do in order to grow in their understanding of those subjects (e.g., do their homework, pay attention in class, ask for help when they need it). Ask them to name the hobbies or sports in which they take part. Again, invite them to share things they do in order to gain greater understanding of their hobby or their chosen sport. Explain that, in the same way, there are things we all can do in order to grow in our understanding of our faith. Have the students name those things (e.g., pray, listen to God's Word, learn about the teachings of the Church). Affirm the students' responses, and encourage them to choose to do something just named in order to grow in their understanding of the faith.

Called to Be Saints

Our life's job description is to share in God's **holiness**. God created us to be holy as he is holy. He created us to know him, to love him, to serve him, and to live with him forever in eternal happiness. God's command to the Israelites is a command to all his people:

"For I, the Lord, am your God; and you shall make and keep yourselves holy, because I am holy . . . Since I, the Lord, brought you up from the land of Egypt that I might be your God, you shall be holy, because I am holy." LEVITICUS 11:44–45

The ability and freedom to live a holy life is a gift from God. He not only invites us to live a life in communion with him, but also gives us the powers to live that life. God gives us the **Theological Virtues**, which help us to live as his children.

Faith, Hope and Charity

The Theological Virtues enable us to grow stronger in holiness, the life of God within us. They are those strengths that begin in God and direct us toward holiness. There are three Theological Virtues: faith, hope, and charity. You may recall that Saint Paul concludes his great hymn to love with this memorable verse,

So faith, hope, love remain, these three; but the greatest of these is love. 1 CORINTHIANS 13:13

These virtues are gifts from God. The more we choose to live according to these virtues, the more we grow in holiness.

Activity Draw a symbol that reflects your understanding of faith, hope, and love.

(157)

FAITH FOCUS
What does it mean to live a holy life?

FAITH VOCABULARY
holiness
The quality, or condition, of a person who is living in communion and in right relationship with God, with others, and with all of creation; being in the state of grace

Theological Virtues
The virtues of faith, hope and charity; gifts of God that enable us to live a life of holiness, or a life in communion with the Holy Trinity

Works of Mercy
Virtuous actions that we do to help others in need, grouped as Corporal (bodily needs) and Spiritual (spiritual needs)

TEACHING VOCABULARY

Faith, Hope, and Charity. Review with the students the meaning of each of these three Theological Virtues. Faith is the gift of God that enables us to believe in God and everything he has revealed to us. Hope is the virtue by which we desire and trust in both the promise of eternal life and the graces necessary to attain it. Charity, or love, is the virtue by which we love God above all else and love our neighbor because of our love for him (*see CCC* 1814, 1817, and 1822).

Key Concept
God created us to be holy as he is holy and gives us the power to do so.

Teach

▶ Point out the three Theological Virtues on the page: *faith, hope* and *charity*. Invite students to define in their own words a definition for each. Then explain that these virtues enable us to live a holy life.

▶ Read aloud the definition of *holiness* on the page. Emphasize the term *communion*.

▶ Read aloud the first paragraph on the page. Then invite a student to read Leviticus 11:41–45 from a Bible. Explain that the ancient Israelites understood that Creation had a unique order and respecting that order helped them stay healthy and alive, especially as they wandered in the desert.

Reinforce

▶ Invite volunteers to read aloud the remaining text on the page.

▶ Have students underline key points in the text that relate to ways in which we can live holiness.

▶ Discuss how the Theological Virtues relate to holiness. *(They show us the ways to be holy.)*

Connect

▶ Ask: What can you do to show that the Theological Virtues are at work in your life?

▶ Invite the students to draw or describe an symbol for each virtue: Faith, Hope, and Charity.

Key Concept
The grace of the Holy Spirit calls and empowers us to freely choose to live a life of holiness.

Teach

▶ Begin by asking the young people to define holiness. Tell them this page may broaden their understanding of holiness.

▶ Invite volunteers to read aloud the text on the page.

▶ Ask: "How does grace help us to be free? What does freedom mean? Does freedom allow us to do whatever we want?" *(Grace gives us the ability to freely choose the good. We can choose to do what is wrong, but that is rejecting God's grace.)*

Reinforce

▶ Review with the class what students underlined as the main points for this page. Emphasis both sanctifying grace and the gift of freedom.

▶ Invite students to explain how grace and freedom are illustrated in each of the photos on the page.

Connect

▶ Have a student read about Job in the Faith-Filled People feature. Explain that grace helped Job be steadfast in faith when everything went wrong in his life.

▶ Ask: In what ways are you a holy person? What qualities does it require to respond to God's grace?

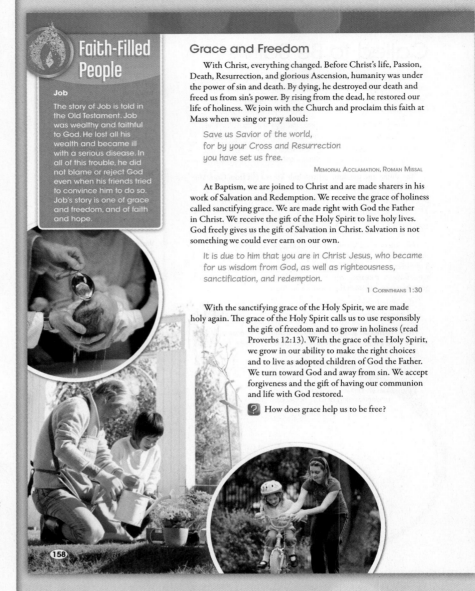

Faith-Filled People

Job

The story of Job is told in the Old Testament. Job was wealthy and faithful to God. He lost all his wealth and became ill with a serious disease. In all of this trouble, he did not blame or reject God even when his friends tried to convince him to do so. Job's story is one of grace and freedom, and of faith and hope.

Grace and Freedom

With Christ, everything changed. Before Christ's life, Passion, Death, Resurrection, and glorious Ascension, humanity was under the power of sin and death. By dying, he destroyed our death and freed us from sin's power. By rising from the dead, he restored our life of holiness. We join with the Church and proclaim this faith at Mass when we sing or pray aloud:

Save us Savior of the world,
for by your Cross and Resurrection
you have set us free.

MEMORIAL ACCLAMATION, ROMAN MISSAL

At Baptism, we are joined to Christ and are made sharers in his work of Salvation and Redemption. We receive the grace of holiness called sanctifying grace. We are made right with God the Father in Christ. We receive the gift of the Holy Spirit to live holy lives. God freely gives us the gift of Salvation in Christ. Salvation is not something we could ever earn on our own.

It is due to him that you are in Christ Jesus, who became for us wisdom from God, as well as righteousness, sanctification, and redemption.

1 CORINTHIANS 1:30

With the sanctifying grace of the Holy Spirit, we are made holy again. The grace of the Holy Spirit calls us to use responsibly the gift of freedom and to grow in holiness (read Proverbs 12:13). With the grace of the Holy Spirit, we grow in our ability to make the right choices and to live as adopted children of God the Father. We turn toward God and away from sin. We accept forgiveness and the gift of having our communion and life with God restored.

? How does grace help us to be free?

FAITH-FILLED PEOPLE

Job. The name *Job* comes from a Hebrew word meaning "hated." Job feared the Lord and shunned evil. His generation saw him as a favored servant of God because of his great wealth and power and his abundant blessing of children. All is well until this hero of the Old Testament suddenly loses everything, including his health. Job is excluded from society and instead of being revered, his own wife finds him revolting. During this time he never loses faith and trust in God. As Job did, we experience suffering, sometimes tragic suffering. The gifts of faith, hope, and charity strengthen us to deal with our sufferings just as they gave Job the vision and strength to deal with his suffering.

Growth in Holiness

God's gift of holiness is not just for us as individuals. It is not something we keep for ourselves. As God shares his life and love with us, we also share our life and love with others. Our growth in holiness involves the way that we live with other people. Holiness is about how we act with others.

Saint Paul teaches,

Put on then, as God's chosen ones, holy and beloved, heartfelt compassion, kindness, humility, gentleness, and patience, bearing with one another. . . . And over all these put on love, that is, the bond of perfection.

COLOSSIANS 3:12–14

The Church gives us the Spiritual and Corporal Works of Mercy to guide us in living the life of mercy and compassion that Saint Paul describes. These **Works of Mercy** are part of the Church's social teachings—a collection of principles that guide us to moral living as a holy community. Yet the Works of Mercy are not just an idea; they are concrete, practical things that we can do to live the Gospel. They clearly show that holiness is not just an idea, but something we must practice everyday. Holiness is a life of true courage, a life that requires God's grace.

Catholics Believe

Sacramentals

Sacramentals are sacred signs that help us give praise to God and live holy lives. The Church uses sacramentals to remind us of God's presence with us. One of the most important sacramentals is blessings. Blessings include praising God for his works and gifts, and the Church's intercessions for people to use God's gifts according to the Gospel.

Activity Read the lists of Corporal and Spiritual Works of Mercy on page 261. Under each picture write the Work of Mercy it illustrates. In the space provided, draw or write how you can live one of the Works of Mercy.

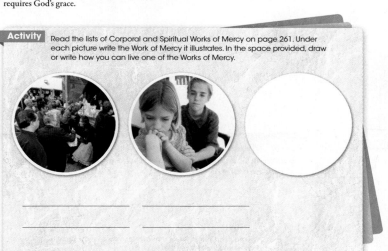

_____

_____

(159)

HUMAN METHODOLOGIES

Learning through Apprenticeship. The *National Directory for Catechesis* explains that learning by apprenticeship is when one is guided throughout his or her entire life to a deeper knowledge of and relationship with Jesus Christ (*see NDC* 29H). This year the children are your apprentices. As you teach the Corporal and Spiritual Works of Mercy, be mindful of how they invite us to grow in holiness, or Christ-like living. Have the students work in two teams to write contemporary versions of the Corporal Works of Mercy and the Spiritual Works of Mercy. Each list should show how sixth graders can care for the bodily and spiritual needs of others. Allow time for each group to share their list with the class.

Teach

▶ Recall with students that God gives us the grace to use freedom to live a holy life. Point out that living the Works of Mercy assist us.

▶ Read aloud the first paragraph on the page. Then have a volunteer proclaim the passage from Colossians.

▶ Point out that the qualities described by Saint Paul are the basis for the Works of Mercy. Refer the students to page 261 for a list of them.

▶ Have students work with partners to develop and present a pantomime for one of the Works of Mercy.

▶ During each pantomime, ask the other students to identify which Work of Mercy is being illustrated.

▶ Explain that sacramentals are another way for Catholics to live holy lives. Point out the Catholics Believe feature. Invite students to share what sacramentals they have and use in their daily lives.

Reinforce

Remind the students that these actions are the way to greater holiness.

Connect

Introduce the concluding activity on the page. Have students complete it and share their responses.

Reinforce

▶ Recall with students the Great Commandment by reading Mark 22:37–39.

▶ Point out that living the Works of Mercy is a way to live the Great Commandment.

▶ Remind students that Ruth lived a life of holiness because she understood her relationship to God. This is why she was able to freely choose to stay with Naomi.

Respond

▶ Introduce and explain the directions for the activity on the page.

▶ Have students complete the activity, inviting them to share their responses with the class.

▶ You may choose to have students complete this activity in groups.

Choose

▶ Have students silently read the last section and complete their faith choices.

▶ Then have students complete the last section to make their commitment in prayer. Encourage students to put their faith choice into practice this week.

I FOLLOW JESUS

Ruth told her widowed mother-in-law, Naomi, "Wherever you go I will go" (Ruth 1:16). Focus on trying to understand how God desires for you to live your life in holiness. Go where God wants you to be. Living the Works of Mercy is a way you can strive to live a holy life. See God in each person you help, for each of us is created is the image and likeness of God.

HOLY LIFE IN ACTION

Develop a list of three activities that you could do with others that would help you to live a holy life. Choose one and draw up a plan to put it into action.

Which Work of Mercy?	With whom?	What we'll do?	When will we do this?	What will we need to do it?
1.				
2.				
3.				

MY FAITH CHOICE

This week I will focus on understanding God's will for me, so that I can know myself better and live a life of holiness. I will

_____

_____.

 Pray, "Lord, help me to know you more, so that I may know myself better, and know your will for my life. Amen."

(160)

CATHOLIC DOCTRINE

Call to Family, Community, and Participation. Remind the students that they learned about this principle of Catholic social teaching in Unit 2. The Works of Mercy are one more example of how we live this teaching. All people have the obligation and the responsibility to participate in society and to work to promote the common good. As the new People of God, the Church lives the Works of Mercy and promotes the equitable, just, and fair participation in community life of all peoples.

Tip: Before having students complete the Holy Life in Action activity on page 160, help them brainstorm how they might more effectively live the Works of Mercy. Help them to see that actions like sharing kind words about someone or welcoming a new student or neighbor are different ways of living the Works of Mercy.

Chapter Review

Match each term with its description.

	Faith Term	Description
D	1. holiness	A. The virtue by which we love God above all else and love our neighbor as ourselves.
B	2. virtues	B. Good habits that enable us to grow stronger in the God-life that dwells within us.
C	3. faith	C. The virtue by which we believe in God.
E	4. hope	D. God's presence in us and our fidelity to him.
A	5. charity	E. The virtue by which we trust that God is looking after us.

TO HELP YOU REMEMBER

1. The Theological Virtues are gifts from God that connect us with him and strengthen us to live a life of holiness in communion with God.
2. The grace of the Holy Spirit helps us grow in our ability to freely make choices to grow in holiness.
3. Living the Works of Mercy is a sign that we are trying to live holy lives.

The Road Ahead

The road to living a holy life is not always an easy road to travel. Yet God always leads us along that road. Quiet yourself and place your trust in God, praying this prayer. Pray it often.

My Lord,
I have no idea of where I am going.
I do not see the road ahead of me.
I cannot know for certain where it will end.
I hope that I have the desire to please you in all that I am doing.
And I know that if I do this,
you will lead me by the right road.
Therefore, I will trust you.
I will not fear, for you are ever with me,
and you will never leave me.

ADAPTED FROM "THE ROAD AHEAD" BY THOMAS MERTON

161

LITURGY CONNECTION

Prayer Option. As an addition to praying "The Road Ahead" as a class, allow the students their own quiet prayer time to pray Psalm 119:1–2, 5, 10, 18, 34, 41 on their own. Create an environment conducive to quiet reflection by darkening the room a bit, if possible, and playing a recording of reflective, instrumental music. Have the students use their Bibles and their journals (or a blank sheet of paper) to write about their road to living a holy life. You and the students could then conclude with Thomas Merton's prayer.

We Remember

▶ Have the students complete the matching activity in the Chapter Review. Then have the class share their answers. Be sure to validate all correct answers.

▶ Now divide the class into three smaller groups: Grace, Theological Virtues, Works of Mercy. Have each group outline the key points they learned from this chapter about their assigned concept.

▶ Allow time for the whole class to compare the groups' key points with those statements in the To Help You Remember section.

We Pray

▶ Gather the students for closing prayer. Introduce the prayer. Tell the students that Thomas Merton was a Trappist monk who left us his writings to assist us in our spiritual lives.

▶ Call students to prayerful silence by inviting them to reflect on the conditions of their own road ahead toward holiness.

▶ Lead the class in the prayer, beginning and ending with the Sign of the Cross.

Preview

▶ Have students carefully tear-out the With My Family page along the perforation.

▶ Encourage them to share the pages with their family and to complete the activities together at home.

▶ If the students did not or were not able to complete the chapter review, encourage them to complete it with their family.

▶ Point out the chapter title and theme of next week's lesson.

Visit www.BeMyDisciples.com

▶ Take time with the students to explore the many activities and resources available at **www.BeMyDisciples.com.**

▶ Encourage them and their families to discover the many resources available at the Web site.

Before Moving On ...

As you finish today's lesson, reflect on the following question before moving on to the next chapter.

What have I done to let the students know that they are helping me to grow in a life of holiness?

With My Family

This Week...

In chapter 17, Our Call to Holiness, your child learned:

▶ Each of us is called to live the way of holiness that Jesus lived and taught to his disciples.

▶ We are joined to Christ and receive the gift of the Holy Spirit, and the grace to live as adopted children of God the Father.

▶ As we strive to understand more about God, we come to know more about ourselves and how we can respond to his call of holiness. Understanding, a gift of the Holy Spirit, helps us know ourselves better and grow in our relationship with God.

For more about related teachings of the Church, see the *Catechism of the Catholic Church,* 1699–1715, 1730–1748, 1803–1845, 1987–2029; and the *United States Catholic Catechism for Adults,* pages 307–313, 315–321, 328–330.

■ Sharing God's Word

Read together Leviticus 11:44–45. Emphasize that every person is created by God and is to live a holy life.

■ We Live as Disciples

The Christian home and family is a school of discipleship. Choose one of the following activities to do as a family or design a similar activity of your own:

▶ Write a family pledge to live holy lives. Be sure that the pledge describes specific behaviors and attitudes that constitute holiness.

▶ During family prayers, remind everyone that God is with you as you journey on the road of holiness.

■ Our Spiritual Journey

Trusting God may not be easy, especially during times of distress and anxiety. During such times, God is there. He might be inviting you to help others in need through Works of Mercy. In doing so, we take up our cross for the sake of others and receive the grace to persevere.

For more ideas on ways that your family can live as disciples of Jesus, visit **www.BeMyDisciples.com**

(162)

PARTNERING WITH PARENTS

Corporal and Spiritual Works of Mercy. As a follow-up to today's lesson, send a note or an e-mail to parents inviting them to review the Corporal and Spiritual Works of Mercy (on page 261 of the student text) with their children. Encourage them, with their children, to choose one Corporal and one Spiritual Work of Mercy they can do in the coming week or two in order to grow in holiness as a family.

Enriching the Lesson

Creating Portraits of Holiness

Purpose

To reinforce that God creates every person to be holy as he is holy (taught on page 157)

Directions

▶ Have the students work individually to create portraits of themselves in their journals.

▶ Invite them to list in their journals the gifts God has blessed them with.

▶ Have them write a self-portrait describing themselves using these gifts and blessings to live a holy life.

Materials

journals

pens or pencils

A Job Description for Life

Purpose

To reinforce that our life's job description is to share in God's holiness (taught on page 157)

Directions

▶ Have the students work with partners to write a job description for a person who wants to work at sharing in God's holiness.

▶ Ask them to include a narrative of the job description, including the things that they will need to accomplish the job; for example, be merciful or pray.

▶ Invite the students to share their job descriptions with the entire class.

▶ Use ideas from the individual job descriptions to create one job description.

▶ Display the class' job description as a reminder of the universal call to holiness.

Materials

chart paper

pens or pencils

Organizing a Food Drive

Purpose

To reinforce that living a life of holiness includes how we treat other people doing the Works of Mercy (taught on page 159)

Directions

▶ Work with the class to plan and organize a food drive to supply a community food bank or to contribute to the collection done in their parish.

▶ Brainstorm a list of the types of canned food or other nonperishable foods appropriate for a food drive.

▶ Have the students decorate a large cardboard box with words and pictures of the appropriate items and place the box in your learning space.

▶ Have them write sticky notes to themselves reminding them to bring in the items.

▶ Connect with the appropriate person in the parish or community and make arrangements to either deliver the food or have members of the class deliver the food when the box is filled.

Materials

large cardboard box

markers or crayons

sticky notes

BACKGROUND

Choosing a Life of Holiness

God has blessed us both with the ability to know what is right and what is wrong and with the ability to choose to do what we know is right and to avoid what we know is wrong. We are free to choose holiness and live a life in communion with God. We are also free to reject God and chart a course toward selfish pleasure and personal gain. God gives us free will to cooperate with his grace and to shape the final destination of our lives.

[handwritten: free will]

Our moral lives may be compared to a journey toward an ever deepening relationship with God—Father, Son, and Holy Spirit. All journeys are composed of steps. We can keep stepping forward, we can go backward, or we can hunker down and refuse to budge. Our pilgrimage toward God is comprised of step-like decisions, those little daily choices between good or evil, between doing the right thing or opting for the opposite.

[handwritten: - "seed" analogy]
[handwritten: - small choices]
[handwritten: - go forward: face on front of head, toes " " " foot (- we are made to go forward)]

Our Pilgrimage Toward God

Our pilgrimage toward God takes place in such common settings as grocery stores, restaurants, the workplace, behind the wheel of the car, on the telephone, in hospitals, in classrooms, and, above all, in our homes. It is in such places, in the ordinary situations of our lives, that we meet God. We meet him in a child, a bank teller, a waitress, a spouse, a mother-in-law, a police officer, a homeless person, a depressed friend, a sick cousin—in all whom we meet every day.

Stop and Reflect

We are to reach out to help others and do what we know the Holy Spirit is calling us to do. We need to stop and reflect on the reason we are acting. We need to be aware of our intention. We perform an act of kindness because it is the right thing to do out of love for God and our neighbor. We share food with the poor because grace freely given to us compels us to freely give of ourselves. When our good actions are motivated by love of God and neighbor, we are progressing on our journey toward the Kingdom of God.

[handwritten: - but don't show off" in y' good works]

Love Builds on Itself

We can also choose to do what is good and right for the wrong reasons. When we do, we deceive ourselves. We can congratulate a classmate for the purpose of gaining public admiration or impressing others. If our good actions are motivated by false pride, by vanity, or by shame, our actions may temporarily appease our egos, but they fail to move us toward God.

[handwritten: - showing off - get attention]

The more good that we freely and generously do out of love for God and for others, the freer we become to do it. The saints, who are acknowledged experts in these matters, give us the testimony of their lives to support this good news. Love builds upon itself, expands our hearts, doesn't keep tabs of the cost, and becomes a habitual way of life.

[handwritten: - or avoid guilt]

[handwritten: "doing good" = love]

For Reflection

What could I do to improve my daily moral decision making?

In my exercise of free will, how generous or selfish am I?

Catechist to Catechist

The Gift of Conscience

Sixth graders know when they have deliberately made either loving or hurtful choices. We usually know when we have deliberately hurt others. We know when we are about to, or have turned our backs on God and sinned. There is something deep inside each person that lets us know that we are in a dangerous place—this is called our conscience.

Examination of Conscience

Learning to identify the morality of our actions is vitally important to the moral development of young people. Take the time to help your students name the sources of morality as discussed in this chapter. This is also a good time to reinforce the use of an examination of conscience. Using the Great Commandment as the structure for an examination of conscience is appropriate for sixth graders. Making a regular examination of conscience will also help them develop the habit of asking and answering the question "How will this action affect my family, my friends, myself, and, most importantly, my relationship with God?" before they act.

[handwritten: on Ellen tebits book & examples ?]

The Church Teaches...

"Christ is the norm of morality . . . Christian moral formation involves a journey of interior transformation in light of Christ's Paschal Mystery, which brings about a deep personal conversion to Christ. Conversion to Christ involves confession of faith in him, adherence to his person and his teaching, following in his footsteps, taking on his attitudes, and surrendering the old self in order to take up the new self in Christ" (*National Directory for Catechesis,* 42).

With strong faith and the grace of God, the children are empowered to make good moral choices. As a catechist, you can help the children turn toward God to choose what is good, true, and beautiful in all their words and actions.

Further Reading and Reflection

For more on the teachings of the Church, see the *Catechism of the Catholic Church,* 1750–1761, 1776–1876; and from the *United States Catholic Catechism for Adults,* pages 311–321.

Catechist Prayer

Holy Spirit,
teach me how
to serve others
with the gifts
of your love and compassion.
Amen.

Lesson Planner

Chapter 18   Making Moral Choices

Focus To explain what is necessary for making moral decisions

LESSON PART	PROCESS	MATERIALS and RESOURCES
EXPLORE **Focus** **To explore the role of proverbs in making choices** 🕐 10 minutes **Pages** 163–164	▶ Proclaim and discuss Proverbs 3:13–14, 18 (Happy are they who find wisdom). ▶ Enjoy the story of students seeking wisdom. **Disciple Power:** Prudence	Bible Pencils Crayons or markers
DISCOVER **Focus** **To discover factors in making good moral decisions** 🕐 30 minutes **Pages** 165–167	▶ Identify the sources of moral actions. **Activity:** Role play a moral scenario. _Skit_ ▶ Review kinds of sin. ▶ Explore the formation of conscience. **Activity:** Solve a moral dilemma.	Index cards **Additional Activities Booklet:** Activities 18a–18b, or see BeMyDisciples.com.
DECIDE **Focus** **To decide on a response to the lesson on making moral decisions** 🕐 10 minutes **Page** 168	**Activity:** Choose how to build one's conscience. **My Faith Choice:** Connect the practice of prudence to good moral decisions. _define_	**Enriching the Lesson Activities:** Catechist Edition, page 275 • Designing Proverb Bumper Stickers • Solving Moral Dilemmas • Creating Conscience Cartoons

Concluding the Lesson   10 minutes

We Remember

Page 169

▶ Review concepts and do the review activity.

▶ **Assessment Tools Booklet:** Chapter Test 18a–18b, or see BeMyDisciples.com.

We Pray

▶ **Prayer:** an Examination of Conscience

Materials: Bible, candle, cross for prayer space

▶ Grade 6 Music CD

Preview

Point out resources for this chapter at

www.BeMyDisciples.com

▶ Preview the With My Family page and next week's lesson theme.

Looking Ahead

In this chapter the Holy Spirit invites you to ▶

EXPLORE how two boys mixed faith and fun.

DISCOVER how to make moral decisions as a disciple of Jesus.

DECIDE on ways you can form a good conscience.

CHAPTER 18

Making Moral Choices

? What are some skills that you would like to develop? What are some qualities about yourself that you would like to improve?

The Book of Proverbs is a summary of maxims, short sayings that guide us in living a moral life. In this proverb, we read about the value of wisdom:

Happy the man who finds wisdom,
*   the man who gains understanding!*
For her profit is better than profit in silver,
*   and better than gold is her revenue . . .*
She is a tree of life to those who grasp her,
*   and he is happy who holds her fast.* Proverbs 3:13–14, 18

? What is this proverb saying about the role of wisdom in making good decisions? In what ways do you seek wisdom?

163

HUMAN METHODOLOGIES

Learning by Heart. The *National Directory for Catechesis* emphasizes the importance of learning the fundamentals of many Catholic teachings, traditions, practices, and prayers by heart (*NDC* **29F**). At the conclusion of this chapter, encourage the students to memorize the list of "Conscience Builders" found on page 168. Knowing these by heart will help the students evaluate and make their moral decisions.

Pray

▶ Begin and conclude by praying the Sign of the Cross together.

▶ Lead an opening prayer:

"God our Father and Creator, send us your Holy Spirit to enlighten our minds and to strengthen our wills so that we may walk in the way of Jesus Christ, your Son. Amen."

▶ Invite the students to add petitions of their own. Respond to even, "Lord hear our prayer."

Reflect

▶ Discuss with the students the opening questions on the page.

▶ Invite students to examine the photo on the page and think about what it means to them.

▶ Have a volunteer student read from their own Bible, Proverbs 3:13–14, 18.

▶ Ask the questions that follow the Scripture passage.

▶ Explain that the beginning of wisdom is "fear of the Lord" (Psalm 111:10). Recall from Chapter 3 that this means being in awe and wonder about the mystery of God.

Focus

▶ Call the students' attention to the Looking Ahead feature. Invite them to read aloud each bullet.

▶ Explain to the students that in this chapter they will learn more about making good moral decisions.

Introduce

▶ Ask the students who they consider to be wise. Explain the good advice of wise people is often passed on through generations. The wisdom of the Israelites was handed on in proverbs.

▶ Explain that wisdom is more than abstract ideas. Wisdom often comes as result of practical experience. Read the Disciple Power feature and point out the connection between prudence and wisdom.

▶ Explain that Saint John Bosco helped youth who lived in poverty by teaching them how to make good moral decisions.

▶ Ask volunteers to do a dramatic reading of the text. Serve as the narrator yourself. Explain that the high school boys are living out the values of St. John Bosco: reason, religion, and kindness.

Reinforce

Remind the class that the proverbs are part of the Wisdom books of the Old Testament. Encourage them to memorize proverbs that can guide their lives.

Connect

▶ Invite the students to list people in their lives whom they can turn to for good advice.

▶ Emphasize that the Church guides us in making good moral decisions.

▶ Discuss what good advice they have been given that helped them make good moral decisions.

Disciple Power

Prudence

This cardinal virtue is also referred to as wisdom. Saint Thomas Aquinas defined prudence as "right reason in action." With experience comes wisdom, and prudence is often the guide for growing in wisdom.

THE CHURCH FOLLOWS JESUS
Mixing Faith and Fun

For the Hebrew people, proverbs were a source of wisdom. In this story, some contemporary students find value in the Proverbs too.

In honor of Saint John Bosco, who was known for mixing faith and fun, the boys at Don Bosco High School have a tradition in which they challenge each other by quoting Scripture while juggling. It keeps their minds sharp and their bodies coordinated. Plus, the fun is a nice distraction from the poverty and turmoil of their inner-city life. The one who lasts the longest is the "new Don." This respectful title means "nobleman" in Italian. A sense of brotherhood among the boys results from the challenge.

"Yeah! Dominic! Get ready to call me Don Roberto!" shouted Robert. "You are on!" Dominic hollered back. "So you think you've got what it takes?" Dominic said, ready to juggle.

Robert and Dominic squared up in front of each other, while other boys circled around them in anticipation of who would be first to drop out. They began to juggle, and Robert started quoting first since he was the challenger.

"Proverbs 29:8—Arrogant men set the city ablaze, but wise men calm the fury!" Robert said confidently. The crowd cheered. Still juggling, Dominic went next, "Proverbs 16:8—Better a little with virtue, than a large income with injustice."

"Proverbs 11:19—Virtue directs toward life, but he who pursues evil does so to his death," Robert said, as he almost dropped a juggling ball. Dominic then moved closer to Robert saying, "Proverbs 15:4—A soothing tongue is a tree of life, but a perverse one crushes the spirit." The crowd waited for Robert's return.

Robert stood his ground saying, "Proverbs 24:3—By wisdom is a house built, by understanding is it made firm." Just then, Dominic lost his balance, and the juggling balls scattered. Dominic was disappointed, but out he went over to Robert and said, "Nice one, Don Roberto!"

? Who helps you to make good moral choices?

DISCIPLE POWER

Prudence. Invite the students to think about some of the life lessons they have learned since they were in kindergarten. For example: if you want a pet you must take care of it; if you want to make good grades, you must study hard; it's important to give everyone on the team a chance to play in the game. Explain that as we learn these life lessons, we are growing in wisdom. Prudence is putting that wisdom into action. For example, we may know that in order to be a good piano player we must practice often. But, if we don't put that knowledge to work—if we never practice—we will not become a good piano player. In the same way, we might memorize the Ten Commandments or the Works of Mercy. Emphasize that if we never put God's Commandments into action, we have not grown in prudence and wisdom.

Christian Morality

Each day we juggle many choices. The decisions we make, as disciples of Jesus, to live a holy and moral life are called moral decisions. Our life is a response to God's invitation and to the grace he gives us as we make our journey. Here are some guide for our journey:

The natural law, the laws written on our hearts. For example, "Do good and avoid evil" and "Treat others as you want them to treat you."

The Bible, especially the Great Commandment and the Ten Commandments

The life and teachings of Jesus Christ and the teachings of the Church

Knowing what determines the **morality**, that is, the goodness or evil of human acts, will also help us make wise moral decisions. Three things determine the morality of an act. They are :

The Object. The object of the act is <u>what we do</u>. It is the good or the bad we do or say. Some things are good in themselves, such as praying. Other things such as murder are evil in themselves. Many evil acts, such as lying, cheating, and stealing, are prohibited by the Ten Commandments.

The Intention. The intention is what <u>the person</u> doing the act wants, or desires to do. <u>Intention is the purpose for doing</u> or saying something. A good intention cannot change an evil act into something good. For example, if a person steals something to give it to someone else as a gift, the act of stealing is still wrong, even if the person had a good intention.

The Circumstances. The circumstances of the <u>act are those things that surround the decision.</u> Circumstances do not change the goodness or evil of an act. They can make something we do or say better or worse. For example, if a person steals out of fear or ignorance, the act is still evil and wrong, but they may not be as responsible for the act.

A morally good act requires all three aspects: the goodness of the object, a good intention in doing the act, and its circumstance.

Activity Discuss with a group examples of circumstances that might make it difficult for people to choose to do something they know is right. Role play one of the situations you discuss.

(165)

FAITH FOCUS
How do you choose to make a good decision?

FAITH VOCABULARY

conscience
The gift of God that is part of every person that guides us to know and judge what is right and wrong.

morality
Refers to the goodness or evil of human acts; the morality of human acts depend on the object, intention, and circumstances of the action.

TEACHING TIP

Sacrament of Penance and Reconciliation. Recall with the students that through the Sacrament of Reconciliation we receive the mercy and forgiveness of God. Share with them the Gospel account of Jesus handing on to Saint Peter the Apostle and the Church the power to forgive sins in his name (Matthew 16:19). Point out the connection between the Gospel story and the Sacrament of Reconciliation: "Since then the Church has never failed to call people from sin to conversion and through the celebration of penance to show the victory of Christ over sin" (Introduction, Rite of Penance 1). Seeking forgiveness for all sins is essential to Christian moral living.

Teach

▶ Ask: "Where do you find guidance in making moral decisions?"

▶ Point out the Faith-Filled People section on page 166. Explain that St. Alphonse wrote practical answers to moral questions.

▶ Write on the board: *object, intention, circumstances*. Briefly assess the students' understanding of these terms.

▶ Read aloud the text emphasizing guides for the moral journey.

▶ Point out that God has given us the ability to understand the goodness or evil of human acts.

Reinforce

Point out the definition of *morality* in the Faith Vocabulary.

Connect

▶ Have students cite examples of a morally good act. Ask them to describe the act (object), the intention, and the circumstances of each. Clarify any misunderstandings.

▶ Summarize, explaining that all three sources must be good for the act to be morally good.

▶ Invite groups of students to role play situations where it is difficult to choose what is right. Move them explore what helps a person to make a good decision, referring to the text on the page.

Key Concept
Sin is to freely and knowingly turn away from God.

Teach

▶ Read aloud the first paragraph on the page. Explain that often if we follow the good advice of others, we can avoid temptations.

▶ Inquire: What do you think are some major sins and what makes them so?

▶ Have students read the remaining text on the page silently.

Reinforce

▶ Review the distinction between mortal and venial sins.

▶ Reinforce that grace is necessary for the full living of any virtue. Emphasize that God's mercy and forgiveness are abundant.

Connect

▶ Have students match up the capital sins and the capital virtues in the activity. Explain that these virtues help us resist these sins. *(pride—humility; greed—charity; envy—kindness; anger—kindness; lust—chastity; gluttony—temperance; sloth—diligence)*

▶ Recall from the previous chapter the Theological and Cardinal Virtues. Discuss how living the moral virtues takes education, deliberate practice, and can be a struggle. Ask the students to describe when living the virtues could be a challenge. *(Peer pressure, opportunity for personal gain)* Remind them that all the virtues and gifts included each week in the Disciple Power feature, if practiced, will give them the skills for discipleship.

Faith-Filled People

Alphonse de Liguori

Saint Alphonse is a Doctor of the Church and the founder of a religious community called the Redemptorists. He was a poet, musician, and author. His writings on the moral life include practical answers to questions about moral decisions for daily living. He is the patron saint of confessors and teachers of moral theology. His feast day is August 1.

Sin: Turning Away from God

The Cardinal Virtues, such as prudence, help us make good moral decisions which are necessary to live a holy and moral life. The decisions we make, however, are not always easy. Sometimes we come close to doing what we know is against God's Law and choose not to do it. At other times, we give in to temptation and choose to do something that we know is wrong.

We sin when we deliberately turn away from God and his love. In doing so, we offend him. To help us understand more clearly what sin is about, the Church speaks about capital sins, mortal sins and venial sins.

Capital Sins. These are sins that lead to other sins. There are seven capital sins (read Proverbs 6:16–19; Matthew 15:18–20). They are usually listed as pride, greed, envy, anger, lust, gluttony, and sloth, or laziness. Each of these capital sins has a corresponding capital virtue to help resist the temptations of these sins. The capital virtues are humility, loving kindness, patience, chastity, temperance, generosity, and diligence (read Galatians 5:19–26).

Mortal Sins. These are serious offenses against God that break our relationship with him (read Mark 10:17–22). If we die in this state of separation from God, we remain separated from him forever by our own choices. Being forever separated from God is what we call Hell. When we are aware of being in a state of mortal sin, we are to seek God's grace and forgiveness in the Sacrament of Penance and Reconciliation.

Venial Sins. These are less serious offenses against God. Because all sins turn our hearts away from God's love, we should seek forgiveness of all sins, including venial sins (read 1 John 5:16–17).

❓ How does the virtue of patience help us resist the sin of anger? How does the virtue of humility help us resist the sin of pride? Discuss with a partner.

166

FAITH-FILLED PEOPLE

Alphonse de Liguori. We might call Alphonse (also Alphonsus) de Liguori a child prodigy. He graduated from law school at age 16 and by the time he was 20, Alphonse was a leading lawyer in his hometown of Naples, Italy. At age 27 he decided to give up his successful law career to study for the priesthood. Ordained in 1717, he immediately became well-known as a compassionate confessor and down-to-earth preacher. In 1732 he established the Redemptorists, an association of priests and brothers who continue to serve the Church today. For more information on Saint Alphonsus Liguori go to the Saint Resource at www.BeMyDisciples.com.

Conscience

Our life is filled with so many things that compete for our attention. We juggle facts and ideas to make our decisions. How do we know what is good and what is evil?

Every human being has another "voice" that constantly calls for our attention. It is our **conscience**. Our conscience helps us to judge what is right and what is wrong. We have the responsibility to train our conscience, and obey our well-formed conscience. The better we train, or form, a good conscience, the better we will be at making decisions that help us live as followers of Jesus Christ.

People can have a conscience that does not correctly judge something to be good or evil. Such a conscience is called an erroneous conscience. An erroneous conscience provides someone with information that leads to decisions that are against God's Law. When a person deliberately chooses not to work at forming a good conscience, that person is responsible for his or her erroneous conscience. That means that the person is also responsible for the wrong caused by actions that are due to erroneous conscience. However, if a person has never been taught what is right, or is not mentally able to choose, then that person cannot be held accountable for the evil he or she does.

Activity
What To Do?

Solve this dilemma. Your friend approaches you with the answers to an upcoming test. What do you do?

1. What is your first response?

_____

2. What will you do?

_____

3. Why would you do it?

_____

4. What might be the consequence of your decision?

_____
_____

Catholics Believe

Magisterium

The Church has the responsibility to guide us to make moral decisions. Guided by the Holy Spirit, the Church fulfills this responsibility to make sure she is faithful to the teachings of the Apostles on faith and morality. We call this teaching office of the Church, the Magisterium.

THE TASKS OF CATECHESIS

Moral Formation. The Church teaches that each of us is guided by an inner voice that is our conscience, inviting us always to choose what is good and to turn away from evil. Our conscience speaks to our hearts as we make choices, letting us know those that are right and those that are wrong. Tell the students that in order to strengthen our ability to hear and to respond to our consciences, we need to take time to reflect upon our actions and choices, and to listen to our hearts. When we realize that we have made wrong choices or have turned from doing what is right and good, our well-formed consciences compel us to take responsibility for our actions, to seek forgiveness, and to turn our hearts and our lives back to God (CCC, 1777, 1779, 1781).

Key Concept
A good conscience helps us to judge if an act is good or evil; and guides us in doing good.

Teach

▶ Ask a student to read aloud the definition of conscience in Faith Vocabulary on page 165.

▶ Explain that each person is created with a conscience. Yet our consciences must be informed and formed.

▶ Invite students to suggest ways in which we inform and form our conscience. Recall Chapter 13 on Penance.

▶ Have volunteer students read aloud the text on the page.

▶ Discuss the difference between comparing a well-formed conscience and an erroneous conscience. Emphasize that we are responsible for the formation of our conscience.

▶ Read the Catholics Believe section. Explain that the Magisterium is that part of the Church responsible for guiding us in understanding the teachings of the Church. We use her teachings to help form our consciences.

Connect

▶ Write on the board, "Right is right, even if everyone is against it; and wrong is wrong, even if everyone is for it."

▶ Have students work with partners to discuss the saying, provide specific examples, and apply the saying to their lives.

▶ Have students compete the activity on the page. Invite them to share their responses to the dilemma.

Reinforce

▶ Remind students that we all have many guides to help us make good moral decisions.

▶ Point out that the Holy Spirit is always with us to teach and guide us and to help us follow our informed conscience.

▶ Recall the Cardinal Virtue of prudence. Explain that grace from the Holy Spirit strengthens our ability to know what is good and wisely choose the good, even in the face of difficulty.

Respond

▶ Introduce and explain the directions for the activity on the page.

▶ Have the students complete this activity individually. Invite volunteers to share how they completed it if they wish.

Choose

▶ Have the students read My Faith Choice silently and respond to it.

▶ Then have students complete the last section to make their commitment in prayer. Invite them to put their faith choice into practice this week.

I FOLLOW JESUS

You make many moral decisions each day. Some are easy to make; others are more difficult. The Holy Spirit is always with you to teach you and to guide you in making good moral decisions. Forming a good conscience will help you make wise and morally good choices.

CONSCIENCE BUILDERS

Look over this list of conscience builders. Mark a ✔ next to the actions you use to help build, or form, a good conscience.

☐ Read Sacred Scripture.

☐ Pray to the Holy Spirit.

☐ Study and follow the teachings of the Church.

☐ Learn from the stories of people of faith, like Saint John Bosco.

☐ Seek the advice of people of faith whom I trust.

How might using these conscience builders help you make good moral decisions?

_____

_____

_____

_____

_____

MY FAITH CHOICE

This week I will practice the cardinal virtue of prudence and make good moral decisions thoughtfully and responsibly. I will

_____

Pray, "Holy Spirit, be my Advocate and guide me in making good decisions. Amen."

168

TEACHING TIP

Adages. Adages are sayings that state a general truth. They are concise and catchy sayings that can help us focus. The popular saying "What Would Jesus Do?" is an adage in question form that captures the truth that Jesus is "the way and the truth and the life" (John 14:6). Asking and answering the question, "What Would Jesus Do?" will help guide the students to make moral decisions. However, refrain from applying this question in situations that are extremely complex. Rather, ask the children what values, such as love, forgiveness, honesty, or fairness, would have guided Jesus as he made his decisions. Remind them that the Holy Spirit is always with them helping them to understand what Jesus taught and guiding them in making decisions to live as followers of Christ.

Chapter Review

Read this situation. Name the object, intention and circumstances. Then discuss the morality of the whole act with a partner.

Sarah and her teammates were playing in the championship game. In the final minutes of the game, Sarah swept by the defender. As she kicked the ball trying to break the 0-0 score, she slipped on the wet grass, and the ball struck the goalkeeper in the face. Stunned from the fall, she looked toward the goal and saw the goalkeeper running toward her.

Object: _____kicked the ball_____

Intention: _____tried to score_____

Circumstances: _wet grass, slipped, ball_

struck goalkeeper

TO HELP YOU REMEMBER

1. Sin is turning away from God and his love, freely choosing to do or say what we know is against God's Law.

2. The sources of morality are the object of the act, the intention of the agent, and the circumstances surrounding the act.

3. Our conscience helps us to judge whether an act is good or evil.

Examination of Conscience

Thinking about and evaluating our moral decisions is important. One way we do this is by examining our conscience.

Leader: Let us look into our hearts and think about the way we have loved or failed to love God and our neighbor as Jesus taught us.

All: **Happy those who observe God's decrees, who seek the Lord with all their heart.**
PSALM 119:2

Leader: Reflect in silence after each question.

Reader: How have you kept God first in your life? *(Pause)*
How have you shown respect to your parents and teachers? *(Pause)*
How have your words and actions shown respect for your body and the bodies of others? *(Pause)*
How have you been kind and helpful to other people? *(Pause)*

All: **Happy those who observe God's decrees, who seek the Lord with all their heart.**
PSALM 119:2

169

We Remember

▶ Introduce and explain the Chapter Review.

▶ Read the moral dilemma to the class. Have each student write the object, intention and circumstances on a separate sheet of paper.

▶ Invite the whole class to discuss what they wrote. Provide the correct answers making sure each student understands the correct responses. Have the students write the correct answers in their books.

▶ Review key points from the chapter using statements in the To Help You Remember section.

We Pray

▶ Gather the students for the closing prayer. Introduce the prayer by reviewing an examination of conscience. Recall the last one in Chapter 13.

▶ Select a leader and a reader and offer them a moment to prepare.

▶ Together pray beginning and ending with the Sign of the Cross.

▶ Encourage the young people to memorize the psalm verse and to include it in daily prayer.

TEACHING TIP

Best Response Extension. After students complete the Chapter Review, invite the class as a whole to come up with other scenarios that present young people with situations where they need to make moral decisions about their actions. Invite volunteers to describe the situations to the class and then have a class discussion to identify the object, intention, and circumstance of each situation presented. In addition, discuss the morality of the act that the students present.

Preview

▶ Have students carefully tear-out the With My Family page along the perforation.

▶ Encourage them to share the pages with their family and to complete the activities together at home.

▶ If the students did not or were not able to complete the Chapter Review, encourage them to complete it with their family.

▶ Point out the chapter title and theme of next week's lesson.

Visit www.BeMyDisciples.com

▶ Take time with the students to explore the many activities and resources available at **www.BeMyDisciples.com.**

▶ Encourage especially them and their families to discover the many resources available the Web site.

Before Moving On ...

As you finish today's lesson, reflect on the following question before moving on to the next chapter.

Do I follow up and ask the children to report on their progress with their faith choices each week?

With My Family

This Week...

In chapter 18, Making Moral Choices, your child learned:

▶ The Church guides us in making wise decisions to live as faithful followers of Jesus Christ. Prudence is the cardinal virtue that helps us make good moral choices.

▶ When we freely and knowingly choose an act that is evil, we sin; we turn away from God and offend him.

▶ These three things determine the morality of our actions: the object of the act, our intention in doing the act, and the circumstances surrounding the act.

▶ A good conscience helps us to judge if an act is good or evil; and guides us in avoiding evil and doing the good.

For more about related teachings of the Church, see the *Catechism of the Catholic Church,* 1750–1761, 1776–1876; and the *United States Catholic Catechism for Adults,* pages 311–321.

■ Sharing God's Word

Spend time reading through sections in the Book of Proverbs with your child. Select proverbs together to memorize. Keep them both in your mind and your heart as you make daily choices in life.

■ We Live as Disciples

The Christian home and family is a school of discipleship. Choose one of the following activities to do as a family or design a similar activity of your own:

▶ Discuss as a family how this statement applies to making moral decisions: "Right is right even if everyone is against it; and wrong is wrong even if everyone is for it."

▶ Spend one on one time with your children doing an activity they enjoy. Offer bits of advice or "kernels of wisdom" to help them in life.

■ Our Spiritual Journey

Discernment is vital to living a moral life and making our spiritual journey. An examination of conscience is one traditional tool that facilitates our use of the spiritual discipline of discernment. In this chapter, your child used an examination of conscience as part of the closing prayer. Use this or another form of an examination of conscience every day.

For more ideas on ways that your family can live as disciples of Jesus, visit **www.BeMyDisciples.com**

(170)

PLANNING AHEAD

Charity and Almsgiving. Two of Chapter 19's suggested activities require advanced preparation. Three pieces of music are suggested as a way to explore the meaning of the theological virtue of charity in the Disciple Power activity. Look ahead to this feature box on page 280 for the suggested songs. The With My Family page suggests that families find new ways to give. Prepare in advance a list of outreach opportunities in your parish and community, and provide Web site information for international outreach organizations. See the Partnering With Parents feature box on page 286 for specific suggestions. Also on page 285 it is suggested that a person who speaks Hebrew be invited to class to share in the closing prayer.

Enriching the Lesson

Designing Proverb Bumper Stickers

Purpose

To reinforce that the Book of Proverbs provides maxims to guide us in making decisions to live as children of God (taught on page 164)

Directions

▶ Distribute Bibles and allow time for children to explore the Book of Proverbs.

▶ Have the students work with partners to design bumper stickers using a proverb from the Bible.

▶ Have volunteers explain how the proverbs guide them in making a difference in their own life and in the lives of other people.

▶ Display the bumper stickers as reminders to the students to live their faith.

Materials

construction paper

markers or crayons

Solving Moral Dilemmas

Purpose

To reinforce that knowing what determines the morality, the goodness or evil, of human acts will help us make wise moral decisions (taught on page 165)

Directions

▶ Present a moral dilemma to the class. Note: You might even invite the students to develop their own moral dilemmas.

▶ Ask the students to work in small groups to write a skit to resolve the moral dilemma.

▶ Have each group present their skits and have the class discuss the effectiveness of the solutions presented in each skit.

Materials

paper

pen or pencils

Creating Conscience Cartoons

Purpose

To reinforce that our conscience guides us to judge what is right and what is wrong (taught on page 166)

Directions

▶ Have the students work with partners to create cartoon-like illustrations with four frames illustrating characters listening to their conscience as they face and resolve a moral dilemma.

▶ Have the students illustrate their cartoons and share them with the class.

▶ Mount all the cartoons on mural paper and display them where others can enjoy and learn from them.

Materials

art paper

fine point markers and pens

mural paper

The Law of Love

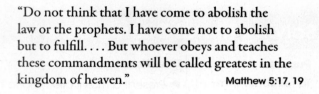

BACKGROUND

A Mandate to Each of Us

The Ten Commandments as found in Exodus 20 contain a curious diversion from the way God usually addresses the people of the Old Testament. In the Old Testament, he generally addresses the people of Israel collectively, as a community. This is not what happens in the rendering of the Ten Commandments.

"I'm Talking to You"

God, using the first person singular, says, "I am the LORD" (see Exodus 20:2), as in "Listen up, what I'm about to say is very important." Then he says, "you," not the plural, collective "you," but "you" as an individual. God, in other words, is addressing each person individually as he speaks to the whole community. In other words, we need to listen up. These Commandments are not "just for others"; they are for me. It is as though he is saying, "Take this personally; I'm talking to you."

In the Revelation of the Ten Commandments, God was not revealing something new. He was not revealing a mystery beyond the comprehension of humans. He was putting in human words what he had already written on every human heart. God was making us aware of what his people, both the community of Israel and each member of it, already should have known and come to understand.

The Fulfillment of the Law

Jesus is the new Moses. He encourages us to seek the fullness of life by loving God and our neighbor as he did. All of the prophets and all of the Law that comprise the legacy and the gift of the Old Covenant are not only summed up but fulfilled in the Person of Jesus, the Son of God, who teaches us the truth and the way to authentic life. Jesus, the Incarnate Son of God, revealed the importance of the Commandments. He taught:

"Do not think that I have come to abolish the law or the prophets. I have come not to abolish but to fulfill. . . . But whoever obeys and teaches these commandments will be called greatest in the kingdom of heaven." **Matthew 5:17, 19**

Parable of the Rich Young Man

The story of the rich young man gives us an insight into how Jesus fulfilled the Law. The young man approached Jesus and asked him, "[W]hat good must I do to gain eternal life?" (Matthew 19:16). Jesus replied, "If you wish to enter into life, keep the commandments" (19:17). The young man then said, "All of these I have observed. What do I still lack?" (19:20). Jesus confounds the young fellow—and us—with his response, "If you wish to be perfect, go, sell what you have and give to [the] poor, and you will have treasure in heaven. Then come, follow me" (19:21).

Jesus asks his disciples to live the Law of God as it is written on the human heart. Always make the love of God and others your motivation in all you say and do. Fulfill Jesus' New Commandment: "love one another as I love you" (John 15:12).

For Reflection

When am I most aware of God speaking to me? How attentive and responsive am I?

In what ways do I strive to fulfill the Law of God as Jesus taught?

Catechist to Catechist

Choosing Wisely

Many sixth graders are very concerned about being accepted by their peers. They want to belong. Sometimes this need causes them to follow someone who may be popular but not very wise. Eleven- and twelve-year-olds are not too young to begin to understand the value of making wise decisions. The gift of divine wisdom gives us the grace to see things from God's perspective and act accordingly. Jesus taught us that living according to Law of Love will help us make us the right and wise choice.

Making Wise Choices

When we keep our eyes fixed on Jesus, we grow in wisdom. One of the signs that young people are growing spiritually is their ability to use their intellect and free will responsibly. During this session, invite the students to role-play and solve moral dilemmas. After each solution help them see the principles underlying their decisions and evaluate the wisdom of their actions. *examples of skits??*

The Church Teaches...

"Life in Christ is a way of being, a way of loving. It is not a plan of action, even action on behalf of justice. Life in Christ shapes human beings a new and provides a new vital principle for all their activity. It is the radical integration of the person with Christ, the indwelling of Christ in the heart and soul of the Christian, a fusion of the Christian with the Son of God. 'Christ lives in me' is the singular confession of the Christian who has been led by God's grace and who trusts, at the deepest level of being, that true life comes only through the redemptive sacrifice of Jesus Christ" (*National Directory for Catechesis*, 46).

Reflect on this powerful statement from the Church and how it can help inspire you to help the children let Christ live in them.

Further Reading and Reflection

For more on the teachings of the Church, see the *Catechism of the Catholic Church*, 1949–2029; and from the *United States Catholic Catechism for Adults*, pages 310–311, 315–318, 327–330.

Catechist Prayer

Holy Spirit,
Spirit of Holiness,
help me reach out
and serve others.
Amen.

Lesson Planner

Chapter 19 The Law of Love

(Focus) To learn about Jesus' Law of Love

LESSON PART	PROCESS	MATERIALS and RESOURCES
EXPLORE (Focus) **To explore the power of God's love** 🕐 10 minutes **Pages** 171–172	▶ Proclaim and discuss Matthew 5:44, 46–47 (Love your enemies). ▶ Learn about Saint Josephine Bakhita. **Disciple Power:** Charity	Bible Pencils Crayons or markers
DISCOVER (Focus) **To discover the significance of Jesus' Law of Love** 🕐 30 minutes **Pages** 173–175	▶ Connect the Natural Law to the Ten Commandments. **Activity:** Compare U.S. laws to the Natural Law. ▶ Explore the foundations of the Great Commandment. ▶ Describe the Law of Love. **Activity:** Apply the Law of Love to everyday living.	**Additional Activities Booklet:** Activities 19a–19b, or see BeMyDisciples.com.
DECIDE (Focus) **To decide on a response to the lesson on the Law of Love** 🕐 10 minutes **Page** 176	**Activity:** Identify concrete examples of living the Golden Rule. **My Faith Choice:** Connect the Law of Love to the Golden Rule.	**Enriching the Lesson Activities:** Catechist Edition, page 287 • Mapping Qualities of a Disciple • Making a Class Rules Banner • Designing Friendship Prayer Cards

Concluding the Lesson 🕐 10 minutes

We Remember

Page 177

▶ Review concepts and do the review activity.

▶ **Assessment Tools Booklet:** Chapter Test 19a–19b, or see BeMyDisciples.com.

We Pray

▶ **Prayer:** The Shema

Materials: Bible, candle, cross for prayer space

▶ Grade 6 Music CD

Preview

Point out resources for this chapter at

www.BeMyDisciples.com

▶ Preview the With My Family page and next week's lesson theme.

Looking Ahead

In this chapter the Holy Spirit invites you to ▶

EXPLORE the life of a person who loved others as Jesus taught.

DISCOVER that living as a child of God is to follow the Law of Love.

DECIDE how you can live according to the Golden Rule.

CHAPTER **19**

The Law of Love

? How do friends treat one another? How do enemies tend to treat one another?

Read how Jesus challenges his disciples to be perfect as the Father is perfect, to love as God loves:

"But I say to you, love your enemies, and pray for those who persecute you . . . For if you love those who love you, what recompense will you have? . . . And if you greet your brothers only, what is unusual about that?"

Matthew 5:44, 46–47

? How did Jesus show love to his enemies? Why should we love our enemies?

(171)

Pray

▶ Begin and conclude by praying the Sign of the Cross together.

▶ Have the students picture in their minds their closest friends. Have them think about how they treat their friends.

▶ Pray aloud a prayer of thanksgiving to God for all of our friends.

Reflect

▶ Ask the students how, on the other hand, enemies tend to treat one another.

▶ Have a volunteer read aloud the Scripture passage. Ask the questions that follow.

▶ Loving one's enemies is a difficult concept for young people. Remind them of the dignity of each person in God's eyes, and of the example of Jesus. Explain to the students that God calls us to love everyone, not just our friends.

Focus

▶ Discuss the photo on the page as related to the chapter title.

▶ Call the students' attention to the Looking Ahead feature. Invite them to read aloud each bullet.

HUMAN METHODOLOGIES

Making a Commitment to Live the Christian Life. The *National Directory for Catechesis* states that Christian living includes doing acts of charity, meeting the needs of the poor, and working for justice (*NDC* 29G). As the students learn more about the Great Commandment in this chapter, encourage them to share in the many ways their parish follows this commandment. For example, talk about how the parish community expresses its love for God by gathering for Mass and other liturgical celebrations. Highlight ways in which the parish expresses its love for neighbor by praying for and visiting with the sick, by caring for the needy, and by taking part in community efforts such as Habitat for Humanity.

Introduce

▶ Acknowledge to the students how difficult it is to love our enemies.

▶ Ask students what they know about St. Josephine Bakhita, a slave from Sudan in the late 1800s.

▶ Invite students to read the fictional journal entries on the page. They are based on an autobiography of Saint Bakhita.

Reinforce

Ask the students to look for the following examples of Josephine's goodness in the diary entries:

- showing respect for her elders,
- a desire to serve God,
- obedience to God's will.

Connect

▶ Have students read aloud the Disciple Power box. Point out that St. Bakhita followed the virtue of charity.

▶ Ask the closing question. *(Possible answers: She was given the opportunity to know and serve him; she was gifted with a spirit of thankfulness, even as she suffered.)*

Disciple Power

Charity = love

To love as God loves is what we call charity, or *caritas* in Latin. This is the standard by which all of us are to live by, and as Saint Paul says, charity is the greatest of the three theological virtues (read 1 Corinthians 13:13).

THE CHURCH FOLLOWS JESUS
Witness of Love

Josephine Bakhita was an African girl from Sudan. She was taken into slavery as a child and became a saint of the Catholic Church. Read these selections from an imaginary diary about her life.

7:30 am October 15, 1878
I write my first journal entry . . . trying to remember my name. I am only nine years old. My friend, Elham, and I were walking around the fields. We noticed we were far from home. Suddenly two strangers appeared from behind a fence. One of them asked me to pick some fruit for him in the forest. I did so out of respect for those older than I. They did not respect me. While in the forest, he grabbed me and threatened me with a knife. He told me, "If you cry, you'll die! Follow us!" They call me "Bakhita." I am now their slave.

9:00 pm February 2, 1881
Escape seems impossible. I think tonight I will die. I do not know if I can take any more cuts. My masters tattooed on my body my age, 13. It still hurts from when they rubbed the salt into my wounds. Why do they do this to me? I feel humiliated.

5:00 am January 10, 1890
Heavenly Lord! I know that you have let me live because you have destined me for great things. I am free now. I live far away in Italy and have now learned about God and the Christian faith. My Master, what blessings you have bestowed upon me in my life! You have washed away all my sins, and I now take part in your heavenly banquet here on Earth. Yesterday was the beginning of my new life as your daughter as I was baptized. Loving Father, you have always been in my heart but now I know your name. May I love everyone as you have always loved me. Perhaps I will become a sister like the ones who instructed me.

7:00 am February 7, 1947
Almighty Father, I am not afraid to see you. Please loosen these chains, they are so heavy! I realize that the pain and suffering all my life, even as I lay dying, has been like that of your Son, Jesus. I am truly your daughter in Christ. All that I am belongs to you. As you desire, my Master.

Saint Josephine was canonized in October 2000.

 How did God bless Josephine, in spite of her suffering?

(172)

DISCIPLE POWER

Charity. To help illustrate the meaning of charity (caritas), use one of the following songs in the opening or closing prayer of today's lesson. Before singing or listening to a recording of the song, have the students read its text and discuss how that text defines charity (caritas).

You will find an instrumental version with a refrain on your Grade 6 music CD. You also may wish to use one of the following versions, that might be found in your parish hymnal.

▶ *Where Charity and Love Prevail* (1961, Paul Benoit, OSB. World Library Publications, Franklin Park, IL).

▶ *Ubi Caritas* (1978, Taizé Community. GIA Publications, Inc., Chicago, IL).

▶ *Ubi Caritas* (1996, Bob Hurd. Oregon Catholic Press, Portland, OR).

Love Like God

Before Josephine learned about God, she tells us that she knew him in her heart. God created us in his image and likeness, calling us to love like him. In God's fatherly love for us, he has etched into our hearts and minds a law that guides us in living as his images in the world.

There is something about the way God has created us that moves us naturally to choose what is good for us and for others. The Church calls this the **Natural Law**. This law, a pattern or design, helps us to discover the way to the true happiness that God has promised us. This law also helps us to recognize evil, which leads us away from happiness and away from God. Here are three principles of the Natural Law:

- Do good and avoid evil.
- Tell the truth to each other.
- Be respectful toward one another.

The Ten Commandments

When God entered into the Covenant with Moses and the Israelites, he gave Moses the Ten Commandments. These commandments reminded the people of the laws that God had written on their hearts. The Ten Commandments named the important ways by which God wants his people to live so that they can create a community of care and respect (read Exodus 20:1–17).

Jesus told his disciples they were to live the commandments. He said that he came to fulfill the commandments, and not to do away with them (see Matthew 5:17).

Activity Which U.S. laws or customs appear to reflect the principles of the Natural Law listed above? Write your thoughts in the space below.

— life
— liberty
— happiness

FAITH FOCUS
What rules or laws does Jesus ask us to live by?

FAITH VOCABULARY
Golden Rule
This is a rule to live by that is knowable by human reason. It is to do unto others as you would have them do unto you.

Natural Law
It is the foundation of moral life for everyone. It enables us by human reason to know what is good and what is evil.

Shema
The Shema is a prayerful rule revealed by God in the Covenant that there is only one God, and the Lord is God.

173

Teach

▶ Ask the students the Faith Focus question.

▶ Remind the students that Josephine tells us she knew God in her heart even before she heard about him.

▶ Have students read the text on the page about natural law.

▶ Point out the principles of natural law and how we can think of it as the "law of the heart."

▶ Explain that natural law is not based on feeling but on reason.

▶ Invite the students to think of other principles or rules common to everyone beyond the list on the page. Examples: fairness, compassion for those in need, respect for human life.

Reinforce

Have students read about the Ten Commandments. Explain that the Ten Commandments are reasonable and good rules to follow. God spelled out for his people what they had forgotten was true.

Connect

Complete the activity and invite responses. (*American principles of "life, liberty, the pursuit of happiness"*)

TEACHING TIP

The Law of the Heart. The Natural Law is just that—natural. Written on the heart of every person, it guides us in living as God created us to live. Emphasize that cooperating with the grace of the Holy Spirit helps us to know and use the precepts of the Natural Law in making decisions to live as children of God. Ask the students to help you compile a list of values that all human beings can understand to be good and true, regardless of their religious or cultural background.

Teach

▶ Invite students to read the Faith-Filled People feature on the page to expand on the story of Saint Josephine Bakhita.

▶ Have students read the page silently.

▶ Explain that the Great Commandment includes both the Shema and the Golden Rule. To love God is an act of faith; to love others as ourselves is reasonable and universally accepted as a good rule to follow.

Reinforce

Recall the definitions from the Faith Vocabulary on the previous page and make word cards for them.

Connect

▶ Write on the board in three columns: Tobit 4:15, Deuteronomy 6:5, and John 15:12. Divide the class into three groups. Distribute Bibles and invite each group to look up one passage. Have volunteers write the passages on the board in the appropriate column when they find them.

▶ Discuss how these passages, though phrased differently, are essentially the same as Luke 6:31.

Faith-Filled People

Canossian Sisters

Saint Bakhita was a member of this group founded by St. Magdalene of Canossa in 1808. This religious group of Catholic women dedicate themselves to education, evangelization, and pastoral care of the sick and health services. The rule of their organization is based on the belief that the good we do for our neighbor comes from being good to ourselves.

The Great Commandment

Jesus told us to live the commandments as he did. We are to love God and one another as he did. Jesus' way of love is the Christian way of life. When the Pharisees, scholars of the Law, gathered to hear Jesus speak, one of them asked him which of all the laws is the greatest. Jesus said:

> "You shall love the Lord, your God, with all your heart, with all your soul, and with all your mind. This is the greatest and the first commandment. The second is like it: You shall love your neighbors as yourself. The whole law and the prophets depend on these two commandments."
>
> MATTHEW 22:37–40

In teaching the Great Commandment, Jesus revealed his authority on the Law. The Great Commandment is a combination of the **Shema** and the **Golden Rule**. The Shema, from the Jewish tradition, is a prayerful reminder of the First Commandment that God is the Lord and God is One.

> "Hear O Israel! The LORD is our God, The LORD alone! Therefore, you shall love the LORD, your God, with all your heart, and with all your soul, and with all your strength."
>
> DEUTERONOMY 6:4–5

A Rule for Everyone

Over the centuries, people have lived by different laws, both just and unjust. Yet God has clearly given us his standard for living in the commandments. Within the Great Commandment, we can detect the Natural Law at work. To love our neighbor as ourselves comes from what has been called the Golden Rule, a principle of the Natural Law. Almost every religion has taught and continues to teach some form of the Golden Rule. It is phrased in different ways in the Bible (read Tobit 4:15; Matthew 7:12). Essentially the rule states that we should "do to others as you would have them do to you" (Luke 6:31).

Jesus teaches that those who faithfully follow him and live the Great Commandment will be invited to join him in the Kingdom that God has prepared since the beginning of creation (read Matthew 25:31–40). This is possible for everyone. God leads us to happiness here on earth within the Church. Yet complete happiness is everlasting life with God and with Mary and all the saints.

❓ How is the Great Commandment a combination of the Shema and the Golden Rule? Explain it to a partner.

(174)

FAITH-FILLED PEOPLE

Canossian Sisters. The motto of the Canossian Sisters is "to make Jesus known and loved." Their foundress, Saint Magdalene of Canossa, once said that "Jesus is not loved because he is not known." Magdalene herself came from a noble family, but she experienced much loss, many trials, and emotional and physical illness in her younger years. During the difficult times she prayed to Mary, Our Mother of Sorrows. She eventually founded the Canossian Daughters of Charity, Servants of the Poor, whose focus is to touch each person, especially the poor, with the love of God. Their ministry of love extends throughout the world. This is the community that brought Josephine Bakhita to faith in Jesus Christ, and it is the community she later joined.

"Remain in My Love."

Happiness with God comes through the grace of love and the freedom found in following God's Law. This grace of love is the grace of the Holy Spirit given to us as members of the Church. When we act out of charity, we are using the grace of love. And we follow Jesus' new commandment, to "love one another" (John 13:34). The New Commandment is the Law of Love. By following this law, we show others that we are Jesus' disciples (read John 13:35).

The Holy Spirit gives us the grace to follow the Law of Love. Jesus taught, "As the Father loves me, so I also love you. Remain in my love. If you keep my commandments, you will remain in my love, just as I have kept my Father's commandments and remain in his love" (John 15:9–10). By following the Law of Love, we are not just being a disciple of Jesus; we are his friends (read John 15:14). By loving God, we are able to love one another, even our enemies.

"I Have Called You Friends."

Loving one another frees us to be who God created us to be—an image of God! This is why Jesus says, "I no longer call you slaves, because slave does not know what his master is doing. I have called you friends" (John 15:15). St. Josephine Bakhita understood Jesus' new commandment, the Law of Love. She understood her freedom came from her relationship with God. Despite her childhood experience of being a slave, Josephine remained in the love of Christ. She was able to see herself as a friend of Jesus and a daughter of God the Father.

> **Activity**   **Applying The Law of Love**
>
> When is it easy to apply the Law of Love to others and when is it hard to do? Describe a situation in which someone applies the Law of Love when it is not easy to do. With a partner, act out the situation for your class.
>
> *ideas?   ⚹ ?*

Christ,
Rembrandt Harmenszoon van Rijn, c.1648/50 (oil on oak panel)

(175)

Catholics Believe

The New Law is the grace of the Holy Spirit received by faith in Christ. This law works through charity. We find Jesus teaching this New Law in his Sermon on the Mount (see Matthew 5–7). It is also expressed through the celebrations of the Seven Sacraments, which impart the grace of love (see CCC 1983).

Key Concept
Being a follower of Jesus means to live the Law of Love.

Teach

► Have students read the first paragraph to learn the meaning of The Law of Love. Point out that we need the love of God in order to love one another. Faith in Christ is the way to accept the love of God.

► Have students read the Catholics Believe box. Address any questions that they may have. Point out that the new Law of Jesus Christ perfects the Law as revealed in the Old Testament.

► Split the class in half, one group is to read the second paragraph and the other group is to read the third paragraph.

► Have each group discuss the main point of the paragraph. Then have a representative from each group explain the paragraph to the whole class.

► Invite students to discuss how the Law of Love applies to their friendships.

Reinforce

Ask the students to make word cards for the Faith Vocabulary terms on page 173.

Connect

Have students compete the activity on the page. Invite them to share their responses with the class.

TEACHING TIP

Working with a Partner. Those who have difficulty thinking of multiple ideas and writing them down may benefit from doing the activity on the page with a partner. After each set of partners has had time to complete the activity, invite two sets of partners to form a small group of four. Give the small groups time to exchange their thoughts and ideas regarding ways to show love to their friends and to those who are not nice to them. Conclude the activity by listing on the board or on a flip chart suggestions from the entire class.

Reinforce

▶ Recall that to act with charity is to love as God loves. Explain that charity is a theological virtue that can help us build and maintain our friendships on the solid ground of respect.

▶ Point out that the Holy Spirit guides us in respecting others and ourselves by living God's Commandments.

Respond

▶ Introduce the activity by recalling the Golden Rule.

▶ Explain the directions for the activity.

▶ Have students complete the activity with a partner, inviting them to share their responses with the class. If time allows, invite volunteers to act out their situations.

Choose

▶ Have students read and complete their faith choices.

▶ Then have students make their commitment in prayer. Encourage them to put their faith choice into practice this week.

I FOLLOW JESUS

Part of being a Christian means to love others as God loves you. Each day you cooperate with the Holy Spirit to show love and respect to yourself and others. Making such decisions according to the Law of Love builds friendships.

LIVING THE GOLDEN RULE

Write several ways you would like others to treat you. Then think of a situation in your school, family, or neighborhood where you could treat someone else in the way you like to be treated. Write the situation here.

_____

_____

_____

_____

_____

_____

MY FAITH CHOICE

This week I will look for opportunities to live the Law of Love according to the Golden Rule. I will:

_____

_____

Pray, "Jesus you call me friend. Help me to be a friend to others as you are to me. Amen."

(176)

THE TASKS OF CATECHESIS

Education for Community Life. Support the students in making a faith choice to live the Golden Rule. Have them write the Golden Rule, Matthew 7:12, on a card and keep it with them this week. Encourage them to be very conscious of how often they treat others the way they would like to be treated. Invite them to take a private inventory, that is, make an examination of conscience, of how they are deliberately trying to live the Golden Rule.

Chapter Review

Match the term in the left column with the description on the right.

1. Ten Commandments — a. the laws God gave to Moses

2. The Shema — b. the law written in our hearts

3. Natural Law — c. Love God, and your neighbor as yourself

4. Great Commandment — d. a prayerful rule revealed through the Covenant

The Shema

The Shema is prayed as a morning and evening prayer by Jewish people today. Praying the Shema is the ancient tradition found in the Old Testament. Below is an abbreviated version of the prayer written in English and Hebrew. Pray these words with your class in English.

Hear, Israel, the Lord is our God, the Lord is One.
Sh'ma Yisrael Adonai Elohaynu Adonai Echad.

Blessed be the Name of His glorious kingdom for ever and ever.
Barukh Shem k'vod malkhuto l'olam va-ed.

(177)

We Remember

▶ Review key points from the Chapter using statements in the To Help You Remember section.

▶ Now introduce and explain the Chapter Review.

▶ Have the students complete the matching activity and check their work with a partner.

We Pray

▶ Gather the students for the chapter's closing prayer. Introduce the prayer by reading the opening sentences.

▶ Pray together beginning and ending with the Sign of the Cross.

▶ If any of the children have a Jewish relative, you might ask that person to visit the class to recite the Shema in Hebrew and have the students echo it in English.

LITURGY CONNECTION

A Profession of Faith in God. Use this information to respond to questions about the Shema. The Shema is composed of three passages from the Pentateuch—Deuteronomy 6: 4–9, Deuteronomy 11: 13–21, and Numbers 15: 37–41. It is common for Jews to recite the Shema twice a day. Since the Shema is not so much a prayer as a profession of faith, Jewish tradition does not speak of "praying the Shema" but rather "reading the Shema." The Shema contains a declaration of Israel's faith in one God, the promise of a reward for the fulfillment of God's laws, and punishment for their transgression.

Preview

▶ Have students carefully tear-out the With My Family page along the perforation.

▶ Encourage them to share the pages with their family and to complete the activities together at home.

▶ If the students did not or were not able to complete the Chapter Review, encourage them to complete it with their family.

▶ Point out the chapter title and theme of next week's lesson.

Visit www.BeMyDisciples.com

▶ Take time with the students to explore the many activities and resources available at **www.BeMyDisciples.com**.

▶ Encourage especially them and their families to discover the many resources available at the Web site.

Before Moving On ...

As you finish today's lesson, reflect on the following question before moving on to the next chapter.

How have I followed Jesus' Commandment to love all of the children as God loves me?

With My Family

This Week...

In chapter 19, The Law of Love, your child learned:

▶ God etched in our hearts the Natural Law. This law helps us to do good and avoid evil.

▶ Jesus taught us that we are to love God and to love our neighbor. This is the Great Commandment.

▶ Jesus challenges us to be perfect as the Father is perfect. We can do this with the grace of the Holy Spirit who enables us to love others as God loves us.

▶ Charity calls us to love others as God loves us.

For more about related teachings of the Church, see the *Catechism of the Catholic Church,* 1949–2029; and the *United States Catholic Catechism for Adults,* pages 310–311, 315–318, 327–330.

■ Sharing God's Word

In John 15:1–17 Jesus teaches the Parable of the Vine and the Branches. Read this Scripture passage with your family reflecting on how this imagery is relevant today. Discuss how your family remains in the love of Christ.

■ We Live as Disciples

The Christian home and family is a school of discipleship. Choose one of the following activities to do as a family or design a similar activity of your own:

▶ Post in your home the family rules. Be sure that each of the family rules follows the Law of Love.

▶ During family mealtime, talk about some major events in the lives of your children. Discuss how the Law of Love is followed or violated.

▶ Select new ways to participate in the life of your parish and greater community that demonstrate the Law of Love.

■ Our Spiritual Journey

Often we struggle with the need to make sacrifices in life. This can limit us in our ability to fully respect others, especially those who we might consider undeserving. Almsgiving is an ancient practice in which sacrifice and charity come together for the good of those in need, as well as for the good of ourselves. Find new ways to give to the needy this week.

(178)

For more ideas on ways that your family can live as disciples of Jesus, visit **www.BeMyDisciples.com**

PARTNERING WITH PARENTS

Almsgiving. This week's "Our Spiritual Journey" activity on the With My Family page suggests that families find new ways to give this week. In order to make it more possible for parents and young people to do so, provide families with a list of outreach opportunities in the parish and in the community, as well as Web site information for relief organizations such as Catholic Charities, Catholic Relief Services, and Operation Rice Bowl.

Enriching the Lesson

Mapping Qualities of a Disciple

Purpose

To reinforce that moral decisions help us to live as disciples of Jesus, (taught on page 175)

Directions

▶ Have the students work with partners to create character maps describing good decision makers.

▶ Invite the students to place their own names in the center circle of the character map.

▶ Have them identify the qualities of good moral decision makers and write these qualities on lines coming from the circle.

▶ Invite the students to share their character maps with the entire class.

Materials

paper

pens or pencils

Making a Class Rules Banner

Purpose

To reinforce that good rules based on the Great Commandment help us to love one another as God loves us, (taught on page 175)

Directions

▶ Have the students work with partners to create a list of 3 practical rules that reflect the Great Commandment taught by Jesus.

▶ Invite the students to write their rules on the board for the entire class to read.

▶ Have the class consolidate the rules on the board to a list of only ten.

▶ Compare their lists to any list of class rules you may have completed earlier in the year.

▶ Invite the students to decorate a banner that includes their list of class rules.

▶ Display proudly it in the classroom as a reminder of how to love one another as God loves us.

Materials

paper

markers

mural paper

scissors

Designing Friendship Prayer Cards

Purpose

To reinforce the teaching about the Golden Rule, (taught on page 174)

Directions

▶ Have the students work with partners to design prayer cards for a friend in need.

▶ Distribute Bibles and have the students open to the Book of Psalms.

▶ Tell the students to write an appropriate psalm verse on each side of the card.

▶ Have them decorate the border of their card.

▶ Invite students to share their prayer card with a friend who is in need.

Materials

Bibles

tag board cut into prayer card size

markers or crayons

BACKGROUND

The Path to True Happiness

Unlike any other creatures, human beings are given the ability by God to act in freedom. We have the ability to choose the path of life or to choose the path of death. The path of life leads to a life of eternal happiness with God, or Heaven. The path of death leads to destruction and, ultimately, to a life of eternal separation from God for eternity, or Hell.

The Ability to Choose

Animals act on instinct alone. Humans have been given the gift of an intellect that gives us the ability to know God, to know ourselves, and to know right from wrong, good from evil. We have the ability to reflect on our actions and to discern whether or not those actions show respect and reverence for God, for ourselves, for others, and for all of God's creation. We can know whether we are building a world of life or a world of death, a civilization of life or a civilization of death. Obviously, we cannot always know the minute details of the end result of every choice the moment we make every choice. What we can know is whether the action taken here and now will promote and uphold life or whether it will diminish or destroy life for oneself or others.

The Beatitudes

Building a civilization of life leads to the happiness God desires and has created every person to have. Sometimes this world is filled with forces, opinions, teachings, and temptations that disguise themselves as ways to happiness.

They confuse and mislead us. They direct us away from the path of life and true happiness. At other times, these same forces, opinions, teachings, and temptations name and try to convince us that the ways to happiness revealed by Christ lead to our destruction and unhappiness. Christ taught that "the poor in spirit," "those who mourn," "the meek," and "the merciful" were blessed by God and were walking the path to true happiness. These Gospel values, lived by Christ, are not easily accepted by many to be the way to happiness.

Fortunately, God assists us with the gift of the Holy Spirit, who dwells within each person and within the Church. The Holy Spirit guides us continually as we try to discern whether our choices are good or evil, whether they will lead us to life and happiness or to death and unhappiness.

Making our journey toward happiness is a struggle. The Son of God himself was tempted to travel a different road. His response to the Tempter was clear: "Choose the way of God." Christ won victory over the forces of evil and sin and gained for all the glorious freedom of the sons and daughters of God. In that freedom we have been given a new life and our ultimate hope of living a life of eternal happiness with God, and with Mary and all the saints.

For Reflection

When have I struggled to choose the path of life and happiness? What were the consequences of choosing the path of life?

Who do I see living the Beatitudes? What difference is it making for them? For others?

Catechist to Catechist

Happiness

A quick answer to the question, "What is happiness?" might be "Having everything I want." The validity of this response usually fades as quickly as it is uttered. The wise person soon learns that the accumulation of possessions brings only the need for more and more. Giving not taking, brings happiness. Living the Beatitudes is the sure road to happiness. Being poor in spirit, merciful and meek, working for justice and peace, keeping God as our top priority, and serving others in need all lead to God and an eternal sharing in his divine love. That's happiness.

Word Game

Have the students name what makes them happy. Write the letters H-A-P-P-Y on the board. Brainstorm things for each letter that make people happy. After the list of words for all letters is completed, evaluate the responses by asking, "How does this relate to the Beatitudes?"

The Church Teaches...

"Both the private practice and the public witness of knowledgeable and committed Christians are indispensable factors in the sanctification of the world, a responsibility to which all the baptized are called. In such an environment, living an active Christian life becomes a crucial element in effective catechetical methodology" (*National Directory for Catechesis*, **30G**).

As a catechist, you are a disciple of Jesus, who is your Teacher. The way Jesus taught is the model of how you are to teach the children, the young disciples of Jesus, entrusted to your care. God calls you to teach beyond the classroom—to teach through all aspects of your life.

Further Reading and Reflection

For more on the teachings of the Church, see the *Catechism of the Catholic Church*, 1716–1729, 1812–1819, 1830–1845, 1965–2029; and from the *United States Catechism for Adults*, pages 307–311, 318.

Catechist Prayer

Creator God,
you made me in your own
image and likeness and
gave me the freedom to
make choices.
Help me use that
freedom to choose good
over evil, life over death.
Amen.

Lesson Planner

Chapter 20 Ways of Happiness

Focus To learn what the Beatitudes teach us about following Jesus

LESSON PART	PROCESS	MATERIALS and RESOURCES
EXPLORE **Focus** **To explore how to live justly and with joy** 🕐 10 minutes **Pages** 179–180	▶ Proclaim and discuss Matthew 5:3–11 (the Beatitudes). ▶ Read about Blessed John XXIII. **Disciple Power:** Joy **Activity:** Write headlines about peacemakers.	Bible Pencils
DISCOVER **Focus** **To discover the true happiness that the Beatitudes describe** 🕐 30 minutes **Pages** 181–183	▶ Learn the meaning of the Beatitudes. ▶ Describe how living the Beatitudes leads us to Heaven. **Activity:** Identify ways to live the Beatitudes. ▶ Learn the connection between holiness and canonization.	**Additional Activities Booklet:** Activities 20a–20b, or see BeMyDisciples.com.
DECIDE **Focus** **To decide on a response to the lesson on the Beatitudes** 🕐 10 minutes **Page** 184	**Activity:** Sketch ideas for peace in the world. **My Faith Choice:** Connect to purity and peaceful actions.	Crayons or markers **Enriching the Lesson Activities:** Catechist Edition, page 299 • Creating a Happiness Word Web • Creating CDs about Holy People • Catholic Social Teaching: Living the Beatitudes

Concluding the Lesson 10 minutes

We Remember	We Pray	Preview
Page 185 ▶ Review concepts and do the review activity. ▶ **Assessment Tools Booklet:** Chapter Test 20a–20b, or see BeMyDisciples.com.	▶ **Prayer:** Psalm 146, a prayer of praise **Materials:** Bible, candle, cross for prayer space ▶ Grade 6 Music CD	Point out resources for this chapter at **www.BeMyDisciples.com** ▶ Preview the With My Family page and next week's lesson theme.

Looking Ahead

In this chapter the Holy Spirit invites you to ▶

EXPLORE the impact of Blessed John XXIII's spirit of joy upon the Church.

DISCOVER how following the Beatitudes is living a life of holiness.

DECIDE on you can live the Beatitudes to gain a sense of joy.

CHAPTER **20**

Ways of Happiness

? What do you do to bring happiness to others?

While ministering to a great multitude, Jesus taught how to live as one of his disciples. Listen for the attitudes of discipleship:

"Blessed are the poor in spirit,
for theirs is the kingdom of heaven . . .
Blessed are the merciful,
for they will be shown mercy.
Blessed are the clean of heart,
for they will see God.
Blessed are the peacemakers,
for they will be called children of God . . ."

MATTHEW 5:3–11

? According to Jesus' words, who are blessed by God? What do you think people thought when they heard these words?

(179)

HUMAN METHODOLOGIES

Learning within the Christian Community. The *National Directory for Catechesis* reminds us of the importance of the consistent witness of parents, catechists and the community of believers in the catechetical process. A vibrant community of faith provides young people with many models, examples, and opportunities to become active participants in the life and work of the Church (*see NDC* 29C). Consider how you live and model the Beatitudes to the students, particularly an invitation to be meek, merciful, and a peacemaker. Reflect, too, upon those things that bring you happiness on Earth, and give thanks to God, the true source of happiness and joy.

Pray

▶ Gather the students for prayer. Begin and end with the Sign of the Cross.

▶ Ask the class to echo you:

"Father, we praise you. You have shown us the path to true happiness through your Son, Jesus Christ."

Reflect

▶ Ask the opening questions and invite responses. Point out that Jesus' rules are often different from the rules that some people practice, especially regarding enemies.

▶ Introduce the Scripture passage and ask a volunteer to read aloud the Scripture passage of the Beatitudes. Ask the rest of the class to listen as if they were hearing the words for the first time, as the crowd did that day.

▶ After a moment of silence, ask the closing questions. Accept all reasonable responses to the second question.

Focus

▶ Call the students' attention to the Looking Ahead feature. Invite them to read each bullet aloud.

▶ Tell the students that on the next page they will learn more about Pope John XXIII and his spirit of joy and peace.

Introduce

▶ Invite students to read about joy in the Disciple Power box.

▶ Share a personal experience when you had a great sense of joy. Describe the experience and then invite volunteers to share when they too have had a sense of joy.

▶ Ask students what they know about Blessed Pope John XXIII. Recall for them that he was the Pope who called the Church to the Second Vatican Council. Explain that they are going to learn more about Blessed Pope John XXIII.

▶ Invite students to volunteer to read the text on the page.

▶ Have students go back through the reading and underline the major issues addressed by the encyclical. Point out the pope's belief that bringing justice would lead to joy and peace.

Reinforce

Facilitate a discussion among the students on how joy, peace and justice are interconnected.

Connect

Invite the students to complete the activity on the page. Point out that peace on earth is limited because true peace will be found ultimately with God in heaven.

Disciple Power

Joy

One of the Fruits of the Holy Spirit, joy demonstrates that we live according to the Spirit (see Galatians 5:22–23). Joy results from moral living and believing in the hope of eternal life.

THE CHURCH FOLLOWS JESUS

A Spirit of Peace

A great sense of joy and anticipation filled the air as the bishops began the Second Vatican Council in 1962. Pope John XXIII called this meeting of all the bishops of the Church to renew the Church with the light of Christ. The Council continued until 1964. Despite the unexpected death of Pope John XXIII on June 3, 1963, the pope's spirit of joy and peace reinvigorated the entire Church.

Not long before his death in 1963, Pope John XXIII released *Pacem in Terris,* or "Peace on Earth." He wrote this encyclical not only to Catholics but to all people of good will to remind the world that all human life, without exception, is sacred. The pope was very concerned about the many ways human life was being abused.

The encyclical listed the rights of all human beings to life, respect, freedom, and education. It also addressed the need to do away with nuclear weapons. Pope John pointed out that when people are left to be poor, or when governments misuse power and make people less free, God's plan for humanity is abused. We must work to correct these injustices and build the kingdom of peace that Jesus announced. We must love one another as Jesus did, according to the natural rights given to us by God.

The road to peace leads to joy. When as individuals and groups, we respect the life and dignity of everyone as sacred, we pave a way for justice in the world. The Holy Spirit teaches us Christ's way of justice. The more we listen, accept his help and act justly, the more we are building a world of peace as Blessed John XXIII taught. Today the Church continues Christ's way of justice with a joy-filled spirit.

Activity Work with a group. Think of situations from your community or from the news where people are building a world of peace. Write headlines for their efforts in this space.

_____

_____

_____

_____

_____

DISCIPLE POWER

Joy. Help students realize the many sources of joy in their lives. Invite them to draw four columns on a blank sheet of paper. Instruct them to give each of the columns one of the following headings: Things I Have; Things I Do; People in My Life; and My Life of Faith. Their task is to list as many sources of joy as possible under each of the headings. To help start them thinking, as a class come up with one example for each column. For example: Things I Have—video games; Things I Do—sing; People in My Life—my parents; and My Life of Faith—the youth group. After giving the students several minutes to complete their lists, invite volunteers to share their responses.

Living as Disciples

(handwritten: 13ᵀᴴ)

In his encyclical *Pacem in terris*, Pope John XXIII taught that the happiness we all seek is not fully possible here on Earth. Because God created us with spiritual souls as well as physical bodies, life on Earth can never fully satisfy us. God created all of us to be with him forever. While we remain on Earth, our work is to prepare the way for God's Kingdom by our works of love, justice, and peacemaking. Following the **Beatitudes** shows us how to do what God intends.

(handwritten: Lesson help others)

The Beatitudes summarize the attitudes and actions of a person living a life of holiness. Jesus taught us the Beatitudes in his Sermon on the Mount. His teachings there are a summary of what it means to live as his disciple. When we follow his way, we are promised the gift of eternal life with God in Heaven.

Understanding the Beatitudes

The Beatitudes give us a grace-filled way to seek true and lasting happiness. They reveal the way to Heaven. If we think of each beatitude as a step on a ladder, we can see our path to God. Jesus teaches us that the first step to eternal happiness is being "poor in spirit." This is the way of the lowly and humble, who recognize their complete dependence on God. This is how we are to live, too. They who mourn a loss also will be comforted by God. Those who are meek will inherit the Kingdom of God.

Several of the Beatitudes speak of "righteousness." To be righteous means to stand in a right relationship with God and other people. This word is related to the Kingdom of God. A righteous person is one who is working to fulfill God's will and prepare the way for the kingdom to come in its fullness. The "clean of heart," as well, are those who are singleminded in their pursuit of the will of God. They are undistracted by anything that could separate them from their desire for God. By taking the Beatitudes as our guide, we can be happy here on Earth while we await the promise of eternal life with God the Holy Trinity.

? What new understanding of the Beatitudes did you gain from this page?

181

FAITH FOCUS
What is the relationship between happiness and living as a disciple of Jesus?

FAITH VOCABULARY
Beatitudes
The teachings of Jesus from his Sermon on the Mount that describe the attitudes and actions of people blessed by God; a word meaning "ways of happiness."

canonization
The process by which the pope declares that a deceased member of the faithful lived a life of heroic virtue and is to be honored as a saint.

THE TASKS OF CATECHESIS

Missionary Initiative. The Beatitudes in the Gospel are criteria by which we measure whether our actions and attitudes reflect a life centered on Jesus Christ. Christian beatitude is intimately connected to our call from God to know, love, and serve him. Beatitude is a gift God gives us freely, and it "confronts us with decisive moral choices . . . It teaches us that true happiness is not found in riches or well-being, in human fame or power, or any human achievement . . . but in God alone, the source of every good and of all love" (*CCC* 1723).

Key Concept
The Beatitudes reveal one path to God.

Teach

▶ Invite the students to discuss what they have learned about being a disciple of Jesus. Ask the Faith Focus question.

▶ Recall from Chapter 8 that the responsibility of being a disciple of Jesus is building up the Kingdom of God. Ask students to identify ways in which this can be done.

▶ Have students read the text on the page. Explain that the Beatitudes are a kind of road map to help instruct us, as disciples of Jesus, on how to build the Kingdom of God. Remind them that the Kingdom of God is the fulfillment of justice, peace, joy and happiness.

Reinforce

Ask volunteers to read aloud the Faith Vocabulary definition of The Beatitude on page 181, and make a word card for the term.

Connect

▶ Inquire: When have you experienced an overwhelming sense of happiness? Point out that happiness is found in our loving relationships because this is how God created us to live.

▶ Have students imagine the following: a place where everyone experiences great joy and happiness. What would this place be like?

Key Concept
Living the Beatitudes brings joy and strengthens us with the knowledge of God's love.

Teach

▶ Ahead of time, use masking tape to create a walking labyrinth on the floor that leads to a center point.

▶ Ask students what it means to "step up to the plate." Explain this phrase is a challenge for us to do something for what is good and right.

▶ Have two students walk the labyrinth that you made on the floor. Tell them to take steps toe to heel, like measuring with their feet. Have them count the steps taken to complete the labyrinth.

▶ Have other students walk the labyrinth. This time place large objects, like a chair or desk, within the labyrinth as obstacles. Repeat the exercise.

▶ Invite students to read the text. Emphasize that the road to happiness is not an easy one because there are often obstacles in life.

▶ Read the Faith-Filled People feature. Emphasize how. Blessed Chiara did not lose her joy despite her obstacles.

Reinforce

Discuss how God calls us to deal with the obstacles. Inquire: "How can we still have joy despite the obstacles we encounter along the way?" *(We accept the words of Jesus that when we follow his way, our joy will be forever.)*

Connect

Invite students to complete the activity and share their responses with a partner.

Faith-Filled People

key-aurah

Blessed Chiara Badano

Chiara was nicknamed "Luce" meaning "light" because of the spirit of joy that beamed from her smile. As a young girl in Italy, she desired to live the Gospel with all her heart, mind, and spirit. Chiara was known for saying that she had nothing but her heart, and with that she could still love. In 1990 at the age of eighteen, Chiara died from bone cancer. Her last words were to her mother: "Be happy, I am happy!"

Living the Beatitudes

You can think of the Beatitudes as the way to live the Law of Love. We cannot earn Heaven. That is why Christ won it for us. In Christ, all our actions are made worthy. We live the Law of Love joyfully because we are so grateful for what has been done for us.

In the Footsteps of Christ

As we live the Beatitudes, we are walking in the footsteps of Christ. The way of Jesus is not always an easy one. Jesus does not hide the fact that the way to eternal happiness often involves hardship and sometimes persecution. Living the Beatitudes strengthens and protects us with the knowledge of God's everlasting love. We can experience joy amidst our hardships, because we have accepted the words of Jesus that our joy will be forever.

Activity On the sole of the shoe in the space write the name of one of the eight kinds of people blessed by God. Then write one way you have tried to live the message of this Beatitude.

182

FAITH-FILLED PEOPLE

Blessed Chiara Badano. Chiara "Luce" Badano was in many ways like any other teen. She had many friends. She loved sports, dancing, and singing. She was good in some subjects at school and weaker in others. She had differences with her parents. But, from an early age, she was a young person full of faith, compassion, and joy. She belonged to the Lay Focolare Movement, also called the "Work of Mary." This international movement, founded in Trento, Italy, in 1943, promotes solidarity and unity. The strong faith of her parents and her participation in Focolare's Gen Movement (New Generation) had great influence in Chiara's life. Her great faith in Jesus was recognized by all who came to know her. She chose to embrace her illness as a sharing in the sufferings of Jesus, and she was often heard to say, "For you, Jesus. If you wish it, so do I!"

Holy Men and Women

There are many people who have walked the way of Jesus with the joy and love of God in their hearts. As faithful members of the Church, they have lived a life of heroic virtue. Some have even died for their faith in Jesus Christ. The Church refers to this faithful group as part of the Communion of Saints. Some of them are officially recognized in the process called **canonization**.

These holy men and women lived the Beatitudes and acted in imitation of Christ. They lived worthy lives because they accepted God in their lives, lived according to his Law and knew that with faith in Christ all things are possible.

Saint Paul knew well the way of Christ. He believed that all things are possible with God (read Mark 9:23). He instructed the Church in Philippi that the ways of happiness involve the joy and peace of Christ:

Rejoice in the Lord always. I shall say it again: rejoice! Your kindness should be known to all. The Lord is near . . . whatever is true, whatever is honorable, whatever is just, whatever is pure, whatever is lovely, whatever is gracious, if there is any excellence and if there is anything worthy of praise, think about these things . . . I have the strength for everything through him who empowers me.

PHILIPPIANS 4:4, 8, 13

Catholics Believe

Communion of Saints

The unity in Christ of all the faithful, here on Earth and those in Heaven, and includes not just holy men and women but all holy things that bring about unity in faith through acts of charity and participation in the Eucharist. Therefore, we practice the Beatitudes and build up the Communion of Saints here on Earth.

Activity Use this checklist to evaluate the current state of your attitude. I have an attitude:

☐ in which I put God first in my life.

☐ where I respond with gentleness when I am hurt.

☐ that seeks the truth of God's plan for love and life.

☐ that leads me to call for peace when I see conflict.

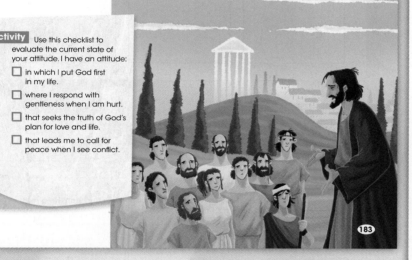

183

TEACHING TIP

Achieving Holiness. Remind students that God's grace is offered to every person to help them live good and holy lives. Point out that the canonized saints are but a few of the many saints who lived ordinary lives doing ordinary things each day out of love for God and their neighbor. By keeping the love of God before them, they were able to overcome obstacles and respond to God's love in remarkable ways. Encourage the students to cooperate with the grace God gives them to live ordinary lives in holy ways.

Key Concept
The Church officially recognizes certain holy men and women as saints.

Teach

▶ Recall the story of Blessed Chiara and how the light of Christ shined in her heart.

▶ Explain that the Church honors such holy women and men to help us on our road to happiness. Have students read the Catholics Believe box.

▶ Then have them read the first two paragraphs silently. ask the students to describe their understanding of the term "heroic virtue" in the first paragraph. Remind them that living the virtues is to form the habits of a Christian.

▶ Introduce the reading by Saint Paul in your own words. Ask a volunteer to proclaim the Scripture passage.

▶ Point out Saint Paul's joy and his knowledge that Jesus empowered him for all that he would ever do.

▶ Read aloud the Catholics Believe box.

Reinforce

Ask a student to re-read the last sentence of the Scripture passage. Remind them that this statement can empower us whenever we face a difficult challenge. Encourage the students to memorize it.

Connect

Have students compete the activity on the page. Invite them to share their responses with the class.

Reinforce

▶ Recall that the spirit of joy comes from the indwelling presence of the Holy Spirit. If we treasure God above all else, then we can prioritize things in life well.

▶ Explain that Jesus taught in the Beatitudes that purity of heart is necessary to be a peacemaker.

Respond

▶ Introduce the activity by recalling the story about Blessed Pope John XXIII.

▶ Explain the directions for the activity on the page.

▶ Have students complete the activity, inviting them to share their responses with the class.

▶ Invite students to explain what they can do to encourage one another to treasure love of God in their hearts so they can keep themselves and others on the road to joy and peace.

Choose

▶ Have students complete their faith choice.

▶ Then have students complete the last section to make their commitment in prayer. Encourage them to put their faith choice into practice this week.

I FOLLOW JESUS

As we live according to the Spirit, the fruit of joy will bring us happiness. In the Beatitudes, Jesus taught that purity of heart and being a peacemaker are essential aspects of the Christian life.

THE JOY OF BRINGING PEACE

Think of a situation to which someone could bring peace. Sketch your idea in the three frames. In the first, show the situation. In the second, show what you could do. In the third, show the outcome.

MY FAITH CHOICE

This week I will focus on being a peacemaker. I will
_____
_____

Pray, "Holy Spirit, may your love dwell in my heart. Help me to keep a spirit of joy. Amen."

184

CATHOLIC DOCTRINE

Purity of Heart. The Church teaches that the pure in heart have "attuned their intellects and wills to the demands of God's holiness, chiefly in three areas: charity, chastity or sexual rectitude; love of truth and orthodoxy of faith" (*see CCC* 2518). Though we receive purification from all sins through the grace of Baptism, we must continue to maintain a purity of heart throughout our lives. With the help of God's grace, we discipline ourselves to live chaste lives. We live with purity of intention, seeking God's will in all things. We maintain purity of vision by guarding our feelings, our imagination, and our thoughts, and we remain faithful in prayer (*see CCC* 2520).

Chapter Review

Complete each sentence based on the eight Beatitudes found in Matthew 5:3–12.

1. Blessed are the ___poor in spirit___, for theirs is the kingdom of heaven.

2. Blessed are the ___merciful___, for they will be shown mercy.

3. Blessed are the ___clean of heart___, for they will see God.

4. Blessed are the ___peacemakers___, for they will be called children of God.

TO HELP YOU REMEMBER

1. The Beatitudes are teachings of Jesus from his Sermon on the Mount that describe the attitudes and actions of people blessed by God.

2. Living the Beatitudes is the way to follow the Law of Love.

3. The spirit of joy comes from the love of God being the treasure kept in our hearts.

Praise the Lord, My Soul

The Book of Psalms is filled with different kinds of psalms. One type is a psalm of praise. Use the following prayer to praise God for the spirit of joy in your heart.

All: **Praise the LORD, my soul; I shall praise the LORD all my life, sing praise to my God while I live.**

Reader: Happy those whose help is Jacob's God, whose hope is in the LORD, their God.

All: **Praise the LORD, my soul; I shall praise the LORD all my life, sing praise to my God while I live.**

Reader: The LORD shall reign forever, your God, Zion, through all generations! Hallelujah!

All: **Praise the LORD, my soul; I shall praise the LORD all my life, sing praise to my God while I live. Amen.**

Psalm 146:2, 5, 10

(185)

LITURGY CONNECTION

Chanting Psalms. The Responsorial Psalm at Mass is meant to be sung, and is most often chanted or sung to a melody. Vary today's closing prayer by chanting the psalm verse marked "All." The chant can be as simple as singing the psalm verse on a single note. Or, the class could sing all the words on a single note and lower their voices for the final word or two. If the Reader is a singer, he or she could chant their lines of the Psalm, too.

We Remember

▶ Review key points from the chapter using statements in the To Help You Remember section.

▶ Now introduce and explain the Chapter Review.

▶ Have the students complete the review.

▶ Encourage the students to memorize the Eight Beatitudes so they can cherish ways of happiness.

We Pray

▶ Gather the students for the chapter's closing prayer. Introduce the prayer.

▶ Select yourself as the Reader and pray together, beginning and ending with the Sign of the Cross.

▶ Suggest that the students wear something as a reminder to hold onto the spirit of joy that comes from the love of God. It could be a Christian bracelet, a necklace with a crucifix, or a Rosary or small cross in their pocket.

Preview

▶ Have students carefully tear-out the With My Family page along the perforation.

▶ Encourage them to share the pages with their family and to complete the activities together at home.

▶ If the students did not or were not able to complete the Chapter Review, encourage them to complete it with their family.

▶ Point out the chapter title and theme of next week's lesson.

Visit www.BeMyDisciples.com

▶ Take time with the students to explore the many activities and resources available at **www.BeMyDisciples.com**.

▶ Encourage especially them and their families to discover the many resources available at the Web site.

Before Moving On …

As you finish today's lesson, reflect on the following question before moving on to the next chapter.

How well do I provide activities that honor the different learning styles in my class?

With My Family

This Week...

In chapter 20, Ways of Happiness, your child learned:

▶ The Beatitudes are teachings of Jesus from his Sermon on the Mount that describe the attitudes and actions of people blessed by God.

▶ Living the Beatitudes is the way to follow the Law of Love. Canonized saints are models of people who faithfully lived the Beatitudes.

▶ Pope John XXIII is one example of this. He was a great proponent of creating a just society so that peace can reign in the world.

▶ The spirit of joy comes from our knowledge of the love of God, the treasure kept in our hearts.

For more about related teachings of the Church, see the *Catechism of the Catholic Church,* 1716–1729, 1812–1819, 1830–1845, 1965–2029; and the *United States Catechism for Adults,* pages 307–311, 318.

■ Sharing God's Word

There are two Gospel accounts of the Beatitudes. The Sermon on the Mount version is found in Matthew 5:3–12. The Sermon on the Plains version is found in Luke 6:20–26. Spend time breaking open the Word of God to let the light of the Gospel shine in your heart so your actions may be worthy of Christian living.

■ We Live as Disciples

The Christian home and family is a school of discipleship. Choose one of the following activities to do as a family or design a similar activity of your own:

▶ On occasion during family prayers, instead of reciting a traditional prayer read the Beatitudes from the Sermon on the Mount.

▶ When there is conflict in the home, take time to pause to reflect on the attitude in your heart. Then act seeing yourself and the other as children of God.

▶ Randomly celebrate a "Beatitude Day" by marking the calendar as such. This celebration is choosing joy no matter what is happening throughout the day and letting the actions of the Beatitudes guide your choices. At the end of the day, discuss your experiences as a family.

■ Our Spiritual Journey

Consider enacting the Works of Mercy as the way to act out the Beatitudes. Let the loving attitude in your heart guide you in offering to others God's merciful love. For example, when you comfort people who suffer, do not attempt to rush them through their sadness. Simply stand with them and let them know you share their sorrow.

For more ideas on ways that your family can live as disciples of Jesus, visit **www.BeMyDisciples.com**

(186)

CATHOLIC SOCIAL TEACHING

Life and Dignity of the Human Person. All humans are created in the image and likeness of God and, therefore, all life is sacred. This is the source of our fundamental dignity as human persons. Every person's basic dignity demands our respect. Because of this dignity, every human has fundamental human rights—a right to life, to the means to live a decent and healthy life, to meaningful work, and to freedom—within the limits required for the common good. Corresponding to these rights are responsibilities to one another. These rights and responsibilities exist side by side, and are not "either-or" choices. The young people reviewed concepts related to this principle in Chapter 17, where they learned more about the gift of God's abundant grace; in Chapter 19, where they learned the Golden Rule; and in Chapter 20, which reinforced the proper behaviors toward those who are most in need of being treated with dignity. Use the last activity on the next page to reinforce this teaching.

Enriching the Lesson

Creating a Happiness Word Web

Purpose

To reinforce that when we live as disciples of Jesus, we learn to live as happy people (taught on page 182)

Directions

▶ Have the students work with partners to write profiles of a happy person who helps them live the Beatitudes.

▶ Have each set of partners read Matthew 5:3–12.

▶ Invite them to construct a web portraying a happy person. Have them write the name of the person in the circle and, on the lines emanating from the circle, the qualities, based on Matthew 5:3–12, that makes that person happy.

▶ Around the web have them add names of people whom they have read about or know who also seem to demonstrate some of these qualities.

▶ Invite volunteers to share and discuss their completed webs with the entire class.

▶ Encourage the students to choose one or several of the qualities on their web and work toward developing that quality of a happy person in their own life.

Materials

Bibles

paper

pens or pencils

Creating CDs about Holy People

Purpose

To reinforce that living the Beatitudes helps us to live holy lives (taught on page 183)

Directions

▶ Have the students work in small groups to design a cover for a CD called "Holy People."

▶ Ask the groups to create a list of song titles for the CD using words and pictures that illustrate holiness in a person's life.

▶ Invite the groups to share their song titles and covers.

Materials

construction paper

markers or crayons

pens or pencils

Catholic Social Teaching: Living the Beatitudes

Purpose

To reinforce the principle of the dignity of the human person addressed throughout this unit

Directions

▶ Using the box on page 298, explain why we treat all people with dignity.

▶ Divide the class into small groups. Ask each group to brainstorm kinds of people in our society whom they believe are treated with the least respect. Have them make lists of their ideas and to write their lists on the board.

▶ Ask the students to vote on a category that they would like to focus on. Together, create an action plan responding to this need. Invite the classroom groups each to devise a poster, a public service announcement, a skit, or some similar idea. Explore the possibility of having the class sponsor a Human Dignity Day for the other classes.

Materials

The Unit Review provides the opportunity to assess the students' understanding of the faith concepts presented in the unit and to affirm them in their growing knowledge and love of God. Here are a few suggestions for using these pages.

▶ Share that the next two pages are an opportunity to stop and review what they have learned.

▶ Provide time for the students to ask questions.

▶ Have the students complete the review alone or with partners.

A. Choose the Best Word

▶ Read the directions for this section.

▶ Then have the student work alone or with a partner to complete the section.

▶ Invite volunteers to share their responses. Clarify and correct responses as needed.

B. Show What You Know

▶ Read the directions for this section. Answer the first question together as a class.

▶ Then have the student continue working alone or with a partner to complete the section.

▶ Invite volunteers to share their responses. Clarify and correct responses as needed.

Unit 5 **Review**

Name _____

A. Choose the Best Word

Fill in the blanks to complete each of the sentence of the paragraph. Use the words from the word bank.

| Cardinal | conscience | holiness |
| moral | Mortal | Venial |

God gives each person the grace to make prudent decisions and to live a life of ___holiness___. Making decisions to live according to God's will is called living a ___moral___ life. By developing and practicing the four ___Cardinal___ Virtues, we develop good habits and grow in holiness. Our ___conscience___ guides us in judging whether an act is right or wrong. When we deliberately choose to do or say something that we know is against God's Law, we sin. ___Mortal___ sins are grave or serious sins that break our relationship with God.

B. Show What You Know

Read each statement and circle the best answer.

1. Which of these virtues is one of the Theological Virtues?
   - A. Wisdom
   - B. Prudence
   - C. Faith
   - D. Courage

2. Which of these describe the morality of an act?
   - A. object, intention, circumstances
   - B. intention, reason, effect
   - C. object, intention, purpose
   - D. object, circumstances, effect

3. Which one of the following is not the result of an informed conscience?
   - A. Judging what is right and wrong
   - B. Choosing to do what is against God's Law
   - C. Living as a follower of Jesus Christ
   - D. Making good moral decisions

187

TEACHING TIP

Self-assessment. Value the Unit Reviews as an opportunity for your own assessment. Sharing the faith of the Church with the students and facilitating their growth as persons of faith is not an easy ministry. Listen carefully to the students' responses. Their incorrect responses or their inability to respond will give you insights on ways to improve your presentation of the material, and help you to realize the students' growth in faith is not your work alone—the Holy Spirit is truly the catechist during your sessions, and you also support the parents who are the primary catechists of their children by their guidance and example.

C. Connect with Scripture

Reread the Scripture passage on the first Unit Opener page. What connection do you see between this passage and what you learned in this unit?

Responses will vary.

_____

_____

D. Be a Disciple

1. *Review the four pages in this unit titled "The Church Follows Jesus." What person or ministry of the Church on these pages will inspire you to be a better disciple of Jesus? Explain your answer.*

Responses will vary.

_____

_____

2. *Work with a group. Review the four Disciple Power virtues or gifts you have learned about in this unit. After jotting down your own ideas, share with the group practical ways that you will live these virtues or gifts day by day.*

Responses will vary.

_____

_____

188

C. Connect with Scripture

▶ Invite the students to reflect on the Scripture passage in the Unit Opener and to write their understanding of how this passage connects with the doctrinal content of the unit they have just completed.

▶ Ask volunteers to share their responses, now or after completion of the entire Unit Review.

D. Be a Disciple

▶ Invite the young people to work independently on the first question about The Church Follows Jesus. Ask volunteers to share their responses.

▶ Divide the students into small groups of three or four for the second part of this section. Ask them to write their personal reflections first, and then to share with their group practical ways of living the Disciple Power virtues or qualities of discipleship in everyday life.

▶ Ask for feedback from the small groups as time allows.

TEACHING TIP

Rest Stops. Strategically located rest stops are part of any long-distance trip. Invite the students to share their experiences of family road trips. Be sure to have them highlight their experience of rest stops. Then share with the students how these Unit Reviews are more like a rest stop than some formal testing. Remind them that rests stops on their faith journey are also an important part of the life of the Church. Ask the students to reflect on their faith journey rest stops. These stops might have occurred during Mass, prayer before the Blessed Sacrament, or just socializing with friends and family.

Objectives

In Unit 6, the students will learn that:

▶ The first three Commandments guide us to love God above all else.

▶ The Fourth, Fifth, Sixth, and Ninth Commandments teach us to love one another as Jesus loves us.

▶ The Seventh, Eighth, and Tenth Commandments teach us to live honest, generous, and truthful lives.

▶ The Lord's Prayer shows us how to live as people who place our faith, hope, and love in God above all else.

Spiritual Insights

"The Kingdom is already here because of the redemption of Jesus Christ. But in another sense, it is 'not yet' here, since Christ's final transformation of individuals, society, and culture has yet to happen in its fullness. That is why we need to pray this petition ('thy Kingdom come' in the Lord's Prayer) every day and work for its coming" (*United States Catholic Catechism for Adults*, page 486).

"If a brother or sister has nothing to wear and has no food for the day, and one of you says to them, 'Go in peace, keep warm, and eat well,' but you do not give them the necessities of the body, what good is it?"

James 2:15–16

Living the Six Tasks of Catechesis

Missionary Initiation: Saint Katharine Drexel (1858–1955)

When Katharine Drexel joined the convent, the headlines in the Philadelphia newspapers called her the "richest nun in America!" Katharine came from a very wealthy family, but was always taught that she had a special responsibility to serve people in need.

Katharine's family frequently traveled throughout the United States and Europe. On one trip, Katharine was saddened to see the poverty of the Native-Americans living on reservations. Later, during a family visit to Rome, the family was granted an audience with Pope Leo XIII. Katharine pleaded with the pope to send missionaries to help the neglected tribes. The pope asked her, "Why don't you become a missionary yourself?"

Katharine knew that God was calling her to a life of service. When she inherited her father's fortune, she donated money to the neglected Native-Americans. The money was used to build schools and to meet the many other physical and spiritual needs of Native Americans.

Yet, it was not enough. Katharine joined the Sisters of Mercy for three years of formation in religious life. With the blessing of the bishop, Sister Katharine left the Mercy order to establish a new religious community, The Sisters of the Blessed Sacrament, dedicated to the education of Native-Americans and Blacks. Over the next six decades, Katharine and her sisters built over 63 schools in 21 states. Mother Katharine, as everyone called her, founded Xavier University in New Orleans, the first Catholic university in the United States for Blacks.

We celebrate Saint Katharine Drexel's feast day on March 3. Saint Katharine never stopped working for justice and equality for all people. Her life reminds all catechists that we are called to continue Christ's work in the world and to do our best to prepare the way for the coming of God's Kingdom of peace, love, and justice.

Sharing Your Faith

Find a partner to work with: a spouse, a friend, a fellow catechist. Come together at the beginning or end of each unit for shared prayer and discussion. Use the questions below as a starting point. As an alternative, record your thoughts in a personal journal.

▶ How do you prepare the way for the coming of God's Kingdom?

▶ If you inherited a fortune, as Saint Katharine Drexel did, how would you use it to serve others?

▶ What are some of the service activities you have planned to enable your students to reach out to people in need?

Unit 6 Opener

Opening Page

▶ Invite the young people to tell you what they see in the illustration. (*Jesus is standing speaking to a crowd.*)

▶ Ask a volunteer to read the Scripture story "Depend on God" aloud. Then ask: "What do you think Jesus means by the advice he gives the crowd? Who will give them these things?" (*Accept all reasonable responses.*)

Getting Ready

▶ Invite the young people to write their responses to the questions and directions under What I Have Learned, Faith Terms to Know, and the other headings in the second column.

▶ Invite a few volunteers to share their responses, but do not correct them at this time. Tell the students that they will return to this page to check their learning at the end of the unit.

▶ For Questions I Have, you might write their questions on the board on a piece of newsprint so that you can refer to them if or when the topics come up in the unit.

▶ Ask the class to look at the next page and begin Chapter 21.

BACKGROUND

"I, the Lord, Am Your God!"

During their wandering in the desert, the Israelites were faced with many life-or-death situations that tested their faith and trust in God. They began to lose hope in his promise that they would live freely in a land of their own. They murmured and grumbled among themselves and complained over and over again to Moses, "Why did you ever make us leave Egypt?" (Exodus 17:3).

During one of those confusing, tense, life-or-death moments in the desert, Moses went up Mount Sinai to renew his faith in God. He opened his heart to God in prayer for guidance, pleading for advice on how to lead his people.

Free Choice

Faith in God is a gift and a free human response. God invites us to order our life in such a way that our whole life is centered on him. God invites us to come to know and believe in his unconditional, infinite desire to have us live in communion with him, now and forever. Faith calls us to make living in communion with God the highest priority in our life. As we hear the words of God to the Israelites, we need to hear him speaking to us:

"I, the Lord, am your God, who brought you out of the land of Egypt, that place of slavery. You shall not have other gods besides me."

Exodus 20:2–3

Love God with Your Whole Heart

The First Commandment might be subtitled "Keeping Our Priorities Straight." This Commandment asks that we respond to God's love and embrace him as the One who is at the center of our lives. The golden calf can tempt us in many ways. Making money, success, fame, our jobs, investments, and pleasure are not unlike the idols God warned the Israelites about.

The Second Commandment is a measuring rod of the depth of our love and respect for God. The manner in which we reverently or irreverently, respectfully or disrespectfully speak the divine name concretely manifests the quality of both our love for him and the honesty of our relationship with him.

Living the Third Commandment manifests that we are proud to call God, our God. We gather with other believers to proclaim his love for us. We thank and praise him for revealing himself to us and inviting us to live in happiness with him forever. All we do on the Lord's Day gives evidence to the priority God has in our lives and the priority that we give to deepening our love for him.

For Reflection

How do I witness that my highest priority is keeping God at the center of my life?

What do I do to support others to center their lives on God?

Catechist to Catechist

Keep the Lord's Day Holy

For some people, keeping holy the Lord's Day means going to Mass and then taking it easy for the rest of the day. For many people, however, work and shopping seem to be a regular part of life on Sunday. Running from one activity to another seems routine. Such demands on our Sunday time together can easily cause us to lose focus of what it means to keep holy the Lord's Day. With such busy lives, we need to focus our Sunday activities so that they contribute to keeping the Lord's Day holy.

Sensitivity to Family Diversity

In presenting the Church's teaching on the Third Commandment, it is important to be sensitive to the needs of families when talking about the prohibition of working on Sunday. In some families, there might be the need for a parent to work on Sundays because of the demands of their jobs, jobs they need in order to support their families. Be sensitive to this reality as you present this lesson.

The Church Teaches...

"The Ten Commandments (or Decalogue) and the Beatitudes are the primary reference points for the application of Christian moral principles. The Decalogue, the expression of God's covenant with his people, is also a privileged expression of the natural law that sums up love of God and love of neighbor" (*National Directory for Catechesis*, 44).

To teach as Jesus did means that every catechists is to do more than present information. This is why we both teach about God's Law and also help the children apply his laws, such as the Ten Commandments, to their daily lives.

Further Reading and Reflection

For more on the teachings of the Church, see the *Catechism of the Catholic Church*, 2083–2195; and from the *United States Catholic Catechism for Adults*, pages 337–371.

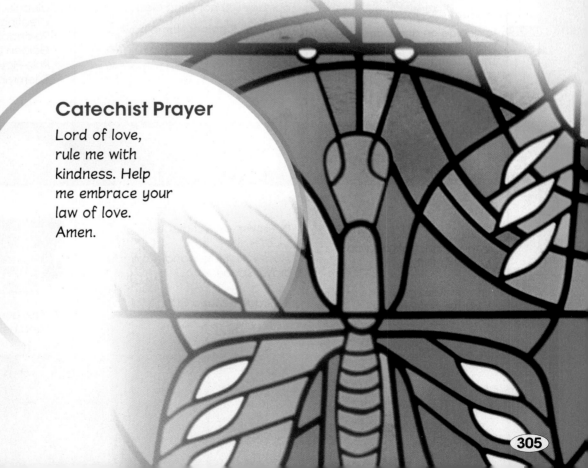

Catechist Prayer

*Lord of love,
rule me with
kindness. Help
me embrace your
law of love.
Amen.*

Lesson Planner

Chapter 21   Love of God

Focus To learn how the first three Commandments guide us to love God above all else

LESSON PART	PROCESS	MATERIALS and RESOURCES
EXPLORE **Focus** **To explore how to put God first in our lives** 🕐 10 minutes **Pages** 191–192	▶ Proclaim and discuss Psalm 19:8–9 (Precepts of the Lord are right). ▶ Learn why love of others is a way to show our love of God. **Disciple Power:** Piety	Bible
DISCOVER **Focus** **To discover how the First, Second, and Third Commandments guide us to love God above all else** 🕐 30 minutes **Pages** 193–195	▶ Review the need to place God first. **Activity:** Explore false idols. ▶ Reflect on the holiness of God's name. ▶ Explore ways to keep the Lord's Day holy. **Activity:** Plan daily ways to honor God.	Pencils **Additional Activities Booklet:** Activities 21a–21b, or see BeMyDisciples.com.
DECIDE **Focus** **To decide on a response to the lesson on the First, Second, and Third Commandments** 🕐 10 minutes **Page** 196	**Activity:** Identity how to overcome obstacles to honoring God. **My Faith Choice:** Name how to make God the top priority.	**Enriching the Lesson Activities:** Catechist Edition, page 315 • Creating Scrolls • Re-enacting the Story of the Golden Calf • Role-Playing Commandment Dilemmas

Concluding the Lesson   10 minutes

We Remember

Page 197

▶ Review concepts and do the review activity.

▶ **Assessment Tools Booklet:** Chapter Test 21a–21b, or see BeMyDisciples.com.

We Pray

▶ **Prayer:** an Act of Love

Materials: Bible, candle, cross for prayer space

▶ Grade 6 Music CD

Preview

Point out resources for this chapter at

www.BeMyDisciples.com

▶ Preview the With My Family page and next week's lesson theme.

Looking Ahead

In this chapter the Holy Spirit invites you to ▶

EXPLORE the sacred space in your parish to nurture the gift of piety.

DISCOVER that the first three commandments teach us to love God.

DECIDE on how you will keep God above all else in your life.

CHAPTER **21**

Love of God

? Do you think laws are necessary for people to be happy? Why or why not?

Laws, decrees and precepts are guidelines to help us keep what is important in life a priority. This psalm attributes God as the source of all that is truly important:

> The law of the LORD is perfect,
>   refreshing the soul.
> The decree of the LORD is trustworthy,
>   giving wisdom to the simple.
> The precepts of the LORD are right,
>   rejoicing the heart.
>
> PSALM 19:8–9

? How are God's laws "refreshing" to the soul? How can you tell that a person places God first in their life?

(191)

HUMAN METHODOLOGIES

Making a Commitment to Live the Christian Life. The *National Directory for Catechesis* speaks of the way in which the secular culture challenges Church teachings (*NDC 29G*). As you begin this chapter, create three posters, one for each of the first three Commandments. Label each poster with the Commandment title. Divide the posters into two columns: "Difficult to Keep this Commandment" and "Live to Keep this Commandment." Divide the class into three groups. Have each group work with one of the Commandment posters by adding their ideas to the columns. Then ask the groups to rotate until each group has worked on all three posters. Discuss responses as a class.

Pray

▶ Gather students for prayer. Begin and conclude by praying the Sign of the Cross together.

▶ Pray aloud:

> "Lord God, thank you for the gift of your law to guide us. Amen."

Reflect

▶ Discuss with the students the questions at the top of the page.

▶ Have a volunteer proclaim the Scripture passage on the page.

▶ Call attention to the image on the page and have them imagine that they are standing in that scene. Inquire: What kind of path do you think the road to happiness is like?

▶ Invite the students to read silently the questions at the bottom of the page. Then share their responses with a partner.

Focus

▶ Invite three students to read aloud the three bullet points in the Looking Ahead feature.

▶ Explain that in this chapter the students will learn more about the first Three Commandments that teach us to place God first in their lives.

Introduce

▶ Ask the students to name ways they have contributed to the needs of others with their money or material goods, such as clothing. When have they done this through the parish?

▶ Point out that we also show our love for God by loving and caring for our neighbor as we would ourselves.

▶ Paraphrase the first two paragraphs of text on the page for the class. Ask what special customs may be a part of taking up the Sunday collection in their parish. In what ways does the Sunday Collection show our love for God? *(It shows our thanks to God for all his blessings to us.)*

▶ Read Disciple Power aloud.

Reinforce

Ask: When is it easy to give of our earthly goods and when is it hard? Remind the students that we show our love for God when we show our love for other people.

Connect

Share with the class any knowledge you have of special collections being taken up on Sunday at this time of year.

Ask the students to brainstorm what they could do to involve youth of their age in the observation of one of these collections.

Disciple Power

Piety

When we worship God, we exercise the gift of piety. Piety is one of the seven Gifts of the Holy Spirit, which helps us give devotion to God. The attitudes of reverence and respect accompany piety and pious activity.

THE CHURCH FOLLOWS JESUS

The Collection at Mass

When we take part in the celebration at Mass, we show our love both for God and for others. The collection of money at Mass is one sign of that love. This ancient tradition of the Church is one way we generously show our thanks to God and provide for the material needs of the Church.

From the earliest days of the Church, wealthy people gave money to the Church. Others brought cheese, hand woven cloth, grain, animals, vegetables, bread, and other goods. After gathering at the entrance of the church, they walked in procession to an area near the altar where they left their gifts. After the celebration of the Mass concluded, these gifts were brought and shared with people in need. In some countries of the world today, that custom is still followed.

In what ways does the Sunday collection at Mass show love for God?

DISCIPLE POWER

Piety. Invite the students to share ways they already show their devotion to God by expressing their love for him, for the world he has created, and for their neighbors. List their examples on the board or on a flip chart. Explain that one of the invitations of piety is to increase their love and devotion for the Lord. Using the students' examples, lead a discussion of practical ways to do so. For example, students might have said that one way they show their love for God is by saying grace at meals. The invitation of piety—a deeper love—is to turn to God in prayer many times throughout the day. Students might give the example of doing their chores at home. The invitation of piety would be to do those chores without being told and without complaining.

Precepts of the Lord

God gave us commandments to remind us what is of most important in life. The first three commandments teach us ways that we are to love the Lord our God with our whole heart, soul and mind (see Matthew 22:37). God gave his commandments to Moses and this was the first and most important of all:

I, the LORD, am your God who brought you out of the land of Egypt, that place of slavery. You shall not have other gods besides me.
Exodus 20:2—3

The First Commandment

This First Commandment teaches us that we are to **worship** only God. We are to place our faith and hope in God and to love him above all else. Atheism, or denying the existence of God, is a sin against the First Commandment. This commandment also warns us about **idolatry**. Idols are those people or things that we place before God. Idols in our lives could be things like power, fame, material possessions, money, even a person. We all know how easy it is to love these things to excess and allow them to take over our lives.

Our Top Priority

There are many things in life that give us a feeling of great pleasure and excitement, especially when they place us in the center of life. Sometimes they may be the newest gadget, the latest trend or the desire to be the "star" of a team. In and of themselves, they are not bad. But when they become our top priority in life, we worship them or ourselves as an idol. Idols consume our time and energy, enslaving us. When God is our top priority, we become liberated, truly free to seek happiness.

> **FAITH FOCUS**
> How do the first three commandments guide us to love God above all else?
>
> **FAITH VOCABULARY**
> **idolatry**
> This is the substitution of someone or worshiping a creature or thing (money, pleasure, power, etc.) instead of God the Creator.
>
> **worship**
> Honor and respect we give to God above all else; faith in, hope in, and love for God above all else is worship.

Activity Work with a small group. Create a list of all the false idols that a person your age might worship. Then think of some practical steps people could take to redirect themselves toward God.

Idols	Solutions
_____	_____
_____	_____
_____	_____

193

TEACHING TIP

Making Time for God. Give the students blank sheets of paper. Have them title their page "My To Do List." Allow five to seven minutes for the students to write down everything they have scheduled for the coming week. For example, dance lessons on Thursday evening, a soccer game on Saturday morning, shopping for new jeans tomorrow after school or getting homework done tonight. Afterward, ask volunteers to share some of their responses. Then invite each student to take a second look at his or her list. Ask if anyone listed anything related to God or to the Church, such as taking time for prayer, going to Mass, or looking through their clothes to see if they have items to donate to the parish clothing drive. Brainstorm other God-centered examples that could be incorporated into a sixth grader's "to do list."

> **Key Concept**
> The First Commandment teaches us that we are to worship only God.

Teach

▶ Read the Faith Focus question aloud and ask the students to silently think about it.

▶ Ask the students to brainstorm their top priorities in life. List their ideas on the board. Note that their individual lists may vary.

▶ Point out that in this chapter they will deepen their understanding of what the First, Second and Third Commandments teach about keeping God first in our lives.

▶ Have students read silently the first three paragraphs on the page and underline what they think the key concepts to each paragraph are. Discuss why it is most important to keep God first in our lives.

Reinforce

Review the Faith Vocabulary words and clarify any student questions.

Connect

▶ Introduce the activity and ask students to work in groups to complete it.

▶ Invite responses and compare to their opening priorities list.

Key Concept
The Second Commandment teaches that we are to treat the name of God with respect and reverence.

Teach

▶ Using the board or a large piece of butcher paper, have students write words that they think speak of reverence and respect. Invite them to explain why.

▶ Have a student read aloud the first section of text on the page. Ask students why it is wrong to use the name of God when we are angry. *(God's name is holy and deserves our highest respect.)*

▶ Explain that a person's name represents the person. God's name was so precious to the Israelites that they did not use it, but instead had a substitution. Point out that many Orthodox Jews write "G-d" out of respect for God's name and to make the word unpronounceable.

Reinforce

▶ Have another student read the remaining text on the page.

▶ Read the Faith-Filled People feature. Emphasize how Moses lead the Israelites to follow God's Commandments.

Connect

Ask the closing questions. Poll students by raise of hands, if they think profanity is a problem for their generation. Discuss how they can become leaders to guide others in respectful speech.

Faith-Filled People

Moses

Moses believed in God above all else. While Moses was on Mount Sinai, the people persuaded Aaron, the brother of Moses, to gather and melt all the gold the people had to create a golden calf. Aaron and the people worshipped this golden calf as the god who freed them from Egypt. Hearing the people dancing and singing, Moses came down from Sinai. He took the golden calf, and threw it into a fire (read Exodus 32).

The Second Commandment

As we prioritize things in our life, we seek to order our lives with the hope that life becomes not just manageable but enjoyable. Often the words we use speak volumes about our attitude toward life.

You shall not take the name of the LORD, your God, in vain. For the LORD will not leave unpunished him who takes his name in vain.

Exodus 20:7

The Second Commandment teaches us that we are to use the name of God and the names of Jesus, Mary and the saints reverently and respectfully. Blasphemy is the use of the names of God, of Jesus Christ, of the Virgin Mary, and of the saints in an offensive way. In fact, all the words we use and our intent behind their use speak to the condition of our hearts.

This commandment also teaches that we are to take an oath only when it is necessary, as in a court of law. Whenever we call God as our witness, we must tell the truth. To use the name of God or Jesus when we are angry, to show off, or to casually say "I swear to God" is against the Second Commandment.

The Power of Words

Each of us knows that our words do affect others, not just because of how we say them but how we use them. We can use words to praise, honoring that which is sacred such as God and one another. We can also use words to curse, hurting others with our profanity. Some words evoke such an impact when used that regardless of our intention, they are powerful. The name of God and Jesus Christ are examples of powerful and sacred words. God, above all, deserves our respect and worship.

? What influences in the world around you show disrespect for the names of God and Jesus? What can you do to stand up to them?

194

FAITH-FILLED PEOPLE

Moses. Share with the class the full biblical story of Moses' reaction to the golden calf created by the Israelites and the renewal of the tablets of the Ten Commandments by paraphrasing the appropriate passages in chapters 32, 33, and 34 of the Book of Exodus. Connect this story to the First Commandment and the "golden calves" that we might be tempted to create in our modern world; for example, the false gods of money, power, fame, and prestige.

The Third Commandment

In the Old Testament, God rested from the work of Creation on the seventh day, or the Sabbath. He commanded his people to do the same:

Remember to keep holy the sabbath day. Six days you may labor and do all your work, but the seventh day is the Sabbath of the LORD, your God. EXODUS 20:8–10

The Sabbath is to be set aside from all the other days of the week as the Lord's Day.

Sunday is the Lord's Day for Christians. It is the day on which the Lord Jesus was raised from the dead. It is the first day of the new creation of the world in Christ. It is the day on which we focus on keeping God first in our lives.

Sunday is to be kept as the most important holy day of obligation. Catholics have the obligation to take part in Mass on Sunday and on other holy days of obligation. We rest from all work that is not necessary. We are to use Sunday as the day to help us keep our hearts and minds focused on God. If we start our week with God first in our hearts and minds, then the work we do for the rest of the week can be out of love for him and in his honor.

Catholics Believe

Sins against God

God is due our honor and praise. When we participate in activities that place our trust not in God, we commit sins against God. Superstition and the occult are such practices that reject faith in God (see CCC 2110–2122).

| Sunday | Monday | Tuesday | Wednesday | Thursday | Friday | Saturday |

Activity

Keeping It Holy

Name some of the ways that you can keep the Lord's Day holy. Log them here. How can you keep Sunday for God?

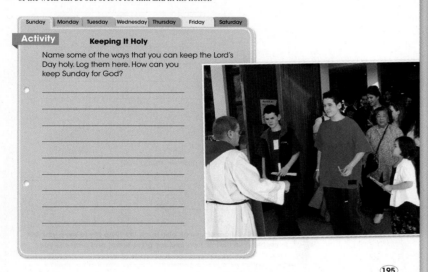

(195)

CATHOLIC DOCTRINE

On Keeping the Lord's Day Holy. In 1998 Pope John Paul II issued the apostolic letter *Dies Domini* (On Keeping the Lord's Day Holy). In it he encouraged Catholics to keep Sunday holy by living the entire day well. He suggested that, in addition to gathering with the Church to celebrate the Eucharist, parents spend time with their children, families enrich their relationships with others, and all spend time in relaxation and prayer. These practices, he said, help cultivate peace and joy in the simple things of ordinary life (see *Dies Domini* 52). Pope John Paul II encouraged us that spending Sunday in this way helps us to keep our worldly concerns in better perspective, and helps us to be at peace in our relationships with God, ourselves, and others (see *Dies Domini* 67).

Key Concept
The Third Commandment teaches that we are to keep the Lord's Day holy.

Teach

▶ Inquire: How many of you have ever read your horoscope? Explain that if these are taken seriously, they would lead someone not to trust in God. Have students read the Catholics Believe box. Address any questions that they may have about how superstition leads one away from trusting in God.

▶ Then have students read the text on the page.

Reinforce

▶ Invite the students to list the first three commandments. Then have a volunteer read Exodus 20:1–11.

▶ Review the Faith Vocabulary terms again. Explain that we set aside Sundays to worship God.

Connect

▶ Invite the class to list ways in which they worship God and keep Sunday holy and sacred.

▶ Have students make a personal response by completing the activity on the page. Invite them to share their responses with the class.

Reinforce

▶ Remind students that we are to love God above all else; we are to worship him alone. Piety is the gift from the Holy Spirit that helps us respect and worship God.

▶ Point out that the Holy Spirit is always with us, inviting, teaching and strengthening us to place our faith, hope and love in the Holy Trinity above all else.

Respond

▶ Introduce the activity and then have students complete it.

▶ Then invite them to share their responses with the class.

Choose

▶ Have students read the last section silently and write their faith choice.

▶ Then after a moment of prayerful reflection, have students complete the last section to make their commitment in prayer. Encourage them to put their faith choice into practice this week.

I FOLLOW JESUS

The Holy Spirit is always inviting you to place your faith, hope and love in the Holy Trinity above all else. This may not always be easy to do. Recognize the temptations and idols in your life that make it difficult to keep God first. Use the gift of piety to help you keep God above all else.

KEEPING GOD FIRST

Think of the obstacles to keeping God first that you brainstormed on page 193. Which of these things is the greatest temptation for you. Draw it on the pedestal. Then write how you can overcome that obstacle.

I can overcome this obstacle . . .

_____
_____
_____
_____
_____
_____
_____
_____

MY FAITH CHOICE

This week I will make God my top priority in my life. I will:

_____
_____

Pray, "Lord, you are above all else in my life. Help me to keep you first in my heart so that all I do and say gives honor and praise to you. Amen."

196

FAITH VOCABULARY

Grace. Recall with the students their understanding of grace. Remind them that grace is God's helping presence, and that God is always with us, helping us to live as his children. If young people believe and trust that God is standing with them in their times of temptation and offering them the help of his grace, they can become more confident in making decisions to live their faith. Take a few quiet moments to allow for the students to consider areas in their lives where they need God's grace, God's helping presence, today (see *Catechism of the Catholic Church* 2000).

Chapter Review

Write First, Second or Third beside the phrase that best describes that Commandment.

1. **Second** We call God to be our witness to the truth of what we are saying.

2. **First** We worship only God.

3. **Third** Catholics take part in Mass on Sunday.

4. **Second** We speak the name of God reverently and respectfully.

5. **First** We love God above all else.

TO HELP YOU REMEMBER

1. The First Commandment teaches us to worship only God and to believe in, hope in, and love God above all else.

2. The Second Commandment teaches us to use the name of God reverently and respectfully.

3. The Third Commandment teaches us to keep the Lord's Day as a holy day, a day set aside for God. Sunday is the Lord's Day for Christians.

Act of Love

There are many traditional prayers that young people are asked to memorize. If you do not already know this prayer, memorize it so that you will always remember your love of God. Pray it now with your class.

**O my God, I love you above all things,
with my whole heart and soul,
because you are all good and worthy of all my love.
I love my neighbor as myself for the love of you.
I forgive all who have injured me,
and ask pardon of all whom I have injured.**

**"Bless the LORD, my soul;
all my being, bless his holy name!"**

Psalm 103:1

197

We Remember

▶ Review key points from the chapter using statements in the To Help You Remember section.

▶ Now introduce and explain the chapter review section. Have students match each statement correctly with the First, Second or Third Commandment.

▶ Review the answers with the class.

We Pray

▶ Introduce the chapter's closing prayer by paraphrasing the opening sentences. Begin and end the prayer with the Sign of the Cross.

▶ Take a moment of silence before beginning the prayer. Then invite all students to pray the prayer together.

▶ Encourage the children to memorize this prayer from the Catholic tradition.

▶ Time permitting, have students create a bookmark with Psalm 103:1 written decoratively on it. Have them use this bookmark as they read from their Bible.

THE TASKS OF CATECHESIS

Teaching to Pray. One of the options in Chapter 17 was to review the Act of Faith, the Act of Hope, and the Act of Love with your students. In today's closing prayer instructions, you are encouraged to have the children memorize the Act of Love. Invite them to memorize the Act of Faith and the Act of Hope as well, reminding them that these prayers highlight the three Theological Virtues of faith, hope, and charity. Begin next week's class by having the students pray the Act of Faith, the Act of Hope, and the Act of Love from memory.

Preview

▶ Have students carefully tear-out the With My Family page along the perforation.

▶ Encourage them to share the pages with their family and to complete the activities together at home.

▶ If the students did not or were not able to complete the Chapter Review, encourage them to complete it with their family.

▶ Point out the title and theme of next week's chapter to the children.

Visit www.BeMyDisciples.com

▶ Take time with the students to explore the many activities and resources available at **www.BeMyDisciples.com**.

▶ Encourage especially them and their families to discover the many resources available at the Web site.

Before Moving On ...

As you finish today's lesson, reflect on the following question before moving on to the next chapter.

How are my words and actions reverent and respectful of God?

With My Family

This Week...

In chapter 21, Love of God, your child learned:

▶ The First Commandment teaches us that we are to worship only God. We are to believe in, hope in, and love God above all else. God alone is and should always be at the center of our lives.

▶ The Second Commandment teaches us that we are to honor the name of God. We are to speak the name of God reverently and respectfully.

▶ The Third Commandment teaches us that we are to set aside one day each week as the Lord's Day. It is the most important holy day of obligation. On Sundays Catholics have the obligation to take part in the Mass. We are to avoid all work that prevents us from keeping God as the center of our lives.

▶ Exercising the gift of piety is a way we can make God our top priority in life.

For more about related teachings of the Church, see the *Catechism of the Catholic Church,* 2083–2195; and the *United States Catholic Catechism for Adults,* pages 337–371.

■ Sharing God's Word

Read together Exodus 20:1–17. Emphasize that we give glory to God when we live the Ten Commandments.

■ We Live as Disciples

The Christian home and family is a school of discipleship. Choose one of the following activities to do as a family or design a similar activity of your own:

▶ Choose one thing this week that your family can do together to show that God is the top priority in your lives.

▶ Visit or call someone who is important to the family so that you can honor God by loving others, especially if they were not present at Sunday Mass.

▶ Create table placemats proclaiming Sunday as the Lord's Day. Use these placemats at your Saturday evening and Sunday family meals.

■ Our Spiritual Journey

Fasting is a form of piety that Jesus emphasized (read Matthew 9:16–18). This is also an obligation for Catholics as a way to prepare ourselves to receive the Eucharist and to help us place God first in our lives.

For more ideas on ways that your family can live as disciples of Jesus, visit **www.BeMyDisciples.com**

(198)

PLANNING AHEAD

The "Partnering with Parents" box. The box at the end of Chapter 22 suggests creating bookmarks with the Canticle of Zechariah (Luke 1: 68–79) and the Canticle of Mary (Luke 1:46–55) printed on them. Gather materials needed to make the bookmarks ahead of time: card stock, a hole punch, ribbon, stickers, markers or crayons, scissors and glue sticks or scotch tape.

Note: You may find it easier and less time consuming to type and copy the texts of these two prayers ahead of time. Students could then tape or glue the texts to the bookmarks they design.

Enriching the Lesson

Creating Scrolls

Purpose

To reinforce that piety is a gift of the Holy Spirit that helps us honor and worship God, keeping him as our top priority (taught on page 192)

Directions

▶ Invite the students to make scrolls containing their own messages conveying encouraging words about keeping God our top priority.

▶ Ask them to choose one of the first three Commandments for their scrolls to point to how the Holy Spirit helps us to worship and honor God in our daily activity.

▶ Have them then create proverb-like messages for their scrolls. The wording should evoke inspiration rather than simply saying what to do.

▶ Invite volunteers to share their scrolls.

▶ Display the completed scrolls in a place where members of the parish might be inspired by reading them.

Materials

shelf paper

pens or pencils

markers

Re-enacting the Story of the Golden Calf

Purpose

To reinforce that we are to worship God alone, thus having no idols (taught on page 193)

Directions

▶ Read or have a volunteer read aloud the story of Moses and the golden calf in Exodus 32.

▶ Have half the class work to prepare a dramatic presentation of the story.

▶ Have the other half work to prepare a contemporary version of the story, using today's idols in place of the golden calf.

▶ Invite the groups to present their dramas.

▶ Summarize by pointing out the meaning of God's word for our lives today.

Materials

Bibles

Role-Playing Commandment Dilemmas

Purpose

To reinforce that the First, Second, and Third Commandments teach us that we are to love God above all else (taught in Chapter 21)

Directions

▶ Have the students work in small groups to identify a dilemma young people might encounter when trying to live the First, Second or Third Commandment.

▶ Have each group create and present a role-play of its dilemma.

▶ Have the class analyze the impact that the media has in creating that dilemma.

▶ Summarize with the students the importance of prayer and cooperating with the grace of God in overcoming obstacles to living the Ten Commandments.

Materials

Commandments of Love

Laws of Human Behavior

God revealed the Ten Commandments to Moses. In doing so, he was actually awakening what is written on every human heart. God was awakening in the Israelites the inner core of what it means to be human, to live a life in communion with God and with one another. To help us do that, God has written the foundational laws of human behavior on every human heart. The Ten Commandments summarize those laws and call us to live as God created us to live.

The Blueprint for Relationships

The Ten Commandments are the foundation of any good social contract and healthy relationships. We are to respect our families, human life, sexuality, the fruit of human labor, truth, purity, and justice. Abiding by the principles and values of the Ten Commandments directs individuals and society in their pursuit of life, liberty, and happiness.

The Fourth through Tenth Commandments are a blueprint for how we are to love our neighbor and ourselves.

The commandments, "You shall not commit adultery; you shall not kill; you shall not steal; you shall not covet," and whatever other commandment there may be, are summed up in this saying, [namely] "You shall love your neighbor as yourself." Love does no evil to the neighbor; hence, love is the fulfillment of the law.

Romans 13:9–10

Life, Liberty, and Happiness

The Fourth Commandment teaches us that we are to honor our parents, to whom we owe our lives. It requires us to show respect, affection, and gratitude to our elders and ancestors and to those who exercise legitimate authority over us and the communities in which we live.

The Fifth Commandment sternly and tersely guides us to respect all human life as sacred. God is the author of life (see *Catechism of the Catholic Church* 2258).

The Sixth Commandment requires us to respect the dignity of women and men and brings into focus our call to self-mastery, chastity, and fidelity.

The Ninth Commandment complements the Sixth Commandment. It enjoins a respect for purity of heart. The pure of heart are those who fix their minds and wills on God's love. The pure of heart aspire to holiness by means of charity, sexual integrity, and love of the truth.

For Reflection

How do I measure up to each of the Commandment's call for respect of others, myself, and creation?

How can I pursue life, liberty, and happiness, using each of the Ten Commandments as my guide?

Catechist to Catechist

Love as Jesus Loved

Jesus revealed that the Great Commandment is the heart of God's Law. At the Last Supper he commanded his disciples, "[L]ove one another. As I have loved you, so you also should love one another" (John 13:34). Later during his final discourse with his disciples, Jesus connected that love to the Ten Commandments. (See John 14:15.)

Living the Commandments

It is important to model living the virtues underlying each of the Ten Commandments. For example, respect the life of each student by affirming their goodness. Show your respect for the truth by instilling discipline appropriately. Modeling these things will show the students the positive difference living the Ten Commandments makes.

As you teach this chapter, particularly the Sixth and Ninth Commandments, the young people may encounter some topics that are beyond their personal experiences. While it is important for them to be aware of God's laws regarding sexual relationships, focus on habits such as self respect, fidelity, and loyalty that will prepare them for adult living.

The Church Teaches...

"In Christ, God reveals how we human beings are to live our lives. God created human beings with the freedom to initiate and direct their own actions and to shape their own lives . . . This human freedom does not, however, entitle the person to say or do just anything. Human beings are not fully self-sufficient. We are capable of sin . . . The more one chooses to do what is good, the more free one becomes . . . Freely choosing to do the good, to obey the universal and unchanging moral norms, in no way diminishes the freedom and dignity of the human person" (*National Directory for Catechesis*, 41A).

Moral formation in Christ calls every person to honor the way Jesus lived—according to the will of the Father. To live according to God's will requires us to love. The source of our love is God, who loved us first. When we love like God, we live according to his will.

Further Reading and Reflection

For more on the teachings of the Church, see the *Catechism of the Catholic Church*, 2196–2400, 2514–2533; and from the *United States Catholic Catechism for Adults,* pages 373–416, 439–446.

Catechist Prayer

Come, Holy Spirit,
help me welcome all people
into the circle of family and
friends.
Help me affirm the sacredness
of all human life.
Amen.

Lesson Planner

Chapter 22 Commandments of Love

Focus To identify what the Fourth, Fifth, Sixth, and Ninth Commandments teach about living the second part of the Great Commandment

LESSON PART	PROCESS	MATERIALS and RESOURCES
EXPLORE **Focus** To explore the power of forgiveness ⏱ 10 minutes **Pages** 199–200	▶ Proclaim and discuss Mark 10:5–9 (Man and woman shall become one flesh). ▶ Learn about promoting the culture of life. **Disciple Power:** Temperance	Bible
DISCOVER **Focus** To discover what the Fourth, Fifth, Sixth, and Ninth Commandments teach about loving ourselves and others ⏱ 30 minutes **Pages** 201–203	▶ Promote a culture of life through the Fourth and Fifth Commandments. **Activity:** Create a poster about a culture of life. ▶ Apply the virtues of faithfulness, chastity, and loyalty to daily living. ▶ Explore the practice of purity of heart. **Activity:** Analyze TV shows depicting marriage.	Pencils Poster board Crayons or markers **Additional Activities Booklet:** Activities 22a–22b, or see BeMyDisciples.com.
DECIDE **Focus** To decide on a response to the lesson on the Fourth, Fifth, Sixth, and Ninth Commandments ⏱ 10 minutes **Page** 204	**Activity:** Create a story supporting a culture of life. **My Faith Choice:** Connect temperance to respect.	**Enriching the Lesson Activities:** Catechist Edition, page 327 • Creating Heritage Booklets • Creating a Discussion Web • Using a Graphic Organizer

Concluding the Lesson   10 minutes

We Remember

Page 205

▶ Review concepts and do the review activity.

▶ **Assessment Tools Booklet:** Chapter Test 22a–22b, or see BeMyDisciples.com.

We Pray

▶ **Prayer:** Prayer of St. Francis of Assisi

Materials: Bible, candle, cross for prayer space

▶ Grade 6 Music CD

Preview

Point out resources for this chapter at

www.BeMyDisciples.com

▶ Preview the With My Family page and next week's lesson theme.

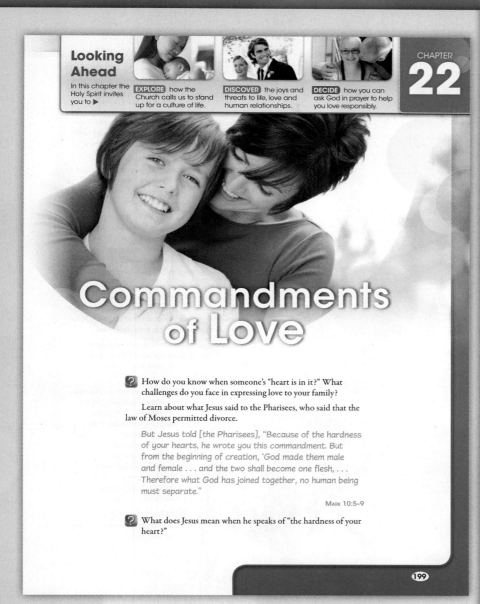

Looking Ahead

In this chapter the Holy Spirit invites you to ▶

EXPLORE how the Church calls us to stand up for a culture of life.

DISCOVER the joys and threats to life, love and human relationships.

DECIDE how you can ask God in prayer to help you love responsibly.

CHAPTER

22

Commandments of Love

❓ How do you know when someone's "heart is in it?" What challenges do you face in expressing love to your family?

Learn about what Jesus said to the Pharisees, who said that the law of Moses permitted divorce.

But Jesus told [the Pharisees], "Because of the hardness of your hearts, he wrote you this commandment. But from the beginning of creation, 'God made them male and female . . . and the two shall become one flesh, . . . Therefore what God has joined together, no human being must separate."

MARK 10:5–9

❓ What does Jesus mean when he speaks of "the hardness of your heart?"

199

THE TASKS OF CATECHESIS

Promoting Knowledge of the Faith. Point out to the students that the foundation of the Fourth through the Tenth Commandments is the revealed truth that all people are made in God's image and likeness. We are temples of the Holy Spirit (1 Corinthians 6:19). We acknowledge the sacredness of the human person when we live these Commandments. Remind the students that the Holy Spirit is always with us, inspiring and helping us to respect and love others as we want to be loved and respected (Matthew 7:12).

Pray

▶ Gather the class for prayer. Begin and conclude by praying the Sign of the Cross together.

▶ Pray together:

"Lord, make me on instrument of your peace."

Reflect

▶ Have the students discuss the questions at the top of the page.

▶ Invite a volunteer to proclaim the Scripture passage on the page.

▶ Invite the students to read silently the questions at the bottom of the page. Then share their responses with a partner.

Focus

▶ Explain that in this chapter the students will learn more about God's plan for love and life.

▶ Spend a few moments imagining the difficulties a "hardened heart" might have beating. Explain that a heart is to flex in order to beat, which is its function. Thus a "hardened heart" is not functioning as God intended.

▶ Then call the students' attention to the Looking Ahead feature. Invite them to read aloud each bullet.

Introduce

▶ Explain that the Church is concerned about how humanity has "hardened its heart," especially when it has come to God's plan for life and love.

▶ Point out that the story on the page depicts a typical parish trying to live a culture of life.

▶ Ask the question at the bottom of the page and jot responses on the board.

▶ Ask: How did the members of St. Luke's parish try to promote a culture of life? *(care for elders)*

Connect

▶ Ask the question at the bottom of the page. Accept all reasonable answers.

▶ Give the students a few moments for quiet reflection before inviting responses.

Disciple Power

Temperance

One of the four Cardinal Virtues, temperance includes other virtuous acts and attitudes such as chastity, self-control and responsible living according to God's plan for life and love. This virtue helps us to moderate our actions so that we do what is good and right.

THE CHURCH FOLLOWS JESUS

Conflicting Cultures

In 1995, Pope John Paul II wrote an encyclical letter, the *Gospel of Life*. He called for all Christians to stand up for the culture of life rather than the culture of death. He asked them to adopt a "new heart," or to have a loving outlook toward life.

The members of St. Luke's Parish studied the pope's encyclical and took it to heart. They thought of all the ways that they were already supporting a culture of life. They wondered what more they could do and asked the children of the parish to assist them.

Ben's class discussed the question. They thought of ways their families supported life by caring for one another and helping the poor and needy. Then Lin Zhang, a Chinese boy, remarked that his Chinese people have great respect for their elders, especially when they can no longer care for themselves. He said, "We respect their wisdom and all they have done for us."

"So do the people of my culture," said Estella, who was Mexican. Our *abuelos* and *abuelas*, our grandparents, are the most respected members of our families. We ask their advice about everything. My *abuela* lives with us and takes good care of us."

Their teacher said, "I have an idea. Maybe we could make the elderly in our parish our special concern. Let's brainstorm some ideas and present them to the parish staff."

Today, St. Luke's Parish is known through out the community for its care for the elderly. They prepare meals and run errands for them. They visit care centers for the elderly to read them stories and entertain them with songs and skits. They send friendship and get well cards to those they cannot visit. All the people of St. Luke's support a culture of life.

 What do you do to show your respect for the older members of your family?

200

DISCIPLE POWER

Temperance. Share with the students appropriately incidents in your everyday life when you get angry. For example, you get stuck in traffic on the highway due to construction. Ask volunteers to share examples from their lives. Perhaps their softball coach rarely lets them play in the games, even though they participate in every practice. At the end of the discussion, point out that the word temperance has hidden within it the word "temper." One of the invitations of the cardinal virtue of temperance is to hold our "temper," to remain mild and modest in our response to everyday situations that can lead us to expressing our emotions.

Respect for Others

Strengthening the Family

Honor your father and your mother. — EXODUS 20:12

The Fourth Commandment is one way that God tells us to build a culture of life. He commands that each family member contribute to the family's well-being. This means that family care for all members, especially the elderly and most vulnerable, is to be a top priority. After God, we are to honor our parents, even as adults. We are to respect and obey them, and offer appropriate assistance when they are in need. We are to care for our parents later in their lives, in honor of their caring for us at the beginning of ours.

Promoting the Culture of Life

You shall not kill. — EXODUS 20:13

The principle underlying the Fifth Commandment is that all human life is sacred. This commandment teaches that we must protect and nurture all human life, from conception to natural death. We are to respect and care for our own lives, health, and bodies, and those of others. We are to act safely and not put ourselves or others in unnecessary danger. We are to live as peacemakers.

The Fifth Commandment forbids abortion, **murder,** suicide, euthanasia, bullying, terrorism, unjust wars, and any act that violates the right to life or disrespects the dignity of the human person. This commandment, however, does not prohibit the defending of human life with appropriate force. All people, a nation or an individual, have the right to safety and security in life. However the nuclear arms race is an evil threatening human life that must be overcome for the good of all. The Fifth Commandment promotes the culture of life.

Activity Work with a group. Brainstorm ideas for a poster inviting families in your parish to support a culture of life. Write your ideas here. Make the poster and ask permission to display it in your parish.

_____

_____

> **FAITH FOCUS**
> What do these commandments teach us about living the Law of Love?
>
> **FAITH VOCABULARY**
> **covet**
> To covet is to unjustly desire what rightfully belongs to someone else.
>
> **murder**
> The direct and intentional killing of an innocent person is murder.

201

TEACHING TIP

Respect for All Life. Respect for all human life without exception is a fundamental revealed moral teaching. In addition to teaching this concept cognitively, we need to teach it by putting our words into action. The adage "actions speak louder than words" is particularly applicable to guiding the students to value and integrate this fundamental moral principle into their lives. Be the first to speak up for the unborn, underprivileged, and abandoned. Show respect for the individuality of each of the students.

> **Key Concept**
> The Fourth and Fifth Commandments teach us to honor our families and respect life.

Teach

▶ Read the Faith Focus question aloud and ask the students to silently think about how they might respond to it.

▶ Point out that this chapter explains four important Commandments about honoring and respecting the dignity of every person, especially within families.

▶ Ask the students to read the text on the page, have them circle unfamiliar words. Invite them to write in the margins short definitions of each.

Reinforce

▶ Review the Faith Vocabulary words and clarify any student questions.

▶ Time permitting, have students read Matthew 5:38–42 and Luke 6:27–36. Inquire: What does this teaching tell us about the Fifth Commandment? *(love your enemies, be peacemakers)*

Connect

Introduce the activity. Divide the class into groups of three or four and distribute art supplies if time allows. Ask the groups to share their work when they are finished.

Teach

▶ Recall with students the sacredness of human life. Point out that this foundational principle also underlies the Sixth Commandment.

▶ Have the students read the text on the page silently. Emphasize that the Sixth Commandment teaches us that we are to share love appropriately.

▶ Note: If specific questions arise regarding sins against the Sixth Commandment, remind the students that details regarding sexual matters should be discussed with their families.

Reinforce

Invite a volunteer to read the Faith-Filled People feature. Discuss how Ruth lived the Commandments in her relationships.

Connect

▶ Divide the class into two groups: boys and girls. Have each group write a list of ways in which they express their relationships to their friends.

▶ Then on the board, have students list their responses.

▶ Explain that the love of friends is a great foundation for the different kind of love necessary between spouses.

Faith-Filled People

Ruth

When Ruth's husband died, she took care of her mother-in-law, Naomi. Ruth left her own homeland and took Naomi back to Bethlehem, where Naomi's family came from. Ruth worked in the fields owned by Boaz to feed herself and Naomi. Ruth and Boaz eventually married. Their son Obed was the grandfather of King David, who was an ancestor of Jesus. Ruth is an example of both faithfulness and respect for elders.

The Commandment of Faithfulness

You shall not commit adultery. — Exodus 20:14

The Sixth Commandment teaches everyone to live a chaste life. Chastity is integrating the gift of human sexuality within the whole person. This involves self-control and modesty. This commandment guides Christians to follow Christ as our model in the way we express our love for our family, friends, and others. We are always to express our sexuality in appropriate ways.

❓ How does a person live a chaste life in words as well as actions?

This commandment also teaches about God's plan for marriage. In their marriage commitment, the husband and wife have promised to love, honor, and be faithful to each other until death. When a person has sexual relations with the person who he or she is not married to, that person violates the Sixth Commandment. Marriage is broken or seriously weakened when this happens. The Sixth Commandment calls for faithfulness in which both spouses freely, fully, faithfully, and forever give the gift of self to the other.

Among sins gravely contrary to the Sixth Commandment are: masturbation, artificial contraception, fornication, pornography, sterilization, and homosexual practices. Everyone experiences temptations to misuse the gift of sexuality. To dwell on these thoughts and desires can easily lead people to disrespect themselves and others. God's grace is always there to help us deal with such temptations.

❓ In what ways can you practice the virtues of faithfulness, loyalty, and chastity now so that you will prepare yourself for the lasting commitments of adulthood?

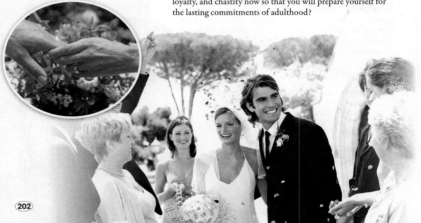

202

FAITH-FILLED PEOPLE

Ruth. The Book of Ruth, one of the shortest books in the Bible, contains the complete story of Ruth's faithfulness to her mother-in-law, Naomi, and the story of Ruth's marriage to Boaz. Two important verses from this book of the Bible are sung at many Catholic weddings. They are: "Wherever you go I will go, wherever you lodge I will lodge, your people shall be my people, and your God my God. Wherever you die I will die, and there be buried" (Ruth 1:16–17). Ruth and Boaz had a son, named Obed, who was the father of Jesse. Jesse was the father of King David. Boaz, Obed, Ruth, Jesse, and King David are all listed in the genealogy of Jesus (Matthew 1:1–17).

Practice Purity of Heart

You shall not covet your neighbor's wife. EXODUS 20:17

The Ninth Commandment teaches that everyone is to respect and honor the promises a husband and wife make to one another in marriage. We are not to do anything, not even desire to do anything that would break up a marriage.

This commandment also guides us to train ourselves to be pure in mind and heart, and in our actions. To **covet** someone or something, which is one of the capital sins, is to have an unjust and inordinate desire for someone or something that belongs to someone else. The Beatitudes and the Commandments correspond to one another. The Ninth Commandment teaches us we are to practice purity of heart.

When we act according to purity of heart, we practice the cardinal virtue of temperance. We demonstrate modesty through patience, decency, and discretion. Not only do we honor and respect others, we protect the "intimate center" of ourselves. This means that we love ourselves as God loves us.

Catholics Believe

The Dignity of Persons

God created us to love and respect one another as persons, not to use each other as objects. In creating us male and female, God gives men and women equal personal dignity. Each of the two genders is an image of the power and tenderness of God equal in dignity, distinct in sexual identity (see CCC 2333–2336).

Activity

Marriage Today

Name a popular television show that depicts people in a relationship. Are the people in that relationship living according to the Commandments? How might the show affect the people viewing it?

TV Show	My Analysis
_____	_____
_____	_____

FAITH VOCABULARY

Respect. Assess and reinforce the students' understanding of the virtue of respect. Write the word *respect* vertically on the board. Invite volunteers to share their understanding of the word. Then use the letters in the word *respect* to have the class work together to create an acrostic, detailing ways that we show respect to one another as demanded by the Gospel. Summarize by pointing out that living the Fourth through Tenth Commandments is, in one important way, about respecting others and ourselves.

Key Concept
The Ninth Commandment teaches us to practice purity of heart.

Teach

▶ Review what the expression "clean of heart" means. (See Chapter 20.)

▶ Explain that practicing purity (cleanness) of heart means following the Ninth Commandment.

▶ Invite the students to read the text on the page. Have them describe in their own words, what "purity of heart" means. Challenge them to give examples of how to practice purity of heart.

Reinforce

▶ Read aloud the Catholics Believe feature. Have students elaborate on how both genders offer something unique in loving relationships.

Connect

▶ Prepare the students for the activity on the page by inviting the class to list examples of popular TV shows that depict people in relationships such as friendships or marriages.

▶ Have students complete the activity on the page. Invite them to share their responses to the class.

Reinforce

Ask a volunteer to read the opening text aloud.

Respond

▶ Introduce The Culture of Life activity and then have students complete it.

▶ Invite them to share their responses with the class.

Choose

▶ Have students read the last section individually and in silence and write their faith choice.

▶ Then after a moment of prayerful reflection, have students make their commitment in prayer. Encourage them to put their faith choice into practice this week.

I FOLLOW JESUS

The Ten Commandments are reminders of how to be in loving relationships. In order to act responsibly in your relationships, you can channel your desires to meet the needs of others first. Prayer is an effective way to refocus your attention on what is most important in life.

THE CULTURE OF LIFE

Choose one of the commandments addressed in this chapter. Create the outline of a story that supports a culture of life. Write or draw three scenes for the story in the boxes.

MY FAITH CHOICE

This week, I will think of the needs of older members of my family. I will respect them by:

_____

_____

 Pray, "Jesus, you show us how to love. Help me to channel my desires so that I can see others to respect, as Jesus does. Amen."

204

TEACHING TIP

People of Prayer. Before having students complete the activity, invite them to reflect on the role of prayer in their daily lives. Ask them to share aloud when they pray during the day. Ask them to name what types of prayers they pray most often, such as the traditional prayers of the Church (the Our Father, the Hail Mary, the Glory Be), spontaneous prayers, prayers of thanksgiving, and prayers of petition. Have them complete the "Pray Always" activity, encouraging them to look through the end-of-chapter prayers and the prayers in the Catholic Prayers and Practices section of their student text for prayers that would fit the activities listed.

Chapter Review

Mark the true statements "T" and the false statements "F." Change the false statements into true statements.

equal

(F) T **1.** Adult children who live away from home have less responsibility to honor their parents as do younger children who still live at home.

F (T) **2.** All human life is sacred from the first moment of conception to natural death.

F (T) **3.** Everyone is called to live a chaste life.

F (T) **4.** The virtues of temperance and modesty help us to live the Sixth and Ninth Commandments.

F (T) **5.** The Fifth Commandment is about promoting the culture of life.

TO HELP YOU REMEMBER

1. The Fourth Commandment teaches that all family members are to contribute to the well-being of the family.

2. The Fifth Commandment teaches that we are to respect all human life as sacred and live as peacemakers.

3. The Sixth and Ninth Commandment teach us to live chaste lives in our thoughts and actions.

Peace Prayer

This well-known prayer of St. Francis of Assisi summarizes the attitude of one who supports a culture of life in human relationships. Pray it with your class and often with your family.

Lord, make me an instrument of your peace:

where there is hatred, let me sow love;

where there is injury, pardon;

where there is doubt, faith;

where there is despair, hope;

where there is darkness, light;

and where there is sadness, joy.

O Divine Master, grant that I may not so much seek

to be consoled as to console;

to be understood as to understand;

to be loved as to love.

For it is in giving that we receive;

it is in pardoning that we are pardoned;

and it is in dying that we are born to eternal life. Amen.

(205)

We Remember

▶ Review key points from the chapter using statements in the To Help You Remember section.

▶ As a review, remind the students of these four points: (1) freedom comes from following God's laws; (2) love is to put the needs of others first; (3) marriage is the place for men and women to express their committed love; and (4) temperance and chastity help us place God first.

▶ Now introduce and explain the Chapter Review. Review the answers with the class.

▶ Encourage the students to memorize the Ten Commandments, found on page 261 in their student book.

We Pray

▶ Gather the students for the chapter's closing prayer.

▶ Introduce the well-known Prayer of Saint Francis. Invite the class to pray it reverently together.

HUMAN METHODOLOGIES

Learning by Apprenticeship. The *National Directory for Catechesis* states that two important aspects of learning by apprenticeship are growing in the knowledge and practice of Christian prayer and taking the Word of God to heart (*NDC* 29H). Learning prayers of meditation, rooted in the Word of God and a part of our rich heritage of Catholic prayer, fulfills both of these demands. As you lead the students in today's closing Peace Prayer, make sure that you allow ample time for silent reflection, decision making, and prayer.

Preview

▶ Have students carefully tear-out the With My Family page along the perforation.

▶ Encourage them to share the pages with their family and to complete the activities together at home.

▶ If the students did not or were not able to complete the Chapter Review activity encourage them to complete it with their family.

▶ Point out the title and theme of next week's chapter to the children.

Visit www.BeMyDisciples.com

▶ Take time with the students to explore the many activities and resources available at the Web site.

▶ Encourage especially them and their families to discover the many resources available at **www.BeMyDisciples.com.**

Before Moving On ...

As you finish today's lesson, reflect on the following question before moving on to the next chapter.

How often do I take time to promote a culture of life?

With My Family

This Week...

In chapter 22, Commandments of Love, your child learned:

▶ The Fourth Commandment teaches that all family members are to contribute to the well-being of the family.

▶ The Fifth Commandment teaches that we are to respect all human life as sacred and to live as peacemakers.

▶ The Sixth and Ninth Commandments teach us to live a chaste life as Jesus did.

▶ The cardinal virtue of temperance helps us to moderate our actions so that we do what is good and right.

For more about related teachings of the Church, see the *Catechism of the Catholic Church,* 2196–2400, 2514–2533; and the *United States Catholic Catechism for Adults,* pages 373–416, 439–446.

■ Sharing God's Word

Read together Luke 1:46–55 (The Magnificat) and Luke 1:69–79 (The Canticle of Zechariah). Emphasize that prayer helps us to recognize God as the source of life and love. In prayer we can turn to God for his loving kindness and tender mercies.

■ We Live as Disciples

The Christian home and family is a school of discipleship. Choose one of the following activities to do as a family or design a similar activity of your own:

▶ Blessed Mother Teresa said, "Prayer enlarges the heart until it is capable of containing God's gift of himself." Invite family members to share how they invite God into their hearts.

▶ Use family prayer time to pray for the specific needs of others. Then form a family action plan to help meet those needs.

▶ Have each family member handwrite a "love letter" to one another.

■ Our Spiritual Journey

Prayer is a way that helps us to persevere in love. Saint Paul calls for all Christians to pray without ceasing. This is possible if our wills are aligned with God's. The Church teaches us that such tireless activity comes from love. Love opens our hearts to faith, making prayer possible. Pray the Prayer of Saint Francis on page 205 with your family.

For more ideas on ways that your family can live as disciples of Jesus, visit **www.BeMyDisciples.com**

206

PARTNERING WITH PARENTS

Gospel Canticles. One of this week's With My Family suggestions is for families to read together the Magnificat and the Canticle of Zechariah. If class time allows, use the supplies you gathered and have the students prepare bookmarks for each canticle. Encourage them to take the bookmarks home, and to pray the Canticle of Zechariah (the traditional canticle for the Church's Morning Prayer) in the morning and the Canticle of Mary (the traditional canticle for the Church's Evening Prayer) in the evening. Suggest that they tuck the bookmarks in their family Bible at Luke 1:69–79 (Canticle of Zechariah) and Luke 1:46–55 (Canticle of Mary).

Enriching the Lesson

Creating Heritage Booklets

Purpose

To reinforce that the family is the domestic Church in which all members are important, especially the vulnerable and elderly (taught on page 201)

Directions

▶ Recall the meaning of the family as a domestic Church.

▶ Have the students work in small groups to create a booklet of memories, stories, and images related to their family. Encourage them to write uplifting messages since this booklet will be shared with others.

▶ Have them share the booklets with their families and together pray for all family members, especially those who are in need, alone, elderly, or estranged from the family.

Materials

construction paper

markers or crayons

Creating a Discussion Web

Purpose

To reinforce that following the Ten Commandments builds a culture of life (taught on page 201)

Directions

▶ Present a scenario in which a group of teenagers intentionally plans to disrespect or bully another teenager.

▶ Write this question on the board: "If you were part of this group of teenagers, what could you do to change the course of events and instill a culture of life?"

▶ Have the students work in small groups and discuss the questions in detail.

▶ Invite a spokesperson from each group to create a web using the key points of their discussion and present the details of their answer to the question.

▶ Summarize with the class the importance of building a culture of life through respect for the dignity of others.

Materials

newsprint

pens or pencils

Using a Graphic Organizer

Purpose

To reinforce the teachings of the Fourth, Sixth, and Ninth Commandments (taught on pages 201–203)

Directions

▶ Have the students work in small groups to identify TV shows, books, videos, and movies depicting marriages, family life, and friendships that reflect the teachings of the Catholic Church.

▶ Invite them to discuss qualities, such as respect, that exist in these relationships.

▶ Ask them then to complete a three-column graphic organizer with the headings "Marriage," "Family Life," and "Friendship." Have them list the positive qualities depicted in the media about these relationships under the appropriate headings. Tell them to note the media situations that reinforce their claims.

▶ Have the groups present their organizers.

Materials

chart paper

pens or pencils

Love of Neighbor

BACKGROUND

I'm Talking to You

The Ten Commandments as found in Exodus 20 contain a curious diversion from the way God usually addresses the people of the Old Testament. In the Old Testament, he generally addresses the people of Israel collectively, as a community. This is not what happens in the rendering of the Ten Commandments.

"You" Singular

God, using the first person singular, says, "I am the LORD" (see Exodus 20:2), as in "Listen up, what I'm about to say is very important." Then he says, "you," not the plural, collective "you," but "you" as an individual. God, in other words, is addressing each person individually as he speaks to the whole community. In other words, we need to listen up. These Commandments are not "just for others;" they are for me. It is as though he is saying, "Take this personally; I'm talking to you."

Awareness of the Law

In the revelation of the Ten Commandments, God was not revealing something new. He was not revealing a mystery beyond the comprehension of humans. He was putting in human words what he had already written on every human heart. God was making us aware of what his people, both the community of Israel and each member of it, already should have known and come to understand.

The Fulfillment of the Law

The Ten Commandments do not only belong to the Old Law. Jesus, the Incarnate Son of God, revealed the importance of the Commandments. He taught:

> "Do not think that I have come to abolish the law or the prophets. I have come not to abolish but to fulfill. . . . But whoever obeys and teaches these commandments will be called greatest in the kingdom of heaven." Matthew 5:17, 19

The story of the rich young man gives us an insight into how Jesus fulfilled the Law. The young man approached Jesus and asked him, "[W]hat good must I do to gain eternal life?" (Matthew 19:16). Jesus replied, "If you wish to enter into life, keep the commandments" (19:17). The young man then said, "All of these I have observed. What do I still lack?" (19:20). Jesus confounds the young fellow—and us—with his response, "If you wish to be perfect, go, sell what you have and give to [the] poor, and you will have treasure in heaven. Then come, follow me" (19:21).

Jesus asks his disciples to live the Law of God as it is written on the human heart. Always make love for God and others your motivation in all you say and do. Fulfill Jesus' New Commandment: "love one another as I love you" (John 15:12).

For Reflection

When am I most aware of God speaking to me? How attentive and responsive am I?

In what ways do I strive to fulfill the Law of God as Jesus taught?

Catechist to Catechist

Respect

There is always plenty of discussion when it comes to the issue of youth showing respect to others. As adults we would do well to ask ourselves what role we play in fostering a healthy environment of respect. For example, does our driving, especially on a busy highway during heavy traffic, model respect? Respect or lack of respect is often a learned behavior.

Modeling Respect

You can help your students learn about and internalize the virtue of respect as you teach them the Ten Commandments. Model virtuous living even in the smallest ways, and be intentional. Your kindness and patience, your encouragement and compassion, your time doing activities and praying together are forms of respect. Continue treating one another with the love that God shows us. Look for opportunities each time you gather to show the love of God for the sake of others.

In this chapter your children will be exploring the respect due to our elders. Use this opportunity to encourage the young people to pay special attention to the way they treat the older members of their families and of the parish.

The Church Teaches...

"Catechesis prepares the Christian to live in community and to participate actively in the life and mission of the Church. . . . [Catechesis] should encourage a spirit of simplicity and humility, a special concern for the poor, particular care for the alienated, a sense of fraternal correction, common prayer, mutual forgiveness, and a fraternal love that embraces all of these attitudes" (*National Directory for Catechesis,* 20.5).

Jesus sets the example of service by his own life. As catechists, our ministry is a work of service to our students and their families.

Further Reading and Reflection

For more on the teachings of the Church, see the *Catechism of the Catholic Church,* 2401–2513, 2534–2557; and from the *United States Catholic Catechism for Adults,* pages 417–438, 447–457.

Catechist Prayer

Holy Spirit of Wisdom, fill my heart with hunger for wisdom and help me choose the good. Amen.

Lesson Planner

Chapter 23   Love of Neighbor

Focus To learn what the Seventh, Eighth, and Tenth Commandments teach about living the second part of the Great Commandment

LESSON PART	PROCESS	MATERIALS and RESOURCES
EXPLORE **Focus** To explore how generosity is a reflection of loving others as God loves us 🕐 10 minutes **Pages** 207–208	▶ Proclaim and discuss Luke 21:3–4 (The poor widow). ▶ Learn about Venerable Henriette Delille. **Disciple Power:** Generosity	Bible Pencils Crayons or markers
DISCOVER **Focus** To discover what the Seventh, Eighth, and Tenth Commandments teach about loving ourselves and others 🕐 30 minutes **Pages** 209–211	▶ Discover the challenges of living the Seventh Commandment. **Activity:** Chart our Time, Talent, and Treasure. ▶ Explore the damage done by lies and gossip. ▶ Learn the relationship between greed and generosity. **Activity:** Choose an act of generosity.	Butcher paper **Additional Activities Booklet:** Activities 23a and 23b, or see BeMyDisciples.com.
DECIDE **Focus** To decide on a response to the lesson on the Seventh, Eighth, and Tenth Commandments 🕐 10 minutes **Page** 212	**Activity:** Create a daily prayer planner. **My Faith Choice:** Connect generosity to spending more time with God.	**Enriching the Lesson Activities:** Catechist Edition, page 339 • Reviewing Faith Vocabulary • Role-playing Moral Dilemmas • Affirming One Another

Concluding the Lesson   10 minutes

We Remember

Page 213
▶ Review concepts and do review activity.

▶ **Assessment Tools Booklet:** Chapter Test 23a–23b, or see BeMyDisciples.com.

We Pray

▶ **Prayer:** a prayer for peace in sign language

Materials: Bible, candle, cross for prayer space

▶ Grade 6 Music CD

Preview

Point out resources for this chapter at

www.BeMyDisciples.com ❯

▶ Preview the With My Family page and next week's lesson theme.

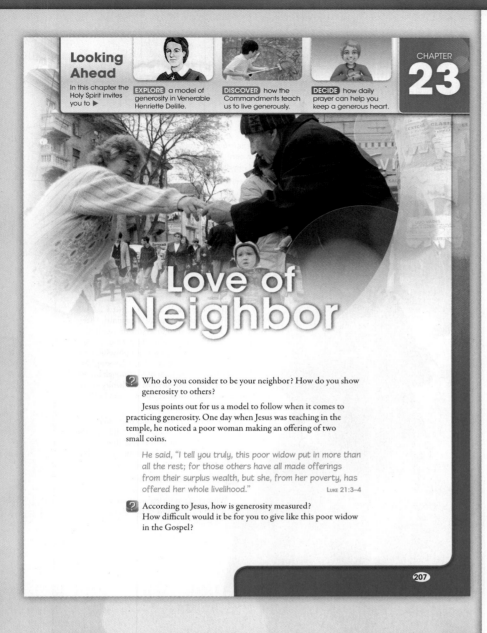

Looking Ahead

In this chapter the Holy Spirit invites you to ▶

EXPLORE a model of generosity in Venerable Henriette Delille.

DISCOVER how the Commandments teach us to live generously.

DECIDE how daily prayer can help you keep a generous heart.

CHAPTER 23

Love of Neighbor

❓ Who do you consider to be your neighbor? How do you show generosity to others?

Jesus points out for us a model to follow when it comes to practicing generosity. One day when Jesus was teaching in the temple, he noticed a poor woman making an offering of two small coins.

He said, "I tell you truly, this poor widow put in more than all the rest; for those others have all made offerings from their surplus wealth, but she, from her poverty, has offered her whole livelihood." LUKE 21:3–4

❓ According to Jesus, how is generosity measured? How difficult would it be for you to give like this poor widow in the Gospel?

207

Pray

▶ Gather the class for prayer.

▶ Begin and conclude with the Sign of the Cross.

▶ Lead the children in the prayer of Saint Francis on page 205.

Reflect

▶ Use the opening questions as a way to continued prayerful reflection.

▶ Have a volunteer proclaim the Scripture passage on the page.

▶ Have the students respond to the questions at the bottom of the page, and then share their responses with the class.

Focus

▶ Call attention to the Looking Ahead feature. Explain that in this chapter the students will learn more about God's plan for love and life, especially involving others who are not family or friends, like neighbors.

▶ Tell them that on the next page they will hear the story of a wealthy young women whose love of neighbor led her to lead a very generous life.

SCRIPTURE BACKGROUND

Love of Neighbor. Saint Paul writes about the importance of loving our neighbor. "[T]he one who loves another has fulfilled the law. The commandments . . . are summed up in this saying, [namely] 'You shall love your neighbor as yourself.' Love does no evil to the neighbor; hence, love is the fulfillment of the law" **(Romans 13:9–10)**.

Introduce

▶ Elaborate on what it means to have a "generous heart." Inquire: What kinds of acts would show a person has a generous heart?

▶ Explain to students that on this page they will read about the first United States native-born African American whose cause for canonization has been officially opened by the Catholic Church. Her name is Henriette Delille.

▶ Have several students read aloud the text on the page.

▶ Then have a volunteer student read aloud the Disciple Power feature about generosity.

Reinforce

Ask the students to identify ways in which Venerable Henriette Delille showed generosity. Ask a student to re-read the opening sentence to summarize.

Connect

▶ Ask the students to list charitable works that they can reasonably accomplish that would show to others their generous heart.

▶ Challenge the students to consider the model of Venerable Henriette Delille. Where could they practice generosity to serve those in need in their local area?

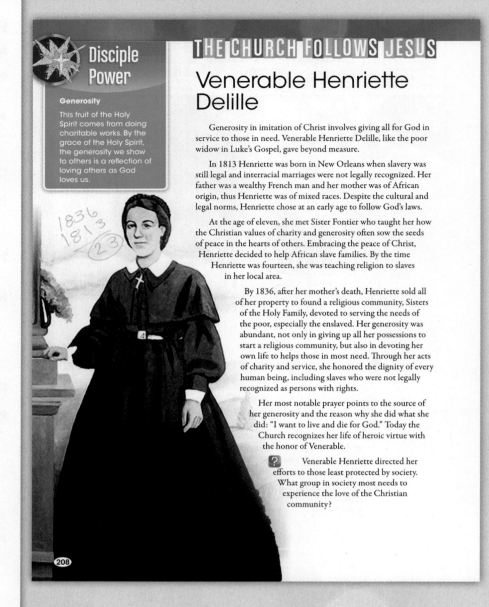

Disciple Power

Generosity

This fruit of the Holy Spirit comes from doing charitable works. By the grace of the Holy Spirit, the generosity we show to others is a reflection of loving others as God loves us.

THE CHURCH FOLLOWS JESUS

Venerable Henriette Delille

Generosity in imitation of Christ involves giving all for God in service to those in need. Venerable Henriette Delille, like the poor widow in Luke's Gospel, gave beyond measure.

In 1813 Henriette was born in New Orleans when slavery was still legal and interracial marriages were not legally recognized. Her father was a wealthy French man and her mother was of African origin, thus Henriette was of mixed races. Despite the cultural and legal norms, Henriette chose at an early age to follow God's laws.

At the age of eleven, she met Sister Fontier who taught her how the Christian values of charity and generosity often sow the seeds of peace in the hearts of others. Embracing the peace of Christ, Henriette decided to help African slave families. By the time Henriette was fourteen, she was teaching religion to slaves in her local area.

By 1836, after her mother's death, Henriette sold all of her property to found a religious community, Sisters of the Holy Family, devoted to serving the needs of the poor, especially the enslaved. Her generosity was abundant, not only in giving up all her possessions to start a religious community, but also in devoting her own life to helps those in most need. Through her acts of charity and service, she honored the dignity of every human being, including slaves who were not legally recognized as persons with rights.

Her most notable prayer points to the source of her generosity and the reason why she did what she did: "I want to live and die for God." Today the Church recognizes her life of heroic virtue with the honor of Venerable.

❓ Venerable Henriette directed her efforts to those least protected by society. What group in society most needs to experience the love of the Christian community?

DISCIPLE POWER

Generosity. Give the students five minutes to write down the names of all the games, clothes, and sports equipment they own. At the end of the five minutes, have the students circle the things on their list they frequently use or wear. Have them underline the things they seldom use or wear. Instruct them to cross out the things they no longer use or wear. Make a class list of all the games, clothes, and sports equipment the students crossed out or no longer use or wear. Ask them if they can think of others who could use those items. Encourage them to be generous, as Venerable Henriette Delille was, by giving their unused items to those in need. If possible, coordinate a collection of those items, and, with their family's permission, donate them to an area shelter or outreach effort.

Truth and Justice for All

The Seventh Commandment

You shall not steal. EXODUS 20:15

The Seventh Commandment teaches that we live the virtues of justice and charity in our relationships with other people. We are to use the goods of the Earth responsibly with generous hearts. How we treat the environment and use natural resources has an impact not only on our own but future generations. God consistently calls us to be good stewards of his creation. We are to use our resources without waste yet out of generosity for those most in need.

This commandment forbids stealing, cheating, human trafficking (slavery), misusing or damaging another's property, and paying unjust wages. If we break this commandment, we have the obligation to repair whatever damage we have caused and to restore what we have unjustly done. This is called **reparation**.

The Seventh Commandment also teaches us about the importance of work. Our virtuous work is a participation in the work of God the Creator. Because we are joined to Christ in Baptism, our work is to be joined to his. One important work of the Christian life is **almsgiving**. In this way, the work we do is an act of generosity and charity—loving our neighbor as God loves all of us. All of our daily activity is to give honor and glory to God.

FAITH FOCUS
What do the Seventh, Eight, and Tenth Commandments teach us about living the Law of Love?

FAITH VOCABULARY
almsgiving
Money, food or material given to the poor as an act of penance or charity

reparation
The process of righting a wrong; making amends

stewardship
The actions of responsibly caring for what God has given in service to others

Activity The Church asks us to give of our time, talent, and treasure for the good of the community. In what ways might you have wasted all three at times, and what will you be willing to give?

	Waste	Give
Time		
Talent		
Treasure		

209

CATHOLIC SOCIAL TEACHING

Human Work and the Dignity of the Worker. We all have the obligation to make use of our talents and to use them to work for the common good. Governments have the responsibility to create a just society. Governments are to guarantee workers a just wage, to provide access to meaningful jobs, and to promote equality in the workplace.

Tip: Lead the class in a discussion that helps them value the work and workers that are part of their daily life and how this principle of Catholic Social Teaching applies to the Seventh Commandment.

Key Concept
The Seventh Commandment teaches us to use what God has provided in a just and charitable way.

Teach

▶ Read the Faith Focus question aloud and ask the students to silently think about how they might respond to it.

▶ Point out that this chapter explains three important Commandments about treating others justly, truthfully, and with love.

▶ Review the Faith Vocabulary words and clarify any student questions.

▶ Ask the students what they can tell you about the Seventh Commandment.

▶ Have the students read the text on the page, and as they do so, have them circle unfamiliar words. Clarify any questions they may have about the content of the reading. Ask them what new understandings they learned about the Seventh Commandment.

Reinforce

Help the students brainstorm examples of stewardship, almsgiving, and reparation.

Connect

Invite them to complete the activity and to show their responses. Ask: "In what way can wasting our 'treasure' be seen as a sin against the Seventh Commandment?" *(It makes unavailable or takes away from others a resource they might need.)*

Teach

▶ Ask the students why a person's name is important. Have them discuss what a name says about a person.

▶ Review their understanding of the term *truth*.

▶ Have the students read the text on the page to learn what the Eighth Commandment teaches us about speaking and living the truth.

▶ Ask the students when they should withhold the truth. (*Example: When the person they are speaking to has no right to know it; for example, a family secret.*)

Reinforce

Invite a volunteer to read the Faith-Filled People feature. Discuss how Saint Paul lived the Commandments.

Connect

▶ Use the question on the page to discuss ways in which the students can actively live and promote the truth in their daily lives.

▶ Caution students about using the Internet or text messaging to spread gossip or rumors about others. Remind them that once a message is sent it never goes away.

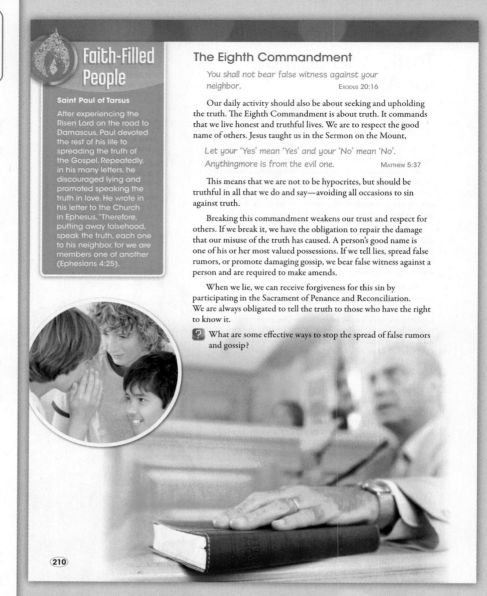

Faith-Filled People

Saint Paul of Tarsus

After experiencing the Risen Lord on the road to Damascus, Paul devoted the rest of his life to spreading the truth of the Gospel. Repeatedly, in his many letters, he discouraged lying and promoted speaking the truth in love. He wrote in his letter to the Church in Ephesus, "Therefore, putting away falsehood, speak the truth, each one to his neighbor, for we are members one of another (Ephesians 4:25).

The Eighth Commandment

You shall not bear false witness against your neighbor.   Exodus 20:16

Our daily activity should also be about seeking and upholding the truth. The Eighth Commandment is about truth. It commands that we live honest and truthful lives. We are to respect the good name of others. Jesus taught us in the Sermon on the Mount,

Let your 'Yes' mean 'Yes' and your 'No' mean 'No'. Anything more is from the evil one.   Matthew 5:37

This means that we are not to be hypocrites, but should be truthful in all that we do and say—avoiding all occasions to sin against truth.

Breaking this commandment weakens our trust and respect for others. If we break it, we have the obligation to repair the damage that our misuse of the truth has caused. A person's good name is one of his or her most valued possessions. If we tell lies, spread false rumors, or promote damaging gossip, we bear false witness against a person and are required to make amends.

When we lie, we can receive forgiveness for this sin by participating in the Sacrament of Penance and Reconciliation. We are always obligated to tell the truth to those who have the right to know it.

 What are some effective ways to stop the spread of false rumors and gossip?

(210)

FAITH-FILLED PEOPLE

Saint Paul of Tarsus. Paul, also called Saul, was born in Tarsus, a city in the Roman province of Cilicia, which is in the southeast part of Asia Minor. Tarsus, which lies northwest of Jerusalem, was a trading center populated by many wealthy citizens. Tarsus had a university, which was more renowned than those in Athens and Alexandria. Saint Paul had studied under Gamaliel, a rabbi, and also learned the trade of a tent maker to support himself. For more information on Saint Paul of Tarsus go to the Saints Resource at www.BeMyDisciples.com.

The Tenth Commandment

You shall not covet your neighbor's goods. Exodus 20:17

We are to share the blessings that God has given to us with others. We are to avoid greed and envy, which are capital sins. The Tenth Commandment teaches us to treat others fairly and justly. We know that we are tempted to violate the Tenth Commandment when we desire too much or are jealous of what others have. This kind of coveting can lead us to placing material possessions before personal relationships. For example, if you feel resentful of a possession that your friend has, that it may be a sign of greed and envy.

The Tenth Commandment also calls us to be thankful for what God has given us, and to be generous in the gifts we have received. All blessings and gifts are from God. Many of the gifts given to us by God are to be used for the benefit and good of others. When we take care of what God has provided us, we exercise **stewardship**. And in our generosity, we live according to the cardinal virtue of justice.

Activity In certain Native American traditions, a person chooses on his or her birthday to give gifts to others rather than receiving them. Think of a friend and a possession of yours they would appreciate. Discuss with a partner what you chose and how difficult it would be to give it away.

Catholics Believe

Poverty of Heart

Jesus celebrated the joy of the poor because their hearts were not set on earthly possessions. The Kingdom of God belongs to those who are "poor in spirit" because their hearts long for the treasures that await them in Heaven (see Matthew 5:3; 6:19–21). So the more we desire the things in this earthly life, the less we are able to focus on the source of true happiness, God.

211

THE TASKS OF CATECHESIS

Education for Community Life. Many Catholic parishes promote three areas of stewardship—stewardship of time, stewardship of talent, and stewardship of treasure. Draw three columns on the board or on a flip chart. At the top of each column, write one of the three areas of stewardship. Invite students to first name the ways they are already being good stewards in each of the three areas. Affirm their stewardship efforts. Then invite students to name other practical ways a sixth grader can be a good steward of time, talent, and treasure. After listing their examples, encourage students to choose a new way to be a good steward of what God has provided.

Teach

▶ Have students read the text on the page. Recall the definition of *covet* from the previous chapter.

▶ Discuss how the image on the page relates to the Commandments and the Beatitudes.

▶ Remind the children that generosity is the antidote to covetousness.

Reinforce

▶ Remind the students that the materialism of our culture makes greed and envy particular problems.

▶ Read aloud the Catholics Believe feature. Recall the Beatitudes and how poverty of heart relates to the Tenth Commandment.

Connect

Have students complete the activity on the page. Invite them to share their responses to the class.

Reinforce

▶ Remind students that prayer strengthens our faith, hope, and love for God.

▶ Point out that the Holy Spirit helps us to pray. Invite students to express the importance of prayer in their daily lives, especially on how it helps them to have a generous heart.

Respond

▶ Recall traditional times and ways in which Catholics pray each day. Note the back section of the student textbook that covers prayers and practices of the Catholic Church.

▶ Introduce the Prayer and Action activity and then have students complete it.

▶ Then invite them to share their responses with the class.

Choose

▶ Have students read the last section individually and in silence, and then write their faith choice.

▶ Then after a moment of prayerful reflection, have students make their commitment in prayer. Encourage them to put their faith choice into practice this week.

I FOLLOW JESUS

The Church teaches us that the Holy Spirit guides and strengthens us in our ability to love our neighbor as God loves us. Works of charity come from a generous heart, and your generosity can sow the seeds of peace. The Holy Spirit invites you to pray often throughout the day, seeking a generous heart.

PRAYER AND ACTION

Take the time to fill-out this daily planner. Set aside several different times during the day for praying. Choose reasonable timeslots in which you can pray for something. In another slot, write something you will do that demonstrates a generous spirit. Write down what you plan to pray for in that slot.

Morning	
Afternoon	
Evening	

MY FAITH CHOICE

This week I will spend more time with God, the source of all love and generosity, in prayer. I will act with generosity. I will:

_____

_____

Pray, "Holy Spirit, guide my heart to love others as you love me. Amen."

(212)

HUMAN METHODOLOGIES

Learning within the Christian Family. The *National Directory for Catechesis* states that children learn the prayers of the Catholic faith and the importance of developing a life of prayer within the family (*NDC* 29D). Before having students complete the activity, invite them to share how and when their families pray together at home (i.e., at meals, at bedtime, before going to school). Ask them to share how and when their families pray together with the parish community (i.e., Sunday Mass, funeral Mass, sacramental celebrations, evening prayer). Ask if any of the families pray the Rosary or the Stations of the Cross together. Then invite the students to think about their own prayer life, and have them complete the daily planner and My Faith Choice.

Chapter Review

For each scenario, identify which commandment is being violated. Then tell how the person could make reparations for their wrongdoing.

1. Jason's parents bought him his own tablet for his birthday. His older sister, Jane, became jealous because his tablet was newer than hers. Jane complained that because she is older, she should have the newest, and that Jason should have hers.

   Jane is violating the 10th Commandment because she is coveting her brother's tablet; she could make amends by first apologizing for her behavior and then suggest great sites for Jason to check out with his new tablet.

2. Sam and Sophie were proud of their new tablets. So they went to school the next day and showed them off to everyone. Then they noticed that George had an even better tablet than theirs. They took George's and left it where it would be damaged by water.

   Both Sam and Sophie violated the 7th Commandment because they stole George's tablet and then intentionally caused it to be damaged; they could make amends by first apologizing to George and then buy him a new tablet.

TO HELP YOU REMEMBER

1. The Seventh and Tenth Commandments teach us to treat others justly.

2. The Eighth Commandment is about speaking and living the truth.

3. We are to make amends with penance and reparation if we violate any of God's commandments.

Prayer for Peace

Peace is one of the Fruits of the Holy Spirit. Learn to sign the word peace by viewing the image here. Conclude this prayer by signing "Peace."

Lord, make me
an instrument of your peace.
Peace.

(213)

CATHOLIC DOCTRINE

Fruits of the Holy Spirit. It is by the power of the Holy Spirit that we are called to bear much fruit, for we are grafted onto the one true vine, Jesus Christ. The Fruits of the Holy Spirit are our "first fruits of eternal glory" perfected in us by the Holy Spirit (see *Catechism of the Catholic Church* 736 and 1832).

We Remember

▶ Invite three volunteer students to report to the class the top three most important points from this chapter's content. Compare their report to the To Help You Remember section.

▶ Now introduce the chapter review section. Explain that they are to read each scenario about "e-reader envy" and identify which Commandment is being violated. Then have the whole class discuss how the person could make reparation for their wrongdoing.

▶ Review the answers with the class.

We Pray

▶ Gather the students for the chapter's closing prayer.

▶ Teach students how to sign the word *peace* by using the illustration on the page.

▶ Remind them that God is always in our midst and that the Holy Spirit helps us to pray.

▶ Lead them in praying the prayer on the page, while signing the word, peace, in "Lord, make me an instrument of your peace."

▶ Conclude with the singing of an appropriate hymn.

Preview

▶ Have students carefully tear-out the With My Family page along the perforation.

▶ Encourage them to share the pages with their family and to complete the activities together at home.

▶ If the students did not or were not able to complete the Chapter Review activity on page 213, encourage them to complete it with their family.

▶ Point out the title and theme of next week's chapter to the children.

Visit www.BeMyDisciples.com

▶ Take time with the students to explore the many activities and resources available at **www.BeMyDisciples.com.**

▶ Encourage especially them and their families to discover the many resources available at the Web site.

Before Moving On ...

As you finish today's lesson, reflect on the following question before moving on to the next chapter.

Do I make a faith choice each week as I encourage my students to do?

With My Family

This Week...

In chapter 23, Love of Neighbor, your child learned:

▶ The Seventh and Tenth Commandments teach us that we are to be just and generous. We are to use and care for all of God's creation wisely.

▶ The Eighth Commandment teaches us to live honest and truthful lives.

▶ If we violate any of God's commandments, we are to make amends with penance and reparation correcting the wrong we have done.

▶ Through almsgiving and stewardship, we can show our generosity and thanksgiving for all we have been given by God.

For more about related teachings of the Church, see the *Catechism of the Catholic Church,* 2401–2513, 2534–2557; and the *United States Catholic Catechism for Adults,* pages 417–438, 447–457.

■ Sharing God's Word

Read together John 14:15–21. Emphasize that faithfully living the Ten Commandments is a sign of a faithful disciple of Jesus. Find strength in knowing that Christ has given us the Holy Spirit as our Advocate to guide us in truth and justice.

■ We Live as Disciples

The Christian home and family is a school of discipleship. Choose one of the following activities to do as a family or design a similar activity of your own:

▶ Talk about how your family lives as good stewards of God's creation. Focus on various "green initiatives" like gardening, conservation, and recycling.

▶ During the holiday seasons, make an extra effort to help those in need before purchasing extra gifts for the family.

▶ Give as a sacrifice—not from your excess but from what you value. Be intentional about using the family's talents and treasures for the good of others.

■ Our Spiritual Journey

Almsgiving is as much a spiritual activity as it is a material one. Giving of our money and material as an act of penance may be a foreign concept. Reflect on ways to take charity to the next level by making the act of giving an act of sacrifice or penance.

For more ideas on ways that your family can live as disciples of Jesus, visit **www.BeMyDisciples.com**

(214)

PLANNING AHEAD

Year-End Letter. As you near the end of the catechetical year, prepare an end-of-the-year letter to go home next week with students. In the letter, remind families to continue to pray the prayers in the Catholic Prayers and Practices section over the summer months. Invite them to take part in any parish summer activities (list dates, times, and other pertinent information found on the parish Web site). Challenge them to do some summer faith-based reading, such as the life stories of favorite saints, a particular Gospel, or a portion of the Book of Psalms from the Bible. Remember to share with the families what you have enjoyed most regarding your ministry as catechist for their children this year.

Enriching the Lesson

Reviewing Faith Vocabulary

Purpose

To reinforce the faith vocabulary from Units 5 and 6

Directions

▶ Have the students work with partners to create their own vocabulary word cards from selected chapters if they have not already done so. Then have them create vocabulary-reinforcing activities, such as codes, crossword puzzles, and word searches, using their vocabulary word cards.

▶ Have partners share their activities with another set of partners and solve each other's activities.

▶ Rotate the activities as needed so that each set of partners uses a variety of reinforcement activities.

Materials

vocabulary word cards

paper

rulers

pens or pencils

Role-Playing Moral Dilemmas

Purpose

To reinforce the teaching of the Eighth Commandment to live honest and truthful lives (taught on page 209)

Directions

▶ Have the students work in small groups to create moral dilemmas that depict young people being challenged to tell the truth.

▶ Have the groups role play their scenario.

▶ Discuss as a class why it is sometimes difficult to tell the truth.

▶ Brainstorm ways that would help young people overcome common obstacles to telling the truth that they might face.

Materials

Affirming One Another

Purpose

To reinforce that each day we are to live the last seven of the Ten Commandments by showing respect for others and ourselves (as taught in chapters 22 and 23)

Directions

▶ Have the students work with partners to create a list of statements that they could use to affirm one another for living the Ten Commandments.

▶ Have them write their statements on sticky notes.

▶ Invite volunteers to share their ideas.

▶ Invite and encourage the students to give out their sticky notes to their friends and family during the week.

▶ Check back with the students about the reactions of their friends and family when they received their sticky notes.

▶ Optional: an alternative to the sticky notes would be electronic text messages. This would reinforce good positive texting between friends.

Materials

sticky notes

pens or pencils

BACKGROUND

Lord, Teach Us to Pray

The Sermon on the Mount in Matthew's Gospel is a summary of what it means to be a disciple of Christ. The Our Father that is found in the Sermon on the Mount is the model of all Christian prayer and a summary of the entire Gospel (see *General Directory for Catechesis* 85). In many ways and in poetic brevity, the Lord's Prayer summarizes Christ's entire teaching. If we were so inclined, we could devote a lifetime to meditating on the Our Father and still not have grasped the fullness of its teachings.

Abba Father

The Our Father consists of three petitions directed toward God's glory ("hallowed be thy name," "thy kingdom come," and "thy will be done") and three petitions for human need (food, forgiveness, and freedom from temptation).

Jesus is saying "Keep first things first" by opening his prayer with words of touching intimacy: "Our Father, who art in heaven." God is our *Abba*, the Father who is above us and watches out for us, in whom we trust unconditionally for our deepest needs.

Ask and you shall receive

What are our deepest needs? Again, notice how Jesus lines up the wording of the prayer. He resolutely points us first toward God. Jesus' words carry us toward God's name, his kingdom, and his will. Therein is our deepest need—to merge our earthly priorities and our pursuit of happiness with God's will. Christ is telling us to "seek first the kingdom [of God] and his righteousness, and all these things will be given you besides" (Matthew 6:33).

Lord, Teach Us to Live

In the final set of petitions of the Lord's Prayer, Jesus guides us to place before our Father in Heaven our human needs of daily bread, forgiveness, strength to overcome all that leads us from loving God and from loving one another as Jesus did, and victory over evil, suffering, sin, and death. As we read these petitions, we quickly notice that power, prestige, money, or life's tempting trinkets that assuage our egos do not make it onto Christ's short list.

Jesus, in so many words, advises us to boldly and confidently approach God the Father in prayer, trusting that "all that you ask for in prayer, believe that you will receive it and it shall be yours" (Mark 11:24). As the Roman centurion did (see Matthew 8:10) and as the Canaanite woman did (see Matthew 15:28), we are to express our needs boldly and confidently to the Lord.

For Reflection

When have I used the Our Father as a guide to structure my prayer?

What are some concrete, specific implications of the petitions of the Lord's Prayer for living my life as a disciple of Christ?

Catechist to Catechist

Intimacy with God

A main goal of the year was to help the students and yourself encounter Christ by sharing, celebrating, and living the Catholic faith together. Deepening your understanding of the Lord's Prayer is a good way for you and your students to achieve this and to bring your time together this year to a close. The Lord's Prayer is a summary of the entire Gospel. When we pray the Lord's Prayer, we express our intimacy with God the Father and our desire to live as his children. We express who we are and how we are to pray and live.

Excitement in the End

As this year draws to an end, these exuberant sixth graders are understandably excited about summer vacation. Sometimes they may become just a little noisy. Use their excitement and exuberance to your advantage. Show excitement about all you have achieved together this year. Affirm the group for sharing their time with the Lord. Be sure to thank the students for helping you grow in faith, hope, and love.

The Church Teaches...

"Catechesis should invite the believer to join Christ in the Our Father. Prayer should be the ordinary environment for all catechesis so that the knowledge and practice of the Christian life may be understood and celebrated in its proper context" (*National Directory for Catechesis*, 20).

This year you have begun to develop the children's understanding and love for God the Father. Jesus is our model and guide in the ways of prayer. This last chapter presents the Our Father as an essential part of the Christian life.

Further Reading and Reflection

For more on the teachings of the Church, see the *Catechism of the Catholic Church*, 2558–2865; and from the *United States Catholic Catechism for Adults*, pages 461–495.

Catechist Prayer

Holy Spirit,
teach me to pray.
Help me center
myself in your deep
and abiding presence.
Amen.

Lesson Planner

Chapter 24 The Summary of the Gospel

Focus To learn that praying the Lord's Prayer teaches us to pray and to live as disciples of Jesus

LESSON PART	PROCESS	MATERIALS and RESOURCES
EXPLORE **Focus** To explore the power of hope 🕙 10 minutes **Pages** 215–216	▶ Proclaim and discuss Psalm 33:20–22 (We put our hope in the Lord). ▶ Learn about Saint Hildegard of Bingen. **Disciple Power:** Hope **Activity:** Identify ways to develop the habit of praying.	Journals Bible Pencils
DISCOVER **Focus** To discover the meaning of prayer, especially the Lord's Prayer 🕧 30 minutes **Pages** 217–219	▶ Explore the three expressions of prayer. ▶ Reflect on the importance of the Lord's Prayer. ▶ Learn the meaning of the Lord's Prayer. **Activity:** Write headlines about people living the Lord's Prayer.	Index cards **Additional Activities Booklet:** Activities 24a–24b, or see BeMyDisciples.com.
DECIDE **Focus** To decide on a response to the lesson on the Lord's Prayer 🕙 10 minutes **Page** 220	**Activity:** Create a web page about the Lord's Prayer. **My Faith Choice:** Pray the Lord's Prayer during the week.	**Enriching the Lesson Activities:** Catechist Edition, page 351 • Writing Prayers of Adoration • Creating a Cinquains • Catholic Social Teaching: Imitating Faith-Filled People

Concluding the Lesson 10 minutes

We Remember

Page 221

▶ Review concepts and do the review activity.

▶ **Assessment Tools Booklet:** Chapter Test 24a–24b, or see BeMyDisciples.com.

We Pray

▶ **Prayer:** the Lord's Prayer

Materials: Bible, candle, cross for prayer space

▶ Grade 6 Music CD

Preview

Point out resources for this chapter at

www.BeMyDisciples.com

▶ Preview the With My Family page and next week's lesson theme.

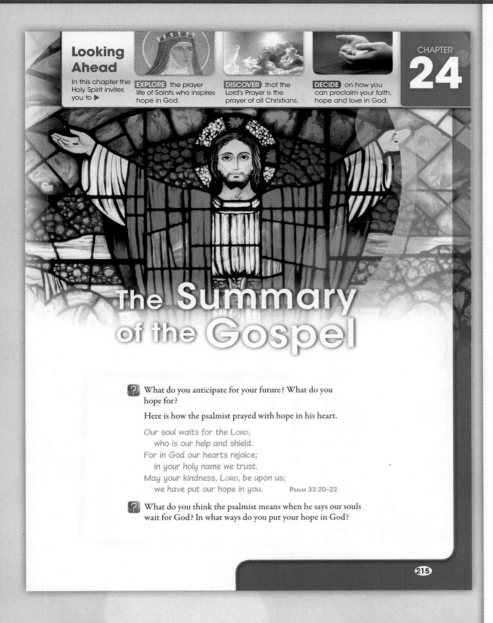

Looking Ahead

In this chapter the Holy Spirit invites you to ▶

EXPLORE the prayer life of Saints who inspires hope in God.

DISCOVER that the Lord's Prayer is the prayer of all Christians.

DECIDE on how you can proclaim your faith, hope and love in God.

CHAPTER **24**

The Summary of the Gospel

❓ What do you anticipate for your future? What do you hope for?

Here is how the psalmist prayed with hope in his heart.

Our soul waits for the Lord,
*   who is our help and shield.*
For in God our hearts rejoice;
*   in your holy name we trust.*
May your kindness, Lord, be upon us;
*   we have put our hope in you.*   Psalm 33:20–22

❓ What do you think the psalmist means when he says our souls wait for God? In what ways do you put your hope in God?

215

CATHOLIC DOCTRINE

The Lord's Prayer. The *Catechism of the Catholic Church* quotes two Doctors of the Church concerning the importance of the Lord's Prayer. Saint Augustine wrote, "Run through all the words of the holy prayers [in Scripture], and I do not think that you will find anything in them that is not contained and included in the Lord's Prayer" (CCC 2762). Saint Thomas Aquinas referred to the Lord's Prayer as "the most perfect of prayers. . . . In it we ask, not only for all the things we can rightly desire, but also in the sequence that they should be desired. This prayer not only teaches us to ask for things, but also in what order we should desire them" (CCC 2763). As you prepare to teach this chapter, take some quiet time to pray and reflect on the Lord's Prayer in light of the words of Augustine and Thomas Aquinas.

Pray

▶ Gather the students for prayer. Begin and conclude with the Sign of the Cross together.

▶ Use the questions at the top of the page for prayerful reflection.

▶ Conclude by having a volunteer proclaim the Scripture passage on the page.

Reflect

▶ Have students select a specific word or phrase from the Scripture passage that touches their hearts or jumps out at them. Ask them to mark them on the page and then explain why they chose those word(s).

▶ Have the students respond to the questions at the bottom of the page, and then share their responses with the class.

Focus

▶ Explain that in this chapter the students will learn more about the Lord's Prayer and how it helps us to live as people who place our faith, hope and love in God above all else.

▶ Call the students' attention to the Looking Ahead feature. Invite them to read aloud each bullet.

Introduce

▶ Ask students to share times when people feel hopeful. List these on the board.

▶ Remind them that through prayer we can have a sense of hope and deepen our relationship with God.

▶ Point out the saints of the Church and other holy people of faith who teach us to pray and have hope.

▶ Invite a volunteer student to read aloud the Disciple Power feature about hope.

▶ Ask volunteers to read aloud the main text on the page. Ask: Why do we honor St. Hildegard today? *(Her love of creation, her prayerful life.)*

Reinforce

Recall with the students that Hildegard of Bingen is a model for us who shows us how to keep prayer at the heart and center of our lives.

Connect

▶ Challenge the students to make prayer a daily habit by using the activity at the bottom of the page.

▶ You may wish to play music or show artwork by Hildegard of Bingen while students work.

▶ If you have been using a journal throughout the year, invite students to write an entry in their journal, that speaks of keeping hope alive in their hearts.

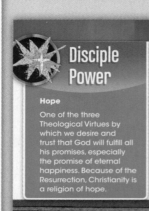

Disciple Power

Hope

One of the three Theological Virtues by which we desire and trust that God will fulfill all his promises, especially the promise of eternal happiness. Because of the Resurrection, Christianity is a religion of hope.

THE CHURCH FOLLOWS JESUS

Saint Hildegard of Bingen

The history of the Church is filled with examples of people of hope. They turn to God in prayer. Some are called saints, like Hildegard of Bingen, who exhibited the virtue of hope. Catholics pray for advice and direction from her and other saints to keep hope alive in their hearts.

Hildegard of Bingen (1098–1179) was blessed with a sense of God's closeness to her, placing hope in her heart. She had a great love of creation as God's great gift to us. At the age of thirty-eight, she was elected abbess, or leader, of a group of women who lived together in a religious community. They had joined together to live their lives according to the Rule of Saint Benedict. They ordered their priorities in life by placing God above all else.

Hildegard kept prayer at the heart and center of her life. Through her example, she continues to inspire people today. She taught that through prayer we deepen our friendship with God, in whom we trust and have hope. The Church honors Saint Hildegard of Bingen on her feast day, September 17.

Activity What can you do to make prayer a regular part of your day? How can this prayer habit give you hope?

_____

_____

_____

_____

_____

_____

216

DISCIPLE POWER

Hope. Share with the students a time when someone gave you hope by helping you through a difficult time. Perhaps you had a parent who was sick, and friends helped by watching your children or running your errands. Perhaps you had to move away from family in order to find work, and people in your new parish helped you feel welcomed. Ask the students if anyone has ever been a sign of hope for them in a difficult time. Invite them to think of others they know who are having a difficult time in life right now. Have the students make suggestions of practical ways they can be signs of God's hope to those they named. Challenge them to find at least one way to be a sign of hope in the coming week.

Being with God

Prayer strengthens our faith, hope and love for God. The Holy Spirit teaches us to pray through the Tradition of the Church. There is no secret to praying. Christians respond to the Holy Spirit by expressing our prayers in three basic ways. They are vocal prayer, meditation and contemplation. They all share one thing in common—all prayer flows from our heart.

Vocal Prayer

How natural it is for us to use words when we pray. Vocal prayer is prayer that uses words. Vocal prayers are prayed aloud or silently. They are prayed alone or with others. **Adoration** is a form of prayer in which our words praise God as the source of all.

The words we speak in our prayers express our thoughts and emotions. They enable us to share with God our joys and sorrow, our achievements and dreams. They give us the power to share with God everything about ourselves.

Meditation

God is a loving Father who every moment is an active part of our lives. In a prayer of **meditation**, we connect our lives more closely with God. We use our imaginations, minds, and desires to live the new life in Christ, which we have received in Baptism. We seek not only to know about Christ, but also to grow in our love and friendship with him. We spend time with God the Father and give him all our attention. We listen as the Holy Spirit shows us how to live as children of God and disciples of Jesus.

Contemplation

Remember, words are not necessary. God knows our innermost thoughts. He knows what we want to say before we put it into words.

Saint Teresa of Ávila (1535–1582), doctor of the Church and Spanish mystic, describes the prayer of **contemplation** as "nothing less than a close sharing between friends; it means taking time frequently to be alone with him who we know loves us." This is what we call communion with God the Father, in Christ, through the power of the Holy Spirit.

? Which form of prayer do you use the most? Which one would you like to try?

FAITH FOCUS
What are some ways in which you pray?

FAITH VOCABULARY
adoration
A form of prayer that declares God is the source of all. We acknowledge God is Almighty Creator, in whom we depend upon for everything.

contemplation
A form of prayer without using words, in which we focus our minds and hearts on God alone

meditation
A form of silent prayer in which we listen to God through our thoughts and imagination, using Scripture, art and music

217

Key Concept
The three major expressions of prayer are vocal prayer, meditation, and contemplation.

Teach

▶ Point out that there are different ways we can express our prayers to God. Invite students to list some of these expressions.

▶ Read the Faith Focus question aloud.

▶ Have the students read the text on the page. Invite them to list examples of each kind of expression.

▶ Read the Faith Vocabulary. Clarify any student questions.

Reinforce

Have each student draw an image that depicts one of the expressions of prayer. Ask volunteers to show their work.

Connect

▶ Prepare the students to do a mix of meditation and contemplation.

▶ Establish a calm atmosphere by: (1) turning the lights down/off (2) play instrumental music, and (3) suggest they close their eyes, clear their minds, and focus on the presence of God. Tell them to simply be with God, without words.

▶ Invite students to express what is on their mind and heart silently to God. Keep this short, three minutes maximum.

▶ Discuss with students this experience, acknowledging the challenges of clearing our minds for these forms of prayer.

TEACHING TIP

Create an Environment for Prayer. We live often surrounded by noise, which constantly competes for our undivided attention. Providing the students with opportunities to step aside from the noisy world is like having them make a mini-retreat, a powerful antidote to that noise. Allow moments of silence for writing and praying. Dim the lights and play quiet reflective music as students work on the various activities suggested in this week's lesson plan. These simple techniques will help students to quiet themselves and connect with God, who dwells within their hearts. Encourage the students to put these techniques into practice over the summer months on a regular basis.

Teach

▶ Read aloud Faith-Filled People. Invite students to imagine what Sarah's life was like, and how prayer might have helped her endure the trials she suffered and the joys she experienced.

▶ Share that Jesus taught his disciples about prayer and how to live as his disciples when he taught them the Lord's Prayer. The Lord's Prayer is a summary of the whole Gospel.

▶ Have the students read the text on the page. Use the question on the page to discuss how the Lord's Prayer helps us to live as disciples of Jesus.

Reinforce

Remind the students that the Lord's prayer is a summary of the whole Gospel. Ask them to identify aspects of Jesus' teaching and example that they see there. *(Examples: Putting God first, accepting God's will, forgiving others and asking forgiveness.)*

Connect

▶ Have students explain the importance of prayer in their own lives. Challenge them to point out how prayer helps them have a sense of hope in their lives.

▶ Invite them to pray a short silent prayer to give glory and honor to God the Father.

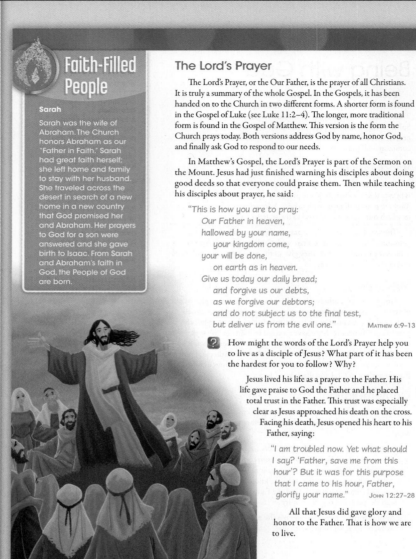

Faith-Filled People

Sarah

Sarah was the wife of Abraham. The Church honors Abraham as our "Father in Faith." Sarah had great faith herself; she left home and family to stay with her husband. She traveled across the desert in search of a new home in a new country that God promised her and Abraham. Her prayers to God for a son were answered and she gave birth to Isaac. From Sarah and Abraham's faith in God, the People of God are born.

The Lord's Prayer

The Lord's Prayer, or the Our Father, is the prayer of all Christians. It is truly a summary of the whole Gospel. In the Gospels, it has been handed on to the Church in two different forms. A shorter form is found in the Gospel of Luke (see Luke 11:2–4). The longer, more traditional form is found in the Gospel of Matthew. This version is the form the Church prays today. Both versions address God by name, honor God, and finally ask God to respond to our needs.

In Matthew's Gospel, the Lord's Prayer is part of the Sermon on the Mount. Jesus had just finished warning his disciples about doing good deeds so that everyone could praise them. Then while teaching his disciples about prayer, he said:

"This is how you are to pray:
Our Father in heaven,
hallowed by your name,
    your kingdom come,
your will be done,
    on earth as in heaven.
Give us today our daily bread;
    and forgive us our debts,
    as we forgive our debtors;
    and do not subject us to the final test,
    but deliver us from the evil one." MATTHEW 6:9–13

 How might the words of the Lord's Prayer help you to live as a disciple of Jesus? What part of it has been the hardest for you to follow? Why?

Jesus lived his life as a prayer to the Father. His life gave praise to God the Father and he placed total trust in the Father. This trust was especially clear as Jesus approached his death on the cross. Facing his death, Jesus opened his heart to his Father, saying:

"I am troubled now. Yet what should I say? 'Father, save me from this hour'? But it was for this purpose that I came to his hour, Father, glorify your name." JOHN 12:27–28

All that Jesus did gave glory and honor to the Father. That is how we are to live.

FAITH-FILLED PEOPLE

Sarah. As God changed the name of Abram to Abraham, he changed Abraham's wife's name from Sarai to Sarah. In the Bible such a change in the name of a person reflected God's choice, or election, of a person to fulfill a role in God's plan. In her old age, Sarah bore a son, Isaac. Through Isaac and his descendants God's promise to build the descendants of Abraham into a great nation was fulfilled.

The Meaning of the Lord's Prayer

The Lord's Prayer teaches us not only how to pray, but also how to live a life of total trust and hope in God the Father, as Jesus the Son of God does.

Our Father. Through our Baptism, we are joined to Christ and become one with him and one another. The Holy Spirit is poured into our hearts, enabling us to call God, Abba (or Father), as Jesus did.

Who Art in Heaven. The word Heaven points to God's majesty and glory. The Church on Earth joins with the angels and saints in Heaven in praising God.

Hallowed Be Thy Name. Glory and praise truly belong to God who creates, redeems, and sanctifies us.

Thy Kingdom Come. We pray that the kingdom announced by Jesus will come to completion when he comes again in glory at the end of time. We promise to prepare a way for the coming of that kingdom by being his disciples now and doing all we can to proclaim the Kingdom.

Thy Will Be Done on Earth as It Is in Heaven. God's will is for all people to live in communion with him forever. When we pray, "thy will be done," we promise to live according to God's will and plan, and to actively seek to do God's will in our lives.

Give Us This Day Our Daily Bread. Our daily bread is Christ himself, who said, "I am the living bread that came down from heaven" (John 6:51). We ask God to watch over our physical and spiritual needs and to keep us honest and attentive about what we really need in order to live a life in Christ.

And Forgive Us Our Trespasses as We Forgive Those Who Trespass against Us. Forgiveness is a two-way street. Those who receive God's forgiveness and mercy must be willing to be as forgiving and merciful toward others as God is toward them.

And Lead Us Not into Temptation. Temptation tries to convince us that there is something better than God's will. We ask God for the courage to face temptation with strong faith, confident hope, and generous love.

But Deliver Us from Evil. Satan and forces of evil in the world try to lead us away from God's love. There is no one, no power, stronger than Jesus. We pray that God's victory in Jesus Christ will be our victory as well.

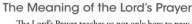

Catholics Believe

Ecumenism

Jesus prayed that his followers would be one as he and the Father are one. The followers of Jesus are often divided, yet all Christians share, in common, the Lord's Prayer. Today many churches exist because of division and differences. Ecumenism is the work of the Church striving to restore unity among all Christians. We celebrate Christian unity during a week in January.

Activity

Living the Lord's Prayer

Write two headlines that tell about people living the Lord's Prayer.

_____

_____

219

THE TASKS OF CATECHESIS

Liturgical Education. "In the Lord's Prayer a petition is made for daily food, which for Christians means preeminently the Eucharistic bread, and also for purification from sin, so that what is holy may, in fact, be given to those who are holy" (General Instruction of the Roman Missal 81). After the words of the Lord's Prayer are prayed at Mass, the priest continues with the praying of the embolism, which the people conclude with a doxology. The embolism enlarges "upon the last petition of the Lord's Prayer itself, begs deliverance from the power of evil for the entire community of the faithful" (General Instruction of the Roman Missal 81). The doxology, "For the kingdom, the power, and the glory are yours, now and for ever," is a prayer that gives glory to God.

Key Concept
The Lord's Prayer teaches us to make our whole life an act of prayer.

Teach

▶ Recall with the students that all Jesus did gave glory and honor to God the Father.

▶ Point out that the Lord's Prayer teaches us how to pray and how to live in a manner that gives honor and glory to God.

▶ Divide the young people into groups and assign a section of the Our Father to each. Ask each group to prepare an explanation of their section.

▶ As you read about each part of the prayer, ask the students to give their explanation.

Reinforce

▶ Explain that the Lord's Prayer teaches us to live as disciples of Jesus, which means sharing the Gospel with others.

▶ Invite the students to write two headlines that tell about people living the Lord's Prayer.

Connect

Read aloud the Catholics Believe feature. Have the students address how they interact with people of other faiths. Ask if any members of their families are of other faiths.

Reinforce

▶ Remind students that we are called to tell the world about Jesus Christ. The Church calls this evangelization.

▶ Point out that the Holy Spirit gives us the power to call God the Father, Abba, and to live as his children.

Respond

▶ Introduce The Lord's Prayer Online activity and then have students complete it. You may wish to have the young people work in groups and give them poster board and markers to use for this activity.

▶ Then invite them to share their responses with the class.

Choose

▶ Have students read the last section individually and in silence and write their faith choices.

▶ Then after a moment of prayerful reflection, have students to make their commitment in prayer. Encourage them to put their faith choice into practice this week.

I FOLLOW JESUS

Jesus gave the Church the Lord's Prayer. That means he gave it to you! The Holy Spirit gives you the power to call God Abba, Father. What a wonderful privilege! Stay in touch with God your Father each day by sharing your faith, hope, and love in God with others.

THE LORD'S PRAYER ONLINE

You have been given the job of Web master of a new Web site. Design a Web page to tell the world all about the hope that comes from the Lord's Prayer.

MY FAITH CHOICE

Each morning this week, I will pray one petition of the Lord's Prayer. I will think about what it means that day and I will:

_____

_____

 Pray, "Heavenly Father, your name is holy. I trust and hope in you and that your will be done. Amen."

220

HUMAN METHODOLOGIES

Learning by Heart. The *National Directory for Catechesis*, quoting *On Catechesis in Our Time* [Catechesis Tradendae] points out: "'What is essential is that texts that are memorized must at the same time be taken in and gradually understood in depth, in order to become a source of Christian life on the personal level and the community level'" (*NDC* 29F). Before having students complete My Faith Choice, have them make a chart, explaining in their own words what each petition of the Lord's Prayer means to them.

Chapter Review

Match the prayer terms in the word box with their descriptions.

| 1. vocal prayer | 2. meditation | 3. contemplation |

___1___ A prayer that uses words that we say aloud or quietly in our hearts.

___3___ A prayer that is a close sharing between friends without words, and being alone with God who we know loves us.

___2___ A prayer that uses our imagination, mind, and desire to live as a faithful disciple of Christ.

TO HELP YOU REMEMBER

1. The Lord's Prayer is the prayer of all Christians.
2. The Lord's Prayer teaches us to make our whole life a prayer.
3. The Lord's Prayer shows us how to live as people who place our faith, hope and love in God above all else.

The Lord's Prayer

The Lord's Prayer is the prayer of all Christians. Take time every day to pray it with a sense of faith, hope and love. Begin your prayer today in silence and a spirit of thanksgiving. Then pray together in the words that Jesus taught us.

Reader: Our Father, who art in heaven, hallowed by thy name;

Group 1: thy kingdom come; thy will be done on earth as it is in heaven.

Group 2: Give us this day our daily bread; and forgive us our trespasses

Group 1: as we forgive those who trespass against us;

Group 2: and lead us not into temptation, but deliver us from evil.

All: Amen.

221

We Remember

▶ Introduce the Chapter Review.

▶ Invite the students to complete the review and share their answers.

▶ Now invite three volunteer students to report to the class the top three most important points from this chapter's content. Compare their report to the To Help You Remember section.

We Pray

▶ Gather the students for the chapter's closing prayer, a prayerful reciting of the Our Father.

▶ Introduce the closing prayer and explain that since this is the last gathering of the year, it is fitting that you conclude the year's sessions by praying the prayer Jesus gave us.

▶ Establish an atmosphere for prayer by playing appropriate music.

▶ Take the role of the reader and divide the class into two groups.

▶ Invite the students to slowly and reverently pray together the Lord's Prayer.

▶ Conclude by sharing a sign of peace, showing that we are all children of God and singing the human "Be My Disciples" from the grade level CD.

LITURGY CONNECTION

Daily Prayer. The early Church prayed the Lord's Prayer three times a day. Have the students think about why, where, and when they might pray the Our Father. Share with them the importance of praying the Our Father daily. Summarize by pointing out that the Church prays the Lord's Prayer every day at Mass and during the Liturgy of the Hours.

Preview

▶ Have students carefully tear out the With My Family page along the perforation.

▶ Encourage them to share the pages with their family and to complete the activities together at home.

▶ If the students did not or were not able to complete the Chapter Review, encourage them to complete it with their family.

Visit www.BeMyDisciples.com

▶ Take time with the students to explore the many activities and resources available at the **www.BeMyDisciples.com.** Web site.

Before Moving On ...

As you finish today's lesson, reflect on:

In what ways could the classroom environment I have created this year be described as positive?

With My Family

This Week...

In chapter 24, The Summary of the Gospel, your child learned:

▶ The Church describes three main expressions of prayer: vocal prayer, meditation, and contemplation.

▶ Jesus' teaching of the Lord's Prayer is part of the Sermon on the Mount.

▶ The Lord's Prayer is the prayer of all Christians and is an expression of our faith, hope and love in God.

▶ When we pray the Lord's Prayer, the Holy Spirit teaches us how to prayer and to live the Gospel.

For more about related teachings of the Church, see the *Catechism of the Catholic Church*, 2558–2865; and the *United States Catholic Catechism for Adults*, pages 461–495.

■ Sharing God's Word

The Christian family is the first place for education in prayer. Read as a family Matthew 6:9–13. Emphasize that Jesus lived his life as a prayer. Discuss how each family member can do likewise.

■ We Live as Disciples

The Christian home and family is a school of discipleship. Choose one of the following activities to do as a family or design a similar activity of your own:

▶ Be sure every family member can recite from memory the Lord's Prayer. Emphasize that you pray from your heart.

▶ This week use the Lord's Prayer for family prayer at least once a day.

▶ Purchase additional items to donate to your local food bank the next time you go grocery shopping for the family. Your parish can give you the location of the food bank.

■ Our Spiritual Journey

Saint Thomas Aquinas called the Lord's Prayer the "most perfect of prayers." He said, "This prayer not only teaches us to ask for things, but also in what order we should desire them." Reflect in prayer on how you can align your will with the will of God the Father this week.

For more ideas on ways that your family can live as disciples of Jesus, visit **www.BeMyDisciples.com**

222

CATHOLIC SOCIAL TEACHING

Solidarity of the Human Family. The Catholic Church teaches that we are all a part of a single human family and that we are responsible for one another. This solidarity is true regardless of national, racial, ethnic, and ideological differences. Solidarity is an interdependence that flows from our common dignity and from Jesus' command to love one another as he loves us. It is a moral virtue that prompts us to commit ourselves energetically to the needs of our neighbor. The principle of solidarity was illustrated in Chapter 23 in the generosity of Venerable Helen Delille, and in Chapter 24 in the teaching about the Our Father, through which we express our willingness to forgive even those who do not treat us well. Use the last activity on page 351 to reinforce this important principle.

Enriching the Lesson

Writing Prayers of Adoration

Purpose

To reinforce that praying a prayer of adoration helps us acknowledge God as the center of life and source of our blessings (taught on page 217)

Directions

▶ Distribute Bibles to the students. Have them locate the Book of Psalms and read several psalms that acknowledge the greatness of God.

▶ Ask them to create a symbol or illustrate on one side of a card something that manifests the greatness of God and demonstrates his glory.

▶ Have them write a psalm verse or their own prayer of adoration on the other side of the card.

▶ Invite the students to share their illustration and prayers with the entire class and with their family.

Materials

poster paper cut into card-size shapes

markers

Creating Cinquains

Purpose

To reinforce the meaning of the Our Father (taught on page 218–219)

Directions

▶ Have the students work with partners to write cinquains based on the Our Father.

▶ Have them copy their cinquains on cards and decorate the border of the cards. Have them then share their cinquains with the class.

▶ Invite the students to take their cinquains home and share them with their family.

Materials

paper

pens or pencils

crayons or markers

Catholic Social Teaching: Imitating Faith-Filled People

Purpose

To review Faith-Filled People studied this year who have stood in solidarity with others

Directions

▶ Present the Catholic Social Teaching principle of solidarity, using the box on the preceding page.

▶ Ask the students to browse through their textbooks and to jot down the names of saints and holy people studied this year who demonstrated a willingness to serve and stand in solidarity with others.

▶ Divide the class into groups of three and ask each group to prepare a small poster highlighting the accomplishments of this person and how he or she exemplified solidarity. Tell them to include the virtue or gift that each exhibited. Encourage them to be as creative as possible.

▶ Collect all the posters and affix them to a long piece of butcher paper, creating a collage. Let the heading on the poster be Faith-Filled People.

▶ Invite the students to come up and admire the work of their fellow classmates. Ask them to reflect silently on what the work of these models of faith inspires them to do.

▶ Post the collage where the whole parish can enjoy it one Sunday and be inspired to stand in solidarity with others.

Materials

small pieces of poster board

crayons or markers

glue and Scissors

colored art paper

butcher paper

The Unit Review provides the opportunity to assess the students' understanding of the faith concepts presented in the unit and to affirm them in their growing knowledge and love of God. Here are a few suggestions for using these pages.

▶ Share that the next two pages are an opportunity to stop and review what they have learned.

▶ Provide time for the students to ask questions.

▶ Have the students complete the review alone or with partners.

A. Choose the Best Word

▶ Read the directions for this section.

▶ Then have the student work alone or with a partner to complete the section.

▶ Invite volunteers to share their responses. Clarify and correct responses as needed.

B. Show What You Know

▶ Read the directions for this section. Answer the first question together as a class.

▶ Then have the student continue working alone or with a partner to complete the section.

▶ Invite volunteers to share their responses. Clarify and correct responses as needed.

Unit 6 **Review**

Name _____

A. Choose the Best Word

Fill in the blanks to complete each of the sentences of the paragraph. Use the words from the word bank.

adoration	communion	contemplation
meditation	prophets	petition

The Christian tradition of prayer has its roots in the Old Testament. Abraham, King David, and the ___prophets___ are some of the Old Testament's models for Christians seeking a prayer life. The Old Testament also reveals that one of the five basic forms of prayer that Christians use is ___adoration___, which declares God as the source of all. We express our prayers in three ways: vocal prayers, prayers of ___meditation___, and prayers of ___contemplation___.

B. Show What You Know

Match the items in column A with those in column B.

1. Which of the Ten Commandments focuses on our relationship with God?
   - A. First
   - B. First and Second
   - C. First, Second and Third
   - D. First, Second, Third and Fourth

2. Which of the Ten Commandments teaches us not to cheat on a test?
   - A. Fifth
   - B. Seventh
   - C. Eighth
   - D. Tenth

3. Which of the Ten Commandments teaches us to live chaste lives?
   - A. First
   - B. Fifth
   - C. Seventh
   - D. Ninth

4. Which of the Ten Commandments teaches us to respect all human life as sacred?
   - A. First
   - B. Fourth
   - C. Fifth
   - D. Tenth

223

TEACHING TIP

Final Review. Use this final unit review to deepen the students' sense of accomplishment this year. Share how much they have learned and what a difference they have made in your life. Take time to remind them that Jesus spent many years in Nazareth with Mary and Joseph, and the people of his synagogue. He spent this time learning the teachings, prayers, and practices of the Jewish religion. Encourage the students to prayer each day so that they might come to know, love, and serve Christ evermore.

C. Connect with Scripture

Reread the Scripture passage on the first Unit Opener page. What connection do you see between this passage and what you learned in this unit?

Responses will vary.

_____

_____

_____

D. Be a Disciple

1. *Review the four pages in this unit titled "The Church Follows Jesus." What person or ministry of the Church on these pages will inspire you to be a better disciple of Jesus? Explain your answer.*

Responses will vary.

_____

_____

_____

2. *Work with a group. Review the four Disciple Power virtues or gifts you have learned about in this unit. After jotting down your own ideas, share with the group practical ways that you will live these virtues or gifts day by day.*

Responses will vary.

_____

_____

_____

224

C. Connect with Scripture

▶ Invite the students to reflect on the Scripture passage in the Unit Opener and to write their understanding of how this passage connects with the doctrinal content of the unit they have just completed.

▶ Ask volunteers to share their responses, now or after completion of the entire Unit Review.

D. Be a Disciple

▶ Invite the young people to work independently on the first question about The Church Follows Jesus. Ask volunteers to share their responses.

▶ Divide the students into small groups of three or four for the second part of this section. Ask them to write their personal reflections first, and then to share with their group practical ways of living the Disciple Power virtues or qualities of discipleship in everyday life.

▶ Ask for feedback from the small groups as time allows.

TEACHING TIP

Family Faith Sharing. Send a note home with the students, encouraging families to use the Catholic Prayers and Practices section of the student book with their children during the off-months. For example, families might use the:

▶ Glossary to share their faith, focusing on some of the key faith concepts that their children learned throughout this year.

▶ Section on the Mass to talk about the families' participation in the Mass, as well as becoming more familiar with the words, gestures and environment of the Liturgy.

▶ Section on the key teachings of the Church to reinforce important key faith concepts or teachings of the Church, and to decide on how the family might work together to make a difference because of their Catholic faith.

The Liturgical Year

Seasons and Feasts

Consistency is important to all of our lives, but from time to time we all need a break. Unswerving consistency introduces monotony and can make things pretty dull. Most people like surprises and festive days once in a while, however, like all things, these need to happen in moderation since endless festivities can wear us down. Experience teaches us the value of balancing the routine and the festive, or the ordinary and the extraordinary.

Through the Liturgy, the Church is uniquely positioned to gather us for celebration. Filled with anticipation during Advent, we prepare to celebrate the festive season of Christmas. Our traditional Lenten practices of fasting, praying, and almsgiving prepare us to enter into the Triduum and the Easter season.

Easter is central to the liturgical year. Because Jesus was raised from the dead on Sunday, the Church gathers to celebrate each week on that day. Every Sunday is a memorial of the Paschal Mystery and a commemoration of Easter.

Festive seasons, such as the Easter season, stand in contrast to the long, steady period of Ordinary Time. Generally, of the thirty-four Sundays in Ordinary Time, about ten occur on the Sundays between the seasons of Christmas and Lent. The remainder of the Sundays in Ordinary Time is celebrated after the Solemnity of the Most Holy Body and Blood of Christ (two weeks after Pentecost) and culminates with the celebration of the Solemnity of Our Lord Jesus Christ the King. This late autumn feast brings the liturgical year to a close

The Rhythm of the Liturgical Year

The seasons of the liturgical year help to keep us balanced as nature's seasons pass. Through the seasons of autumn, winter, spring, and summer, significant changes occur. As time passes from season to season, the Church provides a steady rhythm throughout the calendar year.

Each Sunday the Church calls us to live out the reality of the abiding presence of the Risen Lord among us. Sunday after Sunday from the extremes of deep winter to high summer, we remember with gratitude that all time and all ages belong to Christ, who is Yesterday and Today, the Beginning and the End.

The liturgical year is our way to remember with gladness and joy that every day is the day the Lord has made. We celebrate that God calls us to rejoice in Christ.

For Reflection

How does the liturgical year provide a wonderful balance of ordinary and extraordinary time to live our faith?

Which liturgical season is your favorite? Why?

Catechist to Catechist

Colors of the Season

All through the year, the Church gathers to celebrate the liturgy. We join with Christ and the Holy Spirit to bless and give thanks to God the Father. In our celebrations, we incorporate colors to identify the season in which we celebrate. We see these colors in the priest's vestments at Mass. The liturgical colors also decorate the physical environment of the parish church. For example, violet is used during the seasons of Advent and Lent. During Christmas and Easter, the Church uses white or gold. Red signifies specific feasts days while green is the color of celebration during Ordinary Time. Be sure that the classroom reflects the colors of the liturgical season and day to help celebrate what God has done for us.

Signs of the Liturgical Year

Display signs of the liturgical year in your learning space. Surround the children with reminders that will help set the tone of both the seasons and feasts of the liturgical year. For example, consider using a table runner that is the color of each liturgical season in the prayer area. Place a Bible opened to the Sunday Gospel reading on the prayer table.

The Church Teaches...

"Catechesis is enriched when the word of God shines forth in the life of the Church, especially in the lives of the saints and in the Christian witness of the faithful. And it is made more fruitful when the word of God is known from those genuine moral values that, by divine providence, are found in human society" (*NDC* 18).

During the liturgical year, the feast days of many of the canonized saints are remembered in the celebration of the liturgy. You may wish to celebrate the feast days of some of the saints during your sessions, particularly those who may be the patron saints of the parish and community.

Further Reading and Reflection

For more on the teachings of the Catholic Church on the liturgical year, see *Catechism of the Catholic Church* 1168–1171 and 1172–1173; *United States Catholic Catechism for Adults* 166–179.

Catechist Prayer

God, Father and Creator, through the prayer of Jesus, your Son, may your blessings be poured out on us and keep us safe in your care. Amen.

Based on the opening prayers for Fifth Sunday in Ordinary Time

Liturgical Year Unit Opener

The unit opener pages are designed to assess, through a variety of questioning techniques, the students' prior knowledge about key faith concepts presented in the unit. Processing these pages should not take more than ten or fifteen minutes.

Background

The Greeks had two words for time that we still use today: *chronos* and *kairos*. *Chronos* refers to chronological time and has to do with quantity. *Kairos* refers to sacred time. It has to do with quality and it cannot be measured.

The liturgical year is shaped from both *chronos* and *kairos*. Chronologically, the Church's year begins on the First Sunday of Advent and ends on the last Sunday in Ordinary Time, the feast of Christ the King.

The Church's year is built on *kairos* because it focuses on the celebration of various aspects of the two greatest mysteries of our faith, the Incarnation and the Redemption. It is the active celebration of and conscious participation in those mysteries on the part of the Christian faithful in chronological time that leads communities and individuals to *kairos* and ongoing conversion. Because of this, we call each year of the liturgical cycle a year of grace.

The fifteen two-page lessons in this section give you many opportunities to celebrate the Church's year with your students. The lessons follow the liturgical cycle of major feasts and seasons. The lessons are designed so that you can complete them in approximately twenty minutes as part of your regular class sessions.

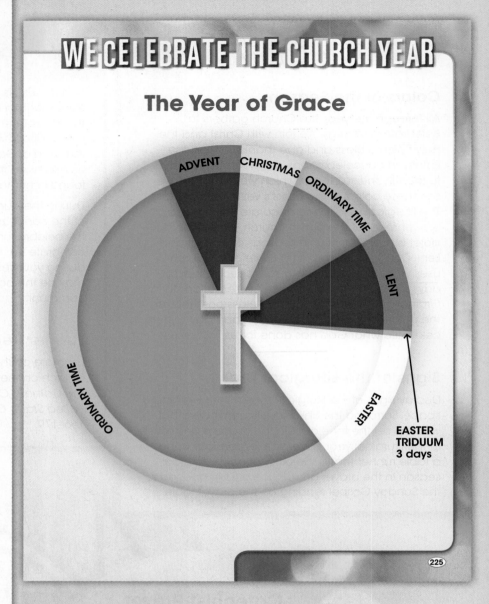

WE CELEBRATE THE CHURCH YEAR

The Year of Grace

ADVENT · CHRISTMAS · ORDINARY TIME · LENT · EASTER TRIDUUM 3 days · EASTER · ORDINARY TIME

(225)

TEACHING TIP

Liturgical Calendar. Make a special effort to mark the important feast days of the Church's year on a classroom calendar or bulletin board. These should include: the Immaculate Conception (December 8), Christmas (December 25), Solemnity of Mary (January 1), Ascension (forty days after Easter), Assumption (August 15), and All Saints (November 1). Also enter children's birthdays on the calendar, as well as any special days your parish celebrates; for example the patron saint of the parish. Pray for those children and pray to those patron saints whose day is to be celebrated during the upcoming week. On the last day of the year, pray for the children who celebrate their birthdays during the summer or off time.

The Liturgical Year

While many things you see and hear at Mass are always the same, other things change. The readings change, as do the colors of banners and vestments. All of the changes help us know what part of the Church's year we are celebrating. Each year is a year of grace because we celebrate the saving presence of Christ in the world.

Advent

We begin the liturgical year by anticipating the birth of Jesus Christ during the season of Advent. It is a time to prepare ourselves through prayer and sacrifice. In these ways, we make room in our hearts for the birth of the Lord.

Christmas

We celebrate the incarnation of Jesus Christ through his birth to the Virgin Mary. During the Christmas season, we also celebrate the Solemnity of Mary, the Mother of God, Epiphany, and the Baptism of the Lord.

Lent

During the forty days of Lent, we pray and make personal sacrifices so that we can turn our hearts more completely toward God. We are preparing for the greatest celebration of the Church year—the Resurrection of the Lord.

The Triduum

The Easter Triduum is at the center of our year of worship. Beginning on the evening of Holy Thursday and ending on Easter Sunday evening, the Triduum is our three-day solemn celebration of the Paschal mystery.

Easter

On each of the fifty days of Easter, we celebrate our new life in the Risen Christ. At the Easter Vigil, we light the Paschal candle in the midst of darkness to remind us that Jesus is the light of the world. Our celebration continues until Pentecost.

Ordinary Time

The rest of the Church's year is called Ordinary Time. We celebrate many events in the life and ministry of Jesus. We also celebrate other great feasts and solemnities honoring Jesus, Mary, and the saints.

226

Focus

▶ At the beginning of the year, take a few minutes and lead the children through the seasons and times of the year using the liturgical calendar on the page. Point out the starting point at the beginning of Advent.

▶ Help them to notice the colors and ask if they have noticed that the priest's vestments and Church banners change from time to time.

Teach

▶ Use the text on page 226 to describe the major seasons and Ordinary Time.

▶ Ask the children to identify the season or time that is their favorite. Ask volunteers to tell why they made their choices.

▶ Tell the children that they will be celebrating each season with their class during the coming year.

▶ As you study the various saints and holy persons in the regular chapters of the child's book, you may wish to add their feast days to your classroom calendar or to a large liturgical calendar. In this way the children can begin to celebrate these feast days as well.

Solemnity of All Saints

Focus

Ask the students to read the Faith Focus question silently. Tell them that in this lesson they will learn that the saints teach us that anyone can answer God's call to holiness.

Discover

▶ Have volunteers take turns reading aloud the text on the page.

▶ Ask a student to write *Communion of Saints* on the board. Ask the students to explain in their own words who is included in the Communion of Saints.

▶ Discuss with the class how the saints give us hope. Help them to understand that we don't have to be famous to be a saint; what we need to do is follow God's call in our lives.

Faith Focus
How are the saints a source of hope for the Church?

The Word of the Lord
This is the Gospel for the Solemnity of All Saints. Read it and talk about the reading with your family.

Gospel
Matthew 5:1–12a

Solemnity of All Saints

The Church is a communion of the holy people of God. When we say that, we express our belief that we are all united, or in communion, with Christ and all the members of the Church, the Body of Christ. We are all a part of the Communion of Saints. The Communion of Saints includes all the faithful members of the Church on earth and those who have died. It includes both the saints living with God in heaven and those faithful in Purgatory who are being prepared to receive the gift of eternal life in heaven.

The Church officially declares someone a saint through a process called canonization. There are several steps involved in recognizing an individual as a saint. Over the course of many years, the person's life and virtue is carefully examined by the Congregation for the Causes of Saints in Rome.

The holy person is first named Servant of God, then Venerable, then Blessed, and finally, in some cases, canonized by the Pope as a saint. Each step requires investigation and evidence.

Although we know the names and life stories of many of the saints and celebrate special feast days in their honor, there are many saints in heaven who are known only to God. The Church teaches that anyone in heaven is a saint. On the Solemnity of All Saints we honor all the saints in heaven, those we know and those we do not know.

We celebrate the Solemnity of All Saints on November 1. This special day is a holy day of obligation in which we honor the saints as a source of hope and renewal for all members of the Church. They inspire us to put God first in our lives and to live as Jesus taught. All Saints' Day is a time to thank God for giving us so many examples of how to live our faith. We remember that the saints pray for us and that we can pray to them, asking them to show us the way to holiness.

Blessed Louis and Zelle Martin, Saint Lawrence, Mary Magdalene

(227)

SCRIPTURE BACKGROUND

The Light of World. The Gospel reading for the Solemnity of All Saints is that of the Sermon on the Mount when Jesus reveals the Beatitudes to the crowds who have gathered (Matthew 5:1–12a). What follows that reading in Scripture serves as a powerful meditation on our call to be saints. *"You are the salt of the earth. But if salt loses its taste, with what can it be seasoned? It is no longer good for anything but to be thrown out and trampled underfoot. You are the light of the world. A city set on a mountain cannot be hidden. Nor do they light a lamp and then put it under a bushel basket; it is set on a lampstand, where it gives light to all in the house. Just so, your light must shine before others, that they may see your good deeds and glorify your heavenly Father"* (Matthew 5:13–16).

The Little Way

Saint Thérèse of Lisieux, a Carmelite Sister, is one of the Church's most well-loved saints. She was only 24 years old when she died and is known as "the Little Flower." She wrote, "What matters in life is not great deeds, but great love." Thérèse wanted everyone to know that love was the way to holiness.

On the page below, write down the little ways that you have shown love to others during the past week. Memorize Saint Thérèse's words and reflect on them often.

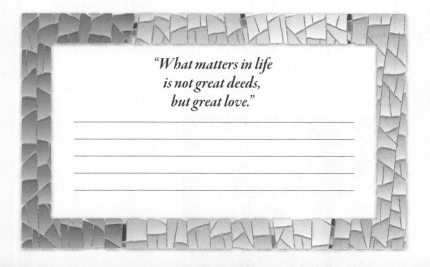

"What matters in life is not great deeds, but great love."

_____

_____

_____

_____

_____

MY FAITH CHOICE

This week I will follow St. Thérèse's little way of doing small deeds with great love. I will

_____

_____.

 Honor St. Thérèse by loving God as she did. Pray, "Dear St. Thérèse, beloved friend of God and friend of mine, help me to love God with all my heart."

228

LITURGICAL YEAR BACKGROUND

Solemnities, Feasts, and Memorials. You may notice the designation of Solemnity or Feast on some of the celebrations in this section. The Church's Universal Norms on the Liturgical Year and the General Roman Calendar provides an explanation of the distinction among all the different kinds of celebrations that occur during the liturgical year. "As it celebrates the mystery of Christ in yearly cycle, the Church also venerates with a particular love Mary, the Mother of God, and sets before the devotion of the faithful the memory of the martyrs and other saints" (*Universal Norms* 8). The celebrations in the calendar are divided into solemnities, feasts, and memorials. Solemnities are the principal days, such as Christmas. They begin on the evening of the preceding day. With only a few exceptions, Feasts always occur within the hours of a calendar day. The observance of Memorials "is integrated into the celebration of the occurring weekday..." (*Universal Norms* 14).

Respond

▶ Ask a volunteer to read Matthew 5:13–16. Invite the students to share how the saints made their light shine before others.

▶ Direct attention to The Little Way. Remind the students that St. Thérèse was very young. Read to the class 1 Timothy 4:12: Let no one have contempt for your youth, but set on example for those who believe, in speech, conduct, love, faith, and purity.

▶ Have the young people complete the activity and share their responses with the class.

▶ Invite the students to respond to My Faith Choice.

▶ After a moment of prayerful reflection, have the young people write their choice on the lines provided.

▶ Encourage the class to put their choice into practice by praying that they grow in love for God.

Pray

▶ Gather the students for prayer. Invite them to quiet themselves and quietly reflect on the Faith Choice they made.

▶ Lead them in prayer with these words: "Lord, we gather today to celebrate all the saints of heaven who share in your glory. We offer you the small choices we make each day to follow their example and please you. May their example help us to live more fully according to your will. We make our prayer in the name of Jesus, your Son. Amen."

Advent

Focus

Ask a volunteer to read the Faith Focus question aloud, and have the class silently think about how they might answer it. Point out that the Church's season of Advent begins the new liturgical year and is a time to prepare to make room in our hearts for Jesus.

Discover

▶ Ask a volunteer to read aloud the introductory paragraph.

▶ Point out the drawing of the family tree of Jesus on page 229.

▶ Invite the group to finish reading the rest of the page silently.

▶ Read Isaiah 11:1–3 aloud. Clarify that this prophecy traces the lineage of David, the son of Jesse.

▶ Share with the young people that Jesus comes from the family of David.

Faith Focus
How does the Jesse tree help us celebrate Advent?

The Word of the Lord
These are the Gospel readings for the First Sunday of Advent. Choose this year's reading. Read and discuss it with your family.

Year A
Matthew 24:37–44

Year B
Mark 13:33–37

Year C
Luke 21:25–28, 34–36

Advent

All families have a history and a story to tell. All the people who are part of your family history make up your family tree—your parents, brothers and sisters, grandparents, aunts, uncles, and family members who lived generations ago.

Jesus has a family tree too. We Christians use it to help us celebrate Advent. We call it the Jesse tree. The tree is named for Jesse, a shepherd from Bethlehem. He lived about one thousand years before Jesus. Jesse was the father of David, who grew up to be the greatest king of the people of Israel. David is an ancestor of Jesus.

During Advent we remember the people—like Jesse and David—who are part of Jesus' family tree. We decorate the Jesse tree with symbols of these Old and New Testament figures. The Jesse tree is like our family tree. Each person on the Jesse tree is part of the long story of God's loving plan of salvation that is fulfilled in Jesus.

Remembering the faith stories of the people on the Jesse tree helps us remember God's great love for us—and for all people.

The Tree of Jesse, from "Heures a l'Usage de Rome," (16th century)

(229)

TEACHING TIP

Create a Jesse Tree. At the beginning of Advent, place an airy, broad-branched bare or evergreen tree in a prominent place in your learning area. During each week of the Advent season, invite the young people to hang the traditional symbols used to decorate the Jesse tree. Post a list with the names of the people of the Bible who prepared the way for Jesus, with an idea for a symbol for each person. For example, an apple or garden for Adam and Eve, a star for Abraham and Sarah, two tablets for Moses, a king's crown or a harp for David, and a quill or pen for Isaiah.

The Story of Salvation

Make a Jesse tree for your class. Use a small evergreen tree.
Make a symbol for each of these figures. Add others of your own.
Put the symbols on your Jesse tree.

When **Adam** and **Eve** refused to obey, God promised a savior would come some day.

Noah is a man to note; while others laughed he built a boat.

Abraham and **Sarah** obeyed God's call. Their faith is an example for one and for all.

When **Isaac** was born, Sarah was old. Her laughter rang out, so we are told.

Isaac's son **Jacob** was rich and able; soon twelve healthy sons sat at his table.

Joseph saved his family from starvation. In Egypt they grew into a very strong nation.

Moses, leader and man of God, led Israel through the Red Sea dryshod.

David, the Lord's shepherd and king, could rule, protect, play, and sing.

Isaiah was one who spoke for his Lord. The faithful listened to every word.

John the Baptist's announcement was clear. "Prepare the way! The Lord draws near!"

On **Mary** God's blessings were abundantly poured. Yes was her response to the angel of the Lord.

Joseph cared for Mary as he promised he would, Joseph the mild, the patient, the good.

Angels came and shepherds adored, **Jesus** is born, our Savior and Lord!

MY FAITH CHOICE

The season of Advent is a time to prepare for the coming of Jesus. To prepare for Jesus' coming, I will

_____

_____

 Rejoice Jesus, the Christ, is coming. Pray, "The LORD, our God, is in our midst"
BASED ON ZEPHANIAH 3:17

(230)

BACKGROUND: FAITH-FILLED PEOPLE

Two well-known feast days occur during Advent: Those of Saint Nichols and Our Lady of Guadalupe. In addition, there is the Solemnity of the Immaculate Conception, that the class will explore in the next lesson.

Saint Nicholas (December 6). Although little is known about Saint Nicholas, he is one of the most popular of the saints. Nicholas was the Bishop of Myra, in what is now the country of Turkey, and he died in the fourth century. Saint Nicholas inspired our modern figure of Santa Claus. He is the patron saint of children because so many stories are told about his generosity.

Our Lady of Guadalupe (December 12). Mary, Our Lady of Guadalupe, is the patron saint of the Americas. Share with the group the story of Saint Juan Diego and the miracle of the roses on pages 233–234 in their texts.

Respond

▶ Ask the young people to describe a Jesse tree and explain why it is an appropriate Advent decoration.

▶ Introduce and explain the directions for the "Story of Salvation" activity.

▶ Invite volunteers to take turns reading the couplets.

▶ Have the young people work with partners. Assign a couplet to each pair of students, and have them make a symbol of the person or persons named in their couplet.

▶ Invite the young people to put their symbols in the prayer area.

▶ Invite the students to respond to My Faith Choice.

▶ After a moment of prayerful reflection, have the young people write their choice on the lines provided.

▶ Encourage the class to put their choices into practice by praying that they will prepare well to welcome Jesus.

Pray

▶ Ask the students to quiet themselves for prayer.

▶ Ask volunteers to read the couplet relating to their symbol, and have the class respond to each by praying, "Come, Lord Jesus, come."

The Immaculate Conception

Focus

Ask a volunteer to read the Faith Focus question. Tell the students that in today's lesson they will learn that Mary relied on God's grace throughout her entire life. She cooperated with God's plan of salvation for his children.

Discover

▶ Ask the students to explain salvation in their own words. *(Accept all appropriate answers, such as save us from sin, lead us to holiness, make all things perfect in Jesus Christ, union with God.)*

▶ Invite several volunteers to read the text on the page aloud.

▶ For each paragraph, ask students to identify one thing in that paragraph that is part of God's plan for us. *(Answers will vary, but may include: Mary, Immaculate Conception, Jesus, worship, prayer, living lives of faith.)*

Faith Focus
Why was Mary always able to say yes to God?

The Word of the Lord
These are the readings for the Solemnity of the Immaculate Conception. Choose one and read it. Talk about the reading with your family.

First Reading
Genesis 3:9–15, 20

Second Reading
Ephesians 1:3-6, 11–12

Gospel
Luke 1:26–38

The Immaculate Conception

On December 8, 1854, Blessed Pope Pius IX declared the Church's belief in the Immaculate Conception an official dogma of the Church. A dogma is a teaching of the faith that is revealed by God and must be believed by all Catholics. The date the teaching was formally announced was also made the day of the liturgical feast of the Solemnity of the Immaculate Conception. A solemnity is the highest ranking celebration in the liturgical year.

In the United States of America, the Solemnity of the Immaculate Conception is a holy day of obligation. This means that Catholics in the United States of America have the same responsibility to take part in the celebration of the Mass on December 8th as they do on Sundays.

God chose Mary to have a unique role in the divine plan of Salvation. He chose Mary to be the mother of the Savior of the world. He chose her to be the Mother of the Son of God who would become one of us in all things but sin.

Because of this unique role, Mary received the unique grace of being conceived without Original Sin and the graces to remain free from all sin her whole life on earth. Mary glorified God by her whole life on Earth from her conception to her Assumption. She continues to glorify God in heaven with all of the angels and saints.

Patroness of the United States

From her earliest days, the Church has expressed her faith in Mary to be the Mother of the Church. Jesus asked us to honor Mary as our Mother. He asked Mary to care for us as a mother cares for her own children. Read the words that Jesus spoke to Mary and to the "beloved disciple," Saint John the Apostle, in John 19:26–27.

The Catholic Church in the United States of America responded to Jesus' words. The United States Bishops chose Mary, as the Immaculate Conception, to be the patron saint of the United States. A basilica, or church, in Washington, D.C., was named the National Shrine of the Immaculate Conception. This shrine honors both God and Mary. Our devotion to Mary gives glory to God, our Father. It reminds us to honor him and thank him, as Mary did. With Mary we praise God,

"My soul magnifies the Lord God and my spirit rejoices in God, my Savior." Luke 1:46–47

(231)

CATHOLIC DOCTRINE

God's Plan. Read aloud the following quote from the *United States Catholic Catechism for Adults* or write it on the board before your session:

The Father of all continues to work with his Son, who is eternal Wisdom, and with the Holy Spirit, who is the inexhaustible source of life, to guide creation and humanity to the fullness of God's truth, goodness, and beauty" (*USCCA* page 56).

Share with the students that God's plan is to bring all of creation into perfect union with him. God fully revealed himself in Jesus, who saved us from sin and made it possible for us to share eternal life in heaven. Mary and her Immaculate Conception were an important part of God's plan. As God's children, we, too, are part of God's plan.

The Miraculous Medal

In 1830, Sister Catherine Labouré, a nun in Paris, had a vision of Mary as the Immaculate Conception. Mary gave Sister Catherine a mission—to have a special medal made for Catholics to wear. Our Blessed Mother described the medal she wanted. The front was to have an image of Mary on it, along with this prayer: "O Mary, conceived without sin, pray for us who have recourse to thee." Mary promised special graces to all those who wore the medal. With the approval of the bishop, the medals were made and a new devotion to Mary was established. So many people who wore the medal received blessings, good health, peace and other graces that people began to call it the Miraculous Medal. It is still worn today. It honors the Immaculate Conception and her special place in God's plan of salvation.

Name three special blessings or graces you would like to receive from our Blessed Mother. Write them on the lines below.

_____

_____

_____

MY FAITH CHOICE

This week I will honor Mary. I will sing her praises by the way I live. I will

_____

_____.

Honor Mary, your Mother. Pray with her and praise God, "My soul magnifies the Lord!"

(232)

SACRED TRADITION

Holy Day of Obligation. "What is a holy day of obligation? A simple answer is that a holy day is an important feast of Our Lord, Our Lady or other saints that Catholics are morally obliged to observe by participating in the celebration of the Eucharist and by abstaining from unnecessary servile work. These days are made solemnities, like a Sunday in terms of festivity and observance, because of their special importance and meaning for the universal and/or local Church. In the United States, we observe six holy days each liturgical year. Holy days do vary from one country to another" (excerpt from *Holy Days of Obligation, Or Holy Days of Opportunity,* by Brother John M. Samaha, S.M., at http://www.catholicculture.org/culture/library).

Respond

▶ Give students an opportunity to answer the Faith Focus question. Remind them that grace is a share in God's life that helps us to respond to God with love, as Mary did.

▶ Read aloud the introduction to The Miraculous Medal. Explain to the class that the word *recourse* means that Mary is a source of help for us.

▶ Have the young people complete the activity. Invite volunteers to share their responses with the class.

▶ Invite the students to respond to My Faith Choice.

▶ After a moment of prayerful reflection, have the young people write their choices on the lines provided.

▶ Encourage the class to put their choices into practice by praying that their lives will give praise to God.

Pray

▶ Gather the students for prayer.

▶ Invite them to reflect silently on God's plan for each of them. How will the way of life they choose give glory to God?

▶ Using your own words, ask Mary to bless them and to help them live a life of love and faith. Then have the students each make the Sign of the Cross.

Our Lady of Guadalupe

Focus

Tell the students that in this session they will learn that people express their devotion to Mary as Our Lady of Guadalupe by visiting her shrine. Her message of love and her promise to protect those who come to her out of love for her Son, Jesus, gives people hope and deepens their relationship with God.

Discover

▶ Explain to the students that symbols are a way of remembering an important event. There are many symbols associated with Our Lady of Guadalupe: the image of Our Lady of Guadalupe, roses, a cloak, a shrine, the outline of Mexico or the Americas, a crown, which appears in the image, and others the students might identify after reading the text.

▶ Write the list of symbols on the board.

▶ Invite volunteers to read the page text aloud: Ask the students to underline references to the symbols on the board, or anything else they might see as a symbol.

▶ Ask the young people to share what they've underlined.

Faith Focus
Why do so many people visit the shrine of Our Lady of Guadalupe?

The Word of the Lord
These are the three readings for the Feast of Our Lady of Guadalupe. Choose one of the readings, and find it in a Bible. Read and discuss the reading with your family.

First Reading
Isaiah 7:10–14

Second Reading
Galatians 2:4–7

Gospel
Luke 1:39–48

Our Lady of Guadalupe

On a cold morning in December, 1531, a peasant named Juan Diego was walking to Mass near the town of Tepeyac, Mexico. Suddenly, he heard music and saw a cloud surrounded by light. In the cloud was a beautiful lady dressed as an Aztec Indian princess. She spoke to Juan in his native language.

The Virgin Mary of Guadalupe asked Juan Diego to tell the Bishop of Mexico that she wished a shrine to be built on that very spot to make her love to all people known. Because Juan did not speak Spanish, and the bishop did not understand the Aztec language, Nahuati, the bishop asked for a sign that the message was from the Virgin Mary.

Three days later, the Blessed Mother again appeared to Juan. She told Juan to gather roses and bring them to the bishop. Because it was winter and roses were not growing, this certainly would be a sign the bishop would believe.

When Juan came to the bishop, he opened his cloak and the flowers fell out. To the astonishment of all, they saw an image of Mary dressed as a Aztec princess. The bishop built the shrine. Today that shrine is known as the Basilica of Our Lady of Guadalupe.

On the feast day of December 12 it is a custom in Mexico for young girls to dress up as Indian girls and young boys to dress up as Juan Diego. Many people carry roses.

Many of our Popes have honored Our Lady of Guadalupe. Pope John Paul II visited her shrine four times. Pope Benedict XVI called the Marian shrine the heart of Mexico and of all America. He entrusted all of the world's families to Our Lady of Guadalupe.

GOOD SHEPHERD

233

TEACHING TIP

Learning Styles. Among the students in your group there will be a variety of learning styles. Some learn by seeing, others by listening, and still others by doing. The more variety in of learning opportunities in a lesson, the more likely students will remember the lesson. Invite children to illustrate the story of Our Lady of Guadalupe in symbols. They might be interested to know that on October 12, 1895, Our Lady of Guadalupe was solemnly crowned, in the name of Pope Leo XIII, as Queen of the Mexican people.

Blessed are They

Our Lady of Guadalupe's message is that Jesus brings salvation to all people, especially the weakest and most vulnerable members of our world. This is the message of the Beatitudes.

Read Matthew 5:3–10 in your Bible. Choose one of the Beatitudes and draw a picture of how you might live this Beatitude in your daily life.

_____

_____

MY FAITH CHOICE

This week I will honor Our Lady of Guadalupe by working for peace and justice for all people. I will

_____

_____ .

 Pray with Mary, "My soul proclaims the greatness of the Lord; my spirit rejoices in God my savior." LUKE 1:46—47

(234)

Respond

▶ Ask the students if they have ever visited a shrine and invite them to share their experience. Remind the group that visiting shrines or praying before statues or pictures of the saints helps us to deepen our prayer life. Emphasize that honoring Mary and the saints enables us grow closer to God.

▶ Explain the directions to Blessed Are They and allow the students time to complete the activity. Afterwards, ask volunteers to share their drawings with the class.

▶ Invite the students to respond to My Faith Choice.

▶ After a moment of prayerful reflection, have the young people write their choices on the lines provided.

▶ Encourage the class to put their choices into practice by praying that Our Lady of Guadalupe will help them grow in being open to others.

Pray

▶ Gather the students for prayer and divide them into two groups.

▶ Using their Bibles, have the young people pray the Beatitudes (Matthew 5:3–10) aloud as antiphons, by alternating lines.

▶ Conclude by inviting volunteers to offer spontaneous petitions for people in need.

Solemnity of Christmas

Focus

Ask a volunteer to read the Faith Focus question aloud. Have the young people silently think about how they might answer it. Point out that this lesson will explore the significance of the angel's announcement of the birth of Jesus to the shepherds.

Discover

▶ Read the first paragraph of the page and then invite the young people to share times when the actions of someone whom they know gave them a new insight into that person.

▶ Point out the picture of the shepherd, and ask volunteers to read aloud the remaining five paragraphs of the page.

▶ Discuss with the group the significance of the presence of shepherds at the manger.

Solemnity of Christmas

Faith Focus
What do we learn from the Gospel story of the angel's announcement to the shepherds of the birth of Jesus?

The Word of the Lord
These are the Gospel readings for Mass on Christmas Day. Choose one reading. Read and discuss it with your family.

Gospel
John 1:1–18 or
John 1:1–5, 9–14

Sometimes the people in our lives surprise us. They do something we do not expect. When that happens, we learn a new thing about them. What happened on the night Jesus was born tells us something new about him.

Luke's account of the Gospel includes the announcement of the birth of Jesus to the shepherds. They were the first to receive the good news of Jesus' birth. As the shepherds watched their sheep, an angel appeared to them and said:

"[T]oday in the city of David a savior has been born for you who is Messiah and Lord." LUKE 2:11

The shepherds hurried to Bethlehem. There they found Jesus and Mary and Joseph as the angel said they would.

Throughout the history of Israel, the writers of the Sacred Scripture used the image of shepherds to speak about God. For the Israelites God was a shepherd who watched over them, his sheep. They often prayed:

The Lord is my shepherd; I shall not want   PSALM 23:1

However, at the time of Jesus' birth, many people thought that shepherds were of little worth. Their hard, dangerous work kept them in the fields day and night. This meant that they were unable to observe religious practices. Because of this, religious leaders thought shepherds were unfaithful, unimportant people.

But it was to shepherds, Luke tells us, that God announced the birth of the Savior. Jesus is the Messiah and Lord of all.

235

TEACHING TIP

Jesus, the Savior of All People. Learning to say or write the name *Jesus* in many languages always interests young people. Invite those who can speak or write the name *Jesus* in a language other than English to do so for the class. This is a memorable and engaging way to help the group come to know that Jesus is the Savior of all people. You might wish to learn in advance how to write and say the name *Jesus* in a language different from your own. This activity can be enhanced by including the singing of Christmas carols in other languages.

The Lord Is Our Shepherd

For each letter of the word shepherd, write a word or phrase that tells us about who Jesus is. Then imagine that you are a newspaper reporter who has been asked to find out more about some amazing events that took place in a stable outside Bethlehem. Use your words and phrases and write a story telling what you discovered about Jesus.

This season of Christmas is a time of joy. I will rejoice in the birth of Jesus. I will

_____

_____ .

 Honor the birth of Jesus. Pray, "For today in the city of David a savior has been born for you who is Messiah and Lord" (Luke 2:11).

236

Respond

▶ Ask the young people to imagine that they are shepherds. Invite them to respond to these or similar questions:

— Why were you the first to receive the good news of Jesus' birth?

— What did you find in Bethlehem?

— What will you tell others?

▶ Have volunteers dramatize this dialogue.

▶ Explain the directions to the acrostic activity and have the students complete it. Afterward, invite volunteers to share their responses.

▶ After a moment of prayerful reflection, have the students write their faith choices on the lines provided.

▶ Encourage the young people to put their choices into practice this week and rejoice in prayer.

Pray

▶ Have the students locate Psalm 23 in their Bibles.

▶ Invite the group to pray the psalm aloud.

▶ Close by singing "Hark! The Herald Angels Sing" or a similar Christmas hymn.

Solemnity of Mary, Mother of God

Focus

Ask a volunteer to read the Faith Focus question aloud. Have the young people silently think about how they might answer it. Point out to the group that the Catholic Church honors Mary many times throughout the year, not only during the Christmas season.

Discover

▶ Read aloud the introductory paragraph and ask the young people to share other times when they honor their mothers.

▶ Ask volunteers to finish reading aloud the remaining four paragraphs of the page to discover the answer to the Faith Focus question.

▶ Summarize by emphasizing that we honor Mary as Mother of God and our mother. We follow her example by seeking to follow God's will for us. We choose to say yes to God as she did.

Faith Focus
How does the Church honor Mary during the Christmas season?

The Word of the Lord
These are the readings for the Solemnity of Mary, the Mother of God. Read and discuss them with your family.

First Reading
Numbers 6:22–27

Second Reading
Galatians 4:4–7

Gospel
Luke 2:16–21

Solemnity of Mary, Mother of God

Each year on Mother's Day we honor our mothers. We thank them for taking us to the soccer game. We thank them for cooking our meals and for keeping us clothed. We thank them for their love each day of the year. What are some other special times when you honor your mother?

The Church honors Mary, the Mother of God, many times during the year. During the Christmas season we think about Mary in a special way.

While the celebration of the birth of Jesus is at the heart of our Christmas season, we also celebrate the feast of the Holy Family between Christmas and January 1. At our celebration of Mass on that day, we pray that through Mary's prayers and the prayers of her husband, Joseph, our families may live in peace and love.

The Church also sets aside the first day of the new year, January 1, as the Solemnity of Mary, the Mother of God. On this holy day and holiday, we gather to celebrate Mass. We ask God to bless our new year. We ask that Mary's prayer and her motherly love bring us joy forever.

By remembering Mary as the Mother of God and our Mother too, we begin the year with blessings. Mary reminds us of what the whole Church desires to do. We all want to say yes to God as she did. We all want to do God's will all our life, just as Mary did.

237

TEACHING TIP

Dramatize the Christmas Story. Use the young people's familiarity with the Christmas story as the foundation to have them dramatize it. Look over the infancy stories in both Matthew's Gospel and in Luke's Gospel and have the students combine them into a simple one-act play. Place the young people's names in a box and randomly select the players for the main roles. Provide simple costumes, such as old colored sheets for clothes. If you do not have sufficient time for the young people to present a play, make available Bibles for the group to read the Christmas narratives.

Mary, Pray for Us

A litany is a prayer of petition in which a series of petitions are followed by the same response. The litany to the Blessed Virgin Mary on this page is based on one that was composed in the Middle Ages.

Pray this litany with your class to honor Mary, the Mother of God.

Group 1: Lord have mercy on us.
Group 2: Christ, have mercy on us.
Group 1: Lord, have mercy on us.

Group 2:	Holy Mary,	**All:**	pray for us.
	Holy Mother of God,		pray for us.
	Holy Virgin of virgins,		pray for us.
Group 1:	Mother most pure,	**All:**	pray for us.
	Mother of our Savior,		pray for us.
	Mother of the Church,		pray for us.
Group 2:	Seat of wisdom,	**All:**	pray for us.
	Mystical rose,		pray for us.
	Morning star,		pray for us.
Group 1:	Refuge of sinners,	**All:**	pray for us.
	Comforter of the afflicted,		pray for us.
	Help of Christians,		pray for us.
Group 2:	Queen of angels,	**All:**	pray for us.
	Queen of all saints,		pray for us.
	Queen of peace,		pray for us.

Group 1: Pray for us O holy Mother of God,
Group 2: That we may be made worthy of the promises of Christ.

Based on the Litany of Loreto

MY FAITH CHOICE

This week I will honor Mary. I will follow her example of saying yes to the Lord's call. I will

_____

_____.

 Honor Mary, our Mother. Pray, "May it be done to me according to your word, Lord" (Based on Luke 1:38).

(238)

BACKGROUND: DOCTRINE

Mary, Mother of God. Mary is truly the Mother of God because she is the Mother of the Incarnate Son of God. For this reason, the Council of Ephesus in 431 proclaimed that Mary truly became the Mother of God by the human conception of the Son of God in her womb (see *Catechism of the Catholic Church* 466, 495, and 509).

Respond

▶ Ask the young people to name the feast day that the Church celebrates on January 1.

▶ Introduce and explain the litany to Mary on this page.

▶ Have the young people work individually to create additional titles for Mary that honor her. Invite them to write their titles in a column on the board.

▶ Tell them you will make their titles part of the closing prayer.

▶ Invite the students to respond to My Faith Choice.

▶ After a moment of prayerful reflection, have the young people write their choices on the lines provided.

▶ Encourage the students to put their choices into practice this week and pray that Mary fills them with her light and love.

Pray

▶ Divide the class into two groups. Invite the young people to quiet themselves for prayer. Gather the class in the prayer center and introduce the litany.

▶ Ask them to pray the litany with you to honor Mary, Mother of God.

▶ Conclude by singing an appropriate Marian hymn together.

Epiphany

Focus

Have a volunteer read the Faith Focus question on the board. Explain to the students that this session will help them understand that Jesus came to save all people of all nations.

Discover

▶ Write the word *Epiphany* on the board.

▶ Beneath it write this teaching from the *Catechism of the Catholic Church:* "The Epiphany is the manifestation of Jesus as Messiah of Israel, Son of God and Savior of the world" (*CCC* 528). Have the students look up the word *Messiah* in their glossary and turn to the chapter page noted there. Have a volunteer read the section on Messiah aloud.

▶ Invite volunteers to read the page aloud.

▶ Invite the students to ask any questions they may have about the reading.

▶ Emphasize that the Ephiphany story reveals that Jesus is the Savior of *all* people, for all time.

Faith Focus
Who did Jesus come to save?

The Word of the Lord
This is the Gospel reading for the Solemnity of the Epiphany. Find it in the Bible and read and discuss it with your family.

Years A, B, and C
Matthew 2:1–12

Epiphany

The word *epiphany* means to make visible, manifest, or make known. The Church celebrates the Solemnity of Epiphany during the Season of Christmas. On Epiphany we remember and celebrate that Jesus was revealed to be the Savior of the world. The Magi were wise men who came from the East searching for the newborn king of the Jews. They had seen a star rising in the sky and recognized it to be a sign that a great ruler had been born.

We do not know how far the Magi had to travel or where they actually lived. We do not know what obstacles they had to overcome. But what we know from Scripture is that the wise men believed that the light of the star that went before them was leading them to a very special newly born ruler.

When the star stopped over the place where Jesus was, the Gospel tells us that the Magi

"were overjoyed at seeing the star, and on entering the house they saw the choild with Mary his mother."

MATTHEW 2:11

The tradition of the Church names the wise men Gaspar, Melchior, and Balthasar. Tradition also identifies them to be kings from different lands and of different races. Though they were kings, when they found the Holy Family

"they prostrated themselves and did him homage. Then they opened their treasures and offered him gifts of gold, frankincense, and myrrh." MATTHEW 2:11

The Epiphany story reveals that Jesus is the Savior of the whole world, of all people and in all lands and of all times. The Magi remind us of the joy of our meeting Jesus both in events of our daily life and especially in the Eucharist and the other Sacraments. The Magi teach us the importance of spending time in adoration of Jesus. They help us remember and trust that we are guided by the light of our faith in Jesus. We will always have that light to find our way to God here on earth and it will lead us to Heaven when our earthy journey is ended.

(239)

TEACHING TIP

Symbols and Mystery. Symbols are an important aspect of our Christian faith. They can spark our imagination, create a sense of awe and wonder, and lead us deeper into the mystery of God. Some of the symbols associated with the Epiphany include gifts, light, a star, a crown, gold, frankincense (incense), and myrrh, a balm used to anoint bodies before burial. Invite the students to works in pairs to choose an Epiphany symbol that is meaningful for them. Using art materials, have the young people create the symbol and work with their partner to write a sentence that explains the symbol's significance, Allow time for the students to share their work with the class.

Kings and Gifts

In the word search below, find the names of the three kings and the three gifts they offered to Jesus. The words may be found in any directions Some words may be written backwards. Gifts don't always have to be wrapped in packages. What gifts do you think Jesus would want you to bring to him today? Discuss your thoughts with your family.

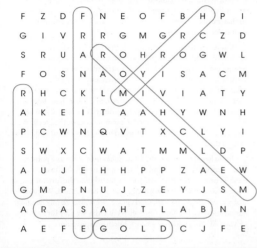

```
F  Z  D  F  N  E  O  F  B  H  P  I
G  I  V  R  R  G  M  G  R  C  Z  D
S  R  U  A  R  O  H  R  O  G  W  L
F  O  S  N  A  O  Y  I  S  A  C  M
R  H  C  K  L  M  I  V  I  A  T  Y
A  K  E  I  T  A  A  H  Y  W  N  H
P  C  W  N  Q  V  T  X  C  L  Y  I
S  W  X  C  W  A  T  M  M  L  D  P
A  U  J  E  H  H  P  P  Z  A  E  W
G  M  P  N  U  J  Z  E  Y  J  S  M
A  R  A  S  A  H  T  L  A  B  N  N
A  E  F  E  G  O  L  D  C  J  F  E
```

MY FAITH CHOICE

This week I will adore Jesus in the Sacrament of Eucharist. I will

_____

_____ .

Worship Jesus, the Second Person of the Holy Trinity. Pray, "Most Holy Trinity; Father, Son, and Holy Spirit—I adore you with my whole heart."

(240)

TEACHING TIP

The Story of the Magi. The Gospel of St. Matthew is the only Gospel that tells the story of the Magi. A careful read of the Gospel reveals that the names and number of Magi are not mentioned. Neither are they referred to as kings. Since Matthew mentions gifts of gold, frankincense and myrrh, tradition developed that three costly gifts must have been brought by three rich and powerful men, perhaps royalty. The names of the Wise Men, Gasper, or Casper, Melchior and Balthasar, stem from an ancient 6th century Greek manuscript as well as a later manuscript attributed to St. Bede the Venerable, which also describes the physical characteristics of the Magi as we see them in Nativity scenes and Christmas cards.

Respond

▶ Remind the students that in the Nativity story, the birth of Jesus was first announced to shepherds, a lowly group of nomads. This honor symbolizes Jesus' coming to serve the poor and the lowly of the earth.

▶ Ask: Who do the Magi symbolize? *(people of all nations and races)*

▶ Introduce the word search activity on page 240. Using the teaching tip on this page, give the class some additional information about the words they are searching for.

▶ When they have completed their work, ask them to share their solutions.

▶ Invite the students to respond to My Faith Choice.

▶ After a moment of prayerful reflection, have the young people write their choices on the lines provided.

▶ Encourage the students to put their choices into practice this week and pray in gratitude for the gift of Jesus.

Pray

▶ Gather the students in the prayer area. Allow them a few moments of reflective silence. Then lead them in prayer:

God, on this holy feast of Epiphany you revealed your Son to be a light for all nations. Just as you guided the Magi by the light of a star, be our light in all that we do, so we may be worthy to be called your children. We ask this in the name of Jesus, your Son. Amen.

▶ Pray together, "Our Father . . .

Ash Wednesday

Focus

Have a volunteer read the Faith Focus question. Ask the young people to think about the many ways in which they live as members of the Church.

Discover

▶ Ask the young people to share what it is like to belong to a community, whether that community is a family, school, or organization. Ask them to consider which ideals and behaviors reflect their membership in that community.

▶ Ask several volunteers to each read a paragraph of the page aloud.

▶ Have the young people work in groups, one for each paragraph. Instruct them to re-read the paragraph once, then close their books and, together, rewrite their assigned paragraph in their own words.

▶ Invite one person from each group to read their paragraph. Add any major points they may have missed.

Faith Focus
How does the celebration of Ash Wednesday help us live as members of the Church?

The Word of the Lord
This is the first reading for Ash Wednesday. Read and discuss it with your family.

First Reading
2 Corinthians 5:20–6:2

Ash Wednesday

On Ash Wednesday you may go to the mall or into your favorite restaurant and see any number of people with grey smudges on their foreheads. Some people may wonder what that's all about. But Catholics from all over the world can tell you that each of those people with the dirty mark on their forehead belongs is a disciple of Jesus Christ. They are all members of the Body of Christ, the Church.

Ash Wednesday marks the beginning of Lent and reminds us of our Baptism and our need to live as disciples of Jesus. It reminds us that we need to become more like Christ. We give the name conversion to our becoming more like Christ.

On Ash Wednesday, when the Sign of the Cross is traced in ashes on our forehead, we remember that we are children of God. Like our first parents, Adam and Eve, we were created out of dust. Like them, we also sin. Beginning on Ash Wednesday and during the season of Lent, Catholics will focus our attention on ways we can live our lives more in line with God's will. We will remember that Jesus began his ministry by spending forty days in the desert, fasting and praying. We remember that Jesus rejected the temptations of the Devil. We remember that Jesus was strengthened by the Holy Spirit and his love of God the Father.

From her earliest days the Church has used ashes as a public sign that a person has sinned and needs to turn away from sin and back to God. When our forehead is marked with ashes in the form of a cross it symbolizes that we acknowledge that we have sinned. We promise that we will cooperate with God's grace. We will work on changing our attitudes and actions. On Ash Wednesday we pray for a change of heart. We join with the whole Church and proclaim.

Rend your hearts, not your garments, and return to the LORD your God, for gracious and merciful is he, slow to anger, rich in kindness, and relenting in punishment."

JOEL 2:13

241

Faithful to the Gospel

When the priest traces a sign of the cross on our foreheads, he may say, "Repent and believe in the Gospel" (ROMAN MISSAL).

On the journal pages below, write a Lenten pledge on how you can be faithful to the Gospel during Lent.

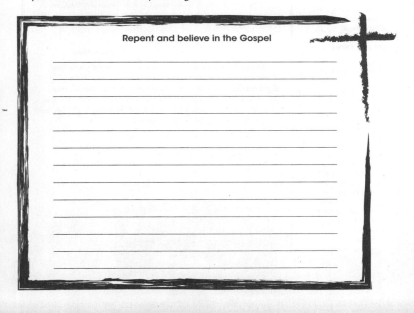

Repent and believe in the Gospel

 **MY FAITH CHOICE**

This week I will try to live out my Lenten pledge by

 Ask for God's help. Pray, "Come, Holy Spirit, help me to resist temptation. Teach me to become more like Jesus."

(242)

TEACHING TIP

Symbol of Time. For the ancient people of the Bible, numbers held symbolic meaning. The number forty signifies a period of trial, testing, and waiting. It also signifies a time of maturing and growing in wisdom and obedience to God. The significance of such symbolism is apparent when we read the stories of Noah and his family, adrift on the flood waters for 40 days, and Moses, who wandered through the desert with the Israelites for 40 years. Jesus was tempted for 40 days in the desert following his baptism by John the Baptist. Invite the children to talk about how they have matured during the past few years. How do they think and act differently than they did as a very young child? Remind them that we mature in our spiritual life as well as our physical life. Lent is an opportunity to grow into a deeper relationship with God.

Respond

▶ Ask the young people to share any new insights that they gained from the rewriting exercise.

▶ Introduce the activity, Faithful to the Gospel. Ask a volunteer to read the instructions.

▶ On the board write the words: *conversion/change of heart and Gospel/Good News.*

▶ Allow time for the students to write a Lenten pledge on the journal page. If you are using the Teaching Tip on page 372, you could ask them to incorporate something about the saint they have chosen into this activity. Encourage volunteers to share their promises with the class.

▶ Invite the students to respond to My Faith Choice.

▶ After a moment of prayerful reflection, have the young people write their choices on the lines provided.

▶ Encourage the students to put their choices into practice by asking God to help them to resist temptation.

Pray

Gather the students in the prayer area. Encourage them to be mindful that they are in the presence of God. While they maintain a prayerful silence, pray aloud the following:

O God, we offer you our promise of repentance during this Lenten season. Instill in us the desire to turn our hearts to you in all things. May our Lenten sacrifices prepare us to celebrate the Passion of your Son and to one day join in your heavenly glory. We ask this in the name of Jesus, our Savior. Amen.

Lent

Focus

Ask a volunteer to read the Faith Focus question aloud and have the class silently think about how they might answer it. Point out that this lesson will help them to explore the different things that we do during the season of Lent.

Discover

- ▶ Have the young people silently read the page, highlighting the key points they notice in the reading.

- ▶ Point out the photos on this page, and ask volunteers to share how these photos are examples of things that we can do during Lent.

- ▶ Reread the last paragraph on this page aloud to the students and ask them to share their ideas about the different ways that they can enter more fully into Jesus' Death and Resurrection during Lent.

Faith Focus
What are we called to do during Lent?

The Word of the Lord
Choose this year's Gospel reading for the First Sunday of Lent. Read and discuss it with your family.

Year A
Matthew 4:1–11

Year B
Mark 1:12–15

Year C
Luke 4:1–13

What You See
In our churches we see signs that Lent is a season of discipline. The color of Lent is purple, the color of penitence. No flowers or brightly colored decorations greet us. We sing no joyous Alleluia or Gloria.

Lent

For many of us, the winter landscape seems bare. Leaves fall from trees, flowers die, and grass turns brown. But we trust that after winter, spring will come and bring new life. Each year during Lent we renew the new life of Christ we received in Baptism.

Lent begins on Ash Wednesday. On Ash Wednesday the Church gathers to begin our Lenten journey. As ashes are placed on our head, we hear the words:

"Repent and believe in the Gospel."

ROMAN MISSAL

During Lent the Church calls us to enter more fully into Jesus' death and Resurrection. We make sacrifices to do this. We may decide to share more of our time and talents with others. We may give up something that we enjoy. We want habits of goodness to live in us. We support one another in our decisions during Lent. Together we look forward to celebrating the joy of Easter.

243

TEACHING TIP

Lenten Resolutions. Lent is a time to reflect on our own Baptism. It is a season during which Christians make serious decisions, or resolutions, to renew living their lives in Christ. Invite the young people to make Lenten resolutions and write them on a piece of paper, place them in an envelope, and seal the envelope. Place the sealed envelopes in a shoe box, and then seal it and keep the sealed shoe box on the prayer table during Lent as a reminder of the students' commitment to turn away from sin and be faithful to the Gospel.

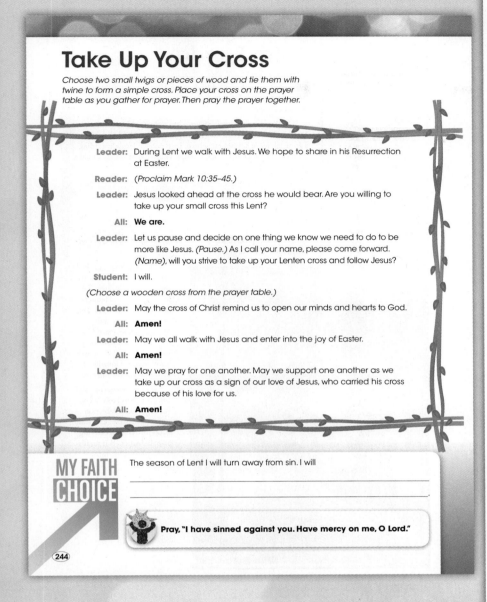

Take Up Your Cross

Choose two small twigs or pieces of wood and tie them with twine to form a simple cross. Place your cross on the prayer table as you gather for prayer. Then pray the prayer together.

Leader: During Lent we walk with Jesus. We hope to share in his Resurrection at Easter.

Reader: (Proclaim Mark 10:35–45.)

Leader: Jesus looked ahead at the cross he would bear. Are you willing to take up your small cross this Lent?

All: **We are.**

Leader: Let us pause and decide on one thing we know we need to do to be more like Jesus. (Pause.) As I call your name, please come forward. (Name), will you strive to take up your Lenten cross and follow Jesus?

Student: I will.

(Choose a wooden cross from the prayer table.)

Leader: May the cross of Christ remind us to open our minds and hearts to God.

All: **Amen!**

Leader: May we all walk with Jesus and enter into the joy of Easter.

All: **Amen!**

Leader: May we pray for one another. May we support one another as we take up our cross as a sign of our love of Jesus, who carried his cross because of his love for us.

All: **Amen!**

MY FAITH CHOICE

The season of Lent I will turn away from sin. I will

_____

_____.

Pray, "I have sinned against you. Have mercy on me, O Lord."

244

TEACHING TIP

Candidates and Catechumens. Point out to the young people that there are people in the parish who are preparing to be baptized or received into full communion with the Catholic Church at the Easter Vigil. These people are called candidates for full communion if they were previously baptized in another Christian denomination. If they were never baptized, they are called catechumens. Make a list of the names of the catechumens and the candidates and post the list in the prayer area. Invite the young people to pray for the catechumens and candidates during Lent. This is one way that you can help the young people develop the habit of practicing the Lenten discipline of prayer.

Respond

▶ Ask the students to recall the words said as ashes are traced on our foreheads on Ash Wednesday: "Repent and believe in the Gospel." Discuss how these words can guide them in making good choices during Lent.

▶ Explain the Take Up Your Cross prayer service. Choose a volunteer to read Mark 10: 35-45.

▶ Gather in the prayer center and pray together.

▶ Invite the students to respond to My Faith Choice.

▶ After a moment of prayerful reflection, have the young people write their choices on the lines provided.

▶ Explain to the class that they will have an opportunity to silently offer their faith choices during the closing prayer.

▶ Allow time for the students to make the twig crosses described in the directions.

Pray

▶ Play instrumental background music as you gather the young people for prayer.

▶ Lead the group in praying Take Up Your Cross.

▶ At the appropriate time, invite the young people to go to the prayer table, silent offer their faith choice and take a cross as a sign of their commitment.

▶ Conclude by having the students repeat the faith choice prayer at the bottom of the page together.

Palm Sunday of the Lord's Passion

Focus

Ask a volunteer to read the Faith Focus question aloud and ask the students to think about how they might answer it. Point out that the celebration of Palm Sunday of the Lord's Passion begins Holy Week.

Discover

▶ Present the opening paragraph of the page. Ask the young people to share ways that we greet national heroes or winning sports teams. Follow up by asking volunteers to comment on why we greet those people that way.

▶ Invite the students to look at the stained-glass image depicting Jesus' final entry into Jerusalem, and ask volunteers to share what they recall about the liturgy of Palm Sunday of the Lord's Passion.

▶ Have the young people silently read the remaining paragraphs of the page.

Faith Focus
Why do we celebrate Palm Sunday of the Lord's Passion?

The Word of the Lord
Choose this year's Gospel reading for Palm Sunday of the Lord's Passion. Read and discuss it with your family.

Year A
Matthew 26:14–27: 66 or 27:11–54

Year B
Mark 14:1–15:47 or 15:1–39

Year C
Luke 22:14–23:56 or 23:1–49

Palm Sunday

When a well-known person comes to your school or town, you welcome them with a marching band and banners and balloons. When Jesus entered the city of Jerusalem, the people gave him a special welcome.

On that day, the people of Jerusalem welcomed Jesus as the Messiah. He did not ride on a mighty horse or in a gilded chariot as a great soldier or a conquering hero. Jesus entered Jerusalem riding a donkey. But as he entered, the people cheered him as they would a great king:

"Hosanna to the Son of David;
   blessed is he who comes in the name of the
     Lord;
hosanna in the highest." MATTHEW 21:9

The people proclaimed "Hosanna", a greeting of joy and praise, which means "Lord, grant salvation."

The people spread cloaks on the road to make the path smooth and less dusty for Jesus. They waved branches taken from palm trees. This welcome of Jesus as the Messiah riding on a donkey reminds us that Jesus is the king of everyone, even the lowly. Jesus is a king filled with compassion and care.

The celebration of Palm Sunday begins Holy Week. We begin our celebration with a procession. Everyone walks into church carrying palm branches. This recalls the day Jesus rode into Jerusalem.

245

SCRIPTURE BACKGROUND

Palm Sunday of the Lord's Passion. Share this background with the young people so that they can better enter into the liturgical celebration of Palm Sunday of the Lord's Passion: (1) Three of the four Gospels mention that people waved branches as Jesus entered Jerusalem. Only John's account identifies the branches as palm branches. Although many of the trees were palms, willows and other trees with supple, small switches also grew in Palestine. (2) As a sign of respect for military leaders and other dignitaries traveling the road, people spread their cloaks on the roadway to keep the dust down. (3) In Jesus' time, military rulers usually rode into the city on horses. Jesus rode on a young donkey or colt.

Hosanna! A Meditation

- Sit quietly.
- Close your eyes and breathe slowly.
- Remember the story of Jesus' entry into Jerusalem.
- Compare the meaning of this story to your own life and share your thoughts with Jesus. Take the time to praise him for the gifts he has brought to your life.
- After a few quiet moments, write down any key words or phrases that will help you remember this prayer experience.

_____

_____

_____

_____

- To close your meditation, pray aloud with your class the words with which the people welcomed Jesus to Jerusalem:

"Hosanna to the Son of David:
blessed is he who comes in the name of the Lord;
hosanna in the highest." MATTHEW 21:9

MY FAITH CHOICE

This day Jesus is welcomed as the Messiah. I will honor Jesus on Palm Sunday. I will

_____

_____.

 Praise Jesus the Messiah, and welcome him into your heart.

(246)

TEACHING TIP

Making Crosses from Palm Branches. Many Christians follow the custom of making crosses using the palm branches that they receive on Palm Sunday. Invite a parent who knows how to weave the palm fronds into designs of crosses to visit with the young people and teach them to make crosses. Encourage the young people to share their new skill with their family and with younger children in the parish—perhaps after the celebration of the liturgy for Palm Sunday.

Respond

▶ Ask a volunteer to proclaim John 11:1–10. Have the students look at the photo on page 245 and compare the Gospel reading with what is depicted in the photo.

▶ Have the young people work in small groups to present tableaux of Jesus' entering Jerusalem. Ask them to imagine that they are among the disciples accompanying Jesus and to present their tableaux from the perspective of the disciples.

▶ Invite the students to respond to My Faith Choice.

▶ After a moment of prayerful reflection, have the young people write their choices on the lines provided.

▶ Encourage the students to put their choices into practice by praising God for Jesus, the Messiah.

Pray

▶ Gather the young people for prayer.

▶ Introduce them to Hosanna! A Meditation and review the steps in the meditation.

▶ Play a recording of appropriate background music, perhaps from the Grade 6 Music CD, and dim the lights if permissible.

▶ Lead the young people in the meditation.

Triduum/ Holy Thursday

Focus

Write the Faith Focus question on the board and ask the students to think about how they might answer it. Explain to the young people that Holy Thursday is the first day of the three day celebration of the Easter Triduum.

Discover

▶ Read aloud the introductory paragraph of the page to the class, and invite responses to the questions that are contained in the paragraph.

▶ Call on several volunteers to read aloud the rest of the page.

▶ Point out the pictures of the foods traditionally prepared for the Seder meal on Passover.

▶ Ask the students to note similarities between these foods and the foods used in the Mass.

Faith Focus
What do we remember as the Church celebrates Holy Thursday?

The Word of the Lord
Choose one of the Scripture readings for Holy Thursday. Read and discuss it with your family.

First Reading
Exodus 12:1–8, 11–14

Second Reading
1 Corinthians 11:23–26

Gospel
John 13:1–15

Triduum/ Holy Thursday

Do you remember eating a special meal with your family or your friends? What made it special to you? Did you eat special food? Did someone say something that made you feel good about yourself? The Church remembers a special meal that Jesus ate with his disciples.

On the evening of Holy Thursday, we remember the last time Jesus gathered the disciples and shared a meal with them. This meal celebrated the Passover. On this special day the Jewish people celebrate their passage from slavery in Egypt to freedom. They remember the Covenant with God.

All his life Jesus celebrated this greatest of Jewish feasts with his family and friends. Now he shared the foods of the Passover for the last time. But at this Last Supper, Jesus did something special. Jesus changed the bread and wine he shared with his disciples into his own Body and Blood. He took the bread and broke it and said,

"This is my body, which will be given for you, do this in memory of me."   LUKE 22:19

After they had eaten, he passed the cup of wine for them to drink. He said,

"This cup is the new covenant in my blood, which will be shed for you."   LUKE 22:20

Later that night, one of the disciples betrayed Jesus and he was arrested.

Traditional food for a Jewish Seder

247

LITURGY CONNECTION

Washing of the Feet: Helping Hands. The rite of washing of the feet is an integral part of the Holy Thursday evening liturgy. Guide the young people to grasp the essence of this rite; namely, we are to serve others as Jesus did. To help the young people understand the meaning of this rite, have them trace and cut out outlines of both of their hands on art paper. In the outline of one hand, have them write their name. In the outline of the other hand, have them write or draw one way they can serve, or help, people at home. Encourage the young people to put their faith decision into action and make a difference.

The Lord's Supper

Today, at the celebration of the Eucharist, the Church continues to do what Jesus asked his disciples to do. On Holy Thursday we especially remember his last Passover with his disciples. We call our celebration on that day the Mass of the Lord's Supper.

Create an announcement inviting your family to join in celebrating the Mass of the Lord's Supper. Point out to them the importance of sharing in the celebration. Display it in your home.

 MY FAITH CHOICE

On Holy Thursday, I will honor Jesus' command to remember the special meal he shared with the disciples. I will

_____

_____

 "Dear Jesus, help me remember the depth of your love for me. Amen."

TEACHING TIP

Invitations to Celebrate Holy Thursday. Work with the young people to create cards inviting their families to participate in the liturgy on Holy Thursday evening. Discuss with the group ideas about symbols that they might use to decorate their invitations, such as a cup, chalice, or unleavened bread on a plate. Write the time of the liturgy and other pertinent information on the board, and have the students include the information in their invitations.

Respond

▶ Invite the young people to share their ideas about the Passover meal and its connection with the Last Supper and the Mass today.

▶ Have the young people work individually to create announcements inviting their families to the Holy Thursday liturgy.

▶ Provide envelopes for their work and encourage them to give the invitations to their families.

▶ Invite volunteers to share their announcement with the class. Consider sharing the completed designs with the appropriate parish staff person for use on the parish Web site.

▶ Invite the students to respond to My Faith Choice.

▶ After a moment of prayerful reflection, have the young people write their choices on the lines provided.

▶ Encourage the students to put their choices into practice and give thanks to Jesus for the gift of the Eucharist.

Pray

▶ Gather the young people for prayer.

▶ Proclaim Matthew 21:26–30.

▶ Encourage the young people to think about and choose one way that they can serve others as Jesus commanded his disciples to do.

Triduum/ Good Friday

Focus

Ask a volunteer to read the Faith Focus question aloud and have the young people think about how they might answer it. Point out that the Church celebrates the liturgy of the Lord's Passion on Good Friday, the second day of the Triduum.

Discover

▶ Have a volunteer read aloud the first paragraph of Triduum/Good Friday, and briefly discuss it with the class.

▶ Point out the photos on this page and describe what they depict.

▶ Invite volunteers to read aloud the remainder of the text on the page.

▶ Summarize by writing the three parts of the liturgy for Good Friday on the board, namely, "Liturgy of the Word," "Veneration of the Cross," and "Holy Communion."

▶ Have the young people name some of the actions that occur during the celebration of the liturgy of the Lord's Passion, and invite them to write these terms under the correct heading.

Faith Focus
How does the Church remember the Death of Jesus?

The Word of the Lord
Choose one of the Scripture readings for Good Friday. Read and discuss it with your family.

First Reading
Isaiah 52:13–53:12

Second Reading
Hebrews 4:14–16, 5:7–9

Gospel
John 18:1–19:42

Triduum/Good Friday

At some time in your life, someone you love will die. This may have already happened to you. You know that when this happens, everyone in your house is sad. People tell stories about the one who has died. The Church does this too, as it remembers the death of Jesus.

On Good Friday our churches have no decorations. The tabernacle is empty; its door is open. There is no altar cloth covering the altar table. The Church gathers to reflect on the Passion and Death of Jesus.

Our liturgy on Good Friday is called the celebration of the Lord's Passion. Good Friday is the only day of the year on which Mass is not celebrated. The celebration of the Lord's Passion is made up of three parts:

- The first part is the Liturgy of the Word. The Gospel reading is a proclamation of the Passion and death of Jesus according to John. After the Gospel proclamation, the Church invites us to pray for the needs of the world.

- The second part of the celebration of the Lord's Passion is the Veneration of the Cross. In this part of the liturgy we show reverence and respect for the cross because Jesus died for us on a cross. We might do this by walking in procession, bowing before the cross, and kissing it.

- The third part of the celebration of the Lord's Passion is Holy Communion. The Church invites us to receive the Body and Blood of Christ, which is consecrated at Mass on Holy Thursday and reserved in a tabernacle as a place of repose, meaning pause or rest.

The celebration of the Lord's Passion ends as it began. The altar cloth is removed from the altar and the tabernacle is empty. In deep silence we leave to begin the long sabbath rest until the celebration of the Easter Vigil.

249

Jesus Asks, You Respond

Each day you do many things to show your love for God and others as Jesus did. You make sacrifices. You give your time. You share your gifts. You take up your cross and follow Jesus as he asked you to do.

On one of the beams of this cross, describe something you have done for someone during Lent. On the other cross beam, describe how it helped the person.

MY FAITH CHOICE

On Good Friday, Jesus died on the cross for my salvation. I will honor his sacrifice of love. I will

_____

_____

 Honor Jesus, who died for us. Pray, "Jesus, you saved all people from sin and death. All glory and praise to you!"

250

LITURGY CONNECTION

Holy Communion on Good Friday. Point out that the celebration of the Lord's Passion on Good Friday does not include the Liturgy of the Eucharist as Mass does on Sunday. Remind the class that the Rite of Communion, however, is part of the liturgy for Good Friday. Tell the young people that the Eucharist that we receive on Good Friday has been reserved from the celebration of Mass on Holy Thursday evening.

Respond

▶ Reread the Faith Focus question aloud, and invite volunteers to answer it, using what they learned in the lesson.

▶ Introduce the Jesus Asks, You Respond activity, and explain the directions to the young people.

▶ Give time for the young people to reflect on the sacrifices that they have made for other people and then have them complete the activity.

▶ Invite volunteers to share their completed crosses.

▶ Affirm the students for their commitment to live as followers of Christ.

▶ Invite the students to respond to My Faith Choice.

▶ After a moment of prayerful reflection, have the young people write their choices on the lines provided.

▶ Encourage the students to put their choices into practice and prayerfully express their gratitude to Jesus for his sacrificial death on the cross.

Pray

▶ Place a large cross in the prayer area.

▶ Gather the young people for prayer, and tell them to make a profound bow before the cross as they enter.

▶ Proclaim John 15:13 to the class and have them respond, "Through the cross you brought joy to the world."

Triduum/Easter

Focus

Ask a volunteer to read the Faith Focus question aloud, and have the class think about how they might answer it. Point out that Easter, the third and final day of the Triduum, is the greatest feast of the Church.

Discover

▶ Present the opening paragraph, and invite volunteers to share how they celebrate Easter in their homes.

▶ Read aloud the remaining paragraphs of the page and have the young people underline key words and phrases.

▶ Invite volunteers to share why "Alleluia!" or "Praise God!" captures the message of the celebration of the Easter season.

Triduum/Easter

Faith Focus
Why is the Easter season a time of rejoicing?

The Word of the Lord
Choose the Gospel readings for Easter Sunday this year. Read and discuss them with your family.

Year A
John 20:1–9
or Matthew 28:1–10
or Luke 24:13–35

Year B
John 20:1–9
or Mark 16:1–8
or Luke 24:13–35

Year C
John 20:1–9
or Luke 24:1–12
or Luke 24:13–35

On our best days, we feel great joy just to be alive. We can do many wonderful things. Easter is a wonderful day in the Church—a day when we rejoice because God has raised Jesus to new life.

Saint Augustine reminds us that we are Easter people and Alleluia is our song. Alleluia is a Hebrew word that means "Praise the Lord." At the Easter Vigil the presider solemnly intones the Alleluia, which we have not heard all during Lent. The Church sings "Alleluia!" repeatedly during the Easter season. We continuously thank and praise God for the new life of Easter. We praise God because we have passed from death to life through our Baptism.

Throughout Lent we focused on turning away from sin to become followers of Jesus. During the Easter season we rejoice in our new life in Christ. We sing "Alleluia!" and may proclaim,

"This is the day the Lord has made;
let us rejoice in it and be glad"　　　Psalm 118:24

LITURGY CONNECTION

The Prayer Area. Easter is the central liturgical time of the Church's year. Every Sunday is a celebration of the Resurrection, a "little Easter." Take the time to decorate your prayer area throughout the Easter season with the symbols and colors of Easter. Cover the prayer table with a white cloth, place a golden bookmark in the Bible to mark the Gospel reading for each Sunday of the Easter season, decorate the prayer table with colorful, fresh flowers, and keep a bowl of holy water on the table to remind the young people of their Baptism. Encourage the young people to use the holy water to bless themselves throughout the Easter season.

Celebrating Easter

Write a cinquain to celebrate Easter. Share the good news of the Resurrection with a partner and with your family.

_____ Easter _____
Title

_____ _____
Write two words
that describe the title.

_____ _____ _____
Write three action words
that describe the title.

_____ _____ _____ _____
Write four words that tell
a feeling about the title.

_____
Write another word
for the title.

MY FAITH CHOICE

Easter marks new life in Christ. I will live my new life in Christ. I will

_____

_____

Honor the new life you have received from Jesus. Pray, "Alleluia, Alleluia, Jesus Christ has risen! Alleluia, Alleluia!"

(252)

Respond

▶ Have the young people look up 1 Corinthians 15:12–24 in their Bibles, read the passage, and compare its teaching with what they learned in the lesson.

▶ Invite volunteers to share their reflections.

▶ Explain the directions for the Celebrating Easter activity.

▶ Give the young people time to complete the activity.

▶ Invite volunteers to share their cinquains.

▶ Invite the students to respond to My Faith Choice.

▶ After a moment of prayerful reflection, have the young people write their choices on the lines provided.

▶ Encourage the students to put their choices into practice and praise God for Jesus' gift of new life.

Pray

▶ Gather the young people for prayer.

▶ Begin the closing prayer by singing "Alleluia," using a melody that the young people know from your parish celebration of the liturgy.

▶ Have a volunteer proclaim John 20:1–9.

▶ Conclude the reading of the Gospel by singing the "Alleluia" together again.

The Ascension of the Lord

Focus

Write the Faith Focus question on the board. Explain to the students that this session will help them understand how the Ascension is part of God's plan of salvation for us.

Discover

▶ Invite volunteers to read each paragraph of page 253.

▶ Ask the students to underline those sentences that refer to the disciples. Invite the young people to share the meaning of those sentences with the group. Provide starter questions such as, "What do you think the disciples experienced, learned, and felt?"

▶ Allow for discussion.

Faith Focus
How is the Ascension part of the Paschal Mystery?

The Word of the Lord
These are the Gospel readings for the Ascension of the Lord. Choose the reading for this year and read it. Talk the reading with your family.

Year A
Matthew 28:16–20

Year B
Mark 16:15–20

Year C
Luke 24:46–53

The Ascension of the Lord

For forty days after the Resurrection, the Risen Jesus appeared to his disciples and continued to teach them about the Kingdom of God. At their last meeting, he gathered them together on a hill near Jerusalem and reminded them that they must wait for the promise of the Father, the Holy Spirit.

Jesus knew he would soon be home in Heaven with his Father. The power of the Holy Spirit would fill the disciples with wisdom and courage to continue the mission of Jesus on earth.

Jesus said to the disciples, "All power in heaven and on earth has been given to me, go, therefore and make disciples of all nations. . . ." (Matthew 28:18). Then, as the disciples looked on, Jesus was taken up into Heaven.

The Ascension of the Lord completes Jesus' Paschal Mystery, the passing over of Jesus from life on earth through his Passion, Death, Resurrection and Ascension into a new and glorified life with God, the Father, in Heaven.

The Church celebrates the feast of the Ascension of the Lord forty days after Easter. This holy day of obligation expresses our belief that Jesus has returned to his Father in glory and majesty to reign with him in Heaven. We believe Jesus has prepared a place for those who love him. We believe that, like the disciples, we must continue the mission of Jesus on Earth.

253

TEACHING TIP

Seek What is Above. It is important for the students to move from understanding what the disciples experienced 2000 years ago to what the Ascension means to us today. They have learned that the Ascension is part of the Paschal Mystery. As such, it is the fulfillment of God's promise to restore all things through Christ. The young people have also learned that Jesus instructed his disciples to continue his mission on earth. Distribute Bibles and have the students read Colossians 3:1–4. Have volunteers suggest what it means to "seek what is above." Help them to appreciate that one way we can continue Jesus' work is by praying for others. By seeking God's healing, grace and blessings for the sick and people in need, we also prepare the way for God's kingdom.

Continuing Christ's Mission

Before he ascended to the Father, Jesus gave his disciples a mission. He asked them to continue his work in the world. Your parish responds to Jesus' command in many different ways.

Look through a parish bulletin. Find four ministries that serve your community. Write the names of these ministries on the church steps. Choose a ministry you would like to participate in and explain your reasons on the lines below.

MY FAITH CHOICE

This week I will celebrate the Ascension by continuing Jesus' mission on earth. I will

_____

_____

 Honor the Paschal Mystery. Pray, "Jesus, your Passion, Death, Resurrection and Ascension are the source of our glory and hope. Alleluia!"

(254)

SACRED TRADITION

Yearning of the Heart. St. Augustine, Bishop of Hippo and Doctor of the Church, wrote in his *Confessions*, "You have made us for yourself, and our hearts are restless until they rest in you." This well-loved quote reflects the words of St. Paul. "If then you were raised with Christ, seek what is above, where Christ is seated at the right hand of God. Think of what is above, not of what is on earth. For you have died, and your life is hidden with Christ in God. When Christ your life appears, then you too will appear with him in glory" (Col 3:1–4). We are made for God and the Ascension is the fulfillment of our hope that we will share communion with God through Christ for eternity.

Respond

▶ Ask volunteers to respond to the Faith Focus question. Help the students recognize that the Ascension celebrates Jesus' return to his Father in heaven and gives us hope of eternal life when Jesus returns again in glory.

▶ Read the introduction to Continuing Christ's Mission. Explain the directions. Have the young people work in teams of two. Give each team parish bulletins to complete the activity. Afterward, invite the students to identify the parish ministries they learned about.

▶ Have the students work alone to complete the activity. Encourage volunteers to share their responses.

▶ Direct attention to My Faith Choice. After a moment of prayerful reflection, have them write their choices on the lines provided. Encourage them to put their choices into practice.

Pray

▶ Explain to the young people that one important way we can continue Christ's work is by praying for the needs of others.

▶ Divide the class into small groups. Distribute paper and ask each group to write two prayer petitions. Have each group choose two readers.

▶ Gather the students for prayer. Pray, "Lord God, we present our needs to you, with trust in your care for all your children." Invite the class to respond, "You are our hope and glory, Lord" to each petition.

▶ Conclude with the Our Father.

The Solemnity of Pentecost

Focus

Write the word *Pentecost* on the board. Ask a volunteer to read the Faith Focus question aloud. Tell the young people that this lesson focuses on what happened on the Pentecost after Jesus ascended to his Father.

Discover

▶ Invite volunteers to read the page aloud.

▶ Ask volunteers to name the signs described in the reading that point to the Holy Spirit at work in the Church.

The Solemnity of Pentecost

Can you think of a day when you felt as if you could do anything you set your mind to? What had happened to make you feel that way? Did someone say something to you or give you a gift?

The disciples knew a day like that. They received a great gift that made them strong in their belief in the Risen Lord. That day was Pentecost.

Pentecost is a Jewish harvest festival. On this holy day the Jewish people offer the first fruits of the new harvest to God. At the time of Jesus, Jews traveled to Jerusalem for this great feast.

The disciples gathered in Jerusalem too. As they prayed together in an upper room, they heard the noise of a great wind. Flames gently settled over their heads.

They were filled with the Holy Spirit. They felt new and strong. They went out and boldly proclaimed the Risen Lord. As they spoke, all the people in the crowd heard the message in their own language. People who could not understand one another before suddenly did! People who were separated drew together. The Holy Spirit came upon the disciples as Jesus promised. The Church was born. The work of the Church, filled with the Holy Spirit, had begun.

255

SCRIPTURE BACKGROUND

Mary and the Holy Spirit. Point out to the young people that Mary was with the disciples in the upper room in the house in Jerusalem when Jesus' promise of the Holy Spirit came true. This is an important detail of the Pentecost event that we often miss. Relate this detail to the role that the Holy Spirit played in Mary's life in the Gospel account of the Annunciation. The angel told Mary, "The holy Spirit will come upon you, and the power of the Most High will overshadow you. Therefore the child to be born will be called holy, the Son of God" (Luke 1:35).

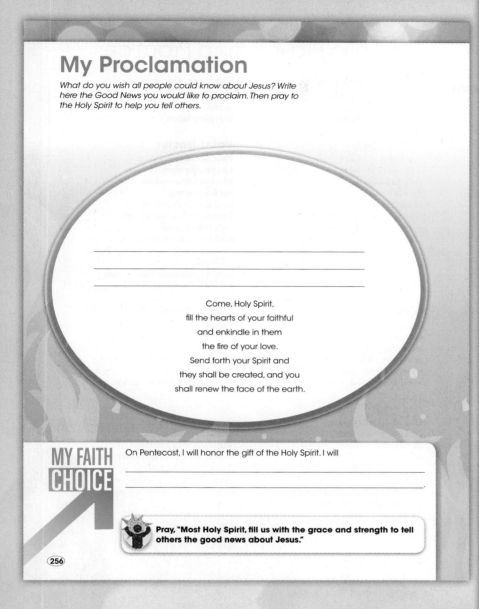

My Proclamation

What do you wish all people could know about Jesus? Write here the Good News you would like to proclaim. Then pray to the Holy Spirit to help you tell others.

_____

_____

_____

Come, Holy Spirit,
fill the hearts of your faithful
and enkindle in them
the fire of your love.
Send forth your Spirit and
they shall be created, and you
shall renew the face of the earth.

MY FAITH CHOICE

On Pentecost, I will honor the gift of the Holy Spirit. I will

_____

_____.

Pray, "Most Holy Spirit, fill us with the grace and strength to tell others the good news about Jesus."

(256)

Respond

▶ Review the Gifts of the Holy Spirit with the young people. Invite them to relate these gifts to the Pentecost event.

▶ Introduce and explain the directions to the My Proclamation activity.

▶ Give the young people time to write the good news that they would like to proclaim in the space provided.

▶ Invite volunteers to share their proclamations.

▶ Invite the students to respond to My Faith Choice.

▶ After a moment of prayerful reflection, have the young people write their choices on the lines provided.

▶ Encourage the students to put their choices into practice and praise God for Jesus' gift of new life.

Pray

▶ Invite the young people to gather for prayer.

▶ Refer the students to page 105 of their texts and pray the prayer to the Holy Spirit together.

TEACHING TIP

A Pentecost Walkway. Discuss this project with the appropriate parish staff person, and ask for permission to create a Pentecost walkway to the parish church. Distribute red, orange, and yellow ribbons or streamers and one sturdy dowel to each young person. Have your group cut the ribbon or streamers into various lengths, curl them, and attach them near the top of the dowel. Plant the dowels in the ground along the walkway to the main entrance of the church, creating a Pentecost walkway.

Catholic Prayers and Practices

This section contains some of the major traditional prayers and practices of the Catholic Church. Refer to these pages during your sessions and integrate them into your presentations and your prayer time with the children. Encourage families to use them with their children as an aid to developing their children's Catholic identity.

Memorization

The memorization of prayers facilitates our ability to pray them spontaneously. Use the prayers in this section regularly throughout your sessions. Encourage the children to pause throughout the day and spontaneously pray. This will deepen their awareness that God is always with them as their divine Companion and Friend.

Latin Prayers

You will notice that the prayers on this page also appear in the right column in Latin. Point out these Latin prayers to the children and tell them that Latin is the official language of the Catholic Church. It is not expected that most children will memorize the prayers in Latin at this age, but the U.S. Bishops encourage us to make the children aware of them from the beginning of their formal faith formation. The children also may have noticed that from at times, certain Mass parts are sung in Latin—for example, the Lamb of God. This tradition reminds us of the history of sung prayer in the Church.

Catholic Prayers and Practices

Sign of the Cross
In the name of the Father,
and of the Son,
and of the Holy Spirit. Amen.

Our Father
Our Father, who art in heaven,
hallowed be thy name;
thy kingdom come,
thy will be done
on earth as it is in heaven.
Give us this day our daily bread,
and forgive us our trespasses,
as we forgive those who trespass
  against us;
and lead us not into temptation,
but deliver us from evil.
Amen.

Glory Be (Doxology)
Glory be to the Father,
and to the Son,
and to the Holy Spirit,
as it was in the beginning,
is now, and ever shall be,
world without end. Amen.

The Hail Mary
Hail, Mary, full of grace,
the Lord is with thee!
Blessed art thou among women
and blessed is the fruit
  of thy womb, Jesus.
Holy Mary, Mother of God,
pray for us sinners,
now and at the hour of our death.
Amen.

Signum Crucis
In nómine Patris,
et Fílii,
et Spíritus Sancti. Amen.

Pater Noster
Pater noster, qui es in cælis:
sanctificétur nomen tuum;
advéniat regnum tuum;
fiat volúntas tua,
sicut in cælo, et in terra.
Panem nostrum cotidiánum
  da nobis hódie;
et dimítte nobis débita nostra,
sicut et nos dimíttimus debitóribus
  nostris;
et ne nos indúcas in tentatiónem;
sed líbera nos a malo. Amen.

Gloria Patri
Glória Patri
et Fílio
et Spirítui Sancto.
Sicut erat in princípio,
et nunc et semper
et in sǽcula sæculórum. Amen.

Ave, Maria
Ave, María, grátia plena,
Dóminus tecum.
Benedícta tu in muliéribus,
et benedíctus fructus ventris tui, Iesus.
Sancta María, Mater Dei,
ora pro nobis peccatóribus,
nunc et in hora mortis nostræ.
Amen.

257

Apostles' Creed

(from the Roman Missal)

I believe in God,
the Father almighty,
Creator of heaven and earth,
and in Jesus Christ, his only Son,
    our Lord,

(At the words that follow, up to and
including the Virgin Mary, all bow.)

who was conceived by the Holy Spirit,
born of the Virgin Mary,
suffered under Pontius Pilate,
was crucified, died and was buried;
he descended into hell;
on the third day he rose again
    from the dead;
he ascended into heaven,
and is seated at the right hand of God
    the Father almighty;
from there he will come to judge
    the living and the dead.

I believe in the Holy Spirit,
the holy catholic Church,
the communion of saints,
the forgiveness of sins,
the resurrection of the body,
and life everlasting. Amen.

Nicene Creed

(from the Roman Missal)

I believe in one God,
the Father almighty,
maker of heaven and earth,
of all things visible and invisible.

I believe in one Lord Jesus Christ,
the Only Begotten Son of God,
born of the Father before all ages.

God from God, Light from Light,
true God from true God,
begotten, not made, consubstantial
    with the Father;
through him all things were made.
For us men and for our salvation
he came down from heaven,

(At the words that follow up to and
including and became man, all bow.)

and by the Holy Spirit was incarnate
    of the Virgin Mary,
and became man.

For our sake he was crucified under
    Pontius Pilate,
he suffered death and was buried,
and rose again on the third day
in accordance with the Scriptures.
He ascended into heaven
and is seated at the right hand
    of the Father.

He will come again in glory
to judge the living and the dead
and his kingdom will have no end.

I believe in the Holy Spirit, the Lord,
    the giver of life,
who proceeds from the Father and
    the Son,
who with the Father and the Son is
    adored and glorified,
who has spoken through the prophets.

I believe in one, holy, catholic and
    apostolic Church.
I confess one Baptism for the forgiveness
    of sins
and I look forward to the resurrection
    of the dead
and the life of the world to come.
    Amen.

258

Apostles' Creed

The word *creed* comes from two Latin words that mean "I give my heart to" that have been joined together to form one word that means "I believe." In the creed we believe in and give our hearts to God. The Apostles' Creed is one of the earliest creeds of the Church. It is called the Apostles' Creed because the teachings in this creed date back to the main beliefs that the Church has professed since the days of the Apostles. Read the words of the Apostles' Creed one line at a time, and have the children echo, or repeat, the words after you.

Nicene Creed

The praying of the creed, or the profession of faith, is part of the worshiping assembly's response to the Word proclaimed during the Liturgy of the Word. The Roman Missal states: "The purpose of the Symbolum or Profession of Faith, or Creed, is that the whole gathered people may respond to the word of God proclaimed in the readings taken from Sacred Scripture and explained in the homily and that they may also call to mind and confess the great mysteries of the faith by reciting the rule of faith in a formula approved for liturgical use, before these mysteries are celebrated in the Eucharist" (General Introduction to the Roman Missal 67).

The Nicene Creed, or more correctly, the Nicene-Constantinople Creed, is the creed often professed during Mass on Sundays. For this reason it is important to guide the children to become familiar with its words so that they can join in professing the creed during Mass. You might slowly introduce it to the children by integrating the use of this creed into your lessons. For example: Point out its Trinitarian structure when you present the Holy Trinity in Chapter 3.

Rhythm of Prayer

▶ Praying is to the spiritual life as breathing is to our physical life. Saint Paul captures the truth of this adage when he recommends that we pray always.

▶ Guide the children to pray always by helping them develop the habit of prayer. Suggest appropriate times in the day for prayer. Help them establish a rhythm of daily prayer.

Morning Prayer

Dear God,
as I begin this day,
keep me in your love and care.
Help me to live as your child today.
Bless me, my family, and my friends
   in all we do.
Keep us all close to you. Amen.

Grace Before Meals

Bless us, O Lord,
   and these thy gifts,
which we are about to receive
   from thy bounty,
    through Christ our Lord.
Amen.

Grace After Meals

We give thee thanks
   for all thy benefits, almighty God,
who lives and reigns forever.
Amen.

Evening Prayer

Dear God,
I thank you for today.
Keep me safe throughout the night.
Thank you for all the good I did today.
I am sorry for what I have chosen
   to do wrong.
Bless my family and friends. Amen.

A Vocation Prayer

God, I know you will call me
for special work in my life.
Help me follow Jesus each day
and be ready to answer your call. Amen.

Prayer to the Holy Spirit

Come, Holy Spirit, fill the hearts
   of your faithful.
And kindle in them the
   fire of your love.
Send forth your Spirit and
   they shall be created.
And you will renew the
   face of the earth. Amen.

Act of Contrition

My God,
I am sorry for my sins
   with all my heart.
In choosing to do wrong
and failing to do good,
I have sinned against you,
whom I should love above all things.
I firmly intend, with your help,
to do penance,
to sin no more,
and to avoid whatever leads me to sin.
Our Savior Jesus Christ
suffered and died for us.
In his name, my God, have mercy. Amen.

259

The Beatitudes

"Blessed are the poor in spirit,
for theirs is the kingdom of heaven.
Blessed are they who mourn,
for they will be comforted.
Blessed are the meek,
for they will inherit the land.
Blessed are they who hunger
and thirst for righteousness,
for they will be satisfied.
Blessed are the merciful,
for they will be shown mercy.
Blessed are the clean of heart,
for they will see God.
Blessed are the peacemakers,
for they will be called children of God.
Blessed are they who are persecuted for
the sake of righteousness,
for theirs is the kingdom of heaven."

MATTHEW 5:3–10

The Angelus

Leader: The Angel of the Lord declared unto Mary,

Response: And she conceived of the Holy Spirit.

All: Hail, Mary . . .

Leader: Behold the handmaid of the Lord,

Response: Be it done unto me according to your Word.

All: Hail, Mary . . .

Leader: And the Word was made flesh

Response: And dwelt among us.

All: Hail, Mary . . .

Leader: Pray for us, holy Mother of God,

Response: That we may be made worthy of the promises of Christ.

Leader: Let us pray. Pour forth, we beseech you, O Lord, your grace into our hearts: that we, to whom the Incarnation of Christ your Son was made known by the message of an Angel, may by his Passion and Cross be brought to the glory of his Resurrection. Through the same Christ our Lord. Amen.

All: Amen.

260

Living Our Life in Christ

This page and the next page contain a brief summary of the ways we are to implement God's Law of Love into daily living. Use these pages to:

▶ Introduce the children to Unit 5 to provide the big picture of what it means to live as a child of God.

▶ Reinforce the teaching of chapters 17 through 22 and prepare the children for the unit review.

The Beatitudes and Works of Mercy

The Beatitudes and Works of Mercy are based on the teachings and life of Jesus. As disciples of Jesus we listen and learn from him so we may live as he taught. Emphasize to the children that when we carefully read and reflect on Matthew 25:31–46, we realize the importance of living these moral teachings of the Gospel.

The Letter of James gets right to the point, admonishing Christians of every age, "If a brother or sister has nothing to wear and has no food for the day, and one of you says to them, 'Go in peace, keep warm, and eat well,' but you do not give them the necessities of the body, what good is it? So also faith of itself, if it does not have works, is dead" (James 2:15–17).

▶ Note that the Works of Mercy are listed on page 261 of the student book.

The Great Commandment and the Ten Commandments

Jesus clearly made the connection between the Ten Commandments and the Great Commandment. Young people sometimes mistakenly think that Jesus gave us the Great Commandment. The truth is that the two parts of the Great Commandment are clearly found in the Old Testament in the Book of Deuteronomy and the Book of Leviticus. When presenting the Ten Commandments, connect each of the Commandments to the Great Commandment and focus on the foundational virtues that help us live as followers of Christ.

Precepts of the Church

These concisely stated guidelines outline concrete ways Catholics are to integrate Church practices into their living of the Ten Commandments.

The Ten Commandments

1. I am the LORD your God: you shall not have strange gods before me.
2. You shall not take the name of the LORD your God in vain.
3. Remember to keep holy the LORD's Day.
4. Honor your father and your mother.
5. You shall not kill.
6. You shall not commit adultery.
7. You shall not steal.
8. You shall not lie.
9. You shall not covet your neighbor's wife.
10. You shall not covet your neighbor's goods.

BASED ON EXODUS 20:2–3, 7–17

Precepts of the Church

1. Participate in Mass on Sundays and holy days of obligation, and rest from unnecessary work.
2. Confess sins at least once a year.
3. Receive Holy Communion at least during the Easter season.
4. Observe the prescribed days of fasting and abstinence.
5. Provide for the material needs of the Church, according to one's abilities.

The Great Commandment

"You shall love the Lord, your God, with all your heart, with all your soul, and with all your mind. . . . You shall love your neighbor as yourself."

MATTHEW 22:37, 39

The Law of Love

"This is my commandment: love one another as I love you."

JOHN 15:12

Corporal Works of Mercy

Feed people who are hungry.
Give drink to people who are thirsty.
Clothe people who need clothes.
Visit people who are in prison.
Shelter people who are homeless.
Visit people who are sick.
Bury people who have died.

Spiritual Works of Mercy

Help people who sin.
Teach people who are ignorant.
Give advice to people who have doubts.
Comfort people who suffer.
Be patient with other people.
Forgive people who hurt you.
Pray for people who are alive and for those who have died.

261

Rosary

Catholics pray the Rosary to honor Mary and remember the important events in the life of Jesus and Mary. There are twenty mysteries of the Rosary. Follow the steps from 1 to 5.

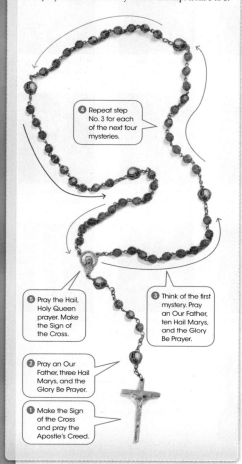

4 Repeat step No. 3 for each of the next four mysteries.

5 Pray the Hail, Holy Queen prayer. Make the Sign of the Cross.

3 Think of the first mystery. Pray an Our Father, ten Hail Marys, and the Glory Be Prayer.

2 Pray an Our Father, three Hail Marys, and the Glory Be Prayer.

1 Make the Sign of the Cross and pray the Apostle's Creed.

Joyful Mysteries

1 The Annunciation
2 The Visitation
3 The Nativity of Jesus
4 The Presentation of Jesus in the Temple
5 The Finding of Jesus in the Temple

Luminous Mysteries

1 The Baptism of Jesus in the Jordan River
2 The Miracle of the Wedding at Cana
3 The Proclamation of the Kingdom of God
4 The Transfiguration of Jesus
5 The Institution of the Eucharist

Sorrowful Mysteries

1 The Agony in the Garden
2 The Scourging at the Pillar
3 The Crowning with Thorns
4 The Carrying of the Cross
5 The Crucifixion and Death

Glorious Mysteries

1 The Resurrection
2 The Ascension
3 The Descent of the Holy Spirit at Pentecost
4 The Assumption of Mary
5 The Coronation of Mary

Hail, Holy Queen

Hail, holy Queen, Mother of mercy:
Hail, our life, our sweetness
  and our hope.
To you do we cry, poor banished
  children of Eve.
To you do we send up our sighs,
mourning and weeping
  in this valley of tears.
Turn then, most gracious advocate,
your eyes of mercy toward us;
and after this our exile
show unto us the blessed fruit
  of your womb, Jesus.
O clement, O loving, O sweet
  Virgin Mary.

262

Devotion to Mary

The Blessed Virgin Mary has a favored and unique place in God's loving plan of Salvation for the world. The twenty mysteries of the Rosary summarize Mary's role in God's plan as intrinsically related to the mysteries of the life of Christ.

Connect the Rosary with your sessions. For example, when a chapter talks about a mystery from the life of Mary and Jesus, such as the Annunciation, the Nativity, the Crucifixion, the Resurrection, the Ascension, or the descent of the Holy Spirit on Pentecost, make the connection with the Rosary.

Introduce the children to the praying of the Rosary. With a rosary, use the information on the page to demonstrate to the children how the Rosary is prayed. Point out the centrality of praying the Hail Mary as part of the Rosary. Draw their attention to the Hail Holy Queen prayer which has been placed on this page so the children can begin to become familiar with it.

Stations of the Cross

When we pray the Stations of the Cross, we are making a mini-pilgrimage. We walk in prayer from station to station visiting the final places on Earth that Jesus walked on his way to Calvary. In the fourteenth century, the Franciscans introduced the Stations of the Cross to meet the desire of those Christians who wanted to visit Jerusalem but were unable to do so.

Living Stations of the Cross

Have the young people develop a dramatic presentation of the Stations of the Cross. One way they might design their presentation is to create a single shadow tableau for each station. Have the young people stand behind a large white sheet to form their tableau. Shine a bright white light on the young people, creating a shadow on the sheet. The people sitting in front of the sheet will then see only the shadows creating the scene for each station. Have a narrator describe each event. Include a prayer for each of the Stations of the Cross. Present the drama for other classes or groups of young people, or present it for parishioners one night during Lent.

Stations of the Cross

1. Jesus is condemned to death.

2. Jesus accepts his cross.

3. Jesus falls the first time.

4. Jesus meets his mother.

5. Simon helps Jesus carry the cross.

6. Veronica wipes the face of Jesus

7. Jesus falls the second time.

8. Jesus meets the women.

9. Jesus falls the third time.

10. Jesus is stripped of his clothes.

11. Jesus is nailed to the cross.

12. Jesus dies on the cross.

13. Jesus is taken down from the cross.

14. Jesus is buried in the tomb.

(Some parishes conclude the Stations by reflecting on the Resurrection of Jesus.)

263

The Seven Sacraments

Jesus gave the Church the Seven Sacraments. The sacraments are the main liturgical signs of the Church. They make the Paschal Mystery of Jesus, who is always the main celebrant of each sacrament, present to us. They make us sharers in the saving work of Christ and in the life of the Holy Trinity.

Sacraments of Christian Initiation

Baptism
Through Baptism, we are joined to Christ and become members of the Body of Christ, the Church. We are reborn as adopted children of God and receive the gift of the Holy Spirit. Original Sin and all personal sins are forgiven.

Confirmation
Confirmation completes Baptism. In this sacrament, the gift of the Holy Spirit strengthens us to live our Baptism.

Eucharist
Sharing in the Eucharist joins us most fully to Christ and to the Church. We share in the one sacrifice of Christ. The bread and wine become the Body and Blood of Christ through the power of the Holy Spirit and the words of the priest. We receive the Body and Blood of Christ.

Sacraments of Healing

Reconciliation
Through the ministry of the priest, we receive forgiveness of sins committed after our Baptism. We need to confess all mortal sins.

Anointing of the Sick
Anointing of the Sick strengthens our faith and trust in God when we are seriously ill, dying, or weak because of old age.

Sacraments at the Service of Communion

Holy Orders
Through Holy Orders, a baptized man is consecrated to serve the whole Church as a bishop, priest, or deacon in the name of Christ. Bishops, who are the successors of the Apostles, receive this sacrament most fully. They are consecrated to teach the Gospel, to lead the Church in the worship of God, and to guide the Church to live holy lives. Bishops are helped in their work by priests, their co-workers, and by deacons.

Matrimony
Matrimony unites a baptized man and a baptized woman in a lifelong bond of faithful love to honor each other always and to accept the gift of children from God. In this sacrament, the married couple is consecrated to be a sign of God's love for the Church.

264

The Seven Sacraments

This page presents an overview of the Seven Sacraments of the Church. As a reinforcement exercise at the conclusion of Unit 4, you might have the children create a mural showing a panorama of the Seven Sacraments.

▶ Invite different groups to draw a picture illustrating the celebration of one of the sacraments.

▶ Have the children use the title and first sentence from the text on this page to label their sacrament drawing.

We Celebrate the Mass

▶ Use this section of the children's book to help the children participate fully and actively in the celebration of the Mass.

▶ This section of the children's book includes photos that will help the children identify with the rites of the Mass, descriptions of the Mass parts, and responses used during the Mass.

We Celebrate the Mass

The Introductory Rites

We remember that we are the community of the Church.
We prepare to listen to the Word of God and to celebrate the Eucharist.

The Entrance
We stand as the priest, deacon, and other ministers enter the assembly. We sing a gathering song. The priest and deacon kiss the altar. The priest then goes to the chair where he presides over the celebration.

Greeting of the Altar and of the People Gathered
The priest leads us in praying the Sign of the Cross. The priest greets us, and we say,
"And with your spirit."

The Penitential Act
We admit our wrongdoings.
We bless God for his mercy.

The Gloria
We praise God for all the good that he has done for us.

The Collect
The priest leads us in praying the Collect, or the opening prayer.
We respond, "Amen."

265

The Liturgy of the Word

God speaks to us today. We listen and respond to God's Word.

The First Reading from Scripture

We sit and listen as the reader reads from the Old Testament or from the Acts of the Apostles. The reader concludes, "The Word of the Lord." We respond,

"Thanks be to God."

The Responsorial Psalm

The song leader leads us in singing a psalm.

The Second Reading from Scripture

The reader reads from the New Testament, but not from the four Gospels. The reader concludes, "The Word of the Lord." We respond,

"Thanks be to God."

The Acclamation

We stand to honor Christ, present with us in the Gospel. The song leader leads us in singing **"Alleluia, Alleluia, Alleluia,"** or another chant during Lent.

266

Additional Suggestions

▶ Have the children examine the photographs of the Mass. Relate what is happening in the photographs with the prayers and explanations. Point out that although there may be some differences in the way each parish celebrates Mass, the main rites of the Mass—the responses, prayers, and actions—always remain the same.

▶ Review the parts of the Mass in relationship to each other. This will help the children see that all the parts of the Mass fit together as one whole prayer.

▶ Integrate the Be My Disciples music, which contains appropriate songs for parts of the Mass. Be sure to incorporate hymns from the CD for each chapter. The hymns and refrains included are all appropriate choices for liturgy.

Additional Suggestions

▶ Review the parts of the Mass in relationship to each other. This will help the children see that all the parts of the Mass fit together as one whole prayer.

▶ Be sure to incorporate hymns from the CD for each chapter. The hymns and refrains included there are all appropriate choices for liturgy.

▶ Take the children on a visit to the parish church. Show them the things that are used in the celebration of the Mass. Let the children see and reverently touch the vestments, books, vessels, and other items used for the celebration of Mass. Allow the children to stand at the altar, the ambo, and the presider's chair so that they can experience the church from that perspective.

The Gospel

The deacon or priest proclaims, "A reading from the holy Gospel according to (name of Gospel writer)." We respond, **"Glory to you, O Lord."** He proclaims the Gospel. At the end he says, "The Gospel of the Lord." We respond, **"Praise to you, Lord Jesus Christ."**

The Homily

We sit. The priest or deacon preaches the homily. He helps the people gathered to understand the Word of God spoken to us in the readings.

The Profession of Faith

We stand and profess our faith. We pray the Nicene Creed together.

The Prayer of the Faithful

The priest leads us in praying for our Church and her leaders, for our country and its leaders, for ourselves and others, for those who are sick and those who have died. We can respond to each prayer in several ways. One way that we respond is, **"Lord, hear our prayer."**

267

The Liturgy of the Eucharist

We join with Jesus and the Holy Spirit to give thanks and praise to God the Father.

The Preparation of the Gifts

We sit as the altar table is prepared and the collection is taken up. We share our blessings with the community of the Church and especially with those in need. The song leader may lead us in singing a song. The gifts of bread and wine are brought to the altar.

The priest lifts up the bread and blesses God for all our gifts. He prays, "Blessed are you, Lord God of all creation . . ." We respond,
"Blessed be God for ever."

The priest lifts up the cup of wine and prays, "Blessed are you, Lord God of all creation . . ." We respond,
"Blessed be God for ever."

The priest invites us,
"Pray, brothers and sisters, that my sacrifice and yours may be acceptable to God, the almighty Father."

We stand and respond,
"May the Lord accept the sacrifice at your hands for the praise and glory of his name, for our good, and the good of all his holy Church."

The Prayer over the Offerings

The priest leads us in praying the Prayer over the Offerings.
We respond, **"Amen."**

268

Briefly talk about the vestments. Share these ideas:

The three basic vestments worn by the priest at Mass are an alb, a stole, and a chasuble. **Alb:** A long, white vestment tied at the waist with a cinture, a sash made of cord or cloth. **Stole:** A long strip of cloth worn over the alb in the color of the liturgical season. Priests hang the stole around the neck. The deacon's stole hangs over the left shoulder and is fastened on the right side. **Chasuble:** The outer liturgical garment worn over the alb and stole. It matches the liturgical color of the season. It is a poncho-like garment that developed from the cloak or poncho-like garment that workers wore.

Additional Suggestions

▶ Explain the prayers, responses, and actions of the Mass so that the children understand what is happening throughout the Mass.

▶ Review with the children your parish's directions for receiving Holy Communion.

How to Receive Holy Communion

▶ Reverently walk in procession to the altar, singing the communion song, to receive Holy Communion from the priest, deacon, or extraordinary minister of Holy Communion.

▶ You may receive Holy Communion either in your hand or on your tongue.

▶ The Consecrated Bread, or Host, is offered to you with the words "The Body of Christ." You respond, "Amen."

▶ If you choose to receive Holy Communion in your hand,

—place one hand underneath the other hand,

—hold your hand out with palms facing up, and

—bow and receive the Consecrated Bread in the palm of your hand.

—Step to the side and briefly stop,

—slowly and reverently take the Consecrated Bread from the palm of your hand, using the hand that is underneath the other, and put the Consecrated Bread in your mouth.

—Chew and swallow the Consecrated Bread, the Body of Christ.

Preface

The priest invites us to join in praying the Church's great prayer of praise and thanksgiving to God the Father.

Priest: "The Lord be with you."

Assembly: **"And with your spirit."**

Priest: "Lift up your hearts."

Assembly: **"We lift them up to the Lord."**

Priest: "Let us give thanks to the Lord our God."

Assembly: **"It is right and just."**

After the priest sings or prays aloud the preface, we join in acclaiming,

"Holy, Holy, Holy Lord God of hosts. Heaven and earth are full of your glory. Hosanna in the highest. Blessed is he who comes in the name of the Lord. Hosanna in the highest."

The Eucharistic Prayer

The priest leads the assembly in praying the Eucharistic Prayer. We call on the Holy Spirit to make our gifts of bread and wine holy and that they become the Body and Blood of Jesus. We recall what happened at the Last Supper. The bread and wine become the Body and Blood of the Lord. Jesus is truly and really present under the appearances of bread and wine.

The priest sings or says aloud, "The mystery of faith." We respond using this or another acclamation used by the Church,

"We proclaim your Death, O Lord, and profess your Resurrection until you come again."

The priest then prays for the Church. He prays for the living and the dead.

Doxology

The priest concludes the praying of the Eucharistic Prayer. He sings or prays aloud,

"Through him, and with him, and in him, O God, almighty Father, in the unity of the Holy Spirit, all glory and honor is yours, for ever and ever."

We respond by singing, **"Amen."**

269

The Communion Rite

The Lord's Prayer
We pray the Lord's Prayer together.

The Sign of Peace
The priest invites us to share a sign of peace, saying, "The peace of the Lord be with you always." We respond,

"And with your spirit."

We share a sign of peace.

The Fraction, or the Breaking of the Bread
The priest breaks the host, the consecrated bread. We sing or pray aloud,

**"Lamb of God, you take away
the sins of the world,
 have mercy on us.
Lamb of God, you take away
the sins of the world,
 have mercy on us.
Lamb of God, you take away
the sins of the world,
 grant us peace."**

Communion
The priest raises the host and says aloud,
 "Behold the Lamb of God,
 behold him who takes away the sins
 of the world.
 Blessed are those called to the supper
 of the Lamb."

We join with him and say,
 **"Lord, I am not worthy that
 you should enter under my roof,
 but only say the word
 and my soul shall be healed."**

The priest receives Communion. Next, the deacon and the extraordinary ministers of Holy Communion and the members of the assembly receive Communion.

The priest, deacon, or extraordinary minister of Holy Communion holds up the host. We bow, and the priest, deacon, or extraordinary minister of Holy Communion says, "The Body of Christ." We respond, **"Amen."** We then receive the consecrated host in our hands or on our tongues.

If we are to receive the Blood of Christ, the priest, deacon, or extraordinary minister of Holy Communion holds up the cup containing the consecrated wine. We bow, and the priest, deacon, or extraordinary minister of Holy Communion says, "The Blood of Christ." We respond, **"Amen."** We take the cup in our hands and drink from it.

The Prayer after Communion
We stand as the priest invites us to pray, saying, "Let us pray." He prays the Prayer after Communion. We respond,
"Amen."

270

▶ If you choose to receive Holy Communion on your tongue,

—fold your hands, bow, and open your mouth and put your tongue out to receive the Consecrated Bread.

—Chew and swallow the Consecrated Bread.

▶ You may also receive the Consecrated Wine, the Blood of Christ. The cup of Consecrated Wine will be offered to you with the words "The Blood of Christ." You respond, "Amen."

▶ If you choose to receive the Blood of Christ at Holy Communion,

—bow and take the cup of Consecrated Wine firmly in both hands,

—using both hands, reverently bring the cup to your mouth,

—take a small sip of the Consecrated Wine from the cup, and

—carefully give the cup back, using both hands.

▶ Reverently return to your place, singing the communion hymn.

▶ Continue singing with the assembly. Then spend some time in quiet prayer and reflection after you have received Holy Communion.

The Concluding Rites

▶ Review with the children the three Concluding Rites: Greeting, Final Blessing, and Dismissal of the People.

▶ Select an appropriate recessional hymn that students can sing together.

▶ Discuss with the children the importance of the dismissal words. Ask the children what those words mean to them.

The Concluding Rites
We are sent forth to do good works, praising and blessing the Lord.

Greeting
We stand. The priest greets us as we prepare to leave. He says, "The Lord be with you."
We respond,
"And with your spirit."

Final Blessing
The priest or deacon may invite us,
"Bow your heads and pray for God's blessing."
The priest blesses us, saying,
"May almighty God bless you:
the Father, and the Son,
and the Holy Spirit."
We respond, **"Amen."**

Dismissal of the People
The priest or deacon sends us forth, using these or similar words,
"Go in peace, glorifying the Lord by your life."
We respond,
"Thanks be to God."
We sing a hymn. The priest and the deacon kiss the altar. The priest, deacon, and other ministers bow to the altar and leave in procession.

271

The Sacrament of Reconciliation

Individual Rite

Greeting
"When the penitent comes to confess [his or her] sins, the priest welcomes [him or her] warmly and greets [the penitent] with kindness" (Rite of Penance 41).

Scripture Reading
"[T]hrough the word of God Christians receive light to recognize their sins and are called to conversion and to confidence in God's mercy" (Rite of Penance 17).

Confession of Sins and Acceptance of Penance
"[The priest] urges [the penitent] to be sorry for [his or her] faults, reminding [him or her] that through the sacrament of penance the Christian dies and rises with Christ and is renewed in the paschal mystery" (Rite of Penance 44).

Act of Contrition
"The most important act of the penitent is contrition...The genuineness of penance depends on [a] heartfelt contrition" (Rite of Penance 6a).

Absolution
"The form of absolution indicates that the reconciliation of the penitent comes from the mercy of the Father" (Rite of Penance 19).

Closing Prayer
"After receiving pardon for sin, the penitent praises the mercy of God and gives him thanks...Then the priest bids the penitent to go in peace" (Rite of Penance 20).

Communal Rite

Greeting
"When the faithful have assembled, they may sing a psalm, antiphon, or other appropriate song while the priest is entering the church" (Rite of Penance 48).

Scripture Reading
"[T]hrough his word God calls his people to repentance and leads them to a true conversion of heart" (Rite of Penance 24).

Homily
"The homily...should lead the penitents to examine their consciences and renew their lives" (Rite of Penance 52).

Examination of Conscience
"A period of time may be spent in making an examination of conscience and in arousing true sorrow for sins" (Rite of Penance 53).

Litany of Contrition, and the Lord's Prayer
"The deacon or another minister invites all to kneel or bow, and to join in saying a general formula for confession" (Rite of Penance 54).

Individual Confession and Absolution
"[T]he penitents go to the priests designated for individual confession, and confess their sins. Each one receives and accepts a fitting act of satisfaction and is absolved" (Rite of Penance 55).

Closing Prayer
"After the song of praise or the litany [for God's mercy], the priest concludes the common prayer" (Rite of Penance 57).

272

The Sacrament of Reconciliation

Review with the children the two rites of Reconciliation. Take the children to church and walk them through the rites of this sacrament. Point out the similarities and differences between the individual and communal rites.

Key Teachings of the Catholic Church

The Mystery of God

Divine Revelation

Who am I?

Every human person has been created by God to live in friendship with him both here on Earth and forever in Heaven.

How do we know this about ourselves?

We know this because every human person desires to know and love God and wants God to know and love them. We also know this because God told us this about ourselves and about him.

How did God tell us?

First of all God tells us this through creation, which is the work of God; creation reflects the goodness and beauty of the Creator and tells us about God the Creator. Secondly, God came to us and told us, or revealed this about himself. He revealed this most fully by sending his Son, Jesus Christ, who became one of us and lived among us.

What is faith?

Faith is a supernatural gift from God that enables us to know God and all that he has revealed, and to respond to God with our whole heart and mind.

What is a mystery of faith?

The word *mystery* describes the fact that we can never fully comprehend or fully grasp God and his loving plan for us. We only know who God is and his plan for us through Divine Revelation.

What is Divine Revelation?

Divine Revelation is God's free gift of making himself known to us and giving himself to us by gradually communicating in deeds and words his own mystery and his divine plan for humanity. God reveals himself so that we can live in communion with him and with one another forever.

What is Sacred Tradition?

The word *tradition* comes from a Latin word meaning "to pass on." Sacred Tradition is the passing on of Divine Revelation by the Church through the power and guidance of the Holy Spirit.

What is the deposit of faith?

The deposit of faith is the source of faith that we draw from in order to pass on God's Revelation. The deposit of faith is the unity of Sacred Scripture and Sacred Tradition handed on by the Church from the time of the Apostles.

What is the Magisterium?

The Magisterium is the teaching authority of the Church. Guided by the Holy Spirit, the Church has the responsibility to authentically and accurately interpret the Word of God, both in Sacred Scripture and in Sacred Tradition. She does this to assure that her understanding of Revelation is faithful to the teaching of the Apostles.

What is a dogma of faith?

A dogma of faith is a truth taught by the Church as revealed by God and to which we are called to give our assent of mind and heart in faith.

Sacred Scripture

What is Sacred Scripture?

The words *sacred scripture* come from two Latin words meaning "holy writings." Sacred Scripture is the collection of all the writings God has inspired authors to write in his name.

What is the Bible?

The word *bible* comes from a Greek word meaning "book." The Bible is the collection of the forty-six books of the Old Testament and the twenty-seven books of the New Testament named by the Church as all the writings God has inspired human authors to write in his name.

What is the canon of Scripture?

The word *canon* comes from a Greek word meaning "measuring rod," or standard by which something is judged. The canon of Scripture is the list of books that the Church has identified and teaches to be the inspired Word of God.

What is biblical inspiration?

Biblical inspiration is a term that describes the Holy Spirit guiding the human authors of Sacred Scripture so that they faithfully and accurately communicate the Word of God.

What is the Old Testament?

The Old Testament is the first main part of the Bible. It is the forty-six books inspired by the Holy Spirit, written before the birth of Jesus and centered on the Covenant between God and his people, Israel, and the promise of the Messiah or Savior. The Old Testament is divided into the Torah/Pentateuch, historical books, wisdom literature, and writings of the prophets.

273

What is the Torah?

The Torah is the Law of God that was revealed to Moses. The written Torah is found in the first five books of the Old Testament, which are called the "Torah" or the "Pentateuch."

What is the Pentateuch?

The word *pentateuch* means "five containers." The Pentateuch is the first five books of the Old Testament, namely Genesis, Exodus, Leviticus, Numbers, and Deuteronomy.

What is the Covenant?

The Covenant is the solemn agreement of fidelity that God and his people freely entered into. It was renewed and fulfilled in Jesus Christ, the new and everlasting Covenant.

What are the historical books of the Old Testament?

The historical books tell about the fidelity and infidelity of God's people to the Covenant and about the consequences of those choices.

What are the Wisdom writings of the Old Testament?

The Wisdom writings are the seven books of the Old Testament that contain inspired practical advice and common-sense guidelines for living the Covenant and the Law of God. They are the Book of Job, Book of Psalms, Book of Ecclesiastes, Book of Wisdom, Book of Proverbs, Book of Sirach (Ecclesiasticus), and Song of Songs.

What are the writings of the prophets in the Old Testament?

The word *prophet* comes from a Greek word meaning "those who speak before others." The biblical prophets were those people God had chosen to speak in his name. The writings of the prophets are the eighteen books of the Old Testament that contain the message of the prophets to God's people. They remind God's people of his unending fidelity to them and of their responsibility to be faithful to the Covenant.

What is the New Testament?

The New Testament is the second main part of the Bible. It is the twenty-seven books inspired by the Holy Spirit and written in apostolic times that center on Jesus Christ and his saving work among us. The main parts are the four Gospels, the Acts of the Apostles, the twenty-one letters, and the Book of Revelation.

What are the Gospels?

The word *gospel* comes from a Greek word meaning "good news." The Gospel is the Good News of God's loving plan of Salvation, revealed in the Passion, Death, Resurrection, and Ascension of Jesus Christ. The Gospels are the four written accounts of Matthew, Mark, Luke, and John. The four Gospels occupy a central place in Sacred Scripture because Jesus Christ is their center.

What is an epistle?

The word *epistle* comes from a Greek word meaning "message or letter." An epistle is a formal type of letter. Some of the letters in the New Testament are epistles.

What are the Pauline epistles and letters?

The Pauline epistles and letters are the fourteen letters in the New Testament traditionally attributed to Saint Paul the Apostle.

What are the Catholic Letters?

The Catholic Letters are the seven New Testament letters that bear the names of the Apostles John, Peter, Jude, and James, and which were written to the universal Church rather than to a particular Church community.

The Holy Trinity

Who is the Mystery of the Holy Trinity?

The Holy Trinity is the mystery of one God in three Divine Persons—God the Father, God the Son, God the Holy Spirit. It is the central mystery of the Christian faith.

Who is God the Father?

God the Father is the first Person of the Holy Trinity.

Who is God the Son?

God the Son is Jesus Christ, the second Person of the Holy Trinity. He is the only begotten Son of the Father who took on flesh and became one of us without giving up his divinity.

Who is God the Holy Spirit?

God the Holy Spirit is the third Person of the Holy Trinity, who proceeds from the Father and Son. He is the Advocate, or Paraclete, sent to us by the Father in the name of his Son, Jesus.

What are the divine missions, or the works of God?

The entire work of God is common to all three Divine Persons of the Trinity. The work of creation is the work of the Trinity, though attributed to the Father. Likewise, the work of salvation is attributed to the Son and the work of sanctification is attributed to the Holy Spirit.

Divine Work of Creation

What is the divine work of creation?

Creation is the work of God bringing into existence everything and everyone, seen and unseen, out of love and without any help.

Who are angels?

Angels are spiritual creatures who do not have bodies as humans do. Angels give glory to God without ceasing and sometimes serve God by bringing his message to people.

Who is the human person?

The human person is uniquely created in the image and likeness of God. Human dignity is fulfilled in the vocation to a life of happiness with God.

What is the soul?

The soul is the spiritual part of a person. It is immortal; it never dies. The soul is the innermost being, that which bears the imprint of the image of God.

What is the intellect?

The intellect is an essential power of the soul. It is the power to know God, yourself, and others; it is the power to understand the order of things established by God.

What is free will?

Free will is an essential quality of the soul. It is the God-given ability and power to recognize him as part of our lives and to choose to center our lives around him as well as to choose between good and evil. By free will, the human person is capable of directing oneself toward the truth, beauty and good, namely, life in communion with God.

What is Original Sin?

Original Sin is the sin of Adam and Eve by which they choose evil over obedience to God. By doing so, they lost the state of original holiness for themselves and for all their descendants. As a result of Original Sin, death, sin, and suffering entered into the world.

Jesus Christ, the Incarnate Son of God

What is the Annunciation?

The Annunciation is the announcement by the angel Gabriel to Mary that God chose her to be the mother of Jesus, the Son of God, by the power of the Holy Spirit.

What is the Incarnation?

The word *incarnation* comes from a Latin word meaning "take on flesh." The term *Incarnation* is the event in which the Son of God, the second Person of the Holy Trinity, truly became human while remaining truly God. Jesus Christ is true God and true man.

What does it mean that Jesus is Lord?

The word *lord* means "master, ruler, a person of authority" and is used in the Old Testament to name God. The designation, or title, "Jesus, the Lord" expresses that Jesus is truly God.

What is the Paschal Mystery?

The Paschal Mystery is the saving events of the Passion, Death, Resurrection, and glorious Ascension of Jesus Christ; the passing over of Jesus from death into a new and glorious life; the name we give to God's plan of Salvation in Jesus Christ.

What is Salvation?

The word *salvation* comes from a Latin word meaning "to save." Salvation is the saving, or deliverance, of humanity from the power of sin and death through Jesus Christ. All Salvation comes from Christ through the Church.

What is the Resurrection?

The Resurrection is the historical event of Jesus being raised from the dead to a new glorified life after his death on the cross and burial in the tomb.

What is the Ascension?

The Ascension is the return of the Risen Christ in glory to his Father, to the world of the divine.

What is the Second Coming of Christ?

The Second Coming of Christ is the return of Christ in glory at the end of time to judge the living and the dead; the fulfillment of God's plan in Christ.

What does it mean that Jesus is the Messiah?

The word *messiah* is a Hebrew term meaning "anointed one." Jesus Christ is the Anointed One, the Messiah, who God promised to send to save people. Jesus is the Savior of the world.

The Mystery of the Church

What is the Church?

The word *church* means "convocation," those called together. The Church is the sacrament of Salvation—the sign and instrument of our reconciliation and communion with God the Holy Trinity and with one another. The Church is the Body of Christ, the people God the Father has called together in Jesus Christ through the power of the Holy Spirit.

What is the central work of the Church?

The central work of the Church is to proclaim the Gospel of Jesus Christ and to invite all people to come to know and believe in him and to live in communion with him. We call this work of the Church "evangelization," a word that comes from a Greek word that means "to tell good news."

What is the Body of Christ?

The Body of Christ is an image for the Church used by Saint Paul the Apostle that teaches that all the members of the Church are one in Christ, who is the Head of the Church, and that all members have a unique and vital work in the Church.

(275)

Who are the People of God?

The People of God are those the Father has chosen and gathered in Christ, the Incarnate Son of God, the Church. All people are invited to belong to the People of God and to live as one family of God.

What is the Temple of the Holy Spirit?

The Temple of the Holy Spirit is a New Testament image used to describe the indwelling of the Holy Spirit in the Church and within the hearts of the faithful.

What is the Communion of Saints?

The Communion of Saints is the communion of holy things and holy people that make up the Church. It is the communion, or unity, of all the faithful, those living on earth, those being purified after death, and those enjoying life everlasting and eternal happiness with God, the angels, Mary and all the saints.

What are the Marks of the Church?

The Marks of the Church are the four attributes and essential characteristics of the Church and her mission, namely, one, holy, catholic, and apostolic.

Who are the Apostles?

The word *apostle* comes from a Greek word meaning "to send away." The Apostles were those twelve men chosen and sent by Jesus to preach the Gospel and to make disciples of all people.

Who are the "Twelve"?

The "Twelve" is the term that identifies the Apostles chosen by Jesus before his Death and Resurrection. "The names of the twelve apostles are these: first, Simon called Peter, and his brother Andrew; James, the son of Zebedee, and his brother John; Philip and Bartholomew, Thomas and Matthew the tax collector; James the son of Alphaeus, and Thaddaeus; Simon the Cananean, and Judas Iscariot who betrayed him" (Matthew 10:2–4). The Apostle Matthias was chosen after Jesus' Ascension.

What is Pentecost?

Pentecost is the coming of the Holy Spirit upon the Church as promised by Jesus; it marks the beginning of the work of the Church.

Who are the ordained ministers of the Church?

The ordained ministers of the Church are those baptized men who are consecrated in the Sacrament of Holy Orders to serve the whole Church. Bishops, priests, and deacons are the ordained ministers of the Church and make up the clergy.

How do the pope and other bishops guide the Church in her work?

Christ, the Head of the Church, governs the Church through the pope and the college of bishops in communion with him. The pope is the bishop of Rome and the successor of Saint Peter the

Apostle. The pope, the Vicar of Christ, is the visible foundation of the unity of the whole Church. The other bishops are the successors of the other Apostles and are the visible foundation of their own particular Churches. The Holy Spirit guides the pope and the college of bishops working together with the pope, to teach the faith and moral doctrine without error. This grace of the Holy Spirit is called *infallibility*.

What is the consecrated life?

The consecrated life is a state of life for those baptized who promise or vow to live the Gospel by means of professing the evangelical counsels of poverty, chastity, and obedience, in a way of life approved by the Church. The consecrated life is also known as the "religious life."

Who are the laity?

The laity (or laypeople) are all the baptized who have not received the Sacrament of Holy Orders nor have promised or vowed to live the consecrated life. They are called to be witnesses to Christ at the very heart of the human community.

The Blessed Virgin Mary

What is Mary's role in God's loving plan for humanity?

Mary has a unique role in God's plan of Salvation for humanity. For this reason she is full of grace from the first moment of her conception, or existence. God chose Mary to be the mother of the Incarnate Son of God, Jesus Christ, who is truly God and truly man. Mary is the Mother of God, the Mother of Christ, and the Mother of the Church. She is the greatest saint of the Church.

What is the Immaculate Conception?

The Immaculate Conception is the unique grace given to Mary that totally preserved her from the stain of all sin from the very first moment of her existence, or conception, in her mother's womb and throughout her life.

What is the perpetual virginity of Mary?

The *perpetual virginity of Mary* is a term that describes the fact that Mary remained always a virgin. She was virgin before the conception of Jesus, during his birth, and remained a virgin after the birth of Jesus her whole life.

What is the Assumption of Mary?

At the end of her life on earth, the Blessed Virgin Mary was taken body and soul into heaven, where she shares in the glory of her Son's Resurrection. Mary, the Mother of the Church, hears our prayers and intercedes for us with her Son. She is an image of the heavenly glory in which we all hope to share when Christ, her Son, comes again in glory.

Life Everlasting

What is eternal life?

Eternal life is life after death. At death the soul is separated from the body. In the Apostles' Creed we profess faith in "the life everlasting." In the Nicene Creed we profess faith in "the life of the world to come."

What is the particular judgment?

The particular judgment is the assignment given to our souls at the moment of our death to our final destiny based on what we have done in our lives.

What is the Last Judgment?

The Last Judgment is the judgment at which every human being will appear in their own bodies and give an account of their deeds. At the Last Judgment, Christ will show his identity with the least of his brothers and sisters.

What is the beatific vision?

The beatific vision is seeing God "face-to-face" in heavenly glory.

What is Heaven?

Heaven is eternal life and communion with the Holy Trinity. It is the supreme state of happiness—living with God forever for which he created us.

What is the Kingdom of God?

The Kingdom of God, or Kingdom of Heaven, is the image used by Jesus to describe all people and creation living in communion with God. The Kingdom of God will be fully realized when Christ comes again in glory at the end of time.

What is Purgatory?

Purgatory is the opportunity after death to purify and strengthen our love for God before we enter Heaven.

What is Hell?

Hell is the immediate and everlasting separation from God.

Celebration of the Christian Life and Mystery

Liturgy and Worship

What is worship?

Worship is the adoration and honor given to God. The Church worships God publicly in the celebration of the liturgy. The liturgy is the Church's worship of God. It is the work of the whole Church. In the liturgy the mystery of Salvation in Christ is made present by the power of the Holy Spirit.

What is the liturgical year?

The liturgical year is the cycle of seasons and great feasts that make up the Church's year of worship. The main seasons and times of the Church year are Advent, Christmas, Lent, Easter Triduum, Easter, and Ordinary Time.

The Sacraments

What are the sacraments?

The sacraments are seven signs of God's love and the main liturgical actions of the Church through which the faithful are made sharers in the Paschal Mystery of Christ. They are effective signs of grace, instituted by Christ and entrusted to the Church, by which divine life is shared with us.

What are the Sacraments of Christian Initiation?

The Sacraments of Christian Initiation are Baptism, Confirmation, and the Eucharist. These three sacraments are the foundation of every Christian life. "Baptism is the beginning of new life in Christ; Confirmation is its strengthening; the Eucharist nourishes the faithful for their transformation into Christ."

What is the Sacrament of Baptism?

Through Baptism we are reborn into new life in Christ. We are joined to Jesus Christ, become members of the Church, and are reborn as God's children. We receive the gift of the Holy Spirit; and Original Sin and our personal sins are forgiven. Baptism marks us indelibly and forever as belonging to Christ. Because of this, Baptism can be received only once.

What is the Sacrament of Confirmation?

Confirmation strengthens the graces of Baptism and celebrates the special gift of the Holy Spirit. Confirmation also imprints a spiritual or indelible character on the soul and can be received only once.

What is the Sacrament of the Eucharist?

The Eucharist is the source and summit of the Christian life. In the Eucharist the faithful join with Christ to give thanksgiving, honor, and glory to the Father through the power of the Holy Spirit. Through the power of the Holy Spirit and the words of the priest, the bread and wine become the Body and Blood of Christ.

What is the obligation of the faithful to participate in the Eucharist?

The faithful have the obligation to participate in the Eucharist on Sundays and holy days of obligation. Sunday is the Lord's Day. Sunday, the day of the Lord's Resurrection, is "the foundation and kernel of the whole liturgical year." Regular participation in the Eucharist and receiving Holy Communion is vital to the Christian life. In the Eucharist we receive the Body and Blood of Christ.

(277)

What is the Blessed Sacrament?

The Blessed Sacrament is another name for the Eucharist. The term is often used to identify the Eucharist reserved in the tabernacle.

What is the Mass?

The Mass is the main celebration of the Church at which we gather to listen to the Word of God (Liturgy of the Word) and through which we are made sharers in the saving Death and Resurrection of Christ and give praise and glory to the Father (Liturgy of the Eucharist).

What are the Sacraments of Healing?

Penance and Anointing of the Sick are the two Sacraments of Healing. Through the power of the Holy Spirit, Christ's work of Salvation and healing of the members of the Church is continued.

What is the Sacrament of Penance and Reconciliation?

The Sacrament of Penance is one of the two Sacraments of Healing through which we receive God's forgiveness for the sins we have committed after Baptism.

What is confession?

Confession is the telling of sins to a priest in the Sacrament of Penance. This act of the penitent is an essential element of the Sacrament of Penance. Confession is also another name for the Sacrament of Penance.

What is the seal of confession?

The seal of confession is the obligation of the priest to never reveal to anyone what a penitent has confessed to him.

What is contrition?

Contrition is sorrow for sins that includes the desire and commitment to make reparation for the harm caused by one's sin and the purpose of amendment not to sin again. Contrition is an essential element of the Sacrament of Penance.

What is a penance?

A penance is a prayer or act of kindness that shows we are truly sorry for our sins and that helps us repair the damage caused by our sin. Accepting and doing our penance is an essential part of the Sacrament of Penance.

What is absolution?

Absolution is the forgiveness of sins by God through the ministry of the priest.

What is the Sacrament of Anointing of the Sick?

The Sacrament of Anointing of the Sick is one of the two Sacraments of Healing. The grace of this sacrament strengthens our faith and trust in God when we are seriously ill, weakened by old age, or dying. The faithful may receive this sacrament each time they are seriously ill or when an illness gets worse.

What is Viaticum?

Viaticum is the Eucharist, or Holy Communion, received as food and strength for a dying person's journey from life on Earth through death to eternal life.

What are the Sacraments at the Service of Communion?

Holy Orders and Matrimony are the two Sacraments at the Service of Communion. These sacraments bestow a particular work, or mission, on certain members of the Church to serve in building up the People of God.

What is the Sacrament of Holy Orders?

The Sacrament of Holy Orders is one of the two Sacraments at the Service of Communion. It is the sacrament in which baptized men are consecrated as bishops, priests, or deacons to serve the whole Church in the name and person of Christ.

Who is a bishop?

A bishop is a priest who receives the fullness of the Sacrament of Holy Orders. He is a successor of the Apostles and shepherds a particular Church entrusted to him by means of teaching, leading divine worship, and governing the Church as Jesus did.

Who is a priest?

A priest is a baptized man who has received the Sacrament of Holy Orders. Priests are coworkers with their bishops, who have the ministry of "authentically teaching the faith, celebrating divine worship, above all the Eucharist, and guiding their Churches as true pastors."

Who is a deacon?

A deacon is ordained to assist bishops and priests. He is not ordained to the priesthood but to a ministry of service to the Church.

What is the Sacrament of Matrimony?

The Sacrament of Matrimony is one of the two Sacraments at the Service of Communion. In the Sacrament of Matrimony a baptized man and a baptized woman dedicate their lives to the Church and to one another in a lifelong bond of faithful life-giving love. In this sacrament they receive the grace to be a living sign of Christ's love for the Church.

What are the sacramentals of the Church?

Sacramentals are sacred signs instituted by the Church. They include blessings, prayers, and certain objects that prepare us to participate in the sacraments and make us aware of and help us respond to God's loving presence in our lives.

Life in the Spirit

The Moral Life

Why was the human person created?
The human person was created to give honor and glory to God and to live a life of beatitude with God here on Earth and forever in Heaven.

What is the Christian moral life?
The baptized have new life in Christ in the Holy Spirit. They respond to the "desire for happiness that God has placed in every human heart" by cooperating with the grace of the Holy Spirit and living the Gospel. "The moral life is a spiritual worship that finds its nourishment in the liturgy and celebration of the sacraments."

What is the way to happiness revealed by Jesus Christ?
Jesus taught that the Great Commandment of loving God above all else and our neighbor as ourselves is the path to happiness. It is the summary and heart of the commandments and all of God's law.

What are the Ten Commandments?
The Ten Commandments are the laws of the Covenant that God revealed to Moses and the Israelites on Mount Sinai. The Ten Commandments are also known as the Decalogue, or "Ten Words." They are the "privileged expression of the natural law," which is written on the hearts of all people.

What are the Beatitudes?
The Beatitudes are the teachings of Jesus that summarize the path to true happiness, the Kingdom of God, which is living in communion and friendship with God, and with Mary and all the saints. The Beatitudes guide us in living as disciples of Christ by keeping our life focused and centered on God.

What is the New Commandment?
The New Commandment is the commandment of love that Jesus gave his disciples. Jesus said, "I give you a new commandment: love one another. As I have loved you, so you should also love one another" (John 13:34).

What are the Works of Mercy?
The word *mercy* comes from a Hebrew word pointing to God's unconditional love and kindness at work in the world. Human works of mercy are acts of loving kindness by which we reach out to people in their corporal and spiritual needs.

What are the Precepts of the Church?
Precepts of the Church are specific responsibilities that concern the moral Christian life united with the liturgy and nourished by it.

Holiness of Life and Grace

What is holiness?
Holiness is the state of living in communion with God. It designates both the presence of God, the Holy One, with us and our faithfulness to him. It is the characteristic of a person who is in right relationship with God, with people, and with creation.

What is grace?
Grace is the gift of God sharing his life and love with us. Categories of grace are sanctifying grace, actual grace, charisms, and sacramental graces.

What is sanctifying grace?
The word *sanctifying* comes from a Latin word meaning "to make holy." Sanctifying grace is a gratuitous gift of God, given by the Holy Spirit, as a remedy for sin and the source of holiness.

What is actual grace?
Actual graces are the God-given divine helps empowering us to live as his adopted daughters and sons.

What are charisms?
Charisms are gifts or graces freely given to individual Christians by the Holy Spirit for the benefit of building up the Church.

What are sacramental graces?
Sacramental graces are the graces of each of the sacraments that help us live out our Christian vocation.

What are the Gifts of the Holy Spirit?
The seven Gifts of the Holy Spirit are graces that strengthen us to live our Baptism, our new life in Christ. They are wisdom, understanding, right judgment (or counsel), courage (or fortitude), knowledge, reverence (or piety), wonder and awe (or fear of the Lord).

What are the Fruits of the Holy Spirit?
The twelve Fruits of the Holy Spirit are visible signs and effects of the Holy Spirit at work in our life. They are charity (love), joy, peace, patience, kindness, goodness, generosity, gentleness, faithfulness, modesty, self-control, and chastity.

The Virtues

What are virtues?
The virtues are spiritual powers or habits or behaviors that help us do what is good. The Catholic Church speaks of theological virtues, moral virtues, and cardinal virtues.

What are the Theological Virtues?
The Theological Virtues are the three virtues of faith, hope, and charity (love). These virtues are "gifts from God infused into the souls of the faithful to make

them capable of acting as his children and of attaining eternal life" (CCC 1813).

What are the moral virtues?

The moral virtues are "firm attitudes, stable dispositions, habitual perfections of intellect and will that govern our actions, order our passions, and guide our conduct according to reason and faith. They make possible ease, self-mastery, and joy in leading a morally good life" (CCC 1804).

What are the Cardinal Virtues?

The Cardinal Virtues are the four moral virtues of prudence, justice, fortitude, and temperance. They are called the Cardinal Virtues because all of the moral virtues are related to and grouped around them.

What is conscience?

The word *conscience* comes from a Latin word meaning "to be conscious of guilt." Conscience is that part of every human person that helps us judge whether a moral act is in accordance or not in accordance with God's law; our conscience moves us to do good and avoid evil.

Moral Evil and Sin

What is moral evil?

Moral evil is the harm we willingly inflict on one another and on God's good creation.

What is temptation?

Temptation is everything, either within us or outside us, that tries to move us from doing something good that we know we can and should do and to do or say something we know is contrary to the will of God. Temptation is whatever tries to move us away from living a holy life.

What is sin?

Sin is freely and knowingly doing or saying that which is against the will of God and the Law of God. Sin sets itself against God's love and turns our hearts away from his love. The Church speaks of mortal sin, venial sin, and capital sins.

What is mortal sin?

A mortal sin is a serious, deliberate failure in our love and respect for God, our neighbor, creation, and ourselves. It is knowingly and willingly choosing to do something that is gravely contrary to the Law of God. The effect of mortal sin is the loss of sanctifying grace and, if unrepented, mortal sin brings eternal death.

What are venial sins?

Venial sins are sins that are less serious than a mortal sin. They weaken our love for God and for one another and diminish our holiness.

What are capital sins?

Capital sins are sins that are at the root of other sins. The seven capital sins are false pride, avarice, envy, anger, gluttony, lust, and sloth.

Christian Prayer

What is prayer?

Prayer is conversation with God. It is talking and listening to him, raising our minds and hearts to God the Father, Son, and Holy Spirit.

What is the prayer of all Christians?

The Lord's Prayer, or Our Father, is the prayer of all Christians. It is the prayer Jesus taught his disciples and gave to the Church. The Lord's Prayer is "a summary of the whole Gospel." Praying the Lord's Prayer "brings us into communion with the Father and his Son, Jesus Christ" and develops "in us the will to become like [Jesus] and to place our trust in the Father as he did."

What are the traditional expressions of prayer?

The traditional expressions of prayer are vocal prayer, the prayer of meditation, and the prayer of contemplation.

What is vocal prayer?

Vocal prayer is spoken prayer; prayer using words said aloud.

What is the prayer of meditation?

Meditation is a form of prayer in which we use our minds, hearts, imaginations, emotions, and desires to understand and follow what the Lord is asking us to do.

What is the prayer of contemplation?

Contemplation is a form of prayer that is simply being with God.

What are the traditional forms of prayer?

The traditional forms of prayer are the prayers of adoration and blessing, the prayer of thanksgiving, the prayer of praise, the prayer of petition, and the prayer of intercession.

What are devotions?

Devotions are part of the prayer life of the Church and of the baptized. They are acts of communal or individual prayer that surround and arise out of the celebration of the liturgy.

Glossary

A–B

adoration *page 217*

Adoration is a form of prayer that declares God is the source of all. We acknowledge God is Almighty Creator, in whom we depend upon for everything.

almsgiving *page 209*

Money, food, or material given to the poor as an act of penance or charity is almsgiving.

Anointing of the Sick *page 129*

The Anointing of the Sick is the Sacrament of Healing that strengthens our faith, hope, and love for God when we are seriously ill, weakened by old age, or dying.

Baptism *page 93*

Baptism is the Sacrament of Christian Initiation in which we are joined to Jesus Christ, become members of his Church, and are reborn as God's adopted children. We receive the gift of the Holy Spirit, and Original Sin and personal sins are forgiven.

Beatitudes *page 181*

The Beatitudes are the teachings of Jesus from his Sermon on the Mount that describe the attitudes and actions of people blessed by God; a word meaning "ways of happiness."

biblical inspiration *page 21*

This is the Holy Spirit guiding the human writers of Sacred Scripture so that they would faithfully and accurately communicate what God intended to reveal.

C–D

canon *page 21*

The word in general means "standard" or "official list." Thus, the canon of Scripture is the official list of books included in the Bible.

canonization *page 181*

The process by which the pope declares that a deceased member of the faithful lived a life of heroic virtue and is to be honored as a saint is canonization.

charism *page 65*

A charism is a grace of the Holy Spirit given to build up the Church and to help the Church fulfill her work in the world.

charity *page 172*

To love as God loves is what we call charity, or *caritas* in Latin. This is the standard by which all of us are to live by, and as Saint Paul says, charity is the greatest of the three Theological Virtues (read 1 Corinthians 13:13).

chastity *page 144*

When we exercise self-control with God's grace in our relationships, the Holy Spirit forms the virtue of chastity in us. This means that we can appropriately integrate the gift of our human sexuality according to God's calling for us. In other words, we respect each other as persons, and not as objects to be used.

Christ *page 49*

This title of Jesus identifies him as the Messiah, the Anointed One, whom God sent to save all of humanity.

Christian initiation *page 93*

Christian initiation is the liturgical process by which a person becomes a full member of the Church.

Church *page 73*

The Church is the new People of God, the Body of Christ, the Temple of the Holy Spirit, and the Bride of Christ, called together in Jesus Christ by the power of the Holy Spirit.

communion *page 137*

Communion is the unity in Christ of all the members of the Church, the Body of Christ; the word is from two Latin words meaning "sharing with." Full communion refers to full initiation into the Church.

complementarity *page 145*

Complementarity is living with and for each other as equal in dignity and unique in gender, helping each other according to God's plan for both genders.

Confirmation *page 101*

Confirmation is the Sacrament of Christian Initiation that strengthens the grace of Baptism and in which our life in Christ is sealed by the gift of the Holy Spirit.

conjugal love *page 145*

Conjugal love is the unique expression of sexual love between a husband and a wife, who freely give their whole selves to each other.

conscience *page 165*

Conscience is the gift of God that is part of every person that guides us to know and judge what is right and wrong.

consecrate *page 101*

To consecrate is to set aside and dedicate for a holy purpose.

contemplation *page 217*

Contemplation is a form of prayer without using words, in which we focus our minds and hearts on God alone.

counsel *page 64*

Counsel, or right judgment, is one of the seven Gifts of the Holy Spirit. This gift, or grace, helps a person sense the moral truth about how to live. The gift of counsel is the ability to judge correctly the daily activity of our lives according to God's will. The source of this gift is the Holy Spirit, who empowers us to form our consciences properly.

Covenant *page 21*

This the solemn commitment of fidelity that God and the People of God made with one another, which was renewed in Christ, the new and everlasting Covenant.

covet *page 201*

To covet is to unjustly desire what rightfully belongs to someone else.

creed *page 13*

A creed is a statement of beliefs, a profession of faith, a summary of the principal beliefs of the Church.

diligence *page 84*

Diligence is the persistent ability to combat laziness. Diligence is related to the cardinal virtue of fortitude. Saint Peter gives advice to a Christian community, to be diligent, or vigilant and steadfast in faith (read 1 Peter 5:5-11). Full participation at Mass requires diligence.

Divine Revelation *page 29*

Divine Revelation is God making himself and his divine plan of Creation and Salvation known over time.

282

E–F–G–H

Eucharist *page 109*

The Eucharist is the Sacrament of the Body and Blood of Christ; the Sacrament of Christian Initiation in which we receive the Real Presence of Christ and are most fully joined to Christ and to the Church.

faith *page 13*

Faith is one of the three Theological Virtues. It is the gift of God's invitation to us that enables us to know and believe in him, and the power God gives us to respond freely to his invitation.

faithfulness *page 108*

This fruit of the Holy Spirit is the steadfast commitment a Christian demonstrates as an act of his or her faith in Jesus Christ as the Son of God, Lord, and Savior. Often faithfulness to God involves a struggle, but Jesus shows us the way to remain faithful to God, especially when it involves sacrifice.

fortitude *page 100*

Fortitude is one of the four Cardinal Virtues. It is the strength of mind and will to do what is good in the face of adversity or difficulty. It enables a person to be a steadfast witness for Christ.

generosity *page 208*

This fruit of the Holy Spirit comes from doing charitable works. By the grace of the Holy Spirit, the generosity we show to others is a reflection of loving others as God loves us.

gentleness *page 128*

When we exercise the virtue of temperance, the Holy Spirit provides us with this fruit, which is related to self-control. A gentle person is one who pardons injury and is free from harshness, even in the face of injury or illness. A sense of gentleness is a sense of calming peace and care in the way we treat others and ourselves.

Golden Rule *page 173*

This is the rule to live by that is knowable by human reason. It is to do unto others as you would have them do unto you.

Gospels *page 65*

The Gospels are the first four books of the New Testament, which pass on the faith of the Church in Jesus Christ and in the saving events of the Paschal Mystery.

holiness *page 157*

The quality, or condition, of a person who is living in communion and in right relationship with God, with others, and with all of creation; being in the state of grace is holiness.

hope *page 216*

Hope is one of the three Theological Virtues by which we desire and trust that God will fulfill his promises, especially the promise of eternal happiness. Because of the Resurrection, Christianity is a religion of hope.

hospice care *page 129*

Hospice care is a ministry of caring for the terminally ill by offering them gentle end-of-life care that respects the dignity of the human person, according to Church teachings.

humility *page 48*

Humility helps us see and accept the truth about God and ourselves. A humble person acknowledges that God is the source of life and author of all that is good. Humility is often described as "poverty in spirit" when the humble person completely trusts in God.

I-J-K-L

idolatry *page 193*

Idolatry is the substitution of someone or worshipping a creature or thing (money, pleasure, power, etc.) instead of God the Creator.

Incarnation *page 49*

The Incarnation is the belief of the Church that the Son of God became fully human in all ways except sin, while remaining fully divine.

joy *page 180*

One of the Fruits of the Holy Spirit, joy demonstrates that we live according to the Spirit (see Galatians 5:22-23). Joy results from moral living and believing in the hope of eternal life.

justice *page 36*

Justice is one of the four Cardinal Virtues. Justice is the habit of consistently giving what is due to God and to our neighbor. We give God what is due to him when we worship him alone. Our worship of God includes loving our neighbor and respecting the dignity of every human person. Through Christian justice, we participate in preparing the way for the coming of the Kingdom of God.

Kingdom of God *page 73*

The Kingdom of God is the fulfillment of God's plan for all Creation in Christ at the end of time when Christ will come again in glory.

knowledge *page 20*

Part of the gift of faith is the desire to know God better. By accepting God's gift of faith, the Holy Spirit perfects our faith with gifts, such as wisdom, knowledge, and understanding. In other words, part of our response in faith is to know God more fully. The light of reason aids us in our journey to love, serve and know God.

liturgy *page 85*

Liturgy is the work by the Church of worshipping God. Liturgy includes words, signs, symbols, and actions used to give praise and thanks, and honor and glory to God the Father.

Lord *page 49*

This title of Jesus indicates his divine sovereignty, or power.

M-N-O

Mass *page 109*

Mass is the main sacramental celebration of the Church at which we gather to listen to God's Word and through which we share in the saving Death of Christ, and give praise and glory to God the Father.

Matrimony *page 145*

The Sacrament of the Church that unites a baptized man and a baptized woman in a lifelong bond of faithful love as a sign of Christ's love for the Church is Matrimony.

meditation *page 217*

Meditation is a form of silent prayer in which we listen to God through our thoughts and imagination, using Scripture, art and music.

mercy *page 56*

This fruit of charity is the loving kindness and compassion shown to one who offends us. Even though our sins damage our relationship with God, he still loves us. Throughout his life, Jesus taught how the love of God is one of mercy. Jesus, the Son of God, suffered and died for our sake. Truly the Paschal Mystery reveals the depths of God's mercy for us.

modesty *page 92*

Modesty is one of the Fruits of the Holy Spirit. These are signs that a person is cooperating with the grace of the Holy Spirit. A modest person protects his or her inner self. Modesty encourages a person to respect the dignity of every human person including oneself.

morality *page 165*

Morality refers to the goodness or evil of human acts. The morality of human acts depends on the object, intention, and circumstances of the action.

mortal sin *page 121*

A mortal sin is a serious failure in our love and respect for God, our neighbor, and ourselves. For a sin to be mortal, it must be gravely wrong, we must know it to be gravely wrong, and we must freely choose it.

murder *page 201*

The direct and intentional killing of an innocent person is murder.

Natural Law *page 173*

It is the foundation of moral life for everyone. It enables us by human reason to know what is good and what is evil.

Ordination *page 137*

Ordination is the Sacrament of Holy Orders in which a baptized man is consecrated to serve the Church as a bishop, priest, or deacon.

original holiness *page 29*

Original holiness is that first state of grace in which Adam and Eve shared in God's divine life. They were therefore in a perfect state of grace before the Fall.

original justice *page 29*

Original justice is that first state of grace before the Fall, when Adam and Eve and all of creation were in harmony.

Original Sin *page 37*

Original Sin is the sin of Adam and Eve by which they lost the state of original holiness, and by which death, sin, and suffering entered into the world.

P–Q

Paschal Mystery *page 57*

The Paschal Mystery is Jesus' passing over from life on Earth through his Passion, Death, Resurrection, and Ascension to a new and glorified life with the Father.

Passion *page 57*

The Passion is the suffering of Jesus on his way to the cross and his death on the cross.

patience *page 136*

One of the Fruits of the Holy Spirit is patience, which is the result of virtuous living. Being patient does not mean doing nothing. Patience involves the wisdom of knowing how to wait for truth while actively seeking grace.

peace *page 72*

Peace is one of the twelve Fruits of the Holy Spirit. Peace on Earth is a reflection of the peace of Christ. Christ has reconciled humanity with God, and made the Church the sacrament of unity and peace. Disciples of Jesus are called to be peacemakers.

Pentecost *page 65*

Pentecost is the liturgical feast and holy day when the Church celebrates the coming of the Holy Spirit on the disciples and the birth of the Church.

perseverance in faith *page 12*

This gift is the ability to remain steadfast in one's beliefs because of the strength and Gifts of the Holy Spirit working within us. This gift is also helpful when someone is struggling with difficulties and doubts.

piety *page 192*

When we worship God, we exercise the gift of piety. It is one of the seven Gifts of the Holy Spirit, which helps us give devotion to God. The attitudes of reverence and respect accompany piety and pious activity.

prudence *page 164*

This cardinal virtue is also referred to as wisdom. Saint Thomas Aquinas defined prudence as "right reason in action." With experience comes wisdom, and prudence is often the guide for growing in wisdom.

reparation *page 209*

The process of righting a wrong or making amends is reparation.

Sacraments *page 85*

Sacraments are the seven sacred signs and causes of grace given to the Church by Christ to continue his saving action among us through the power of the Holy Spirit.

salvation *page 57*

Salvation is the deliverance of humanity from the power of sin and death by God through Jesus Christ, who died for our sins in accordance with the Scriptures.

sanctify *page 29*

To sanctify is to put one in that state of grace in which sin is removed and we are made holy.

sanctifying grace *page 93*

Sanctifying grace is the grace that heals our human nature wounded by sin, by giving us a share in the divine life of the Holy Trinity.

self-control *page 120*

Self-control is a fruit of the Holy Spirit that comes from a steadfast commitment to God. A person with self-control demonstrates that God's will comes first in life. Self-control helps us do what is good and just. When others see self-control in us, we become witnesses for Christ by placing the needs of others before our own and following the will of God the Father, in whom we place our trust.

Shema *page 173*

The Shema is a prayerful rule revealed by God in the Covenant that there is only one God, and the Lord is God.

sin *page 37*

Sin is freely choosing to do what we know is against God's will or freely choosing not to do something that we know God wants us to do.

stewardship *page 209*

Stewardship is the actions of responsibly caring for what God has given in service to others.

temperance *page 200*

One of the four Cardinal Virtues, temperance includes other virtuous acts and attitudes such as chastity, self-control, and responsible living according to God's plan for life and love. This virtue helps us to moderate our actions so that we do what is good and right.

temptation *page 37*

Temptation is anything that tries to move us to do or say something that we know is wrong, or prevents us from doing something that we know is good and that we ought to do.

Theological Virtues *page 157*

The virtues of faith, hope, and charity; gifts of God that enable us to live a life of holiness, or a life in communion with the Holy Trinity are the Theological Virtues.

understanding *page 156*

This gift of the Holy Spirit helps us to know ourselves better as we grow in our relationship with God. Saint Augustine said of this gift, "That I may know You, may I know myself." Ruth in the Old Testament understood the needs of others, and her actions showed it (read Ruth 1:11-18).

venial sin *page 121*

A venial sin is less serious than a mortal sin; it is a sin that does not have all three things necessary for a sin to be mortal.

wonder and awe *page 28*

Often this gift of the Holy Spirit is referred to as "fear of the Lord." This gift of awe before God enables us to be aware of God's mystery and majesty. We are humbled by his almighty power, perfect goodness, and unconditional love. Most sacred art reflects this kind of reverence to God and aids us in the worship due to God.

Works of Mercy *page 157*

Virtuous actions that we do to help others in need are the Works of Mercy. They are grouped as Corporal (bodily needs) and Spiritual (spiritual needs).

worship *page 193*

Worship is the honor and respect we give to God above all else; faith in, hope in, and love for God above all else.

Index

Credits

Cover Illustration: Marcia Adams Ho

Photo Credits
Frontmatter: Page 6, © Jose Luis Pelaez Inc/Getty Images; 7, © Kushch Dmitry/Shutterstock.
Chapter 1: Page 11, © Ilia Shalamaev Wwwfocuswildlife.com/Getty Images; 12, © kolvenbach/Alamy; © Bill Wittman; 13, © Bill Wittman; 14, © Bill Wittman; 15, ©Digital Vision/Getty Images; 17, © Jeffrey Van Daele/Shutterstock; 18, © Design Pics/Design Pics CEF/Jupiterimages.
Chapter 2: Page 19, © Bill Wittman; 21, © Radiant Light/The Bridgeman Art Library; 22, © AP Photo/Jim Mone; 23, ©Jane McIlroy/Shutterstock; 25, © Myrleen Ferguson Cate/Photo Edit; 26, © Design Pics/SW Productions/Jupiterimages.
Chapter 3: Page 27, © Robert Simon/iStockphoto; 28, © The Crosiers/Gene Plaisted, OSC; 29, © MEHAU KULYK/SPL/Jupiterimages; 30, © The Art Gallery Collection/Alamy; 31, © Peter Barritt/Alamy; 33, © moodboard/Jupiterimages; 34, © Paul Burns/Getty Images.
Chapter 4: Page 35, © Jack Hollingsworth/Getty Images; 36, © Art Directors & TRIP/Alamy; 37, © James Shaffer/Photo Edit; 39, © ACE STOCK LIMITED/Alamy; 40, © MBI/Alamy; 41, © Bill Wittman; 42, © IMAGEMORE Co, Ltd./Getty Images.
Chapter 5: Page 47, © The Crosiers/Gene Plaisted, OSC; 49, © Zvonimir Atletic/Alamy; 50, © The Crosiers/Gene Plaisted, OSC; 51, © Bill Wittman; 53, © Vibrant Image Studio/Shutterstock; 54, © James Shaffer/Photo Edit.
Chapter 6: Page 55, © SUCHETA DAS/Reuters/Corbis; 56, © The Crosiers/Gene Plaisted, OSC; © Mary Wiltenburg/The Christian Science Monitor via Getty Images; 57, © Nimejo77/Alamy; 59, © SuperStock/Getty Images; 60, © The Bridgeman Art Library; 61, © The Crosiers/Gene Plaisted, OSC; 62, © Michael Newman/Photo Edit.
Chapter 7: Page 63, © Comstock/Jupiterimages; 64, © Pietro Perugino/Getty Images; © The Crosiers/Gene Plaisted, OSC; 65, © The Crosiers/Gene Plaisted, OSC; 67, © The Crosiers/Gene Plaisted, OSC; 68, © Laurence Mouton/Jupiterimages; 70, © Tetra Images/Alamy.
Chapter 8: Page 71, © John Elk/Getty Images; 72, © The Crosiers/Gene Plaisted, OSC; © Jeff Greenberg/Photo Edit; 73, @Painet Inc./Alamy; © Giorgio Cosulich/Getty Images; 74, © EVARISTO SA/AFP/Getty Images; 75, © Jeff Greenberg/Alamy; 77, © Tetra Images/Alamy; 78, © Myrleen Ferguson Cate/Photo Edit.
Chapter 9: Page 83, © HIROI/a.collectionRF/Jupiterimages; 84, © David Young-Wolff/Photo Edit; 85, © The Crosiers/Gene Plaisted, OSC; 86, © The Crosiers/Gene Plaisted, OSC; 87, © David Young-Wolff/Photo Edit; 89, © Godong/Robert Harding World Imagery/Corbis; 90, © Bill Wittman.
Chapter 10: Page 91, © PhotoStock-Israel /Alamy; 92, © David Lees//Time Life Pictures/Getty Images; © Mike Baldwin /Shutterstock; 93, © Bill Wittman; 94, © The Crosiers/Gene Plaisted, OSC; 97, © Bill Wittman; 98, © Bill Wittman.
Chapter 11: Page 100, © The Bridgeman Art Library; 101, © Clarissa Leahy/cultura/Corbis; 102, © Bill Wittman; 103, © Jeff Greenberg/Alamy; 105, © Bill Wittman; 106, © Inmagine/Alamy.
Chapter 12: Page 107, © Anneka/Shutterstock; 108, © Alain Keler/Sygma/Corbis; © Dennis Cox/Alamy; 110, © The Crosiers/Gene Plaisted, OSC; 111, © Bill Wittman; 112, © Eastnine Inc./Getty Images; 113, © The Crosiers/Gene Plaisted, OSC; 114, © Angela Coppola/Getty Images.
Chapter 13: Page 119, © Bonnie Kamin/Photo Edit; 120, © The Crosiers/Gene Plaisted, OSC; 121, © Bill Wittman; © The Crosiers/Gene Plaisted, OSC; © Bill Wittman; 122, © Bill Wittman; 123, © Fuse/Getty Images; 125, © Tetra Images/Getty Images; 126, © ERproductions Ltd/Jupiterimages.
Chapter 14: Page 127, © Bill Wittman; 128, © MBI/Alamy; 130, © Bill Wittman; 131, © Camille Tokerud/Getty Images; 133, © Fuse/Getty Images; 134, © Con Tanasiuk/Jupiterimages.
Chapter 15: Page 135, © Robert Harding Picture Library Ltd/Alamy; 136, © Hulton-Deutsch Collection/CORBIS; 137, © Bill Wittman; 139, © Spencer Platt/Getty Images; 141, © Myrleen Ferguson Cate/Photo Edit; 142, © Bill Wittman.
Chapter 16: Page 143, © Stockbyte/Getty Images; 144, © Radius Images/Jupiterimages; 145, © Ariel Skelley/Getty Images; © Drew Myers/Corbis/Jupiterimages; 146, © Nic Cleave Photography/Alamy; 147, © Rubberball/Mike Kemp/Jupiterimages; 149, © Daniel Sheehan Photographers/Getty Images; 150, © Radius Images/Jupiterimages.
Chapter 17: Page 155, © Toltek/iStockphoto; 156, © Jim West/Alamy; 157, © Stockbyte/Jupiterimages; 158, © The Crosiers/Gene Plaisted, OSC; © ULTRA.F/Jupiterimages; © Adrian Britton/Alamy; 159, © Bill Wittman; © Ted Foxx/Alamy; 161, © UpperCut Images/Alamy; 162, © Design Pics Inc./Alamy.
Chapter 18: Page 163, © Stockbyte/Jupiterimages; 164, © Thinkstock Images/**Getty Images;** © Odilon Dimier/Jupiterimages; 165, © Steven Puetzer/Getty Images; © SW Productions/Getty Images; 167, © Michael Miller/iStockphoto; © Jose Luis Pelaez Inc/Getty Images; 169, © Corbis Super RF/Alamy; 170, © Jupiterimages.
Chapter 19: Page 171, © Jetta Productions/Getty Images; 172, © Julie Lonneman/Trinity Stores; 174, © Viktor Malyshchyts/Shutterstock; © Anton Balazh/Shutterstock; 175, © The Bridgeman Art Library; 177, © Somos Images/Alamy; 178, © Bill Wittman.
Chapter 20: Page 179, © Hola Images/Alamy; 180, © Hank Walker/Time & Life Pictures/Getty Images; © Ap Photo/Luigi Felici; 181, © Bubbles Photolibrary/Alamy; 182, © Buslik/Shutterstock; 185, © Brownstock/Alamy; 186, © Corbis Bridge/Alamy.
Chapter 21: Page 191, © Paul & Lindamarie Ambrose/Getty Images; 192, © Franco Origlia/Sygma/Corbis; 193, © ilker canikligil/Shutterstock; © Fedorov Oleksiy/Shutterstock; © Thank You/Shutterstock; © Jani Bryson/iStockphoto; 194, © Myrleen Pearson/Alamy; 195, © Bill Wittman; 197, © Fancy/Alamy; 198, © Design Pics/Don Hammond/Getty Images.
Chapter 22: Page 199, © Cultura/Nick Daly/Getty Images; 200, © Glow Asia RF/Alamy; © Image Source/Alamy; 201, © Ariel Skelley/Jupiterimages; © PBNJ Productions/Jupiterimages; © SHAWN THEW/AFP/Getty Images; 202, © Bill Wittman; © Digital Vision/Getty Images; 203, © Joshua Hodge Photography/Getty Images; 205, © Design Pics Inc./Alamy; 206, © Jupiterimages.
Chapter 23: Page 207, © VIKTOR DRACHEV/AFP/Getty Images; 208, Courtesy of the Sisters of the Holy Family Archives; 209, © Chris Cooper-Smith/Alamy; © MIXA/Getty Images; 210, © Odilon Dimier/Getty Images; © Stockbyte/Jupiterimages; 211, © Tim Pannell/Corbis; 214, © Tony Anderson/Getty Images.
Chapter 24: Page 215, © The Crosiers/Gene Plaisted, OSC; 216, © Waldhaeusl Franz/Alamy; 217, © Ted Foxx/Alamy; 219, © djgis/Shutterstock; 221, © Bill Wittman; 222, © Carol Guzy/The Washington Post via Getty Images.
Liturgical Seasons: Page 226, © Dan Porges/Getty Images; © Fameleaf Photos/Getty Images; © The Crosiers/Gene Plaisted, OSC; © Bill Wittman; © Tony Freeman/Photo Edit; 227, © Frederic SOULOY/Gamma-Rapho via Getty Images; © The Crosiers/Gene Plaisted, OSC; © The Crosiers/Gene Plaisted, OSC; 229, © The Bridgeman Art Library; 231, © Philip Scalia/Alamy; © Backyard Productions/Alamy; 233, © Bob Daemmrich/Photo Edit; 235, © Dan Porges/Getty Images; 237, © The Bridgeman Art Library; 239, © The Bridgeman Art Library; 241, © Fameleaf Photos/Getty Images; 243, © Jim West/Photo Edit; 245, © The Bridgeman Art Library; 247, © Tom Le Goff/Getty Images; 249, © The Crosiers/Gene Plaisted, OSC; 251, © Bill Wittman; 255, © PhotoStock-Israel/Alamy.
Back Matter: Page 257, © Fuse/Getty Images; 259, © Andersen Ross/Blend Images/Corbis; 263, © The Crosiers/Gene Plaisted, OSC; 265, © Bill Wittman; 266, © Bill Wittman; 267, © James Shaffer/Photo Edit; 268, © Bill Wittman; 269, © Bill Wittman; 270, © Bill Wittman; 271, © Bill Wittman; 272, © Bill Wittman.

Illustration Credits
Unit 1 Opener: Page 9, Gustavo Mazali
Chapter 2: Page 20, Gustavo Mazali
Chapter 4: Page 38, Gustavo Mazali
Unit 2 Opener: Page, 43, Gustavo Mazali
Chapter 5: Page 48, Gustavo Mazali
Chapter 6: Page 58, Gustavo Mazali
Chapter 7: Page 66, Gustavo Mazali
Unit 3 Opener: Page 81, Gustavo Mazali
Chapter 12: Page 109, Gustavo Mazali
Unit 4 Opener: Page 117, Gustavo Mazali
Chapter 14: Page 129, Gustavo Mazali
Unit 5 Opener: Page 153, Gustavo Mazali
Chapter 18: Page 166, Gustavo Mazali
Chapter 19: Page 173, Gustavo Mazali
Chapter 20: Page 183, Gustavo Mazali
Unit 6 Opener: Page 189, Gustavo Mazali
Chapter 23: Page 213, Cherie Zamazing
Chapter 24: Page 218, Gustavo Mazali
Liturgical Seasons: Page 240, Rachel Clowes; Page 253, Doris Ettlinger

Guide Credits

Cover Illustration: Marcia Adams Ho

Catechist Notes

Catechist Notes

Catechist Notes

Catechist Notes